I0531222

I LOVED
MOVIES, BUT...

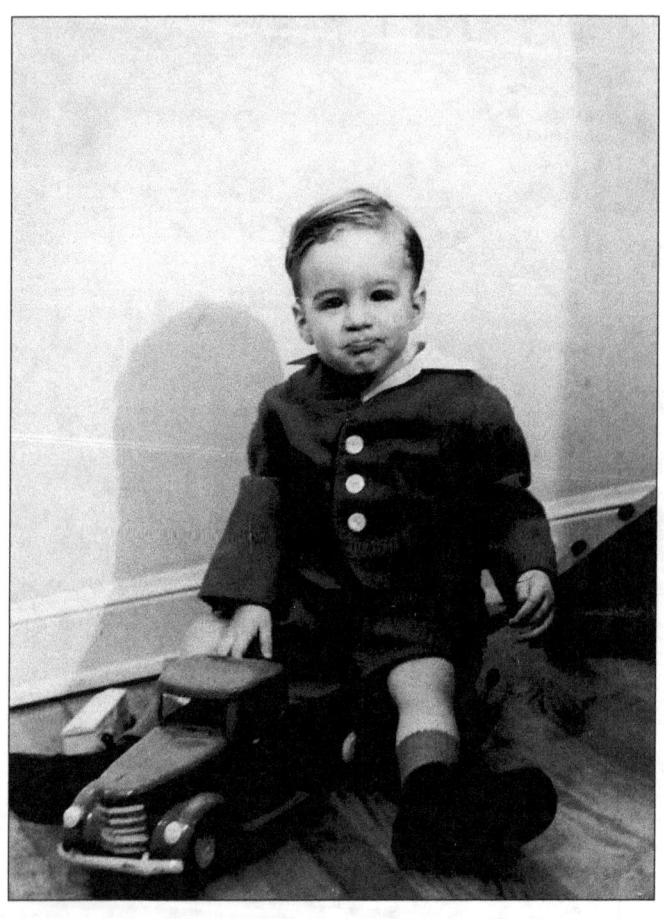

My favorite picture, taken when I was seventeen months old,
in January 1949. I'm wearing my first suit, a red one made by my
mother, while on a semi-truck my grandfather Pierce Joseph Dunne
made me. I loved that truck, but some kid hit me over the head with
it, contributing to my needing an eye operation.

I LOVED MOVIES, BUT...

Joseph McBride

Conversations with Danny Peary

Sticking Place Books
New York

Front cover: Frame enlargement of Joseph McBride writing notes on his wrist as the film critic and historian Mister Pister, from a scene filmed on the first day of shooting, August 23, 1970, for Orson Welles's film *The Other Side of the Wind* (Royal Road Entertainment/Netflix).

Parts of Danny Peary's interviews with Joseph McBride on *Two Cheers for Hollywood* and *How Did Lubitsch Do It?* were published in *Dan's Papers*, the Hamptons, Long Island, New York, in 2017 and 2019.

© Joseph McBride 2025

www.stickingplacebooks.com

All rights reserved.

No part of this book may be reproduced, stored in or introduced into a retrieval system, or transmitted, in any form or by any means (electronic, mechanical, photocopying, recording or otherwise) without the written permission of the publishers, except in the case of brief quotations embodied in critical articles or reviews.

ISBN 979-8-89976-034-1

CONTENTS

ACKNOWLEDGMENTS

With gratitude to people in my life who have been among my mentors and professional allies (a necessarily incomplete list, from the beginning): M. Gertrude Reiman, Lucille Harris, Tom Book, Charles Shinners, Bill Donnelly, Russell Merritt, Michael Wilmington, Errol Morris, Gerald Peary, Andrew Sarris, Robin Wood, Tony Macklin, Ernest Callenbach, Penelope Houston, Fred Curran, Barbara Kaiser, Orson Welles, Peter Bogdanovich, Gary Graver, Jean Renoir, Abe Polonsky, Julie Kirgo, Tom Pryor, Art Murphy, Dave Robb, Bob Thomas, Charles Champlin, Sam Fuller, François Truffaut, Roger Corman, Frances Doel, Todd McCarthy, Joe Dante, George Stevens Jr., Edward Bernds, John Sanford, Penn Jones Jr., Joe Green, Maury Muehle, Virginia Clark, Richard Parks, Jim Goldner, Larry Clark, Steve Kovacs, Steve Ujlaki, Jenny Lau, Sam Hamm, Pat McGilligan, Philip Leventhal, and John Belton.

Ann Weiser Cornell gave the manuscript a thoughtful reading. The Index was well-crafted by Silvia Benvenuto. Andrew Davidson gave valuable help with the photographs. And with thanks to my esteemed and wise collaborator on this book, Danny Peary, and Paul Cronin, who asked me to do the book and shepherded it expertly to completion.

Joseph McBride

I thank my wife Suzanne and, of course, my friend Joseph McBride.

Danny Peary

Writing is a form of therapy; sometimes I wonder how all those who do not write, compose or paint can manage to escape the madness, the melancholia, the panic fear which is inherent in the human situation.

Graham Greene, *Ways of Escape*

FOREWORD
BY JONATHAN LETHEM

Here's the script: my old friend (by now I may surely call him my old friend) Joe McBride, or possibly one of his publishers, contacts me to say that Joe has completed a new manuscript. Would I want a look at it—for comment or review, or simply just to know what he's up to this time? Would I? Surely I would. A galley or stack of pages finds its way to me—increasingly, a PDF file is launched into the ether—and then I go into a kind of aggravated trance, where responsibilities and unanswered emails pile up, my novel-in-progress languishes, and I prepare meals for my children in that distracted way they've come to know, where my attention is torn reluctantly from some priority grasped only by me, like for instance a Mets game in August when they're battling pathetically not to slip out of a wild-card spot. Joe's books aren't mostly short—and they've lately grown, for reasons for which he gives compelling account here, in the book you hold in your hands—but no length can daunt me. Presented with a new Joseph McBride, I can think of nothing else until I finish it.

How did this get started? I was a bookstore clerk, with a young, ravenous appetite for all the books and also all the movies I could get my hands on, and with an instinctual preference for those that had been sorted and aged by time, at least somewhat. I worked (and lived, really) in used bookstores—Moe's, in Berkeley, at that time—and I haunted repertory houses and the Pacific Film Archive. I was also an apprentice writer. I'd given up a brief, diversionary fantasy of being a film critic in favor of writing fiction. As it happened, I was just then working on a collaborative novella (with Carter Scholz) about an alternate future where

Franz Kafka survived tuberculosis, and came to Hollywood and became a screenwriter for Frank Capra. Our principal source, besides Kafka's stories and Capra's films, was Joe's epic Capra biography, *Frank Capra: The Catastrophe of Success*. That book, which forces one to reach for the word "magisterial," I now also see, thanks to these conversations with Danny Peary, as career-transforming for Joe, a pivot point. The biographical study confirmed my instincts about the depressive undertow that drew Capra's ostensibly sunny fables down into the realm of perplexity and despair.

When, by delightful chance, Joe came into the bookshop on a night I was working the register, he cleared out a great number of the most interesting items in our film section. Fortunately, he paid by check, and I was nosey. When I saw his name my eyes grew wide. "Are you *the* Joseph McBride?" I blurted, at which Joe's female companion looked up with an odd expression and then squeezed off a sardonic witticism at Joe's expense, one worthy of Preston Sturges or Robert Riskin: "I've never heard it put exactly that way before."

We then commenced a charming conversation, and the start of a friendship. For, apart from the typical pleasure an author experiences at meeting that rarest of animal in the wild, their own reader, Joe recognized a fellow cinephile when he knew one. My knowledge wasn't then a tenth or even a hundredth of Joe's (it never could be), and I certainly hadn't chatted with Howard Hawks or been directed by Orson Welles (I never would). But we were part of the same "karass," to use Kurt Vonnegut's term for it—a large informal tribe consisting of acquaintances but also strangers linked by their affinity and dedication to some indefinable purpose. Cinephilia is something more uncanny than a mere love of film, I think—it broadens that love to the culture and atmosphere and lore of film production, of filmgoing, and of cinephilia itself, if that isn't too confusing. It dwells partly, but uneasily, within academic contexts—film or media studies—as it does in the money-poisoned realm of film studios and Hollywood. It is more at home in certain film festivals—Telluride, say—and its energies flicker and crackle on websites like Letterboxd, or anywhere commenters are arguing about the extras on a Criterion Blu-ray. And cinephilia finds its truest home in the surviving revival houses, and in places like the George Eastman archives.

Joe then became one of a loose constellation of published writers who became mentors to me; as in the case of another, Paul Williams, I had been instinctively drawn to someone who'd eschewed formal education in favor of autodidactic adventures and hands-on experiences, and transformed themselves into an expert at making self-authorizing forays into multiple writing fields. Joe was an example to me, of discipline, versatility, and abiding with one's obsessions against all odds. Eventually, I hope, I was able to return some part of the favor.

Do either of these things—the cinephilia that unites us, or his kindness in befriending a pesky bookstore clerk—explain why I find his manuscripts impossible to quit reading until I've exhausted them (and the footnotes too)? No. What animates my desire to follow Joe to any lengths, on any subject he engages, whether I already agree with him (Welles! Ford! Hawks! Lubitsch!) or am being seduced into a new exploration (Cukor) or have yet to be fully persuaded (Spielberg) or lack the equipment to judge (Officer Tippit), my response is uniform; I need to know what he thinks; I'm addicted to his form of inquiry and electrified by his gentle ferocity in pursuit of undisclosed or falsified truths. Joe McBride is a seeker, and however disarmingly plainspoken his writing may appear to be, his search, and his rage for truth is a force animating every line he writes. This creates a thrilling energy, a pulse or backbeat in his thought and expression.

In his memoir, in his second book on Capra, which reveals the crises he overcame to bring that book to ground, and now in this book of conversation, we learn the personal underpinnings of Joe's voice. By this I mean the degree to which he has been fighting in every line he writes to convey a suspicion that a world which should be marvelous has in some way betrayed us, or has been betrayed, or both. Joe's hatred of corruption and hypocrisy, and his joy in locating the strength required—in the artists he admires but also in himself—to make a space for human truth in an area of pernicious nonsense, is what unifies his treatment of Hollywood cinema with his treatments of history and his accounts of his own direct experience.

This, then, explains why I neglect my emails when a McBride manuscript lands on my door, and why I burn the food I cook for my children: I can't take my eyes away from Joseph McBride's search, which has gone on much longer than that of Ethan Edwards in *The Searchers*. Joe's writing is highly controlled, and outwardly seemly. But it carries an urgency that asks us to demand to know the deeper story behind every assumption or received notion we've been told to accept. Truth is the captive Joe McBride wants to bring home.

INTRODUCTION
BY DANNY PEARY

When my friend Joe McBride contacted me in Sag Harbor, New York, by Zoom from Berkeley, California, in 2024, I declared I was blissfully retired, having not published anything in years. I was wrong. Because when he asked me to work with him as the Q in this Q&A book, I immediately said yes. How could I resist being able to pick the brain of the person I consider our foremost film historian and critic and even pry into his private life for what would be tantamount to his autobiography? And, most significantly, I would finally complete a 58-year rite of passage from his awestruck admirer to his trusted collaborator, only his second collaborator on a book and his first in over fifty years. It was an opportunity that didn't come along every day.

   I met Joe a few weeks into my freshman year at the University of Wisconsin in 1967, having come to Madison from New Jersey. He had left Milwaukee in 1965 to attend UW, though it was unclear whether he was still a student (which made sense because he was involved in most film activities on campus) or, as was the case, a dropout. He was a good friend of my older brother, Gerald, who had been a TA in the theater department for a couple of years, and both were members of the Memorial Union Film Committee, which I joined that fall but stayed out of the contentious debates over which films to screen. I remember times when I'd be sitting with Gerry in the Union and Joe would appear out of nowhere, talk movies with him, and then rush off to some film-related destination. I had been watching movies since I was three and knew a ridiculous amount about them, but I hadn't found my voice (or pen) yet, so I sat silently during their conversations, soaking it all in. (I would have talked enthusiastically if I'd known back then that Joe was also an avid baseball fan.) I soon discovered that the UW was populated by scores of know-it-all movie fanatics who would make careers in film as critics, teachers, and filmmakers, but to me Joe was on an entirely different level, from them and me. The myth was true: here was someone who had actually watched *Citizen Kane* twenty times! (Sixty eventually, I would learn. And I believed the rumor that after a traumatic breakup, he, like Kane, ripped apart his room.) At twenty, Joe was president of the prestigious Wisconsin Film Society—am still grateful for the education I got watching his hand-picked films that I had only read about—and was already selling articles to the major film magazines that I read. No doubt about it, Joe inspired me. He also intimidated me.

This was through no fault of his own. Joe, a sweet guy, was always kind to Gerry's younger brother, but I didn't think I impressed him with my film knowledge or opinions, so without that validation that uneasy feeling persisted. It increased over the years as he got a real reporter's job with *The Wisconsin State Journal*, started writing books—in those days, any film book author was a star!—and even took a quick trip to Hollywood, where he miraculously met John Ford, Orson Welles, Jean Renoir, and Peter Bogdanovich in one week. Welles even put him in a movie, for heaven's sake. When Joe moved to Hollywood a few years later, he, amazingly, got a coveted reviewer job with *Daily Variety*, and then met virtually every other famous filmmaker, wrote screenplays that were produced or optioned, and eventually was hired by the American Film Institute to co-write their annual Life Achievement Award tributes. (I had no idea until I spoke to him for this book that along with the good times, there was also the very bad and very ugly.)

I dabbled in writing about film when I was in Madison and began publishing books of my own in the late in the late Seventies, but even with all the praise I received, I never felt that I could come close to what Joe was doing. He remained the gold standard, the real deal. Indeed when I edited several film and sports anthologies early in my career, I asked famous people—and I have the rejection letters (and acceptances) to prove it—and all my favorite film critics, including from the "Madison film mafia," to write chapters. But, alas, I never asked Joe. The reason, I deduced, was that I worried he'd think me an imposter among serious film critics and historians, still that unseasoned 18-year-old. Not asking him to contribute to one of those books, and at very least write about his favorite baseball player, Warren Spahn, for *Cult Baseball Players*—for which another of my idols, Andrew Sarris, wrote about Ted Williams—is a huge regret.

I lost track of Joe for a few years but then got a call from him out of the blue to thank me for including a (mostly) flattering chapter on his co-scripted *Rock 'n' Roll High School* in *Cult Movies*. Approval, at last. We lost touch again, but years later, we reconnected and I did several online interviews with him about his critical studies and a lecture he was giving about *Touch of Evil* and Welles at the Film Forum in New York City. It was those detailed Q&As we did together—one film historian interviewer to another—that made Joe think of me to be his partner in crime on this book. Yes, I finally got real validation from Joe McBride.

We both knew from the start that this would be a different kind of autobiography, a not always easy mix of memoir and social, cultural history going back to his youth. We both knew that he would be forced to relive some difficult parts of his long life, and it's not surprising that he had more than his share of emotional times doing so. But I know he also relished the opportunity to take an exploratory journey through his life and career—which were both filled with challenging obstacles—and express his thoughts along the way. Here was someone who followed a turbulent childhood with not one career, but four: journalist, book writer, screenwriter, and teacher. And each career has had many different facets and even sub-careers, as you will discover in this book. And each career overlapped with the others, and every era of his life affected the ones that came after—and affects him even today. Past, present, and future are interwoven and always active in his mind; projects he started sixty years ago are compulsively researched and revised, never put to bed. The one thing that has always prevailed, whether he has been writing about a director or his youth or the Kennedy assassination, is his unwavering determination to uncover the Truth, and then inform us that what we had been led to believe was incorrect. To me that his greatest trait and why he has been so significant for so long.

There were many times during these conversations that I thought, "I wonder what readers will think!" But I never suggested to Joe that he was being too candid. In all his books he has revealed the complete unsanitized picture of his subject as well as himself. They have all been deeply personal, even autobiographical. So it's appropriate that this book also takes readers in unexpected directions yet repeatedly finds its way back to, naturally, the Truth. Joseph McBride's life story is unique so it's ideal that's being presented in this unique Q&A format, And I am fortunate that he chose me to help him tell it.

PART I
EARLY IMPRESSIONS

1. "A secret man"

Joe, I've never told you this, but when we became film buddies at the University of Wisconsin, Madison, in the late Sixties, I knew that your parents were journalists but I initially assumed that you grew up as an only child, lived in a tough working-class neighborhood in Milwaukee, and attended crowded and dangerous public schools. I was wrong. I also pictured you as a loner who pretty much was an adult by the time you were ten, escaped into your own world, and brought yourself up, rebelliously skipping school to see a double feature or ballgame, watching TV past midnight, reading everything you could get your hands on, chasing girls, working odd jobs, engaging in a myriad of intellectual pursuits, and receiving acclaim for your writing. How far was I from the truth?

Some of your early impressions were remarkably accurate, Danny, but some were quite far from the truth. It's fascinating to hear this from you, to see myself as others saw me. I've always been something of "a secret man," as Abraham Polonsky called me when I gave him the first book I wrote, as a teenager, and he was surprised it was about baseball slang. An OSS man in World War II and a Hollywood blacklistee who had to live under the radar for much of his life, Abe was a sharp observer of people. But in college, where I encountered a wider range of people than I had known while growing up, I felt I was often misconstrued as less sophisticated than I actually was.

Part of that misapprehension was that although I was intellectually precocious, I was gauche and ill-equipped to deal with mainstream society, for a variety of reasons, until I was farther along in adult life. As my favorite modern author, Graham Greene, writes in his novel *The Comedians,* "For writers it is always said that the first twenty years of life contain the whole of experience—the rest is observation, but I think it is equally true of us all." Some of my fellow students at the UW, the ones who tended to be comfortable in their conformist regimentation, whether leftist or rightist, looked down on me and didn't realize that I came from an unusually sophisticated intellectual background. But we were not particularly materialistic, and my upbringing was eccentric.

Danny, as you learned from reading my 2015 memoir, *The Broken Places,* we lived in Wauwatosa, a pleasant, tree-lined, outwardly tranquil suburban neighborhood of Milwaukee, during a time when people still left their keys in their unlocked cars. My parents were modestly paid newspaper reporters, and they had seven kids. We didn't have much money. So I dressed in cheap off-the-shelf clothes from J. C. Penney and wore unfashionable horn-rimmed glasses and couldn't afford a barbershop haircut. When I went away to college, I didn't even know how to clean my own clothes or go to the dentist or eat healthily. I looked geeky and seemed odd enough to be ostracized by many students, as I had been in my childhood.

But a couple of years later, this freshman did see you as an unusually sophisticated intellectual.

Because in my second year in Madison, I found my niche and began to thrive. I was welcomed into our lively and congenial film circle, what became known as the "Madison film mafia," including you and your brother Gerald Peary. Our gang of fanatical and vigorously debating cinephiles were proudly eccentric by nature. Cinephilia was considered an odd, fringy kind of behavior at the time, before our "film generation" made it acceptable and then a dominant trend. Our Madison film mafia sent at least twenty-five people into careers in professional filmmaking or film studies as writers and professors.

Loner and renegade

I was also *deliberately* unfashionable in those days and still am. I'm a loner and renegade as a matter of principle, personally and professionally. To help you understand how and why I became a film critic and historian, with careers in journalism and screenwriting and teaching along the way, I first have to explain in some depth the influences that formed me, including those I had to fight against in my boyhood.

I've had four careers: journalist; screenwriter; author; and teacher. In the four parts of this book, my discussion of these careers will overlap to some extent. My varied career in areas often seen as disparate makes me somewhat unusual in the field of cinephilia, and those areas of endeavor have cross-fertilized each other as I've moved along my idiosyncratic path. My diverse career has made me somewhat hard to define, and some people who know me as one thing don't know the other facets of my personality, so I welcome this opportunity to reflect in depth on my more

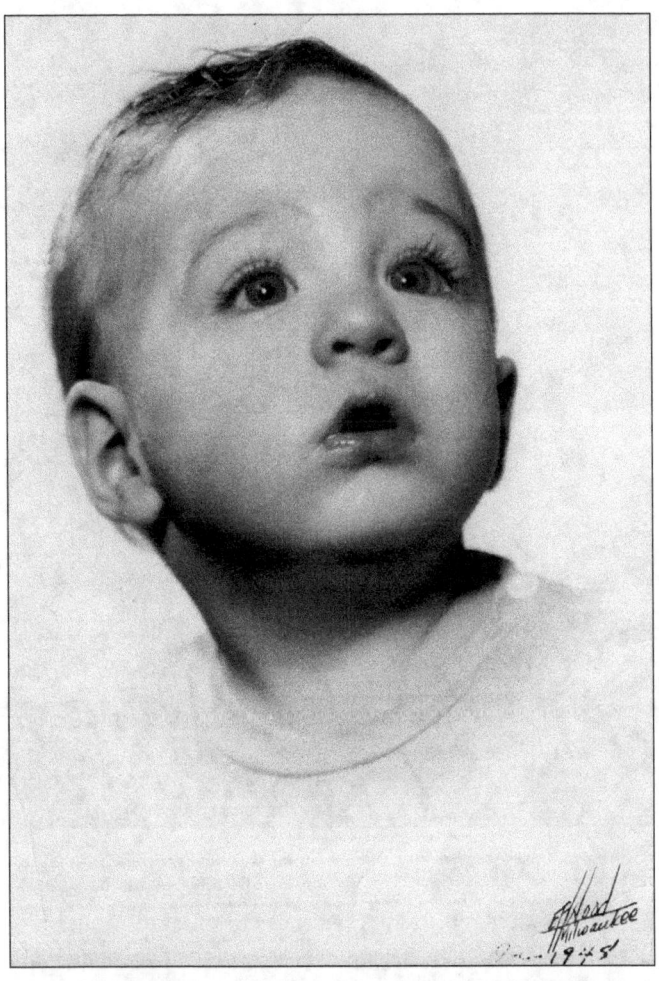

My quizzical approach to life is evident in one of my first studio
portraits, at the age of ten months in June 1948. My mother wrote
that my first year was "a harried and unhappy one" due to health
problems and physical precociousness.

than six decades as a professional writer, in parallel with my
later life of more than twenty years as a teacher.

I have always considered you foremost as a journalist/
reporter, working through the night on fumes, typing a
book with your right hand and an article with your left,
determined to correct the lies and mistakes of others.

When I was interviewed for a video profile as a faculty
member of the School of Cinema at San Francisco State
University a few years ago, videographer Silvia Turchin
asked me to define myself. I found myself replying, "I'm

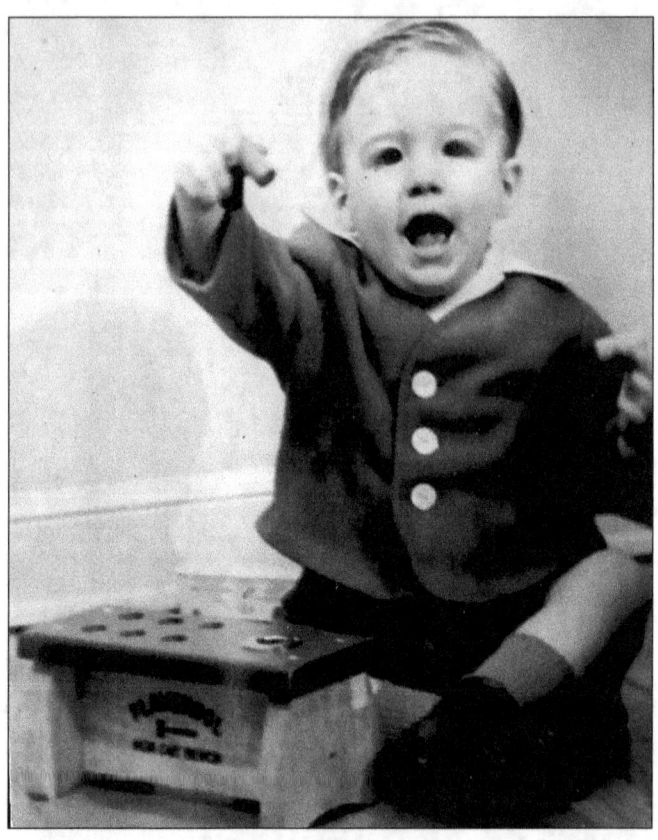

I became more pugnacious by the time I was seventeen months old.

an investigative reporter." I became a professional journalist when I sold my first magazine article at age twelve in 1960. And I was a general assignment newspaper reporter for years with *The Wisconsin State Journal* in Madison and *The Riverside* (California) *Press-Enterprise* and a show business reporter, reviewer, and columnist for *Daily Variety* in Hollywood and weekly *Variety,* which was headquartered in New York. I've always considered being a reporter a high calling and a privilege. It's a job that gives you the opportunity to go up to strangers and ask questions, to seek out the truth from public officials and serve as a witness to public events, to uncover the real story behind the façade of official history.

That search for hidden truth is the common thread that has marked the diverse strands of my four-part career. I've made my parallel careers while looking behind the curtain of the lies we are routinely told by our society, the lies that bedeviled me during my upbringing as a brainwashed Catholic boy and naive believer in our deceitful political system. Reflecting on my tumultuous formative years for this book as well as *The Broken Places* has given me a clear perspective on the familial, social, and cultural influences that made me into the writer I am today. Ernest Hemingway once remarked that the best training for a writer is "an unhappy childhood." Provided that you survive it, an unhappy childhood toughens you up, teaches lessons about the mendacity of the world, and leaves you healthily disillusioned.

As a result, I don't look back at my difficult childhood in sorrow but in gratitude. Although I was raised by two alcoholic parents, bullied by classmates throughout my grade school years, abused by nuns, tormented by Catholic guilt over my developing sexuality, and had a psychological and physical breakdown in high school that landed me in a mental hospital, I managed to come through it more or less intact. I feel I actually was fortunate to go through these hellish experiences, because they purged me of the false and delusional beliefs, both religious and political, that were drilled and beaten into me as a Catholic kid during the Cold War era. If I hadn't gone through that stuff, I would have been trapped in self-destructive patterns of my repressive Catholic boyhood and probably wouldn't have survived. I came through all that a better man and have managed to fashion a prolific writing career. I even became a university professor thirty-four years after I was kicked out of college.

And my youthful experiences gave me fertile material to work with as a writer. I always told my students that if you have a negative experience, write a book about it and get something good out of it. I would add, half-seriously, "And make some money out of it."

Before we get into your difficulties at your Catholic schools and at home, tell me more about your parents and if your self-description as an investigative reporter owes a lot to them.

Let me read you what I wrote in an autobiographical essay at age eighteen:

> Since my parents are both professional journalists, words, particularly of the printed type, proliferated throughout my childhood. Dinner conversation was invariably journalistic shoptalk, which held a certain fascination for me even before I wanted to become a writer.... I could not help but gain from [my father's] respect for economy of style and his

disregard for affectations. He and my mother let my writing ability, such as it was, take its course. Consequently it did not evidence itself at a spectacularly early age, but gradually and naturally developed. I feel that this lack of prodding was remarkably effective in proving my love for and ability in writing. If I had been pushed, and tagged "writer" from the time I began to hold a pencil, I could hold serious doubts about the validity and spontaneity of my career....

Probably the two most important influences in my general writing development in my early youth were the neat, sober prose of the *Milwaukee Journal*, which I read faithfully from the time I was six, and the tricky, witty verbiage of *Time*. The *Journal*'s influence, much more subtle and undoubtedly more beneficial, gravitated me early to a deep, fundamental respect for simplicity of expression.

Because my parents worked for rival newspapers in Milwaukee, and my mother was also a politician, our lively discussions at the dinner table enlightened me about the news of the day. We all expressed our opinions, the kids as well as my parents, and I was fascinated by their sharing of the kind of inside information reporters can't always print. My mother was a voracious reader of books that I also glommed onto, and we subscribed to about a dozen magazines. All this made our house a fertile intellectual atmosphere.

But our family was also blighted by my parents' heavy drinking and the emotional chaos that resulted. A beer truck would come around our neighborhood and drop off a case of twenty-four bottles of beer for my parents every day (some of my friends refused to believe this). My mother would also drink milk laced with vodka. There was constant fighting at night, when both of my parents would get blotto. My father would sit in his easy chair in front of the television and pass out soon after dinner. My mother would scream at him, find a pretext to start hitting him, goad him into hitting her back, and call on me and my siblings to defend her, which tore me apart.

My father, Raymond McBride, was a reporter and columnist on the *Milwaukee Journal*, the afternoon paper, and my mother, Marian Dunne (Toni) McBride, was a reporter for the morning paper, the *Milwaukee Sentinel*. My father started as a sportswriter and cartoonist on the

Joe's father and mother,
Ray and Toni McBride,
both journalists

My father, Raymond McBride, a longtime reporter, columnist, and
rewrite man on the *Milwaukee Journal*, and my mother, Marian
Dunne McBride, a reporter for the *Journal* and, later, the rival
Milwaukee Sentinel, as well as a Democratic Party official.

Superior Telegram in northern Wisconsin. He then spent
thirty-nine years at the *Journal,* where for a while he
was also the Screen-Radio-and-Television editor and
reviewer. (I had some art talent as a boy, and my mother
arranged for me to take lessons from a prominent teacher,
Sister Thomasita Fessler at Cardinal Stritch College in
Milwaukee. I considered becoming an editorial cartoonist
and did some cartooning in our high school Poster Club but
didn't pursue that alternate career path because I discovered
moviemaking.)

Despite my Dad's drinking problem, which caused us a
great deal of disappointment and pain, I admired his qualities
as a journalist and romanticized him as being like Clark
Kent, "a mild-mannered reporter for a great metropolitan
newspaper, [who] fights a never-ending battle for truth,
justice, and the American way." At the end of the day in
high school, I used to go downtown and hang out in the
Journal city room, a setting I found exciting and romantic,
like being on the set of *The Front Page.* I also spent years
delivering the *Journal* in our neighborhood, so from an
early age I considered myself "an old newspaper guy."

My mother was busy in my childhood writing freelance
newspaper and magazine articles to help support our
large family. She had been the valedictorian of a Catholic
girls' high school in Spokane, Washington, and earned a
scholarship to Marquette University's Journalism School
in 1940. Stanford University also offered her a scholarship,
but she wanted to go farther from home to get away from
her abusive mother, so that's why I was born in Wisconsin.

My mother was a journalism student at Marquette during World War II and the editor of the *Marquette Tribune*.

After graduation she worked as a book publicist and then was hired as a reporter by the *Journal*. But she was forced to quit her job in 1946 when my father came back to the paper from the war and married her. If my mother had not been the first member of our family to become a college graduate, we might have wound up as miners, the world's worst profession, like some of my Irish immigrant ancestors. Instead her seven children became teachers, writers, lawyers, and a doctor. And we followed the admonition of my Grandpa John McBride to his children when they left home: "Stay out of jail."

Unfortunately, my Mom was not cut out to be a mother. She suffered because of the Catholic strictures against birth control and because of her frustration over not being able to work outside the home, problems that afflicted so many women in the 1950s. Her plight had made us kids feminists before Betty Friedan's influential 1963 book, *The Feminine Mystique*, diagnosed why women of that era usually felt so unfulfilled, beset by "The Problem That Has No Name." So when my mother was hired by the *Sentinel* in 1963 to cover politics and the White House (ostensibly focused on women's issues, but ranging more widely whenever she could), we were thrilled that it got her out of the house. Life became relatively peaceful when she was replaced by kindly female housekeepers, most of them wise Black ladies.

My Mom was also a pioneering Democratic Party activist and worked on John F. Kennedy's Wisconsin presidential primary campaign. She was elected vice chairman of the state party in 1961. After returning to being a reporter, she covered the Johnson and Nixon administrations in Washington and worked with Helen Thomas, the dean of White House journalists, to spearhead the integration of women into the Washington Press Club. Thomas wrote me about my mother in 2005 that she had "always admired her; great journalist."

I will later ask you about how your mother helped you become a professional writer as a boy, but now can you talk about the notes she kept about you, perhaps in an attempt to be a better mother? What did you learn from them and whatever else she told you about your early life?

The meticulous notes she kept on my physical and mental development over my first three years record that I became a dedicated reader early on and developed a hearty sense of humor. It was rather sarcastic and often directed at my parents. She described me as "a challenge from day 1." She called me that because of my precocious crawling and climbing, and my demanding adult attention and having a vocabulary of 200 words at seventeen months. I was so talkative at two that my Uncle Jack McBride nicknamed me "Windy." I developed into what my mother called "an intense, hypertension child."

I would happily pull some risky mischief, climbing on top of the refrigerator or sitting outside in the snow bare-assed, making snowballs while she was engrossed in a long telephone call. Some of my behavior was more ambiguous. She noted that at seven months I "tried to 'commit suicide' in the toilet... I was taking a bath & couldn't trust he wouldn't hurt himself out of my eye view... so I took him into the bathroom, closed the door, turned to get into the bathtub & heard a strange noise... Joe was upside down in the toilet... put his hands on the seat & did a handstand!"

Only twice in my boyhood did I try to talk frankly to my mother about sensitive subjects. Once I told her, vaguely, that I was "nervous," and she snapped, "Nonsense! Children can't be nervous." And another time, I went into her bedroom and confessed, "I don't think I love you." She exploded with rage, calling me "an ungrateful little whelp." After that I knew I had to hide my feelings. Slowly over time, partly through writing *The Broken Places*, I learned to overcome and shed my sense of taboo and express myself freely and without fear of guilt or shame.

As a kid I had a hard time understanding either of my parents, who were often irrational. I became very upset in the spring of 1954 when they put a "JOE MUST GO" bumper sticker on our station wagon. This was during a recall campaign against our senator Joe McCarthy. But I thought my parents meant me. So I kept pulling the stickers off the car, and my parents kept putting them back on. They thought one of our Republican neighbors was doing the mischief. Finally on his day off, my Dad put the sticker back on the car and waited at the window. He saw his six-year-old son skulking around and pulling off the sticker. I'm told he felt bad about it. As they say, comedy is tragedy plus time.

It's not surprising that you ended up a writer, trying to make sense of all this.

I took a career aptitude test in eighth grade that was uncannily accurate about the way my career turned out.

I scored 47 of 50 as a writer and 46 as a lawyer; my lowest score was as a farmer, the lowest possible score, minus 9— the week I spent on my uncle's dairy farm in 1955 lingers as one of my most miserable, grossest memories. Two of my brothers, Mike and Dennis, became lawyers, and I would have enjoyed that profession. I even considered switching careers in midlife when I was toiling as a screenwriter but thought I had gone too far to make such a drastic change.

A time of trauma

Your memoir The Broken Places *frankly discusses the childhood trauma that led to your breakdown in high school. It is shocking to read about and, of course, it changed your life.*

When I met my future wife Dr. Ruth O'Hara, a research psychologist from Ireland, she said I was "a textbook case of an abused child." My grade school years, from 1953 to 1961, were a hellish existence both at home and at St. Bernard's Grade School in Wauwatosa. I had some disturbed Dominican nuns who were abusive both physically and psychologically; it's no coincidence that Dominicans ran the Inquisition. In the fall of 1953, I got into a violent theological argument with our first-grade nun, Sister Francile. She asked if the Host was bread or the body of Jesus. I said, "Both." She chastised me, yanking my ear painfully. My report card reflects that I was given a D+ for "Social Development" initially before I gradually got with the program and wound up with an A in that category by the end of the semester.

That was the pattern of how I was browbeaten and brainwashed in grade school, when my only real form of rebellion was to tune out in class as much as possible and practice my love of cartooning instead. Once I had to move my desk out into the hall for drawing a picture of Sir Lancelot. My grades were spotty, and I began to miss school whenever I could suffer or feign illness. I was bored out of my mind throughout those eight years at St. Bernard's, because most of the kids were dullards, and the teaching went at their pace. I developed the knack of only half-listening to the lessons as I doodled. When I started first grade, I was so worried that I would be bored that I wrote and illustrated a book about a turtle to take with me.

That's how I began as a writer—under duress. I've always regarded my writing career as a war of survival and a constant battle to maintain my independence and integrity.

Twelve years after the incident with the nun in first grade, I took an advanced theology class at Marquette High. It gave me great satisfaction to learn that my response to her question about the Host was correct in terms of Catholic doctrine, since the mystery of the Host is that it represents the dual nature of Jesus as both God and man. But being smarter than an ignorant nun didn't help me in grade school. Sister Francile told my parents, "We have to decide who's teaching this class, Joe or me." I guess it's natural that I eventually became a teacher.

Did you get along with any of the other kids and teachers at St. Bernard's? Were there any positives?

A few of the girls in my class were smarter than most of the boys, but I was discouraged from socializing with them after an incident in my early grade school years. I had a crush on a girl named Rosalie Daly and walked her home from school at lunchtime a couple of days in a row. I thought that was innocent behavior. But she complained to her mother, who went to our pastor, who called my parents and ordered me to leave Rosalie alone. I got the message, and years would go by before I was able to get to know a girl, at the mental hospital.

Some of the boys in my class beat me up every day after school for eight years, since I was small in those days and I guess because I was smarter and could defend myself only by mouthing off. One fond memory of that abuse sticks out, though: I was so thin and bony that when a kid hit me in the stomach, he broke his hand, and the next day at school he indignantly told me that his parents were angry at me. I had to smile inwardly at the absurd turn of justice.

When I unearthed the autobiographical essay I wrote in 1965 as a college freshman, I discovered what should have been a positive memory of grade school but that I suppressed:

> As an eighth grader I considered it natural to enter a balloting for the editorship of our school paper [*The Saber*], though my career goal at the time was to become a missionary priest. I won the race almost unanimously, though I was the most unpopular person in the class. The paper, which appeared once every two months or so, consisted mainly of atrocious "poetry" written by second graders on up. My major project as editor was to add some prose to the paper; which I did in the

forms of editorials and sports and club reports. I do not recall writing any verse in grade school aside from a few song parodies I was asked to write for a farewell assembly for a parish priest.

My years at St. Bernard's had a bad ending, however. At our class picnic in eighth grade, the boys threw me into a lake. So my last memory of grade school is riding home on the bus, drenched and crying quietly by myself. And another time I had my head held underwater in a pool by my chief bully until I almost drowned. When I went to a reunion of our grade school classes many years later, that fellow came up to me, a small, somewhat fearful-looking man I towered over, and apologized. He told me his father had been beating him at home, so he took it out on me. I was glad we could find a rapport and that I could look on this man with forgiveness and pity. He gave me his phone number, and I meant to look him up, but he died soon after that.

Some of the nuns who taught us were friendly, but the eighth-grade nun, who was also the principal, was a tyrant. She kept telling us how awful we were and how she had applied to be a missionary in Bolivia. We were happy and applauded when she got her wish, but by then it was the end of the year. All day long kids from other classes would come in with notes for the principal, and the highlight of that year was when a third-grader came in with a note from his teacher about how he needed to go home sick. When the poor kid couldn't get his words out ("Sister... Sister..."), she screamed at him, and he vomited all over her. Hilarity ensued.

And I had a psychotic nun in third grade, whom I call Sister Magdalena in *The Broken Places.* She inexplicably tormented me all year. At one point she locked me in a closet with the other students pushing at the door to keep me from escaping. That experience stays viscerally with me as the epitome of my upbringing, a metaphor for why I remain a loner and feel alienated from groups of all kinds and from group beliefs. Part of me is still inside that closet trying to get out. What was worse than that episode, however, was that the nun gave every girl in the class a wooden ruler and told them to hit me over the head whenever I misbehaved. So I was beaten every day that fall semester by most of the girls and couldn't fight back.

I have an aversion to people in groups; Woody Allen said he was once beaten up by a group of Quakers.

When one of the nice girls in my third-grade class, Susan Jones, who had become a teacher at St. Bernard's, met me many years later at the school reunion, she said, "I'm so glad you don't have brain damage." I asked what she meant, and she thought I would have been permanently impaired from the constant blows to my head in third grade. Still worse, in a way, was that for the entire second semester, the nun had me move my desk up next to hers facing the board with my back to my fellow students, a psychological punishment I have never overcome.

No wonder in those years I had so much suppressed anger. Fortunately I survived some dangerous experimentation with my chemistry set and reckless episodes that now seem quasi-suicidal. I bought a two-seater bike at a police auction for five cents and spent a lot of time fixing it up; I was into mechanical tinkering in those days. But I would get a kick out of riding that bike while sitting on the back seat with no one in front, pedaling at high speeds down hills and around curves, sometimes with no hands. And once when I was walking along the wrong side of bridge railings over a river in the Wauwatosa village, a policeman directing traffic spotted me and marched straight over without a word, lifting me to safety. I had a charmed life in some ways, perhaps due to innocence, which helped me survive despite it all.

Toward the end of my spring semester in third grade, another of the nice girls in the class, Mary Sterle, burst into tears while being bathed by her mother and told her how the nun was abusing me and a girl in the class. The mothers began comparing notes, went to the pastor, and the nun was sent to a mental institution by the end of the year. It was a satisfying victory for me, but I paid a heavy price. I had some kind of a breakdown the following fall, but my kindly fourth-grade teacher, Mrs. Lucille Harris, kept me after class each day with the pretense of my practicing my penmanship, but in fact so she could keep company with me and watch over me.

"Solving a division problem by subtraction"

Didn't your parents have a sense of the problems you were encountering in third grade?

Until late in the semester when the mothers began sharing notes, my parents knew nothing of my battles of the will with the crazy nun. I was afraid to tell them anything for fear of further punishment, because I assumed they would think it was somehow my fault. But that March of 1956, sensing that I somehow was feeling disturbed, they sent me to a psychologist, Dr. M. Gertrude Reiman, who suggested I come to her home rather than her office to make me more comfortable. She was a plump gray-haired lady who reminded me of Captain Kangaroo. We had a good time together. Afterward she wrote insightfully to my parents,

> When your son Joseph was given a psychological examination on March 3, the results showed him to be a very bright boy, having a mental age approximately three years in advance of his chronological age. With rare exceptions he did equally well in the exercise of various kinds of mental functions, disclosing breadth of information, alertness to detail, excellent powers of analysis and conceptualization, ingenuity, resourcefulness, and imagination. He was challenged by the tasks presented, and when he succeeded in solving a division problem by subtraction furnished a dramatic example not only of adaptability, but of how much more efficient he could be with the appropriate technique.
>
> There were indications that Joe was, at least temporarily, a rather unhappy youngster. He did not understand people very well and was easily hurt; moreover, his natural sensitivity was currently heightened by the stage through which he was passing. He was trying to learn how to handle negative feelings in a more grown-up way and the effort made him anxious and overly conscientious. What he apparently needed was recognition and support with minimal emphasis on "bad" behavior because he could not at the moment tolerate much pressure and it would be inadvisable to allow his sense of guilt to become excessive. His potentialities for emotional maturity and adult accomplishment were admirable but he could hardly fulfill them without sympathetic assistance.

Did you figure out in your talks with the psychologist why you were targeted for so much bullying and abuse and at times accepted it?

Many years later I realized that there may be an explanation for some, though not all, of the social difficulties I went through as a kid and have continued to go through to some extent as an adult, including during my teaching career. I appear to have some of the characteristics of Asperger's Syndrome. Although I have not been diagnosed with that condition, being "on the spectrum" could account for some of the social difficulties I experienced while growing up, including my inability to "understand people very well." That realization has helped me understand the mysterious hostility I faced from some of my fellow students in grade school, the alienation I felt in my classes, and the abuse by mentally ill nuns who saw me as a rebellious enemy to be vanquished, even though I did not consciously set out to be adversarial. I've found throughout my life that I tend to provoke controversy whether I mean to or not; I'm a contrarian by nature and experience.

Writing biographies and other books, as well as many articles and interviews, and spending part of my life writing and helping produce films and television programs have been my attempts to better understand people and the often baffling world around me. And having some Asperger's traits is a positive asset for an author, especially of nonfiction books, such as biographies, since it fosters a meticulous form of self-discipline, organization, and attention to detail. Being totally on the spectrum might be a hindrance, causing an author to go overboard on detail in self-defeating ways, but being only partially on the scale is a valuable trait.

Before we get into other details about your youth, tell us about the climactic event, your breakdown.

My psychological and physical breakdown in January 1965, due to stress and overwork and my resulting anorexia, led to my institutionalization in a mental hospital. That was the turning point in my life. My collapse occurred on the last Sunday of the first semester of my senior year in high school, the day before I was to take my final exams, and the Harvard alumnus who was interviewing me at his home while I was in the process of falling apart must have found me quite inexplicably strange. Paradoxically enough, my breakdown was the best thing that ever happened to me. It got me out of the house, it got me out of school, it helped lead to my break with the Catholic Church, it kept me out of Vietnam, and it enabled me to finally meet a girl and fall in love.

After my eye operation to correct a muscle pull in my left eye, I wore a patch, so my parents put a patch on my teddy bear and gave me the doctor's kit I'm using in July 1952, when I was almost five. It's ironic that with my bad eyes, I became a film critic and historian.

Although I was terminally bored and alienated in class throughout my grade school years, I went to a scholastically excellent Jesuit high school, where I enjoyed the company of my fellow students, admired most of my teachers, and was successful both in classes and as the editor of our school newsmagazine, *The Flambeau Monthly*. However, I was secretly tormented by conflict over my developing sexuality. And the excessive discipline at Marquette didn't help; when we misbehaved in the halls or in class, we had our asses whipped by a priest with a sawed-off golf club, a punishment I suffered just once before taking pains to avoid it again.

Because of the sexual repression fostered by the church and my school, I compensated by overworking and suffered from acute anxiety and anorexia. I paid my way through Marquette, a tuition fee of $325 a year, which would be $3,241 in today's money, by working as a vendor at Milwaukee County Stadium for Braves and Packers games and a golf caddie during the summers. I was getting so tall and thin that at Blue Mound Country Club, my fellow caddies gave me the mocking nickname "U.N.," for "undernourished." My mother simply sat me down near the end of my last year in grade school and literally told me, "You're going to Marquette, and you're going to pay for it yourself." I certainly did pay for it in more ways than one, but after my breakdown my mother wept and said, "I just wanted you to go to the best school in town," so for that I am grateful.

My teachers at Marquette—let alone my parents—should have realized that I was headed for a breakdown while I was falling apart psychologically and physically. But in those days such signs of distress seemed invisible to adults. My brother Pat, who became a doctor, told me that before my breakdown, "You weren't sleeping." At first I didn't realize what he meant: I literally had not slept for days. My home life for the years before that was spent finding solitude amid the frenzied activity of a household of seven children. My youthful days were not only traumatic because I took my Catholic indoctrination far too seriously, they were also chaotic because of my parents' relentless drinking.

When *Time* magazine ran a feature on the rivalry between the *Journal* and the *Sentinel* in February 1965, it led with a paragraph on my parents. That single paragraph contained seven factual errors, including some downright fabrications, which I realized was standard practice with the magazine. That shattered my naive faith in *Time*, which I had been slavishly imitating with our *Flambeau Monthly*. Even though we won an award for the nation's best high school newsmagazine, we were misled by the influence of *Time*'s slick, breezy approach to journalism, covering the school with shallow boosterism. I found it painfully ironic that I was reading the fairy story about my parents in *Time*—which claimed, among other lies, that they "have been happily married for 19 years"—while I was on the locked ward of a mental hospital.

"Strong at the broken places"

Back in college, I would have been startled to read your unflinchingly candid memoir of your troubled youth, but you held back from publishing it for decades, until 2015. How hard was The Broken Places *to write and exorcise lingering demons from that time?*

The Broken Places took forty-nine years, off and on, and was the hardest of my books to write in a creative sense, as well as the one I had to write. I wrote it as a tribute to the rebellious but self-destructive young woman who liberated me from my repressed Catholic upbringing, Kathy Wolf (as I call her in the book). She saved my life after we met in the mental hospital and she brought me out of my profoundly withdrawn emotional shell. She was half Native American and half Irish, brilliant, sophisticated, sharp-tongued, rebellious, and lovely. But she was seriously disturbed—in the imprecise language of the Sixties, she was diagnosed as schizophrenic—and eventually killed herself by setting herself on fire in a downtown Milwaukee hotel.

My blacklisted writer friend John Sanford, after the death of his wife, screenwriter Marguerite Roberts, wrote only books about Maggie. When I asked why, John said, "Because I couldn't resurrect her, I write books about her." That's how I felt about Kathy. The title of my book is from a celebrated passage in Hemingway's *A Farewell to Arms*: "If people bring so much courage to this world the world has to kill them to break them, so of course it kills them. The world breaks every one and afterward many are strong at the broken places. But those that will not break it kills. It kills the very good and the very gentle and the very brave impartially. If you are none of these you can be sure it will kill you too but there will be no special hurry."

The long, painstaking writing of *The Broken Places* was a form of self-psychoanalysis that enabled me to learn how to cope with the events of my troubled youth. I made an abortive attempt to write it as a jocular manuscript in 1967 called *Holy Joe* but soon realized that tone was inadequate. So I wrote it as a screenplay in 1978 and then spent two years rewriting it as a novel before finally turning it into what it always needed to be, a memoir.

Those pivotal experiences in my youth have left their lasting mark. Because of the bullying and ostracization I faced in grade school, I have a hard time trusting people and tend to keep my friends at something of a distance. And intellectually I always want to be out of step with the mob and with whatever is fashionable, academically or otherwise. As Orson Welles put it, "I think an artist has always to be out of step with his time. He has to be." That tendency as a film scholar, historian, and teacher, has made me rebel against orthodoxy and stake out often unpopular or idiosyncratic positions. That's been helpful in making me original and often ahead of my time.

I didn't talk much about those experiences after I went to Madison, Danny, because I found that people didn't want to hear about them, and that made me feel, if not ashamed, awkward about telling people. Mental illness was less openly talked about in those days. But the long process of writing the memoir eventually helped me get over the feeling of social shame. I am proud that I was able to survive those experiences and not let them ruin my life. During the long process of writing *The Broken Places*, I was buoyed by Tennessee Williams's observation that a writer should never feel embarrassed. Our greatest playwright triumphed over people who maligned him for his bravery in confronting his demons and the flaws in human nature. And the painful process of writing *The Broken Places* finally enabled me to do what Eugene O'Neill said we must do: forgive our parents.

How did you feel in the months after leaving the hospital?

After I left the hospital in May 1965 following four months of treatment, the doctors continued me on Thorazine, a powerful medication for schizophrenia and bipolar disorder that made me groggy and fuzzy. Unconscionably, they kept me on Thorazine when I started my freshman year. Since I couldn't study while taking it, I made a half-hearted suicidal cry for help in the middle of the first semester and was put into the University Hospitals psych ward for two months. I had a good time socializing there and was taken off that drastic medication; it was like lifting a veil so I could see the world clearly. The experience made me vehemently anti-drugs, since I knew how awful it is to be an addict. Taking drugs was seen as a mark of hipness in those days, and my avoidance of drugs made me unpopular in some circles both in Madison and later in Hollywood, but I could see the disastrous results all around me.

At Marquette University High School in Milwaukee, I found camaraderie as well as a first-rate Jesuit education. I was editor of *The Flambeau Monthly* newsmagazine, and for a yearbook photo, we hauled a desk out onto the Wisconsin Avenue median across from the school. Among my staffers and pals in the photo are Tim Marcou, Dan Melton, Tony Machi, and Jim (Luigi) Schmitt.
(MUHS *Flambeau* yearbook)

"A challenge from day 1"

Didn't it take years before you even tried to comprehend the stresses you felt having grown up in an alcoholic household?

Soon after I met Ruth, she asked if I had memories of physical abuse at home during my childhood. I recalled one early incident when my mother became irate and pushed my head into the wall, shattering a glass picture frame; Ruth felt I must have repressed other incidents of that kind. The bad memories I have from those days are more psychological than physical. In her notes about my early years, my mother recalled a time when I was about two years old and soothed her when she was depressed and lying in bed. That was a telling reversal of roles and an indication of how her depression, compounded by drinking, marked me from childhood. Children of alcoholics often find themselves becoming the parental figures at home. And it's typical of dysfunctional families to have one member eventually crack up as the scapegoat for the entire family's pathology.

The worst day of my life

I imagine that your breakdown was the worst day of your youth, maybe your life.

No, the worst day of my life came the month following my childhood meeting with the psychologist. Sunday, April 8, 1956, was the day of my First Communion. I was in a psychological vise, because I had been taught two conflicting things: (1) receiving Communion in a state of mortal sin condemns you to Hell; and (2) everyone is a constant sinner. So before we made our first confession a couple of weeks before our First Communion, Sister Magdalena made us swear "to sin no more and avoid the near occasions of sin." I knew that was a lie. But I felt powerless not to take that oath. So I believed I was receiving Communion in a state of sin that would condemn me to Hell. I literally believed what I was taught about the eternal suffering of souls roasting in Hell and saw no way out of that agonizing conundrum. So I was sick after church during our family celebration of my First Communion and had to go to bed while the rest of us were partying, not knowing what was wrong with me.

What an evil thing it is to teach a child he will burn in hellfire for all eternity if he commits a mortal sin. I had to cleanse my soul by confessing, but confession was a ritual I had come to fear and dread. Many a night and day I meditated on this ghastly admonition until I could almost feel the agony of the flames. I finally forced myself to confess my sin a month later, which brought a measure of relief.

In high school we were visited by an insane Jesuit priest named Father Gene Jakubek, who at our winter retreat flicked open his cigarette lighter in the pulpit and held his finger in the flames. He pulled it out after a minute shaking it in pain, telling us that if he could only keep his finger in the flames that long, what must it be like to have your body immersed in flames for all eternity? It was the doctrine of Hell, above all, that finally drove me from the Church. I realized that I could not believe in a God who created human beings supposedly out of love and then punished them with eternal torture for disobeying the rules he laid down for them. I took heart from Voltaire's saying,

"If God exists, how I hate him."

From 1955 to 1957, I pounded out a family newspaper on my toy typewriter (which printed only in all caps) and pinned it each day to a bulletin board in the kitchen. Most of the paper was strained jollity, with a joke of the day and a cartoon supplementing the reports on family doings. But in going back through those issues of the *McBride Family News* for this book, I found an oblique reference to my torment over living in a state of sin after taking First Communion. A week after that event, below an illustrated report on the 91st anniversary of Lincoln's assassination, my newspaper reported, "JOE FORGETS AND EATS BEFORE COMMUNION ON SUNDAY, APRIL 15." Reading between the lines, it's obvious I did that intentionally to get out of taking Communion again, because we were taught not to receive the sacrament unless we had been fasting. That was my only way of avoiding the ritual without admitting the reason to anyone.

My family newspaper was determinedly bland and contained no direct references that would let on to my family the agony I was enduring. So too the high school newsmagazine I edited, *The Flambeau Monthly,* would be slick and professional-looking but toothless, subservient to the authority of the school, with a studious avoidance of controversy. Until I could escape the hold of the Church, my writing would continue to feel muzzled.

Addressing God

Even though you were such a staunch Catholic boy, did you really consider becoming a missionary priest?

Yes, indeed. While nearing my eighth-grade graduation, I practiced saying Mass at a makeshift altar in my bedroom. Despite, or perhaps because of, the abuse I suffered from the Church, I wanted to enter the priesthood. I served as an altar boy for three years at St. Bernard's and enjoyed the theatrical pageantry of the Mass, including the Latin responses I memorized as part of the ritual, which like most of the liturgy gave me a feeling of incantatory self-hypnosis.

When I was an altar boy, my partner was good at the motions and not with the Latin words, and I was good with the words but clumsy with the motions. So our act together was rather comical. Latin became a favorite subject of mine for all four years of high school. Father Charles Shinners, the smartest priest who taught there, told me I was the only student he ever had who did not have to mentally translate Latin into English and vice versa but could think directly in Latin. We translated Cicero's most famous oration against Catiline and Julius Caesar's *Gallic Wars* in freshman year, Virgil's *Aeneid* in sophomore year, poetry (mostly Horace and Catullus) in junior year, and I forget what in my distracted senior year. Latin helped me immeasurably with my writing of English, which became Latinate in its rhythms and sentence structure. I enjoy writing long sentences with a complex structure, but now when I edit my work, I often break them into shorter sentences.

I did not like the changes Vatican II brought to the Church liturgy in the early 1960s, including masses in English. James Joyce said you have to have a different language for addressing God from the language you use when buying potatoes. And when Vatican II loosened some of the rules about sin and hellfire, I felt betrayed. Other Catholics may not have been fazed by that, but my Asperger's tendencies and the degree of my adherence to what I thought were inflexible rules shook me up. Now that masturbating or eating a hot dog on Friday were no longer punished by being sent to Hell, that exposed the ludicrousness of such rules but also cast a giant question mark over the whole structure of my faith in Catholicism.

I found the reaction of Ruth's grandmother, Sheila Smyth Harris, instructive. I never had the honor of meeting Mrs. Harris, who joined the old Irish Republican Army in 1919 after her brother Patrick, on his way home from serving Mass, was shot in the back by the Black and Tans. Mrs. Harris was jailed for nine months by the British during the civil war that followed the signing of the Anglo-Irish Treaty. When she died in 1983, she received a state funeral with full military honors. But she was so incensed in her old age about the rules of the Church being changed that she refused to see a priest on her deathbed. She and I would have had a lot to talk about.

"The last place on Earth"

I begged my parents to let me enter a seminary instead of a regular high school. Now I see that it was my panic over my approaching puberty that intensified my desire to escape into holy orders. I went so far as to invite a Maryknoll missionary priest to our house in 1961 to give my parents a pep talk on why I should join that order and become a missionary to what we then called Red China. If I had gone down that road, I probably would have been executed in the Cultural Revolution. That's one reason I thought our campus Maoists in Madison were idiots.

My misguided ambition to preach the faith in China helps explain my subsequent devotion to John Ford's great final feature film, *7 Women*. That 1966 film sharply criticizes the condescending, hypocritical American proselytizing of China—one of the missionaries calls it "the last place on Earth"—while counterpointing it with the paradoxically Christian actions of an atheist doctor who joins their insular community. When my parents said no to my ecclesiastical ambition, they told me that if I still wanted to be a priest after I dated girls, they would approve. Naturally, as soon as I met a girl, I stopped wanting to become a priest.

Thinking back, did you become a lapsed Catholic or shun religion entirely because of your school history? And how did that factor into your film criticism and other writing?

I had the damaging habit in childhood of taking Catholic Church teachings literally, which was drilled into me in school and at church. In later years, many so-called "cafeteria Catholics" came to feel they could pick and choose among the doctrines, but I was taught you had to accept everything or not at all. Eventually, with great difficulty, I decided "Not at all." It took a long time to shake free of the baleful influence of the Church. In my case it may also have been a symptom of Asperger's, which tends to make people literal-minded.

My first partial break with the Church came, fittingly, because I was getting passionate about movies. I was back home from college in my freshman year in the fall of 1965 and attending Sunday Mass with my father. That was the annual day when we had to take the pledge not to attend movies condemned by the Legion of Decency, which still had considerable power in those days. I remained seated as a protest, and my father berated me for doing so. It wasn't until I was nineteen in 1967 that I finally made a clean break from the Church, walking out in the midst of a sermon at the campus church in Madison.

In my college movie-going days, because of my backlash against those religious experiences, I was greatly attracted to the blasphemous yet ironically religiously obsessed films of Luis Buñuel, who also had a Jesuit education. But eventually my interest in Buñuel waned as my religious trauma receded into the rearview mirror. Lately I've rekindled my watching of his work for other reasons, finding his Mexican work most appealing for its funky, sardonic humanism, but I am more fascinated now by what Paul Schrader calls the "transcendental style" of Ozu, Bresson, and Dreyer, particularly with my latter-day predilection for aesthetic minimalism. And it took me quite a while before I could

The North Division of the Milwaukee County Hospital medical complex, where I spent most of four months after my physical and psychological breakdown in January 1965. This was the more relaxed part of the complex where I came to know my first girlfriend, Kathy Wolf. My brother Tim took this photo while I was on a return visit to research my screenplay and book *The Broken Places*.
(Timothy McBride)

understand why my favorite Ingmar Bergman film is *Winter Light*—aka *The Communicants*—which I first saw in college. I eventually realized that I identified with the dilemma of the Lutheran pastor played by Gunnar Björnstrand, who feels obligated to continue conducting services even after losing his belief in God.

No doubt my Catholic background also helps explain my intense fascination throughout my life with the films of Alfred Hitchcock, another student of the Jesuits. I share with Hitchcock a Jesuitical passion for order as well as a subversive obsession with guilt and perverse sexuality. While reporting for *Daily Variety*, I interviewed Hitchcock and watched him shoot his last film, *Family Plot*, for three days. I also wrote the last thing Hitchcock ever did in show business, his taped introduction to our American Film Institute tribute to James Stewart in 1980, shortly before Hitchcock died.

Hitchcock, John Ford, and Frank Capra, whose work and lives I've been studying for many years, are Catholic artists. But I've also written several books about Jewish filmmakers—Steven Spielberg, Ernst Lubitsch, Billy Wilder, the Coen Bros., George Cukor—and have always been drawn to the searching intellectual nature of Reform Judaism, a healthy contrast to the rigid indoctrination of the Catholic Church. I read widely about Judaism while researching the Spielberg biography and interviewed thirty-five Holocaust survivors to learn how they responded to *Schindler's List.*

I've sometimes wished I could have been a rabbi, if only I were Jewish and still believed in God. But "rabbi" means teacher, and I've devoted decades to teaching while living my life in quasi-rabbinical devotion to scholarship. After I lost my faith in the Catholic Church, movies became my substitute for religion. But after I lost my faith in movies…

In terms of religious indoctrination, how did you find Marquette High—another Catholic school—in comparison with St. Bernard's?

High school was a relief in many ways. There was no bullying from the other boys, and I found genuine camaraderie due to the school's respect for academic excellence. I had mostly superb teachers, especially in my favorite subjects, Latin, English, Religion, and Chemistry. In a stately old brick building at 34th Street and Wisconsin Avenue, we were divided into seven classes, ranked by achievement, and I was in the top class except when I dropped down to second for my sophomore year. I was amazed by how much more intense the top class was. And I gained valuable experience as a journalist by editing *The Flambeau Monthly* under the wise tutelage of Mr. Thomas L. Book, S.J., a scholastic—i.e., a priest in training—who encouraged my ambitions (Tom Book later left the order to teach in public high schools and to marry).

The best lesson I ever learned in the art of criticism came in sophomore English. Another Jesuit scholastic, Robert H. Fitzgerald, assigned us to write a book report on *Beau Geste,* P. C. Wren's 1924 adventure novel about the French Foreign Legion in North Africa. Assuming that since the teacher assigned it, the book must be great, I wrote a report filled with over-the-top gushing. To my surprise, Mr. Fitzgerald ridiculed the students who fell for his stunt of assigning what he considered a trashy novel to see how they would react. That taught me to think for myself and make up my own mind about what I read rather than falling in line with authority.

When Father Fitzgerald, S.J., died in 2016, the Jesuits wrote, "Bob had the soul and sensibilities of a poet. He loved to tell stories and to hear the stories of others, especially stories connected to families. The complexities of the human person fascinated him. He loved to write, both for his own enjoyment and for others." But Mr. Fitzgerald's methods probably wouldn't fly in today's timid academic climate, as I found when I cited this story to my chair in the San Francisco State School of Cinema in my last year of teaching. I brought it up when he told me that some students accused me of "making them feel stupid." Even after I recalled the valuable lesson I learned from Mr. Fitzgerald, my chair took the side of the complaining students who preferred being coddled to learning to think with Jesuitical rigor. More's the pity. (Revisiting *Beau Geste* all these years later shows me I was not entirely wrong in considering it a rousing read, but I probably raved ridiculously about the quality of its florid prose.)

Even our Religion classes at Marquette, with their doctrinaire underpinnings, were intelligent, especially the fourth-year course called "Heresies," which in fact was a Comparative Religion class. The Jesuits believe that to defend your faith, you have to know how to debate people who don't agree with you. I found that method stimulating and have followed it in my discussions and writing about contentious subjects. And learning about other religions ironically had the effect of hastening my questioning of Catholicism, since it made me reflect that those other religions often sounded more reasonable. It helped that Father Shinners taught that course, since he was such a brilliant and sharply witty thinker.

But on the day President Kennedy was killed in my junior year, the scheduled topic for our Religion class was "The Ethics of Murder." When I heard the news while in our cafeteria line that Kennedy had just been shot, I ran to a nearby drugstore to listen to the early reports on network radio. The Religion class began at 1:30 PM Central Standard Time, and Kennedy's death was announced by the principal on the loudspeaker ten minutes later. We stood in prayer and were left to our own thoughts. Father Shinners must have been in a state of shock, for our discussion of the ethics of murder continued with no mention of what had just happened. It was a surreal experience that lacked a sense of the history we were living through that day.

Our school tended to be weak on History, which would become my favorite subject in adult life; you could tell what Marquette thought of American history, since it was left to the football coach, who simply read from his textbook. In Catholic schools in those days the basic history lesson was not much more advanced than "Communists are godless." So our knowledge of contemporary politics was inadequate as well. My memory of the Cuban Missile Crisis in 1962, oddly enough, is not being terrified of nuclear annihilation but being bothered that President Kennedy had lied to me. Our family was driving to the Milwaukee airport on the morning of October 20 to see the president speak when the radio said he had to return from Chicago to Washington because he had a cold. That's what the French call a *cold diplomatique.* It turned out that Kennedy had to rush back because the Missile Crisis was approaching its climax.

I was always bothered by people lying and still am, with good reason since I grew up in such a mendacious atmosphere; one of my major concerns as a writer is exposing lies, such as in my biography of Frank Capra, a riposte to his thoroughly dishonest autobiography. But in my immature reaction to the Missile Crisis, that preoccupation skewed my sense of proportion. It also helps explain why it took me so long to understand the Cold War itself and the Vietnam War.

We had no Biology class at Marquette, since the Church didn't want us to learn about the human body. I would have to find out about that subject by exploring on my own. On the other hand, I had a superb Chemistry teacher, a legendary veteran named Louis LeMieux, whose lessons have always stuck with me. You never know how your lessons will come in handy, for Mr. LeMieux's class prepared me well to understand what Capra was doing when he studied chemistry in college and wrote his thesis on high explosives.

I also had a good time doing cartoons for our Poster Club, influenced especially by *MAD* magazine, but was kicked out for causing controversy with a couple of posters that were considered in dubious taste. One that brought down the wrath of the school administration featured Miss Beazly, the ghastly cafeteria lady in the *Archie* comics, ladling soup out of a garbage can with flies hovering around it. The drawing had the motto, "Eat at the Cafeteria." I still think it was funny. That kind of irreverent humor suffuses one of my favorite parts of *Rock 'n' Roll High School,* the 1979 punk rock musical I helped write: When the kids trash the school, they tie up the cafeteria ladies and pelt them with their awful food ("No—*not* the Tuesday Surprise!").

Our cafeteria food was so unpalatable that I would sneak out of school every day to eat a burger and fries at a nearby diner, a dubious diet that eventually contributed to my anorexia. A lot of special feeding and vitamins at the hospital were necessary for me to start recovering physically, but in a picture I have showing me in my cap and gown outside my house on graduation day, I still look like a scarecrow.

How do you feel about Marquette High in retrospect, considering you had your breakdown when you were there?

After my four months of hospitalization following my collapse in the middle of my senior year, I returned to Marquette to say my goodbyes on the day before graduation in May 1965. I also attended the ceremony where they gave me my diploma even though I had missed the second semester; I was ranked sixteenth in the class of 234. I remain fond of my time at Marquette, which gave me an education far superior to what I took away in classes at the University of Wisconsin. I learned to write thirty-page papers as a matter of course at Marquette, which in today's academic world would be considered a master's thesis. I had some great teachers who inspired me and fostered independent thinking and Jesuitical intellectual rigor. But I qualify my praise of my high school with full recognition of its damaging aspects that took such a grave toll on my health—the overly intense intellectual competition fostered by Marquette, the crushing load of homework (four hours a night), and above all the debilitating emphasis on sin and punishment.

My fierce drive to overcompensate for my social and sexual anxieties by studying too much intensified after the shock of the assassination of President Kennedy in November 1963. My sense of profound disillusionment with our political system made me depressed, and I recall having the vague sense that I needed to bear down more seriously in school, perhaps to help block out those disruptive feelings. With the college application process looming, it was no coincidence that the goal I set for myself was being accepted by JFK's alma mater, Harvard. (I also applied to Columbia, Yale, and Northwestern, and the University of Wisconsin, Madison; I was accepted by Columbia as well as the UW.) The most damaging pressure I imposed on myself was taking the College Board tests repeatedly to try to achieve perfection. I managed a 774 score on the Scholastic Aptitude Test English exam and 721 in Math, as well as a perfect 800 on the English achievement exam. As my repeated test-taking indicates, I suffered from perfectionism, a drive no doubt linked to my Catholic anxieties over failing to live up to ideals of conduct. Now I took solace from a more sensible comment Joseph P. Kennedy Sr. made to his children: "Do your best and then to hell with it."

Marquette also promoted the Church's crippling emphasis on sexual sin and guilt. Much of that stress came from the school disciplinarian, Father Jerome Boyle, the grinning sadist who carried out his punishment by whipping us for infractions in the hallways or wherever else priests would find something to mark on our demerit cards. Since he was the sickest member of the faculty, Father Boyle naturally also wrote our guidebook on sexuality, *Instructions on Dating for High School Boys*, sometimes known by the more provocative title of an earlier version, *Modern Youth and Chastity*. Although it had some modern touches, such as noting that "Controlling sex" is "like controlling an atomic bomb," that booklet was medieval in its attitudes, preaching what it called "The *FEAR* Rule" about kissing. According to Father Boyle, kissing became mortally sinful if it was *Frequent, Enduring,* and *Ardent (FEAR)*. That sexual brainwashing exacerbated my anxieties as I went through puberty and tottered into early manhood.

Because ours was an all-boys' school, we invited girls from the two Catholic girls' high schools to come to our dances. I had been taught to dance in eighth grade by the mother of one of the boys; she kindly instructed us in basic ballroom dancing. But when I entered Marquette, I was only five-feet-two and self-conscious about looking so immature. I didn't have a growth spurt until the summer of my sophomore year, when I came back as one of the tallest guys in the class. So I felt shy and awkward around girls in my freshman year and hardly knew how to behave. I went to a dance at Marquette that fall, but when I asked a girl to dance and she accepted, she soon started looking around and suddenly said, "I see my friend, I gotta go," leaving me standing there. I was so mortified that I walked out, took a bus home, and never went to another dance. Later I read that when a woman asked Ernest Hemingway if he enjoyed dancing, he said, "Well, it's better than writing."

The nuns had spurred what became my obsessive interest in pornography in fourth grade, in 1957, by forbidding us to look at skin magazines at a nearby drugstore, so of course I did. In my high school years, I felt guilty about obsessively leafing through *Playboy* and airbrushed nudist magazines at magazine stores after school and going to European "art" movies with tantalizingly brief flashes of nudity at the Princess Theater downtown. One highlight of those sweaty, furtive experiences was a glimpse of Jeanne Moreau's naked backside as she got out of bed and went to the bathroom. There was also the occasional Russ Meyer nudie film, but always with almost all of the nudity tantalizingly cut out. Endless frustration and horniness and guilt—quite a combination. On Saturdays I would take long bus rides to steal a copy of *Playboy* at a drugstore and sneak back home with it.

If you were like me, you couldn't have been "reading" only Playboy.

Yup. But the lists I kept then of books I read show that I was pushing myself with my extracurricular reading as maniacally hard as I was in my classes (I was so obsessive that my lists even included the page counts of the books, which I totaled up to keep track of my accomplishments). My range of reading was creative and eclectic, however, and oriented toward my planned future as a novelist and playwright. The list included many plays, books of poetry, classic novels, some contemporary novels, books on Catholicism, and books on ancient Greece. (I read Edith Hamilton's *The Greek Way* in the summer of 1964, the same time as Robert Kennedy was reading it at the suggestion of Jacqueline Kennedy to try to understand his brother's murder.) Call me scattershot or omnivorous, but I was gobbling up everything, not knowing what would stick and desiring a wide range of cultural influences. But a few patterns can be discerned.

As a kid, I read mostly books on baseball. But after I entered high school, I consciously emulated Ernest Hemingway and while at Marquette and in my college years, I read many of his books as well as literary studies and biographies; I read *A Moveable Feast* twice and wrote a screenplay adaptation of it in 1966. Other novels I read in my last couple of years of high school included *The Scarlet Letter* (which I read in a graveyard), *Lost Horizon*, *Mr. Blue*, *The Loved One* (a book I was reading around the time President Kennedy was shot), *Adventures of Huckleberry Finn*, *The Great Gatsby*, *Tom Jones*, *Gulliver's Travels*, *Nineteen Eighty-Four*, and *Lord Jim*. I read *The Iliad* and *The Odyssey*, James Baldwin's *Nobody Knows My Name*, Sherlock Holmes stories and others by Salinger, Hawthorne, and Poe, and dabbled in biography, reading Plutarch's *Lives*, Sandburg's *Abraham Lincoln*, and Boswell's *Life of Johnson* in an abridged version.

When I was put in the hospital in January 1965, I was reading *Pride and Prejudice* frantically in an attempt to prove to myself that I was still *compos mentis* but could make no sense of it because I was so befuddled with medication. That traumatic experience unfortunately put me off Jane Austen for good; I keep staring at a copy of that novel I keep around the house but find it too troubling to go back to her. On the other hand, after reading *The Catcher in the Rye* five times in my formative years, I found that when I went back to it in later life while writing *The Broken Places,* I had trouble reading the Salinger book because I virtually have it memorized. In the summer of 1965, though still sedated, I blitzed through such books as *Paradise Lost* and *Paradise Regained*; *The Grapes of Wrath*; *A Portrait of the Artist as a Young Man*; Dante's *Purgatorio*; *Winesburg, Ohio*; *Moby-Dick*; and *Jane Eyre.* I increased my reading of Shakespeare and the Greeks and some modern plays such as *Becket, Look Back in Anger,* and T. S. Eliot's *Murder in the Cathedral* twice. I admired Eliot's verse and read his essays of literary criticism, a major influence on my development before and after my interest turned to films.

One nonfiction book that has had a great influence on me, oddly enough, is Richard Nixon's 1962 memoir, *Six Crises,* which I first read as a teenager. Although my political views are mostly antithetical to Nixon's, I admire the way he saw his life, somewhat melodramatically, as a series of crises. I have looked at my life the same way. I always tend to prevail by sheer force of will and endurance, my legacies from the masochism of my Catholic indoctrination. Conquering the third-grade nun was the first of the crises in which I prevailed, and I've now passed Nixon in counting a total of seven crises—so far.

Salvation by Television

Other than reading—and I know that you, as did I, played the APBA dice baseball game, which we'll soon talk about— how did you try to keep yourself sane at home throughout your childhood?

Mostly by watching television. So I have never been one to disparage that medium, as it's fashionable to do. I trace my absorption in show business to that childhood need for diversion and gratification thanks to TV and, a bit later, by movies.

We were early to get a TV set, in 1951, because of my father's duties as the Screen-Radio-Television editor and reviewer of the *Journal*; he interviewed stars who came to town, from Cary Grant to Mae West and Marilyn Monroe. Since sets were expensive then, TV appealed more to the intelligentsia than it did even two years later, when the prices came down. By 1953 most homes could afford a TV, so the programming was dumbed-down in a way I could not help noticing at age six. As a kid I was nurtured on *Omnibus*, the innovative Sunday afternoon arts program that introduced me to a wide range of culture in an entertaining way.

From early on, I loved the many intelligent talk shows, enjoying the interviews with authors and political figures that were common on TV in the 1950s. I watched *Meet the Press* with my mother and got a kick out of Mike Wallace's evening interview program with his hardboiled style of grilling his subjects while they were sweating and wreathed in cigarette smoke. Those shows taught me how to interview people, even if I had to learn to be a bit more subtle and less confrontational than Wallace. I also was devoted to live TV drama in what we now call the Golden Age of TV.

Of course, I also doted on kids' shows, from *Ding-Dong School* with Miss Frances, a matronly mother substitute like Kate Smith, the singer whose variety show I watched; *Kukla, Fran and Ollie*, a clever puppet show, and *Howdy Doody*; *Andy's Gang*, with Andy Devine showing jungle serials and bantering in his croaking voice with the evil-minded Froggy the Gremlin; the smartly satirical *Leave It to Beaver*; and most of all *The Mickey Mouse Club*. I was passionate about that lively variety show from its beginning in 1955 and had crushes successively on three Mouseketeers, Karen, Darlene, and Annette, while moving up the scale of puberty; when I wrote my biography of Steven Spielberg, I was tickled to find he had crushes on those same girls, though not in the same order. My sister, Genevieve, said that book was virtually my autobiography, since Spielberg and I had many parallel cultural experiences and bullied our sisters, even though I actually remember getting along well with mine, who was my ally against the craziness at home.

I seem to have watched practically everything on TV while growing up, from the groundbreaking sitcom *The Goldbergs* to *The Many Loves of Dobie Gillis* (I identified not with the bland title character but with the brainy Zelda and the beatnik Maynard) and the spy saga *I Led 3 Lives*, with the odd exception of the ubiquitous "adult" Western series aired in that craze of the late 1950s and early '60s. Although I had liked some TV Westerns as a kid, I mostly shunned those entries as I grew older because I was a fan of theatrical Westerns, preferring their spectacular landscapes to the backlot look of TV Westerns. But I made an exception for *Have Gun—Will Travel*, starring Richard Boone as Paladin, a sophisticated hired gun who lived the good life in a fancy San Francisco hotel and tried to use his gun as little as possible while solving disputes; Ida Lupino directed some of those well-written shows. And I thrived on the haunting

Television kept me sane in my childhood.
I watched almost everything.

Twilight Zone series—anything to do with time travel has always enthralled me, because I want to escape the mundane world—and the droll introductions by Alfred Hitchcock to his anthology series, though I usually skipped the stories.

And like most other TV viewers in the Fifties and early Sixties, I was also a fan of comedy shows, from Milton Berle and Martin & Lewis to *Your Show of Shows* and Steve Allen and Ernie Kovacs. But my favorite show was the wonderfully written—mostly by creator-producer Nat Hiken, a former Milwaukeean—and hilariously acted *Sergeant Bilko* series, originally titled *You'll Never Get Rich.* My Dad said the scams pulled by Phil Silvers's conniving Sergeant Bilko and the rest of that TV show's army barracks atmosphere were exactly like his service as a master sergeant in World War II.

At age nine, I made my first appearance on TV on March 9, 1957, on a Milwaukee "bookworm show" for children called *Billy's Quiz.* I won the spot on the WXIX program by entering a drawing in a contest. They awarded me *A Child's Book of the Theatre* by William M. Hutchinson, which unfortunately didn't make enough impression on me to seriously whet my interest in the subject at the time. But I remember that during a discussion about books with the

Under the influence of TV's Hopalong Cassidy and Western movies
and our family pioneering tradition, I liked to play cowboy in the
1950s, as did many other kids in my generation. No wonder Westerns
are my favorite genre.

host and some other kids, the host was tickled when I used
the word "culprit" in reference to a crime story.

Dancing Waters

*Did that spark any interest in you to pursue a career in show
business?*

My first job in show business was not encouraging. In the
summer of 1961, when I was thirteen, my Dad was covering

the Wisconsin State Fair for the *Journal* and found me a job with a tacky sideshow called *Dancing Waters*. This show took place in a tent and involved water being sprayed rhythmically from pipes with colored lights playing on it to musical accompaniment. The real appeal of this goofy spectacle, I suppose, was to fairgoers who wanted to escape the heat for a few minutes and cool off a bit. I was assigned to go around between shows and pick up trash that the patrons threw onto the gravel. This was a messy job, since most of the trash was sticky stuff—gum, cotton candy, Cracker Jacks, and so forth.

I did this miserable job all day long for two weeks, because I was promised minimum-wage pay at the end. But on the Sunday evening when the fair closed, and the *Dancing Waters* tent was being struck, I asked the boss for my money, and he denied I had ever been promised payment. Fortunately my Dad was still working in the press building, so he rushed over and browbeat the crook into paying me. It's fitting that in my first job in show business, I was almost cheated out of the money I was due and had to beg for it. I should have learned the lesson then and there and gotten out when the getting was good. Much the same pattern of behavior followed me throughout my years as a screenwriter. Almost every time I had a job in Hollywood, I had to go begging for the payment I had been promised. They love to make writers grovel. But at least it's a step up from groveling in the gravel.

The Rosebud Cinema

What was your introduction to movies? Was it love at first sight?

Since our black-and-white TV dominated our living room, provided communal family viewing, and helped drown out my parents' bickering, it was soothing psychologically and therefore more valuable to me than going to the movies in those years. But movies were also a welcome form of escape. The first movie I saw, though, I didn't like. My mother took me downtown to see Walt Disney's *Fantasia* in 1949, when I was two. I remember riding in a trolley car, sitting on a wicker seat, over the rickety bridge that traveled over the valley of the Miller Brewing Company grounds. That was near where I later went to high school; we would get mildly intoxicated by the smell of hops at school once the windows were opened half an hour before the end of classes. The year I saw my first movie also was the year of my earliest memory—an image of a *Batman* comic book on a highly polished wooden table shiny with a slash of late-afternoon sunlight in the home of affluent friends we were visiting on Milwaukee's East Side.

As a youngster, I would use my father's *Milwaukee Journal* passes for the big downtown first-run theaters and take the bus on Saturdays to see serious films such as *The Diary of Anne Frank* and *Compulsion,* as well as William Castle's gimmicky horror movies. My Uncle Jack, who worked for the *Wall Street Journal*, took me to see *Judgment at Nuremberg* when I visited him in Chicago. For my twelfth birthday, I took my friends to our neighborhood theater, the Tosa, to see one of Frank Capra's sadly botched later movies, *A Hole in the Head.* I liked Eddie Hodges, though, and identified with him when he raved about Marilyn Monroe, but my friends mostly spent their time throwing candy and popcorn. In my youth I would go to the Tosa at night to see some great movies, such as *Imitation of Life, Lawrence of Arabia*, and *Dr. Strangelove*, as well as Roger Corman's Edgar Allan Poe movies and social-issue movies such as *On the Beach* and *Inherit the Wind.* (The Tosa Theater now is more felicitously called the Rosebud Cinema Drafthouse.)

The first movie I was impressed enough by to see twice in a theater, in 1957, was *The Spirit of St. Louis*, the most anomalous movie by another director I would write a book about, Billy Wilder. As a ten-year-old I was captivated by Charles Lindbergh's flight but knew nothing of his Nazi sympathies. The movie that resonated most strongly in my boyhood, though, was *Rio Bravo.* I saw it when it came out in 1959 when I was about twelve. I told Howard Hawks while doing my interview book *Hawks on Hawks* that "the only reason I went to see it was because Ricky Nelson was in it. At that time I didn't know who you were." Hawks joked, "I didn't know you appreciated music so much." *Rio Bravo*, moreover, was the first time I saw a film that connected directly with what I was experiencing in my personal life. I found Dean Martin's portrayal of an alcoholic startlingly accurate to what I was seeing every night at home, and I was overwhelmed by the moment when he pours a glass of whiskey back into the bottle ("Didn't spill a drop"). Then I could see what movies could do for me.

This emotional moment when Dean Martin begins to kick the
drinking habit in Howard Hawks's 1959 Western, *Rio Bravo*, startled
me because I was seeing his problem every day at home. This is the
first time a movie resonated with my personal life.
(Armada Prods./Warner Bros./Frame enlargement)

Rio Bravo *is a great film and the lead was John Wayne, now
your favorite actor, but I'm surprised you didn't say a John
Ford-John Wayne Western impacted you most.*

I was also a Wayne fan as a kid, Danny, but somehow
missed *The Searchers* until the late 1960s after your brother
Gerry urged me to see it, and Mike Wilmington and I
took a Greyhound bus to watch an original 35mm print
at the Clark Theater in the Chicago Loop, another of my
formative moviegoing experiences. The only John Ford
film I saw during its first run in theaters was *The Man Who
Shot Liberty Valance* in 1962 — a good introduction to the
director who became my favorite filmmaker, a subject of
endless study and influence, though I didn't become excited
by his work until my Madison days. I missed *Cheyenne
Autumn* because I wasn't going to movies by the fall of
1964. During my later years in high school, I was too busy
studying to go to movies or even watch TV shows.

Since I was a little guy in my childhood and constantly
getting beaten up by my classmates, I developed a strong
and enduring identification with underdogs of all kinds,
and I began to wonder naively why the Indians were always
getting beaten in Westerns. I started longing to see one in
which they won for a change. I used to watch a Western every
day at 4 PM on a local TV program called *Foreman Tom's
Jamboree*. One day, to my great excitement, Foreman Tom
showed a Western with the Indians winning in the end. There
weren't many films of that kind in those days, so it might
have been Ford's *Fort Apache*. His revisionist 1948 Cavalry

film with Henry Fonda and John Wayne is a fictionalized takeoff debunking the "heroic" legend of General George Armstrong Custer. Ford had earlier tried a direct approach with a project about Custer called *Glory Hunter*, but the studios wouldn't go for it, so he took a subversive approach with Fonda as a racist Custer-like commander and Wayne, contrary to his clichéd image, playing the cavalry officer most sympathetic with the Native Americans.

When I saw *Fort Apache* on TV while home for the Christmas season on December 23, 1967, it set me off on my lifelong study of Ford and my mission to correct the record about his work. Not only do the Apaches beat the cavalry troop in *Fort Apache*, but they are the heroes of the film. *Fort Apache*, with its novelistic screenplay by Frank S. Nugent, influenced me more than any other film besides *Citizen Kane*, which first inspired me to study and make films. *Fort Apache* epitomizes for me what a historical film can be. Knowing that it was shooting in Monument Valley when I was born, I looked up the call sheets and found that at eleven in the morning of my birth, August 9, 1947, Ford was filming the climactic scene of Wayne throwing down his gauntlet in futility when Fonda orders his suicidal charge. Part of the tragedy is that Wayne's character fails to arrest or kill his commanding officer. (In Milwaukee on that day when I was born, the city had the first earthquake in its history. No wonder I have lifelong anxiety!)

Ford's OSS unit had filmed the Nuremberg Trials, in which the Allies executed Nazi leaders who had tried to defend themselves by arguing that they were "just following orders." So it is not coincidental that Ford sharply explores that theme with the U.S. cavalry in *Fort Apache*, a film that has been much misunderstood and inadequately recognized for its subversiveness. As Tag Gallagher puts it in his book on Ford, "Conservatives, meanwhile, were blind to Ford's ridicule and revisionism, and saw only celebrations of tradition; their interpretations reinforced progressive rejection of Ford. For example, *Fort Apache*: here is a picture glorifying the Indians and debunking myths of the 7th Cavalry; yet it is incessantly cited as a typical example of exactly the opposite and of everything wrong with John Ford." When I asked Ford about his cavalry films, he replied, "The cavalry weren't all-American boys, you know. They made a lot of mistakes. You just mentioned Custer, that was a pretty silly goddam expedition."

The first Ford film I had ever seen (on television) wasn't a Western but *The Last Hurrah*, his 1958 film based on the classic novel by Edwin O'Connor about the benign but wily mayor of a New England city resembling Boston. Mayor Frank Skeffington, played by Spencer Tracy, has a scene of splendidly controlled rage in which he recalls how his Irish immigrant mother was treated unjustly by her WASP employers. Telling the story to his nephew, a sportswriter played by the Kennedy-like young Jeffrey Hunter, Mayor Skeffington takes pride in how their people are now controlling the city as a way of getting back at the people who used to oppress them. When I saw *The Last Hurrah*, I was especially tickled that one of the characters, a priest played by Ken Curtis, says he went to Marquette University, my mother's alma mater. In early 1964, I learned from Pat O'Brien's autobiography that he and Spencer Tracy had gone to my high school when it was called Marquette Academy. I excitedly told Father Shinners, who scowled and said, "Spencer Tracy—he's shacked up with that Hepburn woman and he's never given a penny to the school." I've always emulated Tracy by never giving a penny to the school. I never managed to shack up with that Hepburn woman, though I did get to meet her and interview her.

Besides Rio Bravo, *what are some other movies that especially influenced you a kid?*

In 1959, I somehow made it into the Tosa Theater to see a movie that greatly alarmed the Legion of Decency, Billy Wilder's *Some Like It Hot*. I had a pubescent passion for Marilyn Monroe and had a copy of the 1956 issue of *Time* with its cover story about her; I kept the magazine in our garage and would pay it surreptitious visits. I found *Some Like It Hot* as captivating as it was hilarious. Beyond the adorable Marilyn and her risqué dresses, that movie opened my eyes to whole new vistas of sexuality, including cross-dressing and what we now call gender fluidity. I regard Wilder as "my sex ed teacher."

But because of the lingering effects of my Catholic repression, when Wilder made his 1963 comedy about Parisian prostitution, *Irma la Douce*, I had to make three attempts to watch the movie after school at a downtown theater before I could make it all the way through. The first two times I walked out because I was scandalized by the bawdy goings-on, the second time just before the end, when Irma is going into labor and delivering her baby during her wedding ceremony at a church. I later did an audio commentary for the Kino Lorber Blu-ray edition of that film, among numerous commentaries I've done for Wilder films, also including *Some Like It Hot*.

The first movie celebrity I met was not John Ford or Jean-Luc Godard but an actor from *Some Like It Hot*, Joe E. Brown. It was shortly after his memorable turn as the randy, sexually adventurous old millionaire who benignly tells Jack Lemmon's cross-dressing "Daphne" at the end of the movie, "Well, nobody's perfect." Brown visited our neighborhood in Wauwatosa to stay with some friends. We kids went to the house and waited for him to arrive. Brown got out of a car and walked past us with a scowl. I should have realized right then and there that I should not go into the movie business. (My brother Pat recalls Brown turning around at the doorway and giving us his trademark grin and a wave, but I don't remember that.)

One of the few movies I saw during my high school years was *Dr. Strangelove*. I saw it at the Tosa one night in February 1964 with my friend Dick Benka, the smartest guy in our class at Marquette; he was always first in the class, and though I tried hard to topple him, once coming in second, I never could. (He went on to become first in his class at Harvard Law School and had a long and distinguished legal career in Boston before becoming a teacher.) I had long been terrified of nuclear war—I ran upstairs and hid under the covers in 1953 when Martin & Lewis joked about it on TV—and I was not familiar with the genre of black comedy, so I experienced *Strangelove* at first as a scary Cold War thriller.

But Dick kept chuckling all the way through it and suggested we sit through it again, as you could in those days. Then I got that it was funny, although Dick had to explain to me why anti-Communists were actually afraid of fluoridation. I left the theater that night a different person: *Strangelove* was a paradigm changer for me. I lost much of my waning respect for authority by seeing that movie and became fascinating with the use of comedy for subversive dramatic and political effect.

Another film that meant a great deal to me in my youth was *My Fair Lady*. When I was in the hospital, they eventually gave me weekend passes during the spring of 1965, and I would go to the big downtown theaters to see movies. I became enraptured with *My Fair Lady* and saw it five times in its roadshow engagement at the Towne Theatre. Not only did this luxurious, serenely wise spectacle help ease me back into the world, but I identified with Eliza Doolittle being made over into (almost) a different person by Professor Higgins, because I was going through the same nearly miraculous experience with Kathy reshaping my life. I also related to Professor Higgins because of my love of language and my amused common ground with his pedantry and the film's satire of his misogyny. It has become fashionable for film critics and scholars to downgrade *My Fair Lady* because of its popularity and because it won George Cukor his only directing Oscar. But it's one of his most characteristic movies with its Pygmalion theme and sure-handed command of a stylized blending of theater and cinema. When I came to write a book about Cukor, I wrote a long appreciation of the film and took issue with its snobbish critics.

One of the other movies I discovered on my forays downtown during that period was *What's New Pussycat*. Those were still the days when you could enter a movie at any time before staying through a second viewing. I walked in at a suitably disorienting moment, during the scene when Woody Allen is having dinner by himself on the bank of the Seine while Peter Sellers is trying to commit suicide by giving himself a Viking funeral. That zaniness captivated me, and I quickly became a Woody Allen fan; like many other people, I responded to his intellectual brand of wit and the way his nerdy character managed to prevail against oafs and somehow get the girls.

I appreciated the flamboyant sexiness of *Pussycat*, which seemed in synch with my newly liberated sense of the world. The stripper played by Paula Prentiss who kept trying to kill herself reminded me of Kathy, who had cut her throat one weekend while we were dating and almost bled to death before she reappeared, horribly pale, with a huge bandage around her neck.

The film's satire of psychotherapy with Sellers's nutty Dr. Fritz Fassbender and his crazy group therapy sessions struck another chord with me. I had a highly negative view of the profession. My parents sent me to a psychiatrist when I was in high school, but he failed to help me. Since he never explained the analytical process, I couldn't figure out why he didn't respond to what I said. So at one session, I just sat there staring at him, and he said nothing for the entire forty-five minutes. Later I heard that he had shot and killed himself next to some railroad tracks. And in December 1964, shortly before my breakdown, my parents sent me to another psychiatrist who stupidly pronounced me "no more neurotic than the average Marquette High senior."

I did have a sympathetic and helpful therapist at the hospital, but I basically came to believe in healing myself. For that reason I deliberately left doctors largely out of *The Broken Places*. That also helped avoid the cliché that writers often use, a cheap device to give their protagonists someone to talk to who can verbalize and analyze their problems. It's more challenging and meaningful to dramatize problems than to have people talk about them.

O Pioneers!

Although you enjoyed films of all genres as a kid, why do you think you were drawn most of all to Westerns, which you would write about extensively?

Westerns always resonated deeply with me, partly because, as I realized only later, the West was a deep-rooted part of my family heritage. My Irish immigrant ancestors on both sides of the McBride and Dunne families were Western pioneers. Like most other kids in the early 1950s, I had a Hopalong Cassidy costume and wore six-guns. Once I saw a cop standing on a corner of our block talking with someone. I went up to the cop, pulled my gun, and said, "Stick 'em up, you copper-eyed copper!" Fortunately he chuckled; today a kid could get shot for doing that.

Besides *Hopalong Cassidy*, the first TV Western series, I enjoyed *The Lone Ranger* and *Cisco Kid* series in those days. I identified with Tonto, the Native American companion played on *The Lone Ranger* by Jay Silverheels. And I'll never forget how disappointed I was when I came down with chicken pox and had to give another kid my tickets to see Cisco, that amiable desperado, and Pancho, his Mexican sidekick (played by Duncan Renaldo and Leo Carrillo), in their appearance at the Milwaukee Arena. But when Western series became a fad on TV a few years later, I preferred the Western features I watched on *Foreman Tom's Jamboree* and often on weekends at Tosa Theater matinees, along with cartoons, serials, and sci-fi and comedy movies.

According to the scholarly and voluminous family history compiled by my brother Dennis, a lawyer who became mayor of our hometown of Wauwatosa, our ancestors on both sides were the kind of pioneers Willa Cather wrote about and Ford made movies about. Some of my ancestors on both sides of our family were coal or silver miners. My great-great-grandparents Patrick and Mary Walsh Gallagher were Irish immigrants who lived and worked in the coal fields of Pennsylvania and Iowa. They went west in 1875 with their daughter Hannah and several male siblings in a wagon train led by General John O'Neill, a Civil War veteran. There were about twenty families of Irish immigrants who stopped and founded the town of O'Neill, Nebraska (then considered quite far west).

My grandfather John Gabriel McBride was born in O'Neill in 1882, the year after the Gunfight at the OK Corral. He worked on an Indian reservation as a young man and studied at the Art Institute of Chicago before spending thirty-nine years as a "Mr. Chips" figure teaching art at Superior Central High School in northern Wisconsin.

The only part of my family background that impressed my Irish wife's family, the O'Haras, was a tale told by my grandfather McBride in a short autobiography he wrote for my benefit in 1950. When his father, Edward McBride, who married Hannah Gallagher, was on his way to O'Neill in a covered wagon, he and his uncle John supposedly were robbed by the Jesse James Gang. The outlaws were benign and only wanted to swap their exhausted horses. Ruth's writer father, Noel, told me that in Ireland, people thought of the James Gang as quasi-mythological figures. Our family tale may have been a myth, alas, since the dates for our ancestors' journey and the gang's history don't coincide. But the yarn entered our family history and seems to have become embellished along the way, perhaps with the notorious outlaws substituted for some run-of-the-mill horse thieves. That's a sign of how important legend is to America's experience in the West, as I've learned from my study of John Ford.

Some of my relatives on my mother's side were silver miners in Idaho during the period of violent labor strife ("the Big Trouble"), which made us staunch union supporters. I was named Joseph Pierce McBride after my grandfather Pierce Joseph Dunne; my third-grade nun mocked my Irish middle name in front of our class. My great-great-grandmother Thursea Cooper Ward ran a beanery for miners with help from her eldest child, my great-grandmother Joy Ward Flynn. Joy and her husband, Dominick Flynn, owned a brothel in Wallace, Idaho.

The Flynns also ran a busing and trucking company. One of Dominick's truck drivers, Pierce Dunne, married the boss's daughter, my grandmother Julia Flynn Dunne. My Grandpa Pierce gave me a large toy semi-truck I cherished when I was two because I could sit in it and roll around; some kid hit me over the head with that heavy truck around that time, exacerbating my poor vision. Grandma Julia drove what was called a "stagecoach" in the early twentieth century but was actually a bus; she was the first woman in the Pacific Northwest to have a license to do so. My feisty, cheerful Great-Grandma Joy also drove a stagecoach for the family company and lived to the age of ninety-six, so I was fortunate to know her before her death in 1975. All these family connections show how close we are to the American frontier period. No wonder I became so fascinated with Ford's work.

Strange to say, I didn't tell Ford much of our colorful Western family history when I interviewed him in 1970. But he said he gave me the interview because he was under the belief that I was a native Irishman: "Otherwise I'd tell you to go to hell." I had written "County Mayo" after my name on the letter I wrote him, one of our ancestral homes. When he quizzed me about what village in Ireland I was from, he was irked when I told him I was born in Wisconsin, so I was somewhat chastened. But I persisted, and we reached some kind of rapport by swapping tales in our blarney-fest.

Ford was suitably impressed when I told him that one of my Irish relatives on my mother's side had come to North America after deserting the British navy. My great-great grandfather John Gavin Carey, a native of Tuam, County Galway, had been impressed into servitude by the British during the Great Famine but jumped ship and spent the rest of his life in Newfoundland. (One of our distant relatives, Valerie Wiseman, has since written a 2021 novel about him, *Harbour of My Tomorrows*.) Ford tried to top the story about my renegade Irish ancestor by telling me about his ancestor who had deserted from the British army and come to America. He claimed his ancestor had beat mine over by thirty years, arriving during the Revolutionary War, and had received a personal letter from George Washington, which Ford said he had in his possession.

Liberté

Besides making you so receptive to John Ford's films, how else did your family's pioneering spirit manifest in you?

Going west to California through Monument Valley and entering the movie business. And like most kids in the 1950s, I dreamed of space travel. I won an honorable mention in a Kellogg's Cornflakes art contest for drawing an advertisement of an astronaut floating through space while holding a box of cornflakes above his mouth. My best friend when I was seven, Dickie Swearingen, had an invisible Martian friend who went around with us for a year, although I was humoring him that I believed in his companion. But in 1955, my longing to see a UFO was so intense that I convinced myself I had actually seen a space ship landing in our backyard. When I wrote my biography of Steven Spielberg, I read Carl Jung's

1959 book, *Flying Saucers: A Modern Myth of Things Seen in the Skies*, which attributes belief in UFOs to "an *emotional tension* having its cause in a situation of collective distress or danger, or in a vital psychic need." Another psychiatrist who has studied the UFO phenomenon, Kenneth Ring, noted that when a child from a dysfunctional family learns "to dissociate in response to the trauma," he is "much more likely to become sensitive to alternate realities." That attraction to alternate realities perhaps accounts for my absorption as a boy in movies and television and my going into the world of filmmaking.

And my pioneer ancestry may have helped me conceive my most grandiose plan of escape from my intolerable home situation. In 1957, when I was ten, I formed my own country. I called it Liberté. What that consisted of was nailing a few posters on trees around my neighborhood proclaiming that I had formed the country of Liberté and that every household would be subjected to a two-cent tax. I actually knocked on some doors to collect taxes, but I don't recall anyone paying me anything.

It was not long before a police car showed up. The cop took down the signs. That was the end of Liberté. It was an early lesson in repression. But I tried.

Comic books

As an at least semi-skilled cartoonist, were you a fan of comics and cartoons?

My fascination with pop culture was already evident because of my absorption in TV and movies as my principal means of escape from my hellish environment at home and school. But it was partly because of Dickie that I also developed a passion for comic books. My favorites included *Superman*, *Uncle $crooge*, and of course our generational bible, *MAD* magazine, which began as a comic book. I also was fascinated by the *Plastic Man* comic books and spent some time in the Sixties working on notes for a movie version, but gave up the idea since it seemed impractical (CGI eventually would make such surrealism possible).

I began working as a door-to-door salesman of greeting cards and stationery when I was ten years old because I needed ten dollars a week to buy records and comics. I was such a comic book fanatic that I would go to the local drugstore and wait for the truck to arrive with the weekly shipments at seven on Wednesday mornings.

When the psychiatrist Dr. Fredric Wertham launched his infamous crusade against the supposedly malign influence of comic books, claiming in his 1954 book, *Seduction of the Innocent*, that they turned kids into juvenile delinquents, my progressive mother wrote a magazine article defending comic books and declaring that reading them had not warped her own children (well…). Later as a film critic, my bounteous absorption in pop culture, including comics and cartoons, led me to become part of the generational movement that rescued the popular art of movies, especially Hollywood movies, from the prevailing critical condescension. That movement, spearheaded by our auteurist guru Andrew Sarris, helped bring about a major cultural shift in the late 1960s.

You told Howard Hawks that you were a Ricky Nelson fan. How much did rock 'n' roll fit into your life as a kid?

Dickie Swearingen was an early hipster. He was into rock 'n'roll from the first week it happened, when Bill Haley & His Comets re-released "Rock Around the Clock" to huge success in May 1955 to capitalize on its use in the movie *Blackboard Jungle*. Under Dickie's influence, I bought my first 45rpm record the following week. I became an avid fan and purchaser of early rock records, especially Elvis, Chuck Berry, the Everly Brothers, and Buddy Holly, and I was a regular viewer of Dick Clark's afternoon music and teenage dance show from Philadelphia, *American Bandstand*, which was broadcast nationally beginning in 1957. I was watching on February 3, 1959, when Clark announced that Buddy Holly, Ritchie Valens, and the Big Bopper were killed in a plane crash—"The Day the Music Died." I didn't realize until much later that their show had played Milwaukee shortly before the crash, but I wasn't going to concerts then.

My interest in rock music waned after I went to high school in 1961, partly because I was too busy studying to listen to music or even go to movies but also because rock became dominated by what Paul Le Mat's character in *American Graffiti* calls "surfer shit." I was fond of the Beatles and vividly remember watching them on the Ed Sullivan show and going to see *A Hard Day's Night* in Milwaukee and being unable to hear the dialogue because of the girls in the audience screaming all the way through. But I lost interest in rock when the heavy metal period came in; I found it jarringly chaotic and preferred songs in which you could follow the lyrics, so I enjoyed punk rock instead. My fondness for the hardcore rock of the formative period of the 1950s and my memories of the 1959 plane crash influenced me to write a screenplay in 1976 based on *American Bandstand*, *Rock City*, the first script I ever sold. It wasn't made into a film, but writing *Rock City* led to my being hired to co-write the 1979 punk rock musical, *Rock 'n' Roll High School.*

Baseball

I know your interest didn't wane in one special area. Like you, Joe, I loved movies, TV, rock 'n' roll, and comics, but most of all, I loved baseball. Including fanatically playing (alone) the same dice game you owned, APBA. We'll talk about your baseball writing soon, but tell us now about your being a fan.

For about three years of my life—before starting to write that book in May 1963—I thought of little else besides baseball. Baseball appealed to me partly because it is a game that follows rules, a soothing contrast to my chaotic life at home and school. And I could further exert the control I was otherwise lacking in my life by managing baseball teams in the tabletop game I played obsessively—another absorption into an alternate reality. I spent much of my free time playing APBA, which, as you know, enables a player to "manage" major-league teams (including some classic teams from the past, such as the 1927 Yankees and the 1934 Cardinals). APBA is surprisingly accurate to the players' actual performances, and I rigorously kept statistics on all the teams I managed, past and present, which taught me how to do long division in my head.

As a fan I loved the lore of baseball, the colorfully roguish history of the sport and its slang. I was fortunate in my time and place of birth, which enabled me to watch so many great players in that period at Milwaukee County Stadium, where the Braves played after arriving from Boston in 1953. I saw my first game there in 1954, but my serious interest in baseball began when my father took me to the fifth game of the 1957 World Series, which Lew Burdette of the Braves won 1-0 against Whitey Ford and the New York Yankees. That exciting pitching duel, which I watched from a prime seat in the first row of the upper deck directly behind home plate, was one of the three games Burdette won in that series as the Braves won the world championship. I went to many Braves games in the heyday of the team, led by Henry Aaron, Warren Spahn, and Eddie Mathews, who were among the greatest players in history.

Spahn, the greatest left-handed pitcher in baseball history, was my idol in those years. I would go see him pitch whenever I could, so I probably saw him win forty or so of his record 363 career victories, including his 300th victory, his second no-hitter, and the first game of the 1958 World Series. I admired his astonishing consistency over his long career, the grace of his pitching motion as he lifted one leg high and his left arm swooped down like a giant bird, his remarkable control, and his impeccable professionalism.

After I saw Spahn pitch a no-hitter against the Giants when he was forty in April 1961, I ran onto the field to join the mob congratulating him but didn't see Spahn. I turned to my right to look into the dugout and saw him all by himself, calmly packing his glove and bat into a canvas bag. When asked why he tended to be so cool and controlled on the mound, Spahn, a U.S. Army Purple Heart–awarded veteran of the Battle of the Bulge and the fight at the Remagen Bridge, said, "No one is shooting at me."

Another memorable game was seeing the great Sandy Koufax of the Dodgers beat Spahn, 2-1, by hitting the first homer of his major league career—Koufax was a notoriously bad hitter and would hit only one more. The ball just barely made it over the fence in left center, and Spahn stomped around behind the mound in a rare display of anger as Koufax rounded the bases. I went with my Dad and siblings to see Spahn win his 300th game on August 11, 1961. That night marked my return to the stadium after my Dad had banned me from baseball for months in 1960 and beyond.

He did that because one night in the second inning of the second half of a twilight-night doubleheader, I jumped the fence—instantly regretting it, but it was too late—and ran around the bases. As I passed second, I offered the Braves' second baseman Frank Bolling a peanut, and he said, "No thanks, kid." The veteran Andy Pafko, who was catching as he warmed up the pitcher, gave me a dirty look as I ran past home, the ball whizzing just past my head. The umpire glared furiously at me. The Braves' radio announcer Earl Gillespie said, "Some nut is running around the field." I climbed back over the fence and escaped without being arrested, heading home, but my parents had spies everywhere in town, and five people turned me in. What compounded my offense was that I was using a season ticket that my Dad gave me that belonged to the *Milwaukee Journal.* I chalk up that uncharacteristic bit of youthful hooliganism to wanting so badly to being part of the game.

One of my enduring regrets in life is missing the historic twelve-inning perfect game pitched by Harvey Haddix of the

Home run king Henry Aaron was one of my youthful baseball
heroes; I saw him hit many of his homers at Milwaukee County
Stadium and took this portrait there on a photo day for fans in 1962.

Pittsburgh Pirates against the Braves on May 26, 1959.
Haddix lost the game in the thirteenth inning in a bizarre
and confusing series of events. I had been headed out the
door to catch the bus to go to the game when my Dad
stopped me and forbade me to go because it was cold.
Imagine how I felt the next day when I read the headline in
the *Journal*, "Haddix Pitches Greatest Game in History, but
Loses in 13th, 1-0." (I still have that newspaper.) When my
Dad tried to stop me from going to another game on a cold
night, I reminded him of the Haddix game, and he let me go,
so that's why I saw Spahn pitch his second no-hitter.

Besides Koufax and the Braves' future Hall of
Famers—Aaron, Spahn, Matthews, Red Schoendienst,
Enos Slaughter, Joe Torre, and Phil Niekro—I saw many
of the other greatest players of the era—Bob Gibson, Willie
Mays, Yogi Berra, Mickey Mantle, Stan Musial, Ernie
Banks, Roberto Clemente, et al.—and I waited outside
the stadium after games to get autographs. Almost all the
players generously gave kids their autographs in those
days before they began to make big money; then most
of the players became standoffish. I also met some great
players from the past, such as Lefty Grove, who was cranky
when I found him sitting in the box seats but signed his

Warren Spahn, the greatest left-handed pitcher in baseball history, was my idol as a kid. He and his son, Greg, a member of my Little League team, were the subjects of my first professional article in 1960. I took this photo of Spahn with another baseball giant, Stan Musial, in 1962.

autograph reluctantly, and, most memorably, George Sisler, who was sitting in the back of the Pirates bus quietly while working as a coach. Sisler was one of the top hitters in the 1920s and batted over .400 twice. He asked me delightedly, "How did you know who I am?" I said I had read about his batting exploits and admired him even more because he had bad eyesight, as I did, although I could not hit.

My obsession with baseball was partly a compensation for my spectacular ineptitude at playing the game. I played a lot of sandlot baseball but was a terrible player because of my bad eyesight. Because of the kid hitting me over the head with the metal semi-truck my Grandpa Dunne had made for me, I developed a muscle pull in my left eye that necessitated an operation to repair it when I was almost five. The problem recurred many years later and required another operation. Along the way, one of my eye doctors told me I am "legally blind" without glasses, which makes my choice of career as a film critic and historian rather ironic, doesn't it? But I think that handicap actually helps account for my keen focus on vision and composition.

I remind myself of a character in a New World picture I acted in, *Hollywood Boulevard*, a half-blind, eye-patched cameraman played by George Wagner who explains, "Uh, well, I-I-I sort of got into my work because I was always interested in the visual side of perception." I think we people with poor eyesight go out of our way to compensate for that limitation. I think growing up seeing life through lenses and being acutely aware of how much I want to see life in focus helped foster my interest in movies, including my preference for sharp rather than murky cinematography. I also gravitated to the visually spectacular films of Ford, who was half-blind himself. Numerous great artists preceding him have also had terrible eyesight, which helps them see the world in a fresh, idiosyncratic way.

As a Little League baseball player, though, I was a hopeless fielder and hitter, and once I got conked on the head while trying to catch a fly ball; I remember the anxious coach and the other players running out to see if I was OK. The only sports I was fairly good at were basketball and long-distance running, although not good enough to make any of the teams at my schools. I had to sublimate my desire to be a professional baseball player into intense fandom.

We have in common a treasured childhood memory of seeing the immortal Satchel Paige in uniform. The night before my seventh birthday, on August 7, 1956, Gerry and I were among a minor-league record crowd of 57,000 at the Orange Bowl to see him pitch for Bill Veeck's Miami Marlins—as part of a huge charity event with Cab Calloway and other acts. Paige arrived in a helicopter, sat in a rocking chair on the mound, and earned a 6-2 victory with seven-plus effective innings pitched and a three-run double. You would see Paige a couple of years later, correct?

Yes, I was fortunate to see Satchel Paige, who may have been the greatest pitcher who ever lived, in the bullpen at a Spokane Indians game in 1958, but I wasn't as lucky as you guys, because he didn't get into the game. But he was seated in his signature rocking chair. We were visiting our grandparents on a brief trip to the city where my mother grew up. That gave me a thrill to be in the presence of one of baseball's genuine legends. I've always tried to live by his "Six Rules for a Happy Life," such as "Don't look back; something might be gaining on you."

That is a cardinal rule for a writer; if you start looking back at your manuscript while writing a book, you will be tempted to give up, so don't do it! Francis Ford Coppola told our students at SFSU that "if you read the pages, there is a hormone injected in the glandular system of young artists that makes them hate what they're doing. Don't go back and read it until you have the whole little pile of ninety-eight pages or a hundred and five pages, and then brace yourself and sit down and really enjoy it and read it through. Then I make a little step outline and rewrite the pages." That sage advice from Paige and Coppola is valuable in every other way too, although someone who's working on an autobiography has to violate the "Don't look back" rule, or there won't be a book.

You said you were a vendor at Braves games. That must have been a thrill for a young boy.

I entered an essay contest to be a batboy for the Braves but didn't win. My brother Pat won a similar contest and became not only a batboy for visiting teams at Milwaukee Brewers games but also an assistant clubhouse manager for baseball and Milwaukee Bucks basketball. Pat wrote about his experiences in his delightful 2021 memoir, *The Luckiest Boy in the World*, written with his twin brother, Dennis. The book also movingly chronicles how Pat used sports to cope with our dysfunctional home life and how the players encouraged him to become a doctor. I had to settle for working as a vendor at County Stadium, and I didn't make as much money selling hot dogs and Cokes as I could have, because I was often too busy watching the games.

I was such a baseball fanatic that during the winter I would watch Cuban baseball on TV; I fondly remember the night when Fidel Castro, a former ballplayer, did color commentary on a game. When the Braves were stolen from Milwaukee and moved to Atlanta in 1966 so the new owners could access a larger TV market, that ranked high among my disillusioning experiences as a kid. I later attended games while living in Southern and Northern California, but baseball never seemed the same.

Today I am not only disenchanted by the entitlement of the wealthy players and the exorbitant cost of tickets but also find that the experience is ruined by the blaring music played to keep the fans hyped up between pitches and between innings (making it difficult to talk with your friends) and by the often uncouth behavior of the fans. At the last game I attended, a minor-league game in Albuquerque with my partner, Ann Cornell, and my old friend Bob Kidera, a drunken young woman in the row behind us screamed in our ears incessantly. Going to a baseball game used to remind me of a relaxing picnic. Now it shows that you can't re-create what is gone from your youthful days.

John F. Kennedy

I'll continue to hold off asking you about your early baseball writings and instead ask you about a hero of yours other than Warren Spahn, someone who only threw out balls on opening days. Talk about the profound and lasting impact John F. Kennedy had on you.

Yes, while my mother was working on Senator Kennedy's 1960 Wisconsin presidential primary campaign, she brought me into it as a volunteer, when I was twelve. That enabled me to meet him twice, at memorable events that inspired my lifelong dedication to solving my candidate's murder. I admired Kennedy for his intellect, erudition, agile off-the-cuff wit, the fast way he talked—unlike President Eisenhower, whose muddled speech after his stroke exasperated me as a kid, leading me to underrate him—and I liked JFK's liberal views. But I didn't realize at the time that Kennedy's liberalism was still a work-in-progress, leading Eleanor Roosevelt and other prominent liberals to question some of his earlier stands. I also admired Kennedy's sense of cool detachment from the vulgar rituals of campaigning, which he mastered yet seemed to regard with a superior sense of amusement—vowing, for instance, never to wave his hands above his head, as Eisenhower and Nixon would do in their corny way. Invigorated by Kennedy's youthful energy, I was blithely unconcerned about charges of his inexperience, which was actually a serious problem, as the Bay of Pigs soon demonstrated.

One job my mother had in 1960 was escorting JFK's mother, Rose Kennedy, around Milwaukee for a day during the campaign. The Kennedys were always briefed on local people they met, and Rose said, "So you have seven children. How many of them are in boarding school?" My mother replied, "None," and Rose was surprised, which is telling. JFK always felt his mother neglected him when he was a boy, dumping him in boarding schools when she would go off to Europe for months to shop for designer clothing.

My job as a volunteer in the Kennedy campaign was helping to build the Kennedy myth. I went door-to-door leaving copies of the *Reader's Digest* reprint of John Hersey's 1944 *New Yorker* article on Kennedy's PT-109 incident in World War II. (In 2008, I also volunteered in

Barack Obama's historic campaign for president, a job that consisted of making phone calls around the country on his behalf.) I met Kennedy at an intimate rally on March 31, a small "Kids for Kennedy" event my mother staged at the Wauwatosa Civic Center two blocks from our house. During his speech, he flattered me when I answered a question he asked about his book *Profiles in Courage*. He described three senators he had written about and asked who they were. I had just read the book in preparation for his visit, so my hand shot up, and I answered, "Webster, Clay, and Calhoun." "Only in Wisconsin!" he said, and quipped, "I hope I don't have to run against you in 1964." Then he launched into a story about a kid who had advised Charles de Gaulle on his foreign policy.

On April 3, 1960, two days before the voting, I went to the climactic rally at the American Serb Memorial Hall on Milwaukee's South Side. Three thousand people showed up and treated Kennedy like a rock star. That rally is the centerpiece of *Primary*, a landmark in the documentary genre as the first major American cinéma-vérité film. It was made by Time-Life Films as a television special and shown later that year on a few stations, though most declined to run it since it was considered campaign propaganda. It was produced by Robert Drew and shot by cameramen Ricky Leacock, Albert Maysles, D. A. Pennebaker, and Terence Macartney-Filgate.

Several of Kennedy's PT-109 crew were onstage that night, and I took photos of them and of Kennedy, but they didn't make it into *Primary*. Because my attention was mostly riveted on the candidate, I was oblivious to the fact that a film classic was being made that night. The filmmakers seemed invisible to me. But my Brownie camera contributed the last of the eight flashes during the famous long-take handheld shot by Albert Maysles with the camera above his head to follow JFK as he enters the hall. That night as captured onscreen was the moment when politics in America turned into entertainment. Norman Mailer's classic *Esquire* essay about the presidential campaign, "Superman Comes to the Supermarket," eloquently described Kennedy's appeal as the first TV-star president. (Theodore Roosevelt was the first movie-star president, a charismatic figure doted on by early newsreel cameramen.)

I can't be seen up close in *Primary* but am in the fifth row in a crowd shot from the candidate's point of view. And with the rest of the crowd at the big rally, I serenaded Kennedy with "High Hopes," his campaign song adapted from the Capra movie *A Hole in the Head*, an ironic connection considering what eventually happened to him.

As I write in *Into the Nightmare: My Search for the Killers of President John F. Kennedy and Officer J. D. Tippit*, while attending the climactic rally as a volunteer on Senator Kennedy's Wisconsin presidential primary campaign in Milwaukee on April 3, 1960, I managed to get him to sign both a name tag and my wrist. "I also stuck my Brownie camera about three feet from Kennedy and blew off a flashbulb in his face [that's why this is out of focus]. He looked startled but quickly recovered and chuckled with a good-naturedness that was amazing under the circumstances." Embarrassed by my rudeness and aware of Kennedy's lack of security, in October 1961 I wrote a prescient short story about his assassination for my freshman high school English class, "The Plot Against a Country."

The campaign version was dropped after Wisconsin when Frank Sinatra's mob ties became an issue. I met Kennedy again at that event. I was taking pictures and fired off a flashbulb three feet from his face; I instantly felt embarrassed when he winced but quickly recovered and flashed a grin. The only security I could see were a few policemen who mostly left the candidate exposed to the crowd.

That moment when I blew off my flashbulb in JFK's face, my awareness of his total lack of security at the "Kids for Kennedy" rally, and my absorption during that period in reading about the Civil War and the Lincoln assassination inspired me to write a short story about Kennedy's assassination two years before it happened. "The Plot Against a Country" was written for my freshman

English course at Marquette in October 1961. It's juvenilia but prophetic and shows my early awareness that such a murder would most likely be the result of a conspiracy; I quote from the story in my 2013 book *Into the Nightmare: My Search for the Killers of President John F. Kennedy and Officer J. D. Tippit* and will discuss it later for this book.

In the reception line at the Milwaukee rally, Kennedy also signed my wrist—my mother made me wash off his signature a week later—and a "Hello, My Name Is" tag. I also managed to get Jackie Kennedy to sign that name tag after nagging her for five minutes. She kept saying "No, no" in her whispery voice; one of his aides finally said, "Oh, for Chrissake, Jackie, give the kid your autograph." Many years later I did a Q&A event in San Francisco with Leacock about *Primary* and their follow-up film on Kennedy, *Crisis: Behind a Presidential Commitment*. Leacock told me that when he asked Jackie how she felt about campaigning, she replied, "Have you ever had to smile a thousand times a day?" He said she would spend most of her time on the trail sitting by herself and reading French books, such as Proust or the *Memoirs of the Duc de Saint-Simon*.

The third and last encounter I had with my political hero came when he was president. On May 14, 1962, I served as one of the "honor guard" for President Kennedy when he gave the annual Jefferson-Jackson Day speech at the Milwaukee Arena. That was where ex-president Theodore Roosevelt was heading when he was shot in 1912 while campaigning for president, the time he went ahead and finished his speech before going to the hospital. All night at the dinner for President Kennedy, I paced back and forth in front of the head table as if guarding it; I'm amazed no one tried to stop me as I continually cast furtive glances at Kennedy and State Democratic Party chairman Patrick Lucey as they huddled in quiet conversation.

My mother was one of the people on the dais as vice chairman of the state party. She and Lucey had been instrumental in turning the support of the majority of Wisconsin Democrats to Kennedy and away from our initially favored "third senator," Hubert Humphrey, the politician they went to for help during the dark days when our senators were the Republicans Joe McCarthy and Alexander Wiley. After his election, Kennedy told Lucey that he wouldn't have become president if he hadn't won the Wisconsin primary. Kennedy had virtually lived in Wisconsin for more than two months during that campaign, and he said at the 1962 Milwaukee dinner,

Whatever other qualifications I may have had when I became President, one of them at least was that I knew Wisconsin better than any other President of the United States. And that is an unchallengeable statement. My foot-tracks are in every house in this state.... I suppose that there's no training ground for the Presidency but I don't think it's a bad idea for a President to have stood outside of [Oscar] Mayer's meat factory in Madison, Wisconsin, just because Senator [William] Proxmire always did it, at five-thirty in the morning, with the temperature ten above. When I read some of those great editorials about labor, I like to think about how it is to go to work at six o'clock in the morning at zero degrees. So I think it's a valuable experience, and I want you to know that I am glad to be back here.

After his speech, when just about everyone had left the arena, I went up to the podium with the presidential seal attached to it. Kennedy had left his copy of his speech with doodles of sailboats on it. I wanted to take it but felt reluctant to steal from the president of the United States. Finally a Secret Service agent came to take away the presidential seal. He picked up the copy of the speech. I asked if I could have it. He said no, because "The president might have been making notes about Berlin." When he left, I became aware of movement and noise behind the curtain in back of the stage. I went over and pulled back the curtain. Just then President Kennedy passed, and I impulsively blurted out, "Hi, Jack!" He smiled and nodded, then turned and walked down a ramp toward the limousine in which he would be killed the following year. For me he was vanishing into history.

The speech I heard Kennedy give at the campaign rally in April 1960 was a bellicose oration on the powers of the presidency, with a warning about how we could "see the campfires of the enemy burning on distant shores." The speech was shot mostly from a low angle, usually the vantage point for treating someone as heroic. But Leacock described the speech in hindsight as Kennedy "declaring war on Vietnam." Kennedy's Cold War rhetoric during the campaign didn't bother me at the time, though, because I had been brainwashed that way, and some of it went over my head. As he evolved as president, Kennedy became more liberal on civil rights, the issue I most cared about, and sought to end the war in Vietnam, which I didn't know anything about at the time. Kennedy's Irishness and Catholicism were a large part of his appeal to me. On the

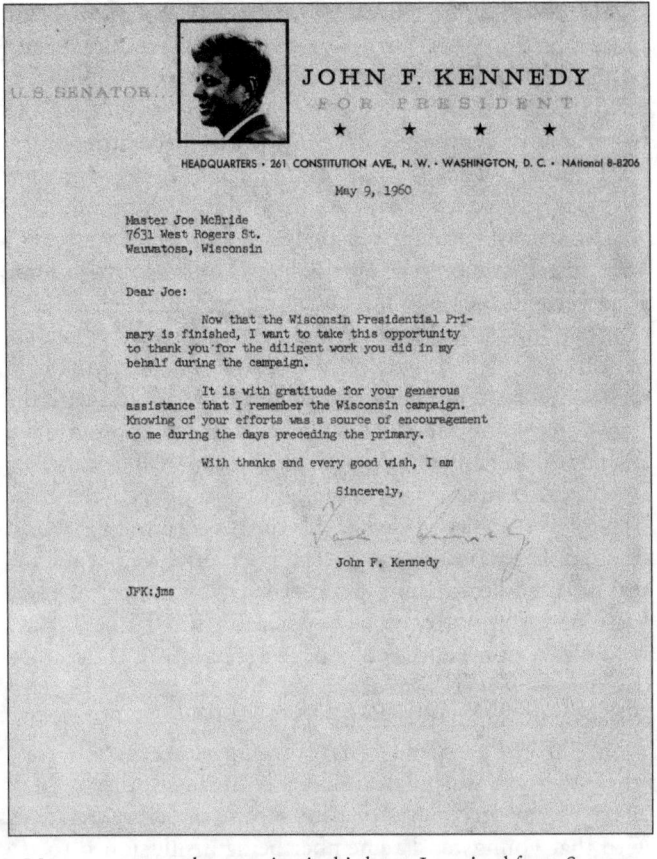

JOHN F. KENNEDY
FOR PRESIDENT
★   ★   ★   ★

U.S. SENATOR

HEADQUARTERS · 261 CONSTITUTION AVE, N. W. · WASHINGTON, D. C. · NAtional 8-8206

May 9, 1960

Master Joe McBride
7631 West Rogers St.
Wauwatosa, Wisconsin

Dear Joe:

      Now that the Wisconsin Presidential Pri-
mary is finished, I want to take this opportunity
to thank you for the diligent work you did in my
behalf during the campaign.

      It is with gratitude for your generous
assistance that I remember the Wisconsin campaign.
Knowing of your efforts was a source of encouragement
to me during the days preceding the primary.

      With thanks and every good wish, I am

          Sincerely,

          John F. Kennedy

JFK:jms

My most treasured possession is this letter I received from Senator John F. Kennedy in May 1960 thanking me for my work as a volunteer on his campaign. His thoughtful gesture and my memories of talking with him gave me an undying sense of loyalty and loss that led me to devote much of my life studying his assassination.

day of his election, I lent my father my "Al Smith for President" button to wear at work in a humorous nod to the only previous Catholic candidate of a major party for president; my mother vividly remembered members of her family crying as Smith lost in 1928 because of vicious anti-Catholic attacks.

When I began seriously researching my candidate's murder in the late 1970s and early '80s, I was increasingly incensed that our government did not want to bring the perpetrators to justice and that the media abrogated their duty. They left the job of investigating the crime to private citizens like me who were often vilified, or worse, for their devotion to Kennedy and the truth. My need to discover what is behind the curtain that our system uses to try to hide the truth about our lives made me a writer whose raison d'être is to do what I can to help solve his murder. My more than thirty years of researching the case resulted in my publishing *Into the Nightmare.* What I learned about the media during those decades and my ongoing research into the crimes of November 22, 1963, led to the writing of my 2021 book *Political Truth: The Media and the Assassination of President Kennedy.* And my investigation continues.

Because of Kennedy's inspiration and under my mother's influence, I planned a career in politics. I was going to become a lawyer and then run for public office, with the ambition of becoming a congressman. I applied to be a congressional page in 1961, which would have been my freshman year in high school, and my mother had worked out a deal with the state party committee to provide me with that opportunity. But another member of the committee, who shall be nameless even though there's now a statue of her outside the State Capitol building in Madison, was late for the meeting, which resulted in my not being chosen. My mother didn't tell me that until I asked many years later why I didn't get to go to Washington. In retrospect I suppose it's for the best that I didn't leave home at the vulnerable age of fourteen and trade that dubious experience for the first-rate education I received at Marquette High. But I missed Camelot.

I did get to spend a day tagging along with a page when I visited Washington, D.C., with my mother in May 1962. I went on the floor of the House of Representatives with that youngster. I remember being disillusioned to see congressmen sleeping in the cloakroom and ignoring the floor discussion on Indian affairs. I particularly remember with distaste one heavyset representative sitting on the brass rail separating the desks from the cloakroom, making the rail sag under his weight as he talked with a colleague. While the page and I made our rounds of the Capitol, he said he would show me something he wasn't supposed to let anyone see. He unlocked a closet that contained the catafalque on which Abraham Lincoln's coffin had lain in state after his assassination. The year after I saw the black wooden catafalque, covered with a dusty tarpaulin, it would be used when President Kennedy's coffin lay in state in the Rotunda. I also went to Ford's Theatre but was disappointed to find that it was closed and that the insides had been gutted along ago; it has since been restored, and I have visited it twice again.

My candidate's murder made me give up my ambition to enter politics. When the federal government showed no interest in solving the crime, I lost my faith in our political system. My ambition changed; I became a writer instead.

My growing disillusionment over how the mainstream media systematically lied and covered up the case influenced the kind of maverick writer I became. And the emotional connection I felt with Kennedy, including the exchange I had with him at our first encounter, helped make me want to solve his murder. That became my life's mission, which I've pursued with my two books about the assassination. Writing about films became my avocation.

Turning pro

Your first professional writing was not about Kennedy or film, but on baseball.

When I was twelve, my mother suggested I write an article about my Little League baseball teammate Greg Spahn and his father, my sports idol, Warren Spahn. One night Spahn came to one of our games at Wauwatosa's Hoyt Park and played pepper with us before serving as our third-base coach. My mother had a friend who worked for a company that published *The Young Catholic Messenger,* a national school magazine. She wrote him pitching the article about Greg, and he went for it. I wrote a serviceable article—with her polishing—and they published it on May 13, 1960, changing my title from "Young Spahn" to "The Lightfeet Top 'Em All!" A *Journal* photographer took some shots of Greg and his Dad warming up together as pitchers on the median strip across from their house in Wauwatosa. One lesson my mother taught me proved unfortunate. She told me I needed Warren Spahn's approval of the article, so I mailed a copy to the Braves' training camp in Florida, which he returned with the inscription, "OK Warren Spahn." It took me years before I realized I shouldn't show my writing to its subjects.

Earning forty dollars for that article—and I still have the check stub—made me a professional writer. Having an article in print was such a heady experience that it gave me the confidence I needed to continue my professional career. The editor, James T. Feely, wrote me, "All of us think you did an extraordinarily fine job with your story on Greg Spahn.... You're a fine writer, Joe. With parents like yours, I know you need no special encouragement from me to continue your efforts in this field." Buoyed with that spirit, I spent the next several years writing and trying to sell articles about baseball to sports magazines. Every day at lunch during the summers while I was working as a golf

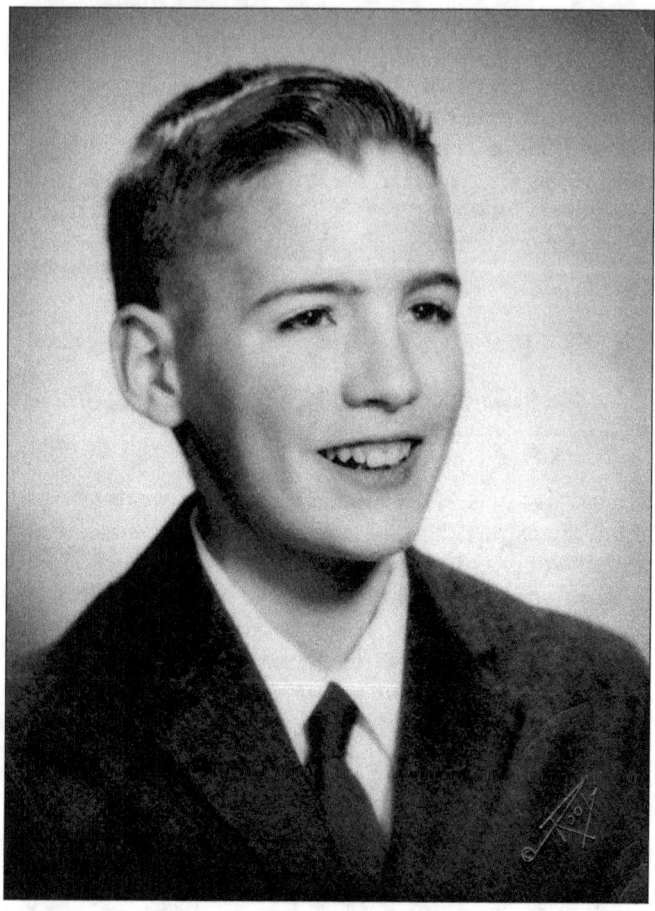

I look much happier in my eighth-grade graduation photo from
St. Bernard's Grade School than I was for most of my trying years
there. (St. Bernard's)

caddie, I used to ride my bike from the country club three
miles and back to see, vainly, if there was any response.
I never had a single reply, not even a letter of rejection. But
since I had done it once, I didn't give up.

The Battle of Cerveza

*After your early success, did your parents actively encourage
you to follow them into becoming a writer?*

Although my mother was always encouraging, my father
always felt jealous and competitive with my career. He
masked that by saying he didn't approve of children going

into the family business, but he was actually worried about being outdone by his children.

When I was ten, my mother sent me out with my Dad so we could jointly cover an event, a church program to give donations of household items to a kid whose home had been destroyed in a fire. She made me give a big stack of comic books to the kid; today they'd probably be worth thousands of dollars. I wrote up the event, and my mother declared that my story was better than the one my Dad wrote for the *Journal.* I'm sure she was just being encouraging, but it hurt my Dad's feelings, showing how sensitive he was to that issue. That made me wary of competing with him, a feeling that held me back as a writer until he died in 1989. I didn't understand at the time but now feel it's no coincidence that my career has been much more successful since then.

When I told my Dad that I was going to study films, he said he would no longer help support me, explaining, "I wouldn't support you if you were studying nightclubs." Well, after many years in Hollywood, I realize he wasn't entirely wrong about that. When he saw *Rock 'n' Roll High School*, though, a film I based partly (and loosely) on his experiences leading a student strike in high school, he told one of my siblings, "It's the first time I've ever been ashamed of one of my children." By then I was beyond hurting, but that's still a chilling memory.

My Dad was an excellent writer with a popular touch but was frustrated because he never got around to writing a book. Since he was a good storyteller, we tried to get him to write a memoir of his years in World War II helping guard the Panama Canal and South America as a master sergeant in the U.S. Army Air Forces, but he produced only two chapters of a hilarious yarn he called *The Battle of Cerveza.* It's fitting that his memoir is titled after a Mexican beer. Although the army personnel in Central and South America performed a vital service during the war, nothing much happened where they were, which was partly due to their presence. If that lent a certain aura of Bilko-like absurdity to my Dad's army years, he liked to quote Milton's line "They also serve who only stand and wait."

My Dad did write a popular column for the *Journal* called "All in the Family" (preceding the Norman Lear TV series of the same title). He spun a folksy series of anecdotes and humorous commentary about us kids that I now realize was beautifully crafted, but at the time it made us acutely uncomfortable to have our foibles spread out for the whole city to read. One by one, we forbade my father from writing about us, until the column degenerated into baby talk about the antics of my two youngest brothers. And it was telling that my mother was so seldom mentioned in the column that some readers assumed my father was a widower raising seven children by himself ("Poor man," one wrote him).

Genevieve suffered a lot of grief at her high school after our Dad wrote his most infamous column, about her first date and how she allegedly was boy-crazy. The title made it even worse: "The Flower Blooms." And I laid down the taboo after he wrote a column in my senior year in high school about how I was overworking so badly that I had to take drugs to stay awake to do my homework. (No wonder: after working four hours each night, I was having trouble getting up in the mornings.) That column caused a priest to stop me in the hall to quiz me about the drugs, which were the over-the-counter caffeine product No-Doz. But the column should have raised a red flag and caused the school—and my parents—to realize that something was seriously wrong.

My first book

How did you, as a teenager, not only write a publishable baseball book but also choose a unique topic?

What I originally called *Baseballese* took four summers to write. I read as many books on baseball as I could find in those days as well as sports magazines, and I was a subscriber to *The Sporting News,* an excellent newspaper for fans as well as professionals. And I had a passion for etymology as a teenager, reading books on the origins of words, which are often fascinating and colorful stories. What impelled me to write a book about the language of baseball was that I was frustrated because I couldn't find a comprehensive book about the game's terminology, nicknames, and quotations. So I decided to write one myself. (My motive for writing a book is usually because I want to read a book on a subject and can't find one.) Knowing slang is a way of becoming an insider in a profession, and I desperately wanted to become a baseball insider, especially since I was hopeless as a player. And being a vendor at County Stadium steeped me in the atmosphere of the subject.

As I wrote in the preface about the book's genesis,

Casey Stengel inspired this book. One Saturday morning in the spring of 1962, when I was a fourteen-year-old baseball fan and the "Old Perfesser" was a seventy-one-year-old legend marking his fiftieth anniversary in the major leagues, I spent an unforgettable hour standing next to the New York Mets' dugout at Milwaukee County Stadium, eavesdropping on a Stengel monologue [that was the Mets' first season, and he was their manager]. Casey gave no sign of being aware of my presence as he rattled on and on to a baffled-looking fellow who occasionally chimed in with a few words of broken English. It was a wonderful monologue, one that would have brought a grin to the saturnine face of Ring Lardner, and I couldn't understand a word of it. Casey Stengel ostensibly spoke the English language, but sportswriters always referred to his rambling, whimsical, sagacious, and thoroughly colorful lingo as "Stengelese." Whatever it was, it fascinated me, and not long thereafter I began jotting down the observations on baseball slang that eventually, years later, came together to make up this book.

High & Inside, as the book ultimately was called, examines the origins of baseball terminology, words that often have intriguing stories behind them. And I explain the origins of the nicknames of many players and managers, not only the leading figures of the game but also some who were lesser known but had wonderful nicknames. And I report on the most famous quotations in baseball history and their context. I was most enamored of the nicknames, since they involve such human stories and are often, by nature, humorous. For quite a while I didn't know how to integrate the quotes into the book but eventually hit on a device that now seems obvious, to scatter them throughout the text.

I taught myself how to write a book by doing it, working by trial and error, first by taking voluminous notes and gradually making outlines and figuring out how to structure it. I wrote baseball teams and some players to find out how nicknames originated, and I scoured many books and articles to track down the derivations of baseball terms and famous quotations. Writing the book kept me out of trouble during the summers of my high school years, sequestered in my second-floor bedroom. I kept the book a secret from my parents all that time because I feared they would stop me from writing it.

Why did you fear your parents would stop you?

Because I always felt that they were holding me back in many ways. Even though my mother was supportive of my writing, I worried that they would discourage me from such an ambitious project on the grounds that it would damage my health or something. And after my breakdown, they always seemed wary that I would have another; they never really understood or empathized with my experience or its positive aspects. I thought they would tell me the project was too difficult or an unhealthy preoccupation. What's astonishing is that they never asked what I was doing up there all that time. For all they knew about what I was doing up there behind my closed bedroom door for three years, I could have been making bombs.

The first summer was entirely devoted to note-taking, out of any order. I was fortunate to have a public library two blocks from our house with an excellent collection of books on baseball and other sports, as well as books on slang and etymology. What little had been written on baseball slang and nicknames was scattered in various sources, usually sketchy. I found other books at the downtown Milwaukee library and elsewhere, as well as scouring periodical files for historical articles.

There had been a doctoral thesis by Edward J. Nichols in 1939, *An Historical Dictionary of Baseball Terminology,* that I obtained from University Microfilms in Michigan. Nichols's scholarly research helped in identifying early sources for terminology, but he did not study the etymology of baseball language, noting that "another investigation [will have] to battle over the origins of much of the terminology," And there had been a pamphlet on *Baseball Nicknames,* written in 1946 by Thomas P. Shea. I tracked down Mr. Shea, who kindly sent me an annotated and corrected copy and answered questions I had about nicknames he did not include in his pioneering work.

I especially got a kick out of my correspondence with players, such as the pitcher Truett (Rip) Sewell. He wrote a delightful handwritten letter on how he came up with his ballooning "Eephus ball" after the big toe on his right foot was damaged in a hunting accident on December 7, 1941, and he had to find a new pitching motion, and how the pitch acquired its funny name. Sewell wrote me, "After I threw my new pitch all the newspapermen wanted to know what its name was. I said, 'I don't name them—I just throw them.' One of the outfielders, Maurice Van Robays, told the sportswriters that the pitch was an 'eephus ball.' They wanted to know what 'eephus' meant, and he told them that 'It don't mean nothing, and that's what that pitch is—nothing.'"

My father, who had been a sportswriter in his early days and was still an avid baseball fan, served as an unwitting source for *High & Inside*. Even though I kept mum on what I wanted the information for, I constantly pumped him in a seemingly casual way for what he knew about baseball terms, players, nicknames, and other lore. Then I'd go upstairs and write down what he told me before checking it out against my other sources, which almost invariably proved him correct. It amused me to get help from my Dad in this surreptitious way, as it did later when I revealed the manuscript to my parents. When I later updated the book for publication, my brother Pat, who had been batboy for all the American League teams, helped me with information on players of the 1970s.

The research and writing of the baseball book in the mid-1960s kept me out of trouble but delayed my maturation process by distracting me from social activities, serving as a kind of protective refuge. It was a deeply satisfying feeling to walk down the stairs at the end of the summer of 1966 holding a box of manuscript and announce, "I've written a book." To their credit, both of my parents reacted favorably to this *fait accompli.* I made a brief attempt to sell the book at that time but didn't know how. *The Sporting News* published some books, but they rejected mine. An exception to my Dad's overall lack of support for my career was his nagging me for years to find a publisher, even when I went through a silly period of thinking that as a film scholar it would be embarrassing to publish a book on baseball. My Dad helped me overcome that notion.

So it was not published until 1980, when I updated it for Warner Books as *High & Inside: The Complete Guide to Baseball Slang* as a mass-market paperback; it was the first comprehensive baseball book of its kind, although others have since been published. The book's editor, who barely brushed through its contents, came up with the title, and when I asked her what it meant, she joked, "It's inside stuff, and you were high when you wrote it." Oddly enough, *High & Inside* is still my bestselling book. It sold 32,000 copies in the first six months, and I was told informally that 40,000 copies were sold before Warner Books let it go out of print. I never received a penny in royalties; all they paid me was a $500 advance. I updated the book again in 1997 with the more modest title *High and Inside: An A-to-Z Guide to the Language of Baseball. High and Inside* is still close to my heart as a happy memento of my early passion for baseball and my not entirely misspent youth. I need to do another edition if I can muster the enthusiasm.

Am I a blockhead?

Even though Dr. Samuel Johnson famously said, "No man but a blockhead ever wrote, except for money," I haven't been pursuing a writing career for more than sixty years now just for money. Even Boswell immediately follows what he calls "that strange opinion" by commenting, "Numerous instances to refute this will occur to all who are versed in the history of literature." Few authors, in fact, are able to earn a living by writing books, although I've managed for some stretches. To continue my career as a writer, I've willingly paid the price of doing without things most people would consider essential, even if they are unattainable for many other Americans as well: I've never been able to own my own home and have spent years without health insurance or credit, buried in debt and living under the radar from paycheck to paycheck while grinding out magazine articles, film reviews, scripts, and other make-work projects to keep alive. Part of me can't help resenting the situation and the fact that so few people buy books, especially books about filmmakers. As Ray Bradbury put it, "You don't have to burn books to destroy a culture. Just get people to stop reading them."

But when the 1981 Fred Astaire AFI Life Achievement Award special—the best work I ever did as a screenwriter—had only a modest viewing audience, as one of my so-called Hollywood friends gloatingly called to point out the next day, my producer and co-writer George Stevens Jr. reminded me somewhat surprisingly, in an even more venerable bit of borrowed wisdom than Dr. Johnson's, "Man does not live by bread alone." Sure, I would have wished to be a bestselling author, but long ago I realized that was not in the cards. I write for a niche audience whether I try to or not. When I was writing film reviews for an Internet site in the 1990s, I asked the editor why he only gave me independent and foreign films to review, when most of my career as an author has been writing about popular cinema. "Because you write about popular films in an unpopular way," he said with some truth.

So I always needed a "day job" (as they call it in the film business) to support my writing habit. I write for the highest reward one can have, the pleasure in the craft. But my long impecuniousness as a writer struggling to make a living before I settled into a teaching job for desperately needed security has contributed to determining some of the ways I have written books, as this one will show. In a sense my awareness that I am writing for a modest audience—or hardly any audience at all, in some cases—has liberated me to write more from the heart and less in an attempt to please others. Hoping to please a wide audience is a chimerical goal at best, and yet, in a strange paradox, some of the books I've written "just for myself"—with what Graham Greene calls "the tone of... secret prose, that sense of a mind speaking to itself with no one there to listen"—have by that strange means connected most strongly with audiences around the world. That was the case when I wrote my biography *Searching for John Ford,* which I was oddly convinced no one would read. My sense of freedom in following the subject wherever I wished is a large part of what makes that book appealing to other admirers of Ford. And yet that book ruined me financially for ten years and drove me to get a regular job.

My necessary development into a solitary, somewhat insular author has made it impossible to sell some of my projects, however, and has not only influenced my subject matter but also my need to self-finance and self-publish some of my most controversial books. Among those have been my dream projects, my most cherished and personal. My decision to become a full-time teacher not only did not slow down my pace as a writer—as one of my colleagues at San Francisco State University, Patricia Amlin, told me it would—but actually spurred me on, especially after I achieved tenure through five years of arduous battle. Her gratuitous warning when she stopped me in a school hallway, delivered with a smug little smirk, actually helped make me more prolific than I ever had been before. I put up with all manner of bullshit in my academia career to concentrate on my greater goal of being able to pay for and write those dream projects.

2. A cinephile's paradise

We can now move on from Milwaukee to Madison, as you did in the fall of 1965, and dip into your stop after that, California. You've mentioned that you developed your own curriculum at the University of Wisconsin after you dropped out. Did that work out for you in the career paths you pursued?

Managing to achieve and sustain a career as a university professor in later life even though I was a college dropout became a matter of great satisfaction for me. One of the highlights of my life was delivering the commencement address in May 2012 for the graduating seniors from the University of California, Berkeley, Department of Film & Media and the Department of Rhetoric. My speech was entitled "Chutzpah: Making the World Realize It Needs You," based on my final class topic each semester for my screenwriting students. Some parents came up afterward and thanked me for telling their kids what they had tried in vain to make them realize, that a film school degree doesn't guarantee you a job in the film industry, and you need a "day job" while you're trying to break in.

The word "chutzpah" (Yiddish for boldness) has a special significance for me, because it was the only piece of advice about the movie business I received before going to Hollywood in 1973. I met a recovering screenwriter who was passing through Wisconsin and asked him for advice. I followed his advice vigorously in my first few years there, going up to people and introducing myself at parties and other events and calling all the directors and others I admired for interviews.

Sitting behind me at the Berkeley graduation ceremony among the faculty members on the stage in a large auditorium was my favorite teacher at the University of Wisconsin, Professor Russell Merritt, wearing his crimson Harvard robes. I remember Russ on the first day of our film class telling us that though most of us would not go on to become filmmakers, the world needs more than just good filmmakers, it needs good audiences.

When I arrived in Madison in September 1965, though, I felt lost among the huge student body and was dismayed to find that the teachers were far inferior to the Jesuit priests and the laymen who educated me at Marquette. I was not prepared for the fact that as a freshman, I was mostly taught by graduate students, who seemed incompetent. Although

I suppose if I had continued and had more full professors teach me, I might have changed my mind.

Joe, please continue, but first tell us about your celebrity TA.

One of those grad students was my teaching assistant in freshman English, Lynne Cheney, the wife of Dick Cheney. They were in Madison so he could keep getting deferred from going to Vietnam. Dick Cheney was also a grad student and was working as an intern for the Republican governor, Warren Knowles; that was the start of Cheney's vile political career. Lynne later became a right-wing political pundit and wrote a bodice-ripper novel. She was at the UW writing her thesis on Matthew Arnold; I found her horribly ignorant and nasty as a teacher.

Though I consider myself a college dropout, I was expelled from the UW after I became disenchanted with the quality of teaching and fed up with the educational system. My attitude resembled that of George Amberson Minafer in *The Magnificent Ambersons*, who brushes off his semester at Harvard before he was invited to go back home to Indiana as just "a lot of useless guff."

I did apply myself for one semester, just to prove to myself that I still could do well in my studies if I wanted to. After withdrawing during my first semester in 1965 because of my second breakdown, once I was off the Thorazine I managed a semester of straight B's in the spring. But I was back to being a grind. My time was consumed by reading a staggering load of Masterpieces of Western Literature, in a Comparative Literature course. Each week we were assigned a classic to read, most of them in translation— *Crime and Punishment, The Trial, Faust, Candide,* French plays, Ibsen plays, Baudelaire's *Les Fleurs du Mal,* parts of *The Canterbury Tales,* and so on and on—all wonderful stuff. One whole week I did nothing but eat, sleep, and read *Don Quixote.* It never occurred to me to skim those books, which some of the other students must have done, and when I became a university teacher in 2002, I couldn't imagine getting students to read even a fraction of that overwhelming workload. But the teacher was terrific (I only remember her first name, Cynthia), and I learned more from that course than from any other at the UW, so I was mildly miffed to earn only a B.

I also took a Philosophy course in Logic, which helped my writing enormously, since I tended to be far more emotional than logical in my early days. And my first-semester Italian course (taught by a TA from Texas, so we spoke Italian with a Texan twang; but he was an exception to the rule about TAs) came in unexpectedly handy when I wrote my biography of Frank Capra, an Italian immigrant. I was able to converse with elderly Italians to some extent and do some translating of Italian material with a University of California, Los Angeles, graduate student I hired to help me with that language and French.

But after desultory attendance for the first couple of years and a spotty record in classes, including failing everything by barely attending in Spring 1967, by that fall I was still officially a freshman. I did well enough that semester, I suppose, with A's in American Literature and History of the Motion Picture, a C in The Symphony (a course I found valuable for my writing, since it helped me understand artistic structure), and an F in First Semester French. But during the second semester in Spring 1968, I arrogantly tried what I considered an experiment to see if I could pass a semester without going to class or doing any of the homework, just taking the final exams.

Such a dumb idea. I received two B's (in American Literature and Film Theory) and two F's (in Renaissance to Modern Art and again in First Semester French). I remember when I went to the last lecture in American Literature out of curiosity, it was on one of my favorite poets, Emily Dickinson, and the professor gave such a captivating talk that I regretted not going to any of his other class sessions.

The dean of students called me into his office in early June 1968 and told me, with regret, that I was being expelled for missing so many classes. (I see in my transcript that the official date of my expulsion was June 8, a Saturday, which happened to be the day of Robert Kennedy's funeral.) In fact, I had dropped out on purpose as my way of rebelling against higher education, so that suited me just fine. I'm still barely a sophomore, with thirty-two credits of the 120 required for graduation; only my three AP English credits pushed me beyond freshman status.

Nevertheless, I had the impression when we met that you eventually became happy about being on campus.

On campus, yes, though not in class. I spent eight years in Madison before going to Hollywood. Madison turned out to be the ideal school for me, because of the lively political and cultural environment that surrounded the buildings where classes were being taught. Even after being kicked out, I hung around the campus until 1969, when I was hired for my first full-time job as a newspaper reporter for *The*

Wisconsin State Journal. Despite some ambivalent feelings I still have about my college days, I like to go back to that beautiful city, which surrounds five lakes and is also the state capital. *Life* magazine aptly called Madison "the Athens of the Midwest."

Alienation

You were so down on the education offered at UW that I wonder you even wanted to go there, especially after doing so well at Marquette High and even winning a National Merit Scholarship.

Initially I was unhappy about going to our flagship state school (the tuition was only $300 a year) because I had wanted to go to an Ivy League school, Harvard or Columbia. As I mentioned, the breakdown I experienced as a high school senior actually happened during my interview for Harvard at the home of an alumnus, the peak of my tension over that process. That was it for Harvard, but I was accepted at Columbia, where I hoped to enter their famous school of journalism. I couldn't afford to go there, though, after I discovered that the National Merit Scholarship I almost literally had killed myself to win was worth only $100 a year. I had naively assumed it would cover my expenses at a top private school, but the scholarship people told me that token stipend was all I needed, because both my parents worked. They didn't factor in that my middle-class parents struggled to support their family of seven children, let alone send any of us to an expensive college. I was so furious that I never bothered to collect the money, and that prompted my disillusionment with so-called higher education.

The problem I had with the quality of teaching at the UW was compounded when I became interested in a career in film. We only had three film courses, which were in the Speech Department, and after taking them all, I decided to set up my own curriculum instead. Besides watching films incessantly, that program included teaching myself how to write screenplays and directing my own increasingly ambitious short films. Madison had extraordinary resources in that regard, a voluminous archive at the State Historical Society of Wisconsin and many film societies, one of which I ran. And I began writing my first book on Orson Welles in Madison as well as articles for film magazines around the world, such as *Film Heritage, Film Quarterly*, and *Sight and Sound.*

I missed some class subjects I now wish I had taken, such as economics and sociology, which I've had to catch up with on my own. I regret not becoming a student of our renowned history professors George Mosse and Harvey Goldberg, the teachers to whom my friend Errol Morris dedicated his documentary film *The Fog of War*. Errol was a member of our Wisconsin Film Society, and we bonded over our shared fascination with the Wisconsin graverobber, cannibal, and murderer Ed Gein, the model for Norman Bates in *Psycho*. Ironically, Errol became the one great filmmaker who emerged from what we called our "Madison film mafia" even though I would have thought him the least likely to become a director, since he was a classical intellectual who didn't fit any of the stereotypes of directors, which is part of his creative originality. I've kept in touch with Errol and am thanked in *American Dharma*, his provocative, important, and unfairly attacked 2018 documentary on Steve Bannon, for which I gave feedback in postproduction.

Another reason Errol stands out is that he studied history and philosophy in Madison and elsewhere rather than being a film major anywhere, although he spent a lot of time watching films at the Pacific Film Archive in Berkeley. You see the profound effects of history and philosophy in his work. So I would hold up Errol to students as an example of how just studying film is not the way to become a great filmmaker.

Autodidact

How do you think not finishing college shaped your future?

My abandoning college as an act of rebellion turned me into an autodidact. That lifelong habit has served me well. The many benefits I received from going to the UW came instead from my extracurricular activities in film and political protests. And being an autodidact marked me forever as an iconoclast, following my own idiosyncratic path in my careers as a writer and later as an academic. That made me more original, although it isolated me to some extent from my colleagues in both fields, a price I have found worth paying.

After my initial feeling of disgruntlement about having to go to Madison rather than a prestigious eastern school, I began changing my mind about the campus environment when I discovered that the UW was a favorite destination for students from New York because of its reputation as a school of radical protest that was welcoming of dissidents. The students from back East and from other countries were fascinating to me, so I gravitated toward them. I admired their brand of sophistication, although some ironically were more provincial than I actually was; I had a different kind of sophistication. Some, but not all, saw me in stereotypical terms as a "hick," a word Peter Bogdanovich also applied to me after I met him in Los Angeles.

Even though I began my career as a film scholar in Madison, I've remained somewhat ambivalent about my years on campus. I've mentioned that I felt ostracized by some of my fellow students because of my poor clothing, clunky haircut, and lack of money. (You can see how I looked in my role as the comically earnest young film scholar Mister Pister in Orson Welles's *The Other Side of the Wind*.) After I dropped out of school, I lived on the edge financially, because my parents cut off my modest allowance.

I spent six months working as an orderly for $1.40 an hour at the University Hospitals, a powerful life experience that cured me of feeling sorry for myself, since I was dealing with people in far worse straits. I was a devoted worker as house orderly, handling a wide variety of chores (even assisting in an operation once), but lost that job because I grew a goatee and quit after being ordered to shave it off; a few years later, a court case brought by another bearded employee ruled against the University Hospitals. And for about three years I washed dishes in fraternity and sorority houses, a dormitory, and restaurants to keep myself fed while living in dumpy rooming houses.

I was often lonely and angry in those years because I was struggling to liberate myself from my traumatic upbringing (one of my girlfriends described me as "an open wound") and because I often felt socially isolated. One of my perverse forms of entertainment while living in a student boarding house in 1967 was playing a two-record set of all the dialogue from the movie of Edward Albee's play *Who's Afraid of Virginia Woolf?*; it was not until years later that I realized I played those records of the ferociously squabbling couple over and over because I missed the atmosphere of home.

My isolation at college was partly due to the hostility I provoked because of my refusal to use recreational drugs. At one point I was tempted to take LSD, but my roommate who took it first ran screaming down the street naked, and that cured me of any desire to experiment. Anyone who didn't use drugs at the time was viewed with suspicion. Some people at parties in Madison and Hollywood angrily called me a "narc." One of my brothers reported that the comedian-activist Dick Gregory told students at the University of Wisconsin, Milwaukee, to stay off drugs, because that was the government's way of keeping them docile so they wouldn't protest the Vietnam War. Unfortunately, many of my generation failed to understand that and fell into the trap of drug-befuddled narcissistic escapism.

I'd get annoyed with people who tripped before seeing movies, including 2001 *in Cinerama, and the next day had no recollection of what they'd seen.*

My avoidance of drugs combined with my lack of interest in money and trendy clothing to stigmatize me as hopelessly square in terms of social status in Madison and Hollywood. A woman I dated (once) in Los Angeles asked me in exasperation, "Don't you *ever* use cocaine?" I find it sadly ironic that in Madison I was guilty of my own snobbery toward fellow Wisconsinites, whom I tended to caricature as a bunch of hicks. That misguided projection was my own self-defensive form of status anxiety.

What, if anything, did you get out of the film classes you took in Madison?

Although the film curriculum was inadequate, I did find two of the three film courses eye-opening. Taught by Russell Merritt and Richard Byrne, both of whom were smart, charismatic, and witty, those were stimulating courses that jump-started my development as a film scholar. The third course, however, was taught by a fellow who had been a male model and seemed to know little about film. His hiring reflected the neglect of the subject by higher education before "film studies" became an academically sanctioned field.

That teacher was amiable and would call on me in class to help fill him in, and I'm afraid that became somewhat embarrassing. When he taught a film history class and came to the subject of American film—which occupied only one day of the semester—he started by saying he had gone to the University Library to bone up on American film and (looking down at his notes) said he had found an article in *"Film Culture"* written by (checking notes and reading more slowly) "Andrew Sarris" on a director named (checking again for another strange name) "Howard Hawks." And once when the professor was lecturing on French film and mentioned Jean Cocteau, he turned to me in the first row and asked, "Joe, what's Cocteau been doing recently?" I had to respond, hunching down in my seat, "He died in 1963," which caused some titters.

I went to Madison expecting to make a career as a journalist and novelist; Hemingway was my favorite writer as well as a role model. But instead I discovered Orson Welles and through him my ambitions to make films and write about them. That epiphany came on September 22, 1966, when Professor Byrne showed *Citizen Kane* in his introductory film class. Byrne had an exciting, eloquent, and humorous style that blended erudition with jokes that kept the class entertaining without lowering its level. As luck would have it—the kind of luck I always seem to have when I become interested in a filmmaker—the Memorial Union was having a Welles series that fall. They were showing six of his films in 16mm in the Stiftskeller, a beer hall. I borrowed the prints ahead of time and first saw *The Magnificent Ambersons* and *Touch of Evil* projected on a wall in a little room at the Union. I found those two films astounding in the ways that expanded what I thought a movie could be. I realized that Welles had made other films that are as good as if not better than *Kane*.

Professor Byrne was also one of the campus's leading theater directors. I wrote a feature for Madison's afternoon paper, *The Capital Times*, about watching him at work on *The Skin of Our Teeth* by Thornton Wilder in our main theater. Byrne directed his cast with verve and enthusiasm, somewhat like Welles himself. Wilder's father had been publisher of *The Wisconsin State Journal*, and Thornton moved with his family to Berkeley as a child and based *Our Town* on both places. No wonder I later gravitated to Berkeley, whose similarity to Madison, beyond its comfortable and funky smalltown atmosphere, includes a major university with its intellectual ferment and political activism. The University of California, Berkeley, set the trend in protesting during the late Sixties; about a week after they would have a protest, we would follow with our own.

Russ Merritt, who became a lifelong friend, also taught film history and was another positive influence on my budding cinephilia. Russ was just a few years older than us and was our enthusiastic advocate with the university. He made us feel that our voices were being heard by the university hierarchy about the importance of film, at least symbolically. He encouraged our appreciation of the then–avant-garde subject

Seeing Orson Welles's *Citizen Kane* in Professor Richard Byrne's film class at the University of Wisconsin, Madison, on September 22, 1966, changed my life. (RKO)

of the American cinema. He also made film scholarship fun, and he punctured our ignorance straightforwardly, such as when he asked whether film was a verbal art form or a visual art form. Under the trendy spell of McLuhanism, I answered "Visual," and Russ replied, "Haven't movies been talking for a long time now?" That was an epiphany about the medium and a warning against glibness.

Russ was already a leading expert on D. W. Griffith and, as you remember, put on a spectacular showing of *The Birth of a Nation* in the campus theater, using an original 35mm tinted print from the Museum of Modern Art along with a fifty-piece orchestra, a choir, and sound effects, including simulated gunshots. That somewhat ingenuous presentation caused an uproar with a Black students' organization protesting. *Birth*'s blatant racism demands that it be shown with a vigorous discussion to frame the still-incendiary issues surrounding it, and even that is difficult now, as I found while teaching excerpts from it with a colleague at San Francisco State. I covered Russ's extravaganza for the *State Journal*, juxtaposing head shots of Griffith and the Black protest leader on the front page. Russ's similarly flamboyant 35mm screening of an original print of *Intolerance* was not controversial but was equally instructive in showing how films were exhibited in the early days of the medium.

"The Madison film mafia"

How did it change your life, as it did mine, to become part of our "Madison film mafia"?

My sense of alienation in Madison was relieved to some extent when I found my niche among our group of cinephiles. A good gang of young men and women indeed, full of intellectual conversation, film lore, and an enthusiastic welcoming spirit that cut through all boundaries. That camaraderie enabled me to make some close and enduring friends and start dating regularly while enjoying the rich Madison film milieu. Still, a major reason I began devoting myself to writing film articles and books was to stand out from even that group. It was my conscious way of creating an identity that would compel respect from my peers, whether they all liked me or not. Out of the need to solve such problems in life comes our choice of an identity. In those years, film became my substitute for religion. When I eventually lost my faith in the world of filmmaking, it was another shattering blow until I gradually recovered from that as well.

I was fortunate to find among the Madison film mafia a wise and sympathetic mentor who recognized my talents and saw through my idiosyncrasies to something deeper. Bill Donnelly was a bearded, erudite, avuncular, slyly humorous graduate student in English literature, about thirty-five years old at a time, who took an interest in me when we were involved in running the Wisconsin Film Society, the oldest film society on campus. Bill made me the head of that group, which had about seven hundred members. We were also the official campus film society until the university stripped us of that status for allowing Stuart Gordon to stage his renegade 1968 production of the "Nude *Peter Pan*" in the auditorium where we had booked a program of Buster Keaton films—more on that later.

Bill shrewdly recognized that I cultivated my apparent lack of sophistication, my image as a hayseed from Wisconsin, as a façade to fool people. I did so out of mischief and self-protection. That attitude masked my disdain toward those who snubbed me. But my approach was too subtle, so I doubt it was effective. It took me a long time to learn to speak out against derision rather than internalizing the rejection.

I certainly did not get that hostile treatment from you and your brother Gerry, who shared my interest in film and quickly became friends of mine. We found we were simpatico as fellow members of the congenial and influential group that gave me a haven from my second year onward. Finding that niche greatly improved my life and helped me develop into an ardent cinephile. I appreciated the background you and Gerry had in spending a lot of time in New York and your experience seeing *The Searchers* in VistaVision in a theater as kids when it came out in 1956. Only later did I learn about your Southern roots as well and discover our common love of baseball, Danny, so at first I didn't fully understand you two guys either. Then I was even more intrigued. (And now we are collaborators! I've always admired how you've written such distinguished books on baseball as well as valuable books on film.)

The Madison film scene

Madison was an extraordinary place to see films in those days, wasn't it?

The campus was one of the best places in the country to watch films during that formative period of film studies. We had an astonishing total of thirty-five campus film societies showing 16mm prints of a wide range of films, classic and recent. As long as I turned a profit for the Wisconsin Film Society by showing Fellini or Bergman films to lure people into buying their semester passes, I could use the extra cash to rent films of lesser audience appeal that I needed to see, such as John Ford's *Wagon Master* and Billy Wilder's *Ace in the Hole*. That was a free double bill I paired mischievously — one of the most optimistic and one of the most pessimistic films ever made in America, shown together.

I showed a lot of mainstream classics ranging widely through film history but also ran some films with shock value, such as a program of *Freaks* with *The Blood of the Beasts*, the Georges Franju short that contrasts fancy Parisian restaurants with graphic scenes inside slaughterhouses. One of the maxims I lived by in my early rebellious days was Picasso's "Good taste is the enemy of creativity." At the Memorial Union, we had a theater called the Play Circle that showed films on weekends in 35mm; we were on the committee that chose the films in impassioned, often angry debates. At the State Historical Society on the library mall, we were fortunate to have collections of the pre-1948 Warner Bros. and RKO 16mm prints as well as paper documents — story and script files, contracts, publicity materials, etc. — in the United Artists collection. The Historical Society also has many collections of filmmakers' papers, notably blacklistees and other luminaries including Kirk Douglas, whom I wrote a short book about in 1976. I gave my papers to the Historical Society when I left Madison in 1973 and have been adding to them ever since. (It's now called the Wisconsin Historical Society.)

The university also generously let me watch the 16mm prints of films ordered for courses in every department. I would go to the basement of the Bureau of Audio-Visual Instruction (BAVI) at 9 AM to watch films all day. Sometimes I would bring along friends, such as my radical friend Ken Mate when he was hiding out from the police; Kenny was also a Ford fan and later served as cinematographer on the last film I directed. After watching films all day, I would grab dinner and watch another film — screenings were announced on posters on walls and telephone poles — before going home to work on my Welles book or a screenplay. I remember going back to the rooming house where I lived and excitedly telling my roommates, "I've just seen two of the greatest films ever made!" They thought I was goofy, but it was true, for one day I saw *Intolerance* and *Battleship Potemkin* for the first time. On another day, I saw *Duck Soup* followed by *The Grapes of Wrath*.

Sid Chatterjee, a friend who ran another film society run by an eating co-op called the Green Lantern, gave me a key to let me watch films in the early-morning hours when I worked at the *State Journal*. Sometimes the neighbors called the cops on me until I turned down the soundtracks. The campus screenings helped me see films I needed for *Orson Welles* (which I mostly wrote from 1966 to 1970; it was published in 1972 by the British Film Institute's Cinema One series) and the critical study, *John Ford,* that Michael Wilmington and I wrote between 1969 and 1971 (it took until 1974 before it was published by the BFI Cinema Two series).

"The annual *Searchers* riot"

As we both remember, the passion surrounding the Union Film Committee over which films to book in the Play Circle could result in debates that were quite heated.

Yes, that for me is a microcosm of the passions surrounding films in those days. I remember walking past your brother Gerry as he exited a Film Committee meeting grinning despite having coffee dripping down his body after it was thrown all over him in some kind of argument, and I remember Mike Wilmington's omnipresent mother, Edna, following Gerry and shouting at him for some reason. We all took that task of choosing films to show in the Union Play Circle with great earnestness. There was a schism in the membership between what were called "Politicos" vs. "Aesthetes." Broadly speaking, those were the hardcore radical Godard vs. the classical Ford-Wayne factions. I was in the latter group. Being in the throes of disassociating myself from Catholicism made me antipathetic to any kind of doctrinaire ideology, and it did not help that Godard had become anathema to me after my attempt to interview him when he came to Madison was met with hostility.

Other than learning that someone bashed him over the head with a hammer, two of my many memories of Michael Wilmington, the future critic of the Chicago Tribune *and* Los Angeles Times, *were how upset he was that I didn't love* The Rules of the Game; *and when he brought a record player into the Play Circle so he could play Gene Pitney's great hit single, "The Man Who Shot Liberty Valance" before and after screenings of the movie, because it wasn't on the soundtrack.*

I remember the memorable meeting of the committee when Wilmington gave a fifteen-minute speech extolling Howard Hawks's autumnal Western *El Dorado* and wound up in tears. Mike's fervent oration stunned the members so much that they voted to bring that John Wayne movie to campus, including even the Politicos. And after vigorous arguing, we also managed to get *The Searchers* accepted by the film committee, despite Russell Merritt inaccurately quipping, "Is that the movie where Natalie Wood plays an Indian?" Unfortunately, the first time we showed the stunning original 35mm print of *The Searchers* at the Play Circle, President Nixon announced his illegal invasion of Cambodia, the students rioted, the National Guard occupied the campus and ringed the Union with rifles and bayonets, and hardly anyone could get in to see the movie. So we managed to schedule *The Searchers* again exactly a year later, but we hadn't factored in that the students would hold another riot to commemorate the previous year's riot, with the National Guard again ringing the Union. I called it "the annual *Searchers* riot" and half-seriously developed the theory that somehow that incendiary film had caused the riots.

I was a full-time student but in at least one year I saw 500 movies, on campus and in our many local theaters. What about you?

Not quite that many! And as I did with books, I kept lists of the movies I watched. In 1967, for example, I saw 379 movies. My totals for other years in Madison are comparable but incomplete. Andrew Sarris's 1968 book *The American Cinema: Directors and Directions 1929–1968* became our bible. We used that paperback as our dog-eared guide for what films to seek out and underlined the titles we had seen. My tastes in movies, like my youthful tastes in literature, were omnivorous, including silents, foreign films, and Hollywood classics of the sound era, as well as new films at downtown theaters. If I liked a movie, I would watch it repeatedly, with *Citizen Kane* popping up over and over. I saw *Bonnie and Clyde* in a theater twice a day on two different days in October 1967, and three more times in November. Although some of our cinephiles talked the managers of the downtown theaters into giving them passes, even though I was barely scraping by, I had the absurd conviction that I should pay for the films I was watching in theaters, to help encourage Hollywood to make good ones. Even today when I see *Bonnie and Clyde* and other films from that era, I find I have them virtually memorized down to the smallest movements of performance, action, and editing.

My eclectic viewing that November ranged from the silent *Variety* and *Storm Over Asia* and several Keaton films to films I saw twice, *Footlight Parade, Sergeant York*, and *Jules et Jim*. Others that month included two W. C. Fields films, *Une Femme est une Femme, Gone With the Wind, Accident, Winchester '73, L'Eclisse, Yankee Doodle Dandy...* you get the picture! I tended to seek out films made by directors I most admired, so my list for the first half of 1968 shows that I watched 23 by Welles, 17 Hitchcocks, 15 Fords, and 13 each by Truffaut and Bergman.

In later years I found that I have gaps with certain popular films with major stars but whose directors I viewed as mediocre, so I've been filling in those gaps on the Criterion Channel and elsewhere. But Madison in those days before cable TV and streaming was a cinephile's paradise, and my autodidactic education in film history was insatiable.

How did you get started reviewing films in Madison?

Introducing films to our Wisconsin Film Society audience of several hundred people in B-10 Commerce was my earliest training for a teaching career. At the suggestion of Bill Donnelly, I began writing the "film notes" we traditionally mimeographed to hand out to our members when they came to see such movies as *King Kong* and *The Passion of Joan of Arc.* That got me started as a film critic in 1966, my second year in Madison. It was my first taste of critical controversy too, especially when I shortsightedly panned *Kong* as "camp junk," which provoked outrage from some of our members. That taught me not to be flippant in my comments on movies and prompted me to take another look at *Kong*, which I recognized is a great achievement in special effects and fantasy storytelling, despite its hokey dramaturgy.

After coming to campus with the ambition of editing our principal student newspaper, *The Daily Cardinal*, I quickly found it too cliquish to bother trying. But I reviewed films and plays and wrote other articles for the paper. The first film I reviewed for the *Cardinal* was some French movie in which the main character falls asleep and wakes up at the end, when it's revealed that the whole story has been a dream. I innocently mentioned the ending in my review and received an irate phone call from some young women in a dorm. That made me understand you shouldn't give away the ending in a review. Unless it's a historical incident, as in *Glory*, the great movie about Black soldiers in the Civil War that I reviewed for *Daily Variety*. I now find that the obsession with not revealing "spoilers"—even in supposedly serious film magazines and books!—is having a damaging effect on film reviewing and film study. But I can see the point of not doing so in newspaper reviews, since, as the Broadway theater critic Walter Kerr once observed, a review is written for a reader who haven't seen the work in question, but a critical analysis is written for a reader who has seen it. That distinction is usually lost in practice, since reviewers like to inflate their importance by calling themselves critics.

In the summer of 1966, I was the second-string film reviewer for the *Cardinal* behind Larry Cohen when much of the staff had gone on vacation. Larry went on to write screenplays, specializing in Stephen King adaptations, including Brian De Palma's hit film version of *Carrie* as well as the disastrous Broadway musical version. (To differentiate himself from the B-movie director Larry Cohen, Larry billed himself professionally as Lawrence D. Cohen.) Larry kicked me out of my job, though, when his friends on the paper returned to campus that fall, which he hadn't warned me about and I found infuriating.

One of my longest and most enthusiastic reviews in the *Cardinal* was of Woody Allen's first full-fledged comedy feature as a writer-director-star, *Take the Money and Run*, in 1969. Since I had first seen him acting in his screenplay *What's New Pussycat*, directed by Clive Donner, Allen was already one of my favorite comedians and modern filmmakers. Like many others of my generation, I identified with his wry and angst-ridden attitude toward life. Although most of my writing seemed serious, a writer for the *Daily Cardinal* who did a feature on me, Elaine Cohen, described my prose with shrewd insight as "quietly merry."

The rise of cinephilia and film studies

How did you see yourself fitting in with the growing interest in cinephilia around the country in that period before film studies became "respectable" and codified in academia?

In those days, our young "Film Generation" of scholars and critics, under the influence of the *Cahiers du Cinéma* critics and Andrew Sarris of *The Village Voice*, were fighting to legitimize the importance of classical Hollywood studio filmmaking. Sarris helped revolutionize film studies, especially the study of Hollywood studio films, with what he called the "auteur theory," which he defined with his "Notes on the Auteur Theory in 1962" in the winter 1962–1963 issue of *Film Culture* and expanded upon in "The American Cinema," his lengthy Spring 1963 section of that journal, which served as the basis for his 1968 book of the same title. Sarris adapted his concept from the young French critics of the 1950s, such as François Truffaut, Jean-Luc Godard, Claude Chabrol, and Eric Rohmer, who created what they called "*la politique des auteurs*" or the policy of authors before becoming filmmakers themselves. But in the process, what the French critics were doing, recognizing how directors with a strong vision could turn even a script they hadn't written into a personal piece of work, became blurred into the misguided notion that someone is an auteur only if he or she both writes and directs a film. That limiting concept still permeates much of academia today, including San Francisco State University's School of Cinema, where I tried to persuade students to learn the art of collaboration, telling them that not every writer can direct and not every director should write.

Our early generation of film scholars in the late 1960s and early '70s laid the foundation for film studies before it became an accepted academic field in the 1970s, when it courted respectability by miring itself in theory and was mostly a hidebound branch of linguistics heavily indebted to French semiologists and Marxists. Our pioneering generation of film scholars, however, tended to be auteurists in the Sarris camp, and we could be faulted in those days for paying insufficient attention to a director's collaborators.

We also were convinced that popular filmmaking had as much artistic value as the foreign films that were then in vogue during the American art-house movement. We had to overcome the deep-rooted American prejudice against popular culture that permeated academia and journalism until we helped to found the field of film studies in the late 1960s. We argued that the traditional cultural distinctions between "high" and "low" art were meaningless, even foolish, particularly in regard to classic Hollywood studio filmmaking, which offered such a rich vein of artistry. We succeeded in our mission beyond our wildest dreams, although in retrospect, we may have been too successful in exalting popular filmmaking and auteurism in particular. Most of the groundbreaking film books published in the late Sixties and early Seventies, including mine, focused around directors. They were necessary but not sufficient. Our myopic tendency to downplay the contributions of screenwriters and others was a flaw that became increasingly evident to me after I entered the industry myself and understood more about the realities of the filmmaking process.

After the brief flowering of the "New Hollywood" of personal screenwriting and directing in the 1970s before the blockbuster phenomenon took hold, the American film industry soon degenerated into making mostly trash for the adolescent male audience, as is the case now. Filmmaking with more adult subject matter and films that feature people talking and having relationships migrated from theaters to cable TV and streaming sites, while the theatrical audience contracted drastically. And already by the late Sixties, the film industry picked up on Sarris's "auteur theory" as a handy marketing tool to promote directors as if they are the sole authors of their films. That furthered the narrow-minded neglect of the director's collaborators by reviewers and academicians.

As our generation of critics and film historians matured, however, we came to offer correctives to auteurism and qualifications of Sarris's debatable categorizations of directors. We found in his "Far Side of Paradise" and "Less Than Meets the Eye" categories such splendid directors as Frank Capra, George Cukor, Samuel Fuller, Leo McCarey, Douglas Sirk, George Stevens, Preston Sturges, King Vidor, Raoul Walsh, John Huston, Elia Kazan, David Lean, William Wellman, and Billy Wilder. Sarris himself became more accepting of those directors later, as Billy Wilder told me about Sarris and other critics, "When I was very successful, they beat me over the head, now maybe some of them are a little gentler because they take pity on me. They commiserate with me. Maybe they are human, at that. They just don't feel like kicking an elderly man in the ass anymore." I've written books about three of those directors Sarris underrated and American Film Institute Life Achievement Award TV specials about two of them. Sarris's book more accurately can be seen now as a jumping-off point for argumentation rather than a bible.

We post-Sarrisites also have championed the work of screenwriters, actors, cinematographers, and other contributors to the filmmaking process. But the damage was already done. And as Jonathan Rosenbaum writes in his 2000/2002 book, *Movie Wars: How Hollywood and the Media Limit What Films You See* (which was originally published with the more accurate and provocative subtitle *How Hollywood and the Media Conspire to Limit What Films We Can See*), most American reviewers regrettably have gone along with commercial imperatives by focusing their attention on the big-budget, highly promoted studio productions at the expense of championing smaller independent films. We used to proclaim that "Film Is the Art Form of the Twentieth Century," and as true as that was and is, we are now living in the twenty-first century.

Our film generation's taste in movies was strongly stimulated by the artistry and creative freedom of foreign films brought to the U.S. in the 1950s and '60s, but in more recent years, the market for foreign films in the U.S. has shrunk to near invisibility. Multiplexes have crowded out smaller theaters, many of which have closed, and film advertising has become prohibitively expensive for all but major distributors. In my opinion, television advertising costs and the trend toward saturation distribution of blockbusters that compounds those costs are a major culprit in the dumbing-down of American films, just as TV ad costs are in the coarsening of American politics. In both cases, promotion, whether of movies or candidates, has been reduced to short slogans and brief video displays.

Streaming services have taken up some of the slack, but cinephilia has suffered accordingly in this country, even though Rosenbaum argues somewhat quixotically that cinephilia is alive and well, if mutated into something more esoteric than it was in our youth; Rosenbaum is special because he travels the world to search out films that are hard to see in this country. Not only do fewer Americans watch foreign films today than we did in the 1960s and '70s, but the passion for classic films tends to exist more among older people now. My own work as a critic and film historian over the years has largely been centered on classical Hollywood films and filmmakers but also includes such modern filmmakers as Steven Spielberg and the Coen Bros. And my work from the mid-1970s onward serves as something of a deliberate corrective to the excesses of auteurism and the over-adulation of what André Bazin called the "genius of the system."

Getting published

When I met you in Madison in 1967, you were already writing your first book on Orson Welles and articles for film magazines. Nobody else I knew at the time was doing that until you influenced others to follow in your footsteps. How did your career path evolve?

After I sold my article about Greg Spahn and his father to a national magazine when I was twelve in 1960 and persisted in writing articles on baseball for the next few years even though I didn't sell any, it wasn't until 1967, when I discovered that I could write articles for film magazines, that I began getting published regularly. That was a fortuitous time to begin, because the rise of cinephilia was leading to a boom in film magazines and publishing lines of film books, so the market was wide open for young beginners. I started publishing articles and interviews for film magazines in the U.S. and England, which established me as a well-known film scholar even before I finished writing what in effect was my scholarly debut, my book *Orson Welles*.

My first article published in a film magazine was a profile of three leading reviewers—Pauline Kael, Dwight Macdonald, and Stanley Kauffmann—for the Summer 1967 issue of *Film Heritage*. F. A. (Tony) Macklin, the editor of *Film Heritage,* kindly gave me that break and ten dollars, and published other articles I wrote. My initial piece was sort of a rumination on what I thought film reviewing should be, nothing profound but an opening salvo, eclectic to a fault, perhaps. My debut piece surprisingly prompted an angry letter to me from Andrew Sarris demanding to know why I hadn't included him, even though I'd written that he deserved a separate article of his own. That perhaps shows the influence of literary criticism on my work as a film critic, since I included Macdonald and Kauffmann while slighting Sarris, who was more purely a cinephile and in retrospect should have taken Kauffmann's place in the trio I studied. That article was an early sign of how I often seem to provoke controversy with my writing even when I don't set out to do so.

As a result, I unfortunately never became close to Sarris, especially after our Ford book preceded his long-delayed book *The John Ford Movie Mystery* in publication by the BFI; I wrote him about it, and he sent back a hostile response, saying he didn't believe in corresponding with rival authors. But I had a brief and pleasant meeting with Sarris in California many years later, and he gave an enthusiastic blurb for my Frank Capra biography and wrote a gratifying letter of support for me when I was advancing to tenure at San Francisco State.

The same year I wrote my article about the film reviewers, I pursued my interests in theater and literature by writing a profile of the veteran British actor Bramwell Fletcher. I interviewed him backstage at the University of Wisconsin, Milwaukee, as he made himself up to do his one-man show of George Bernard Shaw. I tried selling the article to *Life* but wound up finding a more suitable home in the scholarly English publication *The Shavian*. "I thoroughly enjoyed your lively article," Fletcher wrote me. I wasn't yet making more than a pittance from writing articles for publication, but it didn't discourage me, since I knew enough to understand that I needed to establish myself first.

I quickly did. I was asked to contribute articles by Ernest Callenbach, the editor of *Film Quarterly* at UC Berkeley, which was then the leading American film magazine. I wrote film and book reviews for *Film Quarterly* as well as an ambitious 1970 career profile of a subject of one of my later books, Billy Wilder (a piece for which I enlisted Mike Wilmington as co-writer). I also became a regular contributor to *Sight and Sound* in England and New York's *Film Comment*. I was shrewd enough to know that if I planted chapters of my book-in-progress on Welles in film magazines, it would make it easier to sell the book to the British Film Institute's Cinema One series.

So when I finished the manuscript, I wrote Penelope Houston, my editor at *Sight and Sound*, who also edited the book series, and asked her if she was interested in seeing it. She replied that she was familiar enough with my work that she could almost accept the book sight unseen. In short order, it was sold to that pioneering series, which offered a good launching pad for new young writers while helping develop the nascent field of film studies, and the Viking Press picked it up for the U.S. I was told that *Orson Welles* was the bestselling title in the Cinema One series, selling about 15,000 copies. But I didn't receive any royalties until I made a small settlement with the BFI for *Orson Welles* and our Cinema Two critical study *John Ford* when they reverted the rights to those books more than two decades later.

Another big moment in our Madison days was when Swedish director Jan Troell came to Wisconsin and needed extras for his two-part epic, The Emigrants *and* The New Land. *I was in the bunch of students who can be seen as extras. I don't believe you were in them, but you were there. I was in at least three scenes totaling about 45 seconds, playing two or three different characters wearing the same slouch hat and ugly garments. As a farmer, I walk between some cows; then I'm a gambler sitting with a bunch of extras dramatically rolling some dice near the riverboat; and then I am, deliberately on my part, the last passenger walking up a plank onto the boat, feigning interest as Liv Ullmann's character panics because her child is missing. Troell angrily yelled at me for being slow and then walking directly into his camera, but when editing his film, he'd cleverly use the moment I made the screen go black to end the scene. The moments with me and Liv were shown on Oscar night because she was nominated for best actress for* The Emigrants. *(Neither of us won.) Troell also shot my character waving goodbye to my grinning, similarly dressed brother, who for some reason is sitting on a large tree stump, but Troell deleted it, and Gerry didn't make it into the movie.*

I didn't make it into those films either, since I went to the location with Mike Wilmington to write about them. The feature we wrote about the making of that intimate two-part epic was our entrée into *Sight and Sound*. Troell's films about Swedish immigrants coming to Minnesota (which was doubled by Wisconsin) were the only ones I saw shooting while I lived in my home state. Wilmington and I took a bus to the rural site, and true to form, Mike spilled chocolate milk all over his white shirt as we walked along the country road. We found the company in a field near some train tracks and introduced ourselves and were told to talk with the producer, Bengt Forslund. I stupidly felt irked to have to interview a producer but learned a valuable lesson right away, since Forslund was a charming and erudite film scholar as well as an enterprising filmmaker, and he was far more outgoing than the taciturn, somewhat sullen-seeming director.

Troell mostly hid behind his camera while doubling as his own cinematographer. He became upset when I was gauche enough to start by admitting I hadn't seen any of his films. He said they had played at the Chicago Film Festival, as if I should have been expected to go there to see them. But I never made that mistake again. Mike and I rode on a train taking the characters played by Max von Sydow, Liv Ullmann, et al to their new home as Troell filmed them with his handheld camera. The stars were gracious and expansive as Mike and I interviewed them at the end of their workday. Other than that experience, I had only a vague idea of how films were made until I moved to California. I found that the film industry in those days kept the public from knowing much about how the system worked, as a way of protecting itself. So I was fortunate to edge my way inside the system through my journalistic fact-finding process, although many of the most crucial lessons I had to learn were belated and came as a result of my making mistakes out of ignorance or foolish trust in the people I met there.

I continued to write sometimes in collaboration with Wilmington on pieces for magazines, until we had a falling-out in 1971 over our Ford book. I now was making modest amounts of money for my articles to supplement my income, but that was never my goal in writing them. I wrote about films and filmmakers I was passionate about. I was working as a dishwasher and orderly to support myself while also writing my Welles book. I was fired as a dishwasher at a ritzy private dormitory in the summer of 1967 when we workers were talking about the Detroit riots before lunch and I remarked that if I were Black I'd be out rioting too.

Despite the fact that I had found a congenial group of colleagues among my fellow cinephiles in Madison, by writing articles and books on film I was consciously setting out to make my name in the larger world. It became a way of life for me to keep doing so; it stemmed from my need to prove my worth and become acceptable to that coterie among the student body and others who continued to scorn me or find me insignificant. That's one reason my college years are so important to me. I've often reflected on how much we allow youthful trauma to govern the course of our lives, for better and for worse.

"Rough Sledding with Pauline Kael"

Your knack for finding controversy soon got you embroiled in a donnybrook with Pauline Kael.

Besides publishing my chapter on *Citizen Kane* from my work-in-progress on Welles in 1968, *Film Heritage* ran "Rough Sledding with Pauline Kael," my critical response to her shameful 1971 *New Yorker* article, "Raising Kane," claiming that Welles had nothing to do with writing *Citizen Kane*. She falsely charged that Welles's collaborator, Hollywood veteran and former newspaperman Herman J. Mankiewicz, who correctly gets first-position credit on the screenplay, had done it all himself and that Welles, who is billed second for the script, had falsely appropriated a writing credit on the film.

Mankiewicz was always a hero of mine as a fellow reporter-turned-screenwriter whose work gives such sly authenticity to what is, among other things, the best newspaper movie ever made. I spent a month hauling my portable typewriter to the State Historical Society typing an exact copy of the screenplay of *Kane* by Mankiewicz and Welles (in the collection of Welles's lawyer, L. Arnold Weissberger), because I could not afford to Xerox it. In a 2020 article for wellesnet.com that dealt in part with the Kael-*Kane* credit controversy, I wrote that *Kane*

> remains my favorite screenplay, and I have always loved Mankiewicz for his intelligence, sage and cutting wit about Hollywood, savvy journalistic background, and mastery as a screenwriter. But Mankiewicz did not deserve all the credit for the script of *Kane*, as Kael... would have us believe. To pay tribute to this still relatively unknown Hollywood screenwriter (who famously wired [Ben] Hecht and others to come there because

"MILLIONS ARE TO BE GRABBED OUT HERE AND YOUR ONLY COMPETITION IS IDIOTS. DON'T LET THIS GET AROUND") does not require denigrating his collaborator on the best film he ever wrote. Credit is not a zero-sum game, even if Kael, *The New Yorker* (whose vaunted fact-checking system failed spectacularly in that instance), and Hollywood tend to think so.

Kael called my Madison apartment unexpectedly on the day the first installment of her attack on Welles was published, February 20, 1971. She apologized for not using my name in the first paragraph when she mocked "schoolbook...articles" on *Kane* that use hilfalutin' language. Both quotes she mocks were accurately taken from a single source, my *Film Heritage* essay on the film. She said her editor, William Shawn, did not like her penchant for attacking other writers on film and forbade her to do so by name in the magazine. She had overdone that in the past, especially in her denigration of Andrew Sarris. I said I didn't mind being criticized but thought her article was unfair to Welles and one-sided, since she hadn't interviewed him but relied only on Mankiewicz partisans. She said she found no need to interview Welles since she knew what he would say; she admitted she had written "a brief for Mankiewicz."

We had a cordial but spirited talk for about half an hour, and the subject turned general about criticism. She condescendingly told me I would be a better writer if I didn't reach for overly fancy rhetorical language in my writing, a point I took to heart. I recognized I had a tendency to show off and use flamboyant prose that sometimes became detached from meaning or only vaguely connected with analysis of the films I was writing about. An example that jumps out in my mind, from the career overview of Wilder that Wilmington and I wrote for *Film Quarterly* in 1970, is the phrase "a sort of *saftig* Pirandellianism" to describe Wilder's meta satire of his stars. Someone I know wondered at the time what the hell that meant. I should have borrowed Robert Browning's explanation when someone asked him to explain one of his poems: "When I wrote it, only God and I knew; now God alone knows!" The reference to Luigi Pirandello should have been "Pirandellism." And, since I mostly had Marilyn Monroe in mind, I should have written the Yiddish *zaftig*, meaning curvaceous, instead of the German *saftig*, meaning juicy.

As my writing has matured, I believe that concentrating on clarity instead of overt virtuosity has helped me take a more reader-friendly approach rather than preening as some critics do to flaunt their credentials. One of the consequences I find is that my writing ability might be underrated, because it's the showoffy stuff that usually gets plaudits in the field, including the dazzling but somewhat woolly and obscure writing of Manny Farber, the emptily narcissistic verbosity of David Thomson, and indeed the hectoring flamboyance of Kael herself. Someone I know well once told me she thought that taking Kael's advice to avoid excessive language had made me less adventurous in my prose style. I tend to disagree, since I lean more toward emulating the clear and elegantly logical prose of Robin Wood, my role model as a film critic, and the literary critics I learned from in those years, such as T. S. Eliot and Leslie Fiedler. But I can see her point; decisions about what stylistic pathways to take in a writer's formative years often turn out to be lasting and become, in their complexity, part of who you are, for better or for worse.

What were the various responses by you and other Welles scholars to Kael's essay?

I wondered why Kael had bothered to call me on the day her anti-Welles polemic appeared; she reprinted it that October with the shooting script and the cutting continuity in *The "Citizen Kane" Book*. After brooding over her call, I concluded she had made it to try to disarm me from writing a response. I hadn't intended to answer her attack until I realized that's what she was doing. So I turned again to the friendly pages of Tony Macklin's *Film Heritage* to dissect Kael's "Raising Kane" in my fall 1971 article, "Rough Sledding with Pauline Kael." In an unfortunate side-effect I hadn't expected, Tony, who played a key role in helping me get started as a critic, was irked that I agreed with Kael's criticism of my *Kane* article in his magazine as somewhat overwrought, since, as he reminded me, he had done a lot of editing to improve that early piece of mine.

Other Wellesians joined in answering Kael, including Sarris, who wrote a couple of responses and told readers it was ironic that I had written the first sustained piece analyzing Mankiewicz's work on *Kane*, in my appendix on the script in the 1968 book I edited for the Wisconsin Film Society Press, *Persistence of Vision: A Collection of Film Criticism*. Peter Bogdanovich's lengthy, thoroughly researched, eloquent article "The *Kane* Mutiny" in *Esquire* did the best job at the time in demolishing Kael. That is not surprising given that, as Jonathan Rosenbaum later discovered, that article was mostly written by Welles himself under Peter's name! But it was Welles scholar Robert L. Carringer who did the definitive deconstruction of Kael's attack. In his Winter 1978 essay, "The Scripts of *Citizen Kane*" in the journal *Critical Inquiry*, Carringer methodically and thoroughly did what Kael had failed to do: actually study the evolution of the screenplay in its various drafts. He traced how the two writers worked and why their joint credit, with Mankiewicz in first position, is fair and accurate. Kael compounded the shamelessness of her hitjob on Welles by continuing to reprint "Raising Kane" without corrections, including in her valedictory personal monument, *For Keeps: 30 Years at the Movies*, in 1994.

I wrote a further essay on the controversy titled "The Screenplay as Genre" that appeared in the 2009 Harvard University Press anthology *A New Literary History of America*, at the request of the editors, Greil Marcus and Werner Sollors, and I reprinted it in my 2017 collection, *Two Cheers for Hollywood: Joseph McBride on Movies*. And when Netflix released a 2020 film, *Mank*, that purports to dramatize the writing process on *Kane* but hews to the Kael party line, I critiqued that meretricious film for Ray Kelly's scholarly and fan site, wellesnet.com. With Gary Oldman playing the title role of Herman Mankiewicz, *Mank*, directed by David Fincher from a script by his late father, Jack, casts a glowering 39-year-old British actor, Tom Burke, as another caricature of Welles, the 24-year-old wunderkind. I noted that the film portrays him as "a bullying maniac and credit thief, a figure out of Kael's malicious fantasies" and "even goes beyond Kael to portray Welles as an overhyped charlatan as a director."

I analyze *Mank* in the context of the frequent deployment of "pernicious myths" in the American mass media "designed to tear down a great filmmaker." I note that in my 2006 book, *What Ever Happened to Orson Welles?: A Portrait of an Independent Career*, I discuss at length how "the American antipathy to Welles on a more serious, overt level stems from the unflagging radicalism of his work, both thematically and stylistically." And I explain,

> The Finchers' evident thematic intent is to show Mank heroically rallying, for once in his life, to write something of great value but almost being bullied out of credit by a craven, arrogant thief. To pull off that magic trick of storytelling, Fincher and his late father must (1) refer to what Mank is writing as "the first draft"; (2) ignore the previous weeks Mankiewicz

and Welles spent together in Hollywood working out
the structure and characters of what became *Citizen
Kane*; (3) ignore the parallel draft of the script Welles
was working on in Beverly Hills at the same time
Mank was writing his long draft in Victorville, some
of which was being sent down to Welles to revise;
(4) fail to depict accurately the visit or visits Welles
paid to Victorville while Mank was writing (a photo
of him there with Mank and Houseman can be
consulted in [the 1978 *Mank: The Wit, World, and
Life of Herman Mankiewicz*, Richard] Meryman's
biography), even though Marion Davies (Amanda
Seyfried) is shown visiting, which did not happen;
(5) downplay as mere "editing" or "noodling" the
numerous drafts Welles did in reworking their early
work in at least seven drafts; and (6) ignore Welles's
constant revisions even through shooting.

No doubt that will not be my last word on this fraught
subject, for as I observed that "our culture has not progressed
much beyond Hollywood's benighted 1939 view of the still-
troubling *wunderkind*. Perhaps most Americans prefer to
cling to their anti-intellectual view of artists as sinister people
who should be ostracized. We still view maverick artists not
as valiant figures but as egomaniacal monsters who mistreat
hapless underlings and demand credit they don't deserve....
Mankiewicz himself would probably scoff at *Mank*. He
was too smart and self-aware and generous at heart to do
otherwise. But the mythology of Kael and Mank will likely
endure, for it is a tale our belittling culture needs to cling to,
and as Welles prophetically told Bogdanovich, 'Cleaning up
after Miss Kael is going to take a lot of scrubbing.'"

*You had to be industrious to track down or, even harder, do
research on old films in the early days of cinephilia, unlike
today, when so many films are easily available on TV and
homevideo.*

Now a film scholar, as I do on my books, can watch a
film or a sequence over and over to study it, which used
to require numerous strenuous trips, as well as learning
the skill of taking notes in the dark. Back in my Madison
days, I sometimes had to take buses to see films I needed
to see, either with Wilmington to Chicago (usually at the
rowdy Clark Theater repertory house in the Loop, where
legend has it that an usher once shot an unruly patron)
or to Milwaukee (where we argued after seeing Hawks's

patchy final film, *Rio Lobo*, which Mike stubbornly found faultless).

I once even took a bus to another town in Wisconsin, I think Kenosha, and actually rented a hotel room to watch Leo McCarey's *The Bells of St. Mary's* on late-night TV. It took me thirty years to write my essay on that film, finally published in my *Irish America* film column in 2000 as "My Guiltiest Pleasure: *The Bells of St. Mary's*: A Classic That Humanizes Catholicism" and later reprinted in *Two Cheers for Hollywood*. Richard Corliss once asked me to contribute a "Guilty Pleasures" column when he was editing *Film Comment*, but I told him I didn't believe in that concept except in the case of *The Bells of St. Mary's*, since at heart it's a love story between a priest and a nun. But Richard said I couldn't write a "Guilty Pleasures" column on just one film.

Both you and I wrote for the early issues of The Velvet Light Trap, *but did you also write for other local publications in Madison?*

When our friend Russell Campbell started *The Velvet Light Trap* in Madison in 1971, which drew from the resources of the State Historical Society film and paper archives, I was considered one of the founders of that quarterly journal (as the leading film scholar David Bordwell, whom I first met briefly when he first came to Madison, later reminded me). Wilmington and I contributed parts of our work-in-progress on Ford to some of the first issues. Russell's own writing on film is brilliant. The magazine continues today semiannually from the University of Texas Press, edited by graduate students from the UW and the UT Austin.

While hanging around the UW campus, I also sold some anodyne features on campus life to the *Capital Times*, Madison's liberal afternoon paper; I had made that contact with the managing editor, Elliott Maraniss, through my mother. But Maraniss's supposed crusading liberalism proved shallow. His paper published an article I wrote that was critical of the UW's Integrated Liberal Studies program. My mother unfortunately had enrolled me in ILS when I was a freshman, and I found its grouping of courses unengaging. I quoted one of its founders expressing unhappiness to me with how the program had turned out. Then that august professor lied and claimed I had misquoted him, and Maraniss took his side. Maraniss next heatedly rejected an interview I had obtained with the university's new chancellor, William Sewell, which put some hard questions to him about how he would handle campus protests. The interview, which I published instead in the *Daily Cardinal*, proved prophetic when Sewell caused a furor by bringing the Madison police to campus to bust heads during the 1967 Dow Chemical protest.

As you know because you were among them, antiwar students had occupied the Commerce Building in a sit-in to protest Dow's making of napalm for the Vietnam War. The police savagely assaulted the students both inside and outside the building, causing many injuries, and teargassed the campus. That was the incident that radicalized the campus and led to years of unrest. Sewell's brief tenure as chancellor never recovered from that incident, and he resigned the following year. During the Dow protest, I was holding the bullhorn of its leader, Robert Cohen, when he dared the police, who were assembled across the street in riot gear, to charge the building, an unfortunate taunt. I dropped the bullhorn and darted out of the way just in time to avoid being trampled. I helped carry some of the more than forty-seven wounded students to cars to transport them to the University Hospitals (eighteen riot cops were also injured). I was seen in a photo on the front page of the following day's *State Journal* helping three other students carry a bloodied protester to safety.

At 3:30 on the afternoon of the Dow protest, the student union was showing Ford's great World War II movie *They Were Expendable*, and Wilmington later recalled that I burst into the theater beforehand shouting that the police were beating students on Bascom Hill. It was surrealistic, and hardly ideal, to see that film for the first time with tear gas hanging in the small Play Circle theater. The Dow protest became the subject of a Peabody Award-winning 2005 PBS documentary, *Two Days in October*, and a prominent part of another documentary, the Oscar-nominated 1979 feature by two members of our Madison film mafia, Glenn Silber and Barry Alexander Brown (Spike Lee's future editor), about the years of protest in Madison, *The War at Home*. David Maraniss, Elliott's son, wrote the excellent 2003 book that served as the basis for the PBS show, *They Marched into Sunlight: War and Peace, Vietnam and America, October 1967*, which intercuts the story of the Dow unrest with the account of a battle during those same two days in Vietnam.

I'm seen in long shot in *The War at Home* trying to pull down a student who had been seated next to me, Robin David, who was heckling Senator Edward Kennedy's October 1966 speech on campus before Kennedy called him up to debate him on the platform. My physical interference was an action I regret and undertook before I became a Vietnam War protester myself. But I continued to argue for the right of speakers of all kinds to be heard on campus, since I believe free speech and vigorous discourse are vital to a university education.

I often marched in antiwar protests in Madison, but when they turned violent, as they often did after Dow, I opposed those increasingly nihilistic tactics of hardcore activists and their allies in the Weather Underground, which I believe hurt the antiwar movement by playing into the hands of Presidents Johnson and Nixon to help them demonize the left. And I deplored the increasingly bloodthirsty rhetoric of the extreme fringe elements of the movement. But while working on *Daily Variety*, I wrote an article defending the 1976 Emile de Antonio documentary film *Underground*, which was the target of FBI harassment due to its fair-minded portrait of the Weather Underground. I was invited by de Antonio to interview him about it on a local public broadcasting station in Los Angeles. That great radical filmmaker told me that *Variety* was the media outlet that had always treated his work most fairly, since we had to tell exhibitors exactly what was in a film and therefore describe his films accurately.

Stepin Fetchit

Going back to your early writing, you have said that your 1970 interview, in Madison, for Film Quarterly *with, and I quote you, "the much-maligned African American comic actor Stepin Fetchit is one of the most influential pieces I've published, which pleases me because he was so mistreated by Hollywood and by film historians." Tell me about the importance of that rare interview then—and now.*

I won what I considered a moral victory by getting that leftist journal to publish the interview. In an allusion to a line of Preacher Casy's in Ford's *The Grapes of Wrath*, I titled it "Stepin Fetchit Talks Back." I spoke with him on a wintry night in his basement dressing room at a strip club in Madison where he served as the opening act. He proved to be a justifiably angry old Black man, unlike his deceptively shambling public image. He was eloquent in his dissection of Hollywood racism ("Hollywood was more segregated than Georgia under the skin," which unfortunately is still mostly true today), his comments on his creative work with Ford ("one of the greatest men who ever lived"), his comments on how he slyly mocked and subverted racial clichés, and his passionate self-defense against Bill Cosby and other myopic detractors who failed to recognize his artistry.

I love Stepin Fetchit, so I'm pleased you defend his controversial screen portrayals for all of us fans by writing, "that his art consisted precisely in mocking and caricaturing the white man's vision of the black: his sly contortions, his surly and exaggerated subservience, can now be seen as a secret weapon in the long racial struggle." I would think this gut-feeling argument of yours is a challenge to defend, and that's why you added this line: "But whatever one makes of Stepin Fetchit's work, he was one of the few nonwhites to achieve status in American films, and he deserves to be remembered."

In fact, as I reveal in *Two Cheers for Hollywood*, those eloquent introductory words about Stepin Fetchit's importance were written by the late Albert Johnson, not me. He was a respected film critic and festival organizer. I was grateful to *Film Quarterly* for running that interview with such a controversial figure, but they wanted a Black writer to validate the subject, so they asked Mr. Johnson, which was OK with me. He didn't take credit for the introduction at the time, but I wanted to give him credit in retrospect in my collection. I love his words about Stepin Fetchit. Although they may be a challenge to defend, they sum up the essence of his art.

The principal reason I felt vindicated that *Film Quarterly* published the interview was that they had turned down the section from my and Mike's work-in-progress, *John Ford*, on his great 1953 film with Stepin Fetchit, *The Sun Shines Bright*. The magazine angered me by falsely claiming that this heartfelt, deeply moving film about a courageous smalltown judge, played by Charles Winninger, thwarting a lynch mob in Jim Crow era Kentucky is a "racist" film. I had persuaded Films Inc. to send the magazine a 16mm print so they could watch the film, but it influenced them negatively due to their myopic, pre-PC political bias. Other than the Stepin Fetchit piece, I stopped writing for *Film Quarterly* after that. And it was even more gratifying that my interview with the controversial Black comedian was later included in *Film Quarterly*'s fortieth anniversary anthology. In more recent years, for whatever reason, the magazine has been hostile to my work.

Not only was Stepin Fetchit a major cultural figure who managed to become the leading Black male star in 1930s

Hollywood, but he was a brilliant comedian whose work can be viewed as subversive of racial stereotyping. You have to be as hip as John Ford to get what Stepin Fetchit is doing. Most people can't see the artist behind the mask. But watch him in Ford's 1934 comedy, *Judge Priest,* and the director's own remake, *The Sun Shines Bright,* to see trenchant commentary on Jim Crow. Stepin Fetchit was at the lowest rung of show business when I interviewed him, unfairly ridiculed and despised, and I wanted to give him his voice again. I am pleased that the interview has helped inspire two sympathetic biographies of the man.

I'm glad he opened up to you and spoke about his relationships with the most militant Black athletes ever, Jack Johnson and Muhammad Ali, to whom he taught Johnson's "anchor punch," which Ali used—the "phantom punch"—to fell Sonny Liston in their second fight.

Yes, Stepin Fetchit was very proud of his association with those two great men. By the way, Ken Burns once told me he thinks his best documentary is *Unforgivable Blackness: The Rise and Fall of Jack Johnson,* which he made in 2004, and I agree (although when I asked Burns in 2018 if it's still his favorite, he said, "I don't know—there are so many others"). It's an astounding documentary, both for its acute social commentary and because you can see some of Johnson's most important fights in almost real time. Ali also knew what it was like to be an outcast, so he took on Stepin Fetchit as an adviser to learn from him about Jack Johnson's unique blend of grace and power in the ring—and perhaps something about how he was such a free man outside the ring, way ahead of his time.

Do you think Stepin Fetchit appreciated all the other African Americans who played maids and porters at the time in Hollywood? He was glad to become a millionaire, but do you think he had any guilt? Or did he have pride that he figured out a way to take studio money and become rich?

He told me, "A Negro couldn't do anything straight, only comedy. I did more acting as a comedian than Sidney Poitier does as an actor…. They brought Willie Best out there to make him an understudy for me. And he wasn't an actor, he wasn't an entertainer or nothin' like that. I didn't need no understudy, because I had a thing going that I had built my own. And the worst thing you'll hear about Stepin Fetchit is when somebody tries to imitate what I do, the first thing they're gonna say is 'Yassuh, yassuh, boss.' I was way away from that." His hubris was to bask in his prominence and wealth and have Chinese servants in 1930s Hollywood. That pride in his achievements was understandable, but it helped lead to his fall. And he lost some favor with the Hollywood studios at the height of his fame when he started commendably resisting doing some demeaning scenes and went on suspension.

After the war he became victim to what we would now call political correctness, and Ford was one of the few people who would hire him. As Sarris wrote of that instance of blacklisting, for postwar liberals it was "better that Fetchit be permanently unemployed than that he serve as a reminder of a shameful blind spot on both sides of the Mason-Dixon line. But for Ford, Mr. Fetchit was an old friend and a familiar face, and he had to make a living like everyone else."

I laugh when you recall Jean-Luc Godard's visit to the University of Wisconsin in 1970 to show See You at Mao, *because that was the first celebrity I ever sat around with, and it wasn't the best experience! I believe you tried to interview him at a different time, because I don't remember that you were one of the five or six film people who sat with our idol at a table in the Rathskeller at the Memorial Union, and we were all a bit freaked out. I remember almost nothing being said to him by us "brilliant" movie experts, because we were all so intimidated, and he just sat there silently waiting for one of us to dare ask the first question. A few years ago I mentioned this gathering to Anna Karina, and she laughed because it was so like him—she was sure that though Godard came across as aloof and, as you recall, "surly" and "obnoxious and intractable," the reason was that he was too shy to talk about his movies.*

I don't remember you and those others being at the table in the Rathskeller; I am sure I would. When I tried to interview Godard, the other people at the table there were Jean-Pierre Gorin, my friend Ellen Whitman, a Grove Press publicist, and a photographer. I always thought Godard was the biggest jerk I ever interviewed in the movie business, which is saying a lot. I think it's overly generous to call him shy. He barely would talk to me when I did my article on his Madison visit that ran in *Sight and Sound*. Godard was so rude he made John Ford seem like a pussycat. I could barely get a word out of Godard. He mostly glared at me. His few remarks were hostile not only toward me but even to his former collaborators, including the great cinematographer Raoul Coutard. But Godard left most of the talking to his current leftist collaborator, Gorin, a pompous spouter of doctrinaire rhetoric who seemed more like his puppetmaster. I find it fascinating that Anna Karina regarded Godard's monosyllabic rudeness as shyness. Maybe that was part of it. But he was in the U.S. on a publicity tour sponsored by Grove Press for his agitprop documentary *British Sounds,* which they opportunistically retitled *See You at Mao* to exploit the sympathies of American youth on a mindless Maoist kick during the period of the murderous Cultural Revolution.

When I wrote a reflection for *Two Cheers* on that experience and Godard's work overall, I watched *See You at Mao* again and realized it is the worst film I have ever seen except for *Pearl Harbor;* those two abysmal stinkers are closely followed by *Eraserhead. See You at Mao* is maddeningly tedious. It's supposed to stir the working class to revolt, but the only revolt it would stir in a member of the working class, or anyone else for that matter, would be to leave the theater. In my article for *Sight and Sound,* besides the interview, I reported on his pontificating and pandering discussion with the Memorial Union audience who idiotically raved about his film. I'm surprised that the magazine ran it, since I was so hostile in a rather over-the-top way. And they even included it in a collection they later published of pieces they had run on Godard.

I try to put my jaded encounter with Godard in some perspective with my introduction in *Two Cheers* analyzing some of the genuinely groundbreaking qualities I've recognized in him from time to time, including his idiosyncratic and illuminating video essay series *Histoire(s) du cinéma.* And I do still like his, so to speak, early funny ones, such as *Breathless* and *Pierrot le Fou.* Most of all I am moved by *Vivre sa vie/My Life to Live* with Karina's majestic performance and the hauntingly poetic gray tones of Coutard's cinematography.

Did you have similarly difficult encounters in Hollywood?

Usually not, because people tend to be convivial when they want publicity. A few people wouldn't talk. And there were some awkward encounters, but none jumps out as much as my attempt to interview astronaut Buzz Aldrin while I was a reporter with *The Riverside Press-Enterprise* before joining *Daily Variety.* I had an interview scheduled with Aldrin at a mall where he was signing a new book. I arrived, but he wouldn't talk to me for some reason, which made his publicist upset. Aldrin has always been a crank. That was why NASA chose Neil Armstrong to walk on the Moon before him. I encountered some uncooperative people while doing my biographies, but most of the hundreds of people I approached for interviews on those books were helpful. I estimate I have interviewed about fifteen thousand people in my career as a journalist and historian.

Were you pitching ideas to publications in your Madison days or getting assignments?

I've mostly just tended to pick my own subjects, write the articles or interviews, and send them in. I've found that my stubborn, perverse tendency to go my own way as a critic and historian and ignore trends keeps me ahead of the times. One of the editors of *Sight and Sound,* David Wilson, told me, "Every time Ingmar Bergman makes a film, we get fifty articles about it, and maybe we run one. But whenever you send us an article, it's on something no one else has thought of writing about, so we always run it." That happened, most notably, when Wilmington and I sent them our section on *The Searchers* from our Ford book.

Before that article ran in 1971 under the ambiguous title "Prisoner of the Desert," an allusion to the English translation of the film's (feminine) French title, that 1956 Western with John Wayne in a great performance as a racist Indian hater had largely been forgotten. But the year after we called *The Searchers* one of the most important films about America, it appeared for the first time in the top twenty films (tied for number eighteen) in the poll of international critics that *Sight and Sound* conducts every ten years. In the next poll in 1982, the film rose to a tie for tenth place. Stuart Byron, in his 1979 New York magazine article "*The Searchers*: Cult Movie of the New Hollywood," attributed the film's great influence on contemporary filmmakers and critics on how "by the Seventies, the critical floodgates were opened. Most important, Joseph McBride and Michael Wilmington published their seminal article and book." *The Searchers* article and my 1988 articles in *The Nation* exposing the unacknowledged early CIA involvement of George H. W. Bush before he became its director are the most widely influential articles I've written.

Wilson's comment about why he would accept my submissions is good advice I passed on to my students about how to sell magazine articles, although being ahead of the time doesn't help you sell projects in the film business, as I learned while working as a screenwriter. Another example of how being out of step with fashion made me ahead of the times was with my favorite of all my magazine interviews, a 1973 career interview with Richard Lester that ran in *Sight and Sound.* I had not known he was on the cusp of a comeback with *The Three Musketeers* after his career had fallen into eclipse because of his daring black comedy *The Bed Sitting Room;* I missed him and just wanted to talk with him, and I caught him at the turning point of his career. Never again would I have such rapport with an interviewee, and he opened up freely and eloquently. I'll talk more about that interview later in this book.

In Madison, did you think you were on track to make a living writing about film and even becoming famous? Did you consider yourself ambitious?

I was practical enough to know there was little pay in writing about films seriously; I didn't have any interest in the higher-paying jobs of being a mainstream newspaper or TV reviewer, which I considered shallow hackwork. But my film writing did lead to my job as a trade reporter, reviewer, and columnist for *Daily Variety* in Hollywood and weekly *Variety* in New York, which picked up and often mangled our copy. That was a low-paying job when I started there in 1974—I had to supplement my income with my articles for film magazines—but I learned a lot about the business and was able to go on the sets of many films and interview filmmakers. That trade paper and working with Welles were my true film school. (In 1978–1979 at the Directors Guild of America theater in Hollywood, I moderated a two-month "Working with Welles" seminar sponsored by the American Film Institute. Each week for two months we had panel discussions with various collaborators of Welles from throughout his career, and he appeared at two of them, most memorably on his early work in theater—along with his schoolmaster and mentor, Roger Hill—and on *The Other Side of the Wind.*)

I wanted to go from covering Hollywood to being a writer-director. I kept writing screenplays on the side, surreptitiously, while working long hours at the trade paper. I thought I could follow in the footsteps of the French critics who became *Nouvelle Vague* filmmakers after writing for *Cahiers du Cinéma* and other publications. I took heart from Godard's comment that their writing about film was a natural continuum with directing. But I didn't realize until too late that isn't true in the United States. Few film critics or reviewers have ever been allowed to make the transition to becoming directors, although some have become successful screenwriters. Two exceptions are my friends Paul Schrader and Rod Lurie.

Film books

While at Wisconsin I read a lot of film books, and the authors, past and present, automatically became my idols and inspiration. You were just a couple of years older than I, yet were not only churning out film articles but getting film books published! I was more than impressed. Did you think it was just a common thing for someone to be so prolific and to be published so young?

I thought it was natural, because I had been a professional writer since I was twelve and had already been well into writing a book by the time I went to Madison. But I started taking films more seriously when I saw Ingmar Bergman's *The Seventh Seal* at the Play Circle—I remember thinking, "Oh, yes, film is an art form." And when I saw *Citizen Kane* in Professor Byrne's class in September 1966, it changed my life. Rather than wanting to be a novelist and journalist, I wanted to write and direct films and write about them. I even set myself the unrealistic goal of making my first film by the age of twenty-five, as Welles had with *Kane*.

So I went to the university library to find a book on Welles to learn more about him. All I could find then were the rather tabloidish 1956 biography by Peter Noble, *The Fabulous Orson Welles*, and the 1965 critical study by Peter Cowie, *The Cinema of Orson Welles*. I was disappointed in Cowie's bland and superficial analysis of Welles's work, so I thought, "I'd better write my own book." It was the same impulse I had with my baseball book, writing it because I couldn't find one to read on the subject, at least a good one. My horizons on Welles kept expanding the more I saw of his work. In March 1967, I took a Greyhound bus to see *Chimes at Midnight* three times in one night in at a theater in Chicago before it turned into a softcore porno house the next day, and I considered that Welles's masterpiece, as I still do.

Wasn't the first paid lecture you ever gave about Welles?

Well, it wasn't paid, but it was my first experience lecturing at a university. In fact, the Wisconsin Film Society wound up paying for it. That was a strange and somewhat unpleasant experience. In 1969, when I was twenty-one, I was asked to speak about Welles at St. Joseph's College, a Jesuit school in Philadelphia (it later changed its status to a university). The professor who invited me evidently assumed from reading my essay on *Citizen Kane* in *Film Heritage* that I was a distinguished middle-aged academic. So imagine his shock when he came to the airport with a group of young male students to meet me. The students were friendly and seemed amused that I was as young as them, but the professor was a huffy sort who seemed mightily embarrassed and gave me the cold shoulder throughout my brief visit.

I remember feeling nervous but plunging ahead blindly as I spoke about *Kane* the next day from a stage to a large crowd in a lecture hall. I lectured for an hour without notes, and I think I did sort of OK; I don't recall much about it. But Bill Donnelly later told me the St. Joseph's professor had contacted our film society and asked it to repay the money his school had shelled out for my trip. Bill complied; I resented that but said nothing. In those days I had not yet learned how to respond to insults and tormented myself by stewing about them afterward. I was eventually taught by my Irish wife, Ruth O'Hara, how to respond more spontaneously when that happens.

Looking back on what happened in my first brush with academic politics, I realize that the professor should have appreciated my being a youthful prodigy. After Robin Wood came to Madison in 1972—I invited him and got our film society to pay for his visit—he wrote me, "How surprising, when expecting Orson Welles, to meet Tony Perkins!" I had a great time with Robin, who gave lectures on Otto Preminger and Anthony Mann. Robin was my principal role model as a film critic, since he was such a precise, logical, and eloquent writer with such a humanist perspective. I found his later work too heavily doctrinaire and overly concerned with being acceptable in the politically correct world of academic film studies. But my admiration for him otherwise remains strong as well as foundational. I was honored when he also wrote a letter recommending me for tenure.

While I was in Madison, George Stevens, King Vidor, Shirley Clarke, Marcel Ophuls, and Nicholas Ray were also brought to campus to show their films and discuss them with the students. I was deeply impressed by Stevens and his personal 35mm print of *Shane*, which I consider the perfect Western. And Stevens, I believe, is currently the most underrated American filmmaker; his artistry has been neglected in a backlash against his enshrinement by the Hollywood establishment during the 1950s, and he is overdue for rediscovery. I met Stevens a couple of times in California, became quite fond of him as a man and an artist, and with my Madison film mafia friend Pat McGilligan had a memorable interview with Stevens at the Beverly Hills Brown Derby in 1974, just six months before his death. Stevens was garrulous and rambling in our conversation, so the interview took me six months to edit; when it ran in *Bright Lights*, George Stevens Jr. commended Pat and me for capturing how his father talked better than any other interviewers.

Vidor came to campus with *Our Daily Bread*, his vigorous and heartfelt 1934 agitprop film. I later ran into him from time to time in Hollywood, and once, when I told him I thought his best film is *Japanese War Bride*, he seemed startled and said, "But that's one of my minor pictures." The gutsy independent filmmaker Shirley Clarke, who showed us her rawly powerful feature *The Cool World*, was the first director who agreed to read a script of mine. I am not sure which one I sent her, but I remember her kindness and generosity in giving me feedback.

How did you even begin to write all those books while also doing all your other jobs?

I worked on my critical studies of Welles and then Ford steadily after finishing my baseball book in the summer of 1966. I've always been disciplined as a writer, a self-starter who makes my own deadlines, and at that time I had an extra charge of youthful energy. I also did a lot of partying with my pals in a rooming house near campus as well as endless film-watching until I got my first full-time job as a newspaper reporter in 1969 at the *State Journal*.

With the baseball book buried in a box for the time being, the first book I published was *Persistence of Vision: A Collection of Film Criticism*, which our Wisconsin Film Society Press self-published in 1968. It was the fourth book our society published. Bill Donnelly suggested I edit the new collection; the title was suggested by his wife Kelley. It's a lively collection of articles and interviews by members of our society, including Mike Wilmington and your brother, Gerry. I contributed some pieces on Welles, including my long essay on *The Magnificent Ambersons*. That was the first attempt by anyone to "reconstruct" that butchered film in print, comparing the RKO release version with the shooting script, provided to me by the future film restoration specialist Robert Gitt. I also had the benefit of talking with Welles after he read what I wrote in *Persistence of Vision* about some of the changes between the script and the film he shot, but I was lacking the studio cutting continuity of Welles's original version (i.e., a transcription by a studio secretary of the shots, action, and dialogue before the film was drastically altered by RKO). I wish I had pursued a more thorough conversation with Welles about *Ambersons*, my favorite film. I later reprinted the essay in *Orson Welles* and revised it for the 1996 edition of that book, incorporating information from the previously unavailable cutting continuity.

Our film society earned enough through film ticket sales to print copies of *Persistence of Vision*, but after I made a futile attempt to place it in bookstores, I became so discouraged that I gave up on it. Today self-published books are accepted in some stores and can be made easily available through Amazon, as I've done with five of my own that would be hard to place with commercial publishers, but back then it was impossible to persuade bookstores to stock such books. I'm embarrassed to recall that after *Film Quarterly* gave the book a good review, we received dozens of orders from university libraries that I disregarded. I left boxes of copies of *Persistence of Vision* in the basement of the university's Bureau of Audio-Visual Instruction and never retrieved them. I have only myself to blame for it being my rarest book. Some day I may bring it back into print.

I wrote my critical study of Welles at a fairly leisurely pace over a four-year period, finishing it in 1970, although ironically, my anthology *Focus on Howard Hawks*, which I had to put together quickly after finishing *John Ford* in 1971, arrived before the Welles book, also in 1972.

John Ford

What led you and Wilmington to write your critical study of John Ford? Was it actually because his reputation was in eclipse in the late 1960s?

With my Welles book mostly completed, I wanted to tackle Ford, whose work I had become passionate about since I watched *Fort Apache* for the first time in December 1967. Mike and I decided to write the Ford book after we watched *She Wore a Yellow Ribbon* in a UW classroom one afternoon in 1969. Russell Merritt was showing that 1949

John Wayne cavalry Western—bravely, I would say as a fellow teacher, for any glimpse of Wayne on campus during the Vietnam War era provoked kneejerk hostility. To make matters worse, the only 16mm print Russell was able to rent of that spectacular Technicolor film, which won an Oscar for cinematographer Winton C. Hoch, was in black -and-white, which seemed grotesque, a pale echo of its true majesty.

The screening was tense throughout. Mike and I became upset when some of the students, including a prominent campus actor who should have known better (I won't mention his name, because I don't want to give him any credit), hooted at the moving scene of the troopers presenting Wayne's Captain Brittles with a silver watch upon his retirement. So after that screening, Mike and I told each other that we would write a critical study of Ford: "We'll show them what a great director he is."

Ford couldn't get work in Hollywood anymore after he made his final feature, the 1966 *film maudit, 7 Women,* one of his masterpieces, which was popular overseas but not in the U.S. I asked him in our 1970 interview, "Did you expect that the American audience would like it? Were you surprised when it didn't do well?" He said, "Unh-unh. It was over their heads." His reputation was low when Mike and I began working on our critical study, partly because he was not bankable, his classical style out of fashion and his personal themes out of step with the times. Although *7 Women* now seems to capture the apocalyptic zeitgeist of the late 1960s and the disastrous American mission in Asia, at the time it was regarded by reviewers as a studio-bound oddity and, worse, an old-fashioned "women's picture." At the time, that phrase was commonly used, even by film reviewers, as a misogynistic insult, which always struck me as unjust, since as people now belatedly realize, the "women's picture" genre is one of the most acute sources of sociopolitical analysis that came from the Hollywood system. Americans in 1966 were largely oblivious to Ford's subtleties and mistakenly characterized him simply as a conservative, lumping him in with Wayne's reactionary politics. Ford's politics were always complex, and he contributed to that misunderstanding by publicly supporting the Vietnam War even though, as I later learned, he privately thought it was futile and didn't understand why the U.S. was there.

Both times I wrote books on Ford, he was out of fashion with the American public. The same thing was happening before I wrote my biography, *Searching for John Ford,* which I began researching after I finished the critical study in 1971.

The other film that had the most impact on my life was *Fort Apache*, the 1948 Western written by Frank S. Nugent and directed by John Ford. I had always wanted to see a Western with the Native Americans as heroes. Here Miguel Inclán as the Apache chief, Cochise, tells Colonel Thursday (Henry Fonda, at left) their grievances but is rebuffed while seeking peace. Seeing this revisionist film that tells the truth about American history on December 23, 1967, set me on my lifelong study of Ford. (RKO/Argosy; frame enlargement)

My heart would sink when I mentioned his name and get a dreaded blank stare from the average listener. My indignation over the way this great American artist was unknown to so many people was the engine that drove my work on those books. I wrote the biography because I believed we needed a book that would explain how these beautiful, sensitive films emanated from a man who presented himself as something akin to an uncouth old cowhand. I already realized that was a protective self-disguise, but I wanted to understand him better. I agreed with Andrew Sarris that the source of his artistry was "the John Ford movie mystery." To try to solve that mystery, I researched the biography off and on over the years, finishing it in an intense two-year sprint in 2001. Now because of my and Mike's efforts and those of other scholars, Ford has his rightful place as one of the greatest directors in film history.

How did your collaboration with Wilmington work on the Ford book, which seems seamless?

Making it read that way took me a lot of work. Writing the book with Mike soured me on collaborating on a book until I decided to work with you. I knew that since you've published many books of your own, you are reliable, unlike Mike. He and I worked well enough together writing articles for film magazines. But writing a book together was quite another matter. It became a prolonged struggle and burden, though the book doesn't show the stress that went into its writing.

Mike and I had actual physical brawls twice over the writing of our book. The proximate causes were a bit absurd, but they reflected outbursts of my deep frustration over Mike's endless inability to complete his contributions to the book. I had asked him to work with me on the Ford project because I didn't think I had the ability at that stage of my career to tackle such a vast subject without having a collaborator. I also thought it would make the writing go faster. We had many long talks about Ford for a year and a half, often daily, and the book benefited greatly from having two complementary points of view. I assigned different sections of the book to both of us; we worked together on the introduction. But after that period, with Mike continually having trouble doing his share of the writing, I finally had to fire him from the project and finish it on my own, including combining and rewriting all his erratic drafts, which took another exhausting six months.

Mike was so knowledgeable and passionate about film; what did you learn from him along the way?

I especially learned a lot about acting from Mike, who was a brilliant actor of feral intensity. His understanding of acting was profound and greatly influenced our work on Ford as well as my other writing. I directed him at the UW in Edward Albee's *The Zoo Story* (twice, with two different actors, Jon Lamal and Jim Stifter, playing Peter to Mike's Jerry) as well as in a 1969 film called *Close But No Cigar*, a romantic chase comedy co-starring Carolyn Purdy, who became the wife of Stuart Gordon. Stuart was a superb and highly original stage director in Madison before turning to films. He complimented me on *The Zoo Story* for what he thought was my bright decision to have Jerry tell his lengthy story directly to the audience, with his back mostly to Peter. I readily admitted that was Mike's good idea, which rendered Stuart speechless. I guess it's unusual for one director to hear another director giving credit to a collaborator.

The cast of *Close But No Cigar* also included André de Shields, a superb and charismatic theater actor who went on to win Tony, Emmy, and Grammy awards. Mike and I asked André if he would play Othello opposite Mike's Iago under

Michael Wilmington's harrowing death scene as the disturbed Jerry in
my two productions of Edward Albee's one-act play *The Zoo Story*
was so convincing I sometimes thought he had actually been stabbed.
This is the UW Memorial Union production.

my direction on a campus stage, but André said he would
do it only if we made Desdemona a "bitch" who came
between the two men's gay romance. I found that suggestion
misogynistic and beyond my ken, even though in retrospect
it might have been intriguing to direct *Othello* with its gay
subtext foregrounded—Welles emphasizes Iago's thwarted
love for Othello in his film version. But I was so naive at the
time that I didn't realize that *The Zoo Story* is a play about
a disguised homosexual pickup.

Did you also write plays when you were young?

I wrote some very bad short plays in high school and at
college. These experiences made me understand that it
is necessary to have a solid background in the theater to

Directing Wilmington in one of my most elaborate student films, the 1969 chase comedy *Close But No Cigar*. Here Mike is desperately looking for his runaway girlfriend at the construction site of Vilas Communication Hall, the future home of the UW-Madison Department of Communication Arts.

become a good playwright. So I taught myself to write screenplays instead. My only play that had any merit was not produced, a one-act play called *Chessman* about the criminal Caryl Chessman. His execution became a *cause celebre* in 1960, and I had him interrogating himself in his cell; even if the play was rather shallow and muddled, suffering from inadequate research (I simply read his memoir *Cell*

2455, Death Row), the theatricality of presenting a solitary, schizoid character examining his conscience and presenting himself as a pawn in the justice system was fairly effective, even if the symbolism was overly obvious.

After successfully directing *The Zoo Story*, I made a misguided, hubristic attempt to direct Mike in the greatest and perhaps most difficult American play, Eugene O'Neill's *Long Day's Journey Into Night*. My only good idea was to stage it around the altar of the campus Catholic church, but after three weeks, I realized I was hopelessly out of my depth. I turned the direction over to Mike, who was playing Jamie Tyrone and did so superbly, although his wandering around the church while offstage was distracting.

I did venture once more into the theater when I was asked to write *The American National Theatre and Academy Tribute to James Stewart* at the Beverly Hilton Hotel in November 1981. For director Harvey Lembeck—whom I admired as an actor from the *Sergeant Bilko* TV series, as Bilko's henchman Corporal Rocco Barbella—I wrote "What if?" comedy skits spoofing Stewart as if he had appeared as the title character in *Hamlet*, Stanley Kowalski in *A Streetcar Named Desire*, and Tevye in *Fiddler on the Roof*.

Harvey brought in members of his acting classes to play the roles, with a different male and female actor in each skit. The young actors were all hilarious, and it was a delight to help stage the skits with Harvey, the best director other than Welles I had the pleasure to work with. The skits sailed above the heads of the tribute audience at Beverly Hilton. They barely reacted except to a skit in which the old pro Jesse White mostly adlibbed his way through a riff on his role as the mental institution attendant snaring Stewart's Elwood P. Dowd in *Harvey*. It was a terrible loss that Harvey Lembeck, who was a lovely guy as well as a man of rare talents, died shortly thereafter in January 1982, at the age of only 58.

The Nude *Peter Pan*

Our pal Wilmington was also in the cast of the Stuart Gordon stage production of Peter Pan. *I felt guilty but pleased to see it when you bravely presented it on the weekly Wisconsin Film Society screening night, instead of the films that were scheduled. What was your involvement with that controversial production in October 1968?*

Here's what Stuart recalled of its genesis: "I had been protesting against the war in Vietnam, and got tear-gassed by the Chicago police, and it suddenly struck me that you could take *Peter Pan* and turn it into a political cartoon about the whole situation. So, *Peter Pan* became the leader of the hippies and yippies, Captain Hook became Mayor Daley, and the pirates became the Chicago police. We left all of the James Barrie dialogue intact, so when they all went off to Neverland they sprinkled pixie dust on themselves and think lovely thoughts, and up they go. That was an acid trip, which was visualized by a psychedelic light show that was projected onto the bodies of seven naked young ladies."

I was with Stuart on that trip to the Chicago convention and found the preview of his Screw Theater company's *Peter Pan* in the Union Play Circle a terrifically imaginative and involving piece of theater. The following day, October 1, 1968, I saw that the university had padlocked the door of the theater. My mind immediately flashed to the Federal Theatre locking out Orson Welles's company from its premiere of Marc Blitzstein's radical labor opera *The Cradle Will Rock* in 1937. Welles and his producing partner, John Houseman, led the cast and audience in a march through the streets to another theater where the play went on with only Blitzstein onstage playing a piano and the cast members, because of union rules, having to rise instead from the audience. (That historic event was recreated in Tim Robbins's 1999 film *Cradle Will Rock*, which is good on the Popular Front period in the arts but unfortunately offers negative caricatures of both Welles and Houseman.) Welles recalled, "I was very ambiguous in my feeling, and I wasn't sure that we weren't wrecking the Federal Theatre by what we were doing. But I thought if you padlock a theater, then the argument is closed."

Peter Pan was caught in the midst of an anti-nudity crusade by a Madison district attorney, James Boll, who was also trying to shut down a downtown strip joint, and the prudish university administration fell in with Boll on banning *Peter Pan*. When he gave a press conference outside the Play Circle, I asked the last question, "Mr. Boll, do you believe in fairies?" He just looked at me uncomprehendingly. I went to find Stuart in the Rathskeller and told him our Wisconsin Film Society had booked the B-10 Commerce auditorium for that night's screening of Buster Keaton films. I suggested we ask our audience to vote on whether they would like to see *Peter Pan* instead. Stuart asked if he could put on the play even if our audience voted against it. Surprised at his anti-democratic attitude, I said no.

That night I put a sign on the door of the Play Circle advertising the rogue production of *Peter Pan*, and what seemed like two hundred horny guys immediately ran at top speed up Bascom Hill to our auditorium. Only ten people in our packed audience of several hundred voted against seeing the play, and our conservative vice president took them to a small room to watch the Keaton movies. The play went on, quickly re-staged by Stuart on the shallow stage with no set and no special lighting and only two naked girls dancing. But it was electrifying. The mood was enhanced by everyone expecting the police to come barging in at any time, but they didn't, even when the company put on a second show that night.

I was surprised Stuart didn't thank me afterward, but Wilmington, who played John in *Peter Pan*, said it must have been an oversight. The play made the national news, and the next day the campus police chief, Ralph Hanson, called Mike and me to his office and asked us to reveal the names of the two dancers. We refused. *The New York Times* reported on October 13, "Mr. Boll said his investigation has been hampered because witnesses to performances in the basement of the university's Commerce Building have been unwilling to talk to authorities." Chief Hanson was removed from the case by the DA "for his lack of zeal in tracking down the offending dancers," the Madison newspaper *Isthmus* recalled. Our Wisconsin Film Society was stripped of its official status in retaliation for our complicity with Stuart.

Stuart was charged with putting on a lewd and indecent show, and his girlfriend and soon-to-be wife, Carolyn Purdy, was arraigned on October 11, charged with performing in a lewd, obscene, and indecent play. But the DA dropped the charges on December 3 when it turned out that the only accuser he had been able to find was a convicted child molester. The university tried to crack down further on Stuart's plays, so he ran a local independent theater group before leaving town for Chicago in 1969 with Carolyn, and they started the successful Organic Theater Company. He eventually became a prominent film director, celebrated for stylish horror films, some with his wife, Purdy-Gordon, in the cast.

About twenty-five years after the *Peter Pan* episode, I ran into Stuart again at a party in Los Angeles. I expected a cordial reunion. He immediately confronted me heatedly with, "You almost got me put in jail!" I was stunned to realize that he actually blamed me for supposedly making him put on the play. He said he was thinking of directing a film about that incident, and it was clear to me that I would be portrayed as one of the villains. (He didn't get around to making that film before his death in 2020.) Stuart's perspective on my role in that creative escapade reminded me of the story about William Randolph Hearst being told that so-and-so hated him. Hearst said, "I don't remember ever doing him a favor."

The Film Generation

You quoted writer-director Paul Schrader saying, "People talk about the 'Golden Age' of Hollywood in the late '60s and early '70s. It wasn't that the films were better or the filmmakers were better, it was the audiences that were better. It was a time of social stress, and audiences turned to artists for answers." Do you agree with Schrader—and me— that the audiences in the Sixties and early Seventies, who became known as the Film Generation, were the best ever in the sense that they cared about themes as well as stars?
I don't necessarily believe that the films of the Sixties were the best—though they revolutionized the medium—but I think all of us were so lucky because not only were there exciting new directors, but also most of the great American and foreign directors of past decades were still making films. We could see new films by Welles, Ford, Hawks, Hitchcock, Fellini, Kurosawa, Siegel, Fuller, Antonioni, Bergman, Wilder, on and on—and old films to discover—Keaton, the Marx Brothers, It's a Wonderful Life, The Searchers—*were resurfacing. All genres, all countries. That's how I felt when we were in Madison during that time. And I still think it was the greatest decade for becoming a movie—and rock music—fan.*

That was a great time, though I still think the greatest era in Hollywood was the late silent period, when the art form reached its zenith. Mary Pickford said it would have been more logical for silent films to grow out of sound films rather than the other way around. I consider the 1927 film *Sunrise: A Song of Two Humans* the pinnacle of the silent era and indeed of the film medium. For a year when I was writing my Frank Capra biography and living in the San Bernardino Mountains, I would drive to lunch every day at Lake Arrowhead, where F. W. Murnau shot much of that masterpiece. The 1930s and '40s were when many of my favorite films were made, and I saw a lot of great work while growing up in the

'50s. I remember watching a lot of garbage in the '60s and '70s, partly because I had to review so many films, and at *Daily Variety* during the '70s I was mostly relegated to reviewing B movies, many of which were dogs, tawdry horror or revenge pix and the like. Our lead reviewer, Art Murphy ("*Murf.*," as he signed his reviews), hogged most of the prestige pictures.

Nevertheless, in one eight-month period in 1974, we had *The Conversation*, *Chinatown*, and *The Godfather Part II*, and we almost took it for granted that masterpieces would come along regularly. I didn't think much of the audiences then, however, because too many good films were neglected—I am thinking especially of Abraham Polonsky's 1969 radical Western *Tell Them Willie Boy Is Here,* which Abe and I later discussed with an uncomprehending audience in a Q&A reprinted in *Two Cheers*—and pretentious junk such as *Easy Rider* and *The Graduate* was celebrated. Too many of our would-be radical colleagues from that era became stockbrokers, and one I knew from Madison, Mark Rosenberg, even became a studio executive before dropping dead in his forties from a heart attack. But it's true that a climate of cinephilia flourished in that turbulent social period of our youth. A time of unrest tends to lead to some great art. I remember 1968 as being the worst year in American history since the Civil War. But the studios were collapsing then, and along with some horrendous dreck we had some fresh and innovative films until the blockbuster syndrome and the Reagan era pretty much put an end to that.

The nascent field of film studies

You were among the vanguard of young scholars in the foundational days of the field of film studies, yet you opted not to make a career in academia until many years later.

The two British Film Institute series, which published many of the earliest critical studies of major directors, offered good launching pads outside the United States for new young writers in what was still the nascent field of film studies. The opportunities to publish film books were more open in the late 1960s than they are now, when the film book sections in bookstores, even when bookstores remain open, have kept shrinking. I was in on the ground floor of the new film studies movement when I began publishing film articles in 1967 and books in 1968, influenced by such figures as François Truffaut, Andrew Sarris, and Robin Wood. But I did not go on to become part of the academic field of film studies when it became more organized in the 1970s. That was the period when film studies morphed into an academic discipline devoted to rigidly doctrinaire orthodoxy, a mostly theoretical discourse blending semiology and Marxism more than the study of actual films. The field of film studies as it was constituted in making itself acceptable to universities in the Seventies was more an outgrowth of linguistics than about film, and the academics tended to be slavishly governed by the dominant Marxist ideology.

Although I kept publishing articles and interviews in *Daily Variety* and film magazines as well as writing film books during those years—my books were less frequent, since I was largely focused on screenwriting until I began writing books full-time in 1984 with my Capra biography—I was glad to miss that academic development altogether. Richard Corliss, the editor of *Film Comment*, told me when film studies was becoming respectable in academia, "The auteurists have all gone into journalism." He was right, although I never left the field of film studies. I needed a "day job" to pay the bills while I wrote my mostly un-remunerative film criticism and labored in the Hollywood trenches as a trade press reporter and screenwriter.

I found the trendy and influential 1970 *Cahiers du Cinéma* collective text on Ford's *Young Mr. Lincoln* somewhat valuable for its sociological approach, which I learned from, although much of its analysis of the film itself is convoluted or insane. Its approach to American history is ludicrously uninformed: they claim that the film is propaganda for the Republican Party, which they seem to think had not changed since Lincoln's day, and they ignore that Ford called himself a socialist in what was then his Popular Front period. Much of what passed for film studies in those days was hardly about film at all; it was about semiology, symbols and codes and all that, and books and articles were usually written in almost impenetrable jargon. Some of the worst writing I've ever seen continues to be in academic film scholarship, which suffers from a snobbish desire to keep outsiders from understanding its lingo and narrow-minded viewpoints. It's the kind of nonsensical writing Sam Fuller, to borrow one of his pungent neologisms, would call "gibblegabble."

Operating under the slavish influence of French semiologists and roping in the academics who otherwise would have gone into other disciplines such as history, philosophy, or literature, film theory became dominant largely at the expense of studying individual films. I studied film theory in my last film course at the UW and over the years read more work on the subject with little interest. When I was hired by the San Francisco State University in 2002 as an assistant professor in its film department, I bought a bunch of the leading books on film theory to study for my classes. One of them I stopped reading after thirty pages when I realized that the author had not yet mentioned a single film; she explained in her introduction that she was too busy studying film theory to see many films.

Screenwriting

In your 2012 book Writing in Pictures: Screenwriting Made (Mostly) Painless, *you discuss what you said earlier, how you taught yourself how to write screenplays when you were living in Madison.*

I had to do so because I couldn't find a manual to teach me the craft, and our school had no course on screenwriting. I used the script of *Citizen Kane* by Herman J. Mankiewicz and Orson Welles as my bible. Typing a copy of it was good discipline, and I learned how to write a professional-quality script by imitating its format and studying its style.

In my Madison days, I wrote about sixty-five short scripts while also learning to write feature-length screenplays. Most of the short scripts were comedies, ranging from little skits and farces, sometimes suffering from what Woody Allen would call "jejunosity" (including one about a nun finding a vibrator and another about a Chinese girl selling *Mao's Little Red Book* on campus before turning into a vampire) to more ambitious and sophisticated romantic comedies and other short subjects.

At the same time, I did some work on treatments for features on such diverse subjects as Aristophanes' satire about a women's sex strike to end the Peloponnesian War, *Lysistrata* (in modern dress as an anti-Vietnam War protest piece); a Preston Sturges-like comedy about the eccentric aviator Douglas (Wrong Way) Corrigan; a harrowing Western about the cannibalistic Donner Party; the declining years of silent-movie idol John Gilbert after the coming of sound; the surrealistic comic book *Plastic Man*, an impossible film project in those days before CGI; a concentration camp story; and the enigmatic life of Emily Dickinson, *I'm Nobody*. I didn't take Welles's sound advice to approach the BBC with the Dickinson project rather than try to do it as a feature.

In the summer of 1966, I began my self-education as a screenwriter by writing an adaptation of Ernest Hemingway's posthumously published memoir of his life as a young writer in Paris, *A Moveable Feast*. I didn't realize until too late that Hemingway's account of supposedly being poor but happy while working part time as a journalist and writing fiction romantically falsifies his actual financial situation. I didn't factor in the actual cost of the lavish meals and vacations Hemingway chronicles in that book until I went to Paris, followed his path, and realized how expensive it must have been. His first wife, Hadley Richardson, had a trust fund, and his second wife, Pauline Pfeiffer, whom he starts dallying with late in *A Moveable Feast*, had a wealthy uncle, Gus Pfeiffer, who contributed to their support. So I naively thought I could do something like that myself. But poverty was a hindrance. Later if I had looked around in Hollywood more carefully, I would have seen that many of the young people I knew were supported by their families as well, including with trust funds. But by the time I realized how hard it actually is to make a living as a writer, I was too far down that road to go back. My *Moveable Feast* script is not much good but has a few imaginative cinematic ideas.

When I finished, I brashly sent a telegram to Mary Hemingway in Ketchum, Idaho, announcing I had adapted the book. She wired back that I should call her, and when I did, she reamed me out, lecturing me on how I did not have the right to do so. That taught me a harsh but necessary lesson about screenwriting based on other people's material, although I forgot it, to my chagrin, many years later in Hollywood. Oddly, that book still has never been made into a film, although Woody Allen's charming 2011 comedy, *Midnight in Paris,* is partly a spoof, a follow-up on his *New Yorker* satire of *A Moveable Feast* with its running refrain about how Hemingway socked him.

Coming to my senses, I next tackled a short script based on a public-domain short story, Jack London's harrowing and suspenseful classic "To Build a Fire," about a man slowly freezing to death in the Yukon. I mistakenly thought a shooting script should be a shot list, so I wrote one in January 1967 that I planned to use in filming the story in Super 8. I decided against it because it would have been too arduous in the Madison winter. I was sensible in starting with adaptations as exercises while teaching myself how to write screenplays, however, since I knew enough to recognize that before taking the challenge of coming up with original ideas, I would first have to master the craft of this demanding form of writing by learning the professional format.

Meanwhile, I directed seven increasingly elaborate Super 8 films in Madison, also predominantly comedic, although the last one was more dramatic. In those days it cost about $400 to buy enough film to make a twenty-minute short, and it would take me about six months to save up that kind of money.

What else did you study when you taught yourself to write scripts?

Truffaut/Hitchcock was the film book that taught me the most about cinema when it served as my primer upon its first American publication in 1966. Hitchcock was a great teacher and Truffaut a brilliant interlocutor and commentator, and the book's lavish use of frame enlargements to help them analyze sequences was especially illuminating. (And since our audiovisual department had a copy of the sequence from *Sabotage* of Sylvia Sidney murdering her terrorist husband, Oscar Homolka, I must have watched it a hundred times.) But in one way, the *Hitchbook* (as his family calls it) was a bad influence on my early films, because it fooled me into believing the myth that Hitchcock always storyboarded every shot. In fact, as I learned while spending three days watching him shoot his last film, *Family Plot* (1976), he often improvised shots.

While on a soundstage at Universal to write a feature for *Daily Variety,* I stood next to Hitchcock and his cinematographer, Leonard South, in the set of a garage as the director improvised a sequence he originally had planned to shoot more simply. It involved a struggle with Barbara Harris being injected with a syringe full of sodium pentothal by William Devane after his accomplice, Karen Black, passes him the needle from her purse. As Hitchcock became excited by elongating the struggle and the action with the needle, I wrote down every word he told his cinematographer about the shots he wanted and put that in my article for *Daily Variety.* He confirmed to me later that he was indeed making up "a matter of what I would term 'pictorial orchestration'" as he went along: "You improvise a little bit—you have to do that. You rehearse your master operation but you don't photograph it; you select the little moments."

My friend Bill Krohn, the Hollywood correspondent for *Cahiers du Cinéma*, told me that my article, which I reprinted in *Two Cheers for Hollywood*, inspired him to write the authoritative 2000 book, *Hitchcock at Work*. By digging deeply into Hitchcock's papers at the Academy Library, Bill found that contrary to the myth, Hitchcock mostly relied on storyboards for action and special-effects scenes but shot talk scenes and other scenes like any other director, by working with the actors in figuring out the most natural blocking and shot breakdown. When I interviewed the brilliant actor-director Joan Darling about working with Steven Spielberg, she told me when she was hired to direct an *Amazing Stories* segment, she asked him, "How should I decide where to put the camera?" He gave her a profound piece of advice: "Notice where you're standing when you watch the rehearsal and put the camera there."

When you taught screenwriting decades later, were you influenced by your own learning process years before in Madison?

I had to work out my teaching methods by trial and error when I first taught screenwriting at New College of California in San Francisco in 2000. I mistakenly let the students bring in their own stories to write. It turned out that they had little idea what a story is. I gathered that their generation had grown up with such fragmented narratives or non-narratives that they lacked the basic grounding that previous generations had in fairy tales and other children's stories. And the decline in reading habits and skills meant that most had not read much fiction, let alone highly sophisticated fiction. So most of their stories were weak and did not result in good scripts (with a few exceptions). Most of the stories, in fact, were trite rehashes of TV shows or movies they had seen. As a result, only about half of my twenty or so students would learn to write a good script by the end of the semester. Half was not enough; I wanted them all to learn.

So I rethought my approach to teaching screenwriting after I went across town to San Francisco State in 2002. I evolved a new approach, drawn from how I had taught myself to write screenplays, by having the students write an adaptation of an existing short story. That method proved much more successful—the only students who didn't learn the craft were one or two in each class who didn't show up or do the work—and it resulted in my screenwriting manual, *Writing in Pictures*, which I based on how I taught the craft at SFSU.

What other feature-length scripts did you write in Madison?

Once I had written my first two adaptations, I set myself a somewhat broader challenge by tackling two fine books by the erudite baseball pitcher Jim Brosnan, *The Long Season* and *Pennant Race*, which I adapted into a so-so script called *Diamond*, about the mundane world of a journeyman relief pitcher. Only after that did I venture into writing originals, including a dreadfully bad one about a maniacal film director who decides to kill an actor onscreen to make a statement about violence. I called the script *Silverheels* and to play the actor, I wanted to cast Jay Silverheels, the Canadian First Nations and Mohawk actor who was Tonto on *The Lone Ranger* TV series. I sent that muddled script to John Cassavetes to star in and direct. I am still waiting for a response.

Then I wrote a much more ambitious and substantial original called *Hell* in 1969–1970; at one point I considered calling it *The Exorcist* but thought audiences wouldn't understand what that meant. It was based on an actual incident that took place in Indianapolis in 1965, the torture and murder of a teenaged girl by a deranged woman guardian and children in the neighborhood. *Hell* was my attempt to exorcise some of the horror and anger I felt over my Catholic upbringing. I made the mother a religious fanatic and wrote the part with one of my favorite actresses, Julie Harris, in mind. I wanted to direct the film myself and had an old Gothic house on a hilltop in my hometown of Wauwatosa in mind as the location.

I went to New York and talked my way backstage at a theater where Harris was performing in *Forty Carats*. She kindly received me and agreed to read the script. She sent back a note declining the project because she found the subject too horrible to make into a film. I was frustrated that I was not able to make the film myself because it would have cost about $50,000 to film it in 16mm, and I had no idea how to raise that kind of money.

When I met Welles in 1970, I told him about the script. He asked to read it and surprised me on our next meeting in 1971 by telling me angrily that if I weren't the author, he "would do everything in my power" to stop it from being made, since he did not approve of torture scenes (the main one in my script lasted more than twenty minutes). I was surprised and dismayed to find that Welles believed in censorship. But his partner Oja Kodar, with more empathy, asked me why I would write such a script. I explained that it was an attempt to deal with my repressive and abusive religious upbringing. After that I gave up on the script, coming to recognize that Julie Harris was right about it being unfilmable.

Eventually I felt vindicated when the feminist author Kate Millett wrote a 1979 book, *The Basement: Meditations on a Human Sacrifice*, about the original incident, the torture and murder of Sylvia Likens by Gertrude Baniszewski. Millett's other books include *The Politics of Cruelty*, a 1994 work about state-sanctioned torture. She said about the Likens case, "It is the story of the suppression of women. Gertrude seems to have wanted to administer some terrible truthful justice to this girl: that this was what it was to be a woman." In 2007, an independent film was made about the incident and shown on cable TV, *An American Crime*, directed by Tommy O'Haver, written by O'Haver with Irene Turner from trial transcripts and starring Catherine Keener and Ellen (now Elliot) Page. A *New York Times* article on the film was headed, "A Midwest Nightmare, Too Depraved to Ignore."

I know that Keener-Page film didn't get a theatrical release. I tried to watch it when it debuted on Showtime because of the two leads, but found it unpleasant and turned it off early on.

Another film, *The Girl Next Door*, released the same year, somewhat fictionalized the case and is based on a novel by Jack Ketchum. So the material did have some commercial potential. But I tend not to watch movies that I wanted to make; it's too depressing. I wish I could discuss these issues with Welles again now.

How did your self-education in screenwriting translate to your professional work as a Hollywood screenwriter?

Writing *Hell* was my equivalent of what Hitchcock called his belief in "putting the audience through it." In my early days as a screenwriter I was expressing myself by wanting viewers to share my traumatized state. I eventually realized that may have worked in literature but not in a popular entertainment medium such as film, unless one could be as artful as Hitchcock is in expressing his traumatized feelings in an entertaining way. I hadn't learned that yet. Having such a goal was an impediment to my attempt to make a career as a filmmaker. Eventually, though, I managed to both entertain and convey a sense of my repressive educational experiences while writing my five foundational drafts of *Rock 'n' Roll High School*.

I can see in retrospect how out of tune I tended to be with the escapist nature of popular filmmaking, particularly after the New Hollywood with its franker approach to life began to peter out in the mid-Seventies and disappeared in the Reagan era. I was still pitching projects that were considered too challenging for the marketplace, notably my autobiographical drama *The Broken Places*, which I stubbornly kept trying to sell, to the detriment of my career. Many people admired that mental hospital story but found much of it, especially the ending suicide by fire of the female character, unthinkable as a film subject.

Eventually in Madison I wrote a script that I thought was both moving and funny as well as more marketable. It was my fifth feature-length screenplay, *Man Bites Dog*. I took that to Hollywood with me and tried to sell it. It's a seriocomedy inspired by a story I read in the *State Journal* about a mailman's last day on the job. I re-imagined my character as a Black mailman who has always lived a highly conventional, subdued life but is driven berserk on his last chaotic yet liberating day of service. He retaliates against a vicious dog that's been his nemesis and gets into all kinds of other trouble, mostly what John Lewis would call "good trouble, necessary trouble." *Man Bites Dog* has a lot of warmth and believable character comedy. I wrote the script with Redd Foxx in mind, I liked his raunchy nightclub records from what was called the "chitlin circuit" and thought he had the acting chops and the potential to be a movie star. I started writing this script before Foxx became a TV star in 1972 with his series *Sanford and Son*.

Soon after I moved to LA in July 1973, I found an agent who agreed to represent me. He read *Man Bites Dog* but said, "Why are you writing about sixty-five-year-old Black people? Why don't you write about twenty-year-old white people?" The same agent told me that comedies and films about teenagers don't sell; this was shortly before *American Graffiti* opened and became one of the biggest hits in film history. I fired that agent right away and found another but had to do most of the pitching of scripts and ideas on my own. I eventually met Redd Foxx at a Hollywood party and got my script to him. He didn't respond either.

That experience taught me not to write a script that only one actor can do. I suppose I should have retooled it for another Black actor; I tried to get my agent to send it to Sidney Poitier to direct, but for some unknown reason, she never would. My friend Joe Dante and I wanted to do a good film of *Adventures of Huckleberry Finn* together, after we worked together on *Hollywood Boulevard* and *Rock 'n'*

Roll High School, but my agent wouldn't call Joe either, and the Huck Finn project sank on its slender raft. I eventually fired her too, but after too much damage had been done to my career. So it goes, as Kurt Vonnegut used to say.

Making movies in Madison

Oddly enough, despite our atmosphere of intense cinephilia at the UW, we had no cinema department, so aside from you and one or two other students in Madison, people weren't actually making films there in those days.

Back then while learning how to make movies, I wrote and directed my seven short films, photographing the first six of them as well. I also spent a year in Madison getting practical experience working part time as a TV cameraman at WHA-TV for the state educational network on such programs as grade-school arithmetic and cooking shows. We still had those big old-fashioned cameras on wheeled platforms that had to be pushed around, and it was hard going on location with them on the rare occasions when we had to do so. But I learned the basics of visual composition as well as the rigorous tension to get it right the first time—the only time—on live television.

The first film I made was a brief gag comedy, *Papa Takes a Dive*, with Patrick Greene, a stocky, bearded fellow who looked a bit like Ernest Hemingway, running across the Library Mall and throwing himself into a fountain for no apparent reason except that it looked funny. Unfortunately, after I mailed the single roll of Super 8 film to Kodak in Chicago for developing, it never came back; I never made that mistake again, always having my films developed locally. Another actor who looked like Hemingway, my droll *State Journal* colleague George Hesselberg, who was always game, took a pie in the face in another film of mine.

My first completed film, in the summer of 1968, was a somewhat incoherent romantic farce about an encounter in a park, *Coitus Interruptus*, with John Granatir, Kathy Curtin, and Bill Donnelly. It was loosely based on an incident in Jean Renoir's biography, *Renoir, My Father*. I then made a more ambitious chase comedy, *Close But No Cigar*, in 1969, with Mike Wilmington pursuing Carolyn Purdy around campus. I worked hard to make it entertaining with elaborate editing and location work, but the film baffled audiences because I flubbed the shooting of an early expository scene by making it too sketchy. I needed to show why Carolyn runs away from Mike and causes him to chase her around. The scene involves him mockingly putting a cigar band on her hand as an engagement ring, which offends her, but in a mistake Hitchcock never would have made, I filmed the scene too hastily and failed to shoot the necessary closeups.

The film takes place in one afternoon but took four months to shoot because Carolyn rarely deigned to give us more than an hour of her time. At one point I had to resort to using a double wearing her blouse. And though the film is set in the summertime, it started snowing while I was directing one of the ending scenes. After keeping calm for months, I finally lost my temper then and unfairly took it out on Mike, who was always dedicated to the filming process.

Carolyn only finished her role because I went to Stuart Gordon and showed him how I had storyboarded the entire film, which impressed him enough to convince his girlfriend not to bail out on me. At a low point in the filming, when she told me to "Shut up" while I was giving her a direction, I advised her to "Be professional," and she snapped, "I'm not a professional." When I finally showed *Close But No Cigar* at the Memorial Union, Carolyn came to the delicatessen where I worked and told me she was surprised at what a good performance she had given; I'm afraid I reacted with blank indifference.

I did learn from that experience that actors need to enjoy themselves while making a film and not just feel like marionettes in a puzzle composed of many little pieces, as I had designed the film to be. As well as being overly reliant on storyboards, I was too much under the spell of John Ford to move my camera much, so most of my short films suffered from rather rigid camerawork as well as my failure to give the actors enough freedom. Then I made a more elaborate comedy, *The Missionary Position*, in 1971, from a story by Kelley Donnelly, with people trying to rescue Russell Campbell, who looks like a hippie Jesus, from a trance after they mistakenly think he's inhaled glue. The farcical goings-on also include a priest, played by John Davis, falling in love with a nun, played by Ida Jeter, and marrying her. (You can see that I was fond of corny double entendres in those days while trying to exorcise my religious hangups.)

I experimented with documentary filmmaking too. For a 1971–72 film called *Everybody Loves a Parade*, whose political point was rather glib, I intercut footage from an antiwar march with a pro-Vietnam War parade. I linked the parades with John Philip Sousa music and by having my friend Michael Shovers, my comic mascot onscreen, helping

Shooting *The End of a Perfect Day* (1973), the last film I directed.
This romantic drama about a young woman who meets a lonely boy
on the Union Terrace was photographed by my radical friend Kenny
Mate. (Tim Davis)

Jeanne German plays the lead in *The End of a Perfect Day*.
Her strained reading of a heavy-duty text on the Union Terrace is
about to be interrupted. (Tim Davis)

lead both marches. I liked putting my actors in the midst of real events for a cinéma-vérité effect, as I sometimes also did in my comedies. With my first wife, Linda Detra, I co-directed a hallucinatory semi-documentary called *Thin Ice*, with a friend of hers on frozen Lake Mendota near the Union fantasizing that the campus was full of National Guardsmen, as it actually was when we filmed her wandering around in the midst of the rifle-toting troops ringing the administration building, Bascom Hall.

The final film I directed, in 1973 before leaving town, *The End of a Perfect Day*, was based on an encounter my girlfriend Jeanne German had one day when she went frolicking around town with a lonely little boy. I took a looser approach and asked my friend Ken Mate to photograph it so I could have more time to spend with the actors. We made much of the film on the Union terrace where Jeanne and Eric Morse had actually met before they took off for their trip on a double-seater bicycle. I found a book on glamour photography and studied it to learn how Ken and I could photograph Jeanne to her best advantage. The result was a film with more warmth and spontaneity than my previous efforts as well as some moments of lyricism.

After moving to Los Angeles, I tried showing some of the films I directed to some friends but learned that no one there took silent Super 8 films seriously or even wanted to look at anything that smacked of amateur filmmaking. Since then, the films I made have lived in a box in my closet, along with the box containing my Writers Guild of America award and my certificates of WGA and Emmy nominations.

Newspaper days

Though you were writing and making films, you were still a journalist! How did you get your first full-time job on a newspaper in Madison?

I was hired by *The Wisconsin State Journal* as a general assignment reporter in September 1969 and worked there until I left for California in July 1973. I had valuable training in covering a wide range of stories, including three years as "riot reporter" covering battles between the police and militant students.

When I was hired, I was pretty down and out. I was working part time as a dishwasher at Ella's Delicatessen near the campus and living on ten dollars a week and all the bagels and hot dogs I could abscond with. I went from that job to earning a relatively comfortable $175 per week ($1,525 in 2025 money). In those days, because of the Vietnam War, the economy was prosperous, but that did not last long, since President Johnson failed to raise taxes to pay for the war at first, while lying to the American public about its scope, so inflation gradually escalated.

I had to find that job in a hurry. Linda Detra, a Madison girl I had met while we both worked at Ella's shortly before her graduation from high school, became pregnant. Our parents held a summit meeting at the Detras' home in Madison, and my mother ordered me to come to Milwaukee and arrange to get a job by the following week. I was so docile that I followed her command. I applied to the two Madison papers, the *Capital Times* and the *State Journal*, as well as one in the small town of Kaukauna (a hundred miles north of Milwaukee) that was advertising for a reporter. In short order, the *Kaukauna Times* offered me a job (I dreaded moving there), and the *State Journal* called me in for an interview. I took my carefully tended scrapbook of published articles to show the managing editor and was assigned to interview a reporter, the Reverend Bill Wineke (a delightful, subversively funny guy), and write an account of some local issue.

I passed those crucial tests, but another reason I was hired was that the paper's executive editor, Larry Fitzpatrick, said he owed my grandfather John McBride a favor. Larry's brother Dan had been an art student of my grandfather decades earlier at Superior (Wisconsin) Central High School. Dan's overall scholastic record was so weak he was about to be expelled until grandfather told the principal that Dan had talent as an artist and should be given another chance. Dan Fitzpatrick went on to win two Pulitzer Prizes as an editorial cartoonist for the *St. Louis Post-Dispatch*. So I began my newspaper career because, as Portia puts it in Shakespeare's *Merchant of Venice*, "How far that little candle throws his beams!/So shines a good deed in a naughty world." Before I veered into working in the film world, I thought seriously about becoming an editorial cartoonist, which I would have enjoyed. Although I took some art classes my mother arranged for me, I never devoted enough serious attention to that field.

On my first day at the *State Journal*, I was thrown into the arena by being assigned to interview the legendary investigative journalist Clark Mollenhoff and a prominent Illinois congressman, Robert H. Michel, who later became the House Minority Leader. During my four years at the paper, I mostly worked the night shift, six PM to two

AM, covering the Dane County Board of Supervisors and committee meetings and covering late-breaking news events. Some time after I began working for the *State Journal*, I encountered Elliott Maraniss of the *Capital Times* in the street outside the downtown offices of the two Madison papers. He said, "You would have been happier working for us." Rather than asking why, if that was the case, he hadn't responded when I had applied for a job with the *Capital Times*, or telling him that I didn't buy into the myth of the merits of his liberal newspaper, I replied simply that I was happy where I was.

Graham Greene observed in his autobiography *A Sort of Life* that the best training for a young writer was spending some years working on "a rather conservative newspaper. The hours, from four till around midnight, give him plenty of time to do his own work [during his hours off]... He has the company of intelligent and agreeable men [and women, at the papers I worked on before *Daily Variety*] of greater experience than his own: he is not enclosed by himself in a small room tormented by the problems of expression.... Nor is the work monotonous.... [N]o one knows at four o'clock what the evening may produce, and death does not keep a conventional hour."

In my four years on the *State Journal*, I kept writing books in my spare time. I would work until dawn after coming home and then sleep into the early afternoon. I had the energy and drive to keep working double time, but it wasn't good for my first marriage. Linda and I were married in October 1969, just after I began working on the newspaper. I was too immature to be married, and we didn't have much in common, although we had a daughter, Jessica, who was born in March 1970 and is now a journalist and journalism teacher. Linda and I always got along well, even after our divorce in 1973.

On the *State Journal*, I liked to write stories that had cinematic elements. While monitoring the police radio, I often went out late in my so-called "graveyard shift" to cover criminal activity and once I came upon a man shot in the stomach in a hotel lobby, bleeding through a six-pack of beer he was clutching, before the police arrived. All that was good experience for a screenwriter, like Hemingway's youthful stint on the *Kansas City Star*. I felt especially excited to cover some spectacular fires, including one that destroyed a church; my article was accompanied by a series of photos of the steeple toppling over in flames at three AM. I had a creative time working with our superb staff of photographers, especially L. Roger Turner; I learned a lesson in discretion from him early on when he pointedly ignored my suggestion that he take a picture of a young woman kneeling in the grass at a fire scene while keening over her dead parrot.

But my news-gathering instinct nearly always took precedence over such deference: When my friend Mark Jacobson, who later became a well-known journalist and author, and I heard on a radio at the student union at 5:30 PM on December 10, 1967, that Otis Redding had died in a plane crash in Lake Monona, we went to The Factory, where Redding was scheduled to perform that night on a bill with a warm-up band called the Grim Reapers. Before the police showed up to manage the crowd, Mark and I walked up and down the line of people who were waiting to get in, not realizing that Otis was dead. That impulse we had to spread the grim news made me remember watching Dick Clark reporting on *American Bandstand* in 1959 about the plane crash that killed the three rock stars, Buddy Holly, Ritchie Valens, and the Big Bopper.

I assume what Graham Greene also meant that the value of working for a "rather conservative" newspaper has to do with the fact that it takes more finesse to write stories for a publication with stricter standards. Our liberal rival let writers editorialize in news stories and otherwise play fast and loose with their reportage, but the *State Journal* held to serious professional standards and did not let its conservative editorial stance color its news coverage.

The *Capital Times* also was lax in not assigning reporters to evening events, often pirating my reporting on meetings by rewriting it without acknowledgment. Once a member of our staff snuck into the composing room (the two papers shared a building and printing facilities) and inserted a line of type at the bottom of a *Capital Times* story reading "Stolen from *The Wisconsin State Journal*," and no one caught it before it ran in the paper. Through these mundane assignments, I came to understand how government works on a grassroots level. For example, while covering tedious hearings on the issuance of sewer permits on undeveloped land, I realized the importance of those decisions in causing urban sprawl. The school board meetings I covered were a bit livelier, and if I hadn't covered them there would not be the funny school board scene in *Rock 'n' Roll High School*. (I play one of the conservative board members who hire the principal Miss Togar, played by Mary Woronov, to crack down on student unrest; the head of the board was played by the venerable character actor Grady Sutton in his last film appearance.)

I did get some flaky assignments on the *State Journal*. We had a colorful attorney-provocateur in town named Edward Ben Elson, who called himself "a specialist in looney law" and succeeded in getting an important state law passed limiting the ability of family members to get their relatives committed to mental hospitals. Eddie also conducted a "Free Rosemary Kennedy" movement, claiming she was a political prisoner of her family at a Wisconsin Catholic care center for adults with disabilities. But he also pulled a prank by claiming the Comet Kohoutek was going to touch down at his rural home on Christmas Eve in 1973, and he sold tickets to people who wanted to be whisked into space by the comet. Come Christmas Eve, and the executive editor, Larry Fitzpatrick, actually sent me to Eddie's farmhouse to cover the festivities. When I arrived in a snowstorm—naturally I was the only person knocking on the door—Eddie couldn't believe the paper had taken him seriously, so he invited me in to have a hot drink or two.

I learned to write obituaries on the *State Journal,* a practice I enthusiastically continued on *Daily Variety* in Hollywood. I also had the standing assignment of interviewing anyone in Madison who reached the age of a hundred. Invariably, those people told me their secret to living so long was drinking and smoking all their lives. They were clearly unusual, but a valuable life lesson I learned from interviewing people throughout my careers as a journalist and author is that age is no indication of fitness or acuity. Many people in their eighties and nineties I talked with were sharp, and many in their fifties or sixties were wrecks.

What working for daily newspapers taught me most of all was how to write fast and efficiently and to be accurate in quoting people. A Hollywood producer told me I was the only person who had ever interviewed him who quoted him exactly. And though I interviewed many so-called "ordinary" people in Madison, which was helpful training for my biographies, occasionally I was able to meet some extraordinary people who came to town and write features on them. I reported on a talk at the State Historical Society by Jorge Luis Borges and a master class in piano given on campus by Duke Ellington. I spoke briefly with Borges and sat directly below Ellington as he played the piano for an hour. And I heard the fatalistic philosophy of the legendary circus aerialist Karl Wallenda; he died at the age of 73 in a 1978 performing accident.

One of the rewards of working on a newspaper, as Greene noted, is that you never know what will happen when you go to work. And interviewing a wide range of people every day developed my knack for being able to talk with anybody. Since I was somewhat shy by nature in those days, I welcomed the license a newspaper reporter is given to go up and talk to strangers. And it was an immense help to my screenwriting by honing my ability to write dialogue, which I always thought was my strongest suit. I also reviewed an occasional film at the *State Journal* when I felt I wanted to call attention to something special, though without additional pay.

The two biggest scoops I came up with during my time at the *State Journal* were from the same event. In 1972, I covered an appearance at the University of Wisconsin by Henry Kissinger's deputy William H. Sullivan, who would go on to serve as the U.S. ambassador to Iran when the hostage crisis erupted in 1979. As I write in my 2021 book *Political Truth: The Media and the Assassination of President Kennedy*, Sullivan was asked at the Madison event

> why the U.S. was still in Vietnam. He answered that it was because the U.S. needed to control the oil in the South China Sea. That kind of candid public revelation about realpolitik and the economic causations of war is most unusual among government officials. What I reported was picked up by the Associated Press [for which I was a stringer] and went around the world on its wire, although it was eclipsed by another revelation I reported from the same event, Sullivan's comment that the Paris peace talks soon would be resuming. Following the stir both statements caused, Sullivan claimed he had not made them. I produced my notes to prove that he had. Then it was claimed that Sullivan's speech to a university organization had been off-the-record. I produced a letter from that organization inviting our newspaper to cover his appearance on campus. Studies of the Vietnam War rarely discuss the importance of oil in motivating the long U.S. presence there.

What were your experiences covering the student protests in Madison?

My most eventful reporting at the *State Journal* came when I spent three years covering the frequent antiwar demonstrations that often turned into violent confrontations between the local police and demonstrators. Since I was one of the youngest male reporters on the staff, I was the designated "riot reporter." These riots were sometimes provoked by brutal tactics by club-swinging cops with tear gas, causing gangs of students to fight back with rocks and firebombs. The initial police violence at the Dow Chemical protest in October 1967 had begun an endless cycle of escalating confrontations. Once I was even pinned down with a bunch of cops as they engaged in a shootout with students. More often it would begin with a peaceful assembly on the campus library mall of a couple of hundred students before a few dozen hardcore radicals would break away and roam campus and downtown streets, breaking windows and setting fires.

I learned to stay a block ahead of trouble, scout the path ahead, and quickly scan for exit routes. I would take notes on a folded-up bunch of paper while ducking out of sight around the corner of buildings. That way I never was injured, although I often was teargassed; it was more dangerous to be a photographer, since neither side wanted to be caught doing something illegal.

For quite a while I found it exciting to cover these police/student riots. Since I fortunately had not gone to Vietnam, this was how I learned to write action scenes in my screenplays. I also had gone to Chicago with Stuart Gordon and some other Madison friends for the protests at the 1968 Democratic Convention, and on the night when the police viciously broke up a peaceful gathering in Lincoln Park, I was running down a street when I heard gunfire on the next block. Dashing into a vacant lot, I pulled open the back door of an abandoned car and jumped into the back. I landed on top of a girl lying on the floor. She turned out to be a fellow protester from Madison. We hid out there for a while, and I wish I could report that our encounter later led to romance. But if I wrote a screenplay about the protest era, that would make a terrific opening scene, a perfect "meet-cute" for the late Sixties. As Winston Churchill put it when he was in his twenties, "Nothing in life is so exhilarating as to be shot at without result."

Eventually, however, the stress of being a "riot reporter" began to weigh on me; I found my stomach turning ill in anticipation of trouble every time the sun went down. The last time I covered one of those riots, I finally had enough. I confess I stayed in a friend's rooming house all night making phone calls to dorms to get reports on the action and calling in breathless bulletins to the paper. When the editor told me to come in at eleven PM, I realized that though it had rained during the night, I was still dry. So I took a shower fully clothed, and when I arrived back at the paper I was hailed as a hero for my intrepid coverage by staff members pressing beers on me. I am told by an old colleague that the word got around about what I had actually done, which became something of a legend in Madison journalism. By then, in any case, the riots were subsiding.

But for many more years I suffered from PTSD and found myself habitually finding exit routes wherever I went. Finally one day when I walked out onto the quad of our San Francisco State campus, I realized I was no longer automatically scouting an exit.

Going to Hollywood

Tell me about your experience going to Hollywood during this time to interview John Ford. I couldn't believe anyone could be so lucky.

I went to Hollywood in August 1970 to interview Ford for the critical study Mike Wilmington and I were writing about him. That week I also met Jean Renoir, Orson Welles, and Peter Bogdanovich. So I met my three favorite directors on my first visit to Hollywood as well as an up-and-coming young director I admired from watching *Targets* during a break from being teargassed at the Chicago Democratic convention. Peter was about to go to Texas to make *The Last Picture Show*. And thanks to him, I had my first professional film experience with Welles, who put me in his just-beginning film *The Other Side of the Wind*.

Ford gave you quite a hard time, along with showing some warmth and humor. You call him "dour and unruly." It was one of your first interviews with a director, so do you think if you got to do it again knowing what to expect from him, you could have had an easier time?

That encounter in Ford's Beverly Hills office on August 19, 1970, came on what turned out to be the last day of his fifty-six-year career. I was chagrined by Ford's largely intransigent attitude when I attempted to draw him out on his feelings about his work; it was well known that he was virtually impossible to interview, as Lindsay Anderson and many others had learned, but Ford boasted on camera to Henry Fonda shortly after our interview, "I didn't tell him *anything*." Actually, he did offer a few eloquent comments on questions that met his fancy, but more often he pretended not to remember even some of his greatest films or gave me virtually monosyllabic responses.

Were you frustrated that Ford didn't want to talk about individual movies, including The Searchers, *which he recalled mostly because it made money?*

Sure. And it was especially frustrating that he wouldn't say much about *Fort Apache*, the film that made me fall in love with his work in 1967. I was flummoxed by Ford and didn't entirely understand why he was so difficult, though I should have anticipated it. He kept deflecting questions and putting me on, as he was prone to do throughout his career. But I became more stubborn as we continued. Although I knew going in that Ford disdained the interview process, pretending to be an "illiterate cowboy" and refusing to play the game with most journalists and scholars who managed to penetrate his bunker, I was still confused at the time by how difficult he was. Bogdanovich, who had been similarly flummoxed when he tried to interview Ford on camera for his documentary *Directed by John Ford*, reassured me that playing dumb and deaf—he had me sit on his deaf and blind side—was just Ford's way of coping with pesky interlopers.

I later came to admire Ford for refusing to discuss his work. Directors today tend to give a hundred interviews telling you what to think about their new films, but Ford refused to play that game. He respected the audience enough to make us want to think for ourselves. With some distance, I can also see the humor in the interview now. Ford was being mischievous in pretending of *Fort Apache* that he didn't remember "what the hell it's all about," or in claiming it was hard to "get a story" about the Civil War, or saying of *The Searchers* that it's "a good picture, made a lot of money, and that's the ultimate end." For my part, I was overly serious and reverent—Ford told Fonda that I "came in fear and trembling"—but today I would be able to roll with the punches better and find inroads through his armor. Since this was my first interview in Hollywood, though, I was at a serious disadvantage.

After I went back to Wisconsin and played the audiotape, Wilmington observed that I had tended to probe sensitive spots in Ford, which was the worst way to go about trying to interview him. Nor was it possible, at least on that day, to get Ford in a more relaxed and reflective mood. I went there with the fantasy of finding him discoursing eloquently on his view of the world. That fantasy shared by Ford admirers is beautifully conveyed in the imaginary meeting the future Nobel Prize-winning author Peter Handke has with Ford at the climax of his 1972 German novel about a pilgrimage through the United States in *Short Letter, Long Farewell*.

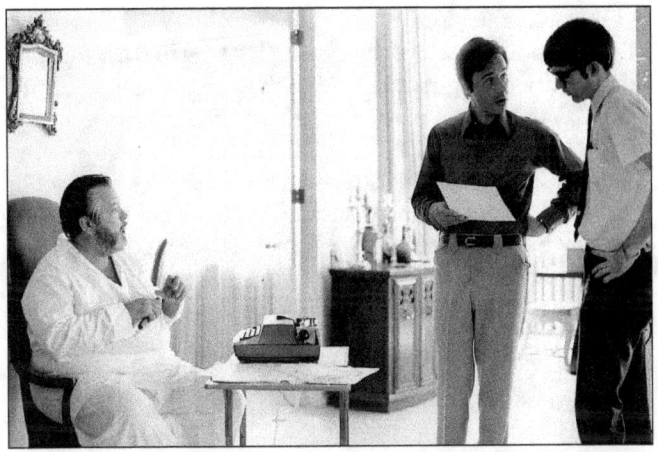

Orson Welles rehearses me and Peter Bogdanovich on the first day of shooting *The Other Side of the Wind* at the director's rented home in Los Angeles, August 23, 1970. I would spend more than five years playing the gauche film critic and historian Mister Pister, a spoof of my earnest young self. (Felipe Herba)

Mike helped me realize that in the midst of his grumpiness, Ford had given me some enlightening material about his working methods, including when to move your camera: "When there's a cause for it.... I like to have the audience feel that this is the real thing. I don't like to have them interested in the camera. And the camera movement disturbs them." His other memorable comments included his defiantly high opinion of his great final feature, *7 Women*, and how it was "over the heads" of the American audience of its day, and his caustic views of studio executives: "You're working with a stupid lot of people, I mean the executive producers, so what the hell, you've got to expect it." And the most stunning aspect of the interview was that he actually announced his retirement in the course of our discussion.

Much later, through studying Ford's papers at Indiana University in Bloomington, I confirmed that the day I arrived in Ford's office was the last day of his career. It was the day he finally gave up after failing to get an Italian spaghetti Western financed with the help of his good friend Woody Strode. During our interview, Ford kept anxiously asking his secretary if "the gentleman from Italy" or "the Italian gentleman" had called or written yet. That was a reference to a producer Ford was hoping would make a deal for his picture. While I was trying to interview Ford, he was coming to the conclusion that the producer would not be calling, there would be no deal, and that had been his last chance at making another film.

No wonder Ford was in a bad mood when I came to ask him about his classic movies. That was the last topic he felt like discussing that day. He tried to shoo me out, but I kept filibustering. Finally, after I asked an inane question about *3 Godfathers*, Ford said, "I enjoyed making it... and that should about finish our interview. Mac, I've got a lot of work to do. Today's an awful busy day for me. I've gotta... I'm way past—I gotta call up Rome. That's a good piece of news." I apologized for asking "some silly questions," and he said,

> Well, it isn't that, but everybody asks the same questions, and suddenly you say, "Jeez, I'm being interviewed." But all you people, I mean, you all ask the same questions, and I'm sick and tired of trying to answer them because I don't know the answers. I'm just a hard-nosed, hard-working... ex-director, and I'm trying to retire gracefully.... I'm just trying to live out my life in peace and comfort and quiet.

That pause before Ford called himself an "ex-director" was heartbreaking.

Despite Ford's intransigence, the time I spent in his presence proved immensely valuable in understanding him, for I learned as much from his affect as I did from what he said. The teenaged Steven Spielberg visited Ford in a similar state of anxiety. When I saw Spielberg's recreation of that meeting in his 2022 film, *The Fabelmans* (with Gabriel LaBelle playing Steven's alter ego, Sam Fabelman), I felt it captured the essence of the crusty but inwardly tender old director. David Lynch was inspired casting as Ford, and Spielberg delightfully prolongs Ford's ritualistic lighting of his cigar with what he humorously noted was "the magic of film editing."

Ford gave Spielberg only a couple of memorable minutes, but that encounter included a priceless lesson about cinematic composition. I was fortunate to spend an hour in his presence, and observing his body language and evasively defensive responses helped me immeasurably when I came to write his biography. I was struck by how insecure this legendary director was around a young admirer. There was so much going on in Ford behind his gruff façade.

My assumption is that Jean Renoir and Orson Welles treated you much differently when you met them!

Later that Wednesday after my interview with Ford, I interviewed Renoir at his home, and temperamentally he was the opposite of Ford, kind, easy to talk with, amusing. But he told me that a director needs to have "an iron fist inside a velvet glove." And when I asked for advice on how to be a director, Renoir said, "Try a little acting." Little did we know I would be getting that chance four days later.

It came about because I called Bogdanovich after getting his phone number from Milt Luboviski at the Larry Edmunds Bookshop in Hollywood. That led to my meeting Welles and being cast in *The Other Side of the Wind*, which was about to start shooting. Peter had been asked to round up some film buff types to appear in the film, and when he noticed that I had written some notes on my wrist, I said I had done so while watching *Fellini–Satyricon* at a theater in Beverly Hills. Peter found that amusing and told Welles, who said he had to have a guy in his movie who writes on his wrist!

That Friday, August 21, I met Welles for lunch and a three-hour chat, which I've written about at length in my three books on him. When I went to Welles's rented house in the hills near Twentieth Century-Fox, I saw he had the copy of *Persistence of Vision* I had sent him on his mantelpiece. He told me, "Finally I meet my favorite critic." I asked why he thought of me that way. And he said, "You're the only one who understands what I'm trying to do."

In *The Other Side of the Wind*, Welles's *roman à clef* about Hollywood, I play a spoof of myself, Marvin Pister, aka Mister Pister, a bumptious young film scholar following John Huston's Jake Hannaford around, asking him intrusive film-buff questions. That was a real Walter Mitty experience. And Welles let me collaborate with him on writing my dialogue for *Other Wind* (as that film was called on the clapper boards). This lasted intermittently for more than five years until the film wrapped in early 1976. Some of the footage we shot that first day, August 23, of me interviewing Hannaford in his car, is in the finished film. But we didn't shoot Huston until he was cast three years later. This string of events on my first visit to Hollywood may all seem like luck, but as Branch Rickey said, "Luck is the residue of design."

Was it a bit surreal meeting such luminaries, including three of your idols, the first week you came to town? Or had you already met enough famous people, including baseball legends and John F. Kennedy, so that it was easy for you?

Orson Welles wrote me this note after I returned to Wisconsin
from the first day of shooting on *Other Wind*,
along with two boxes of cigars.

Good point I hadn't thought of, but I was still in awe
of Ford because I thought so highly of his work, as you
would be if you had been a young journalist meeting Bach
or Beethoven. But when I said that to Sherman Beck, who
directed the USIA documentary *Vietnam! Vietnam!* on
which Ford was executive producer, Beck said it was hard
for him to be in awe of Ford after having to clean his shit off
the floor of the Caravelle Hotel in Saigon. I eventually lost
that awestruck attitude about people in the movie business.
At first when I was in Hollywood and would see a famous
film person at a party, I'd charge over to him or her and
boldly introduce myself and talk. Now I would never do
that. It seems a very youthful thing to do.

*Could you believe you were sitting with Welles, Ford, and
Renoir, that they were real, and your worlds had connected?*

It seemed every week would be like that. I didn't realize that was the pinnacle.

You got into a political argument with Welles on that first encounter, about Lyndon Johnson.

During my fascinating talk with Welles, which was mostly about movies, I angered him by challenging his view that Lyndon Johnson was a great president. Welles was an FDR liberal and admired Johnson's social programs so much that he seemed willing to overlook Vietnam, though I wasn't.

As you describe that discussion, Welles did not enjoy being challenged, and so you didn't get into arguments with him much in the years that followed. When you interviewed other people in Hollywood, on the left and right and in between, how did you approach political issues with them? Did you ever argue politics with Hollywood people, or did you settle into a neutral reporter mode?

After those early experiences with Welles and Ford, I learned to be more diplomatic as I interviewed more people in Hollywood. Generally you get more out of people that way, by not antagonizing them. I might have challenged some of them more, but when you interview someone you're there more to listen than to argue, which can be counterproductive. I was a good listener, so people felt they could reveal themselves to me. That was a byproduct of my early ambition to become a priest; people were comfortable confessing to me in interviews. To give one example, when I was researching my 2013 book *Into the Nightmare: My Search for the Killers of President John F. Kennedy and Officer J. D. Tippit*, I interviewed a retired Dallas police detective named Morris Brumley, who had been a boyhood friend of Tippit. As we talked in a diner with my tape recorder in front of us, Brumley began telling me how he had been a member of the Ku Klux Klan and even showed me his Knights of the Ku Klux Klan membership card. He claimed he had "infiltrated" the KKK for the police, but he boasted about committing violence.

I finally had to say something, so I asked if he had tried to arrest his fellow Klansmen. That more or less stopped him from telling me much more, unfortunately. I wish I had challenged Howard Hawks more about his conservative politics during the seven years I was doing our interview book *Hawks on Hawks*. I tried, but not much resulted. My biographies have a great deal about politics in them, especially my biography of Frank Capra, which I wrote after leaving the film industry. I became more politically conscious as I went along in Hollywood. I am not exaggerating when I say that working in Hollywood radicalized me. I was operating within the heart of what I realized was a criminal enterprise, as I later would call Hollywood in talking with my students.

I would think Bogdanovich, a young cinephile and interviewer himself, was the easiest for you to connect with on your first visit to Hollywood.

Yes, Peter was very helpful in sharing inside information I needed about Welles and Ford. And it was through Peter that I had my first professional film experience. What I learned from working with Welles not only enhanced my books about him, but since he was the greatest actors' director in the history of the cinema and taught me how to act, that experience helped me enormously when I came to write my 2024 book about the much-misunderstood art of film acting in the hands of another great director of actors, *George Cukor's People: Acting for a Master Director.*

Welles died in 1985 with *The Other Side of the Wind* unfinished, and in the 1990s I tried to raise money with cinematographer Gary Graver to finish the film, which was mired for decades in financial, legal, and political turmoil. I eventually suggested bypassing film studios, since they rejected Welles's experimental work when we offered it to them, and taking it instead to the new outlet of cable TV. In doing so and raising interest from Showtime, I managed to help push the project along to completion; I saw the process as a relay race. Eventually I was a credited consultant on the postproduction, along with fellow film scholar Jonathan Rosenbaum, when *The Other Side of the Wind* was released by the streaming service Netflix in 2018.

I'm curious if Ford, like Welles, realized you were the preeminent authority on his work.

When our 1971 *Searchers* essay appeared in *Sight and Sound*, Ford somehow got wind of it and had his secretary write me to ask for a copy of the magazine. I sent it to him with some other essays I had published on his films and asked for his cooperation on the biography I had begun researching. He replied in a handwritten note that November,

Dear Joe,

I appreciate your interest (especially the up-beat kindly way you treated me) but honestly, I'm too old and tired to go for a biog—even with a McBride (My McBride of 52 years [Mrs. Ford, the former Mary McBride Smith] is improving, knock wood). However, let me mull it over.

Sincerely, thanks
John Ford

I'm glad my work made him happy. But as I recalled in *Searching for John Ford*, "Uncertain whether it would be wise to press him further, and intimidated by his bluster, I never pursued that tentative opening, his offer to 'mull it over.' Perhaps it would not have mattered much if I had been able to persuade Ford to talk with me at greater length, because the truth about anyone's life cannot be captured solely in what the person says about it, particularly if that person is a master fabulist like John Ford. I also did not realize in 1972 and '73 that Ford was interviewed at length by his grandson Dan Ford for his official biography, published in 1979 as *Pappy: The Life of John Ford*; I benefited from Dan's donation of those interviews to the Lilly Library, for they offer many insights for subsequent biographers, even while raising as many questions as they answer."

John Ford was dying when Dan was doing his interviews. In 1973 when I moved to Riverside, not far from Palm Desert, I wanted to go see Ford on his deathbed but couldn't muster up the nerve. He died shortly after that. I went to his funeral in Hollywood and wrote an emotional article about it for *Sight and Sound* that divided people who did or did not appreciate my feelings. It frustrated me that our John Ford book did not come out in his lifetime.

The Army Math bombing

The bombing of the Army Mathematics Research Center on the UW campus happened just after you met Ford, Welles, Renoir and Bogdanovich in Hollywood in the summer of 1970. The fairy tale was over. It was a shock to all of us there, in Madison. How did you react to that event and cover it for the State Journal?

By Monday morning, August 24, I was back home in Madison. I discovered upon landing at the airport at 7:30

AM, when I asked a cabbie what had been happening while I was away, that "The students just blew up a building." At 3:42 that morning, a group of four radicals had used a truck bomb to severely damage Sterling Hall, because it housed the Army Mathematics Research Center, which was involved in picking bombing targets for Vietnam. A graduate student, Robert Fassnacht, was killed while working on a physics project in Sterling Hall. He had parked his bicycle outside, so the bombers had to have seen it and continued on their mission with awareness that someone was inside the building. That event, along with the deadly Greenwich Village townhouse explosion that March, helped fracture the antiwar movement by discouraging nonviolent protesters from continuing their actions against the war.

During my somewhat contentious discussion about politics with Welles three days before the Army Math bombing, Welles was also offended when I offered a criticism of the antiwar radicals in Madison. I said they were getting crazy and were about to kill someone. I was on the ground covering the hardcore radicals who were getting increasingly violent in Madison, and I knew what I was talking about. Even though Welles didn't want to hear my criticism of President Johnson's conduct of the war, in a somewhat contradictory way he also seemed to think the protesters were above criticism. Perhaps the real bone of contention was that Welles didn't know enough about what was happening in the streets and felt testy when I knew more than he did about something. And three days later, my prediction came true. I never discussed the subject with Welles again.

The Sterling Hall bombing was my inspiration for the ending of *Rock 'n' Roll High School*, when the students who have taken over their school from the evil principal blow up the building. When I proposed it to director Allan Arkush, he turned down the idea, saying, "It would make the students unsympathetic." But as he admitted in Stephen Armstrong's 2023 book on the film, *I Want You Around: The Ramones and the Making of* Rock 'n' Roll High School, within a week he realized it was the only way to end the film. Allan then started claiming that he had fantasized as a high school student about blowing up his school. He went on claiming that for decades. But if that was true, he didn't say so at the time I proposed the ending. Roger Corman later told Leonard Maltin that the ending was the main reason he approved the project. Allan admitted to Armstrong that the ending was my idea but soon went back to claiming he had thought it up as a high school kid.

That's a case study of how directors often feel they need to claim authorship of everything important in their films. And Allan seems never to have understood the point of my ending, which is to show how legitimate revolutions often turn nihilistic. Instead, he seemed to mindlessly endorse the bombing by having a disk jockey at the end of the film look directly at the audience and tell them to call him "If you want *this* to happen at *your* school."

Heading to Hollywood

When you returned to Madison and your newspaper job, did you already plan to head back to live in Hollywood?

Sure. My city editor in Madison said I was the only reporter he knew who would walk around with a copy of *Variety* under his arm. I had Hollywood in mind from the time I first saw *Citizen Kane* in class in 1966 and became determined to make films and write about them. It took me until 1973 to make the move west, though, and I had to pay my dues by suffering through a year working on a newspaper in the godforsaken, smog-blanketed city of Riverside, California, before I landed the exciting job on *Daily Variety* in Hollywood.

Nostalgia

I have always sensed that you are sentimental about your time in Madison.

Yes, in the same way I am nostalgic for the 1950s even though my childhood was the worst time in my life other than the years I spent later as a professional screenwriter. And the Fifties was a bad time for the country in many ways, even if middle-class suburban white people like us were fairly prosperous, and culturally the landscape had a lot going for it despite the damaging effects of blacklisting and social pressures to conform. Similarly, the Sixties was a time of great turmoil and pain but also tremendous change and excitement. So much of what we feel about our past is subjective in any case, dependent on our individual circumstances and the times of our life we are remembering. Nostalgia is a complex and paradoxical emotion.

When I asked the formerly blacklisted Abe Polonsky what he thought of *American Graffiti*, he replied, "How can anyone be nostalgic for 1962?" In my youthful days in Wisconsin, I was well aware of McCarthyism, I was deeply concerned with racism, and I was even, because of my mother's dilemma, precociously aware of sexism. Yet in strange ways, I am nostalgic for some of the worst times I personally lived through in the Fifties and early Sixties, though not for the period that followed, with the assassinations and the war that drove our country to the brink of civil war.

What I remember with fondness from growing up in the 1950s are the cultural touchstones that kept me sane, the TV shows, the movies, the rock songs, the comic books, the baseball games. And Madison in the late Sixties and early Seventies, when I discovered my profession in films and learned to be more sophisticated about politics, has always seemed the most formative time of my life. In some ways the best things happened to me in those years as well as some of the saddest. I had a hard time leaving Madison because I had been married and divorced and had a three-year-old daughter. Since I was mostly impoverished during my years as an industry reporter and screenwriter, it was hard to get back to see my daughter as often as I would have liked. I felt guilty over that but felt I had to fulfill my career potential by leaving home. I am nostalgic for the Madison years even though they are bittersweet. Despite the fact that I was often lonely there and frustrated romantically and sexually and felt condescended to by some people, in other ways it was exciting and an exhilarating period of growth and self-discovery.

When you left Madison for Los Angeles in 1973, did you leave behind some of your belongings because you worried you might return in a year or two?

No, I was gone for good. I hedged a bit by asking the *State Journal* for a "leave of absence" when I resigned, but it was not granted. I financed my trip to California with the $500 prize I won from the Wisconsin Council for Creative Writers Award for my *Orson Welles* being chosen as the best nonfiction book of 1972 by a Wisconsin writer. I thought it was ironic and rather sad that the award enabled me to leave my home state.

With a friend I moved to Los Angeles in July 1973, taking a memorable detour through Monument Valley, where my Navajo guide took me to the ruins of the ranch house Ford had burned for *The Searchers*. "They left an awful mess down there," he said. I took away some charred wood and bricks as souvenirs and distributed some to fellow Fordians. But I left behind an empty can of the propellant that had been used to start the fire. I also talked with Navajos who had worked for Ford. As I wrote in a 2001 profile of John Wayne for *American Movie Classics Magazine*,

> There I met a young Navajo who had just returned from service in Vietnam and was still wearing his U.S. Army fatigue jacket. When I asked what he thought about Ford, he replied, "Is he the old guy with the eyepatch? He's OK."
>
> Then I asked what he thought of John Wayne. I assumed this was a touchy subject, particularly since Wayne's 1971 *Playboy* interview in which he responded when questioned about the suffering of American Indians, "I don't feel we did wrong in taking this great country away from them, if that's what you're asking. Our so-called stealing of this country from them was just a matter of survival. There were great numbers of people who needed new land, and the Indians were selfishly trying to keep it for themselves."
>
> The young army veteran was so infuriated by Wayne's comments that he told me if Wayne ever came back to make another movie in Monument Valley, "He'd better watch out, because I'll be sitting up there in those rocks with my M1 rifle and I'll pick him off."
>
> .In the next six years until Wayne died, I often wondered what I would do if I heard that he was going back to Monument Valley to make another movie. Would I alert him to the danger looming in the ancient mesas or simply let history happen?

Fortunately, Wayne never went back to Monument Valley, so I was spared that moral decision.

Paying penance

I am surprised that when you went to live in Hollywood, you took a job not in Hollywood or even Los Angeles.

A former Madison colleague, George Mitchell, arranged a job for me with *The Riverside Press-Enterprise*. I looked at a map of Southern California and saw that Riverside was a dot near the big dot for Los Angeles, but I didn't realize that those dots were fifty miles apart. That became a problem when I took the job in Riverside. I was driving back and forth to Los Angeles many nights for film events and getting back home at two or three in the morning, and then stumbling into work in a daze at 8 AM. I've never been a morning person, anyway, and it would take me most of the morning to come to my senses while drinking coffee at my desk and reading newspapers.

Riverside was also one of the smoggiest cities in the world when I lived there. I didn't realize for the first month that the city was surrounded by mountains. I saw them when I opened the door one morning to get my paper, and when I related the experience to my city editor, I said, "It's like having a poison cloud surrounding the city." She corrected me by saying, "It's not *like* having a poison cloud surrounding the city." I made some friends on the paper but had more of a social life during my frequent semi-desperate escapes to Los Angeles.

I came to find life in Riverside almost unbearable. Although the *Press-Enterprise* was a solid newspaper, the city itself was terminally dull, so there was not much to write about, even though I spent a day covering the trial for Riverside's biggest story in years, the 1971 murder of two policemen. My *Press-Enterprise* colleague Ben Bradlee Jr. wrote a gripping 1979 book about that incident, *The Ambush Murders: The True Account of the Killing of Two California Policemen*, and it was made into a TV movie. And once when I was reporting on a would-be jumper at a downtown building under construction, I found myself having to help the police talk him down.

In an odd assignment, I spent a day riding around town in a convertible with The Amazing Criswell, the flaky psychic who is most famous now as a member of the Ed Wood Stock Company. Criswell does his prediction thing in Wood's *Plan 9 from Outer Space*, and director Tim Burton gives Jeffrey Jones the role of Criswell in his funny and endearing 1994 biopic *Ed Wood*, which starts with the wavy-haired, silver-tongued charlatan sitting up in a coffin to invite the viewers into Ed's world. I don't recall any predictions Criswell may have made as we were driving around and I was taking notes on his utterances or why we were doing that at all. That meaningless but goofy assignment epitomizes the year I spent in Riverside. At least it had some connection to showbiz.

Celebrating my last day of work at *The Riverside Press-Enterprise* in July 1974. It was a good paper but in a deadly Southern California town, and I was relieved to escape to Hollywood. (Dana Downie).

Did you do any lecturing or outside writing to help with finances?

While still working in Riverside in the spring of 1974, I took a course on Hitchcock and Truffaut at the UC Riverside extension division. I knew more about the subject than the professor, who asked my friend Rick Thompson how to handle that, and Rick said, "Make use of him." I also was able to teach my first course on film at Sherwood Oaks Experimental College in Hollywood. The guests in my "International Film Directors" course included two pantheon directors, Howard Hawks and Fritz Lang, as well as Roman Polanski, Bob Rafelson, and Maximilian Schell. I found Hollywood in that period a cornucopia of opportunities for a film historian, since some of the last of the Golden Age directors were still working and many other veterans were still around to interview. I watched Billy Wilder filming the classic newspaper play by Ben Hecht and Charles MacArthur, *The Front Page*, at Universal and wrote up my interviews with Wilder, his writing partner I. A. L. Diamond, Jack Lemmon, and Walter Matthau for Boston's *The Real Paper* and *Sight and Sound*. Following on my critical analyses of Wilder's work for *Film Quarterly* and *Film Heritage*, that experience helped lead to my writing the 2021 critical study *Billy Wilder: Dancing on the Edge*.

I also co-hosted a tribute to Hawks with Peter Bogdanovich at the Los Angeles County Museum of Art in early 1974, and I was paying visits to Hawks at his home in Palm Springs so I could learn about screenwriting from this great cinematic storyteller. It was not until I had been doing that for a while that I realized I was accumulating enough material for an interview book, and as good fortune would have it, I was asked to host a "Weekend with Howard Hawks and His Films" for the Directors Guild of America at a Laguna Beach hotel two months before his death in 1977. I used that three-day weekend to fill in areas that remained to be covered in the book, which I finally put together as *Hawks on Hawks* for its first publication in 1982. That book has had the widest issuance of any of my books, with translations in French, Spanish, Japanese, Italian, Finnish, and Iranian, as well as publication in Great Britain.

And a movie came to town while I was working in Riverside, *The Wild Party*. That artsy Merchant-Ivory movie about 1920s Hollywood is based on a poem by Joseph Moncure March. In a loose takeoff on the Fatty Arbuckle scandal, James Coco plays a sympathetic character based on the silent comedian. Probably the only film other than

Shakespeare films that is narrated in iambic pentameter, *The Wild Party* was filmed at the Mission Inn, a bizarrely ornate old hotel that was Riverside's most historic site, a former resort attraction for Hollywood stars before the smog ruined the city. Director James Ivory was intrigued to learn from me that Douglas Sirk had made a 1951 movie at the Mission Inn, *The First Legion*, about Jesuit priests. I found Ismail Merchant as charming as Ivory was chilly, and the producer cooked marvelous Indian food for everyone.

After writing a feature on *The Wild Party* for the *Press-Enterprise* in the summer of 1974, I talked my way into being an extra for two days, outfitted in a period tuxedo and haircut as a party guest. In addition to continuing my acting during that period in *The Other Side of the Wind*—another movie about filmmaking—I was trying to get experience by getting bit parts or extra roles in various films, which was helpful experience for an aspiring screenwriter.

I am among the guys singing "Singapore Sally" with Raquel Welch while she parades on top of a bar in *The Wild Party*. I can actually hear myself singing in the film. (I am the world's worst singer, but I also sing "High Hopes" in *Primary* and "The Glow Worm Song" in *Other Wind*.) And I am part of the orgy that is the centerpiece of *The Wild Party*. But since it is a James Ivory orgy, nothing much is happening. My female screen partner and I are passed out fully dressed on a bed as Coco wanders through the scene. The frenetic screenwriter, Walter Marks, did most of the directing of the orgy while Ivory sat back with a little smile on his face. There was a lot of pot-smoking going on, and when Marks discovered that a newspaper reporter was on the set, he had me thrown out. Hacked up by its distributor, *The Wild Party* was a dismal flop.

From Riverside to Hollywood

Did you feel trapped in Riverside?

Eventually, after a year in Riverside, I was mightily frustrated about living there and being apart from the film business. My slowing pace of production at the *Press-Enterprise* got me in hot water with the increasingly hostile editor. But after receiving a warning, I managed to make a fortuitous and immediate escape to a job as a reporter and reviewer on *Daily Variety*. To affront the editor of the *Press-Enterprise*, who was rude about my departure and enforced a formal dress code, I wore a Mickey Mouse T-shirt on my next-to-last day at work. He issued a memo that I should wear "a regular kind of shirt" for my final day. So I rented a tuxedo and carried a cane and a bottle of juice resembling a champagne bottle, in a bucket wrapped in tin foil. Our photographer Dana Downie made me a present of a series of photos of that Hildy Johnson escapade. I used one of the pictures as the frontispiece for *Two Cheers for Hollywood.*

On my arrival in Los Angeles in July 1973, I had applied for jobs at the two trade papers and as a publicist at Warner Bros. My friend and I were living in a frat house near the UCLA campus in Westwood, and my $500 was quickly running out. But before it did, I had a promising interview with Thomas M. Pryor, the veteran editor of *Daily Variety.* Tom and I hit it off; he was an old *New York Times*man, a solid old-fashioned newspaperman and a tough but sentimental Irishman. He could tell I was savvy about movies and a solid reporter, but he didn't have a job opening at the time. When I mentioned that I had an opportunity to work on the Riverside paper, Tom recommended I take it to become knowledgeable about life in southern California, and he said to keep in touch. A year later, I happened to apply again to Tom just when an opening appeared on *Daily Variety.* He needed me right away, because Lee Beaupre, a reporter and reviewer, was leaving to become a publicist. I met Lee briefly while doing an interview for the trade paper; he was West Coast public relations director for Twentieth Century-Fox when he was murdered by his roommate, a male prostitute, in 1984.

Since I had to find an apartment in a hurry before starting work at *Daily Variety*, I wound up as if by fate in a cockroach-infested dump in Hollywood just down the road from the apartment that the cinematic patron saint of screenwriters, Joe Gillis, initially occupies in *Sunset Blvd.* In a later interview with Billy Wilder, I told him, "Before I came to Hollywood, I thought *Sunset Blvd.* was too cynical a depiction of the film industry. When I moved out here, I realized that it's like a documentary. Everything in it is totally true." He replied, "It's a valentine. But it is not just the picture industry—it is every industry. You make a picture about Exxon vs. Texaco vs. Shell, every industry has got this kind of slush that is underneath the whole thing. *Network.* The newspaper business. Naturally."

PART II
HOLLYWOOD

3. "The business of creating illusions"

As we look back on your early years living in Hollywood, when you churned out reviews and did interviews for Daily Variety, *tried with some success to write and sell screenplays, did some acting in movies, met your cinematic heroes, and published a number of books, how do think those diverse experiences affected what you've been doing—not counting your teaching—since you became strictly an author?*

I've learned to be philosophical, to understand that life generally turns out the way it's supposed to, regardless of what goals you set for yourself. I set out to be a film director but gradually realized I wasn't meant to be in that profession; I learned that from turning down three offers to direct films, wondering why, and eventually understanding my reasons. I prefer to be a writer and was always meant to be a professional writer, as I've been since I was twelve. Back in my Madison days, Mike Wilmington asked me why I wanted to be a director and observed that not every writer should be a director and that maybe being a writer is who I am. I of course resisted his shrewd insight at the time.

I had a reasonable amount of success as a screenwriter, with a couple of movies produced, one of which became a cult classic, and nine TV specials or documentaries. I won the Writers Guild of America award for co-writing one of my five American Film Institute Life Achievement Award specials on CBS-TV and was nominated for the other four as well as being nominated twice for Emmy awards. But film and TV writers are treated with such contempt in Hollywood, and I was so poorly paid, that it was always a struggle. Part of the problem I was having selling my original work, I realized, was that I was taking the job of screenwriter too seriously. I couldn't conceive of doing the work any other way but my best, but that set me up for being vulnerable to more cynical people taking advantage of my comparative lack of defense mechanisms, my seemingly ingenuous sincerity. That's what Shakespeare had Iago tell Roderigo in *Othello* that he would not do, "wear my heart upon my sleeve/For daws to peck at."

As I would learn over and over, to no avail, the writers who survived the blows of the Hollywood system insulated themselves emotionally and professionally by *not* taking their work seriously and being willing to accept almost any form of compromise. Like Iago, they could describe their duplicity by saying, "I am not what I am." I was lectured by well-meaning friends who tried to convince me to bend or abandon my principles as a writer as a means of survival. But I had contempt for that attitude, since the screenwriters who practiced it made life difficult for me and anyone else in Hollywood who did not have a "take the money and run" attitude. That mindset was epitomized for me in the utterly cynical 1997 book by John Gregory Dunne, *Monster: Living Off the Big Screen,* his sneeringly jocular account of the destructive hackwork he and his wife, Joan Didion, practiced as screenwriters. They whored themselves in order to support what they considered their more serious work as book writers and, not incidentally, their lavish lifestyle as power players in Malibu and New York. Their lives and careers could not have been more alien to me.

I found that the path I would be required to follow to break into the industry proved much more circuitous than I had expected. As it turned out, the only way I could break in during the 1970s was to work on the fringes of the industry—specifically for Roger Corman, who made his reputation and fortune by shrewdly hiring talented young people who were blocked from entering the rigidly controlled studio system.

The chicanery, mendacity, and sheer crookedness I faced as a screenwriter eventually made me escape the film business. Since I made the decision in 1984 to write books fulltime, even though that too has had its periods of combat, I have been much happier and have felt more fulfilled in my goals as a writer. I came to see that although I probably would have been relatively happy as a screenwriter in the days of the studio system, I was miscast as a screenwriter in the crass and chaotic modern Hollywood; I was as suited to that way of life as I would be writing liner notes for rock albums. But leaving the film business was one of the two hardest decisions I've ever made. The other was turning my back on the Catholic Church, since both involved escaping cult programming and both literally were life-saving decisions.

When I read over my reminiscences in this book of my time as a screenwriter, I think, "What a chronicle of stupidity." That's my first reaction, how stupid I was to do this and that and the other thing. How could I have fallen for all the lies I was told again and again? And how I paid the price for being gullible and trusting for such a long time, partly out of stubbornness, partly because of a reluctance to face facts. But then I recall my wife, Ruth, telling me in retrospect that I was unsuited for a career in Hollywood because I was too honest. As the corrupt senator played by Claude Rains says of James Stewart's Senator Jefferson Smith in *Mr. Smith Goes to Washington,* "This boy's honest, not stupid." I couldn't help being honest in that world of mendacity, because that was how I was raised, and it became my temperament and character. I was my own worst enemy in my Hollywood years, because I couldn't play the game the way it was played. So even though I did have moments of undeniable stupidity, I suppose I shouldn't blame myself too much. And yet in looking back, I believe I made a mistake by entering that field of corruption.

I hope this chronicle of my misadventures and intermittent successes in Hollywood will be enlightening as well as morbidly entertaining for the reader. It should serve as a cautionary tale, an illustration of how the industry malfunctions. And it provides an explanation for how my experiences have had an invaluable influence on my subsequent books about filmmakers.

"It's over"

When you arrived in Hollywood, I was getting my master's nearby at the University of Southern California Department of Cinema, in the screenwriting division. I wrote a couple of arty Western scripts, but the main script I turned in and got an A+ on was for an outright exploitation film, because I thought that was what was the most marketable for the increasingly dumbed-down movie audience of that time. George Lucas debuted American Graffiti *for our sound class, because he was friends with our teacher from when he was at USC. I asked him what he was doing as a follow-up and he told me that he was working on a space adventure. I wondered if it would be too juvenile for the marketplace.*

I could see a sharp decline from the freer and more open atmosphere of the mid-1970s to when the *Star Wars* era arrived. When I saw the first Hollywood screening of that film at the Academy Theater in May 1977, I was so depressed, I thought, "It's over." When I called my producer friend Jon Davison to share my dismay, he said, "*Star Wars* would be my favorite film if I were six years old." By "It's over," I meant that I realized the American cinema I loved and had lured me to Hollywood had turned a corner into artistic oblivion. I could tell that cardboard juvenilia would be taking over. I stuck it out for seven more years with stubborn self-destructiveness before "ankling the biz" to write books fulltime, as *Variety* would put it.

It took much longer for the irreversible collapse of Hollywood to become apparent to most people. In the late 1990s, I wrote a proposal for a book about the decline and fall of Hollywood, which I called *Twilight in the Smog,* a title I borrowed from a 1959 *Esquire* article on the subject by Orson Welles, who was far more prescient than I was; Gary Graver told me he thought that article was the basis for *The Other Side of the Wind*. Another title I considered earlier when I suggested the book to Knopf was *Hollywood Reckoning,* inspired by David Halberstam's 1986 book, *The Reckoning*, about how Japan overtook the American auto industry. But my proposal was rejected because people thought I was too pessimistic. They didn't realize how behind the times they were. Many years later, when Hollywood's malaise became an unavoidable topic of conversation, a former studio executive I knew suggested I finally should get down to writing that book, and I told her, "It's a moot point."

And yet in retrospect, the mixture of being beaten down and having occasional success, the deadening grief and transient elation I went through as a screenwriter before I retired from the industry in 1984 was worth it because of what I learned in the process about how the film industry works. That made it possible for me to write the books I've been writing about what Irving Thalberg so profoundly described as "the business of creating illusions." And without having covered Hollywood for years for *Daily Variety* before toiling as a screenwriter, I would not have fully understood what the artists I've written about went through and how these extraordinary figures coped or didn't cope with the Hollywood racket. Being an honest investigative reporter is an asset in the field of writing books even if it makes it hard to function effectively in a comparatively insignificant field such as entertainment trade reporting.

"That fucking rag you love so much"

What did you find most gratifying about working for Daily Variety *at that time?*

Before I came to California from Wisconsin in 1973, even though I had an extensive knowledge of film history that allowed me to write my critical studies of Welles and Ford, I had a rather foggy view of how films were actually made, and I was mostly ignorant about the film industry. Working as a reporter, reviewer, and columnist for *Daily Variety* was a dream job for me in many ways, enabling me to learn about the business by interviewing almost everyone I wanted to meet. I was hired by *Daily Variety* in August 1974 for my first tour of duty, which lasted until 1977; I would return briefly in 1980/1981, serving as the paper's business editor as well as a film reviewer, and for a more controversial stint from 1989 to 1992.

Even though my friend and mentor Sam Fuller, an old newspaperman with no illusions, described *Daily Variety* to me as "that fucking rag you love so much," working there was an experience I was fortunate to have. In my first three years with the paper, I was able to go on sets to watch films being made and to interview almost everyone I wanted in films past and present, and I received a thorough education in the arcane subject of corrupt Hollywood business practices. I learned the ropes from our gruff but lovable editor Tom Pryor, who managed to maintain high journalistic practices at *Daily Variety* against considerable odds, and from our cantankerous box-office maven Art Murphy, whom I succeeded for a time as business editor.

Tom Pryor, who looked and acted like James Cagney and similarly came from the Hell's Kitchen section of New York City, began working at the *New York Times* in 1931 and was a show business reporter and reviewer in their home office before becoming Hollywood bureau chief of the *Times* in 1951. He was recruited by *Variety* in 1959 to turn its slick daily edition into a legitimate newspaper. That was a challenging task in which he largely succeeded by keeping the editorial and advertising sides of the paper separate, even though most of the paper's revenue came from the studios it covered. I felt privileged to work with Tom but wished I had known him better and not felt intimidated by him. My background has always made me anxious around authority figures, and I often felt like a "secret man" (as Abe Polonsky called me) because I was leading a double life by writing books and scripts on the side while working at my "day jobs." But Tom always had my back as an editor and taught me a lot by his example.

My friend and colleague Doug Galloway wrote in Tom's obituary in 2001: "Pryor was on a first-name basis with luminaries as diverse as Ernest Hemingway, Robert Benchley, Dorothy Parker, and George S. Kaufman. His experience in showbiz spanned so many decades that he'd often astonish rookie *Variety* reporters with his first-hand accounts of key figures and events. Once in a dispute with

Thomas M. Pryor, my boss at *Daily Variety*. A former *New York Times* film reporter and reviewer and Hollywood bureau chief, Tom was brought in to make a real newspaper out of our trade paper and maintained its integrity as editor until being rudely fired by the British conglomerate, Cahners, that bought the paper and told him they wanted to placate advertisers. Here Tom is being honored by current and former staffers at a 1992 dinner in Studio City.

editors over *Show Boat*, Pryor casually mentioned that he was at the 1927 Broadway opening of the musical. And another time when an editor was researching Charlie Chaplin, it came out that Pryor had had dinner with the comic the night before he was forced to leave the country."

My fellow "muggs"

What were some of the other staffers like when you arrived at Daily Variety?

Most of the staff at the time when I first joined the paper in 1974 was ancient. Whitney Williams told me he had gone to the first Academy Awards dinner with Joan Crawford in 1929, and Jack Hellman had worked with Hemingway on the *Kansas City Star*. I enjoyed being in the company of those characters, even if they had seen better days. I never had a meaningful conversation with Jack, who was mostly non-functional by the time I came. He would arrive at 11 AM, call around to publicist pals to find one to take him to lunch at the Hollywood Brown Derby, and bend the elbow there before coming back to file occasional small items. One reason we had so many old-timers was that there was no pension plan. As soon as one was put into place, a number of people immediately retired, although Jack had already been let go when he started smashing up cars in the company parking lot, and he died of a broken heart a few months later.

Whitney's take on the cinematic medium was antediluvian, and he did damage with some reviews. He panned John Ford's final feature, *7 Women* (1966), calling it an old-fashioned 1930s genre movie, helping set the derogatory tone for American reviewers. In 1964, after *Whit.* reviewed Ford's last Western, *Cheyenne Autumn*, and complained about the best part of the movie, the Dodge City interlude, Warner Bros. cut that segment in half and ruined its point. That example of misused *Variety* power made me resolve never to complain in a review that a film was too long. *Whit.* eventually caused a quiet scandal by grossly misdescribing the plot of a TV pilot he was reviewing. When the producer complained, Tom took Whitney into his office and learned that he had fallen asleep partway through the show. That was his last review.

Although I came on the scene too late to fully appreciate some of those *Variety* "muggs," as we call ourselves, I admired the dauntless professionalism and integrity of our labor reporter, Dave Robb, veteran TV reporter Dave Kaufman, and film reporter Hy Hollinger (who had perhaps the best of all *Variety* "monikers," *Hyho.*), all of whom became pals as well as colleagues. I was fortunate to sit next to another old pro, Armand (Army) Archerd. Army had been the gossip columnist since Sheilah Graham, F. Scott Fitzgerald's former paramour and memoirist, had left *Daily Variety* in 1953. I was fascinated to eavesdrop on Army having his expertly succinct conversations all day long with the top names in the business. Once, like a magician unveiling his tricks, he briefly showed me the rows of miniature index cards he kept locked in his desk with everyone's phone numbers on them; I remember seeing six numbers for Barbra Streisand, including for the phone in her bathroom.

Army was a good guy up to a point, a liberal who took on such issues as blacklisting and AIDS awareness, and he was renowned for his accurate reporting. But he was also a company man who criticized me to my face for defying the paper during the *Patriot Games* brouhaha (which I'll talk about later). He also was a fervent anti-smoker, and I regret now that I puffed away on cigars all day without concern for his (or my) health. Army was allowed to take free junkets and other largesse from studios because he was considered an institution, a double standard that made Tom uncomfortable. Army and his wife, Selma, often appeared in movies and TV shows. But there were different rules for the rest of us. When Tom told me to review Paul Bartel's *Cannonball!*, I said I couldn't because "I'm in it." I play a reporter interviewing David Carradine's race-car driver at the finishing line. Tom became furious and ordered me to stop appearing in movies.

So during your time at Daily Variety *you were getting more acting gigs in addition to* The Other Side of the Wind?

After becoming a screenwriter, I did bit parts in two movies I helped write, *Blood & Guts* for director Paul Lynch in 1978, as a ring announcer, and *Rock 'n' Roll High School* for Allan Arkush, in 1979, as a right-wing school board member. But before that, while still working for *Daily Variety,* I had a slightly longer role as the "Drive-In Rapist" for Joe Dante in 1976, in *Hollywood Boulevard* (which he co-directed with Arkush). That very un-PC spoof of New World Pictures exploitation movies, starring Candice Rialson as a naive actress who's a newcomer to Hollywood, is an ultra-shoestring production, costing only $64,000. Producer Jon Davison bet Roger Corman he could make a movie cheaper than any other he had made, but it went $4,000 over budget to pay for the visual effect of the "H" in the HOLLYWOOD sign falling on Mary Woronov at the end. *Hollywood Boulevard* was conceived as a way for Joe and Allan to break into directing; they split those chores, and their motto was, "Two directors, no waiting."

My character is a hypocritical right-wing father at a Hollywood drive-in theater who, ostensibly out of puritanical outrage, tries to attack Candice Rialson, the star of the sleazy film-within-the-film that's playing there, *Machete Maidens of Mora Tau.* I was told by Jon that the reason they cast me was that I was "the only guy we knew who wore a suit, but you double-crossed us by showing up in a hip-looking shirt," some kind of tropical design I had uncharacteristically purchased in a misguided attempt to fit in with the '70s. While my character is watching *Machete Maidens* with his wife and son, he sees Candice being gang-raped in the Philippines and charges into the projection booth demanding that they turn off the film. When he finds the actual Candice drunkenly making the same demand of the disoriented projectionist, both of us take the opportunity to attack her before we are beat up by her manager, played by Corman stalwart Dick Miller. I asked if I could rewrite my scenes, and they said sure, so I threw in a line to speak while watching *Machete Maidens*—as a meta comment on *Hollywood Boulevard* itself—"*John Wayne* would never make a picture like this."

Among other film appearances in my motley acting career, I am walking past the Hollywood Brown Derby as Harry Dean Stanton kidnaps a dog in the parking lot in *The Black Marble*; part of the crowd at the Hollywood Bowl watching Katharine Hepburn crash a hot-air balloon into the stage in *Olly Olly Oxen Free*; and a pedestrian crossing a street with Christa Fuller, Sam Fuller's wife, as Charles Bronson runs to catch a bus in *Death Wish II*.

Christa and I had gone down Olympic Boulevard during a break in the shooting of Sam's *White Dog*—the scene of a truck crashing into a store front—to see a friend of hers working on the Bronson film. She told me to walk between her and the camera, and I asked why. She said, "I don't want my friends at *Cahiers du Cinéma* to see that I'm acting in a Michael Winner movie." I witnessed Winner—widely regarded at the time as the world's worst director—screaming at his crew, who were openly laughing at him, a sight I never saw before or later. Oddly, Winner was also smiling; he was on his third cinematographer by then. I earned five dollars for my role in that film. Much more rewarding was spending two weeks watching Sam direct *White Dog* at the Wildlife Way Station in Sylmar, scenes in the arena showing Paul Winfield trying to train the racism out of the title character. That powerful film was viciously and misleadingly accused of racism, although as Tom Pryor told me, "It's like a socially conscious 1940s Fred Zinnemann film." Sam was so upset by Paramount shelving the film under pressure that he left the country for Paris until he and Christa and their daughter Samantha eventually returned.

The last time I saw Sam after he returned to Los Angeles, he had had a stroke, and I listened to him "gibblegabble" for an hour while he occasionally interjected, "Do you understand what I'm talking about?" Sadly, those were the only intelligible words from this supremely voluble man.

The Typewriter, The Rifle, and The Camera

I spent several months in the 1970s smoking cigars with Sam many nights in his "Shack" (the book-lined garage where he worked) trying to do an interview book with him, to be titled *The Typewriter, The Rifle, and The Camera*. Usually at three AM, after several hours of recorded conversation, Sam would say, "I gotta kick you out, my boy," and as I staggered to my car, I could hear him typing away on the novel version of *The Big Red One*, which hadn't begun filming yet. I could never keep Sam from digressing, and it was exhausting working on our book while also doing my job at *Daily Variety*. So I abandoned the attempt while we were still talking about his career as a cub reporter in the 1920s, including three hours on his interview with Charles Lindbergh, whom he despised.

I lost a part in *The Big Red One* because I didn't know what to say when Sam woke me one morning by calling and asking, "My boy, can you piss purple?" I mumbled that I just pissed yellow like everybody else. I went back to sleep but a few days later remembered his call and asked him what it was about. He said he had been about to shoot a scene in the San Bernardino Mountains, prior to the overseas filming, with a young soldier getting shot in the groin and pissing blood before he keels over and dies in the snow, and he wanted me for the part. That scene seems to have been only partly retained in a choppy sequence in the restored version of *The Big Red One*, which is far more satisfying in its closeness to Sam's vision than the truncated release version.

That experience taught me to always say "Yes" when a director asks you something, no matter how crazy it may sound.

Who were some of the other memorable people you were able to interview while working for Daily Variety?

In those days, reporters were able to talk with stars and directors and other celebrities at cocktail parties and dinners held for promotional purposes, and we were able to

It was an honor to meet master director Akira Kurosawa at a press luncheon when he came to Hollywood to promote his majestic 1980 film, *Kagemusha*, but it was frustrating not being able to converse other than to convey my respect. (Twentieth Century-Fox)

interview them in their offices and go on sets to watch films being made. But in my final period on *Daily Variety*, I found that the once relatively loose industry had become so corporatized that I found it nearly impossible to visit sets or get interviews. Before that happened, to give a sense of the many people I interviewed, the list includes Alfred Hitchcock, François Truffaut, Claude Chabrol, Terrence Malick, Robert Towne, Roger Corman, John Milius, Maggie Smith, Anne Revere, Neil Simon, Truman Capote, Stanley Kramer, Lee Garmes, Hal Ashby, Ken Russell, John Boorman, Miloš Forman, Andrzej Wajda, Alec Guinness, Toshiro Mifune, Giancarlo Giannini, Alan J. Pakula, Martin Ritt, Samuel Z. Arkoff, James Aubrey, Louis Malle, Robert Wise, Allan Dwan, Sol Lesser, Michael Douglas, Ron Howard, Joan Micklin Silver, Jean-Marie Straub and Danièle Huillet, Don Siegel, Arthur Penn, Wes Craven, Russ Meyer, Lee Grant, Arnold Schwarzenegger, Robert Aldrich, Michael Ritchie, Carl Foreman, Paul Jarrico, Thomas McGuane, Joan Darling, Mike Medavoy, Sid Sheinberg, David L. Wolper, William Friedkin, Paul Mazursky, and John Huston.

On one memorable occasion in May 1975, I covered the unveiling of the D. W. Griffith commemorative stamp. That event in honor of Griffith's 100th birthday took place at the American Film Institute's Greystone mansion in Beverly Hills. The stamp was presented by his leading actress, Lillian Gish, and the pioneer director Allan Dwan. Dwan had begun directing around the same time as Griffith and helped him with the famous crane shot from a balloon descending onto the fabulous Babylon set of *Intolerance,* in which Gish plays the symbolic mother endlessly rocking the cradle of humanity. Meeting her and Dwan made me feel transported back in time. They were such lively characters that it was a joy and sheer ease talking with them, and they made Gregory Peck and Charlton Heston, who also attended the ceremony, seem like youngsters.

When I asked Gish if I could interview her, she asked, "Do you mind coming to Pickfair?" She said she was staying there with Mary Pickford, as she did whenever she came to town. Would I *mind* coming to Pickfair? I could barely believe my good fortune. Gish and Pickford had been friends "since the world was young," as Orson Welles would say of his friendship with John Huston. I had tea with the elegant and charming Gish on the broad, timelessly beautiful lawn of the Beverly Hills mansion renovated for Pickford and her husband Douglas Fairbanks in the silent days (and later razed in one of the worst acts of cultural vandalism among so many in Los Angeles history). I didn't have the chutzpah to ask if Gish would introduce me to the reclusive Pickford, but I could hear Mary playing a soap opera on TV in her second-storey bedroom. It was a scene out of *Sunset Blvd.*

Gish was so considerate that she had the endearingly traditional, and now rare, habit of writing thank-you letters. I cherish the ones she wrote me, including this one. Upon her return to her apartment in New York, which I would visit when I co-wrote her AFI tribute several years later, she wrote me in 1975 on her small notepaper with her boldly graceful signature as its letterhead,

> Dear Joe McBride,
>   Thank you so much for sending me your charming article which I so appreciate having, and thank you as well for coming to Pickfair for the interview, which I hope did not inconvenience you.
>   May our paths cross again soon and meanwhile every good wish for your writing success as well as your work in the new picture *[The Other Side of the Wind]*.
>   Ever gratefully, Lillian Gish

Gish also wrote me in 1976 that she remembered "with much happiness… our lovely afternoon" at Pickfair.

I have written about the amazing Lillian Gish and even have her autograph, but I never met her and am incredibly jealous! I am less jealous but still awed that you met Allan Dwan, someone I can't believe was still around in the 1970s.

I spent many enjoyable hours talking with Allan Dwan about his early days in the industry for a script I was writing about the early days of filmmaking. I did a ninetieth-birthday interview with Dwan for *Daily Variety* in which he reflected on his long view of the industry; he happily told me he received many phone calls about it. I also took Dwan to Paramount for a small screening of the hot film of the day, Robert Altman's *Nashville*. Beforehand, I asked Paramount's veteran publicity chief, Bob Goodfried, to make a fuss about Dwan coming back to the studio he helped create in the silent period. I thought driving the pioneer director onto the lot was similar to Erich von Stroheim driving Gloria Swanson to Paramount in Wilder's *Sunset Blvd*. But Goodfried was not receptive, complaining about how busy he was, etc. Dwan responded politely after seeing *Nashville* but clearly did not enjoy it.

I learned many years later exactly how Dwan felt from reading what my friend Pat McGilligan wrote in an interview with him for the *Boston Globe*: "[H]e had just returned from seeing *Nashville*, which perplexed and disturbed him. He found it a form of 'dramatized carbuncles — all pus and nastiness,' the kind of downbeat movie he sees too often nowadays to suit his taste for happy endings. But he is thinking it over, since the acclaim for such a movie intrigues him."

Working for *Daily Variety* and having the opportunity to ask any questions I wanted of great filmmakers, while simultaneously acting for Welles and helping him write my dialogue for his *film à clef* about modern Hollywood, amounted to the professional training I could not have found at any university. On a single amazing day in the spring of 1975, I met Frank Capra for the first time to interview him over lunch at the La Quinta Country Club; then talked with Howard Hawks at his Palm Springs home in the afternoon; and after driving back to Los Angeles chatted with Samuel Fuller by phone in the early evening; and then went to work again with Welles on *The Other Side of the Wind* that night. For a cinephile, age twenty-seven, I was in a state of bliss.

As I recall in *Frankly: Unmaking Frank Capra*, "I went to the desert to interview Capra on the state of contemporary filmmaking as well as to gather material for his advance obituary [for *Daily Variety*]," and that would lead to my long

François Truffaut talks with Samuel Fuller at the American Film
Institute's Los Angeles premiere party for Truffaut's *The Story of
Adele H.* in 1975, as Todd McCarthy and I look on.
(New World Pictures)

and intense immersion in his life as his biographer. "It was
my practice in my early days in Hollywood to seek out
and interview every venerable director I admired. I was
fortunate that many of the masters of the Golden Age were
still around, and Capra was among those who meant the
most to me, because I was enthralled by his mythic image
as an idealistic, combative filmmaker who made films about
'ordinary' people beating the system."

But that lunch would reveal a stunning discrepancy
between Capra's image and his actual personality, as I will
discuss, Danny, later in this book.

*The second person you listed of film people you met was
François Truffaut. Was it surreal becoming friends with him?
Had he read your criticism?*

Truffaut had read and liked my first book on Welles,
as he wrote in the introduction to André Bazin's *What
Is Cinema?* Truffaut and I were immediately simpatico
when we met at Hitchcock's seventy-fifth birthday party.
That was held in August 1974, shortly after I joined *Daily
Variety*. Orin Borsten, who was Hitchcock's publicist at

Universal, invited me to attend the party at Chasen's, the posh West Hollywood restaurant long popular with the veteran industry establishment. At that event I introduced myself to Truffaut, who was sitting quietly at a table with his publicist, Rupert Allan, a cosmopolitan man who also became a friend of mine. Since Truffaut was hard of hearing, we made plans to get together for lunch so we could talk more easily. We found that we could discourse knowledgeably together about film history, a rarity in Hollywood, while both having ambivalent views on modern Hollywood. (At the Hitchcock party, I also chatted with Cary Grant as well as the guest of honor and his wife, Alma Reville.)

I would see Truffaut whenever he came to Hollywood. He would visit to relax between movies. He would see Renoir and Hitchcock, go to Larry Edmunds Bookshop to buy film books, and sit next to the pool at the Beverly Hills Hotel reading them while smoking cigars (which I was smoking too in those days). At some point, I introduced Todd McCarthy to Truffaut, and we usually saw him together. We interviewed him together for *Film Comment* on *Small Change*. Truffaut and I seemed to speak the same language as cinephiles, so it was a pleasure having our wide-ranging discussions. Although I can read some French and understand some of it when it is spoken, I can't speak that language, so Todd would translate.

I was especially moved by the classroom speech in *Small Change* by the schoolteacher (played by Jean-François Stevenin) after it is revealed that one of the children has suffered abuse at home. Truffaut told the *New York Times* that "even though the spectator's biography has not been the same as the child's, the film turns him back to his own childhood." The teacher's words resonated vividly with Truffaut's and my own childhood experiences: "By a kind of strange balance, those who have had a difficult youth are often better armed to confront adult life than those who have been protected. It is a kind of law of compensation." In the passionate interview Todd and I did with Truffaut about the film and his views on other films about children, he said the teacher's speech drew criticism in France from people who "never made very intelligent criticisms of it. I think it's the truth, line by line. The leftists think it's too conciliatory. The people on the right think it's too left-wing. I thought it was a necessary scene, to have those thoughts expressed." My admiration for Truffaut was due in part to his characteristic stance as an often misunderstood and underestimated maverick opposed to political dogmas from both sides of the spectrum.

I came up with the English title *Small Change*. Roger Corman distributed the film after I advised Truffaut to take his films to him, beginning with *The Story of Adele H.*, but Roger was too cheap to pay $25,000 to clear the literal English title of *L'argent de poche*, *Pocket Money*, which had been used previously for a 1972 Paul Newman-Lee Marvin film for National General. Truffaut proposed calling his film *Tough Skin* or *Thick Skin*, in line with what the teacher says and because he said it is built around "the idea that kids are thick-skinned." I persuaded him that those titles sounded awkward in English. Dido Renoir suggested calling the film "François Truffaut's *Kids*," but Truffaut didn't want it to be compared with Chaplin's *The Kid*. When Jon Davison, Roger's head of publicity, called me in some desperation to ask for a suggested title, I spent half an hour jotting down synonyms before hitting on *Small Change*. (It was given that title in the U.S. and Canada but was called *Pocket Money* in the UK.) Vincent Canby's *New York Times* review noted that *Small Change* is "not a wholly satisfying translation of the film's French title… [but it] is probably as good as one can do, though there is nothing second-rate or of minor importance about it…. *Small Change* is an original, a major work in minor keys."

Once when we met Truffaut in his room at the hotel, he showed us the typewriter he was using to write the script of *The Man Who Loved Women* under a framed photograph of Ernst Lubitsch. I didn't get the hint about how that film is something of a remake of Lubitsch's film about the life of a compulsive ladies' man, *Heaven Can Wait*, but it finally dawned on me when I wrote my book about Lubitsch. Todd and I also arranged for Truffaut to watch Lubitsch's delightful 1931 musical, *The Smiling Lieutenant*, for the first time at the UCLA Film and Television Archive, in a glistening 35mm copy; Truffaut brought Leslie Caron to see it with us. Once in a while I would interview Truffaut for *Daily Variety*, including to get his ruminations on the neglect of women in 1970s Hollywood films, which he blamed on the industry's anxiety over the women's movement. Truffaut sent me a postcard from the Mobile, Alabama, set of Steven Spielberg's *Close Encounters of the Third Kind* when he was acting in that film, and he told us he thought Spielberg should make a movie about "keeds," since he liked them so much and was childlike himself. When we eventually told Truffaut that Spielberg was making his movie about "keeds," but that it was about a kid and an alien, he laughed uproariously.

On one memorable occasion to see a film at the Los Angeles County Museum of Art, Truffaut brought along his teenaged daughters, Laura and Eva; many years later I met Laura again in Berkeley, where we both live, and we became friends. To celebrate the publication of my Lubitsch book, Laura gave me three original lobby cards for his most influential film, the 1924 silent romantic comedy *The Marriage Circle*, that her father had collected. She told me he bought photos or other souvenirs of Lubitsch wherever he went, and she and Eva would watch Lubitsch movies with him and repeat their favorite lines. Laura said hers was the Nazi agent played by Stanley Ridges in *To Be or Not to Be* saying, "It's good to breathe the air of the Gestapo again," and Eva's was spelling Czechoslovakia backwards, as Gary Cooper does while trying to sleep in *Bluebeard's Eighth Wife*. Truffaut also introduced Todd and me to his last love, the actress Fanny Ardant, over lunch at the Polo Lounge, and she was as warm and gracious as he was with us.

Why have you said that among modern directors, Truffaut and Spielberg were the ones "for whom I feel the closest emotional affinity"?

There are many themes and obsessions in their lives and work I share. Truffaut was a school dropout who spent time in a mental institution; Spielberg escaped suburbia and had life-scarring family troubles. Truffaut was fascinated with obsessive love stories; Spielberg is obsessed with dysfunctional families and the search for father figures. I could go on and on. They share some similar stylistic approaches as well, including lyricism and a tendency to cut to a close shot unexpectedly for an emotional *frisson*.

I'll get back to a few others on your list, but since we're talking about a director we both revere, I'll digress and ask if you think about the types of films Truffaut would have made in the many years since he died in 1984 at the age of 52.

I have been heartbroken since that day. For years I saved his last film, *Vivement Dimanche!/Confidentially Yours* (released in 1983), to watch because I figured when I finally saw it, he really would be dead. I felt he died in what would usually be the "middle period" of an artist's career, often a less creative time than the early or late years. His film in which he plays a death-obsessed obituary writer, *The Green Room* (released in 1978), based on two short stories by Henry James, was a powerful exception—but it alarmed me with its morbidity.

That made me sense that something was wrong with Truffaut's health before Jeanne Moreau told me in the spring of 1984 that he was dying and that "He looks like an Auschwitz victim." I wrote Truffaut a five-page handwritten letter expressing my deep affection and respect for him but told him he should not feel he was expected to respond. I learned of his death that October while passing a *New York Times* box on the main street of Middletown, Connecticut, while I was researching Capra's papers at Wesleyan University.

I often recall how Truffaut, in his 1974 essay entitled "Frank Capra, The Healer," described him as "a navigator who knew how to steer his characters into the deepest dimensions of desperate human situations (I have often wept during the tragic moments of Capra's comedies) before he reestablished a balance and brought off the miracle that let us leave the theater with a renewed confidence in life." That shrewd and poignant comment reminded me of the exhilarating effect even the darkest endings of Truffaut's films, such as *Jules et Jim,* have on me. His *film maudit Fahrenheit 451* has always meant a great deal to me. I wrote about it for Philip Nobile's 1973 anthology *Favorite Movies: Critics' Choice*, an especially personal and passionate essay I wrote shortly after my first girlfriend burned herself to death. Renoir told me that the film's ending with the "book people" defying the totalitarian book-burning regime was "one of the most beautiful things I've ever seen." If Truffaut had survived, no doubt would have gone on to make profound films in his later years, as he had made in his youth and intermittently in his "middle years."

The 400 Blows *still is beloved, more so I think than* Jules et Jim, *but do you sense as I do that Truffaut isn't as admired as he once was and young fans don't seek out his films as much as they should? Was he someone, like Preston Sturges and Hal Ashby, perhaps, who made great films that fit perfectly into an era—the right time—and then died as film changed?*

So many great directors are ignored now. It's part of our job as critics and film historians to re-introduce them to new audiences. I enjoyed doing that with my students at San Francisco State. Most were stunned to see classic films they didn't know—such as films by Truffaut, Lubitsch, Welles, Ozu, Renoir, and Wilder—and to realize how good they are and how directly they speak to people today. When I taught a course on Women in the Films of François Truffaut, I brought in Laura as a special guest to share her clear-eyed view of her father and his work.

I visited Jean Renoir on my first visit to Los Angeles in 1970 and reconnected with him in 1975. During the last three years of his life, Todd McCarthy and I would watch films with him each Saturday afternoon at his home and discuss them. Here we are with his wife, Dido, and our friend Linda Strawn. (Greg Giacomo)

Did you stay in touch with Renoir?

After meeting Renoir on my first trip to Hollywood in 1970, I renewed my friendship with him in 1975 when I met him again at a screening of Truffaut's *The Story of Adele H.* at the Academy Theater. Renoir was in a wheelchair by then and couldn't get out much, so every Saturday for the rest of Jean's life, Todd and I would go to his home in Beverly Hills at 2 PM and show him movies in 16mm. We sometimes asked him to show us some of the rarer films among those he directed—such as *Le tournoi dans la cité*, *La nuit de carrefour*, *La Marseillaise*, and *The Woman on the Beach*—and I wish we had asked to do that more often, since he did not regard it as an imposition but enjoyed seeing his work with us.

Although he had many problems making *The Woman on the Beach*, he told us now that he was an old man, he was able to relate much better to its love triangle involving a blind painter, played by Charles Bickford; his younger wife, played by Joan Bennett; and a brooding Coast Guard officer played by Robert Ryan. More often we would bring films by directors Renoir admired, including Ford and Welles, and new films we thought he would like. He especially admired Hal Ashby's *The Landlord*, which reminds me of

Renoir's 1930s films about collectives and his favorite theme of how people from diverse backgrounds learn to "meet each other." Renoir was one of the few directors among the many I met who was happy to talk about other directors without bringing the subject back to his own work. Other directors, in their occupational egomania, reminded me of Hemingway's comment about Gertrude Stein in *A Moveable Feast*, that praising other writers to her "was like mentioning one general favorably to another general. You learned not to do it the first time you made the mistake." Renoir's genuine and deep interest in other people, on the other hand, is one reason that, to borrow a line from *The Rules of the Game*, he "had the quality of making us forget he was a celebrated man."

After each screening, Todd and I and Renoir and his wife, Dido, would have a glass of white wine and discuss the film for half an hour or so, which was always a scintillating experience. Renoir made some surprising observations, such as the time I asked why he suddenly sat straight up in his wheelchair, startled, while watching the ending of Welles's *The Trial*, in which Anthony Perkins's K. is pushed into a pit by men who have come to execute him. Renoir told us he had a dream about death the week before that exactly resembled that scene, so he was impressed that Welles had put it on film. During those final years, Renoir wrote three novels by dictating them to a young man named Paolo Barzman. His continued creativity was impressive, and when I visited Dido after Jean's death, I felt a tremendous sense of emptiness in the room where Jean used to sit and talk under his father's grand painting of his young son as a hunter.

The last person on your list of interviewees—but surely not the least—is John Huston. Huston had a remarkable rebirth and made great films in the 1970s, such as Fat City, Wise Blood, *and especially* The Man Who Would Be King, *long after his heyday and a few years after Andrew Sarris placed him in his "Less Than Meets the Eye" category in* The American Cinema, *so everyone's impression of him might have changed for the better a decade later. What was your relationship with him, including when acting with him for Welles? When he and Welles got together, who would do most of the talking?*

I wasn't privy to their discussions much on the set of *The Other Side of the Wind*, since they tended to talk more in private. Welles was voluble, while Huston tended to be more introspective. I sat next to him for a couple of hours in Arizona in 1974 while waiting to shoot, and he hardly said anything, just puffed on his cigar. He was off in his own world somewhere. I later heard that while making the film, he was brooding over the disintegration of his last marriage.

One of my favorite moments, though, was when Huston's director character, Jake Hannaford, entered the party with a blonde teenaged companion, played by Cathy Lucas, in tow and gave her a lecherous look. I could tell it was too much. I wondered how Welles would handle this with a crowd watching, since Huston was his peer. Welles thought for a moment and said, "John, do you know who you remind me of in this scene? Your father." Huston beamed, as he did whenever his father, the great actor Walter Huston, was mentioned. He said, "Oh, really, Orson? Why?" Welles said, "Because he had that kindly, paternal air—but nobody ever had a higher score." They both roared with laughter, and Huston did the scene again with a sly little smile that gave an ironic tone with "that kindly, paternal air."

I came to know Huston fairly well—though he was an enigmatic, rather aloof man—by co-writing *The American Film Institute Salute to John Huston* (for which I and my writing partner George Stevens Jr. won the Writers Guild of America award), interviewing him a couple of times, and acting with him, all of which deepened my interest in his work. I passed on an offer from a major publisher to write a Huston biography, however, partly because I wasn't interested enough but mostly because it was pitched as an authorized biography with his children having veto power, and I don't write authorized biographies, because doing so would take away my independence.

Huston is one of those good directors whose output nevertheless is very uneven. Welles almost never compromised as a director but often did so as an actor. Huston would compromise as a director by doing crummy projects to keep commercially viable so he could make his occasional masterpieces or highly personal projects. When he was most engaged, he was a splendid filmmaker, and he had an unusually wide range.

Who was the most unexpected person you met in Hollywood?

Ingmar Bergman. After his psychological breakdown in 1976 when the Swedish authorities falsely accused him of income tax evasion, causing him to leave the country, Bergman came to Hollywood in April. The trip was made to discuss his plans to direct two films for producer Dino De Laurentiis, *The Serpent's Egg* (which he made in Germany later that year) and an adaptation of Franz Lehár's operetta *The Merry Widow*, which he had directed onstage in the 1950s. Bergman held a small press conference at the Beverly Wilshire Hotel.

He seemed jovial—as he usually appeared while working, contrary to his image as a gloomy figure—but his wife, Ingrid, sought me out afterward to thank me for what she said was the only part of the event her husband enjoyed. That was when I asked him what he thought of the Erich von Stroheim and Ernst Lubitsch versions of *The Merry Widow*, both of which he admired, with their strikingly different approaches to the material. Bergman had been talking with Barbra Streisand about starring in *The Merry Widow*, but they had a falling-out when she wanted him to rewrite his script; so he had begun thinking that maybe Diana Ross should play the part instead.

I told Bergman as he left the room that I was working on a biography of John Ford and wanted to talk with him about his favorite director. He said to give his agent a call. "We will talk about John Ford," he said merrily. But when I called his agent, Paul Kohner, he told me Bergman would not be giving any interviews during his stay in Hollywood. Nevertheless, he did have an interview with Charles Champlin of the *Los Angeles Times*. I went back to the hotel and left a copy of my and Mike Wilmington's *John Ford* outside the door of Bergman's room. I regret that we never had our chance to talk about John Ford.

Hollywood mavericks

You said it was harder to get interviews in your final tour of duty at Daily Variety, *but were there any who stood out?*

I was able to interview a few important filmmakers who went their own way regardless of what the PR people might have told them, including Streisand, Warren Beatty, Robert Altman, Oliver Stone, Clint Eastwood, and Gore Vidal. The paper would not run my 1992 interview with Vidal about his role in Tim Robbins's political satire *Bob Roberts*, partly because the editors considered Vidal's criticisms of the U.S. government an anathema (and because it is a Paramount film—later I will detail the *Patriot Games* controversy). After Vidal died in 2012, I published the interview on a Vidal website and in *Bright Lights* as "Political Filmmaking and America's 'Poisoned Chalice': The Banned Gore Vidal Interview."

The only other article of mine that *Daily Variety* killed was my interview with Arnold Schwarzenegger in 1976 after he had acted impressively in Bob Rafelson's *Stay Hungry*. They didn't kill it for political reasons but evidently because they couldn't see beyond his beginnings as a bodybuilder when he talked about his ambitions to be taken seriously as an actor. In my final days at the paper, I treated Oliver Stone sympathetically as he poured out his angst about the way he was being unfairly pilloried for making *JFK;* I sought out Clint Eastwood to talk about his masterpiece, *Unforgiven*, at the time it opened; and I had a relaxed lunch with Robert Altman on location for *Short Cuts*.

Barbra Streisand told me she had called the New York *Variety* honchos to complain about how the weekly had eviscerated my favorable review of *The Prince of Tides*. I had especially pleased her by comparing her work as a director with that of her mentor William Wyler. Such mangling with our copy in New York was par for the course. Once they even combined two of my film reviews into one horrible mishmash.

Warren Beatty began our conversation by asking enigmatically, "How can a movie with 78 [if I remember the number correctly] special-effects shots be a home movie?" I didn't know what he meant until he repeated his question and I realized he was still chafing over my review of *Dick Tracy* that called it an expensive home movie he made with his acting buddies. Once Beatty and I got that squared away, I sensed he was in the mood for a genuine discussion. So I told him that despite the technical brilliance of *Dick Tracy*, "It bothers me that a guy who has the ability to direct such a sophisticated historical drama as *Reds* is now directing a silly comic-book movie." Beatty sighed and replied apologetically, "I know, I *know.*"

The Observer

Other than when I was an extra on The Emigrants, *I was on only one movie set before I turned thirty. So were you thrilled at your age to be able to watch legendary or hot young directors shoot their films?*

I was not only thrilled but learned a great deal by seeing how films were actually made. Many film critics and historians lack that experience, and it gives their writing a feeling of unreality. I was able to go on sets of films and watch many directors and actors and others at work, including Alfred

One of the three days I spent in 1975 watching Alfred Hitchcock
directing his last film, *Family Plot*, was in this alley on Los Angeles's
Wilshire Boulevard, where Hitchcock filmed an abducted bishop
being hustled into a car. I'm watching Hitchcock walk past with
his young assistant director, Howard Kazanjian. (Universal/frame
enlargement from the documentary *Plotting "Family Plot"*)

Hitchcock for three days on his last film, *Family Plot*;
Don Siegel directing John Wayne and James Stewart
in *The Shootist*; John Boorman directing the opening
exorcism scene with Richard Burton in a film I consider a
misunderstood masterpiece, *Exorcist II: The Heretic*; and
Hal Ashby for a night on location in Stockton, California,
and a day at the Culver City studio on the Woody Guthrie
biopic *Bound for Glory*.

In fact, I was on location with *Bound for Glory* the
evening when they first used the Steadicam in a feature
film. But I missed that milestone, because the shot of David
Carradine walking through a squatter camp was filmed at
"magic time" while I was interviewing producer Robert
Blumofe over dinner in the warehouse where the hundreds
of extras were being fed and clothed in Depression-era
costumes. I watched the filming of the squatter-camp riot
that night and rode back from location to a hotel with Haskell
Wexler, talking about cinematography and politics. We had
a good rapport, and he responded, "You're into everything,
aren't you?" When I later visited the studio set for the
filming of a violent argument between Woody and his first
wife, played by Melinda Dillon, which resulted in the actors
knocking a hanging lamp into her, Ashby introduced me to
Dillon, but she said, "I can't shake hands, because I think I
just broke my hand." I wrote up the experience for *Daily
Variety* and offered to cover the filming for *Rolling Stone*,

for which I had reviewed Sidney Poitier's Western *Buck and the Preacher* in 1972, but the magazine unaccountably refused, so I sold the article to *Film Comment* instead.

I was also able to watch the filming of many films of lesser interest that also helped me become acquainted with major-studio production methods. But I spent five hours waiting on the set of *The Blues Brothers* before leaving when nobody showed up—that was a notoriously cocaine-blighted production—and I missed a major story about the filming of *Rocky*, starring its unknown writer, Sylvester Stallone. I was invited to the Los Angeles location of a boxing ring but somehow didn't see what was worth writing about, perhaps because I spent most of the time on the set distracted by dallying in conversation with the delightful Talia Shire.

I also felt remiss in my reportorial duties on another occasion, after I covered a dinner honoring Groucho Marx's investiture into a Hollywood social club for actors, the Masquers Club. I realized that I had failed to ask why Groucho would "join a club that would have someone like him as a member." But whenever I saw Groucho at an event, I would make a point of chatting with him. He was still a master quipster—when I first saw him as he was toddling through the outdoor dining area of the Polo Lounge on the arm of his much young companion, Erin Fleming, I dashed up to him and said, "Groucho! I love you!" He looked at me quizzically and said, "I don't blame you."

Every director works differently, and often movie-making can be dull to watch, especially when the lighting is being set up or people are hard to access. George Cukor was a marvelous interview subject—bright, witty, insightful, and profane. But I was disappointed to watch Cukor direct, because with his characteristic discretion, he tended to speak privately with his actresses, Candice Bergen and Jacqueline Bisset, when they were playing longtime friends in his last film, *Rich and Famous*. That's his remake of *Old Acquaintance*, the 1943 Bette Davis-Miriam Hopkins comedy-drama based on the play by John van Druten about two longtime friends who are clashing kinds of writers. I could not hear anything much from Cukor on the set at MGM except him telling the two actresses to "Come on, let's get on with it," repeatedly, and when the cameras rolled, "At a brisk clip, ladies." Once, though, I heard Cukor give a more substantive piece of direction. When Bergen's character is lost in thought at her New Year's Eve party, standing apart from her guests while thinking of slipping away to see her old friend, the actress was having trouble with the focus of the scene. She wanted to know where to look, and Cukor told her, "Look inside yourself." That shrewd and profound piece of direction concentrated Bergen's attention acutely and made for one of the most effective moments in her uneven performance.

Who was the most exciting director to watch? It was a constant circus, drama, and education to watch Welles at work. He was always trying something new, making up brilliant ideas as he went along, and he regaled the cast with funny stories and songs even while he drove the young crew hard. He wanted to make the actors feel happy and entertained, although I was an exception. He was tough on me for the first three years of shooting *The Other Side of the Wind* until a crew member tipped me off that Welles had praised my acting in the rushes ("Joe looks good up there onscreen. But then he *always* looks good onscreen"), so I instantly relaxed for the next two years of our work on the film.

Billy Wilder, one of my heroes, was fascinating and entertaining when I watched him shoot *The Front Page*; I cover that day in close detail in *Two Cheers*. Unlike some directors, Wilder liked having kibitzers on the set. He kept spewing hilarious quips and clever, shrewd, and pithy pieces of direction to Jack Lemmon, Walter Matthau, and the other actors on the press room set, while his writing partner I. A. L. Diamond sat on an apple box, riding herd on the script to make sure the actors didn't deviate from it unless he and Wilder approved.

Watching film history

Talk about the contrast between Jimmy Stewart and John Wayne that you witnessed on the set of Don Siegel's elegiac The Shootist, *Wayne's last film. Did you feel you were watching film history on that set?*

One young crew member told me, "There's so much respect generated around here, the crew is just walking on eggs." Wayne was much more extroverted than Stewart, who sat quietly in his chair (partly because of his deafness) while Wayne made jokes with the crew. Yes, there was a sense of things ending. The scene I watched them shoot for two days was the one in which the doctor played by Stewart tells the gunfighter played by Wayne that he is dying of cancer. It was one of my great experiences to watch my two favorite actors work together. They mostly conferred on timing and technical points like the consummate pros they were. Siegel had his clashes with Wayne, but he was full of respect for both actors and would say, "Action, please."

Siegel told me, "I've directed a lot of stars—even before I was a director, I had Bogart, Cagney, and all the rest when I was doing montage scenes at Warner Bros.—but for the first time in my life I'm conscious of working with a legend. I can't help feeling a bit in awe of the man, but at the same time I can't let it throw me, because you've got to be able to have disagreements." Siegel added only half-kiddingly, "He eats directors for breakfast, but when he eats me he'll get indigestion."

Wayne told you that it would have been impossible for him to play himself onscreen, which his detractors always said he did. Were you surprised he thought about such criticism, or was it so prevalent that he couldn't ignore it?

Wayne seemed surprisingly sensitive to criticism. When I asked if Ford did some second-unit work on *Hondo*, a film Wayne's company produced and John Farrow directed, Wayne said, "Jesus Christ, don't you people ever give me credit for *anything*?" I understand his feelings, because Wayne has been so mistreated by most critics and many film historians, whose lack of understanding of what constitutes good film acting causes them to dismiss him for allegedly just "playing himself." As Wayne thoughtfully told me, "It is quite obvious it can't be done. If you are yourself, you'll be the dullest son of a bitch in the world onscreen. You have to act yourself, you have to project something—a personality. Perhaps I have projected something closer to my personality than other actors have. I have very few tricks. Oh, I'll stop in the middle of a sentence so they'll keep looking at me, and I don't stop at the end, so they don't look away, but that's about the only trick I have." I quote those wise words from Wayne in the introduction of my book on Cukor, in which I analyze the nature of good film acting.

It's a struggle to explain the virtues of Wayne's acting because of the misunderstanding about the nature of film acting that he and I discussed and because too many people let Wayne's reprehensible politics affect their judgment of his work. I am tired of arguing about his talent, which should be self-evident, but I wrote an appreciation of him that's in *Two Cheers* in which I grapple with most of these questions, so I will refer people to that. But if people don't like Westerns, that's another issue—of lamentable myopia.

I met and interviewed one of my idols, Billy Wilder, in June 1974 on the set of *The Front Page* at Universal. This former newspaper reporter's underrated film version offers an acerbic take on the classic comedy play about unscrupulous newsmen by Ben Hecht & Charles MacArthur. (Universal)

It's interesting that the word Wayne's co-star Jimmy Stewart used most when describing his own screen image was "vulnerable." It makes sense but I never thought of that word in regard to Stewart. Maybe he equated "being vulnerable" with "going dark," as some of his strong protagonists do in the films he made with Capra, Hitchcock, and Anthony Mann. What do you think?

Vulnerability stems from anxiety and vice versa, and many of Stewart's roles are filled with both psychological states, even before he went to war, such as in *Mr. Smith Goes to Washington* and *The Shop Around the Corner*. I worked and talked with Stewart several times but never managed to understand him very well, since he was so reticent and inarticulate, even though he went to Princeton. When I would ask about his experiences as a bomber pilot in World War II, he couldn't or wouldn't talk about them.

Capra told me that on *It's a Wonderful Life* Stewart said he wanted to quit acting because it wasn't a "decent" job for a man, so Capra asked Lionel Barrymore to give him a pep talk. Barrymore asked Stewart, "Do you think it's more decent to drop bombs on people?" Capra told me that was "pretty rough" but that it did the job. Stewart admitted to me that he came back a somewhat different man, and his postwar career in that film as well as his films for Mann, Hitchcock, Ford, and other directors contains many brave and disturbing roles in which the actor shows great vulnerability.

I also appreciated Stewart's old-fashioned courtesy, which reflected his upbringing and the era of American life he embodied. I cherish the signed copy he sent me of his charmingly whimsical 1989 book, *Jimmy Stewart and His Poems*. And on two occasions when I wrote articles about him, he sent me notes with his gratitude. In 1976, after I sent him a copy of *American Film* with my cover-story profile, "Aren't You... Jimmy Stewart?," which included, among other observations, my recollections of his work with Wayne on the set of *The Shootist*, Stewart wrote me, "I can't tell you what a fine time I had reading your story on me and on Duke. Your story means a great deal to me and makes me very proud and I am very grateful to you." He signed it, "Sincerely, Jim Stewart."

What kinds of films did Variety *send you to review?*

I reviewed a lot of schlock as well as occasional good movies and TV shows. In those days, *Variety* reviewers weren't credited by name, since the paper wanted to leave the impression that it was speaking ex cathedra. So my first *Variety* "moniker" in 1974 was *Mack*. I had asked for *Mac.*, but Tom Pryor said the rule was it had to be four letters (despite the fact that some reviewers were exempted from the rule). Eventually, a movie came out called *The Mack*, the Black slang for pimp, and I told Tom what *Mack.* meant, calling it an unfortunate name for someone touting films, and that finally convinced him to let me become *Mac. Murf.* told me a moniker was also a form of protection, enabling a reviewer to safely interview the filmmaker.

But when I panned Larry Cohen's *It's Alive*—an ugly 1974 horror film about a murderous baby who goes on a rampage—and had to interview Cohen over lunch that same day at the Beverly Hills Hotel, I was too honest, and pugnacious, for my own good. Over our salads at the Polo Lounge, I told Cohen I was *Mack.*, who had called his film a symptom of the anti-child attitude rampant in the country, a noxious trend that also led to audiences chortling over the child abuse exploited in *The Exorcist.* So the whole lunch was taken up with Cohen heatedly attacking my review and me defending it.

Variety and the *Hollywood Reporter* were the first media outlets to review movies in those days. Since *Murf.* kept most of the top-drawer titles for himself while disdaining B movies, I was fortunate to be the reviewer who discovered that *The Texas Chain Saw Massacre* was a demented masterpiece. (That review shocked the mob-connected distribution company.) I also was delighted to review such offbeat fare as Paul Bartel's *Death Race 2000*, *Monty Python and the Holy Grail*, *Cooley High*, and *Somewhere in Time* (I read in a book about that cult favorite starring Christopher Reeve that I was the only reviewer who had liked it when it came out).

I gave a rave review to the TV miniseries *Sybil*, starring Sally Field as a woman with multiple personalities. But I foolishly hailed her performance as the greatest in the history of television—as if I had seen everything! And I was chagrined when that line wasn't quoted in the ads promoting her for an Emmy; she won anyway, helping her escape the typecasting she had suffered from playing the Flying Nun. *Murf.* did me a favor by letting me review Hitchcock's *Family Plot* after I had written my feature about its filming. I was told that my review surprised Universal executives by being so enthusiastic. Although it's a genuinely charming offbeat Hitchcock comedy-thriller, I did tend to overreact when I actually had the rare opportunity to review a film by a top director.

But I panned William Friedkin's massively overblown *Sorcerer*, a remake of the French classic *The Wages of Fear* that cost $22 million (the equivalent of $115 million in 2025) and involved two studios. François Truffaut later told me he thought *Sorcerer* failed because Friedkin had shot so much of it in rain, which had the subconscious effect of making the audience think the truckloads of nitrogylcerin wouldn't explode.

And I found David Lynch's low-budget debut feature, *Eraserhead*, nearly unwatchable and panned it except for its masterful technical aspects. In my second tour of duty at *Daily Variety* in 1980–1981, I wrote that Scorsese's *Raging Bull*, despite having the best boxing scenes ever filmed, was dramatically tedious. (I was something of a connoisseur of boxing movies and had been a fan of boxing until I saw Benny [Kid] Paret murdered in the ring on live TV in 1962 by the closeted-gay Emile Griffith, who was maddened by Paret calling him a homosexual at the weigh-in.) I agreed with Pauline Kael that when Robert De Niro and Joe Pesci in *Raging Bull* keep calling each other "dumb fucks," they just seem like dumb fucks. As the years passed, I found myself mocked in some critical circles for supposedly missing the boat on *Eraserhead* and *Raging Bull*, but I stand by those contrarian reviews. My strong opinions brought me some notoriety at the time, including from surprising sources: when I met John Wayne's secretary, she said, "Oh, you're that *mean* critic!"

Murf. also tossed me some foreign movies to review, mostly minor ones, so when I was assigned an Ingmar Bergman movie, I was so excited that I overpraised one of his weaker efforts, the cutdown theatrical version of his TV miniseries *Face to Face.* Most of the films I had to review as the second-stringer, however, were the dregs of Seventies American exploitation genres or cornball family pictures, including such depressingly bad films as *Race with the Devil*; *The Great Scout & Cathouse Thursday*; *Mother, Jugs & Speed*; *Hawmps!*; and an abominable Elliott Gould "comedy" about nerve gas called *Whiffs.* But I always tried to review movies on the basis of how well (or not) they fulfilled their goals, not on the basis of genre prejudice.

When I reviewed a Disney potboiler called *Treasure of Matecumbe*, I called attention to how that studio's once-vaunted technical brilliance had deteriorated. Tom Pryor couldn't believe it and angered me by sending *Murf.* to check out the picture; *Murf.* agreed with my assessment, but they ran his review instead of mine, which compounded the insult. Nevertheless, Disney's technical standards noticeably improved after I blew that whistle.

Tom made me fly all the way to Seattle to review Alan Rudolph's *Welcome to L.A.*, after producer Robert Altman refused to trade-screen it. When Altman heard I was making the trip to see its distant premiere, he offered to show it to us in Hollywood, but Tom spitefully refused and made me fly back on the first plane the next day after getting only a few hours of sleep. Naturally, that put me in a foul mood, but I wouldn't have given that pretentious piece of junk with its lousy songs a good review in any case.

Was there pressure at Daily Variety *to be kind to studio films?*

In the time of Tom Pryor, when the paper was still under the original ownership of the Silverman family, we had more editorial freedom than we had later, after the paper was sold in 1987 to Cahners Publishing Company, part of a UK-based media conglomerate. We were paid much better, but the trade-off was that our editorial freedom was circumscribed. The paper's integrity vanished during the editorship of Peter Bart, with whom I came into public conflict after I returned to *Daily Variety* for my third tour of duty in 1989 through 1992. Bart was hired to pander to the studios in a way that Pryor never did, and the paper lost its reputation.

How did it happen that Variety *reviewed porno movies during your first period on the paper?*

I covered the gamut of production from A to B features and beyond. My beats included the Oscars (both in daily coverage of the Academy and as a backstage reporter at the event) and even the porn world, so I became familiar with the seamy as well as glamorous sides of Hollywood. I was acquainted with the underbelly of Hollywood and its marginal characters and viscerally understood the sense of decay in the industry. Addison Verrill, a *Variety* reporter and reviewer in New York who was a connoisseur of the hardcore genre, convinced the paper that the huge financial success of *Deep Throat, Devil in Miss Jones*, and other porno films that played theaters could no longer be ignored. So for a brief time, we had to review porno movies.

That beat led to some absurd moments. In July 1977 I had to cover the Adult Film Association of America Erotic Film Awards dinner at the Wilshire Ebell Theatre, a kind of Bizarro mirror of the Oscars. The surreal highlight in my view was Georgina Spelvin confessing upon winning the best supporting actress award for a movie called *Ping Pong* that she didn't remember making the film, since she often performed sex scenes without knowing what the film she was shooting was called. Spelvin, whose performance in *Devil in Miss Jones* stands out from the genre as truly searing and eloquent, told me how proud she was that Orson Welles had helped edit one of her hardcore movies. He took charge of a lesbian sex scene in a shower in *3 A.M.* when he became impatient with how much time his *Other Side of the Wind* cinematographer, Gary Graver, the director of *3 A.M.* and other porno films under a pseudonym, was devoting to the editing.

But it proved virtually impossible to review porno films, since, unlike with films of other kinds, we weren't allowed to say what happened in them. Some *Variety* reviews I've read of regular films contain little but plot synopses, just as "book reviews" in even some illustrious magazines, such as the *New York Review of Books*, often consist of nothing but a lengthy retelling of the book's storyline, followed by a hasty paragraph of commentary on the book itself. What I always tried to do at *Variety*, from the beginning, was to interweave the telling of plot with the commentary on the creative elements of the film. It takes practice to learn how to do that in a way that seems natural, but it makes reviews far more meaningful than a mere plot synopsis. I've even managed to get away with writing genuine book reviews in the *New York Review of Books* but was careful not to tell that magazine I was doing it.

However, I ran into trouble with the first porno film I reviewed. It was a European film about a pornographic circus (the title of which escapes me now), and I dutifully described the *outré* goings-on, including a scene of a clown penetrating five women simultaneously with five dildos attached to a long pole. That and other graphic descriptions were cut from the review, leaving only vague innuendos about what the film actually contained. *Murf.,* on the other hand, was so intimidating even to Tom Pryor that he got away with some highly graphic language in describing the sadomasochistic content of gay porno films directed by Fred Halsted. When I later had to write Halsted's obit, Tom's son Pete, our managing editor, fiercely wielded his blue pencil to excise every single title of Halsted films I had cited, since they were mostly lewd double entendres.

Another time I described a porno film as having some "arousing" elements, which I thought was within the bounds of accurate critical commentary, since that was surely the *raison d'être* of any successful film in the genre. But Tom came to me, alarmed, pointing to that word in my review and asking, "Do you really want to admit that you were *aroused* by this film?" My explanation failed to satisfy him, but he kept sending me on this dubious mission. Once I had to review a 3-D porno film, which failed in its desired effect because it gave me double vision and a splitting headache. This madness went on until 1977, when Addison Verrill was murdered by a man he had picked up and taken home with him, a medical technician who had a bit part in *The Exorcist.* That gruesome event was referred to by some cynics as *Looking for Mr. Gaybar.* The morning after it happened, Tom walked in and loudly announced, "That's it! No more porno film reviews!"—as if that reviewing policy had somehow caused Addison's murder.

"Scenes from a Relationship"

What was the best film you got to review during your first tour of duty on Daily Variety?

Since *Murf.,* disdained going to film festivals, I was assigned to cover Filmex, the Los Angeles International Film Exposition, and thereby was the first reviewer to recognize what a groundbreaking classic *Annie Hall* was and how deeply indebted Woody Allen was to Ingmar

Bergman (I wrote that the film could be called *Scenes from a Relationship*). That insight was echoed shortly thereafter by former *Variety* mugg Vincent Canby in his *New York Times* review and then by Arthur Knight and Hollis Alpert in *Playboy* and became a critical commonplace.

Nevertheless, I didn't realize I was living through a Golden Age of moviemaking until Stuart Byron, another former *Variety* mugg, asked me in the late 1970s if I realized that had been the case. Because I was so familiar with the underbelly of Hollywood, the marginal characters, and felt the rot in the mainstream industry, I didn't quite recognize how unusual that period actually was before it was snuffed out by the coming blockbuster era. As I wrote in my *New York Times* review of the shallow and gossipy 1998 Peter Biskind book about the so-called New Hollywood, *Easy Riders, Raging Bulls:*

> A Golden Age seldom seems like a golden age when you're living through it. Late in his long career, Melvyn Douglas said he was flabbergasted to hear film buffs talk about the 1930's as a golden age, when he and other actors remembered those years as a constant struggle to escape mediocre projects. I felt much the same sense of surprise when I began to hear people talk about the early-to-mid-'70s as Hollywood's last golden age. When I covered that period as a reporter and reviewer for *Daily Variety,* I felt American movies were in a perilous state of decline, mired in a coarsening process thrown into stark relief by filmmakers' occasional success in slipping masterpieces through the system. For every *Chinatown* and *Godfather,* I had to sit through dozens of schlocky car-chase movies, brutal revenge fantasies, misogynistic buddy pictures and bloated disaster epics. The agent Sue Mengers observed to me back then, "Movies are becoming like dinosaurs—their bodies are getting bigger and bigger and their brains are getting smaller and smaller."

But with the passage of time, the artistic landmarks of a period become clearer and the schlock (even if it presaged the future) vanishes into the mist.

The New Hollywood flowered only briefly before the blockbuster era crushed it and enabled the studios to revert to their old cookie-cutter ways; Roger Corman told me his brand of guerrilla B-moviemaking was doomed when the studios started making big-budget versions of his formulaic monster and sci-fi movies. *Jaws* was the example he gave; but I recognized its artistry from the moment I saw the preview audience at the Cinerama Dome jump in unison during the first shark attack. That was the only time I ever saw a film audience react that way. But it took me a couple of more years and seeing *Star Wars* to understand what was happening to the taste of the wider film audience and the changes in the industry.

I spent most of my time at *Daily Variety* reporting rather than reviewing and covered many press conferences and other events. I was assigned to interview a wide range of producers, directors, executives, and others and took the initiative to write features on veteran directors I wanted to get to know, including Capra. That meeting would give me the seed of the idea of writing his biography, as I'll tell you about when we come to my departure from the industry to concentrate on writing books fulltime.

The perils of a theater reviewer

Besides films and TV shows, what else did you review?

I also reviewed many plays for *Daily Variety* as the second-stringer under our drama reviewer, Bill Edwards, who often assigned me to several a week—I reviewed *Three Sisters* five times. Usually these were at what were called "99-seat theaters," designated as such because the modest productions received Equity waivers that enabled them to avoid paying the actors. Actors did the plays to keep in practice and because they were desperate for notice in the trades, which could help them get paid work in TV or movies. And that went for playwrights, too: my favorable review of a one-act play about childbirth prompted the wife of a TV producer to see the show, and the playwright was hired to write her first script for TV. She called to thank me for getting her the break she had been working toward for many years and said she would throw a party for me in gratitude. (I'm still waiting.) I saw many good actors in these small productions, but sometimes only one was worth watching, so to avoid boredom or exasperation, I would follow that actor with my eyes most of the night.

Orson Welles once said, "Anybody who does theater in Los Angeles is either crazy or Charlton Heston." I worked with Heston (or "Chuckles," as he was known at the AFI) seven times, but I don't think he ever quite knew who I was, even though he eventually started looking at me quizzically. I saw him at the Music Center on his opening night of *Macbeth* with Vanessa Redgrave. She played Lady Macbeth as a kind of spaced-out hippie wandering the stage in a long white gown. Heston, that "axiom of the cinema," gave his role his earnest best, as always, but the director came out at the beginning to ask our indulgence, since the actor playing Macduff had broken his leg at rehearsals and had to play his role on crutches. The audience tried hard to be understanding, but Heston was getting agitated at the incongruity of it all, so there were a few titters here and there. Finally, in his climactic swordfight with Macduff, the exasperated Heston lost it and took a mighty swing of his sword at his rival's crutch, knocking him sprawling. The theater erupted in a tsunami of laughter.

Sometimes my reviews of the zany LA theater scene provoked bizarre reactions. After I panned a silly and pretentious play written and performed by an actress with her little-theater group, the next time I went to her theater, I found that part of her new play was about me. Actors kept coming up to my front-row seat and spouting thinly veiled abuse excoriating my abilities as a critic, and I was strategically stuck in a spot from which I could not leave the theater without crossing the stage. So I had to sit through the invective in silence. I should have excused myself from reviewing that play but could see no way to do so without going into the whole *mishegoss*. I'm afraid I could not help making some harshly sarcastic remarks in print about that production, whose attack on a reviewer would have seemed incomprehensible to the rest of the audience if the regulars had not been accustomed to the company's plays not making sense. I had found myself trapped in something Tom Stoppard might have written, but he would have done it with more wit.

Another time, an actress who played a supporting role in a one-act play tried to commit suicide after reading my review. A friend of hers called to let me know. Fortunately, the despondent actress survived. But I was alarmed and went back and looked at the review, worried about what I might have written. I found that I had given the actress a *good* review! Her friend (also an actress) explained that when the play had been done off-Broadway, the actress in that small part was hailed as stealing the show and had become a star; the actress I reviewed had counted on the same thing happening to her but became distraught when I simply praised her performance without declaring that she had stolen the show. My conscience was assuaged. And my friend gave me a valuable overall insight into actors' psychology: She said actors never believe a rave review (because they are so insecure) or a complete pan (because they have to develop protective armor), but they always implicitly believe a mixed review, because it echoes their ambivalence about themselves.

And then there was the time I reviewed an ugly one-act play about a male psychopath who torments a woman after stripping her naked, gagging her, and tying her to a chair. The poor actress had to face the audience in the raw for the whole evening while the male actor strutted around wearing only pants, his mouth spewing vitriol. I criticized the play not only for being vile and sadistic but also for its sexist double standard, letting the actor keep his pants on while fully exposing the actress and keeping her mute. The day the review ran, the macho actor barged into our office wearing a black leather jacket and planted himself in the chair next to my desk, ranting abusively about my review.

Army Archerd quick-wittedly called the police. The actor demanded to know why I had attacked him for "not being able to get it up." I pointed out I had not written that, but in his deranged mind, that's what he thought I was implying he didn't remove his pants. Bellowing, he jumped up and demanded I go outside and fight. Army shouted, "The police are on the way!," and the guy took off. I mean he beat a hasty retreat. Army asked his name and said he would never mention the actor in his column. He kept that promise for ten years until the actor's name popped up in "Just for Variety," no doubt because Army had forgotten the incident.

From time to time, Bill Edwards did let me review some major stage productions. When I wrote about Ingrid Bergman's return to the Los Angeles stage in Somerset Maugham's *The Constant Wife,* directed by John Gielgud, the *Los Angeles Times* drama critic Dan Sullivan wrote Tom Pryor a letter commending my work, which made my editor treat me with a bit more deference. My growing familiarity with the theater as well as movies would stand me in good stead many years later when I wrote my critical study *George Cukor's People*, a close analysis of the often misunderstood art of screen acting and its difference from stage acting. Cukor, who came from the theater, mastered the art of how to adapt plays into films that use the cinematic medium fully.

As a *Daily Variety* staffer, I was also given free tickets to expensive plays I wasn't reviewing. When I left the paper and eked out a living as a screenwriter, I missed being able

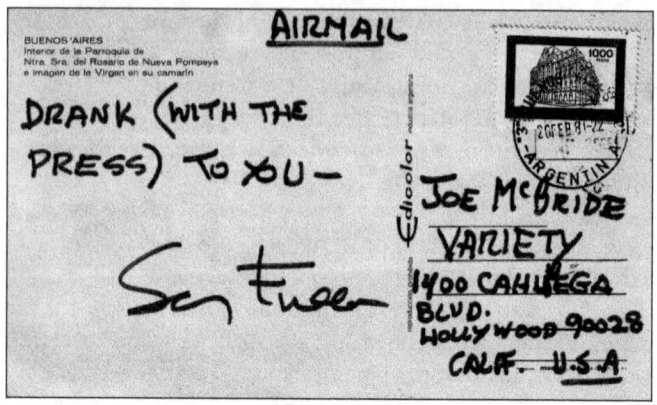

BUENOS AIRES
Interior de la Parroquia de
Ntra. Sra. del Rosario de Nueva Pompeya
e imagen de la Virgen en su camarín

AIRMAIL

DRANK (WITH THE PRESS) TO YOU —

JOE McBRIDE
VARIETY
1400 CAHUEGA
BLVD.
HOLLYWOOD 90028
CALIF. U.S.A

Sam Fuller sent me this card during one of my tours of duty at *Daily Variety*. As old newspaper guys, we had an immediate rapport. Sam was a mentor, and we worked on an unfinished interview book.

to see plays. Despite the perks I received at the trade paper, I became resentful of the grueling hours and miserable pay as a film and stage and nightclub reviewer—we were paid only $7.50 for covering a show at night, less than it cost for gas and a meal out on the town—especially when Edwards kept sending me to cover sleazy theaters run by third-rate companies, often in far-flung locations that caused me to lose my way in the wilds of the San Fernando Valley or Orange County. Even worse, he made me review crummy nightclub acts as favors to his friends at record companies.

In desperation, I finally managed to get out of that corrupt gig by criticizing the noise from bar patrons and the poor sound system at one particularly dubious club in Beverly Hills. I also called attention to the nearly empty house when I strategically went on second nights when the house wasn't papered with fawning record company employees, as was the case on opening nights. But in retrospect, I can hardly believe I was so docile that I failed to protest the paper making me work like a dog and having to supplement my meager income by grinding out articles for film magazines. I attribute that willingness to the long view I've always taken while working at two jobs simultaneously, my "day (or night) job" and my creative writing. But in those days my ambition to succeed in Hollywood was only matched by my foolish masochism.

You mentioned doing an interview with Truffaut about how women were neglected in Hollywood during the 1970s, as Molly Haskell also writes about in her 1974 book From Reverence to Rape: The Treatment of Women in the Movies. *How did you try to deal with that issue on the trade paper?*

When I came to *Daily Variety* in 1974, I was surprised that they didn't have any women on the editorial staff, only in the accounting and circulation departments and at the switchboard. Not only was my mother an acclaimed journalist, but I was accustomed to working with women reporters and editors on the *State Journal* and the *Press-Enterprise.* So I asked Tom Pryor why there weren't any women at *Daily Variety,* and he replied blithely, "We had one once, but she didn't work out." When I returned to the paper in 1980, they did have a woman working as a music reporter and reviewer. She was a large, eccentric woman who wore Mickey Mouse ears in the office and did an excellent job. So I commended Tom on having a woman on the staff. He was surprised and confused. I reminded him of her name. *"Oh,"* he said, "I don't think of her as a woman." (I had run into similar bias while working at McDonald's in 1965. I suggested to the boss that instead of having rude and pimply teenaged males working the windows, he should hire women, who would be more personable and welcoming. The boss became apoplectic and started shouting: *"McDonald's will never hire women!"* His myopia is especially ironic given that fast-food restaurants later seemed to be staffed predominantly by women.)

As a *Daily Variety* reporter and reviewer, in addition to complaining in reviews about the dominance of male buddy-buddy movies and the lack of female protagonists in the 1970s (a situation I also addressed by turning *Rock 'n' Roll High School* into a female buddy-buddy movie in 1979), I sought out important women for interviews who had been given short shrift by the industry and film historians. For instance, I did a rare interview with the legendary film editor Margaret Booth, whose career stretched back to *Intolerance.* That came about after I interviewed the MGM musical director Charles Walters. Booth called me to complain about Walters criticizing her because she had exercised an iron hand over the studio's films. So I did a fascinating and respectful interview with Booth. Ironically, though, she was outraged because I had not referred to her in print as "Miss Booth," an anachronistic style our paper no longer followed thanks to the women's liberation movement. As a result, she did a *second* interview for a British film magazine to complain about our interview. At least that flap got Booth on the record twice.

For *Daily Variety* I also interviewed such upcoming women directors as Joan Darling and Joan Micklin Silver. Darling is an actress who memorably worked with Steven Spielberg on the *Psychiatrist* series in his favorite of his episodic TV work, "Par for the Course," and she directed the celebrated "Chuckles Bites the Dust" episode of *The Mary Tyler Moore Show* in 1975. When I interviewed Darling about her 1977 feature directing debut, *First Love,* we had such a rapport that she asked, "Were we married in a previous life?" My interview with Joan Micklin Silver and her producer husband, Raphael, helped call attention to their maverick distribution plans for their studio-shunned 1975 film about a Jewish immigrant woman, *Hester Street,* which the major distributors shortsightedly considered "too ethnic" to be successful but brought Carol Kane an Oscar nomination for best actress for her deeply truthful performance.

When I was living in Riverside, I helped your brother, Gerry Peary, interview Dorothy Arzner at her home in La Quinta. While we were driving down into the desert, Gerry exclaimed, "What's *that?!*" I casually told him it was a roadrunner that had just dashed across the road. Gerry couldn't believe there actually was a bird called a roadrunner—he thought that was just a cartoon character—so he was astonished he had seen one.

When we arrived at Arzner's comfortable home at the ungodly hour of 9 AM, she was cordial and elegant, but we were a bit bedraggled, so we asked if she could make us coffee. She apologized and said she had never learned how to make coffee, and her maid had the day off. I reflected that was one reason Arzner succeeded as a director—she had never learned to make coffee. Gerry and I had a good time talking with her, filling in areas of her career that he and Karyn Kay hadn't covered with her by mail. Gerry and Karyn, who was also a member of the Madison film mafia, published the interview in a magazine and a booklet on Arzner as well as in their 1977 book, *Women and the Cinema: A Critical Anthology*; and it appears in Martin F. Norden's 2024 collection, *Dorothy Arzner: Interviews.*

I also covered a 1975 Directors Guild of America tribute to Arzner and helped promote it in an interview with its organizer, director Francine Parker. The film clips from Arzner's career were introduced by Ida Lupino. Although Jeffrey Goodman and Tony Slide's documentary *The Silent Feminists* shows that thirty women directed silent films in Hollywood, Arzner and Lupino were the only women to sustain directing careers in talking pictures until others began to make inroads in the 1970s.

When I saw Lupino standing in the DGA lobby beforehand with her husband, Howard Duff, I approached her and said I had had a dream about her the night before.

Lupino's eyes widened, perhaps in alarm. I told her that in the dream I was scheduled to interview her for a film magazine about her directing career and went to her house in the San Fernando Valley at four o'clock. I found her vacuuming the carpet in an apron and rubber gloves. I said she apologized and told me she had to clean the house and cook dinner to leave out for her husband before going to Universal to direct a film at six o'clock. When I finished telling Lupino the dream, her eyes widened some more, and she said, "How do you know *exactly* what my life was like when I was directing films?" I didn't have a ready answer but later realized it was because I had seen my mother carry off similar feats while raising seven children and working for newspapers. I wish I had thought of asking Lupino if I could actually come to her house to interview her. She is a great director. (At San Francisco State, I taught a course on pioneering women directors, Lois Weber, Arzner, Lupino, and Elaine May.)

When I asked to interview screenwriter Alma Reville about her life with and before Hitchcock, her husband initially refused to let me do so. But when I saw them at a party at Chasen's for screenwriter Jay Presson Allen (who had written the script of *Marnie*, a *film maudit* I greatly admire), Alma eagerly agreed and took me over to get Hitch's (grudging) approval. Thirty minutes after we began the interview at their Bel-Air home, however, just as I was about to get into some of the knottier questions, through the window behind her I saw a black limousine pulling up outside. Hitchcock had arrived unexpectedly in mid-afternoon to take over the discussion, and Alma fell mostly silent. I published the somewhat sketchy interview in *Sight and Sound* as "Mr. and Mrs. Hitchcock." She then invited me to dinner at their house, but I was too shy to take her up on the kind offer.

Cuckoo

How impactful were your interviews and reviews in Daily Variety *at drawing attention to movies*?

To give an example showing how powerful *Daily Variety* could be in shaping the fortunes of films and filmmakers, producer Michael Douglas told me I gave crucial early validation and momentum to his 1975 film, *One Flew Over the Cuckoo's Nest*, when I did the first interview about the project with him and his producing partner, Saul Zaentz.

I found them refreshingly independent in their plans to make the film for United Artists with financing by Zaentz, a wealthy record industry mogul from the San Francisco Bay Area. *Cuckoo's Nest* went on to win the best-picture Oscar and the four other top Academy Awards—for director, screenwriter, actor, and actress—the first film to do so since Frank Capra's 1934 *It Happened One Night*. (Zaentz also won Oscars for producing Miloš Forman's *Amadeus* and Anthony Mingella's *The English Patient* and is tied with Sam Spiegel for the most best-picture awards.)

And before the Oscar nominations were decided in 1976, I consciously gave director Forman a boost by interviewing him about his work on the film. I was not especially a Forman fan and found *Cuckoo's Nest* repugnant for its condescending attitude toward insane people and smug encouragement of audience identification with the "sane" Jack Nicholson protagonist. But I sympathized with Forman as a refugee from Czechoslovakia and wanted to help advance his career in the American film industry. When I stopped in the Music Center auditorium before covering the Oscar show, I ran into Forman, who had his arms around his two young sons. He thanked me for enabling him to get them out of Czechoslovakia so he could see them for the first time in years. And when Michael Douglas appeared backstage for a press conference after winning the best-picture Oscar, he singled me out for thanks, reminding the press that I had done the first interview with them about the film. That was all highly gratifying.

Now we dissolve forward to 1996, and I am interviewing Forman again for an online publication about his film *The People vs. Larry Flynt*. I told Forman I fondly remembered what he said while introducing me to his sons at the Oscar show, but he said he had no memory of that. And when I expressed my criticism of *Cuckoo's Nest,* he said, "I'm not going to apologize for having made a commercial film." I also told him I found his Larry Flynt film hypocritical in defending the publisher of *Hustler* while not being frank about what kind of salacious images he published, which should have been the true test of a First Amendment defense of a magazine considered pornographic. By then I was inured to a filmmaker's amnesia and avoidance of difficult issues, such a contrast to the graciousness displayed earlier by Michael Douglas.

Writing obits

You mentioned earlier that you had another important duty at Daily Variety.

Among my contributions to *Variety* as a film historian was my enthusiastic writing of obituaries. I've always felt that the test of a true journalist is how he or she writes obituaries. I learned that from my Dad, who always made a point of finding something good to say about a person who died. He was stymied once, though, when writing an obit on a mob boss, so he typed at the end, "He liked dogs." Too often on newspapers, I found, obit writing was held in disdain, but I felt honored to write them, to have the last word on someone's life and work, and they helped train me for writing biographies. The one job in journalism I wish I could have had was that of Alden Whitman, the chief obituary writer of the *New York Times*, who would go around the world and spend days interviewing important people; they were pleased to cooperate.

Unlike some of the later *Variety* editors, who scorned obituaries as yesterday's news, I was always aware of how important obits were to our readers: in readership surveys, they were second only to film reviews. I often thought of the wonderful exchange between the two old vaudevillians in Neil Simon's play *The Sunshine Boys* about the death of the songwriter Sol Burton: "He died?—Last week.—Where?—In *Variety.*" I took as much time and care with obits of lesser-known craftspeople, writers, and actors as I did with those of the major names in the business.

When Irving Berlin died in 1989 at the age of 101, I recalled what Jerome Kern said when he was asked what place Berlin had in American music: "Irving Berlin has no place in American music. He *is* American music." Fred Astaire, who often worked with Berlin and introduced some of his most popular songs, remained his good friend. When George Stevens Jr. and I went to Astaire's house to prepare for our AFI tribute, I saw that Berlin had done some paintings for him. The songwriter seemed to favor various poses of penguins in human garb, including one in a tux who looked like Fred. And while writing the show, I spent an afternoon on the phone with David Brown, a producer friend of the songwriter. Brown and I kept coaxing Berlin to write something suitable to be read as his contribution, but despite our efforts and Berlin's rewrites, it still felt grudging in its praise of Astaire. After Berlin died on a Friday, I spent an entire weekend in the office writing his obit, but it was such an epic that when I turned it in on Monday, I was told, "Cut it in half."

Usually, though, they let my obits run as long as they needed to run. I often consulted books and did research in the clipping files of the Academy's Margaret Herrick Library. I cherished my many moving conversations with relatives to gather information, and I made sure to mail them copies of the paper after the obits ran. When the deluge of AIDS-related deaths swept through show business, I successfully came to the support of gay activists in lobbying the initially reluctant management of *Variety* to list same-sex partners as survivors.

When the great animator Fred (Tex) Avery died in August 1980 at the age of 71, I learned about it from the City News Wire I monitored. It was 5:50 PM, ten minutes before our deadline. I told the managing editor, Pete Pryor, who said it could wait a day. But I was of the school of reporting that believed news should go in the next day's paper. I argued that Avery was such an important filmmaker that we shouldn't wait. I was fortunate to know his work well and to have heard him speak for half an hour while accepting a lifetime award from his fellow animators. He was so funny and such a good storyteller that no one seemed to mind as he told his life story.

Knowing how little time I had to write Avery's obit, I quickly figured out how to break down the work. I pulled the clipping file from our "morgue" and spent three minutes reading the clips, a minute outlining the obit, four minutes drafting it, and two minutes doing a second draft. The twelve-paragraph obit appeared in the next morning's paper. "Among his peers and film historians," I wrote, "Avery was regarded as a consummate visual stylist and one of the few authentic surrealists in American film."

After I wrote the obituary of Ernest (Sunshine Sammy) Morrison, an original member of Hal Roach's Our Gang in silent films who died at age seventy-six in July 1989, I received a phone call from Joel Fluellen, a venerable actor and activist who was something of a father figure in the Black Hollywood community. Fluellen touched me by calling it "the best obituary of a Black person that ever appeared in *Variety.*" Most of the credit, however, belonged to my friend Karl Thiede, a film historian who was one of my best sources and filled me in on the late comedian's life and work. Fluellen asked if I would write his obituary when the time came. I was saddened but honored by his request, even more so when he committed suicide the following February because of failing health. As well as writing his obituary, I covered a moving memorial service at which the great Sidney Poitier and numerous other key figures in the Hollywood Black community spoke of Fluellen's importance.

I rarely had a negative experience with a source as an obit writer. When Mary Tyler Moore called to report the death of an uncle, a talent agent, I asked her questions to fill some gaps, and she reamed me out, ordering me to print just what she told me. I went right to Pete Pryor to report that encounter, and he wisely counseled me to keep in mind that people respond differently to grieving. So I quietly fleshed out the obit with research in our files. In my last tour of duty at *Daily Variety,* however, the new Peter Bart regime was contemptuous of obituaries. Bart's lackey as the new executive editor, Stephen West, told me to write obits faster ("down and dirty"). I refused and kept doing them the way they needed to be done. After I left the paper in 1992, the annual book collection of *Variety* obituaries published for libraries dropped in size by a third, and the next year that longtime publishing tradition ended altogether. The paper started charging families for most obituaries other than those for the biggest names.

As a trade reporter, where did you fit into the Hollywood pecking order?

When I moved from Hollywood to Beverly Hills soon after going to work for *Daily Variety,* I was treated like a criminal. I was driving on the Sunset Strip in West Hollywood with a car full of appliances and other stuff, and just after I turned down toward my new residence nearby, I was stopped and handcuffed by a cop. He apparently thought I was a thief. He only let me go when a witness protested, but I felt I was jinxed and living in an unpleasant part of the world. The problem was compounded the next day when the cop came to my place of work to apologize, which created another spectacle with my colleagues wondering what I was involved in; I told one it was none of his business. I should have turned around and gone back to Wisconsin, but then I wouldn't have done all that I did later.

Early on, I found that schmoozing with film people on sets and locations, at industry dinners, or at eateries while interviewing them was one thing; casual socializing with celebrities was taboo. I learned a harsh lesson in the rigid Hollywood caste system when I interviewed Glenda Jackson after seeing her onstage locally in *Hedda Gabler,* which she also filmed as *Hedda.* She and I hit it off (and later worked together on a political TV special), and at the end of our interview in her dressing room, she invited me and my girlfriend to a party her film producer was throwing for her at his home. Shortly thereafter a representative for the producer called to disinvite us, making it clear that members of the press were not allowed to mingle casually with show-business royalty.

As that encounter with Jackson showed, people from overseas didn't always adhere to this Hollywood rule. My friendship with Truffaut demonstrated that as well. But I vividly recall that on the way to Chasen's for Hitchcock's birthday party, I got lost and pulled over next to a lady walking her dog alongside a park in Beverly Hills. When I asked the way to Chasen's, she looked askance at my beat-up old Chrysler and said, "Are you kidding?" I don't know if this rude lady was connected to the film business, but I found that transgressing geographical and economic boundaries was frowned upon in Los Angeles and environs. I felt such snubs keenly. Joan Didion called Hollywood "a community as intricate, rigid, and deceptive in its mores as any devised on this continent," and felt that as such it "sometimes presents the appearance of the last extant stable society." That was written when I went there in 1973 and started trying to figure it out.

The ugliness of Hollywood's rigid stratification was further rubbed in by the cutting behavior of some big shots when I and my partners happened to be seated next to them at award show dinners and other such events. Eventually I abandoned the chutzpah that made me introduce myself to people at parties and retreated into a shell out of self-protection. The social barriers I experienced, I came to realize, interfered with my reason for working on the trade paper, which I had thought would be a natural stepping stone to a career as a screenwriter and director. Perhaps that would have been true in the European film industry. I found common ground with old-timers who had been shunted aside by the industry, such as Renoir, Hawks, Dwan, Capra, and many others.

The brutal reality I found was that most people in Hollywood were there not for love of cinema, as I had naively assumed, but for sex, money, and power. In one of Redd Foxx's "blue" records, he says someone asked him what he thought was more important, sex or money. He replied, Money, because if you've got some of that, you can buy the other thing. Sex follows power and money in Hollywood. I found that very few people in Hollywood actually love movies. That's a big difference from the 1930s and '40s. Those people liked movies and though they viewed Hollywood as a business, they also wanted to make good movies in the best way they knew how. Now those running the business only want to make money.

I felt the humiliation and social isolation of being treated as a second-class citizen. Although I had a measure of power as an industry reporter, I ran into fierce opposition from the studios when I tried to exercise it, and I was judged by most people for conspicuously lacking money and being dumb enough to work at a trade paper for less money than I could have earned as a waiter at one of the trendy industry restaurants. Just before Christmas one year at *Daily Variety,* when we were waiting expectantly for our end-of-year bonus, Tom Pryor went around the news room with a brown paper bag of oranges and placed one on each desk. We were all speechless, as was Tom. It seemed like a joke, but it wasn't. Even the paper we worked for seemed to hold us in contempt.

I reached my breaking point when Army Archerd made some snobbish remarks in the *Daily Variety* office about the shabby clothes I was wearing, which were all I could afford on my subsistence-level salary. So I decided to strike back symbolically at him and the rest of the industry that looked down on us lowly ink-stained wretches. I wrote a magazine article for *American Film* for the money I needed, $500 (the equivalent of $5,500 in 2025), and went to the best men's tailor in Beverly Hills to order a gray, pinstriped three-piece bespoke suit. I wore that suit for the rest of my first tour of duty on *Daily Variety* and during the subsequent years when I worked as a screenwriter and appeared in *Rock 'n' Roll High School.* The suit was my overt act of rebellion.

Most of the rest of Hollywood tended to dress "casually" but in expensive duds. And what was worse was that part of the Hollywood caste system was expecting screenwriters to look silly by dressing in sloppy, cheap clothing. I remember how mortified I felt walking a picket line during a writers' strike and seeing how degradingly foolish the older writers looked; witnessing their lack of self-respect was an epiphany, making me vow I would never behave that way and would get out before it was too late. Rather than conform to the stereotype of writers as second-class citizens, I defiantly emulated the true power brokers in Hollywood, specifically lawyers and MCA chairman Lew Wasserman. Wearing a tie and a suit or sport coat was seen as crossing a dangerous line, even a fighting provocation, as I had already found in two incidents when industry people actually challenged me to brawl for dressing that way. Some people in those days were deranged about social signifiers.

My pinstriped suit had the desired effect of making most people in Hollywood treat me with more wariness, if not respect, but it also drew some overt hostility. When I interviewed film producer Max Palevsky, a computer mogul who had become one of the country's wealthiest men, he asked snidely why I was wearing a suit. I found myself saying what I actually thought: "Because I'm tired of rich people dressing like slobs." Jean Firstenberg, the head of the American Film Institute, repeatedly asked me the same question but seemingly with genuine curiosity while I was working on one of the AFI shows. I finally told her, "Because I don't want to look like everybody else." That seemed to make sense to her. I also kept in mind some advice my mother had given me when I was a boy: "Never call attention to someone's clothes or the color of their skin."

Wasn't Beverly Hills a posh address for a reporter in those days?

Actually, for a while I and my roommate, the guy I moved from Madison with, rented a Beverly Hills duplex surprisingly cheaply, for only $125 a month, before prices escalated in the real estate boom. We found ourselves across the street from the residence of Shelley Winters. An apartment complex was going up next to her house, and every morning at eight a food truck would come out and blow its horn to summon the workers to breakfast. Out would come Shelley running across her lawn while screaming at them in her muu-muu. She would wake me up every morning, and my roommate would run out and try vainly to seduce her, but I always managed to get a couple of more hours of sleep before going to work at *Daily Variety*'s cramped and modest old office on Cahuenga Blvd. in Hollywood.

I had a falling-out with my roommate because I was too busy working on a screenplay at night to party with him anymore, so I found another apartment down the block. The landlady, an elegant elderly Chinese American woman, looked familiar. "Were you an actress?" I asked. She vehemently denied it. But I dug into a box in my apartment and found the issue of *Cahiers du Cinéma* with a picture of John Ford directing the cast of *7 Women*, including my landlady, Jane Chang, who plays the Mandarin princess, Miss Ling. I showed Jane that issue, she grinned, and we became fast friends.

She shared memories of Ford with me that I report in *Searching for John Ford*. She told me she had quit acting because every single film or TV director in Hollywood, except Ford, told her the same thing, exact quote: "Orientals don't show emotion." Jane was eternally grateful to Ford for giving her the one big emotional scene of her career. I borrowed the MGM studio print of *7 Women* and set up a small screening for her in a projection room on the Sunset Strip. I also invited my fellow critic Todd McCarthy and directors Joe Dante, Allan Arkush, and Paul Bartel. Imagine my chagrin when Arkush and Bartel giggled and talked derisively throughout the film, even though they knew a cast member was present. I should have told them to leave but didn't want to create a ruckus. Jane graciously did not say anything and was pleased to see the film again. Joe and Todd, who are gentlemen, did not participate in that misbehavior.

"Tell 'em we're all out of souvenirs"

You've written a lot about the Hollywood blacklist in your books on Capra, Ford, and Welles. And you became friendly with the formerly blacklisted Abraham Polonsky. As a kind of outsider in town yourself, did you feel an affinity with him and other blacklisted people you met?

During my first few years in Hollywood, I became friendly with several formerly blacklisted people and came to identify common interests with them, especially with Welles and Abe, a great writer-director with whom I had an immediate rapport. Abe helped educate me about the business and our country. "Because we can't be Stalin, we become movie directors," he said with a wry smile.

I especially admire Abe's radical 1969 comeback film, *Tell Them Willie Boy Is Here*, a Western that deconstructed the white supremacist, pseudo-heroic myths of the genre and the nation. The last line of the film is uttered by Robert Redford's Deputy Sheriff Cooper after he kills the rebellious Native American protagonist (played by Robert Blake) and orders his body buried. But the Natives on the posse defiantly burn Willie rather than allow him to be picked apart by his pursuers. When the sheriff protests to Cooper, "God damn it, Coop—people have got to see *something,*" the deputy says with contempt, "Tell 'em we're all out of souvenirs." Ironically, the astringent honesty of that film in portraying Willie Boy as a doomed participant in an existential dance of death he knows he is fated to lose—Abe described the film to me as "a pavane for an early American"—made the film unpopular with some people

I knew in Madison who failed to find in it their romantic illusions about rebellion.

Abe based the film on a 1960 nonfiction novel, *Willie Boy: A Desert Manhunt* by Harry Lawton, a predecessor of mine as a reporter for the *Press-Enterprise*. As I wrote in *Two Cheers for Hollywood*, while living in Riverside, "I explored some of the locations where the 'Willie Boy incident' had actually taken place. [Later] I sought out Polonsky at his home in Beverly Hills and found him among the handful of the most brilliant people I met in the industry (Welles, Renoir, and Wilder were among his few intellectual peers in Hollywood) as well as a surprisingly droll and cheerful fellow considering his long period of internal exile and the often-bleak themes of his work. Abe was also that *rara avis*, a man of honor in Hollywood. He pointed out that the film of his that he most resembled in person was *Romance of a Horsethief* (1971), an even more neglected work that defied its Czarist Russian setting to become his most joyous celebration of life."

I interviewed Abe about *Willie Boy* after we watched it together in 1975. I mentioned that in reviewing the film upon its release, the future screenwriter-director Paul Schrader, then writing for the *Los Angeles Free Press*, observed that *Willie Boy* is so carefully crafted and constructed that it "looks as if Polonsky spent every one of those twenty years [on the blacklist] mulling over the film, perfecting every nuance, weeding out softness and naivete, making sure that the political references were neither too well disguised or childish." Abe replied with a smile, "They just haven't seen fancy dancing for a while." Our screening marked the first time he had seen *Willie Boy* since it was released. I intended to offer the interview to the Directors Guild of America magazine, *Action*, but he disappointed me by refusing to let me publish it and insisting on keeping the audiotape. I don't know why he did that, for he had said to me in that session, "It's worth making pictures for you, because you see things."

After I moderated a Q&A session with Abe at a theater in Los Feliz following a screening of his 1948 film noir classic, *Force of Evil*, he told me, "If you stand next to directors often enough, people will start to see you as a director." I also moderated a discussion with Abe at Filmex in 1980 about *Willie Boy*, which that audience also largely failed to understand. I incorporated some of our 1975 discussion into the resulting interview, the transcript of which was published with my prefatory notes in Andrew Dickos's 2013 book, *Abraham Polonsky: Interviews*, and *Two Cheers for Hollywood*.

One reason I came to feel a kinship with Abe; the historian, novelist, and screenwriter John Sanford; and other former blacklistees I met was that I felt a similar sense of exclusion in Hollywood. Theirs had been far more violent—as Abe said, "The only more effective tool is execution"—but I still felt that what I was undergoing as a screenwriter was a form of blacklisting, which Abe defined as "a secret agreement to ignore someone's existence." I felt that especially sharply when I found myself unable to get numerous script projects made that had political themes, although I did manage to slip some radical political elements into *Rock 'n' Roll High School.*

I also came to know some informers in Hollywood. This helped lead to my Capra biography, with my discovery that my former hero had been an informer. Capra betrayed the principles of the First Amendment he extolled in his great film *Mr. Smith Goes to Washington* when he, ironically, informed on its principal screenwriter, Sidney Buchman, among others. After Buchman's refusal to name names to HUAC in 1951 and his blacklisting, he was found guilty of contempt of Congress for defying a second HUAC subpoena in 1952. He was a member of the Communist Party when he wrote *Mr. Smith,* a fact that Capra uneasily accepted at the time but later panicked about, eventually leading him to disassociate himself from the film during the Vietnam era.

In some ways, my Capra biography, *Frank Capra: The Catastrophe of Success* (first published in 1992), which I felt compelled to write to grapple with my feelings of betrayal by Hollywood, also contains echoes of two earlier projects, a novel about a young man getting to know a great director in all his dimensions and a drama about an informer, in the vein of Arthur Miller but not as rhetorical. Those projects had been vaguely haunting me before I came across the reality in front of my eyes. When I became the first scholar to dig through Capra's papers, I found that he had preserved documents with evidence of his guilt and that he had decided, for whatever reason, to release them to the world.

When I started work on my Capra biography, I saw that book not only as a way to express everything I had learned about the business but also as the vindication of all I had gone through in that world. Even though I've published overtly autobiographical books, such as this one you and I are doing, my Capra biography in some ways is my most personal. The research and the writing and the four-year legal battle I fought to get the book published encapsulated everything I know about Hollywood. Capra's life and career spanned much of the history of the American film industry, and as a representative figure who betrayed his potential, the ideals of his admirers, and the principles of the Bill of Rights, he embodied the tragedy of a once-great art form.

As one reviewer of my Capra biography put it, I was one of his leading admirers, the head writer of his AFI Life Achievement Award tribute, so my disillusionment when I learned the truth about him, that he became an informer in the blacklist era to try to save his own skin when his loyalty to his adopted country was questioned, was correspondingly shattering. That knowledge destroyed what remained of my faith in moviemaking. Exposing the truth about Capra's life taught me to see the film industry with far greater clarity, without the blinders I wore before that. Ironically, though, I am still an admirer of his work, which I now appreciate more because I understand its conflicts and contradictions more fully. The struggle to write that book and my successful battle to get it published the way I wanted was my proudest achievement. And surmounting that challenge has illuminated my other biographies of Spielberg and Ford and my subsequent critical studies of several great filmmakers—Welles, Lubitsch, Wilder, Cukor, and the Coen Bros. The years I spent working in the business served as preparation for those books, giving them depth and insight they otherwise would lack.

The world's best job?

It must have been hard for you covering as well as trying to become part of a business in which lying is the default option.

My *Daily Variety* colleague Jim Harwood, a veteran journalist, told me the reason newspaper jobs paid so poorly is that it's the best job in the world: "You always get the best seat in the house, and you can get anyone in the world on the phone. If journalism paid well, everybody would want the job." That's no longer true; journalism pays better now, but it's harder to get important people on the phone. That's why you're paid off. Nevertheless, I count myself fortunate to have been able to work for *Variety* when it was still a real newspaper before Peter Bart ruined it by bartering away its integrity to advertisers, which is why he was hired, according to Tom Pryor, who was given that explanation by an executive with the paper's new parent company. I was proud to be on the staff when a trade reporter working for

Tom was taken somewhat seriously. But the TV producer George Schlatter angered me when he was quoted as saying, "The trades are the medium through which Hollywood lies to each other."

Although I realize now that what Schlatter said is mostly true, I always did my best to tell the truth in Hollywood as a reporter and screenwriter, a difficult challenge, until the cost to my psyche became so high that I had to leave the business. The degree of habitual mendacity in the business—a racket in which it's actually considered foolish to tell the truth—became glaring to me when I did a feature for *Daily Variety* on the making of Robert Aldrich's *The Choirboys*. After visiting the indoor set of a city park, complete with artfully scattered plastic dog crap, I was given a steadily escalating set of figures by people I interviewed that day for the supposed budget of the film, which I later learned was exaggerated by fourfold from what I was misled into printing. The ballooning budgets that by now have made Hollywood filmmaking so ruinously expensive are partly due to the creative people taking their cuts up front because they have no reason to trust the infamous "creative bookkeeping" system, with its "rolling break" that some accountant devised to keep most films, even box office hits, from officially going into the black.

That's the principal reason I told my students that Hollywood was literally a "criminal enterprise" and warned them to go there, if at all, with their eyes wide open. The extent of the corruption I found in Hollywood was pervasive. Contrary to the publicity about the huge sums people are paid in Hollywood, that applies mostly to a fortunate few, notably major stars and top executives. Most people in Hollywood are struggling to make a living, especially since the pandemic and industry strikes caused production and employment to plummet. Many of the members of the Writers Guild of America, West, don't work in a given year, and the average writer's salary, factoring in those who are unemployed as well as the lucky few who are well paid, tends to be on a middle-class level. That doesn't even count the tens of thousands of wannabe writers living in Southern California who haven't yet managed to break into the guild, as I managed to do in 1977, when it was easier to qualify.

Talking frankly with Hollywood veterans, as I found, revealed seemingly endless levels of dubious behavior. When I was working on *Daily Variety* in the 1970s, I became friendly with a studio chief—it was a minor studio he was running, but a studio nonetheless. He liked to brag that he got his start as a runner for the Al Capone mob in

Chicago, and he taught me many nitty-gritty lessons about Hollywood. One of his lessons was how to calculate the price of hiring a hit man. It depended on what page in the paper the murder would be reported on—say, $50,000 for a page-one murder (today that would be about $285,000), $25,000 for page two, down to $500 for page forty. Maybe he was having me on about that, but I doubt it. Once when I was royally screwed by a producer on a project I had written, I told my tale to another producer friend of mine. He asked half-seriously, "Have you thought about hiring a hit man?"

Moonlighting

You mentioned earlier that you also wrote pieces for Film Comment *and other magazines while you were on* Daily Variety. *Did you enjoy that extracurricular work?*

Yes, especially when I worked for my friend Bob Thomas, the longtime Hollywood correspondent of the Associated Press and a top-notch biographer of film industry figures. I especially admired Bob's colorful and thoroughly researched 1967 biography of Harry Cohn, *King Cohn: The Life and Times of Harry Cohn*. Capra's notoriously profane boss at Columbia Pictures was one of those monstrous moguls who nevertheless had a genuine love of motion pictures and made good ones in the Golden Age along with the usual quota of dreck. Bob was kind enough to let me access his papers at UCLA and quote from the treasure house of three hundred interviews he had conducted with Hollywood people for his book. That resource was invaluable, especially since many of them had died before I began my research. When I started my Capra book, Bob generously gave me a written series of tips on how to write biographies, which I preserved for posterity in *Frankly*. I followed most of his wise advice but ignored some guidance, such as "Avoid too much attribution," because I was taking a different approach. I made a point of disclosing my sources in the text itself, because it was essential to my book to reveal how I had learned that Capra was not the man he claimed to be.

Bob also moonlighted as the editor of *Action*, the excellent magazine of the DGA, and was always willing to bring me on board. I interviewed George Cukor for the first time for *Action* on the debacle he had just faced making a film in the USSR, *The Blue Bird*. During our 1975 luncheon on the patio of the Polo Lounge at the Beverly Hills Hotel, Cukor and I hit it off with our similarly sly senses of humor, and he impressed me on our short acquaintance by how he perceptively analyzed my character in ways other people could not see. He said, "You're a very determined young man but deceptively mild-mannered. Keep that." And as I write in *George Cukor's People,* to get perspective on the production of *The Blue Bird* and how Cukor had survived in the industry through his remarkable talent for resilience, "I brought up other mishaps in his career and asked how it felt to be fired from a film; I was thinking of the 1947 MGM film *Desire Me*, from which Cukor said he had been 'removed'; it was partly reshot by other directors and has no directing credit. Cukor reacted by touching my forearm lightly with his right hand, leaning over toward his publicist, and saying, 'Notice with what finesse he avoids mentioning the title *Gone with the Wind*.'"

Unfortunately for me and for Hollywood's sense of history, Bob eventually was urged by his patrons at the DGA to run fewer articles about directors and films from the past and more stuff of current interest to the wider membership, who primarily worked in television. I wasn't much interested in that kind of nuts-and-bolts guidance. (I later ran into the same problem after a few years of writing mostly historical pieces, including a series of profiles of great screenwriters, for the Writers Guild of America magazine *Written By.*)

Before *Action* was dumbed down, I did manage to do another fascinating feature Bob suggested, to interview directors who had worked with the imaginative B-movie producer Val Lewton on his 1940s horror films. Those innovative films achieve their remarkable effects mostly through suggestion, in contrast with the 1970s' increasing trend toward gore. For that 1976 piece I watched most of Lewton's films on a holiday trip to the State Historical Society in Madison before interviewing Robert Wise, Mark Robson, Jacques Tourneur (by letter from his home in Paris), and Tom Gries (who apprenticed with Lewton before becoming a director), as well as Curtis Harrington, a Lewton admirer. The only aspect of the article that doesn't hold up well now is Harrington's dissing of *Jaws*, which in retrospect seems positively Bressonian in its discretion and unusually insightful about various modes of masculinity in fighting the mostly unseen shark. *Jaws* actually draws from Lewton's method of keeping the object of menace off-camera, a style Spielberg followed out of necessity when the mechanical shark fortuitously kept refusing to work.

I learned a lot about Lewton's secrets of making modest budgets go far while turning liabilities into assets, a subject I would find increasingly compelling over the years as the scale and costs of Hollywood productions escalated out of control. Privileged to hear that historical perspective from his directors, I was able to look back at a minimalist such as Lewton as a guide out of the misguided path of modern Hollywood blockbuster moviemaking.

Peter O'Toole gave you an eloquent interview in 1980 for Film Comment *at the time he was "a bit frantically overpraising his newest film, Richard Rush's* The Stunt Man*"; you describe him as "such a magnificent ruin." Would you have liked to have interviewed him when he starred in* Lawrence of Arabia *instead or, looking back, was 1981 the ideal time?*

I borrowed that "magnificent ruin" phrase from Orson Welles. He said it to me about Edmond O'Brien when we were doing *The Other Side of the Wind*, to kindly explain why he was taking some dialogue I was having trouble understanding and giving it to Eddie, who did it perfectly. Any time would have been a great time to interview Peter O'Toole, one of my favorite actors. He was marvelously expansive even though he was laid up with a cold in his bed in the Beverly Hills Hotel, imitating Garbo in her death scene in Cukor's *Camille*. He was so witty and smart and incandescent. And I found him reflective and self-scrutinizing about his work and about the acting profession.

He recalled the time David Lean needed him for a handful of more closeups after the location work on *Lawrence* was completed:

> So having been in the wilderness of Zin, we find ourselves in the relative wilderness of Hammersmith in a tiny little room with an old blue wall and a bit of dry ice: "Look there," or "Look there."... Do you remember the scene with a mirage? Which was not an optical, it was *there*. He wanted another closeup to help build the tension of that amazing entrance of Ali. He showed me it and it was extraordinary, for I was twenty-seven in the first shot; cut to the figure coming through the mirage; twenty-nine in the second shot; and twenty-seven in the third. The difference was astounding, it really was. I'd lost the bloom of youth. It was the beginnings of all this. *[Gestures to his face]* It *was*

a shock. But, don't forget, attitudes change as the years change. It doesn't bother me now. We're in a strange situation, film actors. We can watch the process of decomposition of the flesh.

I am glad we had such a rapport, because I was an admirer of O'Toole from the earliest days of his film career, especially of his role as a compulsive Don Juan struggling to settle down in *What's New Pussycat,* one of the films, as I told you earlier, that helped shape me as a young man gradually emerging from sexual repression. O'Toole also asked my advice about what he might do to finally win an Oscar, since he kept getting nominated (five times to that point) without winning. I told him frankly, "You need to show up. Every time you're nominated, you're not there, and the audience sees a little black-and-white picture of you in the corner of the frame. Hollywood feels offended when an actor never shows up, and they admire people who seem like troupers and good sports. That might be why you haven't won an Oscar." He took that advice and began showing up the next three times he was nominated, though he had to settle for an honorary Oscar in 2003.

You introduce your 1973 interview with Richard Lester in London by writing that he was "perhaps the most forthcoming, introspective, and charming director I interviewed." You also write in Two Cheers, *"Today our interview seems tinged with a melancholy I barely sensed at the time." I felt the same way reading it. First thought: Perhaps more directors would reveal their sadness, disappointment, frustrations, and insecurities if they too were so introspective. Second thought: It is almost heartbreaking that Lester didn't understand the impact of his films on his appreciative fans—he didn't even realize the enduring greatness and tremendous cultural significance of* A Hard Day's Night. *I am also a fan of* The Knack … and How to Get It, How I Won the War, Petulia, *the underrated* The Three Musketeers, Superman II, Juggernaut, Robin and Marian, *and parts of* Help! *Yet he tells you that his debut short,* The Running, Jumping and Standing Still Film, *is "the only film that I can say I don't feel too embarrassed by." What are your thoughts about how he underestimated his career? Did he have guilt for trying to make popular movies? And what do you think is his legacy?*

I continue to miss seeing Richard Lester. Yes, I found him extremely self-critical, perhaps dismayingly so, but he is such a serious and modest man, which I found appealing.

He never seemed satisfied with his work—few directors actually are—and he retired for a number of personal reasons, including the death of one of his favorite actors, Roy Kinnear, as a result of a stunt in a film they made together.

I wish Lester were still making films. We need him around, with his blend of zany comedy and biting social satire. Wondering what he had been up to since 1969's *The Bed Sitting Room*, I cold-called Lester at his office at Twickenham Studios on my first visit to London in January 1973. *The Bed Sitting Room* is an amazing film that holds up well today as a surreal comedy about a post-apocalyptic Britain, but it was a flop and hurt his career. I interviewed him when he was having to change to more mainstream fare. It so happened he was in preproduction on what proved to be his return to prominence and bankability, *The Three Musketeers*. His work would never be quite as bold and iconoclastic as it had been before, but it has some high points, such as the sly thriller *Juggernaut* and the lovely, autumnal *Robin and Marian*.

Fortuitously, I even ran into Lester at a movie theater the day after our interview while he was there to study the 1921 Douglas Fairbanks silent version of *The Three Musketeers*. "Rumor has it that there is also a Three Stooges version," he said, "but I haven't run across it yet." An inkling of the tone of the Lester version came when the "All for one and one for all" title flashed on the screen, and he muttered, "And every man for himself."

The interview ran in *Sight and Sound,* and when it was reprinted in *Two Cheers for Hollywood*, I sent a copy of the book to Lester. He told me although he had given most of his papers to the British Film Institute, he had kept a copy of the issue of *Sight and Sound* in which our interview appeared. I was touched by that.

Did Hollywood change you politically?

Hollywood radicalized me in ways Madison never managed to do. The political discussions and turmoil in Madison made me more sophisticated politically, but after a while some of the radicals became so confused and hypocritical and lost sight of effectively opposing the war in Vietnam that they turned to nihilistic destruction. In Hollywood, I was living in the belly of the capitalist beast. Everywhere around me I could see stark evidence of the corruption the student radicals had only talked about in glib, overly generalized terms. Watergate, Vietnam, and my growing attention to the political assassinations of the 1960s raised my political awareness during this period, while Hollywood was in the process of stripping me of my remaining illusions.

(In 1975, while the film version of the Carl Bernstein-Bob Woodward book *All the President's Men* was in production, I had an interview scheduled with its director, Alan J. Pakula, for *Daily Variety*. But when I went to his home at noon on a Saturday, he told me his publicist had not informed him about the interview, and he was just too busy to talk. So I had time for just one question. A friend who was researching the Robert Kennedy assassination had told me Woodward was a CIA agent—actually Woodward was and may still be an ONI [Office of Naval Intelligence] operative—so I asked Pakula if he had heard Woodward was CIA. "Yes," he said, "but if I thought about that while making this film, I'd go crazy.")

Since I was looked down upon in my *Variety* days by the monied show-business and Los Angeles gentry as a newspaper peon with a subsistence salary in a world of glittering financial excess, I felt the stark discrepancies of wealth and poverty more keenly and took them personally. The way people in Los Angeles were judged by the cars they drove and the clothes they wore and other superficial, materialistic attributes repelled me. As I learned about and reported on the rampant corruption of the film industry, my eyes were no longer clouded with my outdated fantasy image of Hollywood.

I had come there with the naive assumption that most people who went to Hollywood, like me, did so because they were film buffs and wanted to make good movies, but I found that relatively few of the power brokers and filmmakers knew much about film history or cared about film as an art form. Like Las Vegas, Hollywood was a company town revolving around the most blatant and unscrupulous forms of capitalism, and it was impossible for me to keep from seeing the facts of life any longer. So when I became a university professor teaching screenwriting, among other aspects of cinema, I felt ambivalent about sending my students out into the film world but did my best to acquaint them with the reality of the "criminal enterprise" they would face if they went to Hollywood.

The results of my exposure to that milieu, which nobody had prepared me for, were painful but ultimately salutary. Once I managed to break free of the industry with great psychological difficulty in 1984—it is always hard to let go of your self-destructive dreams, as I had earlier done by leaving the Catholic Church—that led to my career as an author digging more deeply into the business of creating illusions. All I learned about the industry and its people I poured into my investigative book about how one of my false idols, Frank Capra, had constructed a fraudulent image with the collusion of the media and his naively idealistic youthful admirers. I could not have written the Capra book without having worked as an industry reporter and screenwriter, and I saw that book as my report from the trenches, as well as the justification of my years of struggle in coming to understand and escape from a terminally decadent system.

4. "Too expensive a lesson"

How were you able to break into the film business while working as a journalist? Were you writing and trying to sell screenplays from the time you got to California?

When I arrived in California, I was writing a screenplay for a Western about the early film business, *The Authentic Life of Cheyenne Harry*, based on a story I wrote with your brother Gerald Peary. And I was trying to sell the original comedy-drama screenplay I had written in Madison about a diligent Black mailman going berserk on his last day on the job, *Man Bites Dog*. I kept working on screenplays before and during my time at *Daily Variety*, writing originals. The path I would be required to follow to break into the industry proved much more circuitous than I had expected. As a screenwriter, I was starting at what Orson Welles wryly called "the very lowest ladder of the movie world," and since Hollywood tends to rigorously pigeonhole people, I also had to overcome the barrier of being seen through the stigma of my plebeian job as a trade reporter and reviewer, which had the side effect of making me some enemies along the way.

Writing a Western would seem to be a natural thing for you to do, even if Hollywood wasn't keen on our favorite genre anymore.

The ambitious Western I was writing when I came to Hollywood, also called *California, Here I Come*, was set in 1912. It was a takeoff on Washington Irving's classic short story "Rip Van Winkle" and John Ford's silent film *The Last Outlaw*. That 1919 two-reeler stars Ed "Pardner" Jones (aka "King Fisher" Jones), a sharpshooter who actually had been a Western outlaw and lawman. The film is about an old-timer who gets out of the notorious Yuma, Arizona, "hell hole" prison after twenty years and finds himself bewildered by the modern world of automobiles and movie theaters. (About half of *The Last Outlaw* has been rediscovered, but I hadn't seen it at the time I wrote the script, although I had seen the 1936 remake starring Harry Carey that Ford didn't direct. The 1919 version was written by H. Tipton Steck from a story by Evelyne Murray Campbell; the sound remake credits Campbell and Ford with the story and was directed by another silent-film veteran, Christy Cabanne.)

I added the element of having the old-timer becoming part of a silent film company on location—as a technical adviser and extra—and going to Hollywood at the end to continue working on movies, as many cowboys, outlaws, and former lawmen did in those days. That aspect of the story was influenced by Diana Serra Cary's delightful 1975 book, *The Hollywood Posse: The Story of a Gallant Band of Horsemen Who Made Movie History*. I also spent many enjoyable hours talking with pioneer director Allan Dwan hearing his accounts of his early days in the industry, including his skirmishes on location with thugs hired by the Motion Picture Patents Company trust, and worked those into the script.

My visits to Dwan to research my script ended abruptly when he was told to stop seeing me because he was also a consultant on a similar project for Peter Bogdanovich about early filmmaking, *Nickelodeon*. Dwan was apologetic but said he had no choice in the matter. Bogdanovich's superb 1971 book of their interviews, *Allan Dwan: The Last Pioneer*, and the much longer uncut version I read at the AFI library had helped inspire me to write my script. But another writer managed to get a script on the subject to Peter before I did. Peter told me he didn't think much of that writer's script, and despite his own rewrite, *Nickelodeon* (which was released in 1976) turned out to be a turkey. It forced a farcical tone into material that should have been treated more realistically. Peter should have made my script instead, but he passed on the opportunity; that series of events was a crushing blow for me. Peter and his fellow filmmakers didn't trust the audience to enjoy seeing what had actually happened in the days of the Patents Company wars, the colorful period when Hollywood was being invented. A few years later, a writer to whom I foolishly showed my script ripped it off for a Canadian film that became regarded as a minor classic.

One reason my script didn't sell was that it was an epic—182 pages, a three-hour Western intended as a vehicle for John Wayne. Until I came to Hollywood, I didn't realize that producers judged scripts first and foremost on their length. I often witnessed the primitive ritual of a producer "weighing" a script in his hand to decide if it was too long or not. When my agent suggested I cut *California, Here I Come* to a normal length, I misguidedly removed an entire complex subplot and cut it down to 91 pages. Then people said it was too short for a feature film. Later I thought my script would have been better suited to being a novel than a film. Along the way in this process, I managed to get *California, Here I Come* to Wayne's story editor, Tom Kane. He read it and told me, "At this stage of his career, Duke doesn't want to play saddle tramps." That was a shame and ironic, because I based his character of Cheyenne Harry Ridge on the Cheyenne Harry characters played by Wayne's role model as an actor, Harry Carey, in the early Ford silent Westerns. Ford said to Bogdanovich about those films,

> They weren't shoot-'em-ups, they were character stories. Carey was a great actor, and we didn't dress him up like the cowboys you see on TV—all dolled up.... Carey was sort of a bum, a saddle tramp, instead of a great, bold, gun-fighting hero. All this was fifty per cent Carey and fifty per cent me. He always wore a dirty blue shirt and an old vest, patched overalls, very seldom carried a gun—and he didn't own a hat.

But Duke unfortunately had become too grand in his later years, playing cattle barons and other quasi-legendary figures, and that unfortunately blinded his story editor to the potential of my script, which would have given Wayne a memorable character to play. And Wayne disdained what was then being called the End-of-the-West cycle of Westerns, into which my script fell. Even Ford had trouble trying to get a remake of *The Last Outlaw* made in his twilight years. As I later learned from Harry Carey Jr., Ford pitched the idea to Walt Disney personally, without success.

As a budding screenwriter, was it frustrating that the industry was reluctant to tackle original stories because it was safer to just follow trends?

When I interviewed the already-reclusive Terrence Malick for my *Daily Variety* feature "Bread and Dreams: Young Screenwriters" in 1975 (which I reprinted in *Two Cheers for Hollywood*), he admitted that out of self-protection, "I find myself unconsciously censoring the offbeat when I write." Malick found the courage to break out of that box to make his own highly offbeat films, and it worked for him, even if his work sharply divides audiences and critics. I tried my damnedest from time to time to write scripts I thought might be "commercial" (a fool's errand, for no one can predict what makes a project a hit), but I mostly undercut my own career, to some degree unconsciously, by stubbornly following my instincts to write scripts that were politically or otherwise provocative.

Most of what I wrote was out of step with the prevailing commercial marketplace, which, as I came to realize, I was not suited to penetrate. The more pushback I found, the more perversely I kept following my independent course. In my early days in Hollywood, I went to an event for wannabe screenwriters and heard Mike Medavoy, an unusually smart Hollywood executive, tell an audience that you should only write screenplays that come from your heart, rather than trying to copy formulas. It surprised me to hear that, because after being in Hollywood for a year or so, I had already become jaded about whether writing from the heart would work in Hollywood. For me, it did and it didn't. But I listened and tried to follow his advice, even though Medavoy was an atypical Hollywood executive.

His advice was probably sound, because you did have some success "writing from the heart."

Yes, my track record was pretty good. In addition to the nine TV specials or documentaries I wrote, I turned out fourteen feature-length screenplays before retiring from the industry in 1984. Besides the two feature scripts that were filmed, *Blood & Guts* (1978), and *Rock 'n' Roll High School* (1979), and the partly filmed Roger Corman flying picture *Hard Time Aces*—a bizarre story in itself, but more on that later—I had four other screenplays optioned. This total doesn't include *Prom Night,* the 1980 sleeper hit horror film that was based on a story I wrote but for which I went uncredited. Nor does it include four features and a TV special that were stolen from me.

As you can tell from that long list, not only was I busy writing film scripts from 1966 to 1973 in Wisconsin, I worked steadily on film projects for the next eleven years, from the time I arrived in Hollywood until I finally turned my back on the industry in 1984. I also wrote many treatments and outlines that I pitched to producers and readers at production companies. I tried just about every kind of film I had any interest in, but I kept running into roadblocks of one kind or another. My record of produced vs. unproduced scripts was more or less normal for a professional screenwriter, but I found it frustrating to invest months of creative energy and passion in a project and not see it get made. When I wrote a book, it almost always got published, so eventually I realized that's what I should be doing. When you are writing a book, you are in effect the head of the studio. That kind of control is essential to my talent and sense of self-respect as a writer.

The total of fourteen scripts also does not include my strangest assignment, "writing the script" for *Up in Smoke.*

When that pot-smoking comedy starring Cheech & Chong became a surprise hit in 1978, Warner Books, which was publishing my baseball book, *High and Inside*, wanted to publish the shooting script of their film but learned that there wasn't one—it had been improvised by the stars. So my book editor asked me to quickly whip up a "shooting script" of *Up in Smoke* incorporating the dialogue and revising the scene descriptions from the studio cutting continuity. I went to see the movie on a Friday night and had the script done by Monday for Warner Books, but Cheech & Chong decided to publish a marijuana cookbook instead.

Another odd job I did for Warner Books was to transcribe and edit the book version of the Mel Brooks-Carl Reiner *2000 Year Old Man* records. I was surprised that Brooks and Reiner didn't care enough to be involved, but I did my best to serve their material while taking a free hand in editing their routines in ways that worked best and necessitated writing a phrase here and there to make the conversation flow. I didn't get an editing credit on the 1981 book version but once again was paid $500, the same amount I received for *High and Inside* as well as for *Up and Smoke*. (That $500 figure keeps ominously recurring in my career. It's not for nothing that my favorite cartoon character is Wile E. Coyote in the *Roadrunner* series, that modern version of the Myth of Sisyphus. Wile E. is my Familiar.)

Although my seven years as a full-time screenwriter were the worst period of my life except for my first nineteen years under the burden of my Catholic brainwashing, my life has gone uphill since I made the wise and necessary decision to "ankle the biz," as *Variety* would put it. So on balance, I am fortunate to have gone through all my experiences in Hollywood, the good, the bad, and the ugly. I will relate many of them to you in this and future chapters, Danny. As Nietzsche put it in *Twilight of the Idols,* "Out of life's school of war—What does not kill me makes me stronger." And I hope my account of that period in my career will be instructive (as well as amusing) to others who share the dreams and illusions I labored under and want to avoid the pitfalls I ultimately overcame.

Recalling for this project my misadventures and occasional triumphs in Hollywood has given me a richer perspective on what I learned from all that. I can see that now, even though when I told Irwin Shaw about one of the times a film project was stolen from me, he said it was the worst Hollywood story he had ever heard. I told him at least it had taught me a lesson. He said, "It's too expensive a lesson."

Wrestlemania

You've said that you broke into the industry writing for Roger Corman, and we will soon talk about him, but your first produced screenplay was for an indie Canadian film. How did Blood & Guts, *starring the veteran B-movie actor William Smith, come about?*

After my bad experience with my script about early Hollywood and a few months of despondency from December 1974 onward, I almost quit the business. I should have, but I didn't have enough sense. I was lured back into screenwriting in the spring of 1975 when my agent put me together with the Canadian director Paul Lynch. He was living in Hollywood and looking for suckers to write scripts for him. Paul asked me to write a script about professional wrestling. Paul's previous feature, *The Hard Part Begins*, was a pretty good, gritty film about a Country & Western singer on the road, and the wrestling movie we came up with was somewhat similar.

Was anyone surprised that your first feature film script to be produced wasn't Citizen Kane 2 *but a film about wrestling?*

I actually had a good idea for a "remake" of *Citizen Kane* but have never mentioned it to anybody for fear that someone would do it. I jumped at the chance to write a script about professional wrestling, since as a kid I had been a fan of wrestling on TV, watching such stars as Verne Gagne, 600-pound Haystacks Calhoun, Yukon Eric, and the villain who tore off Eric's cauliflower ear with his knee, 6'7" Killer Kowalski. We kids imitated Kowalski's "claw hold," and my mother didn't like our grabbing and twisting stomachs any more than when we'd pull ears and poke each other in the eye like the Three Stooges. I also went to a wrestling show at Milwaukee County Stadium. All I remember about that night is going on the field afterward and standing next to the dugout, and through the tunnel that led to the locker room, I could see Killer Kowalski in the nude. Probably not many people today could say that.

I can't say that.

Paul Lynch pitched his notion as a takeoff on Gorgeous George, the campy 1950s wrestling superstar I remembered well. He put on a dandified act that deliberately outraged people in that homophobic era. I found the topic fascinating,

The tension is palpable in this photo of the 1977 Canadian location shooting of *Blood & Guts*, as director Paul Lynch listens uneasily to an argument I am having with John Hunter, whose rewrite of my original script I was attempting to fix for a florid scene of an aging wrestler (William Smith) explaining his occupation.
(Quadrant Films/Melvin Simon Productions)

partly because, when Paul and I went to see a wrestling match at an arena downtown, I realized how homoerotic wrestling actually is. We met some wrestlers—including a group of female wrestlers the legendary Mildred Burke showed off from her wrestling school; I felt sad knowing we probably weren't going to cast any of them, so I put a tribute to Mildred in my script that didn't make it into the film— and I realized that the wrestlers were nice folks and honest about their work, but that the fans were often nuts. Many fans in arenas and watching matches on TV took the hokey dramaturgy of pro wrestling seriously and got all lathered up about good vs. evil. I decided to write a script in which the fakery of wrestling is a given (an unusual element for a film at the time, as a particularly knowledgeable reviewer pointed out) and the wrestlers are sympathetic but the fans are dangerously volatile.

This script was written on "spec," meaning no pay until the production found financing. I agreed to that if Paul would come to my apartment each day so we could talk through all the scenes. At the end of that creative six-month process, I wrote the script in six days. In re-reading it recently, I found that the structure and characters are solid, and the dialogue is "crisp and cryptic" (as John Ford

Although *Blood & Guts* is mostly a missed opportunity, some warmth and drama comes across thanks to the acting of Micheline Lanctôt as Lucky and William Smith as Dandy Dan O'Neil, a couple in a wrestling troupe who struggle to keep their relationship from crumbling. (Quadrant Films/Melvin Simon Productions)

said good film dialogue should be) without spelling out the themes of the story. The only dubious elements come in an overly melodramatic and violent series of events in the finale that seem unduly influenced by the pervasive violence of cinema in that period.

Unfortunately, as soon as I finished writing the script, the problems began. Without consulting me, Paul had copies in pseudo-leather maroon covers bound with rivets instead of brads and the title embossed on the covers in silver lettering. That thoroughly unprofessional way of presenting a script screamed "Amateur time!" Paul sent it to all seven major studios at once rather than taking a more measured approach. That tacky presentation helped account for all seven studios rejecting the script simultaneously a week later. But it was also true that Hollywood shortsightedly thought wrestling was horribly déclassé—this was not long before a glitzier version of that ersatz sport became a runaway success with middle America in the 1980s via the World Wrestling Foundation on cable TV, forcing the studios to pay attention—and maybe they didn't like the script, either. Even by 1986, when Woody Allen made *Hannah and Her Sisters*, he had the Max von Sydow character, a killjoy and misanthropic snob, say after he spends a night uncharacteristically channel-surfing TV, "Can you imagine the level of a mind that watches wrestling, huh?" By 2008, however, the fine Mickey Rourke picture *The Wrestler*, which tells quite a similar story to *Blood & Guts* although with better production values, could be released by a major studio and gather prestigious reviews.

But back in the Seventies, we were condemned to spend several years finding funding for our wrestling movie. After I had almost given up, my girlfriend Laurel Gilbert, while we were attending a Malibu party, found a producer of low-budget films who perked up when she told him about our project. He was an amiable fellow but eventually went to prison for reasons unrelated to our project. But before he was incarcerated, he provided a letter of intent that, in the irrational world of film production, eventually helped attract serious interest in Canada. The producer and executive producer who attached themselves to the script found an American tax-shelter company, Melvin Simon Productions, willing to put up enough money (barely) to make the film, with the help of the Canadian Film Development Corporation. Paul Lynch directed *Blood & Guts* in Hamilton, Ontario, and environs.

I liked Blood & Guts *when I saw it in 1978 because of its authenticity regarding minor league wrestling, its acting— I was a fan of William Smith dating back to the TV Western series,* Laredo—*and its sweetness despite pretending to be tough rather than sweet, with a smart script. But you have said the script was butchered.*

Since the tax-shelter laws required one Canadian screenwriter, I reluctantly agreed to let one (and only one) writer revise the script, with the caveat that only necessary logistical changes would be made to switch it to Canadian locations and change it from period, the 1950s, to a contemporary setting. I can hardly believe now, and am ashamed to tell you, that Paul somehow persuaded me, like an idiot, to return $1,500 of my $15,000 fee to pay the other writer. Then, behind my back, Paul betrayed me by bringing in *two* writers who were old cronies of his, William Gray (who was also the film's editor) and John Hunter (who had written and helped produce *The Hard Part Begins* and was co-producer of *Blood & Guts*), to drastically rewrite my script. I did not discover what had been done to it until I arrived in Toronto shortly before the start of shooting in August 1977.

When I told Paul over the phone that I was resigning from *Variety* to work on the film, he put Hunter on to frantically try to talk me out of it. Hunter said, "Joe, no one quits *Variety!*" I did not realize that they simply were trying to keep me away from the production and from finding out how they had mangled my script. In retrospect Hunter may have been right in trying to discourage me from quitting *Variety*, but their motives were base. I was not persuaded but had to do double duty as unit publicist and screenwriter to justify the expense of my plane ticket and hotel room. Paul failed to meet me at the airport as he had promised and avoided me throughout the shooting, which mystified me since we had seemed to have such a close friendship while I was writing the first version of the script.

When I read the shooting script in a state of shock, I found that all my dialogue was gone, even though the characters and plot were mostly the same. I considered dialogue my best quality as a screenwriter, more so than plotting, which I sometimes struggled with. The dialogue in the Gray-Hunter script was awful, on-the-nose, simple-mindedly expository, explaining jokes as well as pretentious in spelling out the movie's populist themes because they didn't think viewers would be smart enough to figure them out themselves. A friend had given me an essay by film theorist Roland Barthes describing wrestling as a morality play for the masses, which I thought was valid and a good organizing principle for the narrative, but I hadn't intended my lead character, the aging wrestler Dandy Dan, to explain that theory to the audience while orating on a dock.

I also complained to Hunter about how they had thrown out one of my favorite scenes—the wrestling troupe's indomitably jovial manager, Red Henkel (Henry Beckman), relaxing in bed in his motel room with a cigar and a wrestling magazine. Wearing only shorts and T-shirt, his wooden leg propped in a chair, Red listens to a radio playing Big Band music while pitching his young phenom, Jungle Jim, over the phone to a promoter ("I'm telling ya, Louie, this is the hottest act since Sally Rand. Hell, yes. They had their goddam dorks in their hands.... Oh, screw Joe Louis! Who the hell remembers him? This is new!"). Red's wife, Shirley, wakes in the other bed with a frowsy female stranger. Trying to remember who it is, Shirley lifts the woman's peroxide blonde head and frowns at the sight of her caked makeup, then thumps the head back on the pillow and tells Red she loves him. Red blows her a kiss and replies, "Love ya, too, baby." When I argued to reinstate that scene, Hunter sniffed that he found it "perverted" and

The stylish poster for *Blood & Guts* is better than the movie, but the executive producer killed the film in order to get a bigger tax writeoff. (Quadrant Films/Melvin Simon Productions)

not only refused to let me put it back in the movie but also dropped Red's wife and his impotence from the script. That's the backward mentality I was dealing with.

The film's line producer, Peter O'Brian, reflected in a 2003 interview about the tax-shelter era in Canadian filmmaking and the so-called "Canuxploitation" films that often resulted, "The era could have produced all kinds of great things, but we screwed it up, exploited it and destroyed and pillaged and desecrated it." O'Brian was sympathetic, up to a point, in encouraging me to improve the script I found in Toronto for *Blood & Guts*, which I convinced him was urgently in need of salvaging. I tried my best to fix it during the first few weeks of filming, so the film would not be too disgraceful for me to leave my name on it as the first-position screenwriter and author of the story. But John Hunter drove me to the location every day in an attempt to counteract my rewriting. We had a pitched battle of words on location over his attempt to rewrite my rewrite of what he clearly saw as the big, Oscar-contender scene of Bill Smith's Dan spouting his platitudes on the dock while verbalizing the themes of the picture in a way that seems terribly false for the man in the arena. We reached an uneasy compromise, eliminating only part of Hunter's purple prose for that one scene in the film that Smith overacted, indulging in the kind of "most acting" that tends to win Oscars or Emmys instead of the more subtle kind of acting that tends to get overlooked.

What were you going for with the characters and situation in your plot about mentorship and romantic rivalry between the old and young wrestlers, Dan and Jim and their love interest, Lucky? I think it follows The Lusty Men, *in which Robert Mitchum mentors Arthur Kennedy on rodeo performing while Susan Hayward loves them both, and precedes* Bull Durham, *in which Kevin Costner mentors Tim Robbins on baseball while Susan Sarandon loves them both.*

During the shooting of *Blood & Guts*, I gave an interview to the *New York Times* describing it as a takeoff on Noël Coward's play *Design for Living,* which he described as "the story of three people who love each other very much." (That play was filmed in high style by Ernst Lubitsch in 1933 with a screenplay by Ben Hecht, who made major changes and improvements.) My interview surprised O'Brian, since by that stage in the convoluted process, the script had morphed considerably away from that kinky romantic approach.

Only years after writing *Blood & Guts* did I realize what had actually inspired it. This is a strange but telling story, Danny, about a writer's subconscious and how it can underlie a story without his realizing it. I had written a key dramatic scene of Dandy Dan returning unexpectedly to the motel room he shares with his girlfriend, Lucky (played by Micheline Lanctôt). Dan, slightly loaded, walks up the stairs to find the young wrestler, Jim (played by Brian Clarke), his protégé and rival, leaving their room. Dan growls an insult at Jim and finds Lucky inside on the bed, nude. Dan slaps her face, and a brawl ensues with Jim. Red's wife joins in as a chimp from Jim's ring act runs madly around his cage, banging his head against the bars. In the film, the guilty couple are surprised in bed together in Jim's room, looking sheepish and anxious, expecting a brawl, but Dan, standing in the doorway, just looks anguished, moaning and growling an insult at Lucky, and walks out. It's more effective without the physical violence.

Little did I realize that during the writing and production of the film that this scene of betrayal, a turning point in the relationship between Dan and the other characters, replicated what had happened shortly before I wrote *Blood & Guts* when I went to my girlfriend's apartment unexpectedly and found her with my roommate in a compromising position. I had repressed that painful encounter so deeply, because I couldn't face the consequences, that I didn't realize why I had written it into the movie. *Blood & Guts* was largely about that friendship, the romance, and the betrayal.

How blind we can be, as people and as artists.

The scene in the motel room is one of the best in the movie, along with Dan's heart attack and the moment when a doctor tells him matter-of-factly that he has to quit wrestling. The doctor scene had been dropped from the script, but I insisted it was essential to the movie and was able to persuade O'Brian to put it back in. That necessitated the overnight construction and equipping of an office set and the hiring of an actor to play the doctor. Even though the spine of *Blood & Guts* is my interior psychodrama about a painful time in my romantic life, the film ends with Dan and Lucky walking out of the arena together arm-in-arm, emotionally battered but resilient as a couple: A fantasy I hoped might come true in my life.

But the best scene that was filmed, one that was fairly close to what I had written, also didn't make it into the movie. Dan takes Jim to visit a beaten-down, punchy middle-aged wrestler named Gus living in a trailer park. In my version, Gus is a religious fanatic who's eagerly preparing for the Apocalypse ("I'm in training for the big one"). The point Dan is subtly making to Jim is that he should quit wrestling before he turns into Gus. The three-minute scene, with Harry Prout, a former football player, as Gus, was beautifully acted and received a good response at a preview. But at the production meeting afterward, O'Brian noted that the most enthusiastic preview card had been filled out by the director's elderly British father, who singled out that scene and related to it emotionally. So, irrationally, that became the reason for the producer cutting the scene with Gus, over my vehement objections. O'Brian promised to give me the cut footage but never did.

You believe that the picture could have been better if it had a bigger budget and was set in the Fifties.

To make matters worse, the executive producer had pocketed half of the already minimal $600,000 budget up front, making it hard to shoot a road picture about wrestling. I had to go into the streets of Hamilton to round up enough extras to play fans and make the wrestling scenes marginally believable (although one reviewer—your brother, Gerry, in the Canadian film magazine *Take One*—charitably called those scenes "Bressonian"). Also, transforming the film from period to contemporary, which had to be done for budget reasons, ruined much of its point. Dandy Dan's fop act, carrying a cane and wearing a shiny gold-colored top hat; gold lamé cape, vest, and trousers; and a curly blond wig, would not have stirred the same kind of conflicted feelings in the late 1970s as Gorgeous George's campy routine did in the '50s.

Was it an unhappy shoot because of the low budget?

Well, some on the Canadian crew sensibly groused about how the film was supposed to take place in the US, a common insult to filmmaking in Canada. Some of the crew also were hostile to me because of my insistence on rewriting the script and changing some of the settings, which required extra work on their part.

What about Paul Lynch? You said he avoided you during shooting, but did you think he was doing a good job directing the film?

During the first week of shooting, Peter O'Brian wanted to fire Paul for his ineptitude. He covered every scene from every angle, mechanically and awkwardly, in effect relying on the editor to direct the film. I stupidly defended Paul, helping him to keep his job. I've sometimes reflected that if I had been smarter and less blindly loyal, I should have lobbied to replace him myself, since I knew the story inside and out and could have directed it more effectively. But I now realize that under the tax-shelter laws, the film needed a Canadian director. Paul Schrader, who read my original script before production began, said it best after seeing *Blood & Guts* at the Cannes marketplace: "I loved the script, but I hated the film."

In my conversations with O'Brian over dinner that first week, I strenuously argued that our young cinematographer,

Mark Irwin, was mistakenly using a shadowy lighting style in the ring, when the wrestling scenes should instead be brightly light and cartoonish in their intensity, unlike the scenes elsewhere, which could be more darkly lit. Mark, whose second feature it was, was too much in the thrall of the great Gordon Willis ("The Prince of Darkness"), but I prevailed in that key matter of style. Irwin went on to a long career, notably working with David Cronenberg, Wes Craven, and the Farrelly Brothers.

Well, I liked Blood & Guts. *I appreciated that it wasn't a look at "glamorous" superstar wrestling but Grade-B, sideshow-type wrestling, long bus rides, small arenas, cheap motels, doing laundry. So it seemed unusually authentic. It got good reviews and won awards in Canada. Maybe Paul Schrader didn't watch wrestling as a kid.*

Thank you kindly. After the film received some good reviews and one poor notice on its 1978 opening in Toronto, the executive producer dumped the film to claim a tax writeoff after it played a one-week engagement in North Carolina under the title *Rasslin'*. And, to cap it all, after the film's uneventful release, Paul Lynch told me, "We should have filmed your script." No wonder screenwriters despair.

The good news about my benighted initial foray into professional screenwriting is that the acting was appreciated. Bill Smith gives a sensitive and beautiful performance; Micheline Lanctôt (a future director) is wry and wise as Lucky; and Henry Beckman received a Canadian Film Award for his colorful and touching performance as Red. I received a writing nomination, one of eleven the film received, including best picture and best director.

I am most happy for Henry, a character actor who had been paying his dues for a long time (including in a bit part in Wilder's *Kiss Me, Stupid*) before getting recognition as the funky, gutsy, warm-hearted manager of the wrestling troupe. I wrote Henry a letter of congratulations for his best supporting actor award and said I was delighted that he understood his character better than I did. What I meant by that was, after Dan has to stop wrestling because of his heart attack, I had written that as their two new station wagons roll on to the next town, we see that the name of the wrestling troupe, "BLOOD AND GUTS," has been painted over on the side of both wagons and replaced with the name of their new young star, "JUNGLE JIM," and zebra stripes. In the script as it was revised for filming, it is Dan's name on the side of the troupe's bus that has been painted over. "Red wouldn't do that," Henry pointed out. How right he was—Red was the soul of loyalty—so we followed Henry's advice. (I later gave that as an example for my screenwriting students of what an actor can bring to a script.) Henry told me he framed my letter and kept it on the wall of his study.

Did Blood & Guts *have an afterlife or did it just disappear?*

It played briefly on the Z Channel, a pioneering cable channel for art movies in Los Angeles. And now it can be watched on Amazon Video. Many years after the film's theatrical release, I also found out that it had been released on homevideo outside the US. An Irish professor friend told me her son, a wrestler, had bought a VHS tape, and they watched it together with pleasure. I bought a copy and enjoyed seeing the B-movie actress Sybil Danning giving an amusing introduction on the tape while wearing a wrestling outfit in a ring, which I had nothing to do with. Naturally, I never saw any money from the back end; I was supposed to receive five percent of the executive producer's share of revenues—*not* five percent of the net profits from the film. Unfortunately, I didn't read the contract carefully enough. And he made sure it took a loss anyway for tax purposes. So my work on the project was a waste of four and a half years of effort.

During this three-year period, was your personal life any calmer than your professional life?

They were interrelated fuckups. In early 1975, before I began work on *Blood & Guts,* when I was living in the duplex in Beverly Hills with my roommate and his girlfriend, he started harassing me with crank phone calls and other hostile ploys to drive me out. One day I came home from work and found that he had moved all the furniture out of the living room. I said nothing, and the next day it had all been put back. I thought he was doing these petty but disturbing things so he could move in a male friend who was starting to spend a lot of time with him; I wondered if they were trying to carry on a clandestine gay relationship.

In my agitated state of mind during that period, my romantic life descended into what Laurel and Hardy would call "a fine mess." I had been dating three women, an actress, a film publicist, and, most seriously, a woman who worked for the film program at the Los Angeles County Museum of Art. Playing the field that way was uncharacteristic of me, since I had usually been monogamous, but perhaps because I felt so distraught and disoriented about my recent screenwriting snafu over my Western project, I was going Hollywood in an unhealthy way. I broke up with the girlfriend who worked for the museum because I suspected she was seeing another man. She confirmed she was but wouldn't identify him. Our relationship was already falling apart when I had gone to her apartment and found my roommate sitting there with her. In those days, rather than have confrontations, I would pretend that problems were not happening. So I left without demanding to know what he was doing there. I somehow managed to put the incident in the back of my mind only to have it resurface when I wrote that scene for *Blood & Guts*.

Years later, at a party at Paul Schrader's, I encountered that former girlfriend, who had married a prominent actor. She immediately started asking me how my old roommate was doing, talking about him in an eager, intimate way that suddenly made me realize what I should have known in 1975, that he was the man she had been cheating on me with. And that was why he was trying to force me out of the house. (I escaped my roommate, as I mentioned earlier, by moving down the block to the apartment house managed by the John Ford actress Jane Chang.)

While being harassed at home, I was taking refuge with the publicist for a few days. That ended when my roommate called both her and the actress, disingenuously asking each if I was with her or the other woman, and helpfully dropping their names. So the upshot was that I broke up with three women in a single day. And in an odd coincidence, that same night I saw a preview of the brilliant satire of reckless Hollywood sexual mores, *Shampoo*, which ends with Warren Beatty's character breaking up with three women he was dating. I learned my lesson the hard way at the same time I saw my romantic bungling reflected in that acerbic yet poignant cautionary tale.

To add to the irony, the girlfriend who cheated on me told me she had once screwed Beatty in his penthouse at the Beverly Wilshire Hotel, and as she was dressing to leave, he was already on the phone to another woman, inviting her up. I realized wryly that when you live in Wisconsin, your girlfriend might be *fantasizing* about sex with Warren Beatty, but in Hollywood, she actually may *be* having sex with Warren Beatty. (Even lower behavior, however, is when a woman boasts of a famous man whose overtures she has rejected, as two women I briefly dated in L.A. did in claiming to have turned down passes from a Middle Eastern king and a winner of the Nobel Prize for Literature.)

After seeing my absurd love life reflected in *Shampoo,* never again would I attempt to live the kind of clandestine lifestyle that had caused me to endure such romantic chaos. I not only wasn't suited for it but wasn't clever or devious enough to pull it off when I tried. And I made another resolution. I had dated a number of actresses after joining *Daily Variety;* I was fascinated by the profession but found that neuroticism and narcissism seemed part of the job description. So I vowed never to date another actress, and that brought some sanity to my love life. I made the mistake of telling my critic friend Stuart Byron about my vow, and he reported it in *Film Comment,* while quoting John Milius as describing most women in Hollywood to me as "mercs," or mercenaries.

I hesitate to ask if your love life in L.A. became more stable.

Yes, for a time. It was in 1976 that I met Laurel Gilbert, the young woman who first found a producer who wanted to make *Blood & Guts,* and we entered into a serious relationship. She was a law student and became the model for the bright and sexy character of Kate Rambeau played by Dey Young in *Rock 'n' Roll High School.*

Scripts for Roger Corman

How did you start to actually sell scripts to Roger Corman's company?

It took ten years of steady work writing screenplays before I sold one. That shows how determined I was. I didn't have luck with major studios until later but, like so many other young people at the time, I managed to break in with Roger, who was a maverick and something of a visionary, as well as a notorious cheapskate. I worked on three scripts for his independent company New World Pictures from 1976 to 1979, including co-writing *Rock 'n' Roll High School.*

While waiting in 1976 for *Blood & Guts* to find financing, I wrote *Rock City,* my fictionalized takeoff on Dick Clark and his *American Bandstand* TV show. It spoofed Clark's manipulation of the teenage audience. The story line involved a handsome but no-talent kid who dances on the show—think Fabian—being groomed as a rock star by the TV impresario. Jon Davison, the future producer who was then working as Corman's head of production, optioned

Rock City for $500, with the intention of Joe Dante and Allan Arkush making their debuts as co-directors. Joe, who came from Philadelphia, would have directed the story scenes, and Allan, a rock music fanatic, would have been in charge of the musical numbers.

But the project abruptly collapsed when Clark came into Corman's office one day, and Roger, without thinking, dashed into the office of his story editor, Frances Doel, and asked her for a copy of the *Rock City* script so Clark could read it. The next day Clark expressed his disapproval over the way I treated him satirically as an exploiter of teenagers. So that was the end of *Rock City*. Otherwise in doing that subject we would have been years ahead of *The Idolmaker* and the various iterations of *Hairspray*.

But at least *Rock City* led to my being hired to write the 1979 punk rock musical *Rock 'n' Roll High School*, since it led Jon, Joe, and Allan to think of me as an expert on teenage movies. Instead of making their directing debuts with *Rock City*, Joe and Allan debuted instead by co-directing *Hollywood Boulevard*, the 1976 spoof of New World that Davison produced and I appeared in. On the strength of the professionalism and verve of that super-low-budget film, Allan was able to make his solo directorial debut for Roger with *Rock 'n' Roll High School*, while Joe made his with *Piranha* in 1978. As you wrote in your book *Cult Movies*, Danny, *Rock 'n' Roll High School*, starring the Ramones, eventually became a cult classic after falling through the cracks on its initial release.

I found it amusing that I got the job because I was considered an expert on teenage movies. Although I had been an early fan of rock 'n' roll, my experiences in my teenage years alienated me from that age group. I felt about teenagers pretty much the same way Sam Fuller did: when I asked Sam what he thought of *Rebel Without a Cause,* he said, "I hate these goddam teenagers and their fucking problems." But I liked the Ramones because their elemental beat and witty lyrics reminded me of the 1950s rock I liked so much. Some of the Ramones' lyrics, such as those of "Teenage Lobotomy," are worthy of Cole Porter: "Slugs and snails are after me/DDT keeps me happy/Now I guess I'll have to tell 'em/That I got no cerebellum."

When you were working on the script for the anarchic Rock 'n' Roll High School, *were you thinking about how the political climate was changing in the country and in Hollywood?*

Yes, when we filmed it in late 1978, I knew we were sneaking in under the wire before Ronald Reagan got into the White house. I deliberately turned what started out as a frivolous teenage comedy into an anarchic political satire based partly on the student strike my father led while in high school and the 1970 Sterling Hall bombing in Madison.

Gabba Gabba Hey

During this time when you were starting to sell scripts, were you looking for the right time to quit Daily Variety *to try to make a full-time career as a screenwriter?*

Yes, but because *Rock City* wasn't made, I didn't leave the newspaper job until July 1977, when I went to Toronto to work on the filming of *Blood & Guts.* Earlier that year I had already started writing *Rock 'n' Roll High School.* Arkush called me back from the location of *Blood & Guts* in the latter stages of shooting to resume work on the script for his film. The evolution of *Rock 'n' Roll High School* is a long and colorful story, so permit me to read an entry—slightly condensed, with a few inserts—from my 1999 *Book of Movie Lists:*

> The project originally was called *Girls' Gym,* the title of a sixty-page treatment dictated into a tape recorder over a two-day period in 1977 by the director, Allan Arkush, and his partner in the New World editing department, Joe Dante. The treatment had no plot, only a series of scenes in which high school kids goof off around the school. In the climax, a chimpanzee drinks a drug concocted by the students, turns into a King Kong-size behemoth, and breaks through the roof of the school. There was no political dimension to the treatment; the students were simply having some reckless fun. Charles B. Griffith, screenwriter of such Corman classics as *A Bucket of Blood* and *The Little Shop of Horrors,* was the first writer hired for the project, but I was told that Arkush found his work unsatisfactory. I never saw his script. Griffith did not receive screen credit....
>
> I was handed the *Girls' Gym* treatment on a Friday afternoon and told that if I could come up with a plotline over the weekend, I could write the script. Since I had attended a strict Jesuit

high school… I naturally thought of making the story revolve around a repressive administration's attempt to control rebellious students. I based the plot on the experiences of my father, Raymond E. McBride, when he led a student strike as student body president at Superior (Wis.) Central High School in 1927, to protest the firing of one of their favorite teachers, Lulu J. Dickinson, for mocking the school board members in her humanities classes; she ultimately was rehired. I combined that real-life event with some anarchic elements from the 1933 Jean Vigo classic *Zéro de Conduite*, about students at a boarding school who rebel against their tyrannical headmaster. My father was excited when I told him about *Rock 'n' Roll High School* but was deeply disappointed when he saw it and realized it wasn't a docudrama about his 1927 school strike.

Since the film industry was churning out mostly male buddy-buddy movies in the misogynistic decade of the 1970s, I decided to make it a female buddy-buddy movie, partly along the lines of some of Roger's other popular genre pieces with female leads. I based the character of the brainy and alluring Kate Rambeau (Dey Young) on my former girlfriend Laurel Gilbert; in her large glasses, Dey Young looked remarkably like Laurel. Wanting to slip a subtle double entendre into the name of this deceptively demure character, I dubbed her "Rambeau" after the town of Ramsdale in Vladimir Nabokov's *Lolita*. Arkush modeled the rock 'n' roll fanaticism of Riff Randell (P. J. Soles) on three girls he knew while working as an usher at New York's Fillmore East and borrowed her first name from a character in West Side *Story*. I drew Riff's bold, rebellious traits from my first girlfriend, the late [Kathy Wolf].

I named school quarterback Tom Roberts (Vincent Van Patten) after the star athlete at my high school, Tom Fox (coincidentally, Kate refers to Tom as a "fox"). Arkush named the sympathetic teacher Mr. McGree (Paul Bartel) after the Belgian painter René Magritte. The principal, Miss Togar (Mary Woronov), was named by one of the other writers, Russ Dvonch, after his high school principal (in my script, Woronov was the girls' gym teacher, Miss McQueen). Arkush named the school *macher*, Eaglebauer (Clint Howard), after the character played by Edward Everett Horton in Ernst Lubitsch's *Design for Living*.

I named the school Ronald Reagan High School (Reagan was still three years away from being elected president). The ending was to include a shot of the students blowing up a statue of Reagan. Corman, however, did not want to offend Reagan, who lived near him in Pacific Palisades. So I came up with Vince Lombardi High School, after the Green Bay Packers' football coach, whom I used to watch in action during his glory days in the early 1960s, when I was selling hot dogs at Milwaukee County Stadium. Lombardi's gung-ho approach and famous saying "Winning isn't everything—it's the only thing" made him a perfect symbol of the militaristic discipline the students disdain. Ironically, in the dismal sequel, *Rock 'n' Roll High School Forever* (1991), the school was called Ronald Reagan High School, but by that time, Reagan had come and gone as president of the United States and was safer to satirize.

I decided to politicize the ending of *Rock 'n' Roll High School*, in keeping with its newfound radicalism. The idea of having the students blow up their school was suggested to me by the 1970 Sterling Hall bombing at the University of Wisconsin, Madison.... In his 1997 laserdisc commentary, Arkush claimed that blowing up a high school "had been a fantasy of mine since I was in high school." If that was the case, he didn't mention it to me at the time, nor did he show me a treatment he claimed to have written containing such a scene. In fact, Arkush was nervous about my ending, telling me he was afraid that blowing up the school "would make the kids unsympathetic." However, "As far as Roger was concerned, [blowing up the school] was the whole reason for making the movie," Arkush recalled. Corman felt that what made *Rock 'n' Roll High School* successful was "the anarchy of the film, the fact that it is so wild and the fact that the students act out every teenager's ultimate dream—they take over the high school, and finally they blow it up in the last scene."

The way I managed to talk Arkush into going along with my ending was by passing him the information (gleaned from a fellow journalist) that director Jonathan Kaplan was planning to end his then-filming *Over the Edge* with kids setting fire to a community center. As I correctly guessed, that whetted our director's desire to outdo a more expensive major-studio movie directed by a fellow Corman protégé. In his 1981 book *Cult Movies*, Danny Peary writes of *Rock 'n' Roll High School*, "This may be a silly comedy but there is no other commercial American film in which an American institution is destroyed and no one is punished for the deed."

After I had written five drafts of the script, Arkush, at Paul Bartel's urging, decided to take the movie in an even zanier direction, handing it over for a rewrite to Richard Whitley and Russ Dvonch, who had written for the TV series *National Lampoon's Animal House*. On the laserdisc, Whitley explained their approach to *Rock 'n' Roll High School*: "Allan was talking about, you know, political and social values, and Russ and I just wanted to get into, like, Three Stooges and Bob Hope jokes." They rewrote the dialogue and added the characters of Eaglebauer and the fascistic hall monitors (Loren Lester and Daniel Davies), among other changes, but kept the other characters and much of the story line, including the anarchic final sequences. Among the discarded elements were a track competition and war games conducted on the school athletic field against students dressed as Arabs ("We may have to fight those Arabs for that oil some day," explains a jingoistic teacher). Whitley and Dvonch added more scenes for the rock group—I had been told we could afford only three songs, but Arkush somehow managed forty-five!—and the amusing sex education lesson Eaglebauer gives to Tom and Kate....

I was told to think of the Tubes for the rock group while working on the script. Before the Ramones were signed, offers were made to other rockers, including Todd Rundgren, who passed because he thought the script should have been more serious in tone, like Lindsay Anderson's *If....,* which was similarly inspired by *Zéro de Conduite.* Cheap Trick asked for too much money; Devo and Van Halen also were considered. The Ramones proved a perfect choice, because their punk-rock style was a satirical throwback to the early days of rock 'n' roll in the 1950s, and we were satirizing '50s movies about teenage rebellion, such as *Blackboard Jungle* and *Rock Around the Clock* (filmed at the same school as our movie).... Dick Miller, the Corman regular who plays the police chief, improvised his funny line "They're ugly, ugly, ugly people" after the director said to him, "Tell us what you think of the Ramones."....

Originally, Arkush planned to blow up the school by using a miniature, but Corman said it would be too expensive and wouldn't look believable. So the director was forced to blow up a building for real. The production rented a Catholic school that had been condemned because it wasn't earthquake-safe, Mount Carmel High School in the Watts section of Los Angeles. On the first of two chilly December nights scheduled for shooting the ending, the veteran special effects man, Roger George (who had a large burn scar across his face), rigged a naphthalene explosion, with powder charges in mortars and propane flame pots arrayed from the ground to the roof. The preparations looked so hairy to me that I decided to play it safe and watch the filming from across the street.

Sure enough, there was a huge explosion, sending out a large fireball and showering glass over the crowd of extras. Arkush said the explosion "was about five times bigger than it was supposed to be." Along with trees and bushes, the American flag caught fire and tumbled spectacularly from its pole, making an impressive shot in slow motion, but one that Arkush decided not to use because it would have seemed "too symbolic." When the explosion took place at three in the morning, dazed and angry neighborhood residents streamed out of their homes in bathrobes, wondering what was happening—no one had warned them. Fortunately, there were no serious injuries, but the explosion gave some people minor burns and also broke windows and left scorch marks on the building.

Parts of *Rock 'n' Roll High School* were directed by Joe Dante (including the title number in the girls' gym, the students trashing the cafeteria, the elegantly shot long take in the girls' bathroom, and Riff winning a radio ticket contest), Jerry Zucker (scenes of the students running wild in the hallway), and Jon Davison (who rigged the ingenious paper-airplane gimmick with Zucker).

Dante took over the first unit for the last few days of shooting after Arkush collapsed in the Van Nuys High School gym and was taken away in an ambulance, brought down by the stress of the twenty-day schedule. Still, *Rock 'n' Roll High School* is a genuinely auteurist work, reflecting Arkush's distinctive vision in every frame.

The cinematographer of *Rock 'n' Roll High School*, Dean Cundey, later shot Steven Spielberg's *Jurassic Park*. Arkush notes, "*One shot* in *Jurassic Park* cost more than this movie."

None of us was paid much for our work on *Rock 'n' Roll High School*, although over the years, the Writers Guild forced Roger to pay the writers some residuals. Under the opening credits, when the name of New World Pictures appears on screen, you can dimly hear bird sounds mixed in during postproduction. The birds are going, "Cheep, cheep, cheep." Corman didn't notice the dig at his legendary cheapness....

Some people were upset about the school insurrection scenes, including Jack Valenti, president of the Motion Picture Association of America. After attacking the movie on a Los Angeles radio station, reviewer Gary Franklin encountered Valenti the next day at an industry function and told him about it. Valenti obliged with a radio interview describing *Rock 'n' Roll High School* as "swill." I told people that what Valenti *really* meant was that the movie was "swell," but with his Texas accent it just sounded like "swill."

Why do you think your father said he was "ashamed" of you for making such a popular movie as Rock 'n' Roll High School?

Although I based it on the student strike he had helped to lead in high school, an event that drew national attention, he wasn't prepared for the fact that *Rock 'n' Roll High School* turned the subject of his rather decorous youthful revolt into a musical about kids getting so turned on by a scruffy punk rock band that they blow up their school. He not only was filled with disdain for what he considered a tawdry exploitation movie but also for the son who, in his eyes, had sunk so low as to make a career in the cultural cesspool that turned out such a debased product. I am hypothesizing his motives; I never bothered to ask.

My mother, on the other hand, who was more sophisticated, liked the movie. She told me she hadn't realized it would be a satire and was pleasantly surprised to find that was the case. When I relayed her praise to Allan Arkush, however, he became indignant and said, "It isn't a *satire!* I meant every word in it!" I guess he doesn't understand the concept of satire.

Were you disappointed that Rock 'n' Roll High School *took a while to find an audience? You were grateful that I called everyone's attention to it with the positive chapter in one of my* Cult Movies *books.*

Roger released *Rock 'n' Roll High School* his usual way, as a formulaic teen exploitation movie, in the southwest, in nabes (as *Variety* called neighborhood theaters) and drive-ins. One was the Texas Theatre in the Dallas suburb of Oak Cliff, where Lee Harvey Oswald had been captured. There was no ready-made audience waiting for a punk rock musical starring the Ramones, who had a passionate following but had a hard time getting their records played on the radio because of their edgy lyrics about child abuse, glue-sniffing, lobotomies, and rebellion. The movie only started drawing audiences after a Chicago theater programmed it as a midnight attraction, and Gene Siskel and Roger Ebert hailed it on their syndicated TV show. Arkush credited them with having "saved the movie." Other theaters around the country began playing it at midnight for months as a cult film. Roger Corman joked that it was "my new *Harder They Come,*" after the reggae film that he turned into a sleeper hit, although ours was not a super moneymaker. But *Rock 'n' Roll High School* kept playing steadily around the country until MTV showed it, the first time that rock network had shown an entire feature.

That was a mixed blessing, because suddenly the theatrical audience dried up. The film disappeared for a few years. But it since has had a number of editions on homevideo, however, most recently a beautifully restored Blu-ray edition from Shout! Factory. I have run into quite a lot of people who tell me it's one of their favorite movies, sometimes their number-one favorite. (I hope the students who told me that were not pulling my leg.) And the most remarkable kudo was supplied by Stephen Armstrong, who wrote a thoughtful, well-researched 2023 book about the film, *I Want You Around: The Ramones and the Making of "Rock 'n' Roll High School,"* as a companion piece for his two entertaining books of interviews with New World veterans, including me. (There are so many great Roger Corman stories, most of which were not told by Roger himself in his somewhat disappointingly sketchy 1990 autobiography, *How I Made a Hundred Movies in Hollywood and Never Lost a Dime.*) What a gas it is to have a good book written about a movie you helped make! And I wrote this in my Amazon review of *I Want You Around*:

> I am pleased above all that the book is fair, a rare quality in a book about a film, since filmmaking is such a contentious endeavor, and it's hard to be judicious. But Armstrong is fair to everyone involved, including the various writers and directors, and pays well-informed and informative tribute to the collaborative nature of film. *RRHS,* which has become a cult classic, is a supreme example of collaboration, with many disparate talents coming together on an unusual project that despite great odds worked out well.
>
> I appreciate Armstrong's carefully researched chapter on my contributions to the screenplay....

On December 1, 1978, during a break from shooting the school board scene for *Rock 'n' Roll High School* at the former Mount Carmel High School, I called my agent from a pay phone in the hallway and learned that Barbra Streisand's Barwood Films and Orion Pictures had optioned my screenplay about the TV quiz show scandals of the 1950s, *Big Money.* I never felt more elated in Hollywood than that moment when I went back into the board room to shoot the scene, not realizing that this would be the peak of my career as a feature film screenwriter.

What is the story of the third project you worked on for Corman, Hard Time Aces? *Why was it partly filmed but then abandoned?*

Hard Time Aces, a longtime pet project of Roger's, was my craziest experience with a film. It was a story about former American fliers in the Philippines in 1946, left over from World War II, who come to the rescue of villagers menaced by bandits. One of the writers I followed on the script was Robert Towne, who sensibly bowed out after two days. When I was hired in November 1977, Roger instructed me, "Get a print of *The Magnificent Seven* and rip it off." He provided me a 16mm projector and a print I studied carefully, along with the original Kurosawa classic *Seven Samurai.*

Director Allan Arkush and lead actress P. J. Soles enlivened
Rock 'n' Roll High School with their dynamism, while Ramones
lead singer, Joey Ramone, provided droll counterpoint with his
laidback eccentricities. (New World Pictures)

Hard Time Aces was to be directed by Cirio Santiago,
a Filipino hack filmmaker Roger liked to work with, partly
because he had good connections with the authorities and
knew how to work them to make low-budget films. An
amiable fellow, Cirio, while visiting Los Angeles, handed
me a treatment he had written that began mystifyingly with
"The naughty airplane heads off down the runway." I asked
what a "naughty airplane" was, and he said, "You know, the
bad guys!"

When I was trying to cobble together a semi-plausible
plot, I casually mentioned that the bandits in the story
would also be political rebels. Cirio was horrified, because,
as I learned from office scuttlebutt, Imelda Marcos, the wife
of dictator Ferdinand Marcos, had once thrown him in jail
for making a movie that was sympathetic to rebels. And
though the regime was supplying aircraft for *Hard Time
Aces*, it currently was in the midst of fighting a rebellion
and reserved the right to recall the aircraft at moment's
notice to use against the rebels (as would happen later with
Apocalypse Now). So I had to do a lot of thinking about
how to make the political aspects of my story safe enough
not to land Cirio back in jail. I came up with the idea that
both sides would be equally corrupt. Jon Davison jokingly
told me, however, "The greatest service you could provide
to world cinema would be to get Cirio put back in jail."

Because Cirio's English was so poor, I was supposed
to go up in the planes to direct the actors—Robert Conrad

of TV's World War II aviation series *Baa Baa Black Sheep* was to be our star—and that made me worried. I thought people might be killed on the project, and I didn't want to be one of them. While I was still working out the plot, the American producer, former singer and B-movie actor John Ashley, called one afternoon and said he needed me to fax him shot lists for the five major action sequences by eight in the morning. I protested that I didn't know where such sequences would fit into the plot, but I stayed up all night and wrote them anyway, realizing I would have to work the story around them. President Marcos was going to hold an air show in the Philippines that day, and an air force officer who had invested $50,000 in our movie would let us stage the five sequences for the Corman movie at the air show without telling the president what we were doing. I was told we would have planes strafing a fake village and soldiers running around on the ground in black pajamas. And afterward I was told the sequences were filmed and would be sent to me in Los Angeles, but I never got to see them.

As I was progressing with the script, Ashley called and told me I could take my time finishing it because a Filipino producer scouting locations for the film had been killed when his helicopter struck a power line. So I dallied for a while until Ashley called again to say I needed to finish quickly because they had found a backer in the Philippines who owned some of the country's largest mango plantations. But as I was rushing toward the conclusion, Ashley told me the film had been called off because a typhoon had struck the Philippines and blown all the fruit off the trees on our financier's plantations. I was quietly relieved, especially given all the dangerous incidents that had already occurred on *Hard Time Aces*. My finished script was filed away, a workmanlike job I designed with Hawksian overtones emulating *The Dawn Patrol, Only Angels Have Wings,* and other Hawks aviation pictures.

Tell me your impressions of Corman then and in retrospect. Did you two keep in touch after you stopped working for him?

I covered Roger's New World Pictures and Concorde-New Horizons for *Daily Variety* and interviewed him a number of times. He was always amiable, smart, and savvy. When I was vice-president of the Los Angeles Film Critics Association, I staged a mini-AFI Life Achievement Award kind of celebration for Corman involving some of his former

When I proposed that *Rock 'n' Roll High School* should end with the students blowing up their school—based on the 1970 Sterling Hall bombing in Madison—Allan Arkush said, "It would make the students unsympathetic." But he soon warmed to the idea and falsely began claiming it as his own fantasy. (New World Pictures)

protégés when we gave him our Career Achievement Award in 1997. Since he gave me my break as well as cheating me financially, I felt somewhat ambivalent toward him. As everyone knows, Roger's greatest contribution to the film world was being virtually the only producer who would hire talented young people in the days when the old system was falling apart. Other producers didn't have the smarts to do so; Roger started so many careers, and some memorable low-budget films resulted. I once asked him why he didn't hold those filmmakers to long-term contracts, and he wisely explained that he knew they would soon go on to better things, so they would resent being tied down, and anyway he didn't want to make bigger-budget films.

That was Roger's limitation too, along with his pathological frugality, which perhaps was a safety mechanism that spun out of control. The price we paid for getting our breaks was being paid like paupers. I remember asking the editor of one of his films how it was coming, and she said very slowly, because the director couldn't afford to buy gas to come to the editing room. Joe Dante and Allan Arkush each received $84 for co-directing *Hollywood Boulevard*. Roger's MO in getting around the Writers Guild of America rules was to get someone in the office to dictate a "script" into a tape recorder for $200 and have a secretary type it up. That way he could hire a WGA member for half of the standard $8,000 fee for an original screenplay, by calling it a "rewrite" instead. So I was paid only $4,000 for my script of *Rock 'n' Roll High School* and four additional drafts until the WGA found out about the scam he was running.

When the guild went after Roger for what he owed me for writing unpaid drafts on all three of our film projects, their arbitration panel ruled that I was due $15,000. He arrogantly skipped the arbitration session but indignantly went in to see the guild executives and somehow got the settlement knocked down by half. That was tough for me when I was struggling to maintain my screenwriting career. Roger was so furious at the guild for going to bat for me and another writer that he stopped being a WGA signatory, which hurt his films, because he could no longer hire professional writers. So *Rock 'n' Roll High School* was just about the last memorably personal film made by his protégés.

I enjoy some of the films Roger directed before he gave up on that part of his career, including *A Bucket of Blood*, the Poe films, *The Wild Angels, The Trip*, and especially *The Intruder,* his powerful and gutsy 1962 film with William Shatner playing a racist rabblerouser, filmed on actual Southern locations (it was written by Charles Beaumont). After Todd McCarthy and I saw a rare 35mm print of *The Intruder* at the Fox Venice Theater, Todd, who was working as New World's head of publicity at the time, complimented Roger on it the next day. He shook his head and said, "It didn't make money." I heard Roger asked in a TV interview why he decided to become a distributor, and he said because you can steal more money that way. Roger amassed a vast fortune doing so. He was offered projects that were riskier but could have paid off more handsomely for him than the films he was making—*Easy Rider* is the prime example— but he always held back from taking chances with his own money. He knew that hiring talented young and hungry filmmakers for little money to make genre films was actually no risk. But he was the only guy in Hollywood back then who realized that and acted on it.

Sam Fuller once said to me of Roger, "You know that smile he always has? It doesn't mean he's happy—it's just an expression he has. Roger is Victor Hugo's The Man Who Laughs." Roger deserved the honorary Oscar he was awarded in 2009 "for his rich engendering of films and filmmakers," and it was wonderful that he kept healthy and working until he died in 2024 at the age of ninety-eight. I think Roger *was* happy, and he left a strong legacy, even if he was not able to take the money with him. Among his achievements was distributing a remarkable array of fine foreign films in the 1970s by Bergman, Fellini, Truffaut,

Kurosawa, Jeanne Moreau and other directors when the rest of the distributors were too dumb to do so. Roger's proudest possession, which he pointed out to me on his office wall, was a letter from Bergman thanking him for enabling him to finally have one of his films (*Cries and Whispers*) playing drive-in theaters. Who else could have done all these things but Roger Corman?

"Strong at the broken places"

The period when you were writing scripts for Corman was also the period when you began to write your most personal project, The Broken Places, *as a screenplay, long before it became a memoir.*

The Broken Places, the story of my troubled youth, both made me as a writer and broke my career as a screenwriter. Beginning in 1978, I spent the greater part of three years writing *The Broken Places,* first as a screenplay and then turning it into a novel, a difficult and painful but ultimately satisfying process. *The Broken Places* is the best script I ever wrote, my own *400 Blows.* It brought me a lot of praise but no sale.

While I was trying to find a buyer, I persisted writing treatments and other screenplays with increasing frustration, and my unwillingness to give up on *The Broken Places* undoubtedly was part of the problem. In the more than five years after I finished writing it, I pitched many, many feature film projects on a wide range of topics during those years before I "ankled" (escaped) the biz, as *Variety* would put it. I kept striking out at endless pitch meetings, though I was successful as a writer of television specials.

What was especially frustrating with *The Broken Places,* besides the fruitless praise it received, was what had impelled me to write it. Walter F. Parkes and Keith Critchlow, who co-directed a 1975 Oscar-nominated documentary about neo-Nazis called *The California Reich,* had both expressed interest in directing my screenplay *Blood & Guts,* but neither could raise the money to make it. That would become ironic after Parkes went on to a long and illustrious career as a production chief for Steven Spielberg. Parkes offered a thoughtful criticism of my work when he read the wrestling script. He said, "I think you're hiding behind genres," and he challenged me to write more openly and personally. That remark rang true; it stuck in my mind as a barrier to break through.

Riff Randell (Soles), the Ramones' "Number-One" fan who becomes
their songwriter, joins them for a rousing musical number, "Do You
Wanna Dance?," in the school corridor. (New World Pictures)

And so I began my first serious effort to write my most
openly personal project, my dramatized account of my
youthful breakdown, hospitalization, and first love affair.
I spent several months in 1978 and 1979 pouring that gut-
wrenching story onto paper, and I was pleased with the result;
the script felt strongly focused and emotionally powerful.

The pain of remembering that I willingly put myself
through for long stretches during the many years I worked
on *The Broken Places* was a necessary process of self-
psychoanalysis. While engaged in that process of self-
revelation, I kept reminding myself that Tennessee Williams,
our greatest playwright, said that a writer should never
be embarrassed. And though I had a doctor at the county
hospital who was sympathetic and helpful, I left doctors
out of the story. I always think they are a dramatic crutch in
stories about mental illness, such as *Ordinary People,* because
they exist mostly to give the protagonists a chance to give
what amount to monologues while getting phony feedback.
I wanted to dramatize my story directly, not by having my
protagonist relate it to someone within the story.

And my openness to psychotherapists had largely
vanished as a result of my interactions with my maddeningly
passive doctor in high school. When I heard that he had
committed suicide—he's the one who shot himself in the
woods next to some train tracks—that seemed to validate
my distrust. Many years later, though, when I had some
problems as a teacher with anxiety about public speaking,
I opened myself up to the thoughtful ministrations of a
cognitive therapist I respected.

The nifty poster for *Rock 'n' Roll High School* was by the celebrated William Stout, one of many he drew for films and rock albums, as well as working in other artistic capacities on films (this poster was also used for the Ramones' soundtrack album). (New World Pictures)

You said your script got a lot of praise. From people in Hollywood?

Jon Davison remarked on what a quantum jump *The Broken Places* represented in my screenwriting ability. But no one would pull the trigger and make the film. One fundamental problem I faced is that unlike in Europe, the American film industry tends to frown on autobiographical projects. Even Steven Spielberg's moving and entertaining semi-fictionalized autobiographical 2022 picture, *The Fabelmans*, was not particularly well-received. Despite his vast success directing many popular and critical hits over decades of work, when he told the story of his own youth, he failed to find much of an audience and was often criticized for allegedly being self-indulgent.

The Broken Places was particularly appreciated by young female readers, who were the principal judges of screenplays in Hollywood for producers in those days. They tended to be bright women in their late twenties who had gone to good schools and were well-versed in literature. My script had a direct and meaningful emotional appeal for that audience. One young woman told me she could not stop shaking for fifteen minutes after finishing it, because the ending of the heroine setting herself on fire brought back the memory of watching a female friend burn to death in a car accident. But these sympathetic readers were candid about not being able to convince their bosses, who tended to be insensitive and conventional middle-aged men, that such material would succeed in the marketplace. Not only was *The Broken Places* a female-oriented story in a time when Hollywood was still mostly mired in the male buddy-buddy business, but it was also about trauma and mental illness. And its horrifying ending made it seem hopelessly un-commercial.

One producer offered to let me and Paul Lynch make the film if I would give it a happy ending and make the girl "less of a bitch." When I found that offensive and refused to comply with his demands, the producer actually pointed his finger at the door and told us to get out of his office. Paul chastised me as we walked out because I had blown a chance to make a film, but I preferred to do that than compromise the project. Another, more sympathetic producer, Norman Lloyd, who wanted me to give the story a happy ending, quoted Picasso's line that "Art is a lie that makes us realize truth." But doing so with this story would have been simply a lie. And I found the Hollywood response shortsighted in that many of the most popular love stories in movies have unhappy endings—*Gone With the Wind*, *Casablanca*, *Love Story*, *The Way We Were*, *E.T.*—because it is more poignant when lovers are parted than when they walk off into the sunset in a corny happy ending. But try telling that to a movie executive back then or today. And I have to acknowledge that it may be asking too much of movie audiences to have the heroine set fire to herself at the end, no matter how poetically the scene might be filmed. For that reason, even if the role is a great part for a young actress, the story's true form may be within the covers of a book.

The closest *The Broken Places* came to being filmed was when I gave it to my friend and favorite modern director, François Truffaut. He made what I consider the best autobiographical movie, *The 400 Blows*. But in retrospect I realize that expecting him to direct my story would have been like Truffaut asking Claude Chabrol to direct *The 400 Blows*. Truffaut said he admired my script's "simplicity," which I realized from his writing and films was one of his highest terms of praise. But he said he couldn't understand some aspects of the American setting—such as my friend Alex, a nihilistic Black arsonist I met at the hospital—and that he felt too uncertain about his English to make a film entirely in that language.

Nevertheless, Truffaut happened to be having dinner with Steven Spielberg and Amy Irving, who were married at the time, and when she complained that she couldn't find any good parts for women in Hollywood, he said he had found one that she should play. When I had written the part of a feisty silent movie actress in *California, Here I Come* for Cindy Williams, she told me I was one of the few writers in Hollywood who knew how to write good parts for women. The serendipitous irony of Truffaut recommending *The Broken Places* to Amy Irving was that I had her in mind while writing the script. I kept her photo—in a scene from Brian De Palma's *The Fury*—above my desk all that time. The morning after Truffaut told her about *The Broken Places*, Irving called my agent. She read the script and said, "Don't do it without me." She let us use her name to help sell it, but she wasn't a big enough star to enable the script to surmount its obstacles. Eventually I also realized that as good an actress as Irving is, since my girlfriend Kathy was half Native American, the role based on her should be played by a Native American actress, someone yet unknown.

Eventually I had to admit defeat in trying to market *The Broken Places* to the movies. I decided to take the plunge of trying to turn it into a novel, thinking it would have a stronger chance to sell in that form. I read numerous classic novels for inspiration—Graham Greene, my favorite modern writer, and Tolstoy were my greatest teachers—as well as E. M. Forster's *Aspects of the Novel*. I learned from Forster that a novel needs both "flat" and "round" characters and that there is no hard-and-fast definition of what constitutes a novel, for the form itself is fluid. And I drew valuable lessons from novelist Patricia Highsmith's splendid 1966 book, *Plotting and Writing Suspense Fiction*.

But when I finished the initial novel version of *The Broken Places* after several months, I had a sobering talk with my agent's junior partner, an agent who was much smarter than her boss. She said there was something lacking from the novel. It took her a while to put her finger on what that was. Finally she had it: "*Texture.*" That's all she needed to tell me. I could see that I had turned the script into what amounted to a novelization, with bare-bones descriptions and not much in the way of psychological depth, mostly just action and dialogue. I took the manuscript back to my desk and spent much of the next two years, 1980 to 1982, rewriting while keeping what I was doing from almost everybody for fear of being spooked into giving it up. Those four drafts were the most difficult writing effort of my life: I stopped taking meetings for scripts while I was turning the story into a real novel, what I considered the big leagues of writing.

I had begun to experiment with fiction in 1978, in preparation for turning the *Broken Places* screenplay into a novel. As I had done while teaching myself how to write scripts, I started with a short story, and with the help of Highsmith's guidebook, I learned how to plant clues and the value of having a "likeable criminal." I drew on my concern about reading stories in the paper about children shooting each other with their parents' handguns. So I wrote "Remember Bobby." It deals with a boy who is killed by a small child and whose revengeful parents wait until he turns eighteen to confront him with a gun; but when they do, a vivid memory of their dead son makes them drop the gun and forgive the youthful killer, who by now is a student at the University of Southern California. I had tried to sell the story to *Playboy*, which rejected it, and then offered it to a film student at USC who had advertised for a film story but foolishly turned it down.

Facing the challenge of *The Broken Places* made it necessary to immerse myself imaginatively into that traumatized time and state of mind, yet still maintaining what Wordsworth called "emotion recollected in tranquility." But I was somewhat misguided: I not only took the protective steps of distancing the story by writing in the third person, changing the names of my heroine and my character (to "Sean Gavin") as well as those of other people in my story, I was brainwashed enough by Hollywood to think there would be more of a chance of getting that movie made if I set it in the present day. Doing so hurt the screenplay, because a tale of such a sexually repressed teenaged boy that took place in the late 1970s seemed anachronistic, even hard to accept. Much later I realized the story had to be set in the period just before the "sexual revolution," the time when it actually happened, in early 1965, when the psychological pressures of a Catholic boys' high school inhibiting my sexual development did not seem as odd as they did in a screenplay set in 1979. But the artistic detours I took were necessary, though mistaken, steps in psychologically and aesthetically distancing the material so I could confront it artistically. I cleared up these problems much later when I turned the book into a memoir, which is what it always should have been.

Although when I went to college, I had started out wanting to be a novelist, I found that form did not come naturally to me. Something about the process of envisioning an entire world for the characters to inhabit was extremely challenging. Eventually it would be clear what the problem was. My Asperger's-ish personality is an asset for writing nonfiction, the meticulous assembling and structuring of factual details, but it was an obstruction to writing imaginary stories. I kept at it relentlessly until I thought I had done a solid enough job, the best I could do in bringing the story to new life as a novel. Yet I was still handicapped (without realizing why) by my artistic mistakes. And for some foolish reason I had changed *The Broken Places*, its perfect title — taken from Ernest Hemingway's moving tribute to Frederic Henry's dead wife, Catherine Barkley, in *A Farewell to Arms* — to *Private Parts*, which sounded like a porno movie. (That title had also been used for a feature by Paul Bartel and became the title of Howard Stern's autobiography and its film adaptation.)

By the time I put the novel on the market, I had abandoned my shiftless principal agent and moved back to the major agency in town, International Creative Management (ICM). I was fortunate to find a young woman literary agent in the New York office who was dedicated to the task of selling my novel. But many publishers passed on the manuscript. Some sent encouraging responses but still rejected it for one reason or another; a couple wrote nasty responses about how little interest they had in the sexual hangups of a teenaged Catholic boy. Even the hostile reactions, however, helped me realize people would understand the story better if it were set before free love seemed ubiquitous and hardcore porno movies were playing in Pussycat Theaters. Finally my new agent sensibly told me there was no point in going on. I was grateful for her valiant effort. At least *she* had believed in *The Broken Places*.

Were there movies you worked on without credit during your days as a screenwriter?

I should have been credited for the original story of *Prom Night*, the 1980 horror hit made in Canada. After we made *Blood & Guts*, I still hadn't learned my lesson about working again with the meretricious director Paul Lynch. Paul wanted to make a horror movie and came to me needing a plot to go with his notion of "a serial killer killing kids on prom night." I asked why he kills them. Paul said, "I don't know, he's a serial killer." I said even a serial killer has a motive. So to my later regret, I told Paul about my short story "Remember Bobby," and I suggested that he have the serial killer be the twin of a girl who was killed in a prank by other children long ago. I added that, like the parents in my story, the young man waits to take his revenge when the ones who killed his sister are grown up, and that he does so on prom night after making himself up as a partial facsimile of his sister. My story is about the desire for revenge turning into forgiveness, but by grafting it onto the notion of a prom night killer, the original idea became twisted into a story about out-and-out revenge. That seems symbolic of the amorality of the movie business, doesn't it?

Paul refused to give me any kind of credit and wasn't going to pay me anything until I forced the issue. But I needed money so badly that I accepted only $2,000. (At least he didn't offer me my usual $500.) That deal proved a bitter pill when the low-budget *Prom Night* became a runaway hit. I asked Paul to share some of his own profits, and he half-promised to do so but kept avoiding me, even giving me a false address, so I never saw him again. After making a few lousy exploitation pictures with poor scripts, Paul turned to a career directing TV shows. The person credited with my story on *Prom Night* wrote two features after that but then spent his career writing soap operas. I did not get any money or credit for the later iterations of *Prom Night*, three sequels and a remake, only the pittance for my original story. I was a non-person on that project. I should not have gone along with that deal, but my excuse was that I was broke at the time. Too many decisions are made for that reason. I found in Hollywood that what you turn down is as important, if not more so, than the deals you accept.

I was acknowledged by Paul naming one of the killer kids in *Prom Night* Nick McBride, but it was small consolation and insulting at that. As a result of consolidating her appeal in *Halloween* and *The Fog* with her lead female role in *Prom Night,* Jamie Lee Curtis became known as a "scream queen" starring in a string of grade-B horror films. Ironically, when I was back on *Variety* and reviewed her film *Terror Train,* released two and a half months after *Prom Night,* I chastised her for slipping into lazy diction. Shortly after the review appeared, I was waiting near Curtis in a pharmacy when my last name was called; her head spun around, and she glared at me. Nevertheless, I was pleased to notice that Curtis's diction substantially improved in her next film and that she has continued to speak distinctly in her subsequent Oscar-winning career.

I also made the mistake in 1978 of going along with Paul Lynch's request that I write a screenplay called *Catman and the Kid,* intended for Bill Smith in the role of Clint Harmon, a circus animal tamer whose wife dies while doing their ring act, mauled by a lion. Paul said the idea was loosely based on a 1935 Wallace Beery-Jackie Cooper film for MGM called *O'Shaughnessy's Boy,* which I still have never seen (the screenplay is by Leonard Praskins & Wanda Tuchock and Otis Garrett based on a story by Harvey Gates and Malcolm Stuart Boylan; Richard Boleslawski directed). Since the story of that film deals with the man's troubled relationship with his son and his attempt to reestablish a family connection, it appealed to me in light of my relationship with my young daughter. I changed the youngster to a fourteen-year-old girl and had Clint descend into what another character calls "a self-pitying lush" while working for a carnival after his wife's death. When Clint takes charge of his daughter from a girls' boarding school ten years later, he tells the nun who runs it, "You know, sister, I've faced wild animals in my time, but I don't mind telling you, this scares me to death."

On the title page of the script, William Gray is the "front" Paul assigned the screenplay credit, with the director taking the story credit. I had taken second-position screenplay credit on the first draft under the pseudonym of Jacob Barnes, a bitterly wry allusion to the hero of Hemingway's *The Sun Also Rises,* Jake Barnes, a writer who can't have sexual intercourse because his penis was blown off in the Great War. But Paul wouldn't even let me keep that half-cocked credit on the final version. Paul and I also worked on a wacky horror film treatment called *Don't See the Doctor,* about a sinister, out-of-control hospital; he used to kid me about how I always have hospital scenes in my scripts — since I spent months living in hospitals and later worked in one — so that treatment was fun to write. But Paul couldn't get any studio interest in *Catman* or *Don't See the Doctor.*

I remember one amusing moment when we were working on the story for *Prom Night,* and Paul mentioned that the killer would pick up one of his victims and sling the person over his shoulder to carry away. "Have you ever tried to lift a dead body, Paul?" I asked. Naturally he hadn't, so I explained that part of my job as a hospital orderly had been transporting corpses from hospital rooms to the morgue, a job that always required the help of at least one other hospital worker to lift it onto a cart, because a dead body not only is unresponsive but becomes waterlogged and forbiddingly heavy. It helps to have some experience in such matters if you're going to write a horror movie.

During this period, producer Peter O'Brian asked if I would be interested in writing a script that used the basic plot and character structure of *Blood & Guts* transposed to a car-racing setting. I said I would but heard no more about it until David Cronenberg made the film in Canada with Bill Smith as *Fast Company,* in 1979. In retrospect, I thought O'Brian only pretended to be interested in hiring me to keep me from objecting to my story for *Blood & Guts* being ripped off. Once again I had been fooled out of desperation to get projects made, but by then it was my fault for still being so gullible.

Big Money

At the risk of bringing up another script story with an unhappy ending, tell me about the genesis and nature of Big Money *and why it was met with both support and resistance in Hollywood.*

That was the only project I tried to market that, for a brief time at least, managed to find a home at a major studio, Orion Pictures. I wrote *Big Money* in 1978 about the 1950s TV quiz show scandals. It was based on a story by my friend Pat McGilligan along with Debra Weiner and Bob Taylor. Ultimately that project also fell through, in spite of or perhaps because of its determinedly entertaining qualities as a Capraesque romantic comedy; essentially, though, it was also a strong critique of the corruption of show business.

Big Money involved an innocent young man who is fed answers to questions on a quiz show of that title by the female associate producer. They fall in love, which causes him to wise up and her to question her own corruption. That was my smart idea, but I ran into some problems with how to keep the contestant sympathetic when he blows the whistle on the show before Congress, a development I felt made him resemble John Dean. I was too much in thrall to Capra films and hadn't fully thought through their ambivalent political messages, as I later would do when I wrote my Capra biography.

My agent was excited when I started writing *Big Money* and kept telling me to hurry up and finish my first draft. She wanted me to dump my friends from story credit, which she thought would make it easier to sell, but of course I refused. Shortly after I gave her my draft, we had offers from Ron Howard to make it as a TV movie and Barbra Streisand to make it as a feature. Both would have directed as well as acted in it; it would have been her directing debut. I went with Streisand, the major female star of that time, over Howard, who still hadn't made his name as a feature director, although he had made a rollicking 1977 car-chase movie for Roger Corman, *Grand Theft Auto*. Streisand's company, Barwood, was considering Jon Voight to star with her in *Big Money*.

In retrospect, before making my decision, I should have insisted on having meetings with both Streisand and Howard to discuss their plans for the project; Howard probably would have made it. When I rewrote the script to tailor it for Streisand in 1979, the process was made unpleasant and somewhat unnerving by the obvious but unspoken distaste for the seriocomic story by her story editor, Carol Baum. I later compared notes with Polly Platt, who did a rewrite of *The Women* for Streisand and described Baum as "that terrible woman who never smiles." I was too oblivious of film-industry politics to realize that a junior executive who sat in on our meetings was the genuine fan of the story and wanted to make his mark by producing it. If I had focused more closely on him, that might have helped.

Eventually *Big Money* was dumped by Streisand's boyfriend, Jon Peters, along with other projects when he took over running the company. To add insult to injury, my agents informed me that if I sold the script somewhere else, I would have to return what I had been paid for the option and rewrite; I hadn't known that was another odious standard operating procedure in Hollywood. When I look back over my years in Hollywood, the aftermath of that shock was my darkest period psychologically and the experience that contributed most to my eventually giving up on screenwriting.

I kept trying to sell *Big Money* for several years and raised a fair amount of interest. At one point Paramount wanted to rush *Big Money* into production as a relatively low-budget film to make a star of David Keith, who had come into prominence with a supporting role in *An Officer and a Gentleman.* I had a meeting with the producer who wanted to make it there, but the plans fell apart because of an ill-considered option my agent and I had given previously to another producer, which included a clause he had slipped into the agreement without my understanding it. The clause stipulated that if that producer had shopped *Big Money* to a studio, and it later wanted to make the film, he had to be involved in a producing capacity even if they had turned him down earlier. So he insisted on being a producer on *Big Money* at Paramount. But the new producer who wanted to make the film for the studio wanted me to simply stiff the previous producer, but I refused out of principle and because I reluctantly didn't think we had legal grounds to do so.

When the would-be producer insisted on enforcing the clause in his old option agreement and had his lawyer make a written threat, that caused Paramount to back away from its offer to make the film. I tried to persuade the studio to pay the claimant $75,000 to go away, but that didn't work, since they had already denied his unalterable demand that he receive a producing credit. I can hardly tell you how painful that was. The situation felt Kafkaesque. It encapsulated the craziness and corruption of the film industry and was one of the final straws that convinced me to leave the business, which seemed rigged to keep me from making the films I wanted to make.

So *Big Money* didn't get made. I was told by one studio boss, Frank Price of Columbia, who had come from television, that he would never make a movie about the quiz show scandals, since they reflected badly on show business by portraying it as corrupt. That of course was part of the reason I was attracted to the story.

But in 1994, the movie *Quiz Show*, written by Paul Attanasio from a book by Richard Goodwin and directed by Robert Redford, finally dealt with this subject. I feel it suffers from its generic title—my title *Big Money,* on the other hand, stirred instant excitement from readers, who could smell box-office—and from not having an important female role, which makes it feel cold and bloodless, unlike the love story

I had written. But I realized that *Quiz Show* deals more believably with its contestant, played by John Turturro, who is less naive and likable than the character I had written (my agent accurately called *Big Money* "a fairy tale"). Billy Wilder told me he admired *Quiz Show* and even offered to give me his VHS copy of the film, but I declined, since it was too painful for me to dwell upon. My efforts to sell *Big Money* preoccupied me unprofitably for three years before I left the business, and my inability to sell *The Broken Places* was even more grueling, and persisting with those two projects kept me from moving on to other stories.

Orson and Peter

During those turbulent years, were you still hanging out with Orson Welles after filming ceased on The Other Side of the Wind?

Not exactly hanging out—I saw him from time to time but not often, though I might have if I had wanted. I would get phone calls from people who wanted to reach him for film roles and to attend film festivals and so forth, and I would pass those offers along to Gary Graver. After a while I became fed up with playing middleman, so if a caller wanted Welles to appear at a festival, I would say, "I'm sure he wouldn't do that, but *I'd* be happy to come instead." That would end the call quickly.

By going through Gary, I managed to get Orson to appear on our 1983 AFI Life Achievement Award show honoring John Huston. When he agreed, I called Orson and said I'd like to come to his house and discuss what he would say on the show. He said in a peremptory manner, "There's nothing to discuss, because I'm going to write it myself." That's not what I meant; I simply wanted to know the content of his speech so I could fit it into the overall scheme of the show and avoid repetition. But I was so fed up with my treatment by the film industry by that time, 1983, that I didn't explain why I had called. He added, "But I would like to see *you.*" I made a noncommittal response and never talked with him again but just saw him at a distance when he spoke on our show.

Of course I now regret not going to visit Orson again, but I had reached my limit of being mistreated as a screenwriter. I couldn't help feeling I was betraying him by not responding to his invitation. But as I came to realize from studying Welles's life and career, he feared betrayal so much that he would always push his friends and colleagues past their limit so they would betray *him* instead. What made that worse for me was that Welles was one of the people I most admired, and it stung me when he showed me disrespect as a scriptwriter.

Welles's speech about Huston was not only the highlight of that AFI show but has been described as perhaps the greatest awards-show speech ever delivered, although one prominent producer told me that Mikhail Baryshnikov's AFI speech about Fred Astaire, which I helped write, deserved that recognition. I wouldn't do Welles's magnificent and witty address on Huston justice by quoting just part of it. I did my bit for Welles in postproduction when the director, Marty Pasetta, wanted to slash into his speech, as is typical with Hollywood when they encounter something unique. I found the only painless cut in the text and presented it to Pasetta as a compromise, preserving all but thirty seconds of his original six-minute speech. Huston told me later that Welles's speech was his favorite part of the show. Marty's wanting to mess with it reminded me of an old Hollywood joke I heard Huston tell to open a 1986 Directors Guild of America press conference to protest Ted Turner's colorization of *The Maltese Falcon*: "A couple of generations back, screenwriters used to tell a story about two producers lost in the desert and dying of thirst. About to give up the ghost, they crawl into view of a miraculous spring of pure effervescent water and they go joyously to drink, when one says, 'No, wait. Don't drink. Wait till I piss in it.'"

When Orson died in October 1985, I helped his former right-hand man, Richard Wilson, put together the public memorial tribute at the DGA theater in Hollywood, a kind of posthumous AFI tribute that drew an overflow, standing-room-only crowd. Peter Bogdanovich ably served as host, and along with film clips in 35mm (which had been assembled by Peter for the AFI show), many of Welles's friends and colleagues paid warm and often hilarious tribute to him. But Oja Kodar startled the audience by ripping into Henry Jaglom and Robert Wise, though not by name, as well as French minister of culture Jack Lang in a speech of fiery rage over how Orson was mistreated by the film industry. "Who is that woman dressed in black?" the shaken Wise asked me after the show. The tribute was videotaped by Gary Graver's crew and edited by Frank Beacham and can be watched on wellesnet.com.

Did you stay friends with Peter Bogdanovich?

For years I felt ambivalent and somewhat resentful toward Peter because I thought, no doubt presumptuously, that he should have given me more help to make it as a screenwriter. I had some reason for that feeling due to ill will over the film project about early Hollywood that I offered him and the way he handled that episode. It was not until much later—after a lot of blood had gone over the bridge, to borrow a phrase from Edward Albee—that we began treating each other as colleagues. Peter signed an inscription for his 1997 book of director interviews, *Who the Devil Made It*: "For Joe—We *have* heard 'the chimes at midnight'—so many good memories when I see you! Good luck—Peter (Bogdanovich)."

Eventually I realized that the bottom line was I should simply be grateful to Peter for getting me into *The Other Side of the Wind* in 1970, helping with my Welles and Ford research, and, indeed, helping inspire my career as a film journalist and historian. Before I moved to Hollywood, Peter had also agreed to my offer to write a book about the making of the epic Western he was planning to direct in 1972 from a script by Larry McMurtry, starring John Wayne, James Stewart, and Henry Fonda, but John Ford spitefully killed that project by telling Wayne not to do it. Too bad; it would have been a good movie and a good making-of book. McMurtry later bought back the script and turned it into *Lonesome Dove*.

I saw Peter a few more times before he died, including when we did a panel discussion with producer Frank Marshall at the North American premiere of *The Other Side of the Wind* (on which Peter was an executive producer as well as an actor) at the Telluride Film Festival on September 1, 2018. I found that event, hosted by Todd McCarthy, warm and nostalgic. I was elated that the film was finally released, but Peter was deeply melancholy, because the whole saga of the film and his troubled friendship with Welles was finally over. That same year, Peter came with his wife, Louise, and mother-in-law to an event I did on Lubitsch at UCLA in conjunction with my book on the director. Lubitsch's daughter, Nicola, and I held a Q&A session after showing a sparkling restored print of Lubitsch's 1926 feature, *So This Is Paris*. Peter got up to say a few words of appreciation about "The Director I Never Met."

Peter had done his best to pay homage to Lubitsch with *At Long Last Love*, the 1975 musical that was unfairly reviled, partly because Cybill Shepherd is so awkward in it but also, I think, because Hollywood was scandalized that someone made a Lubitschean film in such an anti-romantic period in

American life. *At Long Last Love* is gracefully filmed and entertaining, even more so in its recently restored uncut version, which begins spectacularly with a Madeline Kahn musical number running more than five minutes in a single shot. Peter had unwisely cut that opening when panicking because the film was getting bad responses at previews. It is a much better way to put the audience into the 1930s Cole Porter mood than the off-putting song number by Cybill in a bathtub that opened the original release version.

What other kinds of roadblocks did you run up against in your last few years of trying to sell ideas for feature films?

My basic problem with Hollywood screenwriting, I realize when I look back on that period, was that I took it too seriously and could not roll with the punches. I was unlike Ben Hecht, who wrote in his autobiography *A Child of the Century*—Terry Malick cited this quote as a cautionary tale for my article on young screenwriters—"For many years I looked on movie writing as an amiable chore. It was a source of easy money and pleasant friendships. There was small responsibility. Your name as a writer was buried in a flock of credits. Your literary pride was never involved. What critics said about the movie you had written never bothered you. They were usually criticizing something you couldn't remember." I could never be that blasé. Raymond Chandler said the problem with the Hollywood system is that it was designed to "destroy the link between the writer and his subconscious." A fellow screenwriter told me many years later that to survive in the business, you have to fundamentally not care too deeply if your scripts are mangled or stolen. But for better or for worse, I could never *not* care. My literary pride was always invested in my work, and if that hurt me as a screenwriter, it would help me when I devoted myself to writing books fulltime.

One story editor told me in the early 1980s after I pitched something to her, "You know, I don't think you really want to make movies anymore." I realized, "You know, you're right." Her perceptiveness showed me a truth I had been resisting and crystallized something in me that led to my understanding that it was time to depart. But before getting out for good, I found that, as Welles once observed, the less money you have to make a film, the more freedom you have. Working on a shoestring for Corman enabled me to be genuinely subversive in ways the major studios would never have tolerated, such as showing the kids blowing up their high school.

But you couldn't survive on what Corman paid his writers. Or on what I made for writing AFI shows. When I qualified for a Writers Guild pension based on my earnings over several years as a screenwriter before my retirement, a guild staffer quipped that my monthly check would be "enough to keep you in beer and potato chips."

Hollywood postmortem

Pitching is an art form I never mastered. Probably the greatest pitch in film history was Ken Russell's one-line sales job to United Artists for his Tchaikovsky biopic, *The Music Lovers*: "It's the story of a homosexual who falls in love with a nymphomaniac." You can almost hear the guy in the suit taking out his checkbook and asking, "How much do you want?"

I belatedly concluded that I was not good at pitching but was more successful when I wrote a script first and then marketed it, as I did with *Big Money*. On most occasions when I was asked to pitch a story idea to a producer, he—producers were almost invariably men when I was an active screenwriter—would spend the first half hour telling me what he had done over the weekend. The spiel was usually about hunting, fishing, watching football and beer drinking, macho pursuits in which I had no interest. I would try to feign interest while anxious to get into my story idea, but I am sure my efforts were transparent. Only rarely did my pitch succeed. The other problem with the ritual was that producers would call in numerous writers to discuss a project and take what they liked from the improvised ideas. I had better luck discussing my ideas with the readers for producers. Those bright young women were my real fans in the business, but that didn't do me much good in selling scripts. But one of the smartest and most congenial people I worked with in Hollywood was Corman's story editor, Frances Doel, with whom I had creative working experiences on three screenplays.

About thirty years later, after leaving the business, I woke one day having an epiphany about why it was that I hadn't understood the pitching process. It occurred to me that the first half hour of seemingly wasted banter with a producer was the time when you did or did not sell your script. That part of the meeting was to find out if you were the kind of guy the producer would like to hang around with on location in some motel in Nebraska, drinking beer. I wasn't that kind of guy. When I met a woman who was writing a book about pitching ideas, I told her my theory, and she said I was exactly correct.

William Goldman, one of the most successful screenwriters, in one of his entertaining and enlightening books on that field, said he had only pitched a script once and realized he was no good at that, so he would just write the script and sell it. After all, most of us writers are better at writing than talking, or we wouldn't have become writers. I wish I had had the sense in Hollywood to do what Goldman suggested on a regular basis, although it worked once with *Big Money*. Billy Wilder offered me a good piece of advice, to find a director to partner with who had the clout and connections to sell the script (as he had done with Ernst Lubitsch), but when I tried to take his advice, I made the mistake of partnering with a lousy director— Paul Lynch—who took advantage of me because I had neither money nor clout. Wilder didn't add the advice, "But don't be a dope about it."

I understand now, however, that I lacked guidance from the people I most needed to listen to, sensible people in my generation who were in the same boat as I was, trying to launch film projects in Hollywood. Instead I spent most of my time talking with filmmakers from previous generations whose advice would have been valuable during the heyday of the studio system but was mostly irrelevant in the dysfunctional modern Hollywood. One of the ways Hollywood controlled writers in my day was to keep them in the dark about its mostly secretive practices, forcing writers to ferret out the information through painful experience. That problem persisted through my time as a screenwriter. I did the best I could to learn about the law, as I later told my students a writer must do, though that doesn't always help in a lawless environment.

For example, I listened to agents who insisted that pitching was the way to sell projects to producers. But usually that process was pointless or tended to drain you of the desire to actually make the project after it became bent out of shape from pitching it too often. After a story editor liked a story I had written about a rich kid who contrives his own kidnapping to get back at his domineering father, a role I designed for Jeff Bridges to play, her producer boss kept bringing me back to revise the idea according to his suggestions. After several such meetings, a practice that I didn't realize was outlawed by the Writers Guild of America unless the writer was being paid, she finally told her boss to stop, because "You're just jerking him around." And on one especially grueling day, I successively pitched five film ideas to a producer, a former big-name agent whom I finally realized was just toying with me for sadistic pleasure; he eventually managed to obtain just one executive producer credit on a forgettable movie before retiring from the business. I should have stopped my pitching much earlier that day, but I was stubbornly locked into the way I thought the system was supposed to operate. When I would come home from pitch meetings, I usually would be worn out, frazzled, and unable to work.

Another time Sam Fuller and I wrote a treatment together. *Grass Roots* was about two old friends in the newspaper business who had gone their separate ways, one in effect becoming William Allen White, the editor of an honest smalltown Midwestern newspaper, and the other in effect becoming the mogul William Randolph Hearst. When the Hearst character dies at the onset, he leaves his empire to his old friend and says in his will to take his flagship New York City newspaper "and make an honest newspaper out of it." My agent liked the idea and set up a lunch with John Foreman, the distinguished producer of, among other films, *Butch Cassidy and the Sundance Kid* and *The Man Who Would Be King*. As I sat there in the MGM commissary, I listened as Foreman and my agent turned *Grass Roots* into a film about television and basketball, since they thought newspapers were passé. After a while, I said simply, "That's not the film I want to make. Our story is about newspapers." My agent was surprised and upset that I was not interested in their twist on our story. (Years later I discovered that Sam had not told me that Columbia Pictures had already made a version of that story, which he wrote with Robert Hardy Andrews in 1943, *Power of the Press*, starring Guy Kibbee and Lee Tracy. So it was not ours to sell.)

Late film projects

Nevertheless, I kept plugging away on scripts. Leaving the film industry would mean giving up on a dream that had ruled my life since 1966. So I persisted with increasing frustration, except for the satisfaction of the five AFI Life Achievement Award specials I worked on, until I retired from screenwriting in 1984. Many stories I wanted to make as films were political, which I found out was a virtual taboo in Hollywood during that period. I could tell after seeing *Star Wars* in 1977 that mindless cardboard juvenilia would be taking over the industry, as the industry came to regard its target audience as adolescent males. As the Reagan years were looming, Hollywood turned its focus to churning out safely escapist fare.

The kinds of stories I wanted to tell were not welcome in the early Eighties, including a film about the Montgomery Bus Boycott and how it turned the young Dr. Martin Luther King Jr. into a civil rights leader. My main theme was drawn from Mahatma Gandhi's statement, "There go my people— I must hurry up and follow them, for I am their leader." I also brought up the idea of making an epic film about the Battle of Stalingrad, but my ICM agent just laughed in my face. And there was what I call my "Castro trilogy." Those ideas included a funny and illuminating idea I had for a biopic of the young Fidel Castro; a *Battle of Algiers*-influenced film about the Bay of Pigs invasion; and a black comedy about the CIA's bumbling attempts to kill Castro with the help of the mob. Imagine the horror with which those pitches were greeted in Hollywood offices. The more hostility I faced, the more obstinate I became and more brazen about pitching impossible projects. (After Castro died in 2016, a producer I know told me he was interested in hearing my idea for a biopic, but I declined, telling him I was happily out of the biz.)

To illustrate the political climate I was up against in my final days as a screenwriter, when I told my agent at ICM about my idea of doing a film on the Bay of Pigs invasion, she became alarmed and said, "You can't do *that!*" I asked why. She sputtered, "It's—it's—*political!*" From her mainstream point of view, that's all that needed to be said to kill the project. I belatedly understood the lasting damage the blacklist era had done to Hollywood in making people terminally afraid of making the kind of political films that emerged in the studio days from such filmmakers as Ford (*The Grapes of Wrath*) and Capra (*Mr. Smith Goes to Washington*).

If I had read more about the blacklist when I lived in Wisconsin, I might have thought more carefully about going to Hollywood. Instead, I found it shocking and instructive to read Victor Navasky's 1980 book *Naming Names,* a thorough and judicious analysis of what led to the blacklist, how it worked, and the moral issues involved. Reading it helped lead to my launching my biography of Capra after I learned that he had been a secret informer in the blacklist era.

In 1982, I wanted to remake George Cukor's 1940 MGM film *Susan and God*, a satire based on a play by Rachel Crothers about a shallow society woman, played by Joan Crawford, who finds Jesus and drives her friends crazy with her moralistic meddling. I had based my idea for updating it on my misbegotten romance with a Southern belle who was a right-wing zealot; I barely escaped from that experience. I pitched the idea to an executive at MGM who not only had never heard of *Susan and God* but was horrified when I described that film to her. She rejected my idea of making it a contemporary story lampooning the Religious Right, saying that would bring down the wrath of that pressure group on the studio. That panicky reaction by the MGM executive showed me how far Hollywood had sunk. The studios were actually more daring when movies were a habit audience for the whole family, and executives could afford to take risks once in a while without undue fear of a backlash.

I have a couple of signed cards of one of our childhood idols, Ray Bradbury, but the only time I nearly met him, the car in front of me picked him up when he was hitchhiking in L.A. But you got to know him and almost adapt one of his short stories?

On the night of the AFI Orson Welles Life Achievement Award show in February 1975, which I was covering for *Daily Variety* at a hotel in Century City, I found myself in a Mexican restaurant across the street from the hotel having drinks with Ray Bradbury and Sam Peckinpah, who were old friends. Bradbury was quietly cheerful, but Peckinpah, who had embarrassed himself at the tribute dinner, was bombed. Wearing a rebel head band, he kept drinking tequila, and at one point he put his head on the table and passed out while a mariachi band serenaded the maker of *The Wild Bunch*. My girlfriend said she was terrified at the end of the evening when Peckinpah got down on both knees outside the restaurant and kissed her hand.

While we were socializing, I told Bradbury that I wanted to write and direct a short film based on a story of his that I loved, "The Utterly Perfect Murder," a story that had resonance with my childhood experiences with bullies, but that I couldn't afford to buy the rights. Bradbury surprised me by saying he would give me the rights, declaring, "I have many short stories but very few lovers." I wish I had made that film but didn't have any money to do so, and a weak adaptation of it later turned up on the TV anthology series *The Ray Bradbury Theater*. But I never forgot Bradbury's generosity. I used to go hear him speak whenever he appeared around town—often at libraries, his favorite places—and he was kind to my son when they met at a bookstore in Pasadena. In the 1990s I tried to raise interest from publishers in a biography of Bradbury, but they shortsightedly saw no potential in the life story of one of our most popular storytellers.

"An Irish *Godfather*"

Because of your long-time connection to John F. Kennedy, did you write any Kennedy scripts?

Among the many other projects I worked on besides the one about the Bay of Pigs, I wrote a treatment for a biopic of Joseph P. Kennedy Sr. That was the one pitch I made that instantly succeeded. I needed to say only three words: "An Irish *Godfather*." When I spoke those words over breakfast to producer Herb Jaffe, he said, "We'll do it." As you can tell, due to my intellectual awakening by the assassination of President Kennedy, I was and am fascinated by political power and some of the calamitous ways it affects the history of our country and our adversaries.

I called the Joe Kennedy project *Hostages to Fortune*. I would have started with the first Kennedy leaving Ireland in 1849—Patrick, a cooper who was Joe's great-grandfather—and taken Joe from his youth in Boston as the son of a saloonkeeper and Democratic politician, Patrick Joseph "P. J." Kennedy, to Joe's swashbuckling and ruthless days as a banker, financier, and government official. Then I would have dealt with his tragic comeuppance as American ambassador to the Court of St. James's and his departure in disgrace as a Hitler sympathizer. I wanted to end the film with Old Joe, reduced to muteness and a wheelchair due to a stroke, staring out a window in his home in Hyannis Port as the American flag is lowered after his son Jack is murdered.

I approached Robert Wise, a two-time Oscar winner as best director, telling him, "This is your chance to make your *Citizen Kane*," and that immediately won him over too. Wise had edited *Kane*, as well as, infamously, *The Magnificent Ambersons*, carrying out the studio-ordered butchery of that film in Welles's absence. One of the great human ironies I found in my time in Hollywood was that Robert Wise, the man who destroyed my favorite work of art, and whom I came to know well, was otherwise a nice man. And he was like the guy who took a hammer to the *Pietà*. That was an object lesson in how people have different and conflicting parts. It's a lesson that needs to be taught in today's simplistic age of cancel culture. My ambivalence about Wise and willingness to work with him on *Hostages to Fortune* was a sign of my complex and perhaps foolhardy attempt to persevere within the Hollywood system at this late stage in its decadence. In retrospect, I should have approached the system with more caution and less romanticism, but I did learn a lot of chastening lessons in the process, even if they were "too expensive." As I've mentioned, those lessons would serve me well as a film historian.

My ambitious Joe Kennedy project fell apart when the parties involved became so worried about possible negative reaction from the Kennedy family that they said they'd make it only if I would change the names and fictionalize it. I didn't see any point in doing that. It had been done, and badly, as a novel by Taylor Caldwell, *Captains and the Kings,* which had been made into a TV miniseries.

I belatedly came to understand that well before the time I became a Hollywood screenwriter in the mid-Seventies, the industry had become terminally cowardly, which was largely due to the lingering effects of the blacklist. Since I didn't realize when I lived in Wisconsin how the blacklist had changed the industry, my ignorance, or innocence, led me to enter the wrong industry at the wrong time. To put it another way, as Graham Greene writes of his title character in *The Quiet American*, "Innocence is a form of insanity." Not only was the industry timid, but I was only dimly aware of how alienating the system was for most people who worked in it. I was made to feel that my problems were mine alone rather than endemic to a system that discouraged freshness and did everything to keep its workers from sharing notes about their status and finding common ground. The dogged means I had used as a journalist to pierce the walls surrounding the Hollywood system were less available to me when I was just another of the thousands of semi-unemployed, easily interchangeable drones in a largely impenetrable system.

Back in Wisconsin I had always dreamed of some day having an office on a studio lot, and I finally thought I had the opportunity in 1978 when I was hired to rewrite *Big Money* for Streisand's Barwood Films and Orion Pictures. Orion, then considered a major studio, was affiliated with Warner Bros. and headquartered at the Burbank Studios. But I was turned down when I made what Streisand's story editor seemed to think was an incomprehensible request for an office. They expected me to work at home like most people in Hollywood. The industry was so atomized that you rarely saw others in the same profession. No wonder I and other Hollywood writers felt so isolated and helpless. In dealing mostly with studio executives in their offices for pitch meetings or story sessions, I was made to feel like a salesman peddling products that had no discernible use to the potential purchasers.

Most of my friends were, like me, film buffs on the fringes of Hollywood who watched movies at the Los Angeles County Museum of Art and the many other venues around town showing Golden Age classics. We were a subculture living in the past, in a remote time detached from our daily lives. Our interests were not widely shared by the rest of Hollywood and environs. When one of my friends, a studio accountant, mentioned casually over dinner one night that she had just cut a $14 million check as part of a star's gross participation for a recent hit, it seemed unreal. *Big Money,* my critique of the entertainment business, squeaked through the system briefly, but it would take a (male) star and director of the magnitude of Robert Redford to turn such a project into an actual film, *Quiz Show,* years after I had spent years struggling to do so.

In their 1978 study of Hollywood political scene in that period and earlier, *Creative Differences: Profiles of Hollywood Dissidents,* David Talbot and Barbara Zheutlin wrote, "One of the main factors militating against progressive change in Hollywood is the absence of community among film workers.... [But] this has not always been the case. The structure of the industry in the 1930s and '40s brought film workers into close, ongoing contact with one another." As Abe Polonsky told the authors, "Every studio had a writers table where all the writers sat and ate together; writers hung out in the same building and exchanged ideas. So even if you're working on nonsense, you're working *together.*" But as Talbot and Zheutlin put it in that same year I optioned *Big Money* to Streisand, "Today, however, there are only the vague outlines of a movie community in Hollywood and no organized radical life on an industry-wide scale. There is no formal political context in which these people can come together on a regular basis. Until one develops, the power relations within the entertainment industry will remain largely the same."

What was the last script you wrote?

No More Mr. Nice Guy, in 1981, was my last completed feature screenplay. It's a black comedy about nuclear war that tries to out-*Strangelove* Kubrick. I wrote the script in only ten days, a single draft. When I finished, I remember telling myself, "I really know how to write a screenplay." I felt liberated at that point, enjoying writing just what amused me, whether other people would like it or not. And sure enough, the script was too provocative for the increasingly timid marketplace.

The premise is that the elderly Adolf Hitler—brought back from his postwar hideout in Paraguay—joins forces with Idi Amin and Muammar Gaddafi to destroy Israel. The plot is foiled by a young Jewish American musician, a flautist named David, who enlists an Israeli nuclear weapon to destroy the underground bunker in the African desert where the villains are operating. A director friend of mine who read *No More Mr. Nice Guy* said he literally fell on the floor laughing when Hitler is being smuggled to Africa on an airplane and starts frothing at the mouth when the in-flight movie that is playing is *Fiddler on the Roof*. The opening gag of the movie is that Hitler is painting placidly on a mountaintop in Paraguay when a neo-Nazi agent tries to lure him back into action, and after a strenuous sales pitch, Hitler finally gives in with the old joke, "OK, but this time no more Mr. Nice Guy."

When I gave the script to Allan Arkush, he huffily said he couldn't go on the set of a movie every day with an actor made up as Hitler. I said, "So you don't like *The Great Dictator*, *To Be or Not to Be*, and *The Producers*?" He replied, snobbishly, that the only one of those films he liked was *To Be or Not to Be*. Before I sent Allan my script, his agent told me, insultingly, that Allan did not want to make any more silly comedies like *Rock 'n' Roll High School*. Allan preferred to direct an inert and unfunny robot comedy called *Heartbeeps*, a failed attempt at pseudo-Chaplinesque humor that bombed. After another fizzled feature based on his youthful experiences working on rock concerts, Allan wound up spending the rest of his career directing TV shows, the same fate that awaited Paul Lynch after I stopped working with him.

For *No More Mr. Nice Guy*, I wrote the lead role of David with Dustin Hoffman in mind. I read an interview in which Hoffman said he wished writers would deliver their scripts directly to him rather than through agents. So I got his home address and left a copy of the script in Hoffman's mailbox. When I told my agent, she said, "And you *believed* that?" I was suitably chastened. I wanted to direct *No More Mr. Nice Guy* as a low-budget comedy in the desert around Palm Springs—standing in for Libya—and with only one major set, a nuclear bunker. I pitched it to Frances Doel at Corman's company. Roger, who had done some graduate work at Oxford University, had found Frances by asking the English literature department for some people to interview as his story editor, and he "thought Frances was the brightest." She liked *No More Mr. Nice Guy* and recommended to Roger that they should make it. But he said it was "too sophisticated."

Before giving up on *No More Mr. Nice Guy*, I foolishly mailed a copy to Stanley Kubrick's home in England and of course never had a response; it's probably filed away in Kubrick's archives now. Arthur Penn told me that after making *Bonnie and Clyde,* for the next year all the scripts he received were for gangster movies, even though that was the last kind of movie he wanted to make again at that point. Instead he was looking for something quite different, and the project he chose to follow *Bonnie and Clyde* was *Alice's Restaurant*. That should serve as good advice for young screenwriters.

How did you feel—I'm sure I know—when your scripts were optioned or were on the verge of being produced but then went nowhere?

I remember the exact words I told myself about how I felt: "like a woman who has had so many abortions that she can't conceive anymore." That was an awful feeling of bottomless futility. I became ill for long stretches in the early 1980s, mostly with respiratory problems, and clearly because my body was rebelling against the punishment I was inflicting upon it by my involvement with the Hollywood system. Something had to give. Psychologically it was as protracted a struggle for me to give up on the film industry as it had been for me to abandon the Catholic Church. But the philosophy I have evolved about a career is that you get the jobs you're suited for and not the others. Although I was not in terms of taste and temperament suited for being a screenwriter in the modern Hollywood, the job I am suited for is writing books, and I've been doing that more or less happily and successfully since 1963.

But it was not until I was writing books fulltime, devoting complete concentration to that craft from 1984 onward, that I realized my long experience as a screenwriter and journalist has greatly enhanced my work as a film historian, enabling me to understand the hidden realities of the industry and both sides of its uneasy balance between business and art. Those of us who study Hollywood history, particularly the history of the studio era, aspire to see it three-dimensionally, like F. Scott Fitzgerald's idealized hero, studio executive Monroe Stahr, in *The Last Tycoon*.

As the book's narrator Cecilia Brady, the college-educated daughter of another executive, puts it, "You can take Hollywood for granted like I did, or you can dismiss it with the contempt we reserve for what we don't understand. It can be understood too, but only dimly and in flashes. Not half a dozen men have ever been able to keep the whole equation of pictures in their heads."

It sounds like you lost your desire to be a screenwriter.

I stopped writing screenplays abruptly in August 1981 while I was in the early stages of writing one called *Red Gold*, about the actual dispute between Navajos and Hopis over uranium rights in the Monument Valley area. It involved a love story between a Navajo cop and a white woman I wanted Jane Fonda to play. It was the kind of idea that later would become identified with novelist Tony Hillerman. Robert Wise was interested in the project when I told him about it, but when Sam Fuller sensibly asked me, "Is he paying you for an option to write it?," I realized how little that expression of interest actually meant. Maybe Sam and I were being too cynical. Although the script was going well, when I had written about thirty pages, I took a break to go out for drinks one night at a piano bar in Beverly Hills. I stopped working on the script at that point and never resumed. I didn't know why it happened at the time I was enjoying working on a script, but I finally just had enough.

Were you thinking of supplementing your income during this period by giving film lectures or teaching film courses?

During the mid-1970s, I had a job offer to teach screenwriting from California Institute of the Arts (CalArts) in Santa Clarita, a highly respected school for the visual and performing arts. I was only twenty-seven at the time. My friend F. X. Feeney, a critic and screenwriter who was a graduate of the school, told me about the opening and arranged for me to visit the campus. I got along well with the head of the program. But I didn't take his offer because I thought I wasn't ready to teach, which I realized requires being selfless and focusing more on your students than on yourself. I was saddened by the enthusiasm I felt coming from some of the young male students I met, since I didn't think I was up to the opportunity they presented. I was only able to reach that point later in life, after I had put my screenwriting career far behind me. But now I wish I had taken the CalArts job back then, which would have enabled me to survive being a freelance screenwriter with much less stress and would have eased me into the dual-track life I later spent as a professor and author.

When you look back on what you learned from being a Hollywood screenwriter, how do you analyze the causes and effects of those "expensive lessons"?

As I reflected on what I considered the somewhat mysterious problems I was having selling scripts, I blamed not only the Reagan era's increasing conservatism but also my depressed state when I went in to perform the excruciating ritual of pitching scripts and the increasingly onerous burden of continuing to grind out material that didn't sell. I had to weigh the alternatives. I began to consider that when I write a book, it almost always gets published. And I had always enjoyed writing books, as hard as that can be. President Kennedy, shortly before his death, defined what makes such a challenge so gratifying: "The Greeks once defined happiness as full use of your powers along lines of excellence."

So with that alternative in mind, when I got to the point where I couldn't stand writing any more scripts or outlines for films that were not made, I realized I had to abandon working in Hollywood. I just could not do it any longer. I had to devote my life to something more fulfilling. I began to find that satisfaction while writing my Capra biography, which drew from everything I had learned about the film industry and the craft of writing. But even so, for the next few years as I was changing professions, I still could not help feeling an aching hole in the pit of my stomach over abandoning my screenwriting aspirations.

My life vastly improved after I gave up screenwriting to write books fulltime. Even though I went right into writing my Capra biography, another fraught experience which I chronicle in my 2019 book *Frankly: Unmasking Frank Capra*, I was working to the fullest of my capacity on a project that I thought would justify the bleak times I spent as a screenwriter. And though it was ironic that the seven and a half years I spent working on the Capra book proved to be an even tougher time than any I had gone through in Hollywood, it had a more satisfying conclusion, vindicating my decision to fully dedicate myself to my career as an author. And that it did, after much *mishegoss* along the way; I could not have written that book without the deep understanding of the film business I gleaned from my years toiling in the trenches.

5. Film History for the Masses

How did you get what would seem like a dream job for you, writing American Film Institute Life Achievement Award specials?

Those were my happiest, most rewarding, and most successful experiences as a screenwriter, the five AFI award specials for CBS-TV from 1980 through 1984, honoring James Stewart, Fred Astaire, Frank Capra, John Huston, and Lillian Gish. These shows made it all worthwhile. (Well, almost.) I wrote them with the producer, George Stevens Jr., and we received Writers Guild of America nominations for all five. We won the WGA award for the Huston show; we also received Emmy nominations for writing the Astaire and Gish shows, which were nominated for Emmys in the category of outstanding variety, music or comedy program (one of those years while sitting in the audience at the Emmys, I had the thrill of hearing my name read out on national TV by two singers I had always idolized, Ella Fitzgerald and Dinah Shore, who were presenting the award in our category). It was a rare privilege to help pay tribute to the truly legendary people we honored with AFI awards and to work with them and their colleagues when many of the greatest names in film history were still with us. And we were able to humanize these pantheon figures and showcase the quality, nature, and range of their achievements.

I considered these shows "film history for the masses." It was a rare opportunity to present film history on primetime television, including a ninety-minute special about silent movies starring ninety-year-old Lillian Gish, perhaps the greatest actress in the history of film. You couldn't get overly arcane while discussing the careers of the honorees, but you could deliver valuable background and insights along with the emotions offered in tribute as well as the abundant film clips. An AFI board member told me I brought a new level of historical awareness and sophistication to the shows, which the board member said had previously been considered "a joke," slick and superficial.

I got the job on the Stewart show in 1980 when my agents suggested me to Harrison Engle, a documentary filmmaker who was editing the film clips. Harrison was and is extremely knowledgeable about film history and agreed that I was the perfect choice to write the show. When I was first hired, it was just three weeks before the tribute to Stewart was scheduled to be videotaped in front of a live audience of about a thousand industry guests in the ballroom of the Beverly Hilton Hotel on a set decorated with large blowups of Stewart in some of his iconic roles. But the AFI was panicking because they had no script. The writer, Peter Stone, had bailed because he had to work on something else, so they scrambled and found me. I also was recommended by, among others, Hal Kanter, a master of writing awards shows, and Robert Blumofe, the producer and former studio executive I had met on *Bound for Glory*. Luckily, my newspaper training taught me hssow to work fast, which is necessary for such complex TV specials. I find a tight deadline exhilarating, and it puts me at my best. And I already knew Stewart's work well, since he and John Wayne are my favorite actors, and I had met them and watched them at work together on *The Shootist*.

Did you help choose the host?

I asked who was going to host the show. George told me they hadn't been able to think of the right person. I thought for about three seconds and said, "Well, Henry Fonda." That seemed a no-brainer, but I was treated like a genius for suggesting him. George picked up the phone and called Fonda, who immediately accepted. Then George called Stewart, who was hard of hearing, and said in a loud voice that we had "Hank" to host the show. "Hank Potter?" Stewart asked, unaccountably recalling the name of an obscure director he had worked with. It was a heady feeling to suggest a star of Fonda's magnitude and to have him hired as quickly as a snap of the fingers.

Fonda provided the two most satisfying moments of my screenwriting career. The first came the next day, when George and I and Susan Winslow, the assistant film editor, were having a production meeting at our office in West Hollywood. Susan nudged me to turn around and look out the picture window. There was Henry Fonda striding down the sidewalk from his Rolls-Royce, wearing cowboy boots, with his stiff but graceful walk that John Ford loved to film. Robert Towne, in his essay on screenwriting, cites Fonda's walk as an integral part of his iconic image: "His way of moving itself embodied paradox: at once awkward and graceful, diffident yet full of purpose, his ambling walk would shift effortlessly—like a powerful thoroughbred changing gaits.... With each step he took, Fonda could display an astonishing number of character traits, including but by no means limited to integrity, sense of purpose and thoughtful courage."

My second greatest moment came at the rehearsal when I actually heard an actor deliver almost all my lines just the way I wrote them, which hadn't happened much on *Blood & Guts* or at all on *Rock 'n' Roll High School*. And the actor speaking my lines was the man I consider the greatest American actor of his generation. So you can imagine the thrill I felt. I asked Fonda how long it had taken him to memorize his opening speech about his friendship with Stewart, his pal's personality, and his film career. Fonda said he had memorized it in the car coming over to the rehearsal. And he delivered all his other speeches verbatim too, except once when he went up on a line (that is, blanked momentarily) but then improved it. I had written something prosaic about Stewart having come from a small town in western Pennsylvania. Fonda lifted up his eyes, paused, and told the audience that Stewart had come from "the lowlands of the Allegheny Mountains."

Sheer poetry. No doubt Fonda, unlike me, had been there with Stewart. I used this story with students as another prime example of what an actor can do for a writer.

What was your overall approach to working with the stars and other people who spoke on the AFI shows?

At the onset, I asked George naively, "How does this work? Do the stars bring in their own speeches, or do we write speeches for them?" George laughed and said, "Joe! These are *actors!* They need a *script.*"

Towne once said a screenwriter has to know how to talk with stars. I wrote most of the speeches for the shows, with input from the speakers if possible while visiting them at their homes, but sometimes entirely on my own, adopting their voices. The trick in writing the speeches was to make each sound as if the star (or director or other colleague) was speaking off the cuff, from the heart and in the person's own highly recognizable style. Since I had written screenplays and more importantly had interviewed literally thousands of people and faithfully but succinctly written up what they said, I was adept at mimicking the voices of any of a wonderful range of stars from the Golden Age of Hollywood to the present who a youngish screenwriter otherwise would not get to work with. Sometimes stars would come in with something they had prepared, which was rare but usually welcome, sometimes with adjustments. When a star would bring along her own perfect speech, as Audrey Hepburn memorably did for Fred Astaire, that was heaven.

Among my most satisfying collaborations were with David Niven, Claudette Colbert, Eleanor Powell, Donna Reed, Bob Fosse, Robert Blake, and Jeanne Moreau. Others in the diverse array of delightful stars I had the privilege of working with included Princess Grace of Monaco, Colleen Moore, Peter Falk, Bill Mauldin, John Houseman, and Sam Jaffe. And we had rousing and unexpected cameo appearances that required no writing, by James Cagney—who phoned us to ask if he could talk about Astaire, calling him "the greatest dancer I've ever seen"—and Pelé, the world's greatest soccer player. Pelé had been in John Huston's World War II movie *Victory* and delighted the audience by recalling how Huston made him do one of his rarest feats (his overhead "bicycle kick") repeatedly by running instant replays in slow motion.

Sometimes a star had nothing to say, such as when we asked Bette Davis to speak about Frank Capra. The problem was that Davis had come to hate Capra (and vice versa) when they made his abominable final feature, *Pocketful of Miracles.* "Write me something," she told George. So I took on the task, deciding to have her be the one to tell the audience what a director does and why Capra is a great director. I incorporated some thoughts Davis had articulated eloquently in interviews about her favorite director, William Wyler. When George read the speech to her over the phone, she said, "Perfect!" When she came to the rehearsal the night before the show, this surprisingly tiny woman asked deferentially if I would mind if she changed a few words. "Mind?" I said. "You're Bette Davis." Naturally her small changes improved the speech, but if they hadn't, I would have sat and worked with her on a revised version, as I did with many of our speakers.

My worst moment, bar none, on any of these AFI shows was when I heard George in our office at the hotel, behind a closed door, reading my speech for Davis in a mocking tone for some friends of his. I barged in and demanded to know what he was doing. He tried to backtrack unsuccessfully. I stormed out and went to the hotel bar with one of the women working on the show, but knocking back a couple of drinks didn't help. I decided to pack up my things, clean off the desk, and leave as a way of registering my protest. As much as I would have wanted to actually quit, I couldn't afford to do so. The next morning when I came in, there was a note of apology from George on my otherwise empty desk.

On the positive side, no experience for me could top that of spending three days in 1981 working closely on hosting remarks with David Niven. He was not only an old friend of Astaire but a delightful writer himself who had published a pair of witty memoirs. Niven's droll reminiscences and observations set a gracefully relaxed and nostalgic tone as well as offering keen understanding of what made Astaire one of the true geniuses of the cinema, akin to Charlie Chaplin in his eloquent use of movement and body language. Niven dropped in some self-deprecatory references on our show to a problem with his voice, which was not apparent to me but stemmed from his early awareness of what would become his case of Lou Gehrig's Disease, from which he died in 1983. After David went home to Saint-Jean-Cap-Ferrat in France, he wrote me,

> My dear Joe,
> ...I'm sorry about my voice but you of all people made things very easy for me and thanks to those geniuses with the boards [cue cards] somehow I muddled through and apparently was understandable!!
> I was so happy to meet you and to get to know you and hope to see you the next time I come back to California.
> Again my thanks for making things so comfortable for me in every way.
> Yours ever, David

It seems that you did a lot more than write the shows—what were your other duties?

I was the principal person doing the research and persuading stars, directors, and other colleagues to be on the shows. That is usually a producer's task, but it was one I volunteered to take on from the second show, the Astaire tribute, onward. Sometimes rounding up the speakers was a challenge due to old animosities with the honoree. For instance, I went to New York to persuade Claudette Colbert, who didn't get along with Capra on their two films together, to fly in to honor him from her other home in Barbados. I also spent several memorably bizarre weeks on the phone with Ginger Rogers in Oregon trying to persuade her to come honor Fred. But she refused, because, as I found, he had snubbed her when photographers asked them to pose together after his Lincoln Center award show. And I learned to my surprise that Ginger and Fred, the greatest romantic couple in movie history, had a frosty relationship while making their films together. Afterward I thought of writing a script about that but realized Neil Simon had already done the subject with *The Sunshine Boys;* Fellini later touched on the theme more affectionately with his fictionalized *Ginger and Fred.*

I watched all the films involving the honorees, which was a treat, especially when we were able to get 35mm prints to watch on a Steenbeck, and I helped the editors choose the film clips so we could ensure that the shows were thematically illustrative and comprehensive as well as entertaining. And I did a myriad of other jobs on the shows, even editing the program books for the last four. Compiling the filmography for the Gish program book while traveling the country to see her films and TV shows took much longer than writing the show itself. When I left after that contentious program, the AFI had to hire five people to replace me.

The director of our shows, Marty Pasetta, did a smooth job with the cameras but had no interest in working with the cast. So I rehearsed the speeches with each of the speakers at the runthrough the night before the videotaping at the award dinner and spent more time than that with the hosts—Fonda for Stewart, Niven for Astaire, Stewart for Capra, Lauren Bacall for Huston, and Douglas Fairbanks Jr. for Gish.

We always cut the shows down to size on the day after the taping, a process in which I was always involved. The film editors of the AFI shows never bothered to show up for the day of postproduction, but I always did; I saw myself as the protector of the film clips and speeches and fought to keep from being cut too heavily. I would get a transcript of the live show prepared overnight by secretaries and make the preliminary cuts before we started work in the editing suite, and then I would suggest ways of fine-tuning the speeches, almost all of which George accepted, as we went through the show. I made many other editing suggestions that were followed, including creative suggestions about the choice of reaction shots, which had an important but subtle effect on the film clips and speeches and how they were received. I tended to want as many clips to play as possible, so I would suggest cutting down some speeches to accommodate them. I didn't realize that placing greater emphasis on the clips for the Astaire show would cost me my industry health insurance for a year. I was belatedly informed of a rule that if a TV special was less than one-half talk, as ours just barely was, it would not be credited for insurance purposes; fortunately, I didn't get seriously ill that year.

How did you establish the tone of the shows you did, which often were more irreverent than the typical overly sentimental award-show?

I was determined to bring a lot of humor to these shows. Because most film industry award shows are pretentious, overly solemn, and larded with shallow and repetitive praise, I decided to tease the honorees in affectionate ways. I also vowed to avoid writing anything about how much the speaker loved the honoree or how the speaker had a wonderful time working with him or her, knowing that some of that kind of flatulent talk would leak into the shows as ad-libs anyway. The teasing element and low-key humor I wrote into the speeches made the shows a lot of fun and brought out lively and sometimes spontaneous moments of character-based humorous insight.

Although I am good at writing that kind of speech, I am not adept at coming up with one-liners. When I tried a couple of those on AFI shows, they fell flat, although one worked. We dealt with Stewart's World War II record as a bomber pilot in the U.S. Army Air Forces by having that history unexpectedly related by a fellow soldier in his squad, Staff Sergeant Walter Matthau. As he came out to the audience's delighted surprise, I had him order them "At ease." That brought out a hearty laugh before he got down to more serious business. The character humor balanced and leavened the sentimental aspects of the shows in a believable and pleasing way.

For the speech by Mikhail Baryshnikov honoring Astaire, I took an audiotape of a conversation with George in which Baryshnikov made a string of hilariously tongue-in-cheek references to how dancers really feel about Astaire: "It's no secret, we hate him. He gives us complexes, because he is too perfect." I enjoyed the conversation so much that rather than twist his remarks into conventional praise, I constructed a speech around his wry, backhanded approach. The audience loved it, as did Fred, whose face showed intense delight as Baryshnikov teased him in such a warm and loving way.

While joshing Astaire, Baryshnikov was simultaneously making serious points about the older dancer's mastery: "You know, you give your own performance and receive applause and you think, maybe, just maybe it was successful. And you go home feeling good and turn on television to relax, and *there he is*—making you nervous all over again. *[Pause]* You remember the remark by Ilie Nastase about Björn Borg—he said, 'We are playing tennis, he is playing something else.'

[Laughter] It's the same with Fred Astaire—we are dancing, but he is doing something else." Then Baryshnikov went into a more straightforward expression of his impassioned appreciation for Astaire's influence and legacy. At first I thought the shift in tone might break the spell, but George persuaded me that Baryshnikov needed to make his heartfelt personal tribute, and it struck just the right balance.

Did CBS try to persuade you and Stevens to make the Astaire tribute in particular but all the AFI tributes into glitzy variety shows?

There was some of that pressure, and some of the later AFI shows I didn't write fall into that trap rather embarrassingly, but we resisted. CBS always wanted live musical numbers, even though most of our tributes weren't for musical stars. George did tell me to write a spoof of the song "They Can't Take That Away from Me" for our Astaire show. He wanted a demo audiotape sent to male stars who would sing it in honor of Fred. I argued that no one would want to do that in front of Fred. But he insisted. So we recorded the song with Hermes Pan, Fred's longtime choreographer partner, and I singing it while our composer, Nelson Riddle, who had been the arranger for Frank Sinatra and Judy Garland, played it on the piano. When Nelson told me to sing the song, I protested, "I can't sing." He said, "Nonsense. Everybody can sing." Then when we finished the song he said with a look of pained wonderment, "You're right. You really *can't* sing." We sent the tape to eight or ten stars, and I was right—only that dauntless and infallibly generous trouper Jack Lemmon agreed to do it. So thankfully a bad idea was shelved.

An even more potentially disastrous development we dodged while working on the Astaire show came when I was driving through the Beverly Hills business district one afternoon and made a right turn. Just then an elderly man jumped off the curb in front of my car. I hit the brakes. It was Fred. He glared at me, I looked at him sheepishly, and we both went on. In that surreal moment, I could see the headline flash before my eyes: "ASTAIRE TRIBUTE WRITER KILLS FRED." If I had turned a moment or two later, this book would never exist.

Was the show honoring Capra difficult to do in light of what you learned about his being an informer?

That was a difficult show for a number of reasons. George seemed to loathe Capra, which I guessed might have been a legacy from his father's problems with their postwar Liberty Films partnership and their relationship during the blacklist era, when George Sr. fought blacklisting and Capra was an informer. The AFI shows were easy to write when George Jr. liked the honorees: Stewart, Astaire, and Huston; the tribute to Huston was especially delightful to work on, because George adored him. The shows were hell, by contrast, when George disapproved of the honorees, meaning Capra and Gish.

I learned about Capra's informing when I was researching the show and went to Wesleyan University for the first time to study his papers. It was a shock, and I didn't know how to process it yet, let alone how such an insight into his character and downfall could possibly be worked into a show honoring him. When I told George what I had discovered about Capra being an informer, he actually put his hands over his ears, broke into a pained grin, and said, "Stop!" I realized that this kind of TV show, designed as a tribute, proved antithetical to the task of presenting the full story. Jean Firstenberg, the head of the AFI, told me after my biography was published, "If we'd known, we wouldn't have honored him."

George had never even seen *It's a Wonderful Life* and refused to do so. But the editor and I insisted he needed to at least see a key clip we were planning to use, the scene of Jimmy Stewart angrily proposing to Donna Reed, which Capra told me he thought was the best scene he had ever directed. George watched it but said he didn't understand it. I said, "You need to understand the subtext." He said, "What subtext?" George never seemed clear about what he wanted the Capra show to accomplish and turned down many of my ideas for guests and speeches. I was struggling to find a way to deal with Capra's complexities and to avoid being simplistic. One idea I had was to invite a wide range of speakers of differing political persuasions to show how Capra meant many things to many people. Perhaps George was right in vetoing that idea, which might have become confusing and evasive, but he simply scoffed at the idea of asking Democrats, such as California Governor Jerry Brown, as well as Republicans to talk about Capra as a political figure (on the AFI tribute to Warren Beatty in 2008, the speakers included former president Bill Clinton and George McGovern, two politicians for whom Beatty had worked as a fundraiser; Jerry Brown was seen in the audience, but that casting was conventional, since they were all Democrats).

George told me when we started work on the Capra tribute that it would "rise or fall on the quality of Capra's speech," since he generally was a poor speaker. He tended to be halting and inarticulate, looking down and not at the audience, mostly showing the camera his bald pate. So I spent two months working hard with Capra in writing and rehearsing the speech. I didn't realize until later that some of the parts he claimed he wrote were the product of a ghostwriter, John Culhane of the *Reader's Digest.* Capra was eager to make it as good as possible, "because it's the end." Going down periodically to his home at the La Quinta Hotel to work on it together and talking at length over leisurely dinners helped me to get to know him much better.

As I write of his speech in *Frankly: Unmasking Frank Capra,* "His ending invocation of being held up by his father to see the Statue of Liberty upon entering New York harbor as a six-year-old immigrant and his thanking his dead parents and siblings were deeply moving, as was his final line, with its suggestive ambiguity: 'But for America, just for living here, I kiss the ground.'" I devised the optimum camera angle to minimize the bald-head problem and suggested we pre-tape the speech on the afternoon of the show so we could intercut it with the live event in case Capra stumbled. That all worked beautifully, and we were able to use more of the live part than we had expected while saving the tape for complicated parts he found more difficult to articulate in front of the audience. The syndicated columnist Liz Smith wrote of the speech, "I haven't cried so hard since Bambi's mother died."

But I admit that the show, unfortunately, did its part in helping perpetuate the Capra myth that I later dismantled in my biography. I added the final touch to the myth when he brought in some lines about how "The art of Frank Capra is very, very simple: It's the love of people. And add two simple ideals to this love of people, the freedom of each individual and the equal importance of each individual, and you have the formula upon which I've based all my films." I gently suggested that "principle" would sound better than "formula," a change he eagerly embraced. But I now regret my suggestion, since those humanistic values really *were* a formula to him, not a principle.

We made a short video about Capra's life story, which drew mostly from what I eventually came to realize was his thoroughly specious autobiography. I had Jimmy Stewart say cryptically in introducing the video, "But you know, I can't help feeling that for all the great pictures he's made, the best Frank Capra story is the story of his own life. It's got more highs and lows than a rollercoaster. It's heartwarming. It's kind of hard to *believe*, really." I don't like to watch that half-hearted tribute anymore.

Did you try to enlist your favorite actress and Capra's, the reclusive Jean Arthur, to appear at the Capra tribute? Did you ever meet or interview her in person?

I was fortunate to spend a lot of time with Jean in the 1980s at her home in Carmel, thanks to an introduction by Capra. I first went to see her to try to persuade her to speak at or at least attend our AFI salute to Capra, but she could not be lured out of hiding to do so. I was one of only a handful of people she would see in her later years, and we had a lot of fun talking. "I don't know what you did up there with her," Capra told me, "but I think she wants to marry you!" *Life* magazine once wrote that she was so reclusive she made Garbo look like a party girl. I interviewed her for my Capra and Ford biographies; she had much more to say about Capra, *her* favorite director, than about Ford, for whom she made her film debut in the 1923 silent *Cameo Kirby* and later starred in his 1935 comedy, *The Whole Town's Talking*. That delightful film pairing her with Edward G. Robinson and written by Jo Swerling and Robert Riskin (who were frequent Capra screenwriters) from a story by W. R. Burnett established her star persona before Capra cast her in *Mr. Deeds Goes to Town*. I suggested to Jean that I would write her biography; she agreed at one point to cooperate but soon changed her mind.

She told me some revealing things, such as when I asked why she left Hollywood. She said that when she was under contract to Columbia in 1944, the female stars' dressing rooms were in a row, with a dark hallway connecting them. There was a secret entrance, and studio chief Harry Cohn would come in there and attack the actresses. Jean decided to kill Harry Cohn. She thought she could shoot him in the hallway and get away with it. But she told me that she walked the backlot for three hours and decided to quit the business instead. Jean left Columbia for the theater and made only two more films, *A Foreign Affair* for Billy Wilder and *Shane* for George Stevens, plus her short-lived TV series, before she retired for good. Sexual harassment in Hollywood did not begin with Harvey Weinstein; it's always been an odious part of the movie business.

Which of the AFI shows you wrote do you think was the best?

The Astaire show was the best of the five I worked on. That was my second show, and unlike the preceding tribute to Stewart, it was not thrown together in a rush but carefully planned and executed. I had months to plan the casting, themes, and elegantly restrained look of the show in advance, and to work with editor Susan Winslow on choosing and editing the film clips. During the dinner that preceded the program, Susan and I sat at the table with Robert Wise, who had worked as a sound effects editor on two of Fred's RKO films, and he complimented her on the editing of our show.

George had made a brilliant producer's decision to omit clips of Fred acting (aside from a few comic bits used as transitions) but to concentrate instead on his dancing and singing. So in the course of researching and writing our Astaire show, I watched all two hundred song and dance numbers from Fred's movies and TV specials and was awed by his virtuosity and ambition, since they all are different and adventurous in their own ways.

The full scope of Astaire's genius was on display on our show, and the clips were sensational. The mood in the ballroom kept building into the most exhilarating, sometimes almost breathless genuine adulation I have ever witnessed for a Hollywood figure. Our montage of Fred doing some of his most astonishing solo numbers brought the audience rising to its feet, the only time that happened in the five shows I worked on. The audience was truly stunned to witness the evidence we assembled of Fred's genius—they seemed to recognize that he was indeed as great a film performer as Chaplin. And virtually all of the cast of speakers rose to the occasion; even Fred, notoriously shy on such occasions, gave a warm and funny acceptance speech. It was touching that the hard-to-please and modest Fred admitted he thought the clips looked really good.

When I was writing the show, Fred's close friend Hermes Pan was our unofficial technical advisor on all things Astaire. Hermes was a wonderful and brilliant man. I told Sam Fuller I was working with Hermes, and Sam said cryptically that "Hermes Pan *was* Fred Astaire." I knew the two men were so similar and so close as collaborators as to seem symbiotic, but Sam said he meant it literally. I asked him to explain, and he said that while he was a scriptwriter in the 1930s at RKO, he spent some time watching the filming of an Astaire-Rogers musical number and witnessed Hermes Pan doubling for Fred in part of the number. I asked Hermes about this, and he loyally denied the story. I went back to Sam, who swore it was true.

Fred seemed diffident beforehand about our show, which he had resisted agreeing to do because of his characteristic modesty and anxiety. When George and I went to his home at the start of our work, Fred was sighing about having to invite his sister and early dancing partner, Adele, and Ginger Rogers. He rolled his eyes to the ceiling as he said, "I guess we'll have to have Ginger." As it turned out, Adele died of a stroke shortly afterward.

Susan Winslow, while struggling to put together a montage of stills showing Fred and Adele in their youthful act together, told me she desperately needed just one more still to make it work. So I volunteered to go to Fred's house to see if I could coax one out of him. As I stood in the entryway, his svelte young wife, Robyn (a former jockey), raced through after a shower, clad only in a towel and giggling. Then Fred emerged. When I told him what we needed, he snapped about how demanding "you people" were. He went into his bedroom and came out a few minutes later holding a shoebox and grumpily handed over a picture of him and Adele. When I went back to the office and told Susan what had happened, she said, "Why are we honoring this guy?" I wondered about that as well but also thought, "Why did I stick myself with the job of her errand boy?"

Ginger was another matter. I found it frustrating to deal with her, for though I understood her resentment of Fred for having snubbed her and acting condescending toward her, I thought it lowered her stature to take her revenge on him by not appearing at his tribute. (Robyn topped her later by withholding clips of Fred and Ginger from his Kennedy Center honors, a peevish move much criticized by the press.) But Ginger's absence from the AFI show, as she told me, had the virtue of enabling us to give more time to Fred's other dancing partners, who usually were eclipsed by the Astaire-Rogers partnership, or, as Ginger insisted on calling it with me, the "Rogers-Astaire" team.

Fred was too much of a gentleman to name his favorite dancers publicly, but Hermes Pan told me that the ones Fred preferred were those with ballet training, Cyd Charisse, Leslie Caron, and Barrie Chase. They and many others were featured in the film clips, and we had Charisse and Chase as speakers. When we had to have Niven announce that Ginger wouldn't be coming, there predictably was a moan of disappointment from the audience in the ballroom. So he then read a brief message I coaxed out of Ginger that I could not help embellishing a bit (to avoid even more acute embarrassment), and we quickly followed that up by having Niven read a telegram of congratulations from President

Reagan, who was in the hospital following his attempted assassination. And then he introduced Eleanor Powell.

The exuberant "Queen of Tap" received a thunderous standing ovation, led by Debbie Reynolds, which was much deserved but no doubt was enhanced by gratitude that Powell, unlike Ginger, had the good grace to come to honor Fred. Powell had not been active for quite a while but told me she did the show to demonstrate to her grandchildren that she had been a star. She devoted herself enthusiastically to working with me on her speech, rehearsing it carefully and repeatedly, and delivering it with aplomb. One critic pointed out that lackadaisical modern stars could learn something from the highly professional way stars from the Golden Age such as Powell dedicated themselves to their work. The clip we showed of her dancing "Begin the Beguine" with Fred from *The Broadway Melody of 1940* was one of the spectacular highlights of the show, and as my young daughter shrewdly observed at the time, Powell was the only dancing partner who made Fred follow *her* style of dancing.

As the date of the event neared, I was concerned and presumptuous enough to write a proposed acceptance speech for Fred and send it to his house. I was worried about his diffidence and thought his speech might bring an anticlimax to all the wonderful film clips. But he ignored what I wrote, fortunately, and seemed to ad lib his remarks, which made them all the more memorable for being heartfelt in his own eccentric style. I was touched, as was everyone else watching, when Fred, who was both a perfectionist about his art and modest to the point of self-deprecation, gave his take on his movie career, riffing on the stunning array of dance numbers we had presented.

After recalling how he went into movies after Adele had retired to get married, Fred said, "I went on by myself and did *all that.*" He gestured toward the twin movie screens behind him and said, "I didn't realize I did all that stuff. Yeemie, Christmas!" As the audience laughed with him, he added, "I saw things up there that I don't remember *doing.* And—and then—I'm glad to say I liked what I saw. I did. I said, my gosh, I didn't know that was that good. And really, it looked good to me." And then, in keeping with the lack of sentimentality that distinguishes his romantic persona on screen, Fred parodied the convention of award-show lovefests. He thanked his colleagues who had come from afar to honor him, saying, "I could cry—I really could—but I mean, if I had a, you know, a little thing that I could squirt in my eye"—he pantomimed squeezing a bottle of glycerin tears—"I could cry." We cut to Audrey Hepburn—who had come the farthest to honor Fred, from her home in Rome—cracking up.

Compared to the brilliantly structured and presented Astaire show, I remember the John Huston tribute being somewhat looser, more relaxed in style, sardonic and even somewhat funky, like Huston himself.

That tribute had a lot of raucous humor and some surprising sentiment, since Huston had recently survived serious surgery, and speakers expressed heartfelt love and concern. After George and I won the Writers Guild of America award for writing that show, I told Huston I thought it was as much an honor to him as it was to us, since he was a hero to his fellow screenwriters as one of the first from our ranks to become an important director. He was pleased to hear that.

For that show, as part of my job of rounding up what is called on TV the "talent," the only person Huston requested we contact was Mary Astor, who starred in the first film he directed, *The Maltese Falcon*, but she was living at the Motion Picture Home, and I was told she wasn't well enough to attend. However, I recruited a record total of thirty-two stars, because so many people were eager to help honor him. So we persuaded CBS to expand the show from the usual ninety minutes to two hours. That probably resulted in an extra $125,000 or more for the AFI, which reportedly received $350,000 per show from CBS in those days. The taping of the Huston special ran for several hours because of the plethora of stars and partly because we had sound problems. At the end of the evening, AFI director Jean Firstenberg and board member Robert Wise sought me out to chastise me for letting the show run so long. I held my tongue but felt like saying to them, "OK, then just give *me* all that extra money I earned for the AFI!"

Anjelica Huston, John's daughter, hosted the part of our show involving brief remarks by some of her father's collaborators who stood up at their tables. But she nervously bobbled some of her introductions, and George had to come out onstage and pretend that we had trouble in the editing truck, so she could start again. I had to direct her at a studio early the following week to redub some of her lines; I also directed Dudley Moore, whose microphone had malfunctioned during the show. He was charming, and I found Anjelica entirely at ease when she didn't have to perform in front of her demanding father, whom she had struggled with while acting as a teenager in *A Walk with Love and Death*. The experience of doing our show helped lead to her coming into her own as an actress in her father's *Prizzi's Honor*, for which she won an Oscar as best supporting actress, and in her beautiful and poignant performance as Gretta in his majestic final film, *The Dead*.

We even had Huston's jockey friend Billy Pearson as a speaker, but he gave a rambling, somewhat incoherent talk that didn't make it onto the air. That was the only time we cut a performer from a show, breaking what George said was a rule of his. Barrie Chase, Fred's last dancing partner, double-crossed us on the Astaire show. She dropped the speech I had written for her and gave a sour speech badmouthing him as a "monster." George resisted my plea to drop her from the televised presentation. Since I had come back from my meeting with Chase filled with enthusiasm about how much fun she was, George joked that in the future when I returned from an interview, he would have me take a saliva test.

I don't like inhabiting their world, but I have always been surprised that few celebrities I've met or interviewed have been unkind or snooty to me, even big stars and directors. Were any of the famous speakers on the AFI show uncooperative or unruly or otherwise a problem?

Jack Lemmon surprisingly was a problem on the Stewart show. He was enlisted to introduce a montage of Stewart doing romantic scenes with various actresses. I have always been a great admirer of Lemmon as perhaps the finest actor of his generation in both comedy and drama. But when his turn came to talk on our show, Lemmon was drunk. Taking a cue from Truffaut's response when I asked what current American actors he liked—he said Sam Waterston, because "Sam Waterston is not macho"—I had written a speech for Lemmon built around that same observation about Stewart being genuinely romantic *because* he was not macho. But in mid-speech, as Lemmon read the cue cards, he seemed to realize he didn't agree with that notion and started adlibbing, defending Stewart's honor against what he mistakenly regarded as a slur on his manhood. The speech became perfectly incoherent, and did we ever have a hard time cobbling together a semi-coherent facsimile in the editing room the following day.

I saw Lemmon sitting forlornly by himself on some stairs in the ballroom after the show, so I went over and introduced myself and, to make him feel better, thanked him for his speech. He brightened up, half-believing me. Over the years, I would have more encounters with Lemmon, who could be strangely moody and introverted in the presence of Billy Wilder (as I witnessed twice) but also a wonderfully observant storyteller when giving me a long interview about John Ford. After the debacle of Lemmon's appearance on the Stewart show, I realized how crucial it was to rehearse with the speakers before turning them loose.

We broke that rule twice with Robert Mitchum. Earlier when I had interviewed Mitchum for *Daily Variety* in his Sunset Boulevard office at ten one morning, the jovially laid-back Mitchum and I knocked down bottles of Dos Equis together. When he agreed later to talk about Huston—a suitably raucous combination—I asked George if I should go up to Santa Barbara and talk with Mitchum about what he might say. "You don't suggest to Robert Mitchum what he might say," George replied dryly. So we had to take a calculated gamble. But I did ask George to suggest to Mitchum that he might like to incorporate his imitation of Huston, which I had heard during our interview and thought was the consummate Huston imitation.

Todd McCarthy was seated at Mitchum's table during the dinner and later told me the actor had arrived with his own bottle of tequila and drank it all before the show. By the time his name was called, Mitchum was blotto, his head reclining on his chest. Hearing his name called, he gradually unwound and ambled *verrry slowly* up to the stage; we cut his minute-and-a-half walk to ten seconds. As he began talking, he didn't quite know where he was. Then he made a joke about Huston not bothering to direct him in a scene involving explosions in *Heaven Knows, Mr. Allison*; a reaction shot revealed Huston glowering. But something clicked in Mitchum, he got going, and he made some wonderfully funny remarks that captured the essence of working for Huston and offered one of the most profound comments I've ever heard about the movie business:

> You know, I tell people that I was led down a garden path when I first signed on. They said you get to meet a lot of pretty people and you make a lot of money, and you have a lot of fun. *[Deep sigh]* Well— the pretty people all go home at six o'clock, the Man comes and takes the money, you know, but John made it fun, and he continues to make it fun. And he, honest to God, is one of the few people who sees the *real basic fun* in the genre of motion picture making and communication. And I adore him for that.

The following year, we were more relaxed in letting Mitchum wing his tribute to Lillian Gish based on their experiences working on *The Night of the Hunter.* Mitchum proved to be a perfect gentleman with his eloquent and gracious remarks on that occasion. He recalled the casting process when he asked director Charles Laughton who was going to play "Rachel, 'the tree with many limbs for many birds.' I envisioned a large stalwart woman that we had been accustomed to seeing in a lot of the American Westerns. And he said, 'Lillian Gish.' And I said, 'But, Charles, she belongs as a decoration on top of a Christmas tree. *[Holding his hand above his head in pantomime.]* You know, she has a fragility, and she smiles like an angel.' And he said, 'I'll *show* you fragility.'"

Laughton took Mitchum to the studio and ran Griffith's *Way Down East,* with its sequence of Gish lying semi-conscious on an ice floe in the midst of a roaring river during a blizzard as she is about to go over what looks like Niagara Falls. Mitchum said, "That's not the sort of thing that *I* would do. And I was impressed. She arrived—and she was the *essence* of grace, and she *did* smile like an angel. She was the cement that held the whole thing together." Their film's lasting impact, Mitchum concluded, "is due in great part to the grace and that inner fiber of *steel* which lies within the character of Miss Gish."

In one of those fortuitous accidents of planning that sometimes brought magic to our shows, the next part of our tribute featured that sequence from *Way Down East* before George presented the Life Achievement Award to Miss Gish and quoted her remark about her career as an actress, "What you get is a living; what you give is a life."

I assume Huston wanted to write his own speech for his AFI tribute.

Huston brought in the text of his acceptance speech ahead of time to show me, a gracious gesture to a fellow writer. I read it quickly as he sat there next to me. It was a picaresque reminiscence of wild and funny and moving incidents that had taken place while he was making his films. Some of them seemed outlandish, such as the time on *The African Queen* when he and his script clerk were floating in a boat down a river in Africa and began to rise slowly above the water. They looked down and found themselves balanced on a hippo's back. Huston paid a felicitous tribute to his script clerk: "I looked to see how Angie was taking it: she was making a note in her script."

Trying to think of a suitable compliment as I finished reading his impressive script, I said it reminded me of Othello's speech to the Senate, that warrior's tale of how he wooed and won Desdemona with his improbably heroic exploits. Huston immediately responded, "The men whose heads do grow beneath their shoulders — the *Anthropophagi*." I thought he would be happy that I compared what he wrote to Shakespeare — and one of Shakespeare's most marvelous speeches at that. But I could tell he was displeased. He seemed to take my compliment as a veiled way of saying his speech was a lot of bullshit, colorful but still bullshit. Over the years, though, I learned that Huston's tall tales actually checked out. When I spoke at the National Film Theatre in London to open a Huston retrospective, his longtime script clerk, Angela Allen, was in the audience. I called her up to participate, and we had a lively Q&A session with the audience. She said it was true that they were riding on the back of a hippo and that she was jotting it down in her script.

Huston's giving me his speech beforehand proved invaluable. Then I could make sure a camera was focused on Mitchum to catch his reaction when Huston talked about his bravery on *Heaven Knows, Mr. Allison*. Huston related that Mitchum raised no complaint doing the Marine crawl on his belly, naked from the waist up, through a field of grass on the island of Tobago. "He did it three times until I was satisfied with the take. Then and only then, when he turned around, did I see that he was bleeding out of every pore. The grasses were stinging nettles." Mitchum broke into a charmingly modest smile. And when the director recalled how the native hunter hired to feed the company on location for *The African Queen* had stocked their stew pot on location with "long pig" (a euphemism for cannibalism), we received a bonus as the camera unexpectedly caught Mitchum delightedly mouthing the words "long pig" along with Huston.

Did the honorees express their appreciation to you?

Lillian Gish did. After she gave her surprisingly hilarious acceptance speech for her Life Achievement Award and the show was over, she gamely posed for a gaggle of photographers in the otherwise deserted ballroom of the Beverly Hilton. But I watched with growing concern as the *paparazzi* became increasingly frenzied. I dashed into the kitchen and found a worker to help me. Together we lifted Miss Gish by the arms and bore her to safety a few steps ahead of the chasing *paparazzi* and deposited her in the freight elevator. My last glimpse of Miss Gish as the doors closed was her giving me a little smile and a wave with her fingers. Seven months later, I received an endearing handwritten letter from Miss Gish. I had written to tell her that our show had been nominated for an Emmy but didn't win, and I sent her an AFI Life Achievement Awards calendar that I wrote. Her letter was dated "October 10th, 1984, on United above the Rockies on the way to Vancouver, B.C.":

> Dear Joseph McBride—
> A triple thank you, kind sir, for the beautiful calendar which I not only will use but enjoy and for the writing of the tribute. Truly beautiful.
> Thirdly—and most importantly—to me you did win the Tony [she meant the Emmy nomination] and it was a thrill and an honor to even be nominated.
> Your talent deserves acclaim—and more acclaim is exactly what I wish you which comes with all my gratitude and love.
> Ever gratefully,
> Lillian Gish

Next to her signature was a colorful image of a floral bouquet. To receive such a letter is accolade enough for an entire career as a screenwriter. It makes it all worthwhile, more than making up for the times when I had to work with people who lacked the grace and courtesy of that rare lady who represents the bygone best of the art form.

I think the guest speaker you were most excited to meet was Jeanne Moreau, whose speech was a highlight of your tribute to Lillian Gish.

Indeed. I always had a crush on Moreau ever since my youthful erotic *frisson* seeing the brief glimpse of her nude backside when I was panting through a European movie at the Princess Theater in downtown Milwaukee. More seriously, Moreau in her mixture of elation and glumness onscreen, and her physical appearance, reminded me of my first love, whom I call Kathy Wolf in my memoir *The Broken Places*. I've always found Moreau's incandescent performance as the free-spirited Catherine in Truffaut's *Jules et Jim* one of my cinematic touchstones. But I was startled many years after I first saw the film by realizing that that female character I found so alluring in my college days is

My long erotic obsession with Jeanne Moreau had a seriocomic
denouement after I became involved with her on some film and TV
projects, including spending a week writing her speech together
for our AFI salute to Lillian Gish in 1984. This shot is from Orson
Welles's 1968 film *The Immortal Story*. (ORTF/Albina Productions/
frame enlargement)

actually a sociopath. Catherine sets her nightgown on
fire while burning her love letters and ominously keeps a
bottle of sulfuric acid "for the eyes of men who tell lies."
Euphemistic 1962 subtitles had partly caused my confusion,
as had my somewhat blinkered youthful romanticism.

Moreau was mercurial in her own maddening ways,
but she and I hit it off so well when we met back in 1975
that she told me about her difficulty getting her first feature
as director, *Lumière*, distributed in the United States.
As I had with Truffaut when recommending that he take
his 1975 film, *The Story of Adele H.*, to Roger Corman,
I suggested she approach Roger with her film. She did, and
he distributed it with some success in 1976, as he did with
Truffaut's 1976 film about children, *Small Change*. Moreau
also asked me to write a screenplay for her. She told me she
was "dreaming" about a movie of a French woman coming
to the American West and falling in love with a cowboy, who
figuratively speaking is "the Marlboro Man." She asked me
to do my own imagining about that idea and come up with a
story. For some reason, perhaps because the male character
seemed alien to me, I kept temporizing about working on
her suggestion and never contacted her about it. When we
came back together for the Gish program nine years later,
I didn't bring up the earlier project, and she seemed to have
forgotten it.

Moreau had directed an affectionate 1984 documentary about Gish (an affectionate portrait I wasn't able to see until many years later), and I recommended her as the person we needed to give weight to the AFI show to explain to the audience why Gish is a great actress. I told George we should get the world's greatest contemporary actress to carry out that mission, as the cornerstone of the show. So I spent a happy week working on the speech with Moreau at her rented home in Los Angeles. We shared thoughts and impressions before blending them into a tribute that authoritatively interwove analysis and admiration. She was wonderfully impassioned and eloquent about the older woman, calling their first meeting in a restaurant in New York "a *coup de foudre* — love at first sight." In discussing technical aspects of Gish's working methods, Moreau wanted to introduce a clip from a 1913 Griffith short in which she gives a comical performance, *The Lady and the Mouse*. I told our film editor about Moreau's desire, but when it came time for the show, I found she had not bothered to get a clip from the film. That was one of the things that infuriated me about that show.

So instead a clip was chosen of Lillian and her sister Dorothy Gish from Griffith's 1921 feature *Orphans of the Storm,* about the French Revolution. It was good, although it kept the show's focus almost entirely on Lillian's tragic side without recognition of her considerable comic talents. I strongly suspected that in the editing process, our director, Marty Pasetta, would try to cut that lengthy but mesmerizing silent clip from *Orphans.* So I protected the clip by writing into Moreau's speech words of introduction for it and also making sure the speech would have no ending if they cut those words; and for extra protection, I instructed Carl Davis's orchestra to begin playing his music for *Orphans of the Storm* while Moreau was still talking about it.

Orphans and Moreau's speech went over wonderfully on the live program. But sure enough, in the editing studio the next day, Pasetta said, "Can we lose that clip?" I pointed out the reasons we couldn't do that. Pasetta and George exchanged looks. I could tell what they were thinking: "He fucked us." Marty exhaled and said, "OK, let's move on." That was one of my most satisfying moments as a screenwriter. (Ironically, the film editor of the Gish show won an Emmy but wasn't there during the final editing.)

There was a tragicomic, or perhaps merely absurdist, anticlimax to my relationship with Moreau: *My Date with Jeanne Moreau.* When I was assigned to cover a black-tie dinner at the University of Southern California honoring

Fred Astaire and Stanley Donen in November 1975 while Moreau was in town (the annual Delta Kappa Alpha national honorary cinema fraternity tribute), I invited her to come with me, and she accepted. With romantic fantasies dancing in my head, I rented a tuxedo, bought Moreau a bouquet of red roses, and borrowed a friend's convertible that was more presentable than my old beater so I could pick her up in style at her hotel that Sunday night at six PM. I confided in a couple of friends that I would be bringing Jeanne Moreau.

At ten to six, the phone rang in my apartment. In her most languid tones, like her jaded Fraülein Bürstner talking with Joseph K. in Welles's *The Trial*, Moreau told me she regretted she was too tired to go to the event and hoped that I would have a good time. That served me right for breaking my rule not to date actresses. When I arrived and saw my friends with their quizzical looks, at least I had the presence of mind to quote a quip by Woody Allen, "I'm still striking out with women, but now I'm striking out with a better class of women." But I got so drunk I couldn't remember anything about that program years later when I wrote the AFI tribute to Astaire and suddenly realized I had attended an earlier event in his honor. I racked my brain, but all I could recall was arriving at the event and then going to Moreau's hotel afterward and dumping the bouquet on her doorstep, without knocking.

There was an epilogue to this absurd story. Christa Fuller, who occasionally tried to play matchmaker, advised me, "Jeanne Moreau only goes to bed with her directors or young men who tell her they want to be a director. So tell her you want to be a director." I muttered something noncommittal. The next time I saw Moreau, during the week in 1984 when I worked with her on the Gish program at her house in the hills above Sunset, she asked, "So tell me, do you want to be a director?" "No," I said. "I'm happy to be a writer." She frowned and said, "Are you *sure* you don't want to be a director?" Again I swore I had absolutely no interest in that profession. She looked mystified. And we left it at that.

Was it your choice to stop working on those AFI shows?

Most of the time, I found the process of writing the shows rewarding and stimulating, even if George later told me, "Your problem was trying to make those shows better than they could be." That comment conflicts with his remark elsewhere that one of the most important lessons he learned from his father was to always have respect for the audience. But once while we were editing one of the AFI shows and I was trying to improve something, George said dismissively that television is just "skywriting" that people instantly forget.

Well, I actually did succeed in making the shows much better, but it was sometimes a battle. I quit Hollywood in disgust in 1984 after the horrible experience of working on the Gish Life Achievement Award show. I struggled against heavy internal opposition to make it a worthy tribute to a great actress and the silent film medium. I succeeded but finally decided to leave the business after I received a WGA award for the Huston show, WGA and Emmy nominations for the Gish program, and becoming vested for a film industry pension, all in a short period of time.

My friend Mike Kaplan came up with the idea of honoring Gish, partly out of his friendship with her and partly to promote her to further his own plans of producing the film *The Whales of August*, in which she went on to star with Bette Davis. (Mike asked me to give the script to Jean Arthur, but I wouldn't, because she told me she would not act again.) I connived with Mike about how to get Gish the award, suggesting that he quietly lobby AFI board members. He did so, and when Gish prevailed by a 10-9 vote, one of the board members who voted for her told me that George "looked like a wall had fallen on him." The board member added, "This finally shows that the AFI has integrity."

The AFI has always had a terrible record in giving the Life Achievement Award to women. Of the first fifty award winners through 2025, only eleven have been women. Gish was the second, after Bette Davis; they were the only two women among the first twelve recipients (Garbo and Katharine Hepburn had been offered the award but turned it down). George at one point in the early 1980s asked me to prepare dossiers on a number of possible candidates for the award, and I added Ingrid Bergman and Audrey Hepburn, names that should have been no-brainers. But George asked me of Bergman, "Has she made that many great films?" I said, "Only about seven of the greatest films in history." And as for Audrey, he told me he thought she was too young to receive the award. I said she was semiretired, had already made numerous classics, and probably wouldn't make many more films. As it turned out, she made only made one more feature and a TV movie before dying prematurely at age 63.

When Gish was chosen as the recipient, George basically tuned out of working on the show and let me perform most of his producing chores as well as my own writerly duties. We

My co-writer, producer George Stevens Jr., and I working on one of
the five American Film Institute Life Achievement Award specials we
did together. This is a rehearsal for the 1981 tribute to Fred Astaire
with fellow dancer Mikhail Baryshnikov, whose droll and ironic talk
was described by a prominent film producer as "the all-time greatest
awards show speech." (American Film Institute)

had quite a brouhaha over his refusal to show a clip from
what I consider Gish's greatest role, in D. W. Griffith's 1919
silent masterpiece, *Broken Blossoms*. George was worried
about backlash over her character's interracial romance
with a Chinese man (played by a Caucasian actor, Richard
Barthelmess): George didn't think the film is PC; or maybe
the problem was that it's too PC. I enlisted the silent film
expert Kevin Brownlow, an advisor on our show, to get on
the phone from London to George while they both watched
on their editing machines a scene Kevin had chosen from
Broken Blossoms. George still refused, saying: "All I see is
a Chinaman running through the streets." Exasperated,
I protested by coming to work wearing a button with a picture
of Gish in that film. When she arrived at our production office
at the Beverly Hilton Hotel and saw my button, she rushed
over with arms outstretched to hug me. My girlfriend wore a
spectacular Chinese dress to the show as her form of protest.
I registered a pseudonym for myself with the Writers Guild
of America—Lucy Burrows, the name of Gish's character
in *Broken Blossoms*, who is abused and eventually beaten
to death by her father—in case the show turned out to be a
disaster, as seemed possible until the final week.

Because George temporized until almost the end about
casting the show, while spending much of his time skiing
in Aspen and leaving me and the film editors to do all the

work, it was thrown together willy-nilly in the final week shortly before the show taped before a live audience. I had prepared for that eventuality by compiling a notebook with a hundred single-spaced typed pages containing possible material for speeches. On the Friday prior to the week when the live show was to be taped on Thursday, March 1, CBS pressed the panic button because the script contained only one speech, the tribute I had written with Moreau. At that point, AFI director Jean Firstenberg, who liked Gish and was sympathetic, asked me how I was doing, but when I opened my mouth, no sound came out. I was getting quite ill.

The upshot was that I had to write almost all of that show in the last two days while suffering from pneumonia. My doctor told me not to go to the Sunday technical rehearsal "or you might die." That was the third time I had come down with pneumonia while writing AFI shows, and this marked two years in succession. (I also had pneumonia twice as a child and have always been susceptible to respiratory problems.) My body was rebelling in the early Eighties, when I was often laid up with illness; it was telling me to quit Hollywood.

In the late 1970s and early '80s I had struggled vainly to give up my foolish habit of smoking expensive cigars, which I enjoyed for a while. Mark Twain supposedly declared, "Giving up smoking is the easiest thing in the world. I know because I've done it thousands of times." But when my health took a serious hit from the bout of pneumonia I suffered in 1982, the mere thought of putting a lit cigar in my mouth again made me sick to my stomach.

My absence from the Sunday tech rehearsal for the Gish AFI show finally caused George to panic. He told me if I didn't come in Monday, he would have to hire another writer. So I made it in, carrying a large bag of over-the-counter cold and flu medicines; the secretaries in our office at the Beverly Hilton were wide-eyed as I laid out all the bottles on my desk. Meanwhile, George finally got down to business and started calling stars. And I quickly wrote speeches for the cast, which I couldn't have pulled off without anticipating what a rush it would be at the end. When a man called me in a controlled panic without identifying himself to say that Eva Marie Saint was *very* nervous because she didn't have her speech yet—obviously this was her husband, Jeffrey Hayden, a TV producer-director—I wrote the speech in half an hour and faxed it to them. He called right back and said it was fine; Saint's appearance on the show was among its many highlights. Another was a droll speech by John

Houseman about Gish's distinguished stage career; he took what I wrote and embellished it with firsthand knowledge and his own wit, which was a great help, since I was so punchy by the time I wrote it that I was almost incoherent when we spoke on the phone after I sent him my draft.

Unfortunately, most of the cast got sick too in a wave of the flu that swept through town, and we had to re-cast those speakers at the last minute. I had suggested Carol Burnett as the host, and she agreed, but when she fell ill, George cast Douglas Fairbanks Jr. without consulting me, the first time he had done so in choosing the host in the five shows we did together. I was irate and felt like not trying to help Doug when he seemed wooden in rehearsal. But my bedrock professionalism kicked in, and I decided to make him work as the host. I asked George what the problem was with Fairbanks, figuring I would get some advice channeled from his father, who had directed him in *Gunga Din*. George Jr. said, "Doug's problem is that he's not Cary Grant, and he knows it."

I had sworn never to flatter another actor again after James Mason behaved rudely to me before our Huston show. When I told him how much his performance in *A Star Is Born* had meant to me, he sniffed, "Let's get on with it, shall we?" But for two days I shamelessly flattered Doug. I decided to treat him as if he were Cary Grant, telling him how *witty, suave, debonair, charming*, etc., he was. At first he looked incredulous, but gradually he began to believe it. His performance came alive and became witty, suave, debonair, etc.

On the night of the taping, I did a reconnaissance sweep of the backstage area and found a stool with a bottle of white wine and a glass on it. I asked the stage manager what that was, and he said Mr. Fairbanks had requested it so he could take drinks between his appearances on the show. I recognized disaster in the making and told George. He put on his producer hat and impressively took charge of the situation, calling Fairbanks and saying, "I'm going teetotal until the party after the show" and suggesting Doug do the same. The bottle vanished from backstage. Doug was flawless and held the show together with charm and authority. I had him call himself an "emissary" from the people Lillian called "all those charming ghosts" of the silent era, including his father and stepmother, Lillian's longtime friend Mary Pickford.

So I called on my professionalism and made the show work. Against all odds, it was a triumph. But toward the end of our work on it, George and I had sharp words in a phone call we did with the editor, who had neglected to order the film Moreau wanted to talk about, her comedy *The Lady and the Mouse*. And I complained in that conversation about the show's narrow focus on film clips of Gish as a tragic actress even while leaving out the summit of her work, *Broken Blossoms*. George stonewalled me by putting on a mocking German accent. That was the final straw. I told him I wouldn't do another AFI show.

When I learned you were writing AFI specials, I marveled that my Madison friend had hit the big time, and I was surprised that AFI would be so smart as to hire someone with out-of-the-mainstream tastes and with such knowledge and passion for film. But I wasn't surprised that the shows were so entertaining and was pleased that you received wonderful recognition for your work and even won awards.

Thank you. It was gratifying to receive such recognition from our peers. But after four WGA nominations, I decided I didn't want to go to those award shows anymore, because I was ashamed that I kept feeling disappointed at not winning. In brighter moments I realized that the true honor is to be nominated by your peers. I believe that, because the winner often gets the prize for political reasons, and it's foolish to consider one show or movie better than another that is nominated.

So when a Writers Guild official called me and asked why I hadn't RSVP'd the April 5, 1984, awards dinner when I was nominated for the previous year's Huston show, I made up a transparent excuse, that I was "going to be in Santa Barbara." The official strongly hinted that George and I were going to win. I still decided not to go. She was irked. But I was afraid I would emulate Norman Maine's speech in *A Star Is Born*: "I need a job," etc., and make a fool of myself. So, as John Ford put it on one of the four occasions he didn't show up to receive an Oscar as best director: "I was taken drunk."

I woke at 9:30 the next morning, hung over, to read in the *Los Angeles Times* that we had won the Writers Guild award. Reading the news only depressed me further. Ten days later, I remembered that I had won and called the guild, asking the same official if there was "some kind of plaque or something" that went with the award. I can't blame her for seeming peevish when she replied that there was. When I went to the office to pick it up, she met me in the lobby and somewhat sarcastically staged a little presentation ceremony for me.

I have never been able to put that plaque on my wall, nor any of the certificates I received for WGA or Emmy nominations. It would be too painful to look at them. So they reside in a cardboard box in my closet. Some time ago I pulled out the box to look at them. I found that the engraving on the WGA award plaque has almost entirely vanished. That seems symbolic.

How do you feel about those AFI shows in retrospect?

When I look back on my checkered career as a film and television writer, I am deeply grateful to George Stevens Jr. for involving me as a collaborator on those five AFI shows, despite the frictions we encountered. Few youngish screenwriters would have had the opportunity I had to work with so many legendary figures from throughout the history of American film. Probably the stigma of being a TV writer, a second-class citizen in those days, contributed to my difficulty selling feature ideas after *Big Money,* though, since Hollywood always has been a rigid, stratified class environment. However, my involvement on those shows has greatly enhanced my subsequent work as a film historian, especially on *Frank Capra: The Catastrophe of Success*, the book I consider my most satisfying and important achievement. For all his irritating qualities, George stands out for me in retrospect as an uncommonly intelligent, capable, and tasteful television producer who helped bring a wealth of genuine cultural achievements to the medium Newton Minow had called a "vast wasteland." I learned the hard way that such producers are rare indeed.

Despite the intermittent problems I encountered, those shows were my most fulfilling work as a screenwriter. And I consider the Astaire tribute by far my most fully realized achievement in that field. Although *Rock 'n' Roll High School* is a cult film, and my influence on it was strong, other writers were involved as well, and its vision was just as much shaped by Allan Arkush's supple and imaginative work as a director. Television is more of a writer's medium, and *The American Film Institute Salute to Fred Astaire* bears the stamp of my artistic involvement all the way through, while serving as a fitting and enlightening honor for one of the greatest of film careers.

Can all your AFI shows be seen today?

All five shows I co-wrote were released on VHS, and the Astaire, Huston, and Gish shows on laserdisc as well (copies

Working closely with the witty and urbane actor and writer David
Niven when he hosted our tribute to his old friend Fred Astaire was
one of my happiest experiences as a scriptwriter.
(American Film Institute)

can be found on ebay), but unfortunately none has been
released (officially) on DVD, evidently because of rights
issues involving film clips, but bootleg DVDs are around
the Internet for those who care to check them out. So the
shows I wrote are often hard to find, although they also
pop up sometimes on YouTube, but with some or all of
the film clips missing. When the Capra show played on the
Criterion Channel, even the music was missing as he enters
the ballroom and later as he walks to the stage to accept
his award. We played an orchestral version of the Oscar-
winning song "High Hopes" from his film *A Hole in the
Head* both times as Capra walks through the audience, but
on the streaming version, applause instead keeps playing
maddeningly on a loop.

*I find it bittersweet that so many people that I interviewed
decades ago are now dead. I imagine you had mixed feelings
about interacting with all these famous people whose careers
were already over or ending and didn't have long to live,
like David Niven.*

Yes, there were times I found myself writing the last
appearances of legendary figures. That happened with Alfred
Hitchcock. He came in one afternoon with his helper from
MCA to tape an introduction to our Jimmy Stewart award
show. I had Hitchcock make his cherished joke about how
he had been accused of saying that actors were cattle, while

adding, "What I *really* said was that actors should be *treated* like cattle." Then he remarked, "But an exception should be made for the actor who is being honored tonight...." Even such a lighthearted tribute caused umbrage from the *Daily Variety* reviewer! What made the little speech special for Hitchcock, though, was that in having him introduce himself, I varied his usual sonorous "My name is Alfred Hitchcock" by having him say "My name is Sir Alfred Hitchcock." He had been knighted by Queen Elizabeth that January, and his surprise when he read the word "Sir" from the cue card made me think he had never had the occasion to call himself that before. Sir Alfred's eyebrows and voice went up with delighted surprise. I was glad to please him. He went home and died a month after we aired his tribute to Stewart.

Tell me about Let Poland Be Poland. *Writing a worldwide live TV special for the U.S. government when Reagan was President must have been quite an experience.*

I had a clash with George over that show in 1982. While I was writing the AFI tribute to Capra, our director, Marty Pasetta, hired me to write *Let Poland Be Poland* for the United States Information Service (aka the United States Information Agency). This was a tribute to Poland's Solidarity labor movement, one of the few times I found myself in agreement with the Reagan administration, so I was happy to do it. I began writing the script and suggested Glenda Jackson and Max von Sydow as co-hosts, along with the inevitable Charlton Heston. Working on more than one show at a time was not uncommon for TV writers (or directors), so I didn't see any problem with my taking this assignment, but when George found that I was working on *Poland* on the side, he became irate. He demanded that I be at the AFI office in Los Angeles to work with him on the Capra show for a week when I was needed in Washington. So I had to allow the USIA to hire two additional writers to do the work I wasn't there to do and had to surrender part of my pay as well. Then when I showed up to work at the AFI at nine on the Monday morning, George wasn't there. He didn't show up for the entire week, just to fuck me over.

But *Let Poland Be Poland* was a pleasure to write. I worked closely with Jackson, a great actress and a strong left-wing politician who later became a British MP. She was wary at first because it was for the Reagan administration, but I told her I liked her appearance in a 1968 British film protesting the Vietnam War, *Tell Me Lies*, directed by Peter

Brook. She said of our show about Poland, "I don't want to poke the Russian bear." I reassured her that we would focus on human rights and minimize the propaganda angle, a goal I did my best to accomplish, although some of that was an unavoidable given. The show had twenty-two heads of state sending taped messages, including Reagan and Margaret Thatcher, and some other dubious characters. We were criticized as well, not unfairly, for having a lot of showbiz people on the program. That decision was made by Charles Z. Wick, the political appointee who headed the USIA and a Reagan crony and film producer whose credits had included *Snow White and the Three Stooges*. I made it a point to avoid frivolity, however, and kept the speeches serious, including the ones delivered by Frank Sinatra and Bob Hope, who for perhaps the only time in his career, at least by design, was not at all funny.

My best experience on that program was working with Kirk Douglas, about whom I had written a short biography. Our lively collaboration began when my phone rang in the office at the ungodly hour of 9 AM, and I picked up the line to hear that hyper-energetic voice: *"Joe??!! KIRRRK!!!!"* Previously, when I had met him at a party, he asked why I hadn't contacted him for an interview for the book, which he told me he liked so much that he bought fifty copies, signed them, and sent them to fans who wrote him for his autograph. He had only one reservation: there were a few errors he could have straightened me out on, if only I had called him for an interview. He wondered why I didn't. I said I regretted that decision, but my editor told me not to ask for an interview out of concern he might try to stop the book. Douglas was surprised, saying he would never dream of doing such a thing. I told him I knew that because of his staunch liberalism and support for civil liberties, one of the reasons I admired him. That made him a strong contrast to Frank Capra and his minions when I wrote my biography of Capra. Douglas's talk on *Let Poland Be Poland* is a touching reminiscence of his hearty visit with the students of the Polish national film school at Lodz, complete with film clips.

With the help of Gary Graver, I also wrangled Orson Welles to appear on the *Poland* show. At my suggestion, Welles read some quotes from celebrated people about freedom. I had thought of having him speak back-and-forth with Jane Fonda, to which Welles readily agreed, but the USIA made noises about banning Fonda from the show. I told the producer, Eric Lieber, that we should resign in protest if that happened, and he agreed, but that was not

GLENDA JACKSON

....waar mensen zich solidair
verklaarden met Solidariteit.

Glenda Jackson, a great actress and future British politician,
co-hosted *Let Poland Be Poland*, the worldwide live TV special I
co-wrote for the United States Information Agency in 1982.
The other hosts were Max von Sydow and Charlton Heston. (USIA)

necessary since Fonda declined to be on the show, declaring
that it was just a lot of words and no action. Welles came
in a wheelchair to record his remarks at a small studio in
Hollywood one afternoon, and we all had a chance to visit
and reminisce with him for a couple of hours. But Pasetta
cut most of Welles's lines from the show, leaving only his
quote from John Donne's meditation on how "No man is an
island" along with the show's most eloquent reading of the
words, "Let Poland—be—*Poland*."

*Did the USIA censor anything on the show for political
reasons?*

I was told that the Swedish pop group ABBA refused to
appear on the show after saying they would if they could
also discuss El Salvador. However, the circumstances were
quite different. I learned while working on this book,
Danny, that on January 27, four days before our show was
broadcast live in fifty countries (with radio transmissions
in thirty-nine languages on the Voice of America), ABBA
members Benny Andersson and Björn Ulvaeus actually
recorded a one-minute video message in Stockholm that the
USIA refused to include.

Benny said, "Our thoughts are with Poland with
all the rallies taking place in so many parts of the world
this weekend in support of the Polish people. But I think
this should also be a reminder that there are many other
countries around the world, for example: Chile, El Salvador,

Afghanistan, and Iran, where people are not able to express themselves openly and freely like we're doing now."

And Björn said, "Human rights, things that we take for granted. And yet we are surrounded by so many examples of how easily they can be crushed and wiped out. I hope that this show can be something to help us keep up the constant vigil necessary to help us realize how very delicate and vulnerable democracy is."

When a Swedish TV reporter later asked Björn, "And this wasn't suitable for the American authorities?," he said, "We had a weak suspicion that it might turn out this way, and it turned out this way in the end." The spot aired on Swedish TV shortly after *Let Poland Be Poland* and can be found online on the group's website.

I introduced some sly elements into the otherwise solemn program. The remarks I wrote for another staunch Hollywood liberal, Henry Fonda, who delivered his talk at home while he was dying, constituted his last appearance before a camera. The bearded Fonda said, "I'd like to read the words of one prominent political thinker who couldn't be with us on this program." Those words: "The restoration of an independent, strong Poland is a matter which concerns not only the Poles but all of us.... For the workers of all the rest of Europe need the independence of Poland just as much as the Polish workers themselves." After reading that declaration, Fonda held up a copy of *The Communist Manifesto* by Karl Marx and Friedrich Engels and identified Engels as the writer of those words, from his preface to the Polish edition. We also had the Polish pope, John Paul II, on the program. When he declined to make an appearance just for us, we "stole" some footage of his customary weekly address from the Vatican balcony, which amused me as a renegade ex-Catholic. That's showbiz.

I worked mostly with John W. (Jock) Shirley, the erudite and diplomatic number-two man at the USIA and its former acting director, who still seemed to be running the agency in effect, as many career government officers do in such secondary positions. He briefed me on Polish history and agreed when I said I thought we should encourage resistance but not revolt, in light of what had happened when the USSR crushed the Hungarian revolt in 1956. The show seemed to have a positive effect on helping legitimize the Solidarity movement in the eyes of the world. I spoke with the renowned Polish poet Czeslaw Milosz about his contribution and helped write a speech for the former Polish ambassador to the US, Romuald Spasowski, who spoke with me via a circuitous telephone connection from a safe house.

A member of the Polish resistance in World War II, Spasowski had defected in 1981 as a result of his support for Solidarity. He recalled, "In the times of our greatest peril, [our] hope was affirmed by words.... When I was a young man in Warsaw at the beginning of the Second World War, I built with my own hands a radio to hear the words of the BBC from London." Still pictures of the war and the invasion of Poland ran with audio of Winston Churchill declaring, "Poles—the heroism of your people standing up to cruel oppressors shall not be forgotten. Your country shall live again." Spasowski, whose family harbored Jews during the war, took my suggestion to remind the viewers that "nearly all of Poland's three million Jews" were exterminated in the Holocaust, including at death camps on Polish soil, Auschwitz and Treblinka.

There were limits to my political influence on the show, however. When I asked Jock Shirley if we could include in our telegrams to foreign leaders suggestions about what they might say on camera, he laughed and said the U.S. government couldn't presume to do that. But I did persuade him to *ask* the foreign leaders if they would say something about their countries' special relationships with Poland. British Prime Minister Margaret Thatcher was the only leader who took up my suggestion, beginning her speech by declaring that "Poland has a special place in British history and in British hearts" because of their alliance during World War II when Polish fliers, soldiers, and sailors fought alongside the British armed forces. (Thatcher did remark later that if she had known she would be speaking alongside Frank Sinatra and other Hollywood stars, she might have reconsidered.)

It was exhilarating on January 30, the day before the show aired worldwide, to run up and down the stairs of our production building across from the United Nations, from screening room to screening room, with batteries of translators helping fill me in on the content of rallies being held around the world, so I could write summaries and commentaries on the montages we put together from each country. My training as a journalist helped immensely in enabling me to write those segments speedily and accurately. But as a USIA publicist predicted, we received little attention in the press and most of that negative, since reviewers wrote critiques of Reagan rather than of the program, despite our aim to appeal more broadly. The review I found most amusing was in the Warsaw army newspaper, which declared that the show was written by that "degenerate cowboy Ronald Reagan." I give that publication high marks for coming up with the best two-word description ever made of Reagan.

At the end of my work on the program, Jock Shirley said he could get me jobs in Washington either as a speechwriter for President Reagan or as a staff writer for the USIA. I was gratified by his kind support, but it took me hardly any time to reject both offers. I couldn't write speeches defending death squads in El Salvador and other heinous Reagan policies. Nor was I ready to give up my Hollywood career, such as it was, to move to Washington to write for the USIA. But I am somewhat embarrassed to recall that I didn't return a call from the president's speechwriter while I was working on *Let Poland Be Poland*. I didn't want to be influenced, yet I was being not only cheeky but rude.

Did your agent attempt to find you more projects while you were doing the AFI shows?

Unfortunately I stuck with a lousy agent for most of my years as a Hollywood screenwriter. She was wealthy and lazy. I learned, too late, that she had a reputation for *not* getting work for her clients. One of the flaws in my personality in those days—a tendency for blind loyalty—not only kept me tied to her far too long but even caused me to follow her when she was let go by ICM. At that major Hollywood agency, my principal agent, who was her boss, was the first-rate Jeff Berg, and I should have stayed there with him. I eventually went back to ICM, but by then it was too late to get anything going with another one of Jeff's assistants, who had little interest in my work. ICM was mad at me, though, when I dropped them in 1984 because I decided to concentrate on writing books and found an independent book agent.

What was the last straw for you in the film business?

The proximate cause in May 1984 was a meeting I had with a story editor working for an independent producer. I had pitched him *The Broken Places* and said I wanted to direct it. The story editor laughed and told me that reminded him of a *New Yorker* cartoon about a trained dog in a circus saying, "But what I really want to do is direct." I found that so insulting that after stewing about it for a while, I wrote a sharp letter of protest to the story editor and copied my agent. The crowning touch was that my agent criticized me for writing the letter because she said it would offend the producer. She meant that it would cause her to have to suck up to the producer.

I finally became completely fed up with the mendacity and criminality of the film industry. I could have continued, but the bottom line is that I didn't like what it was doing to me. It took me quite a while to reach that stage, since it entailed giving up on both my illusions and my dreams about making films, which had been only partly gratified in Hollywood. By that point I also had four screenplays and a TV special stolen from me, which is about the worst experience a writer can have in the film industry. Among the films that were stolen from me, I am not counting another project that I neglected to mention earlier, one that was taken away from me because of my own foolishness.

On that occasion I forgot the lesson I had learned while adapting Hemingway's *A Moveable Feast*: Never try to film a book unless you own the rights. In the early 1980s, I had a meeting late one afternoon with a producer who claimed to be interested in my work. So I brought along a book about sports history with a treatment I had written of it. Shortly after nine the next morning, she called to tell me she had read the book but concluded that "It's not for us." I wondered how she could have read it that quickly. But I was emotionally numb by that point in Hollywood, so I shrugged it off. Even when the producer and her partner later made a film of the book, I didn't dwell on it.

But when the film (which shall remain nameless here) opened, I read an interview with the producer in the *Los Angeles Times* saying that a writer had come in to see her with the book, and she immediately became excited by the story but didn't want to work with the writer. Instead she and her partner took the idea to a writer-director they knew, and he made the film with them. More years went by before I brought myself to watch it. It turned out to be good, but at least by then I had pretty well cauterized the wound.

Once I tried to avoid that kind of problem by actually taking an option on a book. In 1965, shortly after Patricia Neal began playing the lead role in *7 Women,* which became John Ford's last feature, she suffered three strokes in one night. Gravely ill as well as pregnant, she had to be replaced by Anne Bancroft. Although initially unable to talk or walk, Neal eventually gave birth to a healthy daughter and was brought back to health by the strenuous, tough-love ministration of her husband, the writer Roald Dahl. Neal made a remarkable comeback by starring in the 1968 film *The Subject Was Roses* under the direction of Ulu Grosbard and receiving an Oscar nomination.

A few years later, I was in an airport when I found a mass-market paperback book on that subject, *Pat and*

Roald by Barry Farrell. I bought it out of curiosity to read on the plane, not expecting much, but was surprised to find it a deeply moving love story. I located Farrell, an amiable freelance writer with an office near *Daily Variety* in Hollywood. I told him I thought his book would make a good movie, and he said, "I always thought so too, but you're the first person who's said that." When I told him I didn't have any money to purchase an option, we agreed to a six-month option for one dollar so I could try to raise interest in filming his book.

I wanted to start the film on the Chinese mission set at MGM with Ford directing Neal as Dr. Cartwright in *7 Women* and thought of casting Bancroft as Neal and Robert Shaw as Dahl. Sam Fuller had a more audacious casting idea—he suggested asking Neal to play herself. He thought that would be good therapy for her, but I felt (perhaps mistakenly) that it would be too strange. I met Grosbard by chance, and he immediately agreed to direct the film. But when I pitched the project as a feature to various story editors and producers, I was met with repeated turndowns, since they all thought it would be a "downer." I argued unsuccessfully that it would be the opposite, an inspiring love story. Eventually I went back to Farrell and admitted failure. But I should have asked him for another option. I had not reckoned with the fact that so-called "disease-of-the-week" stories were popular on television. *Pat and Roald* was adapted as a TV movie in 1981 as *The Patricia Neal Story*, starring Glenda Jackson and Dirk Bogarde and co-directed by Anthony Harvey and Anthony Page. They didn't show her working on *7 Women* but on some other film. I turned it off shortly after that.

The final blunder

And I made one last mistake... the last time I took a meeting as a screenwriter came when I was distracted because I needed money in late 1986. Ruth O'Hara and I had been married in 1985, and this was shortly after our son, John, was born. I was told by my agent that producer Samuel Goldwyn Jr. wanted to hire me to write the 59th annual Academy Awards show. While driving to see Goldwyn, I was delayed—John was ill, and I was reluctant to take the meeting—and I took notes in the car, filling a page with innovative ideas for improving the show, ones I'd been thinking about for years. I apologized to Goldwyn for being late and told him my newborn son was ill. "Then why did you come?" he asked brusquely. A valid question; I should have turned around and gone home. But since I had been led to assume I had already been hired, I spent an hour telling Goldwyn about ideas I had for the show, and he kept pumping me for more. Eventually I realized he hadn't said when I would start writing the show and hadn't even asked for my phone number. I had the awful suspicion that he had only asked for the meeting to pick my brain. I belatedly recalled that Robert Towne had advised me in 1975 to stay away from Samuel Goldwyn Jr.

I tried to put the experience out of my head, but when I saw the Oscar show in March and realized Goldwyn had used many of my ideas, I filed a complaint with the Writers Guild of America. I was told by one of the guild staffers that the WGA was worried about my complaint because Goldwyn had hired the current president of the guild and a past president to write the show. The day before the hearing, I called the guild counsel about the procedures it would follow, telling her I assumed I would talk first to lay out my case and then would answer questions from the panel. She agreed that's the way it would work. The morning of the hearing, my agent, Michael Hamilburg, called me unexpectedly and told me cryptically to "Be a mensch" at the hearing, which I thought doubly odd, since we hadn't even discussed that there was going to be a hearing.

It was obvious to me that the hearing was fixed. The three screenwriter panelists seemed in the bag against me and advocating for the guild and the producer instead, and the counsel kept interrupting to prevent me from making a coherent case. Meanwhile, a court reporter was transcribing the hearing, a procedure to which I agreed. The guild counsel started by saying that my agent had failed to return several calls from the guild—which surprised me—and that made my complaint difficult to prove. At that point I realized my agent was not on my side either. (I bided my time before firing him at an opportune moment.) When I called as a witness the official who had told me why the guild was so worried about my complaint, he denied telling me that but was sweating profusely as he testified, clearly lying. The panelists said I should have asked for a signed receipt from Goldwyn for the notes I orally presented. At the end, the guild counsel refused to give me access to the court reporter's transcript, though I had assumed they would provide it. It was no surprise when the WGA panel quickly ruled against me.

That betrayal by my own guild redoubled my determination to stay out of the industry. I had also been involved in two WGA script arbitrations, once as a writer on *Rock 'n' Roll High School* and once as an arbitrator on another film in 1984, and both of those times I had also found the guild procedures to be corrupt. New World Pictures' initial credit determination on *Rock 'n' Roll High School* was for me to receive first-position screenplay credit, followed by Richard Whitley & Russ Dvonch, with Allan Arkush & Joe Dante receiving story credit. But when the three WGA panelists were presented with the voluminous material to read for the arbitration, one panelist, a screenwriter with prominent credits, decided he didn't have time to read the material and called a member of the film crew, asking him how he thought the credit should be allocated. The crew member told the panelist to put me in third position. That was a gross violation of guild rules, but I didn't learn about it until too late to file a complaint.

When I served as an arbitrator on the other movie, a remake of a popular Hollywood youth comedy, I was told by the WGA that the producer wanted story credit but that the guild did not like to award producers story credit. That attempt to influence me was a violation of guild rules. When I read the surprisingly good, and surprisingly political, novel on which the original film was based as well as the ten drafts of the screenplays for the two film versions, I found that after the political context was jettisoned when the adaptation process began, each script became progressively worse until the final result was utter crap. I did believe the producer had changed the story sufficiently to receive story credit. The WGA told me the other two panelists disagreed and asked me to change my decision. I refused. Since then I have never been asked to serve on a WGA arbitration panel.

I think I would have enjoyed being a screenwriter in Hollywood's Golden Age, when writers, however disparaged and often disgruntled, worked more steadily. But I came to Hollywood too late, after the studio system had essentially collapsed, and the business had degenerated into a dogfight. I feel sorry for my friends who didn't have the sense to get out when I did, before Hollywood descended further into the toilet. Despite my moderate degree of success in the industry during my years as a screenwriter in 1977–84 before I began work on the Capra book, I was often despondent. I drank too much, to self-medicate, and was mostly alone in my cheap West Hollywood apartment. I experienced what Bertolt Brecht wrote in his "Hollywood Elegies":

The village of Hollywood was planned according
    to the notion
People in these parts have of heaven. In these parts
They have come to the conclusion that God
Requiring a heaven and a hell, didn't need to
Plan two establishments but
Just the one: heaven. It
Serves the unprosperous, unsuccessful
As hell.

My double life writing books

You wrote several books during your years at Daily Variety
*and your period as a screenwriter, but I believe you think
they were mere warm-ups for your ambitious biographies
and later critical studies.*

I've always led a double life as a writer, not only because
of the necessity of having a "day job" but also because
I've felt the need to conceal my creative activities from my
bosses and colleagues in those jobs that paid the rent and
kept me from starving. My book writing slowed as a result
of my concentration on screenwriting. And it did become
less ambitious, which nagged at me until I left the industry
behind and began work on my Capra biography, a book that
drew on all my resources as a writer and that I felt would
serve to justify all the years I had spent in the industry.

While still on *Daily Variety*, I wrote two short books
for editor Ted Sennett and his Pyramid series on movie
stars: *Kirk Douglas* (1976), which I cranked out in five days
(two days of research at the Wisconsin Historical Society
and a weekend of writing) and *Orson Welles: Actor and
Director* (1977), which took six weeks of film viewing and
writing. That is still the only book entirely about Welles's
acting career. And I was working on *Hawks on Hawks* from
1970 until 1977, without fully realizing what the end goal
was until the final stages of interviewing Howard Hawks.
I didn't get around to putting that book together until 1981
and '82. It was also during my screenwriting period that I
began the long process of turning *The Broken Places* into
the book you read, Danny.

One book project I proposed in those years was a critical
study of director Hal Ashby. I had the idea of getting paid to
write it as part of the publicity campaign for one of his films,
but this ill-conceived idea was shot down by Ashby, who

said, "That's not ethical." I was chastened to realize he was right and that I had succumbed to Hollywood corruption to such an extent. But after learning that lesson, I didn't make that kind of mistake again and always wrote unauthorized books on directors. I turned down overtures from two major Hollywood figures—Rouben Mamoulian and Yakima Canutt—to work on their autobiographies, and later Fred Zinnemann, who appreciated my Capra biography, asked me to write his biography, but unfortunately I lacked the interest.

Five million words

Another job you did for the American Film Institute was editing books based on their seminars.

During the gap between the 1982 and 1983 AFI shows honoring Frank Capra and John Huston, they asked me to edit its seminars into two books, *Filmmakers on Filmmaking: The American Film Institute Seminars on Motion Pictures and Television, Volumes One and Two.* I read 40,000 pages of transcripts, a total of five million words, to choose the best twenty-four seminars with filmmakers from the five hundred the AFI had held for its Fellows since 1969. My task was edit two percent of those millions of words into volumes that would be entertaining as well as educational.

I welcomed the six-month assignment because (1) I enjoyed reading the seminar transcripts and learned a lot from them; and (2) I could do the job while lying ill on the couch in my apartment with a stubborn respiratory problem. Each night I aggravated my allergies with an entire pizza. I became ambulatory mostly to drive once a week to the AFI headquarters in Hollywood to pick up copies of seminar transcripts Xeroxed for me by their beleaguered education services staff. They made their resentment known by giving me the cold shoulder as soon as that laborious process came to an end.

I decided to structure the books around important and eloquent representatives of different branches of the art form—the first volume had Hal Wallis as the studio executive; Richard Zanuck and David Brown as producers; Ingmar Bergman as director; Billy Wilder and I. A. L. Diamond as screenwriters; Sidney Poitier and Lucille Ball as actors; James Wong Howe as cinematographer; Leonard Rosenman as composer; Polly Platt as production designer; Verna Fields as editor; Anthea Sylbert as costume

designer; and Sue Mengers as agent. That colorful roster
was matched with names of similar quality for the second
volume—Norman Lear, Joseph E. Levine, Jean Renoir,
Robert Towne, Charlton Heston, Bette Davis, John A.
Alonzo, Jerry Goldsmith, Harry Horner, Edith Head,
Joyce Selznick, and Stan Brakhage—and because I had to
leave out so many seminars worthy of inclusion, I picked a
selection of pungent quotes from those for "Short Sections"
in each book.

Each seminar ran considerably longer than I could
include, and sometimes I combined more than one by
a person into a single entry. While doing a lot of quiet
rearranging and cleaning-up of syntax to make spoken
words readable yet still sounding conversational, I found
I also had to rewrite virtually all of the AFI Fellows'
generally lax and inarticulate questions. I did so to avoid
the acute embarrassment they otherwise would have caused
the Institute if they had appeared in book form; I included a
discreet acknowledgment of that exercise.

I had the pleasure of working with a smart, delightful,
and creative editor, Janice Gallagher, whom I met with
periodically at the Sunset Boulevard office of the publisher,
J. P. Tarcher, Inc. Jeremy Tarcher was a slick fellow whose
tastes ran to trendy self-help and woolly volumes of
mysticism. The only interference I encountered from the
AFI was when its director, Jean Firstenberg, objected to
my leading the Introduction with a quote from Nicholas
Ray, "You can't teach film. I don't give a goddamn who says
it, *you can't teach film.*" Jean sensibly put her foot down,
because that sentiment from the maverick filmmaker seemed
to negate the work done at the AFI's Center for Advanced
Film Studies. I was being cheeky to highlight such nihilism
as well as more sensibly dismissive of the mostly bunkum
academic field I would enter twenty years later. Jean let me
lead off the first "Short Subjects" section with Ray's quote
anyway.

Janice and I thought these two books were terrific, as
I still do. Reading them together will give anyone a lively
crash course in the collaborative art of filmmaking; the
epigraph for both books is producer-director Alan J. Pakula
eloquently describing how "The best of film for me, and the
worst of film, is that it is such a collaborative process. You
are dealing with incredibly different kinds of people and,
even worse than that, you are dependent upon incredibly
different kinds of people.... It is enraging at times and it is
also the most exciting part of it at times. In the end, if the
film is successful, it is a synthesis of so many people that it

is impossible to remember who did what and when." That sentiment expressed my growing understanding, evolved from my experience as a trade reporter and screenwriter, of the complexity of the filmmaking process and the concept of "joint authorship" rather than the solo authorship promoted by the more simplistic auteurist critics.

Those books are rather obscure today. What happened after their publication?

Hardly anyone has ever read these two *Filmmakers on Filmmaking* books, because the AFI and the Tarcher firm (which distributed them through Houghton Mifflin) inexplicably bungled their release. These were not the first books drawing from AFI seminars and would not be the last, and some had also appeared in the AFI magazine *American Film.* But the *Filmmakers on Filmmaking* volumes were intended as staples of libraries and film curricula, and the working assumption Janice and I had was that their publication would be backed with ads paid for by Tarcher and the AFI in *American Film* and elsewhere, along with suitable sales promotions.

But when it came time to release the books in February 1983, neither half of the publication team lifted a finger. I complained and set up a meeting in Jeremy Tarcher's office with Jean Firstenberg so we could work out a rapprochement. But the two principals basically just stared at each other and talked around the subject. I also persuaded the AFI to hold a publication party, with Hal Wallis and Anthea Sylbert as amiable centerpieces, but only one member of the press showed up, the loyal Todd McCarthy, whose rave review in *Daily Variety* was the only notice the books received. A cluster of trees fell in a forest to make those two books possible, but few people heard the sound.

Although I was paid modestly for my work and benefited from reading those five million words, this experience was a letdown that still leaves me baffled. It showed me that the publishing world could be as irrational and self-defeating as the film industry. That proved a valuable warning for what I was about to face.

We've touched on your giving up your dream of going to Hollywood to be a director, but how do you see it now?

Although I started out wanting to be a director and made seven short films in Madison, I surprised myself by turning down three actual offers to direct films, so I guess that means I really didn't want to be a director. Early in my time in Hollywood, my friend Alex Ameripoor, an Iranian cinematographer I had met at John Ford's funeral, took me to the set of a low-budget softcore porn film he was shooting. It looked terribly dull and clumsy. Alex said he could get me a job directing one of these pictures. I was mulling whether I could use that as an entry-level springboard and make something fun out of it when I mentioned the offer to Peter Bogdanovich. He made a face and advised me not to go down that route into the business.

Ironically, although it wasn't even softcore porn, Peter had made a sexploitation picture for Roger Corman, *Voyage to the Planet of Prehistoric Women*, starring Mamie Van Doren. That Ed Wood-level piece of schlock blended Peter's footage of semi-naked women on the beach in Malibu, wearing mermaid costumes with seashell brassieres, with footage culled from two Russian sci-fi pictures. Peter directed it in 1966, two years before it was dumped out as a TV movie under his pseudonym of Derek Thomas, and it didn't hurt his career but helped lead to Corman financing his brilliant official debut picture, *Targets*, a 1968 theatrical release.

In 1974, I had a more serious offer that I am still flabbergasted I didn't accept. When I was talking with Howard Hawks at his home in Palm Springs, he offered to finance and produce a short film I would direct. He had read about a motorcyclist who had become lost in the desert for three days but survived, and thought that would make a good film. As it happens, the reporter who sat next to me at *The Riverside Press-Enterprise*, my friend Diane Milliken, had written a feature about that incident. The subject matter didn't do much for me, but the opportunity to work with and learn from a great filmmaker would have been priceless and a genuine stepping stone. Hawks had only one condition, that I involve his young son, Gregg, like him an avid motorcyclist, in the production. That made me balk, because Gregg was so introverted I found it hard to talk with him. I surely could have found a way of working with Gregg, but some deep-seated insecurity about my ability to work with people kept me from trying.

Another time some friends of mine had shot material for a half-baked documentary on the Hollywood blacklist but didn't know how to finish it and asked me to do so. They had brought together a group of formerly blacklisted people at a Hollywood party in and around a picturesque old house and filmed them talking about politics and moviemaking. I was part of that event, delegated to socialize with the actress and activist Frances Williams, with whom I chatted about her experiences in the Soviet Union and with her colleague Paul Robeson. Not only did I find my friends' approach to the material amorphous, but I realized that one of them had such strong notions about controlling the film that he would try to interfere with whatever I might do to shape the material. So I passed on that offer too.

Mike Wilmington's argument that I might not to be suited to being a director was correct. It was an unrealistic fantasy based on my love for the Golden Age of Hollywood and Ford movies in particular. But for one thing, my chronic health problems since childhood—respiratory difficulties and a diagnosed sleep disorder—would have interfered with my career as a director. I've been able to work around them by becoming a professional writer and teacher. The scattered episodes when I passed on the opportunity to direct reveal that something in me subconsciously recognized that my goal of becoming a director was only a pipe dream.

After you quit doing AFI tributes, were there other offers over the years that kept you from leaving the Hollywood scene entirely?

It was satisfying to go out on top, and I preferred to write books fulltime, a career I find much more rewarding. Since then I've been adamant in turning down opportunities to work in the industry and have turned down several feelers or offers over the years to allow a feature film, a documentary, or a cable TV miniseries to be made from *Frank Capra: The Catastrophe of Success*. That prospect would fill me with horror. I spent seven and a half years laboring on, fighting for, and protecting that book and would not want to surrender any control over it to anyone else.

You have done some other film work after quitting the business, though. Why did you return from time to time?

I weakened a bit in my resolve to stay out of the industry entirely by writing a handful of treatments for documentary films intended for DVD or Blu-ray releases (including a documentary I proposed to Sony about the life and work of Jean Arthur, "The Star Who Ran Away"), none of which managed to attract the backing that would be required. And I reluctantly accepted some other jobs to help pay for the writing of my John Ford biography. I worked only on documentaries, and on two of them, I made a point of not taking writing credit—that would have been too traumatic—but taking a producing credit instead. I was co-producer on Harrison Engle's *Obsessed with "Vertigo": New Life for Hitchcock's Masterpiece* (1997), which I actually wrote, and on Tom Thurman's *John Ford Goes to War* (2002), which was loosely based on the World War II chapter of my Ford biography.

The *Vertigo* documentary, which deals both with the production of the film and its restoration, has some good points, but I regret that we allowed ourselves to be conned by restoration producers Robert A. Harris and James C. Katz into buying their rationale for replacing the sound effects on Hitchcock's film when they restored the visuals. They falsely claimed the redubbing of sound effects was necessary because they were using the original stereo music tracks. Thurman's documentary on Ford's war service is fairly good and has had wide exposure on cable TV and DVD, but I argued against Tom's loading it so heavily with clips from the familiar Ford documentaries *The Battle of Midway* and *December 7th* and not showing more from the scores of rarely shown films I discovered that Ford made during the war with his Field Photographic Branch of the Office of Strategic Services (OSS). Nevertheless, I did persuade Tom to at least touch base with the Holocaust and the Nuremberg trials.

For Engle, I also wrote the segment on war movies, modestly titled "War and Peace," for the 1998 AFI/TNT series *100 Years...100 Movies*, which was limited to safely familiar titles chosen in an AFI poll. No Sam Fuller movies! And he made the best war films. They were too real for the people who voted in the AFI poll. Despite my best efforts, our show turned out rather banal as it kept getting whittled and watered down in postproduction; the best of the fifty edits, I thought, was about seven steps removed from the final. I was tempted to use my WGA-registered pseudonym (Lucy Burrows), but in the end I found the program barely acceptable, so I accepted the writing credit and earned more for working on that show than on anything else in my film career.

I was an unpaid consultant on the partially restored 1998 version of Welles's *Touch of Evil*. I was basically enlisted by producer Rick Schmidlin to give my imprimatur along with other Welles experts to the changes made by Walter Murch. He brilliantly incorporated fifty of the changes requested by Welles in his famous fifty-eight-page memo to Universal-International in December 1957. I am particularly proud that Murch, the world's greatest editor and sound technician, accepted one small but significant suggestion of mine. In the famous opening shot, Murch removed the distracting credits the studio had laid over the bomb-laden car wending its way through the streets and replaced Henry Mancini's music with diegetic sound that Welles intended we hear from nightclubs and cars. I suggested that Murch boost the sound a bit in that shot when the car is moving too slowly from the distance toward the foreground. I didn't ask to receive screen credit on the film but was given one anyway. Ironically, that's my only production credit on a major studio theatrical film, unless you consider Netflix a major studio, since I am a credited consultant on the 2018 release of another Welles film, *The Other Side of the Wind.*

Universal also asked me to write and direct a documentary on the filming and restoration of *Touch of Evil.* I said I would, though I doubted they would follow through on their offer, so I spent only a couple of hours writing a treatment for the documentary. By then I had learned the hard way to take the precaution of faxing the outline (to get a time-coded receipt) along with a cover letter reminding Universal that they had asked me to write it. Sure enough, two weeks later, they called and said they would assign the job instead to an in-house documentarian. Fine, I said, but now you need to pay me for writing the treatment the studio requested. There was a moment of silence, and then the person said, "Someone will get back to you."

The next day, a studio lawyer called and asked me the question all screenwriters would love to hear: "How much do you want?" At the time I was in Ford's old neighborhood in Portland, Maine, researching my biography, and I needed money for the book, so I simply asked for the WGA minimum for a treatment, $3,667. I should have bargained for more, but I thought getting paid that much for not making a film was a good deal; if I could do so twenty times a year without having to make any movies, I'd be very happy. As it turned out, Universal made the documentary, *Restoring "Evil,"* but after a single screening on cable TV, its release was blocked on dubious legal grounds by Welles's daughter Beatrice. So I was fortunate not to have been involved. They used an idea of mine in the documentary, but I had taken the precaution in my legal agreement of making sure I didn't get any credit.

I spent decades helping push along the completion of *The Other Side of the Wind*, a dream come true when it was finally released forty-eight years after we began filming in 1970 and proved to be even better than I had hoped and expected it would be. I worked hard to try to make a deal to complete *Other Wind*, and Gary Graver (the film's cinematographer) and I made a tentative deal with Showtime in 1999 for $3 million, but then I was fired from the project by Oja Kodar and Peter Bogdanovich, who thought they didn't need me. I didn't make a fuss because I didn't want to hurt the film, but I washed my hands of any more direct involvement with it. The project then immediately collapsed. I used to think that if I had remained part of it then, it would have been out by about 2004. But I am not sure of that now, since the postproduction proved to be so fiendishly complex technically that it would have been hard if not impossible to finish it back then.

I helped the final producers of *The Other Side of the Wind*, Frank Marshall and Filip Jan Rymsza, and editor Bob Murawski (who is credited with Welles) with whatever advice and encouragement I could offer. And I was (modestly) paid for being a consultant on the postproduction, along with my friend and fellow Welles critic Jonathan Rosenbaum. After we watched a semifinal version with Murawski at a Netflix screening room and discussed it afterward with him and Rymsza, I wrote a singlespaced, twenty-six-page memo in January 2018 with recommended changes, some of which were made.

Some of the original soundtrack recordings made during production were lost, and they had to work with dupes, so they used sound-alike voice actors when necessary. I was one of the few surviving cast members, so they had me dub seventeen lines of my dialogue with optimum recording equipment. I didn't change the words but welcomed the opportunity to improve my line readings now that I have more experience. Even though I am much older and used to smoke, they told me, surprisingly, that I still sounded about the same, but just to make sure, I raised my pitch a bit.

When I redid my lines as Mister Pister entered the bus filled with Hannaford cronies and dummies on the way to Jake's party, I was in a studio in Berkeley, hooked up with Murawski in Los Angeles. I had trouble walking and talking at the same time when that scene was filmed in 1971. Welles had turned in despair to Paul Stewart, who was acting in the scene and was also a director, to coach me on how to say the lines. Paul did so succinctly, and I nailed the scene in one take. Welles began jokingly calling me "One-Take Pister." But in the dubbing, Bob asked me to read the lines in a different rhythm to help him with his editing. We had to redo them seventeen times to get what he wanted. "It took three directors to get that line reading," I told Bob, and he said jokingly, "That tells you something about the performance." But then he said, "This is a historic moment—that's the last re-recording on *The Other Side of the Wind*."

On my return visit to the Milwaukee County Hospital Mental
Health Center as research for my screenplay and memoir
The Broken Places. By then the North Division building was
abandoned. (Timothy McBride)

I thought Murawski did a brilliant and conscientious
job editing the film according to Welles's plan and his own
artistic judgment. But I regretted that the sex scene in
the car, which I consider one of the greatest sequences in
Welles's body of work, was diminished in the final editing
process by being reduced from seven minutes to four and
a half. I argued strenuously against that shortening, as did
Jonathan, but to no avail. In Welles's original edit, that
tour de force sequence of rapid, rhythmical editing and
expressionistic color changes, coupled with the intense
action of Oja Kodar humping Bob Random in the car in a

rainstorm, amounts to a cinematic equivalent of an orgasm. But in the shortened version, it becomes a scene about a woman's sexual frustration, an entirely different mood. The digital version also loses some of the subtle color qualities Gary Graver brought to the original 35mm film. I hope if *Other Wind* ever gets a Blu-ray release, Welles's cut of that sequence will be included as an extra.

I received "special thanks" for my participation as an interviewee and adviser (and supplier of photographs) on the Morgan Neville documentary for Netflix about the production history of *The Other Side of the Wind, They'll Love Me When I'm Dead* (2018). I had mixed feelings about the documentary, since it seems to argue, absurdly and arrogantly, that it is more important than Welles's film, as some of the Netflix publicists also seemed to think. Neville didn't accept my urgent suggestion to identify the interviewees presented in artsy and often confusingly framed shots onscreen. I warned him that critics would find the lack of names confusing, and they did.

I contributed as a consultant and interviewee on *Becoming John Ford*, the enlightening and lively 2007 documentary directed by Nick Redman and written by Julie Kirgo for the *Ford at Fox* boxed set. I've been friends with Julie, a wise film historian and scriptwriter, since she was a student in the first course I taught in 1974 at Sherwood Oaks Experimental College in Hollywood. The two most comfortable on-camera interviews I've done are that one with Julie (filmed in Darryl Zanuck's personal screening room at Twentieth Century Fox) and my interview with director Sam Pollard for his 2006 PBS American Masters documentary, *John Ford/John Wayne: The Filmmaker and the Legend*.

For the *Ford at Fox* set, which was chosen by *Time* magazine as the best DVD of 2007, I also contributed audio commentaries for his great films *Pilgrimage, The Grapes of Wrath,* and *How Green Was My Valley*. I have recorded commentaries for more than forty other films, including many others by Ford as well as by Ernst Lubitsch and Billy Wilder. I consider these a form of teaching as well as film criticism and history, with similarities to the books I've written on these filmmakers.

And I have been interviewed in many other documentaries, usually on subjects I've written books about, both on filmmaking and on the assassination of President Kennedy. I ask Welles a question during his Q&A with the audience in his uncompleted 1981 documentary *Filming "The Trial"* and am a silent audience member in his TV talk show pilot, *The Orson Welles Show*. In addition to being a member of the crowd at the climactic rally in Milwaukee for Senator John F. Kennedy in the 1960 documentary *Primary*, I help explain the murder of Officer J. D. Tippit while on-site in a documentary called *King Kill '63*. That film played only once at the Texas Theatre in Oak Cliff, but since has been held up for financial reasons.

My former student Hart Perez directed a 2011 documentary feature about my career, *Behind the Curtain: Joseph McBride on Writing Film History*. That began as a class project with Hart interviewing me about Welles, and I suggested we expand it into an hour-long documentary with me also talking about my Capra, Ford, and Spielberg biographies. Hart built rudimentary but attractive sets as backdrops for our interviews and borrowed a classroom from St. Mary's College in Moraga, California, as the studio for our two-day shoot. The total cost of the project, which Hart and I shared, was forty dollars, which went for chips and soda to feed the two crew guys and ourselves. They and Hart did good work. We showed *Behind the Curtain* at a local festival and sell it as a DVD on Amazon, and though it hasn't had many buyers, I am glad to have it out there.

Have you ever thought of writing a screenplay based on your Kennedy-Tippit book, Into the Nightmare?

I call myself a recovering screenwriter and am happy to be out of that racket. What I've always avoided, you'll notice, is any further involvement with writing a feature film. That is anathema to me. If I get a good idea for a film now, as I occasionally do, I suppress it.

Liberating *Let There Be Light*

I'm curious why you returned to Daily Variety *in 1980, for only about a year.*

I rejoined the paper because I ran out of money after being paid only $5,000 for writing the AFI tribute to Jimmy Stewart earlier that year; I later found they had budgeted $15,000 for the writer, but my agent took their first lowball offer, and the incremental raises I received for the AFI shows in the four years after that, until I reached $17,500, kept me barely solvent. I left the paper again in 1981 to write the Astaire show, and Tom Pryor was unhappy. I felt somewhat bad about doing so but couldn't resist the opportunity.

Was there a highlight during that brief time you spent back on the paper?

As I wrote in a 2017 article for *Two Cheers for Hollywood*, when I went back to *Daily Variety*, "I asked myself, 'What good can I do in the short time I plan to stay on the paper?' Since the Freedom of Information Act now existed—a response to the public's discontent with not being told the truth about the Vietnam War, the assassination of President Kennedy, and other clandestine government operations—it occurred to me it might be possible to use FOIA to free [John Huston's long-suppressed World War II documentary] *Let There Be Light*." I had been deeply moved seeing a bootleg 16mm print that Paul Bartel had "liberated" from the U.S. Army while serving in the Signal Corps at Fort Monmouth, New Jersey. Huston made that documentary about "psychoneurotic" soldiers suffering from what we now call post-traumatic stress disorder (PTSD) for the army at the end of the war in 1945. I found *Let There Be Light* an important work of art, and the soldiers' traumatized state called forth memories of my own institutionalization for psychiatric problems.

Although the purpose of the documentary was to demonstrate to employers that men with PTSD could be successfully rehabilitated, the footage Huston shot at a U.S. War Department psychiatric hospital on Long Island was so harrowing that the film was banned from public viewing. Huston, who was furious over that decision, once declared, "I think it boils down to the fact that they wanted to maintain the 'warrior' myth, which said that our American soldiers went to war and came back all the stronger for the experience, standing tall and proud for having served their country well. Only a few weaklings fell by the wayside. Everyone was a hero, and had medals and ribbons to prove it. They might die, or they might be wounded, but their spirit remained unbroken."

James Agee wrote in *The Nation* in 1946, "I don't know what is necessary to reverse this disgraceful decision, but if dynamite is required, then dynamite is indicated." Agee lamented that "Huston's intelligent, noble, fiercely-moving short film about combat neurosis and some of the more spectacular kinds of therapy, will probably never be seen by the civilian public for whose need, and on whose money [$150,000], it was made. The War Department has mumbled a number of reasons why it has been withheld: the glaring obvious reason has not been mentioned: that any sane human being who saw the film would join the armed services, if at all, with a straight face and a painfully maturing mind."

As I wrote in *Two Cheers,*

> I've always felt that part of the job—the obligation— of a film historian is to rediscover and, if necessary, liberate lost films. While studying the careers of great directors, I've managed to fill in some missing pieces. I found Orson Welles's previously unknown 1934 short film *The Hearts of Age* in the late 1960s (on a tip from my University of Wisconsin film professor Russell Merritt), discovered ten unknown Frank Capra World War II documentaries at the National Archives (which were released after my Capra biography was published), and documented several dozen previously unreported films made by John Ford's OSS unit in the war (many of which have since surfaced on YouTube and elsewhere). The many gaps I have found in the official histories, and the always-maddening fact that so much film history is inaccessible, have compelled me to this task of scholarly sleuthing. I also feel a drive to right injustices in the cases of films that have been mislaid, ignored, slighted, or, in some cases, banned. Among the latter, for thirty-five years, was John Huston's *Let There Be Light....*
>
> I figured [in 1980 that] enough time had passed since 1946 that, perhaps, the film could be released, since it might no longer be regarded as so controversial.

I saw my opening when my friend Ronald Haver, the director of film programs at the Los Angeles County Museum of Art, announced that he would show *Let There Be Light* as part of his John Huston retrospective that November, in conjunction with the publication of the director's autobiography, *An Open Book.* So I decided to mount a press campaign at *Daily Variety* to convince the army to free the film.

After Haver showed *Let There Be Light* without incident in his LACMA retrospective on November 8, I wrote in an article/review for *Daily Variety*: "In some cases, legendary 'lost' films turn out to be overrated when they are finally rediscovered. But this is not the case with *Let There Be Light*. The film is a masterpiece, one of the greatest films ever made on the subject of war's impact on the human spirit. And even beyond that, it is a profoundly moving meditation on the fragility of the mind and its ultimate powers of resilience." The morning the article with that review appeared, I received phone calls from Jack Valenti, the head of the Motion Picture Association of America, and producer Ray Stark, a friend and colleague of Huston's. They asked me what they could do to help free the film, and I said they could give me repeated interviews calling for its release.

I began dealing with a U.S. Army FOIA officer who was sympathetic to the request. He told me I also could help free another Huston World War II documentary, *Report from the Aleutians*. I did not know that film had been suppressed more quietly, because it showed a top-secret bomb sight that was no longer a matter of concern. So I wrote him a letter making the request, and that film was quickly freed. But legal and other resistance within the Army still had to be overcome in the case of *Let There Be Light*. Eventually, with the intercession of Vice President Walter Mondale and Secretary of the Army Clifford L. Alexander Jr., *Let There Be Light* was finally freed for release on December 29 in a partly censored version with a few names of patients removed. As I wrote in *Two Cheers*, "I knew that if *Let There Be Light* were not released before Ronald Reagan became president—he had been elected on November 4—it might never be released. So we came in just under the wire."

Let There Be Light received its theatrical premiere at New York City's Thalia Theater on January 16, 1981, and (ironically) was made available for purchase from the army on VHS and in 16mm and even went on sale in the gift shop at the Dwight D. Eisenhower Presidential Library, Museum and Boyhood Home. *Let There Be Light* was selected by the United States National Film Preservation Board for the National Film Registry in 2010, mandating its preservation and storage in the Library of Congress. It was restored in 2012 from an acetate fine-grain master, the best surviving source, with the support of the National Film Preservation Foundation (NFPF) through Chase Audio by Deluxe and the National Archives and Records Administration. The film can now be seen online, entirely uncensored, on the NFPF website, filmpreservation.org.

Were your students impressed that you, literally, helped Let There Be Light *see the light of day?*

My article in *Two Cheers* also noted one of the reasons I decided to assign my screenwriting students at SFSU two short stories to adapt about soldiers with PTSD, Ernest

Hemingway's "Big Two-Hearted River" and Flannery O'Connor's "A Late Encounter with the Enemy." I did so "because I wanted to focus the students' attention on the fact that we are a nation involved in endless wars that too seldom have the direct impact on the home front that the mass mobilization of World War II compelled. And I use *Let There Be Light* as a teaching tool to show the students the reality of PTSD, that it is not a minor neurosis or affliction but a soul-shattering experience."

Another instance when I helped "rescue" an almost-lost film was more unplanned, even bizarre. Over the years I have frequently been mistaken for the director Jim McBride, whom I had never met until the late 1990s but vaguely resemble. Once at Filmex, a young woman told me she had dated me in Berkeley (I had never been there at the time), and she wouldn't take no for an answer while pursuing me as I tried to escape. Then when Jim McBride's remake of Godard's *Breathless* was about to come out, I kept getting approached in public by young actresses looking for work; the film flopped, and that abruptly stopped happening. I began to become offended by the situation, with its implied insult that a director is more important than a writer. When the Serbian director Dušan Makavejev told me how much he liked my work, I just thanked him, thinking of how Ford and Hawks accepted compliments for each other's Westerns. At the same party, when an irritatingly obsequious film editor lobbied me for a job, I let him go on for half an hour about his work before casually indicating I was someone else.

But one day the UCLA Film and Television Archive called to ask my help in preserving "my" film *David Holzman's Diary*. I told them I was not Jim McBride, and they should find and ask him. That 1967 classic, which cost only $2,500, is a landmark no-budget independent film and precursor of the "mockumentary" genre. Strangely, that same night I went to a small Hollywood party and met Jim McBride for the first time. I told him about the call from UCLA and said I assumed he had the materials they needed to preserve his film. He said all he had was a 16mm print (the film was shot in that ratio) and that the original materials had been lost. But he called UCLA the next day, and they began a search for what was needed. So with the help of the Pacific Film Archive and the Berkeley Art Museum, UCLA managed to find original materials and make a new preservation dupe negative, rescuing *David Holzman's Diary*.

Let There Be Light *premiered before you quit your second stint at* Daily Variety. *But you came back to the paper in 1989 and stayed longer, until 1992. How did that come about?*

I went back to the paper as a desperate move to support myself and my family while I was going through my legal struggles over my Capra biography. Being rehired by *Daily Variety* at a surprisingly good salary, starting at $40,000 a year, enabled me to save the book in my four-year legal battle with the publishing firm of Alfred A. Knopf and its parent company, Random House; Jeanine Basinger, Capra's archivist at Wesleyan University; and some members of the Capra family. It was a strange and initially depressing experience going back to the industry after my disenchantment as a screenwriter, but I gradually came to enjoy the work until I ran on a collision course with the corrupt new editor of *Variety*, Peter Bart, which came to a head with the 1992 controversy over my review of *Patriot Games.* As the veteran Hollywood reporter and reviewer Ezra Goodman wrote in his 1961 book, *The Fifty-Year Decline and Fall of Hollywood*, the "journalist is not resented in Hollywood. He has his price and the community is more than willing to meet it.... What the Hollywood operatives are wary of is the occasional journalist who may gum up the works with a misplaced sense of integrity."

I gradually realized that the job at *Daily Variety* was the salvation of my Capra book. As my lawyer, Maurice L. Muehle, said of my book publisher, "It's terrible how they are trying to starve you into submission." But Knopf could no longer do so once I had a regular job. Now I could not only contribute regularly to our upkeep but could also work my way out of our considerable pile of debt, including by volunteering for overtime assignments. By then, however, *Variety* had been taken over by Cahners Publishing. The relative editorial freedom we enjoyed when the paper had been owned by the Silverman family, who founded the paper in 1905 and upheld relatively high journalistic standards, had evaporated under the new ownership and the Bart regime.

My colleague Dave Robb observed that under Tom Pryor, *Daily Variety* had been a writer's paper, but now under Bart, it became an editor's paper. Look around the news room, Dave told me, and see that there were more editors than writers now. When Tom ran the paper, he did so with only about four sub-editors. Bart once called a staff meeting, standing on a chair, to tell us that since a survey showed the average *Daily Variety* subscriber earned $300,000 a year, we should start thinking more like that reader and stop being so critical. I felt like calling out sarcastically, "Yeah, sure, why don't you pay each of us $300,000 a year, and we'll probably start thinking like the average *Daily Variety* reader." Bart was a former film industry executive who was fond of pompously lecturing the studio suits in his column about how they should run their operations; I'm sure that gave them a big laugh. A Cahners executive told Tom that Bart had been hired to keep advertisers happy so the paper could increase its ad sales revenue.

Nevertheless, for a while I thoroughly enjoyed my work back at the paper. It was a relief from agonizing all day over my legal problems, even if I still had to juggle those in my off hours and sometimes by phone during the workday. And I felt more secure dealing with Random House from a less dependent position. As well as being able to pay my legal bills more easily, I was less isolated than I had been during what Gary Graver called my "dark period" working secretively at home on the Capra book, and Ruth and I enjoyed going to Hollywood award dinners and other social events.

Was it the same reviewing movies again after being away from the business for so long?

I wondered when I started reviewing movies again after my years working on the Capra book if I might be tempted to be overly harsh as a reviewer. I had become so disenchanted with the industry that I had seen almost no new films in theaters in years and confined my film viewing mostly to Capra films and other films I used for research. I did make an exception to go to a theater in Milwaukee over Christmas 1987 to see Steven Spielberg's *Empire of the Sun*, which I greatly admired. Ernest Callenbach of *Film Quarterly* asked me in 1988 to review *Bull Durham*. Although I liked that funky romantic comedy about baseball, I felt I had nothing to say about it. On a deeper level in that period, I felt emotionally blocked by the mere idea of writing a film review. And I was dismayed by how junky the trailers for other films looked. The film business repelled me in those years when I was going through my difficult process of withdrawal.

At first when I returned to *Daily Variety* in 1989, I was given nothing to do for two weeks, since Rich Bozanich, then the managing editor, seemed to resent my presence, as continued to be the case, mysteriously, until he left the paper a couple of years later, under duress from Bart. I spent the idle time catching up on the last few years of entertainment news in our archives. I was given only schlocky movies to review initially, but gradually I took over the role of first-string reviewer when Todd McCarthy left the paper. His departure was only temporary, it turned out; when he returned, he took back his top position. When I began reviewing again, I was surprised to find myself more generous than ever before. As the cliché goes, I had learned how much effort goes into even a bad movie, and having abandoned screenwriting, I was looking at the industry from a more detached viewpoint. My lack of ambition to make films anymore freed me of many unhealthy emotions, including any sense of competition or resentment of others in the business and even a degree of anger over encountering poor work in movies. But some capacity for indignation remained, as I would find later.

Were you doing anything besides reviewing films in your final tour of duty there?

I reported on the box office and some other beats, including the Academy of Motion Picture Arts and Sciences. And I was assigned to spend one day a week putting together the film production chart, which was mostly mindless activity, although I made a lot of phone calls to figure out what films were actually shooting and which were phony items. I would find imaginary or wish-list projects or listings of films that had already been completed but were falsely claimed to be in production to fool the unions. I liked that make-work duty and the detective work aspects of the job, because it helped me decompress and relax from the intellectual challenges of my legal battle with Knopf.

Bart eventually also compelled me to write a biweekly column that I called "Straight Shooting," which I didn't tell him was the title of John Ford's first feature, because he would have made me change it. I was wary of writing a column since I thought I would eventually run into trouble over it. He gave me the helpful advice that a good column should consist of reportage and opinion, not merely opinion. So I tackled various issues, with a focus whenever I could on film history, such as the evisceration of Welles's *The Magnificent Ambersons* fifty years earlier; Disney's dubious updating of *Fantasia;* and Ernst Lubitsch's hundredth birthday and why his delicate comic "touch" was so hard to recapture in modern Hollywood. That column brought an appreciative phone call from Lubitsch's daughter, Nicola, who later became a good friend of mine after I wrote my critical study of her father.

Since you, a stickler for the truth, were well aware that studios cook the books, did you worry that your box-office reporting could cause controversy?

I was compiling the box-office charts and writing articles every Monday about how films had grossed over the weekend. I had already volunteered to work on Sundays rather than Fridays, and I came up with the idea of doing box-office estimate articles on Sundays. The idea hit me on Saturday, March 31, 1990, when I saw an enormous line of kids and parents waiting to get into a theater showing *Teenage Mutant Ninja Turtles*. I had reviewed that hokey but enjoyable movie and predicted it would be a hit. So when I went to the office on Sunday and checked to see how much *Turtles* had grossed in its first two days, I found it was running up a record for an independent film, on its way to gross about $25 million that weekend. My story for Monday's paper scooped everyone with the news. The distributor told me they had received calls from 235 journalists who read my article that morning. The film ultimately grossed $135 million.

That scoop convinced me to propose doing a regular box-office estimate article, extrapolating the weekend figures on Sunday from the Friday and Saturday receipts. I thought the news shouldn't wait until Tuesday, since those involved in distribution already knew by Sunday how films were doing and whether a new movie was a hit or DOA. My idea was welcomed by the paper, even though the traditionalist Art Murphy hated it, and the practice soon caught on throughout the world of show business journalism. That was partly to my regret, since it added a new level of frenzy to the obsession over box-office returns at the expense of movies' artistic value.

The studios also complained at first, but I developed a source with access to the telephone hotline reporting the raw figures and estimates the studios shared with each other. They changed the phone number every week to try to outwit us, but my source and I drove the studios crazy by continuing to get access. That enabled me to obtain information they didn't want outsiders to know until they could settle on final figures on Monday. Eventually the studios decided to try to exercise more control by giving out estimate figures themselves on Sundays, and the practice I had created became official. Still, by having access to the uncooked raw data, I could learn whether the estimates I was given officially were padded or realistic.

Eventually I was emboldened to put into print my reports that studios were playing games with some of their figures. That led to some confrontations with studios and, I suspect, played a role in my eventual departure from the paper in 1992. Later the studios figured out a way to exclude reporters from the process by creating a data service that collects and reports the industrywide box-office figures each week.

In regard to your leaving Daily Variety *for good, tell us the story of* Patriot Games, *which you've mentioned with a sense of foreboding.*

In my 1999 *Book of Lists*, I gave out "The Jedediah Leland Memorial Award: To 6 Critics Who Lost Their Jobs Because of Their Reviews." I listed the founder of *Variety*, Sime Silverman (*New York Morning Telegraph*), Graham Greene (the British magazine *Night and Day*), Frank S. Nugent (*New York Times*), Pauline Kael (*McCall's*), and Pat Dowell (*Washingtonian*); each of their stories is unique. The sixth critic was me. I explain that my negative review of *Patriot Games* on June 3, 1992,

> prompted Paramount to pull its ads from *Daily Variety*. That was hardly an unprecedented reaction, but my editor-in-chief, former Paramount executive Peter Bart, reacted by writing a letter to Paramount Communications chairman and chief executive Martin S. Davis apologizing for my review and promising that I would not be allowed to review any more Paramount films. After Bart's letter was leaked to the *New York Times*, I defended my First Amendment right to my opinion. *Daily Variety* tried every possible means of retaliating, such as canceling my assignment to review *A League of Their Own* and assigning me only children's movies until my lawyer [Maury Muehle] forced the paper to let me resume reviewing adult movies. Receiving [virtually] unanimous public support from my colleagues in the media [aside from a handful of Bart lackeys at *Daily Variety* and a right-wing journalist who attacked my political views], I stuck it out for five months before obtaining a financial settlement from *Daily Variety* and resigning to concentrate on writing books.

There is some backstory to what happened to me over *Patriot Games*. My Capra biography was given the lead review in *The New York Times Book Review* on May 3, 1992, under the headline "It Wasn't Such a Wonderful Life." The rave by Barry Gewen, an editor of that section, called my book a "masterly, comprehensive and frequently surprising" debunking of the myth Capra had created about his life with the help of the media and his fans and his autobiography, *The Name Above the Title*, which, as Gewen noted, "appears to have been a lie practically from beginning to end.... Yet among the elements that make this book [my biography] so rich is its intertwining of the bad and the good, so that while we may be appalled at the way Capra turned his back on his parents, we can at the same time admire his sheer determination to make something of himself in the face of huge obstacles. Similarly, if the themes that once provided Capra's films with their resonance no longer hold up, other qualities in them emerge clearer than ever," especially his great talent in bringing out the best in his actors.

Bart called me at home from New York early in his Sunday morning hours when that edition of the *Times* hit the streets, ostensibly to congratulate me but actually to whine that he had never had a book of his reviewed on any page higher than page seven of that section. From then on, *Daily Variety* started giving me nearly impossible punitive assignments with absurdly short deadlines. I managed to pull them off, but the paper clearly was trying to find an excuse to fire me or a means of making me resign. Bart earlier had written a column taking issue with my criticism of the Central Intelligence Agency in my review of the 1990 film *Air America*, and though he didn't use my name, that was an oblique warning shot showing where his political allegiances lay.

About a month before the press screening of *Patriot Games*, I was assigned to review it and read the Tom Clancy novel in preparation. Shortly before the screening, however, I was pulled from the assignment, and it was given to Todd McCarthy. But then I was abruptly reassigned, again without explanation. To quote my review of that Paramount movie, *Patriot Games* is a "morally repugnant... ultra-violent, fascistic, blatantly anti-Irish" adaptation of Clancy's novel. I described the film as "a right-wing cartoon of the current British-Irish political situation" that takes "the side of the British occupying forces and their CIA allies against what it continually labels as 'terrorists.'"

The scathing review I filed has been vindicated, in my opinion, by time and events in Ireland. And as I wrote in *Frankly: Unmasking Frank Capra*, "After having to exercise such restraint for years while writing the Capra book, and gratified by the vindication I had received with its publication, I was feeling liberated and had the illusion I would be able to express myself more freely in my journalism."

The day I submitted the review, I heard Jonathan Taylor, Bart's servile managing editor, describe it to Bart via phone to New York by saying, "Hated it, hated it, *hated* it." When Taylor hung up, he turned to his colleagues on the copy desk and said, "The Bartperson is very happy." So my assignment to review the film was clearly a setup, a political trap Bart had laid in Machiavellian fashion, hoping I would walk into it. Bart accused me of allowing my Irish ancestry and family relationships to improperly influence the review. No doubt there was another reason for the harsh reaction I received. *Variety's* parent company, Cahners Publishing, was a division of Reed International P.L.C., and that prominent British media conglomerate (whose annual report boasted pictures of its executives hobnobbing with Prince Charles and Prime Minister John Major) couldn't have been pleased by my critique of the film's propagandistic depiction of the Irish Republican Army and how the CIA and the British government were dealing with the hot-button political situation in Northern Ireland.

Paramount pulled its advertising from the paper, as it had during a recent flap with our rival, the *Hollywood Reporter.* Tom Pryor, who had earlier been displaced by Cahners in a crude and distressing power play, told me that in the past when a studio had pulled its ads, *Daily Variety* would not bother to respond, and eventually the ads would return. Bart's pandering and public response to Paramount, by contrast, was highly unusual and proved controversial with my fellow film reviewers throughout the country, who saw it as a threat to the entire profession.

Someone (probably Bart himself) tipped off Bernard Weinraub of the *New York Times* about Paramount's ire and leaked him Bart's correspondence to me and the studio. That was an extraordinary breach of a newspaper's usual way of handling a piece of writing internally. *Daily Variety* could have killed the review, reassigned it, or changed it in the editing, but they ran it intact. And they reprinted it in the weekly *Variety* with only a few relatively minor cuts that did not substantially alter its content or tone, and indeed continued to run it unchanged for many years on their website. But in the *Times* article, Bart made the inflammatory remark of calling my review "unprofessional" and was quoted as having told the film's producers that he was especially disturbed by "the political nature of the review." Weinraub called me for a comment, and I defended myself by saying:

> I have been covering this business for almost 20 years. I don't write anything that is not heartfelt and substantiated by facts. I have a reputation in the industry and elsewhere of a high degree of professionalism in all aspects of my coverage. I am bothered by Mr. Bart's statement to me that I should not have reviewed *Patriot Games* because I am an Irish-American. I would find it hard to believe that members of other ethnic groups would not be allowed by *Variety* to review movies about their people. For example, would a Jewish reviewer not be allowed to review a movie about the Holocaust?

I'm sure it was gratifying that you received support from your fellow film reviewers.

The National Society of Film Critics and the Los Angeles Film Critics Association (an organization I had helped found in 1975) issued strong statements of protest in my behalf and defending the rights of critics in general. Through its chairman, Peter Rainer of the *Los Angeles Times*, the National Society issued a statement that it "strongly objects to the aspersions cast by *Variety* against its staff reviewer Joseph McBride. By implying that a critic's ethnicity and political beliefs are antithetical to his professional duties, *Variety* disserves the cause of honest, opinionated criticism—a cause which can only exist in an atmosphere free from destructive fiats and advertising pressures."

Jonathan Rosenbaum wrote in his review of my Capra biography for the *Chicago Reader*,

> Recently McBride wrote a review of *Patriot Games* for *Variety* that dared to attack the movie's politics—a position deemed so out-of-bounds by the studio that it promptly withdrew its advertising from the paper. The fact that McBride was the only reviewer to bring up the film's politics made his comments automatically enlightening, but he was clearly violating a central taboo in contemporary film reviewing by assuming that a movie has political meanings and a political impact in the first

place. His Capra book is both shocking and useful for similar reasons.

Charles Champlin, the influential *Los Angeles Times* film reviewer and LAFCA president, wrote Bart that the organization was "dismayed and angered" by the situation, which

> seems particularly disturbing at a time when First Amendment rights are under constant siege.... McBride responded, honestly and undoubtedly passionately, to what he felt the film could be interpreted as saying or doing: specifically that it was exploiting and trivializing a tragic situation. But, at that, the question is not, of course, whether McBride is "right" or "wrong" (such absolutes being scarce in the art of criticism), but whether he or any responsible critic must be muted so not to offend an advertiser, or bruise a handful of tender egos.... No critic's reputation is made or unmade by a single review. It is won or lost over any number of reviews and reportings over a period of time. McBride's widely and positively reviewed biography of Frank Capra—described as definitive in more than one of the reviews—is simply the latest testimony to his professionalism, sound judgment and felicitous writing.

Did you want to leave Daily Variety *immediately or fight back against Bart and his bosses?*

I briefly felt like leaving but went in to work as usual the next morning, determined to fight it out, even though I knew my remaining time on the paper would be limited. I had an open-and-shut case against the paper for defamation and for how they continued to handle the matter by disparaging my professional reputation. I refused to follow direct orders from Cahners to remain silent about the controversy. I bedeviled *Daily Variety* that summer and fall by giving many interviews to the media defending my First Amendment right to express my critical opinions. Among the interviews was a national NBC television appearance on *Sunday Today*, in which I pointedly told the viewers why Sime Silverman had founded *Variety* in 1905. He did so after being fired by the *New York Morning Telegraph* when a vaudeville comedy team whose act he had panned retaliated by canceling its Christmas advertisement. Silverman declared in the first issue of *Variety* that it "WILL NOT BE INFLUENCED BY ADVERTISING.... The reviews will be written conscientiously, and the truth only told."

I took some enjoyment from the process of defending myself and the principles upon which *Variety* was founded, but as I write in *Frankly,* it was a stressful period overall, and "in retrospect I should have treated the whole episode as a farce." It was hard, though, to restrain my frustration when Bart continued to malign me. *Daily Variety* engaged in an intensified campaign of petty harassment in the workplace, including the paper's refusal to run the review they had assigned me to write of Columbia's feminist baseball film, *A League of Their Own.*

My favorable review of that film directed by Penny Marshall stated that its "amiable crowd-pleasing approach gives it the potential to hit a home run" at the box office; *Daily Variety* ran a review instead by Todd McCarthy, who thought it would face "an uphill marketing struggle." *A League of Their Own* went on to become a hit, grossing $132 million. After the *Los Angeles Times* reported that *Daily Variety* had killed my review, Robert L. Krakoff, chairman and CEO of Reed Publishing (USA) Inc., wrote a published letter to the paper falsely claiming that had not happened. On the advice of my lawyer, I held back with great difficulty from prolonging that issue, since our legal negotiations were in a sensitive stage.

My last day at the paper was November 6. As I write in *Frankly,* "Todd McCarthy, as numerous people told me, spread the false claim that I had been fired (ironically, Todd was fired as the paper's chief film critic in 2010 in a shortsighted cost-cutting move). It had been rumored from day one of the *Patriot Games* controversy that I might be fired. But some people failed to understand that if *Variety* had tried to fire me, I would have had grounds for an even more damaging legal case. The paper thought I was doing everything possible to try to get fired, when I felt I was trying hard *not* to give them any ulterior motives to do so. I wanted to do my work well and keep the focus on the *Patriot Games* issue. The settlement clearly stated that I had resigned voluntarily."

The financial settlement Maury Muehle reached with Cahners in November enabled me to go to Dallas for my most intense research trip into the assassination of President Kennedy and the murder of Officer J. D. Tippit for what eventually became my book *Into the Nightmare.* That was a satisfying denouement, and I found that my critical reputation was only enhanced by the controversy. Bob

Bender, the editor of my Capra book at Simon & Schuster, also strongly supported me throughout the controversy, calling Bart's criticism of me "ludicrous. It defies the intelligence.... I talked to a couple of people at Simon & Schuster who are amazed at the differences between the film industry and the book industry. A publisher would not pull all ads from *Publishers Weekly* for a bad review—it's unthought-of." Bob and I made an agreement for another book, *Steven Spielberg: A Biography*, which was published in 1997.

The *Patriot Games* episode led to blistering exposes of Peter Bart by Dave Robb in the *LA Weekly*, as well as similar pieces in the *Washington Post*, *Los Angeles Times*, and *Los Angeles* magazine. *Variety* never recovered from the blow to its reputation. The day after Weinraub's article appeared, *Daily Variety* publisher Mike Silverman, a good friend and ally of mine who was also at odds with upper management, was talking with me in his office. He indicated the portraits on his wall of Sime Silverman, his great-grandfather, and his father, former *Variety* publisher Syd Silverman. Mike said, "This makes me want to cry and turn those two people's pictures to the wall. This is destroying *Variety*." Art Murphy, our longtime box-office expert and my crusty mentor who left the paper in 1993 to concentrate on the producing program he ran at the University of Southern California, told me, "Somebody ought to do a book on the death of a newspaper." Since then, *Variety* has become markedly inferior to its formerly second-rate rival, the *Hollywood Reporter*, as well as the relative newcomers *IndieWire* and *Deadline*.

Were you worried that your career as a film reviewer and critic would be on shaky ground after the controversy?

Yes, for a little while, but ironically, as a Cahners lawyer ruefully pointed out to Maury, *Daily Variety*'s attacks and my pugnacious response had made me into a "First Amendment hero." I rebounded from the *Patriot Games* donnybrook with the help of Ray Greene, the intrepid editor of another trade publication, *Boxoffice*, who hired me to contribute film reviews. And I went on to review films for various web sites, write a film column for *Irish America* magazine, and contribute articles to numerous other magazines while I was back to writing books.

My stint at *Irish America*—which had chosen me as one of the top Irish Americans of 1993 after the *Patriot Games* episode—went smoothly until May 2001, when I reviewed the film *Thirteen Days*, about the Cuban Missile Crisis, and observed that we wouldn't be here today if George W. Bush had been in the White House rather than John F. Kennedy. The editor, Patricia Harty, who had been invited to stay in the Lincoln bedroom by President Clinton and was currying favor with Bush, tried and failed to get me to take the quotes off "president" in referring to him as "our new non-elected 'president' George W. Bush." Relations between Harty and me became so tense as a result that I soon decided to leave the magazine. (Surprisingly, I am gratified to find that the magazine is still running that column on their website and retaining the quotes around "president.")

For *Written By*, the magazine of the Writers Guild of America, West, I especially enjoyed researching and writing profiles of major screenwriters, including Billy Wilder, Abraham Polonsky, Robert Riskin, Frank S. Nugent, Marguerite Roberts, Gavin Lambert, and Michael Wilson. But when the editor, Richard Stayton, asked me in 2004 to write an article about dystopian books and films and their relevance in predicting the world situation at that point in history, the piece I submitted caused him to panic. "Thoughtcrimes: George Orwell and Other Futurists Warned Us" analyzed how writers and directors had anticipated the repression that was being caused by the Bush/Cheney regime. Stayton seemed to think he might go to jail if he ran my article, and he begged me to let him kill it while still paying me, but I shamed him into publishing it in October 2004 by pointing out that the Screen Writers Guild, as the WGA was previously called, had supported the Hollywood blacklist.

Stayton then refused to let me write any more articles for *Written By*, so I was blacklisted by my own guild. (The magazine did run my profile of Gavin Lambert in 2005, but that had been written, approved, and paid for before the flap over "Thoughtcrimes.") Stayton's agitation over "Thoughtcrimes" did not stop him from taking a bow when Tim Robbins visited the office and asked how the magazine found the courage to run such an article. It inspired Robbins to try to make a new film version of Orwell's *Nineteen Eighty-Four*, but when he couldn't raise the money, he did it as a stage production instead.

I published those controversial articles and my profiles of screenwriters among the sixty-four pieces from throughout my journalistic career that I collected in my 2017 book *Two Cheers for Hollywood*, whose title is a nod to E. M. Forster's 1951 essay collection, *Two Cheers for Democracy*. He wrote, "We may still contrive to raise three cheers for democracy, although at present she only deserves two.… So Two cheers for Democracy: one because it admits variety and two because it permits criticism."

"Schmucks with Underwoods"

In your first published book, Persistence of Vision, *you have a section on the screenplay of* Kane, *so you were already focused on screenwriters then.*

Yes, and as I've mentioned, I typed an exact copy of the *Kane* script by Herman J. Mankiewicz and Welles and used it as my guide to teaching myself how to write a script. The *Kane* script and Frank S. Nugent's screenplay for *Fort Apache* are the two that have influenced me the most. Adapting a crudely racist short story by James Warner Bellah, Nugent reversed its viewpoint on Native Americans. He turned the story of a vainglorious, Custer-like commander who leads his men to be massacred into a passionately pro-Indian screenplay, making the Apaches the heroes of the story. Nugent also gave a richly layered portrait of life at a cavalry fort, the men, the women, and the officers' children. His screenplay showed me how to approach history through screenwriting as well as how a film can be novelistic in its approach to depicting a social milieu with a wide array of characters.

The *Kane* script is brilliantly kaleidoscopic storytelling whose complex structure, including flashbacks and the newsreel that sets up the quest for the deeper truth about Kane's life, showed me how the medium can be used most daringly. And the dialogue is colorful, witty, and insightful. With my background in journalism, I also appreciate the critique of newspapers (thanks largely to Mankiewicz) and how the press can be misused. It shows what journalistic integrity means, through the negative example of Charles Foster Kane and the more positive but humanly flawed example of Joseph Cotten's Jed Leland, the reporter and reviewer and best friend of Kane whom the publisher fires for writing a bad notice about his "hopelessly incompetent" opera-singing wife. I will be talking more about *Kane*, Welles, and my books on him as we move forward.

As your career progressed, you began writing more and more about screenwriters—partly because you had become one yourself—but what also motivated that evolution, and how did it affect your work as a biographer and film historian?

Covering Hollywood as a reporter made me much more aware of the collaborative nature of filmmaking. When you go on a set and see all the people who are needed to help make a film, as I did so often in my years at *Daily Variety,* that fact becomes inescapable. And as a reporter, while interviewing screenwriters, directors, and producers, I followed the development of film projects from literary properties and screenplays (original or adapted) into movies. Naturally I became more acutely conscious of how important screenwriters are when I worked with directors who took credit for my ideas or encountered producers and others who ripped off my work.

But even before I worked as a Hollywood screenwriter myself and was subjected to the usual ill treatment and grievances that are common to that profession, I came to know other screenwriters and felt a shared sense of indignation over how writers are treated in the business. It's symptomatic that Jack L. Warner called screenwriters "Schmucks with Underwoods." While writing my *Daily Variety* feature "Bread and Dreams" about the leading young screenwriters of the New Hollywood, I became friendly with some of them, such as Paul Schrader, Robert Towne, and John Milius. I was invited repeatedly by Gloria Katz and Willard Huyck (who had written *American Graffiti* with George Lucas and doctored the script of *Star Wars)* to hang out with their well-connected crowd of young movers and shakers, but I felt too insecure to take them up on it. That kind of inhibition was part of the reason I did not do more of the necessary networking to make it in Hollywood. I also kick myself for not taking Clint Eastwood up on his offer, when I was interviewing him for a film magazine in the 1970s, to come back, hang out, and have a "brewski" with him.

My admiration for the formerly blacklisted writers I came to know was another element that heightened my awareness of the role of screenwriters. I began studying the history of Hollywood more carefully, and that made me realize that Irving Thalberg was right when he (allegedly) said, "Screenwriters are the most important people in the business, but we must never let them find that out." Welles considered Thalberg "the biggest single villain in the history of Hollywood," because he started the system of the so-called "creative" producer controlling everything, including the script and the director.

You see the impact of all this fresh understanding in my biography *Frank Capra: The Catastrophe of Success,* which discusses in detail how Robert Riskin and other screenwriters, such as Jo Swerling, Sidney Buchman, and Myles Connolly, were as much the authors of Capra's work as Capra was, if not more so. I write a lot about screenwriters in all three of my biographies of directors, which critically examine and qualify the auteur theory by studying how reliant directors are on their writers and other collaborators. I even wrote an article for *Written By* about how screenwriters are the "secret weapons" of film historians, for they know where the bodies are buried and are more willing than most other people in the industry to tell the truth about how movies are actually made. I also noted that screenwriters are grateful to talk with authors and other interviewers precisely because they are usually neglected.

And beyond the biographies, the critical studies of directors that I've written in recent years pay detailed attention to their collaborators and the industrial context of filmmaking. I couldn't have written my biographies and later critical studies in such depth if I hadn't paid my dues while working in the Hollywood system. So that makes the turmoil of those years worthwhile and a fair price to pay for such growth in my career.

PART III
BACK TO BOOKS

6. Welles, Ford, and Hawks

Orson Welles

When we first met in 1967, you were twenty and already working on the first of your three books on Orson Welles. How did you get started on your lifelong mission to tell the true story of Welles and his films?

Although I was always a film buff, I saw mostly new films when growing up and didn't see a Welles film until I first encountered and became thrilled by *Citizen Kane* in Professor Richard Byrne's class at the UW in September 1966. That made me want to read about Welles, but I was disappointed by what I found at the university library. Today there are so many volumes of Welles biography and criticism, but back then film scholarship was in its infancy, and sensible readings of the works of great directors were mostly lacking. The books I found were inadequate in conveying the essence of his achievements. As I mentioned earlier, I was especially disappointed by Peter Cowie's critical study, *The Cinema of Orson Welles*, which I found pedestrian and thought missed many key points about Welles. So I felt I needed to write the book on Orson Welles that I wanted to read.

Although I soon began seeing *Kane* in the context of his other cinematic achievements, I spent the first two years of my work on the Welles book intending it as a full-length study of that single film. Only gradually did I realize I needed to expand my focus and cut back on the *Kane* material to cover his whole body of work as it was known at that point. I wrote about all the feature films he had directed that had been released, which, in reality, was a small subset of his voluminous work as a maker of films and television programs. At the time, we Welles scholars had little idea how rich a vein that was. My book was virtually finished when I began acting in *The Other Side of the Wind* in 1970, so I added a chapter on my experiences meeting Welles and acting for him on the first day of filming.

The Cinema One series published by the British Film Institute was busy in the 1960s making up for the yawning gap in the scholarly literature on most major filmmakers, so during my four years on the Welles manuscript, I designed it with that series in mind. My youthful literary background, strongly influenced by T. S. Eliot's criticism and my study of Shakespeare, was evident in the Welles book's concentration on the thematic structure of his work, particularly his tragic sensibility, his humanistic ideology, his passion for justice, and his love of paradox, a Chestertonian tendency I shared, thanks in part to my questioning response to my Catholic upbringing.

Looking back on the original edition of my first book on Welles, which was published in 1972 when I was twenty-five, it seems solid and reliable but rather basic. That's its limitation as well as its strength. It's a meat-and-potatoes meal of what I considered essential Welles criticism. That kind of analysis of Welles's films was what I believed was needed at the time, and as such it was influential on other scholars in helping establish the field of study. *Orson Welles* was relatively light on stylistic and visual analysis, despite the bravura nature of Welles's style. It was not so much that I did not appreciate that aspect of Welles but that I felt my principal task was to explicate his world view as a cinematic dramatist. Welles was, in my view, a badly misunderstood figure, distant from America in those years and with a reputation clouded by myth, so clarifying him and his work was my primary task with what I intended to be a groundbreaking book.

No doubt I felt somewhat hesitant in my early career as a critic about exercising my analysis of visual storytelling. I consciously set out to explore and develop that side of my critical sensibility more ardently in my next book, the critical study *John Ford*—about the consummate master of landscape in the cinema—that I would write with Mike Wilmington from 1969 through 1971. Acting was another major aspect of cinema I needed to learn more about so I could better analyze and describe it. My work with Welles as an actor from 1970 through 1976 helped me greatly in developing those critical skills, which had a salutary influence on my books and articles. I wrote a small book about his acting career, *Orson Welles: Actor and Director*, published in 1977, but I would not fully concentrate on acting until almost fifty years later, when I wrote *George Cukor's People: Acting for a Master Director*, published in 2025.

So the reason you again wrote books about Welles is that you didn't think your first book stood the test of time?

Not exactly. I didn't have access to Welles's unfinished work for my first book on him, but by the time I wrote the third book I'd seen almost everything he made, except for much of his long-in-the-works *Don Quixote*, which he considered a hobby rather than a film he owed to the public. A fuller look at his career was needed, and I set out to encompass his whole career in *What Ever Happened to Orson Welles?: A Portrait of an Independent Career.* That 2006 book, a combination of critical study and memoir, was complicated for me to structure and keep within a reasonable length so it wouldn't go off the rails like Simon Callow's multi-volume biography of Welles. So it took me five years to write, from 2001 on. For four of those years, I was also teaching fulltime at San Francisco State University.

In writing that ambitious book, I was trying to do several things simultaneously, including recalling how I had worked with Welles as an actor and how I dealt with him as a critic and interpreter from the dual vantage points of participant and observer. Leon Edel in *Writing Lives: Principia Biographica*—a book that taught me many valuable lessons when I began writing my Capra biography, and that I frequently re-read—believes that dual perspective is necessary for a biographer. Although *What Ever Happened to Orson Welles?* is not a biography per se, I wanted to cover all or virtually all of his unfinished work and other hard-to-see material, so that readers would have a clearer overview of his career, which was still widely misunderstood as a failure.

Seeing Welles as a tragic (or ridiculous) failure is the myopic way he is viewed in the American mainstream media, which unfortunately tends to set the parameters of public perception. I wanted the book to make people reconsider their flawed and fragmentary and myth-ridden views on Welles, and I think I largely succeeded.

Your second book on Welles, about his acting, was part of Ted Sennett's Pyramid *series of short works on movie stars. Your* Kirk Douglas *book was also a* Pyramid, *so were they connected?*

In a way. I had earlier written the Pyramid volume on Douglas, whom I've always admired as an impassioned, pugnacious actor and gutsy producer. That 1976 book, however, had to be written under strange conditions, since I was so busy at *Daily Variety* that I kept putting it off until shortly before the deadline. I had gone to Wisconsin to do some research in Douglas's papers at the Wisconsin Historical Society, but with the book due on a Monday, I still had not begun writing it by the Friday night before. Out of despondency, I had a few drinks before calling the series editor, Ted Sennett, to tell him I couldn't do the book. Ted freaked out and insisted that I meet my obligation.

Gary Graver, Orson Welles's cinematographer, suggested we pose
for this 1978 portrait during a break from shooting *The Orson Welles
Show* in a Hollywood TV studio. When I positioned myself at
Welles's left, he said, "Where's your training?," and moved me to his
other side. The unsold talk show pilot, in which I was an extra, later
popped up on YouTube.

So I shot down some cups of coffee to sober up and
moved into the *Daily Variety* office in Hollywood at nine
that Friday night. I took along my notes that I had organized
in a portable file drawer, a box of expensive cigars, and a
bottle of bourbon. Although I rarely drank while writing,
I needed the bourbon to lower my inhibitions so I could
write that book over a single weekend. And I wanted to
write it at the office to avoid distractions at my apartment
and so I would have access to our clipping files and bound
volumes of back issues for reference. I started banging out
the manuscript—while also going home for eight hours of
sleep each night and working all day Sunday despite other
staffers putting out the paper around me—and managed to
finish the 25,000-word book at six on Monday morning.
I put the manuscript of *Kirk Douglas* in the mail and with
a couple of hours of sleep dragged myself back to the office
for another day's work.

Even though I was young, I was so wrecked by the
experience that I could do no outside writing for months.
Some years later, when the courtly and erudite director
Rouben Mamoulian asked me to write his autobiography
with him, I demurred, mostly because I was so busy at
my day job but also because I was allergic to the cats that
crawled all around him and because the constant cloud of
cigar smoke surrounding him clashed with my attempts to

quit smoking. While trying to persuade me, Mamoulian said, in a jocular allusion to the Douglas book, "I'll give you *ten* days."

I was less than satisfied by *Kirk Douglas*, but when Sennett asked me to write another Pyramid book, this one on Welles, I told him I would do so if I could focus entirely on his acting career. I was determined to write that one in a much more methodical way than the *Douglas* book. My breezy but well-informed little book on Welles's acting, which I had fun researching and writing in a relatively relaxed six-week period, remains the only volume dedicated entirely to Welles's prolific but checkered acting career. But there is also Michael Anderegg's 1999 superb book, *Orson Welles, Shakespeare, and Popular Culture*; one of the most original studies of Welles, it offers many insights into his acting. Anderegg considers Welles's dedication to both "high" and "low" culture—arguing accurately that the culture Welles disdained was middlebrow culture, the kind that wins Oscars—and analyzes his position as a mediator between those usually disparate modes in various media.

In my more impressionistic study of Welles's acting career, I managed to see virtually all the films and TV shows he acted in, many of them dreadful, and while surveying them, the book performs the service of letting readers know exactly when Welles makes his appearances, so they can tune in and out accordingly. Unlike John Huston, who was willing to direct some routine films to remain bankable so he could make an occasional personal film, Welles generally was unwilling to compromise as a director yet was unabashedly willing to do so as an actor in virtually all cases. He did so to remain visible and earn money to spend on his own "handmade" films, as his cinematographer Gary Graver called *The Other Side of the Wind*.

How did you approach the revised edition of your first book on Welles when you brought it back into print in 1996?

I updated *Orson Welles* and expanded it by 30,000 words when it was picked up by Da Capo Press, which had previously published *John Ford* in the U.S. For the new edition, I added a lengthy preface based on an article I wrote for the *New York Review of Books* about the Welles-Peter Bogdanovich interview book, *This Is Orson Welles*. I brought further research to bear on my chapter verbally reconstructing *The Magnificent Ambersons*, revised the sections on *It's All True* and *Macbeth* in light of more recent developments, and added a chapter on *F for Fake* as well as a second report on the filming of *The Other Side of the Wind* that I had written for *American Film* magazine. I was blindsided and disappointed by the poor reproduction of photos in the 1996 edition of the book, since in my books on film I always work hard to include a solid array of stills, often ones that haven't been published before.

By then it seemed to me as if someone else had written the original *Orson Welles*. Often as an author I have the odd sense in re-reading my books that I don't recall having written a particular sentence and wonder how I came up with it, although I have a contrastingly good memory for my sources. It's a strange but pleasing feeling that your writing seems to have come from some mysterious place within you, or (literally) from a person you once knew who distantly resembled yourself. For the new edition, I tried to retain and recapture the somewhat overly earnest, if not arch, tone of my youthful prose style, which was an amusing task. Since I have a facility for pastiche, which served me well in writing speeches for the AFI shows, I was able to do a fairly seamless approximation, although the *F for Fake* chapter is noticeably different in style.

I was elated by the process of writing that new chapter because I hadn't tackled a piece of pure film criticism for quite a while—a film review has a far different purpose—and found it went considerably beyond the range of the rest of the book. It's looser in style, and its tone is more mature and sophisticated than my earlier voice, which is natural since I wrote it with far more experience behind me. I approached that kaleidoscopic film from a variety of angles, as you must do to fully understand and appreciate it, and that piece of writing encouraged me to write more critical studies in the years ahead, after I put the writing of biographies behind me because I couldn't afford to do them anymore.

With the help of the RKO cutting continuity of Welles's original version of *The Magnificent Ambersons*, I was able to revise my long chapter on that film and make it more precise, rather than relying on the shooting script as I had done in my earlier attempt to clarify Welles's intentions. The *Ambersons* chapter remains my most detailed piece of analysis of a single film, and I consider that my best piece of film criticism, one that shows in detail how much deeper Welles's version was in every respect, thematically and stylistically.

My friend Roger Ryan put together his own partial cinematically "restored" version of *Ambersons* in 1993 using stills and frame enlargements to cover many of the missing scenes and having amateur actors deliver the missing dialogue, which we know from the cutting continuity for the Welles version. Roger also uses the parts of the Bernard Herrmann score that had been cut from the film — Herrmann took his name off it when another composer redid part of his work. The result of this "restored" version is shocking — it's such a different film from the release version. It's far darker and far more political. RKO tried to cut as much of the critique of industrialization and its prescient view of air pollution as it could, although some remains. There were many more Chekhovian overtones of the family lamenting the changes in their town and their lives; it was an American *Cherry Orchard.* What a disturbing and challenging film about our society *Ambersons* would have been if it had been left alone.

Roger's admirable attempt to show us what it was like leaves out some scenes, because he couldn't find stills or frame enlargements to illustrate everything, but we can get from it a clear idea of what the film was and a greater sense of its stature. Roger has generously helped in my research and supplied images from the original version when I taped my half-hour interview about *Ambersons* for the Criterion Blu-ray edition. Roger wanted to revise his "restoration" with the help of additional stills and more frame enlargements he keeps finding and with more professional actors, and Stefan Drössler of the Munich Film Museum was going to help him. The current owners of the film, Warner Bros., were supportive, but Criterion decided against including the restoration because it would have necessitated a second disk. A Criterion producer agreed with me in retrospect that the company's decision was unfortunate. I like the amateurish fan nature of the job Roger did with himself, his wife, and some friends doing the voices. As Welles liked to point out, "amateur" comes from the Latin word for love, and in Roger's reconstruction, his labor of love comes across. And having professional actors imitate the cast would be hokey. If the opportunity comes up again, I will try to talk him out of that while lending my encouragement to upgrading the imagery and sound.

Will you be putting out yet another edition of your original Welles book or writing another book on him?

After the revised edition of *Orson Welles* went out of print, I reacquired the rights, and I have on my agenda (in my copious spare time, as they say) to do another edition, with some fresh material added. I have carted along boxes of beautiful Welles stills with me through life that I will use to enhance the next edition. Welles's career is still active, too, with films being rediscovered and restored and more facets of his amazingly prolific creative life being understood. I learned in writing my early books on Welles and Ford that when you write a book, you have to keep working on it and researching the subject for the rest of your days. I am sure that when I am ninety, I will be writing a book entitled *Orson Welles: The Last Word.*

You often appear as an expert on documentaries about Welles. Which are those?

I was happy to be able to ask Welles a question in his 1981 documentary *Filming "The Trial,"* which he didn't complete but has been assembled by the Munich Film Museum. It's a fascinating 82-minute discussion about the film and other topics with an audience at the University of Southern California. While we were waiting to go into the auditorium that night, Welles told me he planned to shoot documentaries on all the films he had directed, starting with *The Lady from Shanghai.* He said that was not his best film, but it had the best stories. Unfortunately, he was unable to achieve that goal due to the financial failure of his 1978 documentary *Filming Othello,* the last theatrical release of a Welles film in his lifetime. He blows off my question in *Filming "The Trial"* about whether he dubs eleven voices in the film to demonstrate his ubiquity, the kind of question that no doubt irritated him.

I've done audio commentaries on two Welles films, *The Trial* and *Macbeth,* as well as his starring vehicle *Jane Eyre,* and my videotaped interviews on his films *Othello, Chimes at Midnight,* and *Ambersons* are on the Criterion editions. Among the documentaries on Welles in which I appear as a pundit or talking head or witness, I am seen in interview footage as well as outtakes from *Other Wind* in Morgan Neville's erratic 2018 documentary, *They'll Love Me When I'm Dead.* And I pop up briefly in the fascinating Frank Marshall-Ryan Suffern documentary on the postproduction, *A Final Cut for Orson: 40 Years in the Making.*

When we met, you were already were deeply knowledgeable about movies and obsessively watching classic movies and booking others for the Wisconsin Film Society that you hadn't seen before. How much of your eagerness to see all the great films was fueled by your new obsession with Welles?

Every so often, Welles would moan to Gary Graver, "Why did Joe have to discover that film?" The 1934 short *The Hearts of Age*, co-directed by Welles with William Vance in Woodstock, Illinois, is an amateur takeoff on avant-garde films, with the nineteen-year-old Welles (seen here) playing Death. "I don't know how it has entered the *oeuvre*," said Welles: I found the 16mm film in the Greenwich, Connecticut, Public Library, thanks to a tip from my professor Russell Merritt. (Frame enlargement)

Indeed it was, but I didn't discover Welles until I was nineteen, so I still had much to learn! Welles was such an inspiration that he changed my life, as he has for many other cinephiles and cineastes. When he came to Hollywood in 1939, he famously marveled, "It's the greatest railroad train a boy ever had." And as Jean-Luc Godard wrote, in words I use as a second epigraph with that one for *What Ever Happened to Orson Welles?*, "May we be accursed if we ever forget for one second that he alone with Griffith—one in silent days, one sound—was able to start up that marvelous little electric train. All of us, always, will owe him everything." My scholarship on Welles and the publication of my BFI book on him led to my entire career as a film historian and critic. The year after I first saw *Kane*, I discovered John Ford's greatness by seeing *Fort Apache* and began writing about him as well. When I learned that Ford was Welles's favorite director, it all seemed fitting. Ford has long been my favorite—I think he's the greatest of all filmmakers—but Welles always has that special place in my heart.

Looking back, why do you think you, a kid from Milwaukee, became so enamored by Welles? Could it have been because he was from Wisconsin, too?

Actually, it *was* partly because he was from Wisconsin. When I learned that surprising piece of news soon after seeing *Kane*, it seemed fitting. I was trying to move into the wider world, and I was pleased that such a genius had come from what I then viewed as our somewhat backward state. I've since come to realize I was being patronizing about Wisconsin, from which so many great people have emerged. But we do have to *emerge*. As Lenny Bruce wrote about Milwaukee, it's the kind of town where "The cab drivers ask *you* where to get laid."

I knew that Welles, as a boy, had spent a year in Madison, at a summer camp run by a psychology instructor at the UW and his wife and as a boarder in their apartment while he attended Washington Grade School, the only time he ever attended a public school. The school was located where a drugstore was during my time on campus. Now the drugstore is gone, and across the street is Vilas Hall, the headquarters of the Department of Communication Arts, a building that was being erected while I was making the ending of my film *Close But No Cigar* at the construction site. But I didn't realize while I was writing most of *Orson Welles* in a student rooming house on N. Frances Street that he had lived a block away, around the corner on State Street.

Remembering Madison as "a wonderful city," Welles told me in 1970, "I'm not ashamed of being from Wisconsin. Just of being from Kenosha. It's a terrible place." As I wrote in *What Ever Happened to Orson Welles?*, "Hearing him say that, Oja Kodar interjected that all Welles remembered from his boyhood in Kenosha was the day of his mother's funeral, when he was nine and the rain fell all day long. 'Of course you would remember it as a terrible place if that's all you can remember,' she said, and he grunted his assent." My Madison film mafia friend Pat McGilligan wrote a wonderful 2015 biography, *Young Orson: The Years of Luck and Genius on the Path to "Citizen Kane,"* which takes Welles up to the moment when he began shooting *Kane* and spends many pages on his remarkable parents before Orson arrives in the narrative. It is the definitive account of those early years that for so long were shrouded in myth and mystery.

The Magnificent Ambersons is my favorite film in part because it so profoundly captures the spirit and tragedy of life in the Midwest. Based on the Booth Tarkington novel, the film has a character, the inventor Eugene Morgan (Joseph Cotten), who Welles believed was modeled partly on his own father, Richard, an industrialist and playboy who knew Tarkington. And there is evidence that Tarkington did know Mr. Welles. Welles saw in the book and film much of his own upbringing and heritage and personal loss. So the film is unusually close emotionally to its director, such a loving but clear-eyed recreation of the vanished time just before his birth. I think we are all nostalgic and filled with curiosity about how the world was before we came into it. I feel I missed out on World War II, and it's clear that Steven Spielberg (who was born in 1946) feels that way too, since he keeps making movies about our fathers' war.

Did the fact that Welles was so young when he burst onto the movie scene with Kane *and* Ambersons *impact you because you were young in Madison?*

Yes, indeed. Given Welles's youth when he made *Kane*—twenty-five—it is not hard to see why he is such an inspiration to young would-be filmmakers and critics, as he was for me when I was getting started. I also wanted, rashly, to make my first feature film by the time I was twenty-five. When I told Welles that in 1970, I was twenty-three. He kindly said, "You will." I didn't sell my first screenplay until 1976, though, and I never directed a feature film. There's only one Orson Welles, and as Truffaut noted, *Kane* "consecrated a great many of us to the vocation of cinéaste."

John Houseman and Richard Wilson, Welles's two most important early professional associates, called me over at a film premiere party in 1975 to tell me they had been discussing my *Orson Welles*, which they thought was the best book on Welles up to that time. They made the observation that it seemed fitting that the best writing on Welles tended to be by very young men—they also mentioned *Orson Welles: A First Biography*, a slender but lively volume by Roy Alexander Fowler, an Englishman who wrote it in 1946 when he was only nineteen.

In Sight and Sound's *2012 critics' poll,* Vertigo *famously replaced* Citizen Kane *as the greatest movie ever made. I think* Vertigo, *for all its virtues, is about Hitchcock's twentieth best film, so I was disappointed. You've told me that you no longer think* Citizen Kane *is Welles's best film, but what was your reaction to the poll?*

Polls are somewhat frivolous, and the magazine's 2022 poll polemically elevated Chantal Akerman's *Jeanne Dielman, 23, Quai du Commerce, 1080 Bruxelles* as the best film in history, but they at least stimulate discussion, and I was glad to be asked anyway. I felt somewhat guilty not putting *Kane* in my top ten in 2012 or 2022, but Welles is the only director who had two films on my 2012 list—*Ambersons* and *Chimes at Midnight*. Also on my 2012 list were *The 400 Blows*, *A.I. Artificial Intelligence*, *Dr. Strangelove*, *Late Spring*, Renoir's *The River*, *Some Like It Hot*, *Trouble in Paradise*, and *Wagon Master*. On my 2022 list, I included *Ambersons* and *The Other Side of the Wind* (along with *Wagon Master*, *Trouble in Paradise*, *Tokyo Story*, *Sunrise: A Song of Two Humans*, Cukor's *A Star Is Born*, *7 Women*, *Avanti!*, and *The Thin Blue Line*). I wrote that year, "Quite possibly the greatest film ever made before RKO started hacking it up, *Ambersons* is still my favourite film. Capturing the dark essence of my native Midwest, this film about a rich boy killing his mother and destroying his family as his town falls apart looks like no other film; Welles directed in the freshest and most innovative of styles. And as this list shows, I feel protective toward a *film maudit.*"

I love *Vertigo* and wrote and coproduced the 1997 documentary *Obsessed with "Vertigo": New Life for Hitchcock's Masterpiece*, which is included on the Blu-ray edition of the feature. But among Hitchcock films, I prefer *Psycho* and *Marnie*. Nevertheless, I think it's idle to rank films of that level of quality, as polls, for all their pleasantry, compel us to do. And I would add that I believe we have David Thomson to blame for *Kane* being displaced from the top spot, since he had pompously written a *Sight and Sound* piece urging people to do just that. Thomson wrote perhaps the worst book on Welles, the grossly under-researched, sloppy biography *Rosebud*, in which he wrote that he hoped *The Other Side of the Wind* would never come out, so he was irrationally biased. But then you can blame me too, since I didn't put *Kane* on my *Sight and Sound* lists. I think I wore out *Kane* after watching it more than a hundred times. I know every shot and every line before they appear onscreen, which spoils it for me to a large extent. Unfortunately, I loved it too much!

When I first met you in 1967, I believed you were already the top expert on Welles. But, Joe, from this conversation, in which you've expressed the need to write future books about him, I believe it didn't take long for you to feel that you had much to learn about him and his films and that your opinions about both have kept evolving.

Yes, Welles scholarship was still in its formative phase back when I began. In the process of continuing to study and write about him, I have learned a lot more about his astonishingly rich career, thanks to my endless research and the fine work

I handled the clapper board for the filming in the car on the first day of shooting *The Other Side of the Wind* in Los Angeles, August 23, 1970. Some of these scenes made it into the film, although I was able to re-dub my lines, and John Huston's closeups while driving were inserted later. (Royal Road Entertainment/Netflix)

of many other researchers. He has so many more facets than I could have dreamed of at the time. Even decades after his death, he keeps surprising us with new dimensions and new discoveries, not only in film but also in radio and theater and television and print and other media. And his career is not over, since he left a number of unfinished films for his admirers to complete, perhaps partly by intention to keep us working for him. We members of the cast and crew of *Other Wind* called ourselves members of VISTOW, or "Volunteers in Service to Orson Welles." That term was coined by producer Frank Marshall, and crew member Lou Race had VISTOW buttons made up for us at the time of the 2018 release.

My absurdly long involvement with *Other Wind*—throughout what became the longest (intermittent) production history of any film ever made—finally played an integral part in the herculean task of getting it completed and released. That denouement had often seemed unlikely over the decades that had passed since that first magical day of shooting. It was a sort of relay race with the baton being passed from one Wellesian to another. I was glad in the end that I had been fired as a producer, since Filip Jan Rymsza had to spend nine agonizing years negotiating with Oja Kodar to release her rights to the film that she had inherited from Welles. And for anyone who, unlike me, has forty-eight years to spare, there is still *Don Quixote* waiting to be finished properly... but no one has stepped up to the plate. Jonathan Rosenbaum, who has probably seen more of the *Quixote* footage than any other Welles scholar, told me he thinks that is *the* great unfinished Welles film and prefers it to *Other Wind*.

Over the years I also dreamed of doing what I could to search for the complete print of *Ambersons* that Welles may have left in Brazil, but I never got around to it. Joshua Grossberg did make that strenuous pilgrimage, though, and I am a talking head in a documentary, *The Lost Print*, that he has been making. It's a long shot that it might be found, but who would have thought Welles's unfinished 1938 film *Too Much Johnson* would have turned up in an Italian warehouse as it was about to be thrown away?

I wrote about that rediscovery of Welles's delightful silent comedy, which demonstrates he had a considerable facility for directing well before *Kane*, for the online magazine *Bright Lights* in 2014 and revised the essay for *Two Cheers*. And while writing *Orson Welles* and discovering his amateur short *The Hearts of Age*, a spoof of avant-garde cinema, in the Greenwich, Connecticut, Public Library with Russell Merritt's help, I published an article about that discovery, "Welles before *Kane*," in the spring 1970 issue of *Film Quarterly*, including a discussion of the making of *Too Much Johnson*. Welles was irritated that I unearthed *The Hearts of Age*. According to Gary Graver, every few months Welles would say, "Why did Joe have to discover that film?" Welles preferred the world to think he had sprung fully formed as a great director with *Citizen Kane*, but I have a passion for cinematic archeology.

What kind of relationship did you have with your idol after meeting him and immediately being cast in The Other Side of the Wind?

I allowed myself to be putty in Welles's hands while he was directing me. In any case, after we collaborated before each scene in writing the dialogue I had to speak and he typed up the pages, he was dictatorial about exactly how I moved and spoke. He would often say, "It's terrible when a director gives line readings, but—," and then give me a line reading. I was pleased, because he was teaching me. But he bullied me a lot to keep me in an intimidated mood to fit the character—until belatedly hearing Welles's compliment of my acting from a crew member made it possible for me to relax for the last two years of shooting.

Our relationship was always friendly but a bit prickly on occasion since I didn't hesitate to disagree with him, such as when I criticized both LBJ and violent antiwar radicals during our long conversation on the first day we met. There was some truth in Ben Hecht's observation that Welles had "no friends, only stooges." So I think he always felt somewhat on guard with me. But except when he was bullying me, we were polite and usually cordial on the set; I didn't see him much off the set, though, since I wasn't as reflexively flattering as Bogdanovich was.

I know that your writing about Welles's films differed at times from what Welles said about them himself. Would he argue with you? Did you ever teach Welles anything about his own films that he had never thought of?

Welles often called me over during shooting to explain what he was doing. I think one reason he put me on the set was that he wanted a historian there who would report accurately what he was doing, since so much that was written about him was false. I am not sure if I taught him anything about himself; he was one of the most self-aware of artists. We did have differences of opinion on some of his films. One time during the making of *Other Wind*, I heard Welles say loudly from another room, "*Joe* would like Christopher Plummer. *He* doesn't like my Shakespearean performances either." I hastened to Welles's side and reminded him that I thought his Falstaff in *Chimes at Midnight* was his greatest performance and that I also thought he was good as Macbeth but that he was miscast as Othello. That didn't seem to mollify Welles. He didn't try to argue these points with me, though. He was thin-skinned about criticism, as most directors are, but I think he ultimately, if grudgingly, respected the fact that I wasn't a sycophant and didn't simply praise his work but had complex opinions about it and drew distinctions.

The first time I met him, he pointed out that in my essay on *Chimes* in the Autumn 1969 issue of *Film Quarterly*, I had misunderstood a key scene, when the newly crowned King Henry V (played by Keith Baxter) rallies his people with "No king of England if not king of France!" I had written that the war, which Shakespeare presents as "the God-given and ancestrally determined right of empire, becomes in *Chimes at Midnight* a totally unmotivated, madly willful action.... Hal, on accepting responsibility, immediately puts it to blindly destructive ends. Welles does not invoke, as Shakespeare does, a higher imperative for Hal's action, presenting it solely as a function of his will."

Welles didn't tell me what I was wrong about but made me study the Shakespearean text to find out for myself, a gesture I respected. I then realized Henry is making a Machiavellian move to consolidate his fragile hold on power by rallying the country behind him to follow the dying advice of his father, King Henry IV: "Therefore, my Harry,/Be it thy course to busy giddy minds/With foreign quarrels, that action, hence borne out,/May waste the memory of the former days."

I was reminded of that scene when I spent a day with Baxter in Spain on the location of the Cardona church where they had shot thirty percent of *Chimes*. We were there as part of a 2015 Welles conference at the Filmoteca de Catalunya in Barcelona organized by the Spanish Welles scholar and archivist Esteve Riambau. Keith told me that he was so taken with the role of Prince Hal that he told Welles he hoped to star in a stage production of Shakespeare's *Henry V*. "Why would you want to do that?" responded Welles. "He was such a terrible shit." Keith did go on to play Henry IV onstage, the role John Gielgud embodies so magnificently in *Chimes at Midnight*. When I told Keith I thought he and Agnes Moorehead in *Ambersons* give the greatest non-Welles performances in Welles's films, he immediately added the name of Gielgud, as I had unaccountably failed to do.

I think Welles's movies are about flawed men, betrayal, bad choices, hubris, and failure. Do you consider these essential to Welles? And what have I foolishly left out?

Yes, those are key themes in his work. He would say they are key themes in *all* serious drama—as he did when a French interviewer noted that each of his films is a story of a failure with a death in it. I would add that a constant theme of Welles's work is the intense friendship between two men, one of whom ends up betraying the other. This can be traced back to Welles's feeling that he betrayed his father by abandoning him when he was drinking himself to death; Welles actually believed he had killed his father. And perhaps this theme stems from Welles's feeling that his mother and father betrayed him by dying in his youth. There is a homoerotic element to the male relationships in Welles's films that is one of the two great taboos in Welles criticism. The other point you're not supposed to acknowledge is that he was blacklisted. I discuss both of those topics in *What Ever Happened to Orson Welles?* and have drawn some of the expected flak for doing so, but I am glad to have broken the taboos.

If you asked Welles if he was proud of his movies and happy with his film career, what would his honest answer be?

Welles was always dissatisfied with his work and would still be reediting all his films now if he had the chance. But he knew his worth. He would say such things as, "In handling a camera I feel that I have no peer." He was proudest of *Chimes at Midnight*. It expresses his worldview most fully, and there is little distance between him and Falstaff. It's such a profound and beautiful and haunting film. *Ambersons* probably would be his greatest film if we still had all of it. He said it was much better than *Kane* before RKO started hacking it up.

But he said on numerous occasions late in life that he should have left the film business, which treated him so badly and made him spend much of his life begging money men in restaurants to fund his work. Still, he said he fell in love with movies, the most expensive mistress a man can have, and couldn't leave her. His first wife, Virginia Nicolson, advised him not to go to Hollywood and stay in the theater instead. Their daughter, Chris Welles Feder, told me he acknowledged late in life that Virginia was right. He would have been happier in the theater and would have had an easier time of it. (His Mercury stage production of *Julius Caesar* cost only $12,000 to mount.) But then we would not have all those great movies.

Was he pleased that you, Peter Bogdanovich, and most film critics of the Sixties and Seventies, and film historians, revered him or did he humbly—the wrong word for Welles—think he didn't deserve such acclaim?

I don't know how humble he was, but I'd say he actually was humble to some extent. When Welles was once accused of being vain, he responded precisely, "I am *conceited*—I am not vain." He also said once that since he didn't command the popular audience that Doris Day pictures did, he needed serious film magazines such as *Sight and Sound* to keep him viable. So he appreciated what Peter and I and others wrote about him. Still, I believe that need caused him to resent us critics as well. He shouldn't have had to depend on us to the extent he did. That's one reason he mocks my Mister Pister and other critics in *The Other Side of the Wind*. I was aware of that when we colluded in satirizing the foolishly earnest young critic I was playing. I sympathized with Welles's point of view and shared his sense of the absurdity of the situation, that a Mister Pister could be important to the career

While not on camera, I would watch Welles at work directing
Other Wind. In this scene filmed at Producers Studio across from
Paramount, Welles and Eric Sherman operate cameras while cinema-
tographer Gary Graver and Peter Pilafian handle sound and future
producer Frank Marshall wields a sun-gun. I am on the porch, and
in the distance Cameron Mitchell chats with fellow cast member
Edmond O'Brien. (Tremolo Productions/
Royal Road Entertainment/Netflix)

of a Jake Hannaford, the legendary director played by John
Huston. But in fact, critics and historians are important to
careers and to analyzing and to some extent judging them;
we just have to avoid being too self-important and power
mad about it, as, for example, Pauline Kael was. That's an
occupational hazard.

*Was he slightly embarrassed that "Rosebud" caused such a
reaction in the film world?*

He thought "Rosebud" was the weakest element in *Citizen
Kane*. That's why he wrote that line in which the reporter,
Thompson, our surrogate investigator, says near the end,
"I don't think any word can explain a man's life." But it is
thrilling when the camera then leaves the reporter and reveals
the Rosebud sled. That explains *parts* of Charles Foster
Kane, but far from everything. Rosenbaum has said, and
I agree, that *Kane* is about the impossibility of completely
defining a human being. Welles tried to put as much of that
into *Kane* as he could, but felt somewhat stymied by the
"Rosebud" theatrical gimmick, as he considered it, and by
people seizing on it to think they understood Charles Foster
Kane once they knew he had been deprived of his childhood
sled. And yet it represents his loss of his childhood, his
Eden, and that *is* critical. His mother actually sells him to a
bank (one of the film's profound mysteries). That means a
great deal in the scheme of things.

Kane did not have had a happy childhood in Colorado — there is the implication his father beats him, and his mother is severe, though anguished — and Welles mourned Lost Edens while still recognizing they are imperfect. But I would not necessarily say the sled is his favorite possession, since we see the glass ball (which also represents a snowy scene of his childhood) on a table behind his mother when it is revealed with a slight panning movement at the exact moment she signs him away. This object is also mysterious, since it turns up in Susie's apartment where she lives when Kane meets her in New York and later at his Florida castle, Xanadu. It's another symbol, and it pops up in her apartment as if by magic, although at the beginning of the film when Kane says "Rosebud" before dropping his glass ball and dying, the script notes that it's "one of those glass balls which are sold in novelty stores all over the world." We don't literally have to think he carried the ball from Colorado to Xanadu, but it links him (and Susan) emotionally/thematically with his mother (like the stuff he keeps at the warehouse and/ or moves to Xanadu, including the sled). Very few viewers even notice the ball in Colorado — or in New York. It took me multiple viewings to spot it in those scenes, though in New York it's more visible since it's in the foreground (our view is directed into the background through a mirror, though, so the magician is using indirection). The film does say a lot about possessions not equaling happiness, but this possession is a vestige of happiness.

And yet let me play devil's advocate: I can't help feeling that the sled was not only his favorite possession but his only playtoy in a non-Edenic childhood before he suddenly became rich and could buy anything or anyone he wanted and yet was miserable. The snow globe is a nostalgic reminder of his mother but not a toy he plays with. The sled is an object of play that gets him out of his unhappy home. The snow globe, on the other hand, encloses his childhood in a frozen scene. So I actually think Rosebud does tell the full story of a man's life, at least in our imagination — not the life Kane actually had but the life he could have had if he hadn't become rich but instead had the opportunity to realize his potential and become a truly great man.

I would agree with you in one sense—when Rosebud is revealed as the sled at the end, the rush of emotion we get from that revelation does seem to convey that we now understand Charles Foster Kane on a profound level. And yet Welles also wants us to question the simplistic nature of that symbol. He said he wrote that line of Thompson's "to take the mickey out of" Rosebud: before we see the sled at Xanadu, the film has just cautioned us to be wary of Rosebud on an intellectual level. Welles is challenging the audience in the way F. Scott Fitzgerald meant when he wrote, "The test of a first-rate intelligence is the ability to hold two opposed ideas in mind at the same time and still retain the ability to function."

The Magnificent Ambersons is so unlike Welles's other films—though you have pointed out connections to Citizen Kane—*so I wonder: why did he want to adapt the book into a movie? Was it the story or the filmmaking possibilities that most intrigued him?*

In addition to finding in Tarkington's novel the evocations of his own Midwestern background, George Orson Welles saw his dark side in the devilishly charming but destructive young George Amberson Minafer. And the death scene of his mother, Isabel Amberson Minafer, is drawn from Welles's memory of his own last meeting with his mother, who died when he was nine. Welles's belief that he had caused his father's death made him suffer from lifelong guilt, much as George does after his mother dies, knowing that he literally killed her, and he begins to understand all the damage he has done. Making a film dealing with a young man's role in causing his mother's death may have been Welles's displacement of his feelings about his father, which he was able to deal with more directly as he aged, as he does in the great scene of Hal's rejection of Falstaff in *Chimes at Midnight.* The town in *Ambersons* is another of his Lost Edens. It can't get any more personal than that, even if someone else wrote the book. And George is Welles as he feared he was, much like the demonic youthful title character he portrayed himself as in his semi-autobiographical 1934 play, *Bright Lucifer.*

Do you agree with those who believe Tim Holt is the weak link in the movie, or do they underestimate him?

Welles played George poorly in the 1939 radio version, putting on a pouting little-boy voice. He was too old to play George in the film, so he narrates instead, with unparalleled eloquence. It's fortunate he cast Tim Holt, who gives one of the film performances I value the most. I want to write an essay on how good Holt is in that film. People have always underestimated him because they find his character objectionable. You have to differentiate between an actor and the character he or she plays. Over the years I have come to appreciate just how fine and nuanced Holt is. He somehow manages to make us empathize with George despite his egomania and all the despicable things he does, including destroying his mother's life. He's a classic tragic protagonist.

I want to explain how Holt carries off that difficult feat of acting. His George manages to charm people who should know better, such as Lucy and Eugene Morgan. That trait is critical to the success of the performance. For contrast, see Jonathan Rhys Meyers as George in the abysmal 2002 TV remake of *Ambersons*. He is so monstrous and loathsome that no one would want to be in the same room with him. Holt's George, by contrast, is very human. He compels people to want to be with him, if only to try to understand him, as we do with tragic characters.

I also identify with Holt because Welles would shout at me when I was acting in *Other Wind*, "Don't act!" I read in a 1942 *Los Angeles Times* article that Welles would do that with Holt as well. But Holt was an accomplished actor—he is also fine in *The Treasure of the Sierra Madre* and *My Darling Clementine*, among other films—and Welles was a master psychologist as a director, giving each actor what he or she needed individually. So he drew great performances not only from John Gielgud and Jeanne Moreau but also from Holt and Dorothy Comingore and many other actors of varying range.

Would you have liked Welles, if he had the money, to have done a remake of Ambersons *to his liking later in his career with an entirely new cast?*

Not a remake, but he was thinking of redoing the lost ending in the boarding house with Joseph Cotten and Agnes Moorehead naturally aged into their roles. That would have been wonderful. I saw the frame enlargement of the final shot when Bogdanovich had it in 1970. It's since been lost. It shows an overhead long shot of the polluted city with Eugene's little car vanishing around a corner. There is an elevated train in the background, the car is surrounded by tall impersonal buildings, and smoke wreathes the atmosphere. It's a hellish vision of what happened to our country in the modern machine age.

Mark Robson, Robert Wise's assistant editor on Ambersons, *expressed regret to me that RKO forced Wise and him to re-*

edit the film after it ran into trouble while being previewed. As you know, RKO, which kicked Welles's team off the lot and assigned Robson and Wise to Val Lewton's B-horror film unit, spread the word that Welles had abandoned ship on Ambersons.

Welles did not "abandon ship." He was shooting *Ambersons* when Pearl Harbor was attacked in December 1941, and the U.S. government told him it was his urgent patriotic duty to go to South America to make a documentary in conjunction with RKO, *It's All True,* to celebrate our alliance with that part of the world and to help combat fascism. He was reluctant to go but felt he had no choice, especially since the Hearst papers and others were calling him a draft dodger. Welles had Norman Foster finishing *Journey Into Fear* at the same time *Ambersons* was finishing shooting. Welles made arrangements for Wise, who had edited *Kane* and was now editing *Ambersons,* to go to Brazil to complete the fine-tuning of the editing with him. Wise either couldn't get a plane because of the war, or RKO reneged on the agreement, or both. RKO also fought with Welles over his duties to the U.S. to serve as a goodwill ambassador during the shooting of *It's All True* in 1942 and blamed him for production problems, not all of which were under his control.

In his forced absence, *Ambersons* had a preview in Pomona at which mostly youthful yahoos hooted at Agnes Moorehead's Aunt Fanny (as, indeed, they did until the women's movement arrived in the late 1960s) and were restless over the film's somber nature and harsh social commentary. So while they kept previewing the film, RKO got Wise to cut fifty minutes out of it and have parts of it reshot; assistant director Freddie Fleck shot the ridiculous happy ending. Then RKO dumped the film on the market, deliberately sabotaged the release after it opened well in some places, and kicked Welles's production unit off the lot. Welles always blamed Wise for the ruination of *Ambersons.* When I told Welles I thought I might have been too hard on Robert Wise in my essay on the film in *Persistence of Vision,* since it was a more complicated situation than laying it all on one man, he said, "You can *never* be too hard on Robert Wise. Wise was the real villain."

Wise does deserve some of the blame. He no doubt was advancing his career by doing the studio's bidding, as Welles believed, but when I spoke with Wise more than once about the situation, it was clear that he sincerely believed he was saving a film that was almost unreleasable, even though he recognized Welles's version was better. The problem with

Wise's involvement with *Ambersons* was that Wise was a Hollywood guy through-and-through and Welles was not; Welles was an artist. Jean Renoir captured Welles's dilemma best when he observed that he was an aristocrat working in a popular medium. He was a democrat (small "d") and progressive politically but an aristocrat by temperament. Welles also had the misfortune to be making a film attacking American industrialization and pollution at the precise time the country was gearing up its industrial production massively for its entry into the world war. In that climate, *Ambersons* was seen as subversive, which, in a way, it is. And Welles was the fall guy for a change of regimes at RKO and for a board of directors that never believed hiring a leftist artist from the New York stage was a good idea.

Was it a goal of yours when researching Welles to find out why he was fired by RKO? Robson guessed Welles was fired because, and I'm quoting what he said to me, "He was in South America with his It's All True *production in shambles,* Ambersons *in trouble, and* Journey into Fear *incomplete."*

In researching *What Ever Happened to Orson Welles?*, I found what I consider the "smoking gun" of Welles's Hollywood career, documentation that clears up a key mystery about his career. This was a major research discovery, still little-understood, a missing piece of the puzzle about Welles's firing from *It's All True* while he was filming that documentary in Brazil for the U.S. government. Even after RKO pulled the plug, Welles still managed to get the studio to let him complete the Jangadeiros segment with a silent 35mm Mitchell camera and a budget of only $10,000. That was the end of the filming, but fortunately the material he shot in their fishing village of Fortaleza was found and included in the 1993 documentary *It's All True: Based on an Unfinished Film by Orson Welles*.

Welles's Mercury Productions was thrown off the lot before Welles could return to the studio from Brazil. Writers hostile to Welles have always claimed that he was fired from *It's All True* for his supposed extravagance and irresponsibility, and that is often cited as a key exhibit in the supposed downfall of his career, the cornerstone of that myth, but I was able to prove just *how* false that charge is. What I discovered was that RKO lied to Welles about the budget for *It's All True*. They deliberately concealed from him that the film was budgeted at $1.2 million. And because of the studio's chicanery, he didn't know when he was fired for allegedly being over budget that he actually was

$447,452 *under* budget when he was doing his final shooting in Fortaleza. I learned this by going through RKO and U.S. government documents. It changes everything about the myth that Welles was run out of Hollywood for extravagance. Among the documents I found were transcripts of telephone conversations between RKO executives in which they admit that they were lying to Welles and didn't want him to know the actual budget. Welles later came to understand that "We spent only a little over half of the money that was supposed to have been spent." But when RKO spread their lie about Welles being fired for supposedly going over budget, that seriously damaged his career and his reputation, and that lie is still believed by many people. Ironically, my detailed discovery about the depths of RKO's dishonesty caused consternation and incredulity among some posters on the wellesnet.com website, since even many Welles supporters are so wedded to the myths about his career that they can't get their heads around it when those myths are corrected. One would think Welles admirers would be pleased to learn that the source of one of the most damaging myths about Welles—his alleged profligacy as a director—was a lie, yet some Wellesians had trouble processing the reality, since it changed the story fundamentally.

Catherine Benamou's 2007 book, *It's All True: Orson Welles's Pan-American Odyssey*, which is largely authoritative and drawn from extensive research, nevertheless misses the story about the film being so far under budget when Welles was fired under false pretenses. When Benamou wrote a follow-up piece on the film for the 2018 anthology *Orson Welles in Focus*, I was one of the manuscript readers for the publisher and provided the accurate information to correct what she wrote, but in a footnote she added about the budget for the published version, she nevertheless was still confused and inaccurate about that key issue. My reporting on my discovery in *What Ever Happened to Orson Welles?* is an example of how my work on *Daily Variety* covering the financial aspects of the industry and learning how to read contracts and other legal and financial documents proved beneficial to my books of film scholarship.

My late friend Michael Schlesinger was head of repertory for Paramount and helped get the 1993 *It's All True* documentary green-lit with its partial reconstruction of Welles's film and the story of the shooting. Mike told me that when the suits who ran the studio finally saw the documentary, *he* was fired. He said two guards wearing guns showed up in his office and escorted him off the lot for making the film. When I asked why the studio executives were

Somehow Mister Pister wound up in Peter Bogdanovich's clothes and body by the end of *The Other Side of the Wind*; it must have been a really wild party! Actually, when I saw the semifinal cut, I told them Peter was in two places at once, so I suggested ILM put someone else's head on his body in this shot, not realizing it would be mine. I am glad to be in this late scene with Jake Hannaford's final words unspooling on a tape recorder before the film goes to the last shot of the empty screen in the drive-in theater.
(Royal Road Entertainment/Netflix)

so upset, Mike said they hadn't realized that half of the documentary, the Jangadeiros segment, is a silent picture and that it is about poor fishermen, people of color. This proved again the truth of what Stepin Fetchit had told me, that "Hollywood was more segregated than Georgia under the skin." There has been some progress in that sense, but not much.

I saw you as the guest speaker for a screening of Touch of Evil *at the Film Forum in New York, so I know how passionate you are about that film, too. Do you think we're fortunate to have three versions of* Touch of Evil *in circulation now, or would you prefer only one version being available to the public?*

The preview version is available on the Universal DVD and Blu-ray sets with the other two versions, the release version and the reconstruction. It is good for film history to have all three versions available. The revisions made by Walter Murch in 1998 follow some of Welles's suggestions in the memo he wrote upon seeing a version of *Touch of Evil* the studio had put together after barring him from the editing process. That version already contained additional scenes shot by another director, Harry Keller. The studio followed only a few of Welles's requests, but the fixes Murch was able to make, given what material remained, help the film immensely. The preview version contains some footage by Welles that was not retained in the 1958 release version, but it also contains more of the Keller footage than made it into the release version, so it's a mixed bag. The preview version is not the "director's cut." Nor is the Murch version, though both have mistakenly been described as that. The director's cut has vanished. Universal-International, which Welles said had been positive about the shooting and the rushes, was horrified by the film as he assembled it, so they reedited and partly reshot it. As Murch put it, "The film committed perhaps the worst sin in the Hollywood book: it was a decade or so ahead of its time."

Including Moses and Ben-Hur, do you think, as many do, that Ramon Miguel ("Mike") Vargas in Touch of Evil *is Charlton Heston's most significant role?*

Heston was described in France as "an axiom of the cinema," and he deserves cinematic immortality for getting Welles to direct *Touch of Evil,* not to mention his admirably solid body of work as an actor. I also particularly admire his General Gordon in *Khartoum,* in which he out-acts Laurence Olivier. Heston is fine as Vargas, but he doesn't get enough credit for being non-stereotypical and heroic as the Mexican government official, a role for which he is unfairly disparaged by today's PC police. When I was hosting a panel on *Touch of Evil* with Heston, Janet Leigh, Dennis Weaver, and second assistant director Terry Nelson, I thoughtlessly asked Heston how he felt playing a "Chicano" in the film. He sharply corrected me by pointing out that Vargas is not a Chicano but a Mexican. Heston and Welles went out of their way to make the character strong and dignified, and Heston noted that he thought it is an actor's job to play different kinds of people, including of different nationalities. He specifically cited his El Cid and Cardinal Richelieu as other examples. I agree with him.

How many times did you have to see the three-minute opening shot before you fully appreciated it?

The very first time, in the little room at the Memorial Union in Madison… it blew me away! It is enhanced in the Murch version by not having the titles superimposed to distract us from the visuals. And by having the sounds of the border town play in a complex Murchian aural collage (as Welles intended) rather than being drowned out by the former Henry Mancini title music. Welles told me, on the other hand, that the first interrogation scene in the apartment (lasting five minutes and twenty-three seconds) is "the greatest use of the moving camera in the history of cinema." He said that while "Everyone talks about the opening shot," he felt that interrogation scene is more impressive. He was right. There are more than sixty camera moves and several characters moving balletically from room to room, along with their shadows. The other two interrogation scenes in the apartment are also done in unbroken long takes, although they are shorter. These three interrogation scenes are subtler than the spectacular opening shot, so most viewers don't realize how astonishing they are technically and artistically.

Today Touch of Evil *is regarded by a multitude of critics as one of Welles's masterpieces, but for him it was another disappointing experience because of studio interference.*

After *Touch of Evil* was taken away from Welles, which he called a "terribly traumatic experience," he was lastingly resistant to working for major studios. I don't know how he went on after *The Magnificent Ambersons* was mutilated, but he did. Still, after it happened again, though to a lesser extent, on *Touch of Evil*, he never wanted to direct a studio film again and went totally independent, literally making "home movies" for the rest of his time in America.

Many decades have passed since we first became Welles fans. And now we're past Welles's age when he died.

That's a sobering thought! And I'm older now than he was when I met him.

Has your aging changed how you look at him and his work?

Films change as we grow; they seem to change for better or worse. We can see layers and depths we may have missed before. But my view of his work has remained relatively consistent. Like Welles, I was into the themes of old age when I was very young; I did not identify with my generation but with older people, including the elder statesmen in the art form. Perhaps I am less wrapped up with old age now that I am getting to be a certified geezer.

If you loved or disliked any old-time director back in the Sixties, are you likely to feel the same about them?

Usually I do. I love Welles as much as ever, as I do Ford and Renoir. I am less interested in Luis Buñuel now, though, since I've largely worked through my old hangups about Catholicism. He is still great, of course, and he inspired me in my anticlerical rebellion period, but I no longer feel the need to revisit his work as often. I've grown more interested in some directors I didn't know as well back then because of the vagaries of distribution or because of my youth. Yasujiro Ozu is now one of my favorites, as is Ernst Lubitsch, partly because I've now managed to see all their films. It was hard to see their work in the 1960s. Ozu, with his concentration on the deterioration of family and society and, like Welles, on old age, means more to me than he would have when I was young.

When I met you, you were equally a John Ford fanatic and expert. If I said that Welles and Ford have nothing in common, what would be your response?

No, they have a great deal in common. Both were intensely nostalgic and critical of American history, for starters. They mourn a Lost Eden that they know didn't actually exist. Truffaut wrote, "Orson Welles has made films with his right hand (*Kane*, *Ambersons*, the three Shakespeare adaptations, *Immortal Story*, *The Other Side of the Wind*) and films with his left hand (the thrillers). In the right-handed films there is always snow, and in the left-handed ones there are always gunshots; but all constitute what Cocteau called the 'poetry of cinematography.'" The snow films, especially *Ambersons* and *Chimes at Midnight*, are the most Fordian among his finished works. But I saw an impressive 40-minute compilation of beautiful scenes put together by Costa-Gavras from Welles's still-unfinished *Don Quixote* that justifies Bogdanovich's description of it to me in 1970 as "Welles's most Fordian film." Welles was asked what directors he most admired, and he said, "The old masters. By which I mean John Ford, John Ford, and John Ford."

Did they often cross paths in Hollywood?

They had a sort of artistic kinship from the beginning. Ford came to the set of *Kane* to wish him well and to warn him against his assistant director, Eddie Donahue, who was a front-office spy. Welles arrived in a stagecoach at the wrap party, which had a Western theme to honor Ford. Welles famously had studied the filmmaking craft before making *Kane* by screening *Stagecoach* over and over. Ford later wanted Welles to play Mayor Skeffington in *The Last Hurrah*, but the Red-baiting Ward Bond interfered with Columbia Pictures and evidently discouraged them from letting Ford cast Welles. Ford was furious at Bond; Welles mistakenly thought, or said he thought, that his agent had bungled the deal.

Early in Welles's time in Hollywood, Ford and his pals, including John Wayne, sent Welles a makeshift cardboard certificate festooned with beer-bottle labels that said simply, "Orson Welles has been elected." Welles said it was the only award he ever kept on his office wall, until someone stole it. I'm not sure how much time Welles spent with Ford; probably not a lot, especially if Bond was around. But Welles pumped Ford collaborators such as Gregg Toland and Tim Holt at great length about the master's working methods and learned much from Ford, such as how to avoid closeups and stage scenes in long uninterrupted takes. I believe *Ambersons*, for example, shows the deep influence of *How Green Was My Valley*, which opened the same day Welles's film began shooting. But Welles moves his camera much of the time, and Ford rarely moves his. You don't have to be identical with your master to learn from him.

John Ford

When you and Mike Wilmington began writing your critical study, John Ford, *in 1970, how did you break down the responsibilities for writing sections of the book? And how did you choose which Ford films to focus on?*

Ford had a career the likes of which can never happen again. After starting at Universal in 1914 as a laborer and prop man, Jack Ford was an assistant director, stuntman, and actor for his brother Francis, who was a leading actor and director at the studio with his partner Grace Cunard. Jack became a director in 1917. In a career that lasted until 1970, he directed 136 films—112 features and 24 shorts—as well as supervising more than 90 documentaries for his Field Photographic Branch of the Office of Strategic Services and the U.S. Navy in World War II. When Mike and I did our book, only twelve of Ford's sixty-five silent films were known to exist in whole or in part, and now we have twenty-seven in various states of survival. Given that Ford's body of work is so huge and unwieldy, we decided to focus on a dozen or so of his most important and characteristic films and analyze them in depth. In the end, we wrote about fourteen films, from his first feature, the 1917 *Straight Shooting*, which had to represent his silent work, to his last feature, the 1966 *7 Women*.

Although I had taken the lead in planning the book, and we divided our work into sections on key Ford films, we had many long talks about Ford for a year and a half, often daily, and the book benefited greatly from blending two complementary points of view. Ford is such a complex artist that I felt it needed that dual perspective to see him in sharp focus, which is why I invited Mike to collaborate with me. Like Walt Whitman, Ford could say, "I am large, I contain multitudes." When I read the book now, I often find it impossible to know who wrote what. We felt that going into depth on relatively few films was preferable to a superficial survey. But the shape of our *John Ford* continually evolved. We would have included some other key Ford films, but we had a policy of only writing about films on whose stature we agreed. That was necessary to make the section on each film coherent and to ensure that the book fairly represented both of our viewpoints. This led to some difficulties.

When I assigned the primary responsibility for sections, we decided neither of us would sign them, other than my interview with Ford and my chapter on his funeral. We contributed equally to the book's Introduction, which took a lot of discussion and drafting to provide an in-depth overview of Ford's themes, style, and evolution, and I thought that part of *John Ford* was our most successful collaborative effort. I took the lead on films I felt I could handle better and/or felt more passionate about, including *Straight Shooting, Wagon Master, Fort Apache, The Rising of the Moon, Sergeant Rutledge*, and *7 Women*. Mike also contributed material to those sections, which enhanced them. We shared the work on the sections on *They Were Expendable, The Sun Shines Bright*, and *The Searchers*. Mike did an excellent job taking the lead on *Stagecoach, My Darling Clementine*, and *The Man Who Shot Liberty Valance*, but I made a mistake in assigning him *The Quiet Man*. His shrewd understanding of the plot and character dynamics of that film far outpaced his sketchy knowledge of the culture and history of Ireland, which made his drafts, as they often were for the book, seem scattered and sometimes confused.

I wanted the book to include *The Grapes of Wrath*, which I consider one of Ford's greatest films, as most people do. But Mike didn't like it at the time, for reasons that I found rather vague, other than that it was out of fashion with auteurist critics because it is a literary adaptation from a celebrated novel. That didn't bother me, and I think Nunnally Johnson's screenplay, Ford's direction, and Toland's cinematography actually improve on John Steinbeck's novel. In later years, Mike told me he had come around to recognizing why *Grapes* is a masterpiece. I found his belated recognition frustrating, as I did his gradual appreciation of *They Were Expendable*, another film on which we differed at the time.

No amount of persuasion could move Mike in my direction on *Grapes* back then; he was a doctrinaire, hardcore auteurist in those days, as a heated argument we had over Howard Hawks's last film, *Rio Lobo*, demonstrated. We took the Badger Bus to Milwaukee when it opened in 1970. Mike was a fanatical Hawks admirer, and I regarded Hawks with some ambivalence. Mike couldn't see any flaws in *Rio Lobo*, even though the lead actress, Jennifer O'Neill, is inept, and Jorge Rivero has trouble with English dialogue. But one of Mike's firmly held beliefs was that a film cannot ever be considered "miscast," and you simply have to accept whoever is in it at face value. My belief is that while you have to approach a film as it is, not how you wish it might be—as I did, for instance, in recording the audio commentary for Ford's studio-compromised, dramatically flawed, and yet hauntingly poetic Western about Native Americans, *Cheyenne Autumn*—you still can and should acknowledge any problems you find in the film, casting or otherwise.

I found that Mike's viewpoints could be simplistic and overly emotional. But when he was at his best, as he was, for example, on *Stagecoach* and *Liberty Valance*, his analytical skills were profound, acutely conveying how those landmark Westerns draw from both legend and history, and his phrasing was eloquent and moving. After I gave James Stewart a copy of our Ford book on the set of *The Shootist*, I visited his home the following week for an interview. He told me he had read the section on *Liberty Valance* with our analysis of the ending sequence in which his character's wife looks out a train window and asks him, "Aren't you proud?" about how he transformed the wilderness into a garden. Stewart said he agreed with us that the bleak look on his character's face after she asks him that is the point of the film, and that Ford is asking the audience, "*Are* you proud?" of what has happened to America.

The climactic moment of John Ford's *Fort Apache*, when John
Wayne's Captain York vehemently protests what he calls the suicidal
order by Lt. Col. Thursday (Henry Fonda) to split the command and
attack the entrenched Apaches. The principled York's failure to stop
Thursday is tragic. This scene in a film that helped change my life was
shot in Monument Valley at eleven AM on the morning I was born,
August 9, 1947. (Argosy/RKO)

On the other hand, Mike faltered when it came to
analyzing another Ford classic, *Young Mr. Lincoln*. After
we published what he wrote as an article in *Film Heritage*
under both our names, as we had agreed we would do on
the book, I belatedly found, to my horror, that Mike had
virtually every plot point wrong and every line of dialogue
misquoted. That kind of sloppiness turned out to be a
problem in his other sections as well, so I had to repeatedly
study every film he wrote about so I could doublecheck
every line and plot description.

*How did you two manage to study Ford's films in detail
in those pre-VCR, pre-cable TV days? The Searchers must
have been especially difficult to access back then.*

It was a challenge to see the films repeatedly. We had to
take the Greyhound bus to Chicago to see *The Searchers*
at the Clark Theater in the Loop, go to Milwaukee to see
other films on TV, and find ways of renting Ford films for
the Wisconsin Film Society and persuading other campus
groups to show them. We later brought to Madison the
beautiful original 35mm print of *The Searchers* from
Warners' Chicago exchange that we had first seen at the
Clark. I vividly remember how that print looked after

seeing it numerous times, so I can still compare it in my mind with the currently available Blu-ray edition, which valiantly but imperfectly attempts to replicate the original color quality. The archival materials have partially faded, necessitating adding some artificial coloring, and the Blu-ray fails to replicate the subtlety of Winton C. Hoch's day-for-night cinematography, including in the closeup on Ethan's anguished face when he tells Brad what happened to Lucy as well as in the tour-de-force sequence near the end leading up to the attack on the Indian village. It's a sad fact of life that as you get older, sometimes films you love literally change too as they age.

Why did Mike have a problem with They Were Expendable, *which is perhaps Ford's most overlooked great film?*

Mike and I could not agree on the merits of that elegiac World War II saga. *They Were Expendable* is now one of my two favorite Ford films, along with *Wagon Master*. I used to put *The Searchers* or *The Quiet Man* at the top, but I wore them out, to some extent, by seeing them so often, as also happened to me with *Citizen Kane*.

Perhaps Mike and I got off on a bad foot with *They Were Expendable* because our first viewing was through a cloud of tear gas on the day of the Dow Chemical demonstration in 1967. As a result, I didn't fully embrace the film immediately. But soon enough I found it deeply moving in every respect, including Robert Montgomery's magisterial performance as the disciplined, mature, wise, yet intrepid commander of the PT boat squadron (who was based on Lt. Cmdr. John Bulkeley, the Medal of Honor winner I later interviewed for my Ford biography). Mike's fierce anti-authoritarian nature and the rebellious atmosphere of the times made it impossible for him to relate to Montgomery's character and performance or to the military ethos of the Navy PT boat squadron. Yet he could understand, to some extent, their camaraderie—an element that seemed Hawksian to him—and their sacrificial nature during what was at the time the greatest military defeat in American history, the loss of the Philippines.

So we tried our best to cobble together a version we both could agree on, drawn from drafts we both wrote, but I always found that section of our book unsatisfactory, since it seems somewhat equivocal on the film's themes and performances. Mike remained unhappy that in our critical study we didn't cover all the films he wanted to include. When I put the *John Ford* manuscript into shape for publication, I had to discard some sections he wrote that I found unsatisfactory and therefore deemed, well, expendable. And for the 2023 revised edition of *John Ford*, I revised the section on *They Were Expendable* extensively to reflect our eventual unanimity on the high quality of the film, the only section of film analysis on which I made major changes. I think Mike would have approved.

You mentioned that you and Mike had actual physical brawls while writing the Ford book. How did the tension between you guys get so bad?

Mike was usually dilatory about turning in his drafts, and when he would do so, they were intermittently eloquent but also messy manuscripts that I had to make him rewrite over and over. What was most frustrating about that process, beyond his inability to finish the work, was that with each draft he would add some good new material while cutting some of the valuable material from the previous draft. His revisions tended to perpetuate and exacerbate the disorganized, often illogical state of his sections, and I found their factual errors maddening.

This state of affairs went on for about five Wilmington drafts per section until, in despair over getting him to do his work after a year and a half, I finally had to give him an ultimatum. Realizing that the book would not be finished otherwise, I said that either I would abandon it or complete it on my own by revising and polishing his sections and that I would have the final say over what went into the book; we would still share credit. By that point I was so exasperated that I was genuinely willing to let it go if necessary. But he agreed to let me finish the book. It took me six months of hard work to do so, a grueling chore, especially given that I was doing most of it in the wee hours after coming home from a long night at the *State Journal*.

When I finished *John Ford* in January 1972, I had only one month to fulfill my contract with Prentice-Hall to edit an anthology called *Focus on Howard Hawks*. The publisher had rejected my first two anthology choices, on Elia Kazan and Billy Wilder, and I rejected their suggestion of doing one on Ford, not wanting to compete with Mike's and my own critical work-in-progress. I agreed on Hawks largely because I thought a need for it existed. I managed to finish that book on schedule, even though I wound up spending more than my meager $250 advance to license the rights to some of the essays, including $350 to Robin Wood's publisher for the chapter on *Rio Bravo* from his BFI

My Portrait of the Artist as an Old Man: John Ford during our interview in his Beverly Hills office on the last day of his career, August 19, 1970, when he announced his retirement while realizing his project to make an Italian Western had fallen through.
(Joseph McBride)

Cinema One book, *Howard Hawks*. After that siege, I could barely do anything but drag myself through the work at the paper for the next six months while I recuperated, and the ordeal of writing the Ford book was partly responsible for the breakup of my first marriage, and that made me resent Mike even more. Having *Focus on Howard Hawks* published by Prentice-Hall proved invaluable, though, because it opened the door for me to pay visits to Hawks at his home in Palm Springs, which led to my interview book *Hawks on Hawks.*

The first fistfight between Mike and me came in the Memorial Union when I confronted him over his refusal to return my copy of the novelization of *The Man Who Shot Liberty Valance* so I could use it in revising what he had written about that film. (I told you the proximate causes were absurd.) The second donnybrook was when I realized he hadn't taken a bus to the Films Inc. office in Evanston to see *Donovan's Reef*, as he had agreed to do. That particular dereliction of duty was why I finally had enough and fired him so I could get the book finished. Years later Wilmington admitted that he had deliberately drawn out the work on *John Ford* because he knew he would never be able to do that kind of project again and that I would go on to other and better things. In fact, he never wrote another book.

But it was remarkable that Mike eventually was able to carve out a solid career as second-string film reviewer for the *Los Angeles Times* and the lead reviewer for the *Chicago Tribune*. Mike's skill was in writing short pieces, which were often brilliantly insightful, but he lacked the discipline and the kind of skill to write anything longer.

How do you feel about your first Ford book in retrospect?

I am proud that we two young critics were able to pull off a critical study that has been recognized as both comprehensive and mature in understanding and conveying the nature of Ford's great artistry. That *John Ford*, despite all the craziness involved in its creation, turned out so well is a gratifying testament to the passion Mike and I brought to the project as youthful cinephiles wrapped up in the excitement of discovery. Peter Bogdanovich called *John Ford* "The first intelligent, informed, and informative critical study in English on one of the only American directors who was also a poet"; Roger Greenspun described the book in *Film Comment* as "an achievement as close to classical ease in critical writing as some of Ford's films are in cinema"; and film scholar John Belton told me recently that he thinks it's still the best book on Ford. (Belton was among the major scholars who wrote letters of recommendation when I went up for tenure and promotion at San Francisco State; his approbation and analysis of my work were especially gratifying in their range and depth, and he later became my editor on my books for Columbia University Press.)

Mike and I were determined to impart our love of Ford's work to a public that had passed him by and to a critical establishment that grossly undervalued him. I had to laugh when the British magazine *Movie* panned our book because it said we had succumbed to "the myth of personality." That phrase sums up what we former auteurist critics found ourselves up against in the academic climate of the 1970s. Fortunately, we were marching to our own drummer and thus were able to defy the myopia of the field of film studies in that period when it was bypassing its beginnings in auteurism and reaching for the dubious status of respectability in the larger world of academia.

You have often said that the essay you and Mike wrote on The Searchers *for* Sight and Sound *is the most influential piece of film writing either of you ever did.*

That's right. The essay ran in the Autumn 1971 issue of *Sight and Sound* under the title "Prisoner of the Desert," (which was a comment on the film's obscurity and an play on its French feminine title, which is quoted that way in the English subtitles of Jean-Luc Godard's *Weekend*). The distinguished British fiction writer, biographer, and screenwriter Gavin Lambert, who became a good friend of mine in Los Angeles, had been an early champion of Ford in England when he edited *Sequence* and then *Sight and Sound*. Gavin not only gave our book on Ford a generous review in *Films and Filming* — calling it "An important and engrossing study… There will be other books on Ford, but this one will not be superseded" — but also warmed my heart by engaging his longtime friend and colleague Lindsay Anderson in a half-hour argument over our essay on *The Searchers*.

Our essay was influenced to some extent by Peter Wollen's insights into Ford's film in his 1969 book, *Signs and Meaning in the Cinema*, notably his observations on how Ethan and Scar are mirrors of each other, as well as by Bogdanovich's quoting of the film as the bookends of his 1971 documentary, *Directed by John Ford*, and Andrew Sarris's Spring 1971 essay on the film in *Film Comment*. In bringing *The Searchers* back from obscurity, we went beyond those sources to break fresh ground in analyzing the themes and style and characters in ways that would become critical commonplaces and foundational in the literature that soon grew on the film.

The influence of our essay was measured by the fact that for the first time, *The Searchers* vaulted onto the magazine's top-twenty list in its decadic poll of international critics, tying for No. 18 in the 1972 poll. Stuart Byron summarized the phenomenon in a 1979 article for *New York* magazine, "*The Searchers:* Cult Movie of the New Hollywood." He traced the profound influence Ford's film had on the new generation of major filmmakers, including on such landmark films as *Taxi Driver*, *Star Wars*, and *Close Encounters of the Third Kind*, and numerous others, including *Hardcore*, *Mean Streets*, *The Deer Hunter*, *The Wind and the Lion*, and *Ulzana's Raid*.

"You could construct half the syllabus for a course on contemporary American cinema just from films that, consciously or not, have been influenced by *The Searchers*," Byron wrote. "'All modern American literature comes from one book by Mark Twain called *Huckleberry Finn*,' said Ernest Hemingway, and I think that in the same broad sense it can be said that all recent American cinema derives from John Ford's *The Searchers*.... And yet its claims to such status continue to rest on an unholy alliance of critics, buffs, and filmmakers. The revival-house public has yet to admit *The Searchers* to the pantheon." Byron quoted our essay calling *The Searchers* "the story of America" and our belief that the film "has that clear yet intangible quality which characterizes an artist's masterpiece." Byron noted that although a few critics and filmmakers had paid attention to *The Searchers* earlier, "by the Seventies, the critical floodgates were opened. Most important, Joseph McBride and Michael Wilmington published their seminal article and book."

The most vocal dissenter on *The Searchers* was Lindsay Anderson, both in 1956 and beyond. The critic and filmmaker had been a passionate admirer of Ford through 1953's *The Sun Shines Bright* but could not understand Ford's progression after that and regarded *The Searchers* with antipathy in his *Sight and Sound* review, calling John Wayne's Ethan Edwards "an unmistakable neurotic" and asking, "Now what is Ford, of all directors, to do with a hero like this?" In reading through Ford's papers, I learned that Anderson had been writing to him asking for a job in the early 1950s, but Ford rebuffed him. That might have contributed to Anderson's sourness over the director's subsequent artistic development and the tone of condescension, sometimes tipping into outright contempt, that Anderson adopts toward Ford in his 1981 book, *About John Ford*.

The only critical comment by someone about my work that has ever actually angered me was Anderson, in that book, following one of his derisively deployed quotes from our *Searchers* essay by calling Mike and me (and Sarris and J. A. Place, the author of two books on Ford) part of "the lunatic fringe [that] becomes the voice of received opinion." He laments how "the infection spreads" and claims, "This is a critical approach that tells us more about the critics, their personalities and their pretensions, than it does about the films."

I took those as fighting words, as a personal affront. They made Gavin's support in challenging Anderson all the more gratifying. And when Paul Schrader said that the Ford films he most admired were not the mainstream classics but the ones he considered the "crazy Ford," such as *The Searchers,* the ones that penetrate most deeply into unresolved American psychic dilemmas, I recognized a further degree of kinship with the screenwriter of *Taxi Driver*.

I have always contended that the flaws in The Searchers *are more than compensated for by all the great things in the film. Of course, over time you recognized those flaws that you had dismissed when you first saw and were excited by the film.*

I now have second thoughts about some aspects of *The Searchers*. My friend Jonathan Lethem, the novelist, wrote a superb essay on the film, and after discussing it for three hours while I was working on my Ford biography, we agreed that the film is somewhat incoherent. That problem paradoxically is bound up with the film's strengths, since Ford, as Mike and I wrote in 1971, "has gone beyond his customary limits, submitted his deepest tenets to the test." Ford's limitations show in his inability to fully develop Debbie's character and face all the realities of her situation; the depiction of the crazed white captive women at the fort deepens the confusion by taking the viewer into Ethan's warped perspective on miscegenation; and the treatment of Look, Martin's Indian "wife," is disturbingly inconsistent. Our original essay acknowledges the film's contradictions while arguing that the contradictions in Ethan, the image of heroism, his poisoned quest, and the history of our country are partly what the film is about. But as time went on, I was able to recognize even more clearly the absurdist aspects of the film's deconstruction of "heroism," and I emphasize those more fully in *Searching for John Ford*.

Why did it take so long after you and Wilmington wrote your critical study to get it published?

Even though Mike and I wrote *John Ford* from 1970 until January 1972, the British publisher for the BFI Cinema Two series, Secker & Warburg, held *John Ford* back from publication for nearly three years. They did so on the grounds that they couldn't find an American publisher to share their exposure. That was not part of the contract, however; it was a deep frustration, and why I put up with that delay for so long is now a mystery to me.

Finally I flew to London and arrived unannounced at the Soho office of the managing director, T. G. (Tom) Rosenthal. He put on a jovial front, told me how fortunate we were to have a $500 advance, and quickly managed to find a U.S. publisher. Da Capo Press, as its name suggests, specialized in reprints. It was a matter of deep regret to me that *John Ford* was not published during the director's lifetime. Ford died in August 1973, shortly after I moved to California, but the book was not published until 1974 in England, 1975 in the United States. Da Capo kept it in print for a long time but eventually reverted the rights; the book is now published in a revised and expanded 2023 edition by the University Press of Kentucky.

Did you and Mike ever reconcile?

Mike and I later patched up our old quarrels and became friends again while working as fellow reviewers in Los Angeles. We didn't see a lot of each other, but it was good talking with him as in the old days. I was happy for Mike that after our falling-out in Madison, he had done well for himself by making a notable career for himself as a reviewer for major publications. Mike kindly offered to sponsor me for membership in the National Society of Film Critics, but I was not interested in joining another critics' group.

The Los Angeles Film Critics Association turned inhospitable to me over the years. I served as LAFCA's vice-president for a while, which mainly involved running the annual awards events, but after my esteemed friend Leonard Maltin decided to leave the presidency, I was passed over for succession. And when I moved to Berkeley, I was expelled from the group, even though when we founded it we promised each other that would never happen. The excuse given for my ouster was that I had left Los Angeles, so I could hardly argue, even though Mike had managed to talk LAFCA into letting him remain a member despite his moving to Chicago to work for the *Tribune*. In any case, belonging to these professional groups meant more to Mike than it did to me. I found the heated arguments in LAFCA meetings over awards-giving (our main function) aggravating and often ridiculous, although I was honored to be able to give the speeches presenting our career achievement awards to Billy Wilder and Abraham Polonsky and to stage our mini-AFI Life Achievement Award kind of tribute to Roger Corman when we gave him our top prize.

When I was vice president of LACMA, I also argued successfully that we should not give our career award to Elia Kazan, since despite his great talent as a filmmaker, he had built his career on betraying his colleagues. That decision was controversial—we were attacked in a *New York Times* editorial for allegedly "blacklisting" Kazan—but I considered the moral nuance worth defending. In a letter to the *Times*, I wrote, "I can assure you that no one in our organization would want to prevent anyone from working because of his political beliefs. That is what blacklisting means, and that is what Mr. Kazan helped to do by informing on his colleagues to the House Committee on Un-American Activities in 1952.

> Choosing to honor someone for his career achievement in the arts is a discretionary act by which a group expresses its own moral and esthetic principles.... Honoring a career means honoring the totality of what an artist represents. In addition to his stature as a film maker, a large part of what Mr. Kazan represents is the shame of blacklisting. The blacklist remains the most important moral issue of postwar Hollywood, and its legacy continues to have a chilling effect on the industry's willingness to deal with controversial subjects. It would compound and perpetuate the moral wrongs of the blacklist era for film critics to honor a career built upon the ruination of other people's careers.

I can still appreciate Kazan's work, as I did in writing an appreciation of *Wild River*, his 1960 film about the Tennessee Valley Authority, for *Oxford American* magazine in 2002. When I reprinted that essay in *Two Cheers for Hollywood*, I wrote, "I am able to make the distinction between a good

John Ford's funeral at Holy Cross Cemetery in Culver City, California, September 5, 1973. Among the mourners are actors John Wayne, Elizabeth Allen (in black hat), George Murphy, and Harry Carey Jr., along with (seated) Ford's sister Josephine Feeney and Wayne's wife Pilar. Ford's nephew Father John Feeney officiates. I am second from right (adjusting my glasses). (Don Schneider)

film and the personal moral bankruptcy of the director who made it. Furthermore, it is one of the many ironies of the blacklist era that Kazan's work as an artist improved after he informed, as I demonstrate in this essay. Before he turned in his colleagues, he made safe liberal movies that conveniently divided people into good and bad characters and morality into a black-and-white affair. Those beliefs and films seem facile in retrospect. His work after informing, by contrast, is full of understanding for complex nuances of human nature."

I also recorded an audio commentary for Kino Lorber in 2023 on Kazan's last film, Harold Pinter's adaptation of F. Scott Fitzgerald's unfinished novel about Hollywood, *The Last Tycoon*, an uneven but fascinating work. I had requested Kazan to let me watch him direct it in 1975, but he called and asked if he could talk with me "man to man," an unusual and disarming phrase to hear in Hollywood. He said he had an insecure young actor (Robert De Niro) in the lead role of studio executive Monroe Stahr who had never before worn a suit in a movie or played a businessman, and that it would make De Niro nervous for a member of the press to watch him at work. In fact, De Niro had won an Oscar for a 1974 film in which he plays a character who wears a suit and is a businessman, the young Don Vito Corleone in *The Godfather Part II*. I acquiesced to Kazan's wishes but still managed to crash the set of *The Last Tycoon* by inviting Jeanne Moreau, a member of the cast, to lunch at a Mexican restaurant across the street from Paramount. As I arrived, though, the company was just breaking, and Kazan and producer Sam Spiegel gave me strange looks.

What prompted you to put together a new edition of John Ford and add some fresh material to it?

Mike Wilmington's death in January 2022 helped motivate me to fulfill a long-term goal of revising our book and bringing it back into publication. By adding four essays for its revised and expanded edition, I took the opportunity to offer more thoughts on key issues that keep coming up in debates about Ford and are the elements of his work that his detractors tend to use against him unfairly. Although Ford's name doesn't draw a blank stare anymore, the enduring hostility in some quarters was reason enough for me to take a pugnacious stand on such issues.

Most people who don't like Ford complain, almost reflexively, about his sense of humor. They find his love of brawling too raucous and vulgar and miss the deeper levels of his comedic sensibility, which I believe underlies all his work. Ford's tragicomic view of the world and his absurdist view of history are very Irish traits. So I decided to focus on that provocative and unsettled topic when I was invited to give the keynote address at the first John Ford Ireland Symposium held by the Irish Film & Television Academy in Dublin in 2012. I adapted and expanded my lecture, "John Ford, Poet and Comedian," as one of the Addenda in the new edition of *John Ford*.

The other essays I added included my thoughts on a related and equally contentious question, the influence of his Irish heritage, "John Ford, Irish American Poet," based on an essay I wrote for *Irish America* in 1999 when I was that magazine's film columnist; and "John Ford and Race: 'We Were on Both Sides of the Epic,'" which was written in 2015 for a collection on race in the American cinema. That essay was rejected because the publisher evidently found my views too complex for the project's academic approach in following "politically correct" ideological imperatives. For the new edition of *John Ford*, I also wrote an ambitious survey entitled "Rediscovering John Ford's Silent Years," drawing on the extant fifteen silent features and twelve fragments now known to exist as well as on material about films that are still missing. The archival rediscoveries and restorations since the book was first published enabled me to provide a more informed and comprehensive overview while benefiting from other research, including the erudite and insightful findings of British scholar Steve Mayhew in his 2013 PhD thesis for Kingston University, "Becoming John Ford: The Silent Period 1914–1930." Steve and I shared copies of existing films, and I gave him other help and encouragement with his indefatigable research, which turned up a plethora of archeological findings on the missing Ford silents.

And I included an expanded chapter on my 1970 interview with Ford, which I had edited too tightly originally, out of frustration mixed with some embarrassment. Forty-plus years later, I no longer felt embarrassed by the interview but enjoyed my sparring, partly humorous, unexpectedly moving give-and-take with Ford and wanted to make it all available for other scholars and Ford fans. In *Two Cheers* I published virtually the entire unedited transcript of the interview, and I expanded it a bit more for the revised edition of *John Ford*. I also let a podcaster put the unedited audio on her website, as well as allowing Kino Lorber to use it as an extra on their restored Blu-ray edition of *Hell Bent* and Eureka! Masters of Cinema to include it on their edition of that film and *Straight Shooting*. (My audio commentaries on those silent Ford Westerns also appear on those Blu-rays, as well as on Kino Lorber's edition of *Straight Shooting*.)

For the new edition of the book, I wanted to preserve the youthful flavor of the original prose while making a few small changes I found necessary. One was adding a paragraph explaining the controversial "Dragging Home the Bride" section of *The Quiet Man*, a playlet deliberately set up by Maureen O'Hara's Mary Kate that has been misunderstood in recent years as a serious act of spousal abuse. Ford, who knew the difference, gave Frank Nugent a book on spousal abuse in the west of Ireland as part of his research material for the script.

Ford the "badass"

How have your partner, Ann Weiser Cornell, and your son, John, responded to your Ford obsession through the years?

I was fortunate to meet Ann when I moved to Berkeley in 2000, shortly after I moved to the San Francisco Bay Area. She is a teacher who gives workshops around the world and has written widely read books on self-help methods called Focusing and its later evolutions, Inner Relationship Focusing and Untangling. We call ourselves "a book-writing factory." Our mutual admiration for Ford films was one of the shared traits that brought us together. Her own longtime fondness for his work was kindled while she was attending DOC Films screenings when she was a PhD student in Linguistics at the University of Chicago. When we were becoming acquainted, I was especially delighted that she appreciated *The Quiet Man*, a kind of acid test of mutual understanding!

Ann was a great help throughout the final editing stages of my Ford biography, which I was finishing when I moved to Berkeley. During the proofreading process, St. Martin's asked me to cut exactly forty-one pages from the book for practical production reasons, and with Ann's help I was able to do so. I found that those cuts actually helped the book but that they were the absolute maximum that could go without starting to hurt it. Ann's insights into psychology and aesthetics have always been valuable to my work on Ford and other filmmakers I have written about in the years since then. We watch many movies together, and she has read and thoughtfully critiqued the manuscripts of all the film books I have written since we met.

I now have a better understanding of Ford's perverse sense of humor than I did when I first wrote about him, which is reflected in my essay on the subject that I added to *John Ford*—and I owe that understanding partly to my son. John said with admiration after watching Ford jousting with Bogdanovich in Monument Valley in *Directed by John Ford* that Ford was a "badass." When he was seven in 1994, John watched forty Ford films with me and his mother,

Ruth O'Hara, in one month during a 35mm festival of the director's work at UCLA and the Los Angeles County Museum of Art. John enjoyed them up to a point, although he kidded us by calling the experience "a cinematic form of child abuse." Years later, though, he said he was grateful for that experience. But John sure was game as a little boy to sit through, say, a screening of *Hell Bent,* a poor dupe of what was then the as-yet-unrestored 1918 silent Harry Carey film with German intertitles translated by a young woman with a microphone.

While becoming a bit OD'd on Ford films that month, John said he tired of the repetition of long shots of cavalrymen riding horses through desert landscapes, so his favorite Ford films were the "town" Westerns, especially *The Man Who Shot Liberty Valance*, as well as *The Grapes of Wrath* and *3 Godfathers*, because they were "different." And he adored Harry (Dobe) Carey Jr., who made his debut as a Ford regular with *3 Godfathers*; I had the pleasure of introducing John to Dobe at a LACMA signing of his marvelous 1994 book, *Company of Heroes: My Life as an Actor in the John Ford Stock Company.*

I have his autograph on a mini 3 Godfathers *poster that he signed "Harry Carey," but you call him by his familiar nickname, Dobe. Tell me about your friendship with Harry "Dobe" Carey, who helped you on your biography of Ford.*

Not only is *Company of Heroes* the best account of Ford's working methods, it's also hilarious, especially his uproarious yarns about the making of *3 Godfathers* when Ford rode Dobe mercilessly to teach him the ropes and ribbed Pedro Armendáriz into a frenzy for wanting to glamorize his outlaw character. I read the book straight through the first time and still keep going back to it with pleasure. Kevin Brownlow told me before I knew Dobe that he was "the nicest person you'll ever meet," and I found that to be true.

Dobe was the closest friend I had among the members of the John Ford Stock Company. I think we bonded not only because of our shared fascination with Ford but also because on a visit to Ford's hometown of Portland, Maine, for a celebration of the director in 1998, I shared with Dobe while we sat in a pub that, like him, I was a recovering alcoholic. We were able to talk with complete frankness after that, and I benefited immeasurably from his insights into the mentor he understood so well. Dobe's mother, Olive (Ollie) Fuller Golden Carey, who knew Ford longer than anyone else I had met, also opened up her bank of memories to bring him alive for me. Ollie had a delightfully candid sense of humor, such as when I asked why she hadn't acted in more films for Ford. She said with her raucous laugh, "Because I'm a lousy actress!" And after I came to know them both well, Dobe and Ollie finally decided to tell me the real story behind the sad break in the friendship of Jack Ford and the elder Harry Carey after they had made so many early films together. That painful and revealing story, which can be read in *Searching for John Ford*, sheds invaluable light on Ford's personality and why he felt it necessary to hide the sensitive side of his nature.

My partner Ann and I were fortunate to spend more time with Dobe and his wife, Marilyn (the daughter of Western actor Paul Fix), when we invited them to appear with me in 2006 at the San Francisco Silent Film Festival for a showing of *Bucking Broadway*. That's a charming early comedy Western Dobe's father made with Jack Ford in 1917, his first year as a director. After one of my interviews with Dobe for *Searching for John Ford*, he signed *Company of Heroes* "To my good pal Joe: Remembering 'Himself' together was great fun. Best of luck on your new one! Fondest regards, 'Dobe.'" And after he read the biography, he gave me a generous comment I cherish: "John Ford was the most complex and fascinating man I have ever known, and Joe McBride captures that. *Searching for John Ford* is the best book about him that I have read."

How did the final stage of work on that biography go?

The final writing, the fruition of thirty years of research, took eighteen months (not counting the editing process), and it was one of the most intense and creatively satisfying writing tasks of my life. Ironically, as I've mentioned, I was convinced while writing the Ford biography that no one was going to read it. I say ironically because that book, more than any other I have written, has been received warmly and enthusiastically by readers throughout the world. But when I wrote it, I was so bothered by the state of eclipse into which Ford had once again fallen that I actually believed that my book would not find an audience. That delusional state helped the book immensely, since I told myself I was writing just to please myself.

Therefore I didn't care what anyone else thought about the quirky paths and bypaths into which the story of Ford's life was taking me. Nor did I worry about how non-Ford specialists would take the fairly extensive critical analysis I interwove of his films, major or minor, with my study of his personality. My mission was to find out for myself how the life of this man who masqueraded as an "illiterate cowboy" accounts for his great works of art, and how those beautiful, sensitive, deeply complex films are the only way this almost pathologically secretive man was able to address the world.

Some readers, my coauthor, and our agent complained that one of my baseball biographies took too long to get to the baseball stuff and that I shouldn't have insisted on devoting so many pages to background material in order to explain who the subject was and why he became that way, psychologically. My guess is that you can relate to that with your experience writing Searching for John Ford.

I rebel against the modern trend in biography to avoid psychological analysis of the subject. Book reviewers in mainstream outlets tend to criticize such writing as "Freudian," as if that is an insult. I found it ironic when I entered academia that it's *de rigeur* to cite Freud and use psychoanalytic language in writing about films and filmmakers. I think it's simply dereliction of duty for a biographer to avoid exploring why his subject behaved in certain ways or made his or her characteristic works of art. Many contemporary biographies are frustratingly opaque because they refuse to probe into the conscious or subconscious motivations of their subjects or to connect their lives to their work. Such biographies are not only dull but unenlightening in the extreme. And I believe it's pointless to write a biography of an artist without examining the work that makes the artist worthy of our attention (or, in your case, the ballplayer's skills). That's one reason my biographies of three major, and prolific, directors are so long.

Searching for John Ford *is such a massive book and took so long to research and write that it must have been a challenge supporting yourself when you didn't always have a day job.*

I did a fair amount of research into Ford's life and work during the 1970s and '80s, including a major research trip to the National Archives and the Library of Congress in Washington, D.C., and my interview with Admiral Bulkeley at the Washington Navy Yard, during a hiatus in the work on the Capra book in 1988. But I still had much library research ahead of me—including in Ford's surprisingly rich collection of papers at the Lilly Library of Indiana University in Bloomington—and many interviews to do while I was writing the manuscript from 1997 to 1999.

I continued my research during the last stages of editing in 2000 before the book's publication in 2001.

I somehow managed to pace myself productively on the Ford biography despite also having to write about a hundred film reviews and magazine articles to help supplement my insufficient advance from St. Martin's Press. I can hardly believe I accomplished all that while writing the book at top speed, though my side work provided entertaining diversions from what would otherwise have been an unhealthy degree of monomania. I even had to break my resolve against any more screenwriting by writing the script for a TV show I mentioned before, producer-director Harrison Engle's segment on war movies, "War and Peace," for the 1998 AFI/TNT cable series *100 Years...100 Movies*.

Meanwhile I had to keep cranking out two fully polished, publishable pages of the Ford biography per day to stay on schedule. One relative who asked about my writing pace responded, *"Only two* pages?" She didn't realize that would amount to 730 manuscript pages per year; civilians usually don't know nothin' about writin' books. Once I finished my pages by dawn each morning, I didn't have time for rewriting, so in effect *Searching for John Ford* is a first draft, the only time I've done that with a finished book other than my rush job on *Kirk Douglas*. I'm amazed that the Ford biography came out so well under the circumstances, but by then I knew and understood his work and life thoroughly.

I've never read Scott Eyman's 1999 Ford biography that was published while you were still writing yours. Was it discouraging to have a competing book?

The reason for the tight schedule I was working under was partly financial but was also because St. Martin's Press and I were in what we considered a race with Eyman's biography at the time. His book for Simon & Schuster is *Print the Legend: The Life of John Ford*, the worst possible title for a biography of Ford. I was determined, by contrast, to sort out the differences between Ford's fables and the truth about his life.

Back in 1992, when my Capra biography came out, I ran into Eyman at a film festival and book-signing event in the Hollywood Roosevelt Hotel, and he pumped me relentlessly on my plans for future books. I finally told him I was first going to write a biography of Steven Spielberg and then would finish my long-in-the-works Ford biography. Eyman became agitated and offered me $10,000 for my interviews and other research materials if I would drop my

Ford project, an insulting offer I rejected. Not content with trying to buy me off, he later persuaded Ford's grandson and biographer, Dan Ford, who had authorized *Print the Legend* as the executor of John Ford's estate, not to cooperate with my book. Dan had told me only the day before at the 1998 Portland tribute to Ford that he was "honored" I was also writing a biography and that he would give me any cooperation he could. Eyman hosted the opening event at those Portland festivities, and his learning that I was busy on my own Ford biography accounted for Dan's sudden change of mind and opposition to my book.

In the late summer of 1999, while Eyman and I were working on our rival Ford books, Dan Ford, through a lawyer, contacted St. Martin's Press in an attempt to stop my book. The lawyer made an implicit threat that they would consider suing us after my book was published. The lawyer also disparaged my Capra biography as "a slash-and-burn job" and asked why we would want to do a biography of John Ford in competition with Eyman's authorized biography. Dan back in Portland had irrelevantly brought up his similarly simplistic view of my Capra biography, but I replied that Ford and Capra were two different people. Dan subsequently wrote St. Martin's, stating that the Ford family was not cooperating with my unauthorized biography and that I had no permission to quote previously unpublished material by John Ford. He threatened that the family would try to stop the publication of my book if I did so and would seek damages if I harmed Ford's reputation.

I considered these moves by Dan Ford, his lawyer, and Scott Eyman to be, in a word, un-American. They were quickly rebuffed by the St. Martin's Press legal department, which admirably supported my First Amendment rights, completely opposite to the corrupt way Random House had treated me on the Capra book. On September 15, Paul J. Sleven, vice president and associate general counsel of St. Martin's, wrote Dan that his suppositions were wrong and unfair and that they had full confidence in my accuracy and objectivity as a serious biographer who had also co-authored a well-received critical study of Ford. Sleven dismissed Dan's threats as ungrounded in legality and pointed out that I would be able to quote some copyrighted material under the legal doctrine of fair use without permission of the copyright holder. Dan and Eyman immediately backed off when faced with my principled publisher, which also, unlike Random House, had immediately and fully notified me of the threats against my book. And I had a productive relationship during the writing of the Ford biography with the wise, empathetic, and supportive lawyer vetting it for St. Martin's, Henry R. Kaufman. I've found that it's crucial who the lawyer is on a book project.

But Eyman finished his manuscript two months before I was able to finish mine in September 1999, and his book was rushed out that November. That ill-advised race caused my blood pressure to become an enduring problem, although that malady is one that runs in our family. And when I finally shipped my edited manuscript of the biography in 2000, I was down to twenty-five cents and was $35,000 in debt. At least I had more in my pocket than when I finished the first version of my Capra biography—at that time I was down to eleven cents. St. Martin's was disappointed that Eyman's book came out first and decided to put some distance between the books by moving mine to a June 2001 publication date. In the end I considered that a smart move, since following Eyman gave me an edge in having my book regarded as the "definitive" Ford biography, as it was called by reviewers for both the *New York Times* and the *Irish Times*. I managed to persuade St. Martin's to let my book run much longer than planned, 838 pages. That was needed because Ford's life and work are so rich and mulitfaceted, and because my book, unlike Eyman's, is a critical biography, i.e., one that analyzes the work in depth along with the life.

Even so, when I turned in my final chapter and asked my editor, Tim Bent, who had been sympathetic and enthusiastic up to that point, for his reaction to that chapter, he simply told me, "It's long." It was, and that was the reason I finished behind Eyman. But I told Tim, as Ford had told me about one of his films, that I thought "The finish is really good." I am particularly proud of that bittersweet finale, which I consider a revealing and important study of how Ford went beyond his earlier boundaries in his later work to make some of the finest and most challenging films of his career—before being sent into internal exile, a deplorable state of affairs I also document in depth.

Dan Ford's opposition to my biography was a decision he later told me he regretted, since he believes it has more warmth and sympathy with his grandfather than Eyman's biography and he considers mine a thorough and accurate account of Ford's complex life and work. I am glad to report that Dan and I were able to become friends again, and he came up to the Bay Area a couple of times to be a guest in my Ford classes at San Francisco State. But I haven't spoken with Eyman since 1992, the same year he also gave my Capra book a mixed review in the *Palm Beach Post* and told me he was "grinding my teeth in jealousy" over that biography.

How did you approach in your biography what Andrew Sarris called "the John Ford movie mystery"? Did you find Ford in your search?

Anna Lee, one of the beloved members of the Ford Stock Company, was a delightful lady I came to know well in the 1970s and later worked with when we did the audio commentary on her first film for Ford, the 1941 classic *How Green Was My Valley.* Anna was British and proudly described herself as a "Winston Churchill conservative" despite being devoted to the filmmaker who was a professional Irishman and yet came to deeply admire the British during World War II, as she pointed out. She told me she liked our book *John Ford* but thought we had made Ford out to be more liberal than he actually was.

While working on my Ford biography, I came to realize she was right, since Ford's political views were so complex and often contradictory. I could see that Mike and I had been trying, not entirely consciously but as part of our agenda, to "sell" Ford to the skeptical 1970s audience. That need to convince readers that Ford was not the caricatured reactionary figure some thought he was caused us to focus more on his liberal and anarchic sides and less on the conservative side of his personality. In my biography I worked harder to face and accept Ford's political contradictions as well as the many other clashing aspects of his personality, since we can't understand him fully without recognizing his various parts.

One reason *Searching for John Ford* had such a long gestation was that I struggled so long with trying to reconcile his contradictions. I was somewhat disillusioned when I began interviewing people in Hollywood about him and heard stories about his cruelty toward his colleagues and even his friends and family. But he could also be generous and compassionate, and his films tend to draw on those sensitive parts of his character as well as his authoritarian and militaristic sides. The key to unlocking the "John Ford movie mystery" was eventually provided for me in the late Seventies by Abe Polonsky, a left-wing admirer of the director who corrected me when I described Ford as "conservative." Abe pointed out that you can't make such generalizations about Ford's personality, because that tends to render simplistic what in fact is so complex about him and his work.

Abe's observation enabled me to see and accept all of Ford's conflicting sides without feeling the need to reconcile those conflicts, as I had been struggling to do. I realized that the enigma of Ford's personality was that he was the sum of all his different and often disparate parts. As I've commented in my Ford books, it is true of Ford what Walt Whitman wrote,

Do I contradict myself?
Very well then I contradict myself,
(I am large, I contain multitudes.)

So while in working on the biography, I stopped trying to force Ford into a coherence he didn't have, his personality became more understandable, and the book started to come alive.

One way Ann has helped me better understand Ford over the years—and he remains a subject of endless fascination to me—is directly related to what Abe told me about him. Ann's self-help method of Focusing teaches that people are made up of parts; those can take over a personality with negative results or be accepted into a complex but more harmonious personality. She said after getting to know me that I had come to that realization intuitively in being able to analyze my own personality honestly and clearly. (Your brother Gerry, though, once compared my political views to the inscrutable plot of *The Big Sleep!*) Ford was a man of many parts, and, as is also the case with some other great artists, those parts often seem in stark contradiction to each other but together make up a highly complex and empathetic creative personality, if also a rather unhappy man.

It's definitely surprising that you managed to get Richard Nixon to comment on Ford for your biography.

Talk about another man of many parts! I sent an interview request to former President Nixon, who dubiously claimed at Ford's AFI Life Achievement Award ceremony that he had seen all of Ford's films (many of which no longer exist), but who otherwise was a sincere and thoughtful admirer of Ford's work. Partly I just wanted to meet a political figure who has always fascinated me. Nixon replied that he was too busy writing a book on world peace to sit for an interview but would write me something about Ford, adding, "John Ford is one of my heroes in every sense of the word."

A week later in January 1988, I received in the mail an envelope from Nixon's office in World Trade Center 7 with his essay, "Reflections on John Ford." It was partly a Nixonian rant about his and Ford's points of agreement on the Vietnam War but also made the observation that "John Ford was to motion pictures what Tolstoy was to literature." That was an apt comparison to another great artist whose personality seemed maddeningly contradictory to those around him but whose many parts enabled him, like Ford, to create a wide gallery of disparate characters. When my editor suggested cutting parts of Nixon's 535-word essay, I trotted out a successful defense an author can use only once in his career, "Are you suggesting we cut an original piece of unpublished writing by a former president of the United States?"

And it's not often that an author can thank such contrasting people for insights that are crucial in helping him write a biography, Polonsky and Nixon—a filmmaker who had been blacklisted after being accused before HUAC of being "a very dangerous citizen" as well as a former member of HUAC who defended Ford's 1940 film of *The Grapes of Wrath* in a 1947 hearing. Nixon said that film version of John Steinbeck's novel about Dust Bowl migrants pointed out "the weak features of our own American system" while being made by "people whose loyalty, insofar as communism is concerned, is absolutely unquestioned." This is how I sum up Ford's complexity in *Searching for John Ford*:

> What made Ford a great popular artist is that he reflected so many facets of the people he addressed. He was able to do so because he had so many warring factions within himself. Like Whitman, he "contained multitudes." In the final analysis, Ford's artistic personality has to be seen as one of perpetual conflicts, contradictions, and paradoxes. If he never entirely resolved the issues that obsessed him, if he often seemed to dispute himself and sometimes acted against his own principles and ideals, that was part of the fuel that powered his creativity. What made him such a flawed human being was also what made him such a great artist. Those who expect artists to be ideal human beings fail to understand the nature of art. Often the greatest art comes out of torment, and some of the most important artists, such as Mozart and Tolstoy and Ford, lived in a riot of complication and frequent public absurdity. In Ford's case, his films are usually far more complex than his public stands were on the issues of his time.

William Butler Yeats could have been commenting on Ford when he wrote, "We make of the
quarrel with others, rhetoric, but of the quarrel
with ourselves, poetry."

Hawks on Hawks

You state in your 1982 book, Hawks on Hawks, *that you
didn't start out intending to do an interview book with
Howard Hawks but that your talks gradually grew into
that. How did those talks with Hawks begin, and how did
they develop into a book?*

I had met Hawks in November 1970 with Mike Wilmington
at the Chicago Film Festival. We recorded and edited his
Q&A session with the audience and published it in *Sight
and Sound.* After I moved to California and was living in
Riverside, about fifty miles from Hawks's home in Palm
Springs, I called his house to request an interview (he was
listed in the phone book), and he answered. His voice sounded
so young that I was taken aback and thought it might be his
son, Gregg, so I asked, "Is this *Mr.* Hawks?" Having *Focus
on Howard Hawks* as a credential was helpful, and he readily
agreed to let me come down to interview him.

My principal motive in interviewing him repeatedly
over the next three years was to learn about screenwriting
and storytelling. He was a master storyteller in his films,
and his reminiscences about his work made the book
colorful, pungent, and wise. And he was unusually secure
enough to admit, when I asked why he thought most of his
movies, even the oldest ones, still look fresh and modern,
"Most of them were well written. That's why they last.
I've always been blessed with great writers. As a matter
of fact, I'm such a coward that unless I get a great writer,
I don't want to make a picture." When I asked why he rarely
took credit as a writer, as he had done on some of his early
pictures, he said, "Because if I did, I couldn't get such good
writers to work with me." As I would later learn by talking
and working with other directors, the ones who denigrated
writers and/or took credit with them, Hawks was wise in
realizing that credit in films is not a zero-sum game.

*You tried to get Hawks to discuss his political views, but he
was stubbornly reluctant to go there.*

Hawks was deeply conservative, but he steered clear of explicitly political subject matter in his films. I didn't get deeply into political discussions with him, although I did try to elicit his views of the Vietnam War when he told me about a film he wanted to make on it. When I asked about the plot and whether the film would have made a statement about the war, he gruffly responded, "I've *never* made a statement. Our job is to make entertainment. I don't give a God damn about taking sides." I felt he was trying to shut the door on the subject, but I persisted by asking, "In a situation like that, though, wouldn't it be hard *not* to make some kind of statement?" Hawks deflected by launching into a complaint about how it had become hard to make films because ethnic humor had become controversial, and he bemoaned that "There's more goddam *minorities*." Now I wish I had delved more insistently with him into such sensitive topics, because even such offhand political comments were revealing.

And there's a fascinatingly outrageous interview with Hawks arguing at length about politics with some intrepid left-wing interviewers for *Jump Cut* magazine, Constance Penley, Saunie Salyer, and Michael Shedlin. They talked with him when he visited Berkeley in 1974 for a retrospective of his work at the Pacific Film Archive (at which, the PFA's Tom Luddy told me, Hawks charged into the projection booth and unsuccessfully tried to grab the rare print of his late-silent 1929 film *Trent's Last Case* so he could destroy it). I'll read to you part of what Hawks's interviewers wrote:

> He wields a penetrating blue stare and a 78-year reputation for no bullshit. He is not the kind of man you niggle with. We were, however, determined to probe into his personal philosophy and get beyond the anecdotal response. We decided to discuss our perspective straightaway and to ground all of our questions in our passions and our politics rather than attempting to set up a "comfortable atmosphere" in which he could be "drawn out."
>
> … Hawks speaks quietly and forcefully. He laughs often, interrupts often, listens intently and asks few questions. He is a curious mixture of taciturnity and loquaciousness. He seems to be a strong silent type and yet he talks almost continuously. During lunch we were perversely enchanted as we found ourselves hanging batedly on every scabrous John Wayne anecdote. "If I want to have fun at a party," said the master over his

chef's salad, "I'll tell the Duke, 'See that guy over there? He's a Red!'"

As that anecdote and the rest of the *Jump Cut* interview showed, Hawks's political views were myopic and crudely reactionary, a world apart from his nuanced view of human nature onscreen. Midway through he said, "This is the first discussion of politics that I've had, and I might say it's going to be my last." Manny Farber, who admired much about Hawks's style, mocked attempts to take the director's view of society seriously, observing in a 1969 essay in *Artforum*, "The feeling of snobbery in any Hawks work is overpowering, whether it is a Great White Father ([Cary] Grant) patronizing a devitalized native with a gift watch or the female Jimmy Breslin (Rosalind Russell) breezily typing a socko story. This romance which wraps the fliers-reporters-cowhands in a patina of period mannerism and attitude makes for a film that isn't dated so much as removed from reality, like the land of Tolkien's Hobbits.... This operetta seaport [in *Only Angels Have Wings*], with boas of smoke hanging in swirly serpentines and pairs of extras crisscrossing through the fake mist, might be good for a Douglas, Arizona high school production."

Yet Farber notes, in pinning down what makes Hawks, in his way, so masterful, "the deep quality in any Hawks film is the uncannily poetic way an action is unfolded.... Not many moviemakers have gone so deeply into personality-revealing motion, the geography of gesture, the building and milking of a signature trait for all its worth. Hawks's abandon with his pet area, human gesture, is usually staggering, for better or worse."

What are some other limitations you find in Hawks's work?

Like Farber, I admire Hawks's way with actors and dialogue, including his imaginative ability to evoke feelings and psychological insights through the close orchestration of the details of human behavior. But I was always skeptical about certain aspects of Hawks's work. I find him less of an artist than Ford because of the lack of interest Hawks displayed in the world outside his narrow concerns and limited social compass; his characters' arrested development; his disdain for families; his preference for women who look and behave like young men; the painful unfunniness of most of his so-called comedies, unlike his often hilarious adventure films; and his tendency to "steal from myself all the time," which made him continually reshuffle the same compact deck of

The last of my nine discussions with Howard Hawks that went into
my book *Hawks on Hawks* was two months before his death in 1977,
at a "Weekend with Howard Hawks and His Films" sponsored by the
Directors Guild of America that October at a hotel in Laguna Beach.
"The timing of it was perfect," Hawks's daughter Barbara McCampbell
(foreground) told me after his death. "And of all the things like that
he'd done, I think that was the one he appreciated the most."

plot and character cards. In those days when I was spending
time with Hawks, however, I was less interested in exposing
his mythmaking than in exploring his skill in storytelling
(even if I sensed he was spinning tall tales about himself)
and in his expert analysis of his working methods with his
collaborators.

*Were you frustrated that he was so willing to talk yet
remained silent on certain topics?*

In a 1978 *Film Comment* reminiscence of Hawks following
his death the previous December, I wrote that despite his
willingness to sit for extensive questioning, "the more one
saw him, the more tightly guarded his inner personality
seemed to be. His emotions were expressed, if at all,
obliquely, and with the clear implication that they were,
finally, a very private matter. It was not hard to draw the
conclusion that beneath the surface pleasantry he was a cold
and distant man. I don't think it was our age difference that
led to this impasse, because as a newcomer to Hollywood,
I found that I had a natural kinship with older men who
were outside the mainstream of the industry whether
because of retirement or forced inactivity." Hawks's second

wife, Nancy (Slim) Gross, the model for the Lauren Bacall's "Slim" in *To Have and Have Not,* described the director as "a great pillar of nothing."

I came to feel about Hawks the way he felt about Hemingway, with whose work and personality he had many affinities: "He interested me. Strange guy." But as I wrote in that *Film Comment* article, which later struck me as overly critical but now seems mostly on target, "Hawks, like most of his peers, resisted any attempt on an interviewer's part to discuss the thematic underpinnings of his work, and one delved in vain for any acknowledgment that his films had been shaped by peculiarities of his own psyche…. Certainly one has no right to demand of an artist that he be fully conscious of the effects he creates, or able to expound on the themes of his work, but it was vexing that Hawks, who showed such keenness in dissecting other people's personalities, had so little perspective on his own."

Were you reluctant to ask him pointed political questions because you didn't want him to disappoint you with his opinions?

That wasn't it. I wasn't under any illusions about his political point of view. But I blame myself for not probing him more deeply. Consciously or not, I also didn't want to risk my welcome by disagreeing too much. In retrospect, that concern was somewhat mistaken, for as Hawks told me when we met in 1970, "One thing you'll learn about me is that I say what I think and I don't give a damn if anybody gets mad about it." My reticence showed the influence of being a relatively passive newspaper reporter too long, in my formative period when reporters were supposed to keep their viewpoints hidden out of a false concept of "objectivity." It took me a while longer to grow a tougher spine with filmmakers I mostly admired and to pursue a more aggressive stance in exposing truths behind the façades of people and social structures.

Hawks himself could be quite caustic about people. When I asked about Jennifer O'Neill, the ingenue in *Rio Lobo*, whom he blamed for that picture's failure, he snapped, "I thought she was a goddam fool." Although Bogdanovich had been his leading acolyte, Hawks told me, "Peter's trouble is that he's no good at writing and directing dialogue." That was an accurate, if harsh, analysis, even if it was prompted by Hawks's belief that Peter was no longer listening to him enough. And Hawks said of Peter's inamorata, Cybill Shepherd, with whom the younger director was making spectacular flops, "Cybill's a nice girl, but she's just no good." Even John Wayne, whom Hawks believed had more strength onscreen than any other actor, came in for some jibing, although of a more good-natured sort: "Have you ever heard Duke sing?" Hawks asked me once. "He's really bad."

Hawks told me he had standing offers from Steve McQueen and Clint Eastwood, the two biggest male stars in movies at the time, to appear in his project *When It's Hot Play It Cool*, about a pair of world-traveling oil riggers. But even though those two actors would have fit Hawks's cool approach to filmmaking, he said, "The trouble with those two fellas is that neither one has a sense of humor. They're both good at what they do, but they'd be deadly together." Hawks complained that a problem he saw with many male stars of that time was that they looked "effeminate," especially with their long hair. When I put that remark into a Hawks interview for *Daily Variety*, Art Murphy, who was gay, angrily slashed it out of the text, even though I argued it was a sign of Hawks being out of touch with the modern scene.

As I reported in *Film Comment*, "When I asked Eastwood if it was true that he had called Hawks and volunteered to act for him ('He wants to study the way I work,' Hawks claimed), a look of surprise came across Eastwood's face. Then, obviously embarrassed and trying to avoid saying anything which would hurt Hawks's feelings, Eastwood made a politely noncommittal comment about how it might, indeed, be interesting to work with Hawks, but the chances were doubtful now, etc. It was painful for me to realize that Hawks, in his prime one of Hollywood's most consistently commercial directors, had succumbed in his old age to hyping himself beyond his true level of 'bankability.' In the last few years, it was increasingly obvious that he would never make another film, yet every time I saw him he'd say, 'I'm working on a story.'"

I did make a futile attempt to dig into a fraught area with Hawks when he related the ending of *When It's Hot Play It Cool*, his late film project in which his two male buddy-buddy characters, abandoned by the woman they both love, fall drunkenly into the same bed in a South American room lit only by moonlight, throw each other out, but then agree to sleep together. That project was a remake of his 1928 silent film *A Girl in Every Port*, a very queer yarn about two roistering sailors who travel the world together, one interested in girls, the other interested only in his buddy. The plot consists of the obviously gay character played by

Robert Armstrong, who is named Bill but is called "Salami," continually trying to stop his pal "Spike," played by Victor McLaglen, from chasing women by deliberately provoking fights so that they will wind up safely in jail together. After they brawl, the queer friend holds out his hand and says in an intertitle to his straight friend, "Pull my joint, Spike." That would have been the title of an article I thought of writing about gay themes in Hawks but put aside because it would have been funny, and a jocular approach might have been considered offensive.

Hawks told me that when he related the ending of *When It's Hot Play It Cool* to a bunch of French directors, he said, "'You Frenchmen are going to think that I've got a couple of homosexuals there.' They all laughed. And I said, 'That's about the way you're gonna interpret it.' No, they love to study this stuff. They know my pictures better than I do." Seeing my opening, I asked in a gingerly way, "Well, what do you think when critics say, as some in fact have, that the male characters in your films border on homosexuality?" Hawks snapped, "I'd say it's a goddam silly statement to make. It sounds like a homosexual speaking. People attribute all kinds of meanings and everything." I found that remark defensively homophobic. It didn't bother me personally, but I didn't pursue it further. Hawks's way of ending that particular discussion was a sign of how threatening he found that largely unconscious subtext in his work.

About most topics other than that and his political views, Hawks was generally tractable and often fascinating, even if he tended to tell the same stories repeatedly. When I finally edited the transcripts of our seven taped conversations, I found I could combine several versions of many stories to make up the best ones. And I did elicit from him many shrewd and practical tips on how to handle cinematic construction, dialogue, and actors. I've heard from many people who find the book a valuable instructional manual on directing, and *Hawks on Hawks* was chosen as one of the "100 Best Books on Hollywood and the Movies" in 1993 by the Book Collectors of Los Angeles, an honor celebrated at a ceremony in the Academy library. (A book was published at the time to commemorate the choices, but I couldn't afford to buy it.) Lawrence Kasdan, who said he had tried to give his script for *Raiders of the Lost Ark* "a Hawksian spine," told me he was reading *Hawks on Hawks* for inspiration every night on location in France while directing his 1995 romantic comedy, *French Kiss*. So the book fulfills the circumscribed goals I and other people have for it, although I would approach it quite differently today.

How did you handle the problem interviewing a book subject who was known to be a fabulist?

Even at the time, I was aware to some extent that Hawks was an unreliable narrator. Todd McCarthy and I had interviewed screenwriter John Lee Mahin, who had collaborated with Hawks and Ford and was described by F. Scott Fitzgerald as one of "the half dozen best picture writers in the business." Todd and I sought material from Mahin for our biographies of Hawks and Ford, and *Film Comment* generously gave us eleven pages for our candid interview with the screenwriter. We also pinned him down, to his discomfort, on his role in helping lead the Hollywood blacklist. When we told Mahin about some of the tales Hawks had been spinning about *Scarface* (which Mahin helped Ben Hecht write) and Hawks's supposed involvement in the writing of three major Victor Fleming films—Mahin was Fleming's favorite screenwriter, and Hawks was an old friend of Fleming's from their days as auto racers—Mahin responded, "Did Howard say *that*? Jesus! He's a complete liar! A complete liar, bless his heart!"

And when we told Mahin that Hawks claimed he had suggested to Hecht an analogy between the Camonte family and the Borgias for *Scarface*, Mahin exclaimed emphatically, "*Ben* said that to *Hawks*. I heard him say that. The Borgias have always been Ben's favorite characters. Howard, bless his heart, probably knew who they were, but I think he looked them up in the encyclopedia. Howard was such a liar! That's a typical example.... Vic Fleming and I would kid Howard about his lying. He just pretended we never said it, he'd just change the subject. I loved the guy, I think he was a lot of fun. But you know Howard."

Robin Wood, because of his excellent critical study of Hawks, was asked to be a reader of the *Hawks on Hawks* manuscript for the University of California Press. Robin questioned the reliability of Hawks's accounts and actually cited our Mahin interview (without naming us as the interviewers) to back up his point. But I brushed aside that concern in cavalier fashion other than to insert a few caveats here and there about Hawks's stories being dubious or contradicted by other people. I did make an effort to check out some of Hawks's anecdotes. Hawks told me he had criticized William Friedkin for making "lousy" pictures such as *The Boys in the Band* and *The Night They Raided Minsky's* and told him to make a chase picture that audiences would want to see. When I asked Friedkin if Hawks really planted the idea of his doing *The French Connection*, he said, "Absolutely true. Before I met Howard Hawks, the entire body of my work was masturbatory."

I didn't do enough of that kind of fact-checking, though. How inadequate my approach to film history in *Hawks on Hawks* too often was I came to understand from Todd's lively and authoritative 1997 biography, *Howard Hawks: The Grey Fox of Hollywood* (a phrase I had passed along from Ford, who called Hawks "the goddam grey fox of Brentwood"). I cooperated fully with Todd's biography because I hoped he would get to the bottom of the actual events. I let him use the raw, uncut transcripts of all my interview sessions with Hawks, and Peter Bogdanovich gave Todd access to his Hawks interviews, so the director's voice is vivid throughout the biography.

Todd had participated in the last of the sessions I had with Hawks for the book, the Directors Guild's "Weekend with Howard Hawks and His Films" I moderated in October 1977 at a hotel in Laguna Beach. By then I realized I had virtually enough material for an interview book, so I used those sessions to fill in gaps. That was a relaxed, warm, friendly weekend attended by younger DGA members as well as by members of Hawks's family, including his daughter Barbara Hawks McCampbell, who has story credit for *Rio Bravo* as the once-mysterious B. H. McCampbell. (Hawks told me, "She thought of the dynamite and a few other things.") Todd found that exposure to Hawks invaluable as a future biographer. Hawks seemed to be in an especially kindly, good-humored, mellow mood that weekend, and the event had an intimacy we all shared, making us feel the same kind of relaxed camaraderie he creates in his films. "The timing of it was perfect," Barbara told me after her father's death that December. "And of all the things like that he'd done, I think that was the one he appreciated the most."

As I wrote in the book, Barbara had also come to other public events I did with her father and "quipped that Hawks and I were beginning to resemble a vaudeville team, with me feeding him straight lines and him responding on cue as if he'd never heard the questions before." Though I think she intended her quip as a compliment, it was a bit double-edged, because I can now see that the interviews tended toward glibness, despite the sharper exchanges here and there. Hawks occasionally even asked me before an event to cue him with a lead-in question, such as "Why don't you ask me how I talked Ben Hecht into writing *Scarface*." My cinematographer friend Alex Ameripoor observed that when we talked with old directors such as Hawks who

Before going onstage for a Q&A with me and Peter Bogdanovich at a February 1974 retrospective of his films at the Los Angeles County Museum of Art, Hawks was in a jolly mood, giving some stage directions. With me here is the host, LACMA film curator Ronald Haver, a prominent film historian. (Rick Alton)

enjoyed reminiscing, it was like putting a quarter in a jukebox and hearing Judy Garland sing "Over the Rainbow" for the umpteenth time.

Truffaut called Hawks an intellectual, but he was a director who claimed to disdain intellectual approaches to this work. How did you approach that paradox?

When my editor at the UC Press, Ernest (Chick) Callenbach, told me *Hawks on Hawks* needed an introduction, I resisted that obvious suggestion at first, protesting that I didn't have any particularly original views on Hawks. But Chick persuaded me to fill in the essence of what people needed to know about him. I wrote a succinct overview and asked Truffaut for a comment to incorporate. Truffaut had told me in 1974 that he wished a book could be done about Hawks along the same lines as his interview book on Hitchcock. After I finished the manuscript in 1981, Truffaut gave me a most welcome blurb: "I read *Hawks on Hawks* with passion. I am very happy that this book exists." And for the introduction, he referred me to this statement he had made in 1977 to the magazine *Grand Illusions:*

Something I feel that's very interesting with Hawks is that in all those interviews, he always criticizes, he raps the intellectuals, and in my opinion he is one of the most intellectual filmmakers in America. He often speaks in terms of film concepts. He has many general theories. He doesn't belong to the school of instinctive filmmakers. He thinks of everything he does, everything is thought out. So somebody ought to tell him one day that despite himself he is an intellectual and that he has to accept that.

And yet, as you note, Hawks didn't present himself as an intellectual and showed little evidence of reading serious literature. Although he cited Willa Cather, a fellow Midwesterner, as one of his influences (along with the more obvious Hemingway and Raymond Chandler), when I suggested he make a film of her classic novel about a Nebraska pioneer woman, *My Ántonia*, Hawks said, "It would be a good movie but I don't know if anyone would go to see it." (That book would be adapted in 1995 as a TV movie.) Hawks's reading material, as far as I could tell from looking at the magazine racks in his living room, mostly seemed to be about automobiles and car racing. But when a studio executive wondered in the 1920s why Hawks had such a fine story sense, John Ford replied simply, "He reads books." Hawks had helped produce films based on Joseph Conrad novels in the silent days and kept his friend William Faulkner solvent with screenwriting chores so he could write his more esoteric books. But Hawks's reading regimen nevertheless seemed to lie in the distant past. He knew all about how he was lionized by French cinephiles and filmmakers but professed to find such adulation a bit baffling—an obvious pose.

Yet if a genuine intellectual is someone with clear, articulate ways of working and a solid yet flexible attitude toward his *métier*, as well as an ability to discuss his work thoughtfully, then Hawks, as Truffaut asserted, could be considered an intellectual. Being an overt intellectual, however, would have been suicidal in the old studio days and still was to some extent in the modern Hollywood. And though Hawks's career was over by the time I started seeing him, which helped bring me such access, he didn't entirely give up on wanting to make films. He simply complained about the modern marketplace and the problems involved in making independent productions without the studio backing to which he had been accustomed; the old studio directors found themselves adrift without such support. Ford's

Hawks was a casual fellow, as seen in this still of him being interviewed by me for the book at his home in Palm Springs. (Dix Bruce)

masquerading as an uncouth illiterate despite reading voraciously on the sly (his research assistant, Katherine Cliffton, told me he had her catalogue his six thousand books) was also not Hawks's mode.

Hawks could not have been more different from Ford in the way he treated a young admirer and interviewer with courtesy, expansiveness, and a willingness to give him all the time in the world. It was good for his ego to talk with people who knew his work well, a substitute for actually working. Every time I went to see Hawks, who was my elder by fifty years, our sessions seldom lasted less than five hours. I staggered out in a state of exhaustion, and he always looked great. Pleasant though Hawks was, it was disconcerting that his social skills were lacking; he didn't show much interest in the people he was talking with and didn't offer drinks or snacks to me or the friends I brought along on some of my visits.

But when Alex Ameripoor had the chutzpah to ask Hawks for something to eat, Hawks sprang up and did an elaborate job of making sandwiches for us. Others I took along to talk with Hawks included your brother, Gerry; Pat McGilligan; and photographer Dix Bruce. Another of the sessions that went into *Hawks on Hawks* was a discussion Bogdanovich and I hosted with Hawks at a February 1974 retrospective at the Los Angeles County Museum of Art. And Hawks made a memorable appearance with actress Charlene Holt to show their film *El Dorado* and talk with the students at the first film course I taught at Sherwood Oaks Experimental College in Hollywood in May 1974.

You have a special kinship toward that film, appreciating it even more than its predecessor in the trilogy, Rio Bravo, *although that film was pivotal in your youth.*

I'm somewhat of a maverick among Hawksians in regarding *El Dorado* as my favorite of his films, both because it is so funny and also because, with the character of Wayne's aging gunfighter, it so movingly explores the subject of mortality. Welles once told Bogdanovich, "Hawks is great prose; Ford is poetry." That's usually true, but *El Dorado,* which borrows its title from Edgar Allan Poe, is also poetry.

Was Hawks on Hawks *difficult for you to finish?*

It took me several years to get around to putting *Hawks on Hawks* together, because I was always busy working on screenplays, but when I buckled down to do it, I edited the book in just one month (not includng the introduction). *Hawks on Hawks* was published in 1982 and has subsequently appeared in more foreign editions than any of my other books. There have been translations in France, Spain, Japan, Italy, Finland, and Iran, as well as a British edition from Faber and Faber. I briefly thought of doing a similar interview book with Capra before realizing what an absurd idea that was. Capra, as I later learned while interviewing him for more than a year for my biography, lied even more relentlessly than Hawks, and the biography was structured as an exposé of the deceitful image Capra had spent decades selling to a gullible public with the help of the media.

I learned from these experiences about the limitations of doing director interview books, despite their popularity and utility in the formative days of film studies. Even Truffaut's wonderful book on Hitchcock falls into the trap of promoting the myth that Hitchcock storyboarded everything and was basically bored when he actually had to shoot his films, a myth I helped discount after watching Hitchcock at work making up shots as he went along on *Family Plot.* The sobering evidence of my credulous treatment of Hawks and my early susceptibility to Capra's lies, as well as my utter disillusionment with Hollywood during my years as a trade reporter and screenwriter, eventually helped make me a much better film historian.

7. Capra and Spielberg

Capraesque/Kafkaesque

Let's finally talk about your magnum opus as a biographer, Frank Capra: The Catastrophe of Success. *You invited controversy by exposing Capra, a hero to us cineastes, as an informer during the blacklist era and a fraud in many ways. And later you wrote a book about the book, explaining how you wrote the biography and all the legal troubles you had getting it published.*

I spent seven and a half years, from 1984 through 1992, researching, writing, and fighting a legal battle to publish my biography of Capra. I poured all I knew and all I had into it. I was ultimately successful in that struggle, which I was determined to win at all costs, and it was gratifying that the book became a critical success. I debunked Capra's mythic account of his life and work with thorough and impeccable research and exposed him as a covert informer during the blacklist period. As someone at the AFI said while I was writing the book, it set a new standard for film biographies. (I wondered, *But how did they know? It hasn't been published yet.*) Screenwriter-director Philip Dunne, whose last piece of writing was a review of my book for the *Chicago Sun-Times,* told me, "It would be a shoo-in for the Pulitzer if it weren't about a movie director." I regard my Capra biography as the fulfillment and vindication of my experiences covering Hollywood and toiling in the trenches as a screenwriter. It was tough but made it all worthwhile.

And many years later, in 2019, I wrote a 601-page book, *Frankly: Unmasking Frank Capra*, my account of my interactions with him and other players in my struggle to get the book published. *Frankly*, which in effect is Volume II of my Capra biography, tells how I researched and wrote the biography while becoming embroiled in a four-year, Kafkaesque legal battle with my publisher, Alfred A. Knopf; its parent company, Random House; my editor at Knopf, Robert Gottlieb; and Jeanine Basinger, Capra's archivist at Wesleyan University. Ironically, in many ways the situation I faced with that biography was much worse than anything I had experienced as a Hollywood screenwriter, more treacherous and more damaging and more prolonged.

As I discuss in *Frankly*, while I was fighting that legal battle, I had to keep what was happening a secret for strategic reasons: I wanted the public focus to remain on the finished book. Or in intelligence lingo that John Ford was fond of using about his work in the OSS, I felt it necessary to be "inky." So those years of my work on the Capra biography were, as my friend Gary Graver so perceptively put it, "your dark period." But when I told my story in confidence at the time to a distinguished fellow author, a future winner of the Pulitzer Prize, he said, "This is the most bizarre story I ever heard. The worst thing I ever heard.... Offending Frank Capra is the least of it. It's a real mystery. I've never heard a story like this."

It felt liberating to finally get it off my chest twenty-seven years later; anyone who wants the whole story in exhaustive detail can read *Frankly,* but I will summarize it here and offer some reflections as I look back from today's vantage point, assessing the pivotal role the biography played in my life.

Go back to the beginning, when you switched from being a fan of Capra, which you were from your Madison days, to a biographer of Capra.

I was and still am an admirer of Capra's work, especially *Mr. Smith Goes to Washington,* but until I learned better I also regarded him as a role model. I thought of him as an idealistic filmmaker who managed to make socially conscious films within the Hollywood system, and my screenplay *Big Money* was designed, somewhat to its detriment, as "Capraesque." But at the same time I was troubled and concerned over the collapse of Capra's career in postwar Hollywood, one of the most precipitous downfalls of a great American filmmaker since D. W. Griffith. I wondered why Capra self-destructed. I began to find the answer when I met him in 1975.

I went to his home in the desert near Palm Springs to interview him for *Daily Variety.* Capra took me to lunch at the La Quinta Country Club and was giving me one of his familiar populist raps—"I've always had a hatred of rich people, since I was a kid. And you have a hell of a time selling comedies to bankers, because they don't laugh much"—when a middle-aged man in a tie and blazer approached our table with a folder of photographs. "Frank," he said, "here are the pictures of you playing golf with President Ford." He spread the photos on the white tablecloth in front of Capra, who sighed, "Ah, wonderful." One especially struck me: the president holding the pin and flag as Capra bent over to putt. I thought this is the ultimate immigrant dream, to have the president of the United States serve as your caddy.

The man left our table, promising to send the photos to Capra the following week. Capra turned back to me and asked, "Where was I? Oh yeah, I was telling you that I've always had a hatred of bankers and rich people."

As I later told the *New York Times*, "Then he just continued, without losing a beat. That illuminated something for me about Capra: there was a contradiction between the image and the man." I realized that his populist image as the champion of the common man was merely a façade; this revered filmmaker was a phony who enjoyed hobnobbing with the elite but pretended to hate them so he could curry favor with his gullible admirers. "I was stunned," I write in *Frankly*. "And I realized I had discovered a great story, one that had been missed for decades by everyone in the media—an American icon who was seen as a representative of all that was best about the country but whose stature was largely based on a cleverly sustained fraud…. I made a mental note: 'Find out more.'"

It took many years for you to publish your Capra biography, but did you decide to start researching him after your Daily Variety *interview, with a book in mind?*

Not at first. But I began to focus my thoughts both on what it was about Capra's character that caused his tragic downfall and how that catastrophe had been influenced by problems in Hollywood and American society. The more I became disillusioned about Capra and about Hollywood itself, the more I felt betrayed by him, since he misled me and his other admirers about how he and Hollywood operated. And he perpetrated injustices against his collaborators, especially his screenwriters. My belated understanding of how the postwar Red Scare and the ensuing blacklist permanently damaged Hollywood filmmaking as a medium for social criticism enabled me to understand the context of Capra's informing on and stigmatizing his writers for providing the vaguely liberal thrust of his best work. When his loyalty to his adopted country was questioned during the postwar Red Scare, he claimed to the U.S. government, in effect, "Those writers made me do it." In the process he destroyed himself. It's a Greek tragedy. Or, looking at it another way, if Capra's autobiography is a captivating Hollywood novel, my biography is akin to a Russian novel. He was a Dostoevskian figure.

But for nine years I resisted the growing imperative I felt to write that biography, because I was wrestling with my feelings to reach the conclusion that I had to get out of the film industry. I was not ready to give up my dream of Hollywood but was faced with the painful decision to abandon the industry to concentrate on my other career as an author. I finally realized that writing books was what had always made me happy. When you write a book, you are, in effect, the studio boss, even if you may have to answer to a publisher, but when you work on a film or TV show, you are a disposable employee. I wanted control of my life and work.

How did you discover that Capra was an informer?

That moment of truth came in December 1981 when I went to Wesleyan University in Connecticut for an initial four-day visit to dig into Capra's papers archived there. Thanks to Jeanine Basinger, I was the first outsider allowed to see his papers. She had arranged for their donation as well as for Capra to receive an honorary degree from Wesleyan. Basinger was also an AFI trustee who had volunteered to help with the Capra Life Achievement Award show. Like many other people before and since, I fell under the influence of her seemingly warm and dedicated scholarly spirit and the image she projects of a motherly figure nurturing film students, scholars, and filmmakers. When I first went to Wesleyan during my work on the Capra tribute, she opened the papers for me in the basement of the archive and let me borrow one of the longer documents, Capra's so-called Security Board File, to read overnight at my motel.

With my reporter's instinct, I began by asking to see the box of Capra's papers for the period around the time of his participation in an international film festival in India in January 1952. I zeroed in on that specific period because of what I had read about it in his 1971 autobiography, *The Name Above the Title*. In what seemed to be a strange stylistic and thematic departure from the general tone of the autobiography—which mostly portrays Capra as a sentimental humanist, though with odd lapses into bigotry—Capra relates his involvement in the film festival as a representative of the U.S. State Department. He presents himself in his book as having served as a vigorous anti-Communist combatant and spokesman for American values. The episode is written in a jarringly strident fashion. His autobiography elsewhere contains a brief and enigmatic suggestion that he was never a Democrat but does not go into much detail about his positions on political issues. He had also been cagey about revealing himself politically to interviewers and others during his heyday and beyond.

As I learned, Capra was in fact a lifelong Republican, a hardcore conservative and fierce opponent of the New Deal

I spent more than a year interviewing Frank Capra in a sometimes
contentious, sometimes cordial process for my biography
Frank Capra: The Catastrophe of Success. Here we chat at one of his
last public events, a January 1985 luncheon tribute from Columbia
Pictures at Chasen's restaurant in West Hollywood. (Columbia)

who admitted to me that he hated President Franklin D.
Roosevelt. That would have stunned most of his latter-day
admirers, who tended to buy his act as a New Deal liberal and
a cinematic champion of the Bill of Rights, an inspirational,
Gandhi-like dispenser of humanistic bromides. His benign
image was further belied by the rampant bigotry he displayed
in our interviews; Capra was actually a misanthrope, biased
against just about every ethnic group, including his own as
an Italian American, and he blamed his career difficulties
partly on Jews in Hollywood.

Within half an hour of opening that first box of papers
at Wesleyan, I began finding the answers about what had
happened to him. Capra's Security Board File stunned me.
What he later described to me as "this *mea culpa* book...
a book about my life" was an anxiously self-justifying
225-document he submitted to the Army-Navy-Air Force
Personnel Security Board in December 1951 in response to
his security clearance being revoked. He had been serving as
a civilian member of a top-secret think tank, Project VISTA,
at his alma mater, the California Institute of Technology
(Caltech) in Pasadena. Capra was VISTA's director of
motion picture production, heading its documentary films
group and in charge of planning psychological warfare
filmmaking in the event of World War III breaking out in

Europe, the focus of the overall study. (I later obtained the final VISTA report, which had been partially declassified in 1980, at the National Archives and studied VISTA documents in Capra's papers and his Army Intelligence and FBI files.)

Capra's autobiographical 1951 document elaborately presented his political, professional, and social history, including what he considered his bona fides as a patriotic, fiercely anti-communist American citizen. The immigrant filmmaker who had come from Sicily as a boy in 1903 set out to prove his loyalty in that document by naming the names of several colleagues whom he considered Communists or possible communist sympathizers and by declaring that he had been an FBI informant. I later found out he also informed on colleagues to the State Department. Although I obtained his Army Intelligence file through the Freedom of Information Act early in my research, it took seven years to obtain his FBI file, which I used as the principal basis for a new appendix in the revised 2000 edition of my 1992 biography. Unlike Elia Kazan, his fellow director who had publicly named names while brazenly attempting to justify his cooperation with the House Committee on Un-American Activities, Capra, as I discovered in his papers, had hidden his collusion with the witch hunt out of apparent shame. I always found it an intriguing question, which approach is more deplorable morally.

I had the basic story about Capra's life already on that initial visit to Wesleyan and knew I was sitting on a major scoop. And yet I resisted the challenge of getting down to telling the story, partly perhaps because I knew how arduous the job would be. And it took the next couple of years of psychic struggle to purge my remaining need to pursue my longtime goals as a screenwriter. I didn't mention this before, Danny, but while writing the AFI shows, I made some attempts to get out of Hollywood and go back to newspaper work. I applied for jobs with the *Capital Times* in Madison, Wisconsin; the *Milwaukee Journal* (they wondered why I wanted to leave such a "glamorous" occupation); and the *San Diego Evening Tribune*. I came close to getting the job in San Diego before someone they contacted who knew my work as a screenwriter told them I was "difficult," the Hollywood code word for "has integrity." Looking back, I am fortunate that I escaped being hired. Returning to the grind of newspaper work would have changed my life for the worse, not for the better, as concentrating all my time on writing books would do for me. I wouldn't have been able to write the Capra book while working on a newspaper.

The buffeting I took as a screenwriter finally eroded my remaining drive to practice that profession. Even the rare and relatively good experiences I had as a writer of the AFI Life Achievement Award shows, enabling me to work with so many fascinating people from the so-called Golden Age of Hollywood, served to distance me further from the corrupted modern industry. And it was ironic that the opportunity to celebrate Capra while writing his AFI Life Achievement Award special in 1982 served as the catalyst for my departure from the industry to write the book. Getting to know him better while helping him write and rehearse his acceptance speech, seeing more cracks in his façade, and learning what his colleagues thought of him galvanized that feeling of urgency. Capra said after the show, "You did wonderful work, Joe, I was pleasantly surprised." And he asked, "What can I do for you?"

So in 1984, nine years after I first interviewed Capra and a couple of years after starting to read his papers at Wesleyan while writing his AFI show, which provided such a fortunate opportunity to study him up close, I finally buckled down to that task of writing my Capra biography. By then my experiences in Hollywood had given me the clear-eyed ability to write about the rise and fall of a representative Hollywood character in the studio system and to analyze how a major director lost his ability while squandering his appeal to audiences.

How did your discovery of Capra's informing help you focus on the central themes of the book?

The Capra biography was the product and expression of my disillusionment with an industry and art form I had loved but that I felt had betrayed me, as it had so many others. Capra's inability to understand the need to give screenwriters the credit they deserved was a major factor in ruining his career, because after a while, Robert Riskin and other top writers refused to work with him anymore. And when Capra informed on several of his writers to the U.S. government after being accused of disloyalty, he in effect was blaming them for the somewhat liberal tinge of his best work in the 1930s, which succeeded partly because of its social criticism. Despite being a hardline conservative who hated FDR and his New Deal, he was savvy enough to know what audiences wanted to see during the Depression era. So he was able through his liberal or leftist screenwriters to tap into his otherwise vestigial sympathies with ordinary people. After *It's a Wonderful Life* failed to connect with audiences in 1946 and the postwar political climate turned hostile, Capra compounded the problem of his self-defensive right-wing turn by consciously refusing to work with liberal writers anymore and relying mostly on the blinkered right-wing ideologue Myles Connolly.

Among the people betrayed by postwar Hollywood were the blacklisted screenwriters I empathized with, including the writers Capra informed on, especially Michael Wilson. Wilson was a U.S. Marine Corps veteran of World War II who had worked on *Wonderful Life* and other projects for Capra, including his adaptation of Jessamyn West's book of short stories about Quakers in the Civil War, *The Friendly Persuasion*. Capra wrote in the uncut, unsanitized version of his autobiography that he had abandoned *The Friendly Persuasion* after he learned that Wilson was accused of being a communist. Capra wrote in the document he submitted to the U.S. government in 1951, "I was bowled over by Michael Wilson's connection with the party. He wouldn't have lasted two minutes with Liberty Films [Capra's independent company with William Wyler, George Stevens, and Sam Briskin] had I the slightest inkling he was a Red."

William Wyler made the film in 1956 as *Friendly Persuasion*. In West's story about the war, the Quaker youth joins Indiana neighbors who join to resist marauding Confederates. But the raiders bypass the area, and the boy is able to go home without having to test his principles in combat. In Wilson's adaptation, although the boy goes into combat, feeling he has a higher duty to his country, he finds it impossible to kill and becomes a stretcher bearer instead. Wilson's script demonstrated that an American, even in a time of war, can choose to remain loyal to his principles. But Wyler had the story changed to make Quaker youth become a killer. The Quakers in the film, as Pauline Kael observed, "are there only to violate their convictions." Wyler and Allied Artists released the film without any screenwriting credit at all, the only such instance in the history of Hollywood. (Wilson nevertheless won a Writers Guild of America Award and received an Oscar nomination for the script but was ruled ineligible by the Academy of Motion Picture Arts and Sciences.) Wilson sued Wyler, Allied Artists, and the vestigial Liberty Films over the denial of credit. The case, settled out of court, became a landmark in the ongoing battle to destroy the blacklist. The WGA restored Wilson's credit for the screenplay in 1996, and the Academy restored his nomination in 2002.

Five days before his HUAC appearance in 1951, Wilson wrote his mother and father, who expressed dismay over his defiant stand, "Have Americans been sold on the Big Lie—that the principles on which our country was founded sound 'un-American'?... If I have any worth as a writer it is because I have been a worthy citizen." He quoted the words of Thomas Jefferson: "It behooves every man who values liberty of conscience for himself, to resist invasions of it in the case of others, or their case may, by change of circumstances, become his own. It behooves him, too, in his own case, to give no example of concession, betraying the common right of independent opinion, by answering questions of faith, which the laws have left between God and himself."

I later realized that Wilson was the hero of my Capra biography, the man Capra should have been but failed to be. Capra had been a hero of mine, but under false pretenses. When I learned that he had betrayed the ideals his films stood for, and in the process betrayed the ideals of the Bill of Rights that *Mr. Smith Goes to Washington* so eloquently defended, my reporter's instincts told me I had an important story on my hands, a story I knew had to be told. And what I had learned from my failure to report with sufficient energy and dedication on Hawks and other Hollywood figures, and on the industry itself, redoubled my desire to do this story right. I was determined to concentrate all my time and talent into telling it honestly and well. I came to it with a tremendous amount of pent-up creative energy.

Did you write a detailed proposal to sell the book to a publisher?

What finally made me focus on selling the book to publishers was (1) my last straw as a screenwriter, the insulting meeting I told you about with that story editor in May 1984; and (2) happening upon an interview with Capra on local TV, an otherwise inconsequential chat with a reporter at the La Quinta Hotel, his latter-day home in the desert. After consulting with my friend Bob Thomas, the longtime Associated Press Hollywood correspondent and seasoned film biographer, I wrote the book proposal. I told Bob in confidence what I had discovered and wondered whether I should reveal the whole story in the proposal. His advice was to put it all in as the best way of attracting interest from publishers and receiving a workable advance to carry me through the research and writing.

I listen as Capra addresses a Directors Guild of America weekend on his films that I hosted in 1981 at a hotel in Indian Wells, California. With us is the great cinematographer Joseph Walker, who shot twenty Capra films and participated throughout that seminar.

While mulling over the structure of my story, I studied the 1966 biography of Mark Twain by Justin Kaplan, *Mr. Clemens and Mark Twain*, and Robert A. Caro's 1982 biography, *The Path to Power: The Years of Lyndon Johnson, Volume I*, both of which make clear how important the early formative years of a life are to a biographer. But I found that biographers of film people often skimped those years, since they seemed impatient to get their subjects to Hollywood and relied on only a handful of interviews with stars. Those shortsighted biographers ignored so-called "ordinary" people such as those who bring Caro's portrait of Johnson's Texas roots so powerfully to life; I sought out such people in Capra's life. I also learned from those books and from Lytton Strachey's *Eminent Victorians* how crucial it is for a biography to have a strong theme rather than hiding behind a weak pose of neutrality, and these biographers helped show me how to examine the discrepancies between the public image and the man.

Leon Edel's sagacious 1984 guidebook, *Writing Lives*, proved invaluable when I read it while going through Capra's papers over two months at Wesleyan in the fall of that year. Edel observes that "a biographer, choosing his subject, tends to be chosen by it." It's often said that a biographer finds a subject because of emotional identification. Although I saw Capra's story as a cautionary tale, I could relate to his drive for success while understanding his feelings of humiliation and self-doubt, which reminded me of how Richard Nixon portrays himself in my quirky role model of a memoir, *Six Crises*.

I already knew that telling Capra's story would involve deep probing into his early years when he clawed his way up the social ladder from what he considered a degrading working-class background while leaving his immigrant family behind. I did not know yet how he had exaggerated their supposed poverty or how, when I asked when he had gotten over being ashamed of his parents, he admitted, "I haven't yet." His attempts to deny his identity became the primary source of his downfall. It was not coincidental that this Italian immigrant filmmaker cast quintessentially WASP stars, such as Gary Cooper and James Stewart, as his idealized leading men, the figures through whom he projected himself as the 100% American he wished to be or at least wanted people to accept him as being.

Some time earlier I had thought of writing a tragic drama about an informer, which I thought would be more fascinating than the lives of victims that tended to be written instead as heroic sagas. I realized I would have to examine Capra's whole life to find the roots of his anguished and vengeful response to the questioning of his loyalty by his adopted country, a country that he deeply loved but had kicked him in the teeth, resulting in his betrayal of his colleagues and himself. That capitulation, I realized, was what destroyed Capra's career when he turned his back on the collaborators who had been largely responsible for his success—his writers, who had threatened his stubborn and dubious claim to solo authorship—and in the process had lost his courage and ability to make meaningful films while, in effect, he blacklisted himself. The first half of Capra's long life was a triumphant chronicle of success, but the second half one of devastating failure. I borrowed my title from Tennessee Williams, who wrote of the "catastrophe of success" that followed his early acclaim. Capra was dogged by lifelong feelings of inadequacy masquerading as egomania, by the belief that being a director was not as important as being a writer, and by his crippling feeling of being a fake, a victim of what is called the "imposter phenomenon."

So I set out to explain how I would tell this quintessentially American tragedy. I wrote my proposal in the form of a letter to my new book agent, Michael Hamilburg, who suggested that helpful approach. I wrote the twenty-three-page, single-spaced proposal in sixteen hours straight in a rush of creative energy on May 17 and 18, 1984. It was strong enough to attract offers from three publishing companies, and that July I chose to go with Alfred A. Knopf when its editor, the celebrated Robert

Gottlieb, outbid Simon & Schuster. I was overly impressed by Gottlieb because he was Caro's editor and because he convinced me how much he wanted the book, declaring, "To me, Frank Capra is the most fascinating person in the world." Even after years of further research into Capra's life and work and dogged labor over the manuscript; after four years of legal battling with Knopf and its parent company, Random House, facing down attempts to stop or gut the book by Gottlieb and Basinger; and after the book was finally freed from Knopf and found its way back to Simon & Schuster, I found that it still resembled the proposal remarkably closely, although filled in with a wealth of evidence, detail, and other revelations.

Tell me about your research process on your Capra book. It must have been prodigious, given that, as one reviewer put it, the book has a surprise on every page.

I found interviewing Capra over the course of a year, until he suffered a series of incapacitating strokes in 1985, a difficult process, since he was often captious and resistant to my questions. Yet just as often he seemed to welcome the opportunity to reminisce about his life and even to confess truths about his life that were not revealed in *The Name Above the Title,* which, as the *New York Times Book Review* would put it in its review of my book, "appears to have been a lie practically from beginning to end." But I had to play a game with Capra, first finding out the truth from my research into documents and interviews with other people before he would admit the truth. Such was the case when a woman he knew well in high school, Esther Gleason Schlinger, told me, "He was ostracized; people never invited him anywhere. Because he was a foreigner, they didn't think of including him in their parties. He was a nice boy. He was just a terrible wop."

That jarring moment made me angry on Capra's behalf for the first time in my work on the book. Her bigoted remarks helped me empathize with him, a necessity in writing a good biography. Edel advises, "No good biography can be written in total love and admiration; and it is even less useful if it is written in hate." When I told Capra what Schlinger said, he admitted that his earlier claim that he had a happy time in high school was false. Those years, I realized, were crucial to his social development and left lasting scars, since it was then that he first ventured out of his East Los Angeles neighborhood—not the Italian ghetto he claimed, but a place where mostly working-class people of various ethnicities lived, as I learned by going to the National Archives and obtaining a copy of the 1910 U.S. census—and making his perilous way into middle-class, Anglo Los Angeles society.

"Well, she was right," Capra responded when I asked him about Schlinger's comments. "I didn't have much to do with the girls—I was ashamed of myself. The girls all looked so pretty. I was a little ashamed of my clothes and my big shoes and everything like that.... I was constantly fighting.... if somebody said a word about my clothes I'd kick him right in the ass or right in the balls." My Irish immigrant wife, Ruth O'Hara, also helped me empathize with the feelings of exclusion Capra gradually discussed and his ambivalence about American life that I learned more about and made me more fully understand his desperate drive to succeed.

I began my research by interviewing members of Capra's loyal crew, starting with his venerable cinematographer on twenty films, Joseph Walker, who was 91 and an excellent source. Capra's sound mixer, Edward Bernds, who became a writer-director himself, was another of my most valuable sources, along with Chester Sticht, Capra's longtime secretary. Chet knew almost everything about him and was willing to talk, because Capra had let him go on six weeks' notice after thirty-nine years of loyal service. Capra's crew gave me a sense of Capra's working methods that was much different from the self-promoting version of frugal efficiency he claimed in his book. His downfall began when he went wildly over schedule and over budget on his woolly 1937 fantasy, *Lost Horizon*, a story that had never been fully reported. And they were eager to set the record straight because they felt Capra had been so "ungenerously skimpy" in his book (as *Sight and Sound* reviewer Elliott Stein put it) in crediting Walker's crucial contributions to his work.

My most extensive research task, however, was devoted to uncovering the years of apprenticeship Capra had served in the industry before 1921, which is when his autobiography falsely claims he began directing with no previous experience. I turned up a wealth of information about his early film work in Hollywood, Reno, and San Francisco. I chronicle Capra's dogged climb from "cleaning up the horseshit" at the Christie comedy studio (as he admitted to me after I learned he had been a janitor there from a friend from his old neighborhood) through his rise to success with a series of odd jobs in the film business. I found these stories more genuinely inspiring than his false "creation myth" of reading a newspaper column in San

Francisco and conning his way into becoming a director.

Another key element of Capra's story was his intensely creative but ultimately fraught relationship with screenwriter Robert Riskin. Capra's anxious lifelong need to misappropriate credit and denigrate his writers led the director to angrily downplay Riskin's contribution to their work together. I concluded, after carefully studying that controversial topic, that Riskin especially had as much and probably more claim to authorship of "Capra's" films than the director did.

I found that Capra did not even believe wholeheartedly or, in some cases, believe at all in the themes he was espousing in the years of his great success, the Depression years, but was giving the public what they wanted, making films that would sell. But part of Capra, the better part that could still relate to the struggling immigrant youth he once had been, could emotionally share the feelings of even his humblest characters. And despite his misanthropic tendencies toward humanity in general, his principal talent was that he was a splendid director of and audience for his actors. The actual collaboration between Capra and his co-workers was a highly complex exchange, one he disguised under his defensive "One man, one film" philosophy of authorship even though, when laid out in detail in my biography, the reality tells much about the nature of filmmaking. My understanding of the collaborative process throughout my years in Hollywood came to fruition in this book.

Were Capra and Basinger cooperative at first?

Before approaching publishers, I had taken the precaution of getting assurances of cooperation from Capra, who agreed to give me interviews but seemed wary of what I would write and asked, "What's in it for me?" I made no concessions to him and reminded him that it would be an unauthorized biography. Those are the only kind I write, since, as Gottlieb put it, with authorized biographies, "There is always a price to be paid." Gottlieb falsely claimed that Knopf did not do authorized biographies, but in reading the acknowledgments, I found that most of them were. As it turned out, Capra was making a deal with Random House behind my back to reprint his autobiography (a stark conflict of interest for my publisher) and had other ideas of how he might benefit. I also obtained verbal promises from Basinger of full access to Capra's papers before anyone else and unlimited permission to quote from his unpublished works. She said the formal written permission would come later.

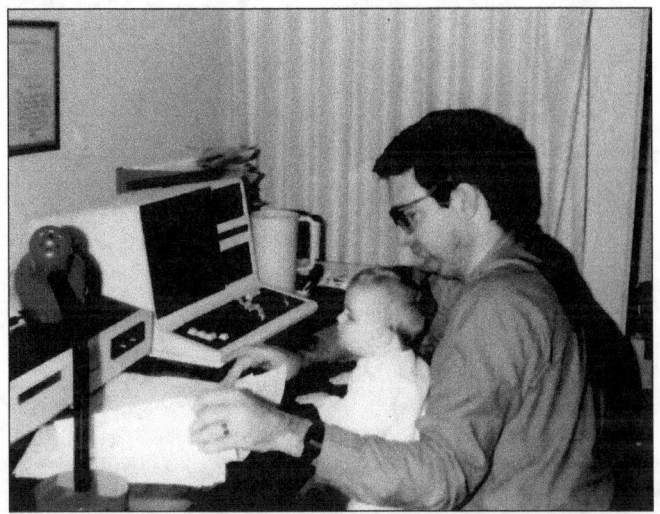

During the lengthy ordeal of writing my Capra biography, one of my great comforts was the companionship of my son, John. This future mathematician and teacher showed admirable cheerfulness helping me at work, as seen here in 1987. (Ruth O'Hara)

As it turned out, that permission never came, and my dealings with Basinger and Gottlieb became a Kafkaesque nightmare, like that of Joseph K. in *The Trial.* She and her archive kept going back and forth with Random House in claiming they did or did not own the copyright to his unpublished writings, even though the 1980 Deed of Gift by Frank Capra and his wife, Lucille, specified that all right, title, and interest in the papers was given to Wesleyan University and its successors. Basinger had her own financial stake in the deal-making with Random House, as I learned in February 1985 when Gottlieb told me that he and Knopf were going to publish *The "It's a Wonderful Life" Book*, which she drew from the Wesleyan archive, another conflict of interest for Random House and for Gottlieb himself. She also began to hide away some materials before I went through the papers methodically in 1984, including hiding the crucial Security Board File, which I had made the mistake of telling her about in 1981.

So once you sold the proposal, it stopped going smoothly?

By early 1985, I realized that I was in trouble, but just how deeply I didn't realize until that October. My own editor and publisher were working against me and in cahoots with Capra's archivist, who not only saw her role as controlling or deep-sixing my revisionist biography but also managed to wheedle her way into a close friendship with Gottlieb. "You know it all—you may know too much," my editor shockingly told me after I turned in the first four chapters in October 1985. "You will regret you ever met me. The Slasher will go to work." How did Gottlieb know I knew it all? And why on earth would the editor of a biography tell the author that "you may know too much"? As it developed, those were not idle remarks, even though he delivered them in a jocular tone.

Gottlieb's thinly veiled threat, so out of keeping with his inflated reputation, was contrary to the advice Dr. Samuel Johnson gave honest biographers: "If a man is to write *A Panegyrick,* he may keep vices out of sight; but if he professes to write *A Life,* he must represent it really as it was." My last chapter of *Frankly* is an exploration of and defense of the art of biography against those who, following the lead of Joyce Carol Oates, malign honest biographers who delve into their subjects' serious failings; Oates labeled such books as "pathography." I call the promiscuous misapplication of her term by "many intellectuals and others who ought to know better... a convenient tool to stigmatize biographers whose truth-telling puts their own personal, ideological, or economic agendas at risk."

How did the writing go? Were you on schedule before it went badly with your publisher?

I began writing the first chapter—about Capra's return to his native Sicily late in life—on a notepad in my doctor's office on March 1, 1985, while suffering from another case of pneumonia. As I wrote in *Frankly,* I was so fanatical about working on the manuscript that "when Halley's Comet appeared over our Los Angeles apartment house on February 9, 1986, I didn't take a break to go outside to watch it (my next chance will come in 2061)." I had estimated the writing would take three years, but I was dogged by dwindling funds and shipped my supposedly finished draft to Knopf well ahead of schedule on February 17, 1987. The manuscript then was 1,610 pages long, and I realized that in any case it would have to be shorter. One side benefit of my four years of legal battling to get the book published was that I had all that extra time to hone and polish the manuscript as well as I could possibly do.

I managed to keep going by extracting more money from Random House by selling back parts of my rights to the book until there was nothing more to sell. The financial and physical toll it took on me and my family was excruciating.

Fortunately, throughout the battle, I was sustained by my belief in the importance of the project and my absorption in the craft of writing. Ruth, who earned her PhD from USC as a research psychologist during that time before joining the faculty at Stanford University, was heroically supportive throughout the writing and the legal process. She was an expert editor and adviser on all matters involving the book and on Capra's convoluted psyche. She kept up the fight for the book with me throughout that grueling process, realizing I was right in my belief that Knopf would never publish the book but pretending otherwise to keep up my spirits. I was also cheered by the daily companionship at home of our son, John, for the first three years after he was born in December 1986. One of the worst setbacks came that July when I barely survived an auto accident when my car went off a cliff in the San Bernardino Mountains. I had moved there for a year to make progress on the book in relative peace and quiet. We lived in ten separate places during the time I was working on the book.

When did you realize Knopf had no intention of publishing the book?

That sinking moment came on September 30, 1986, when Knopf's publicity department read me their press release, calling Basinger's *"It's a Wonderful Life" Book* "the definitive book on the classic… the entire story of the film's production… [containing] a wealth of original material."

Literally years of more legal back-and-forth ensued as Knopf and Wesleyan dug in on their corrupt positions about denying me permission to quote from Capra's papers. And a month before I turned in my manuscript in 1987, Gottlieb, in a move that surprised almost everyone, took a new job as editor of *The New Yorker*, which he would describe in his autobiography as "a rest cure" from the "constant turmoil" in which he had been living at Knopf (perhaps I did my part to add to that turmoil). His departure, turning my book over to another editor, Lee Goerner, didn't do anything to liberate it from what appeared to be a sticky situation into which Gottlieb and Basinger had dragged Random House.

During my painfully attenuated negotiations with the firm's querulous legal counsel, Ellis Levine, he asked in February 1989 with self-righteous indignation, "Do you realize how much time this wastes?" I'm glad I had the presence of mind to respond, "Yeah, it's wasting a lot of my life."

The cover of my first published book, from the Wisconsin Film Society Press, 1968.

And the first book I wrote, although it took seventeen years to get published by Warner Books in 1980.

What finally enabled you to take the book away from Random House?

I wasn't getting anywhere until three constructive things happened in 1989: (1) I fired my agent, Mike Hamilburg, who admitted he had been working against my interests in dealing with Random House; (2) I found an honest, highly experienced, and brilliant attorney, Maurice L. Muehle; and (3) I went back to work at *Daily Variety,* a decision I found difficult to make at first. I felt a sense of temporary defeat going back to a field I thought I had escaped but now realized was a financial necessity. My new job saved the book by putting us back on our feet and giving me a source of income independent of my publisher. No longer could Random House starve me and my family into submission, as Maury observed that they were trying to do. Maury proved a rock of integrity and a fount of solid legal advice, as well as an expert negotiator in enabling me to free the book from Random House. For years from that point on, I went without an agent. Random House had not only had corrupted Hamilburg but also tried to make deals behind my back with other dishonest representatives (another agent as well as two lawyers and possibly a third lawyer) I tried to bring on board but kept discarding until I found Maury, who was incorruptible.

Eventually, however, to break the impasse, I had to propose removing all the quotes from the unpublished material Wesleyan controlled and summarizing them instead (summarizing, not paraphrasing was the one good piece of legal advice I received from the Random House counsel). While I was writing my book, two unfavorable legal rulings came through, involving books about J. D. Salinger and L. Ron Hubbard, seriously limiting the freedom biographers and other authors of non-fiction books previously had to quote from unpublished letters and other manuscripts. So I had no choice but to revise those parts of my book. But even if I had to sacrifice some of Capra's voice, the loss was minimal, since the reader hears plenty from him otherwise. The facts are retained, and since I am a better writer than Capra, the rewriting process actually helped the book.

Ultimately, I prevailed in my duel with the largest publisher in America and other forces arrayed by the keeper of Capra's flame. Fortunately, book authors have more legal rights than screenwriters. But it took a whole year of legal wrangling to get the book away from Knopf and for it to be acquired by Simon & Schuster through an honest editor, Bob Bender, in 1990. I had to pay $25,000, half of my advance from my new publisher, to exit Random House, which bitterly galled me, but it was worth it. I took a partial leave of absence from *Daily Variety* to make the revisions, which also had to be done because Bender told me it would have been the longest book Simon & Schuster ever published. The book, which I had titled A*merican Madness: The Life of Frank Capra*, had been set in galley proofs by Knopf in 1988 after I revised it down to 1,350 manuscript pages. Ruth scanned the entire set of proofs in Maury's office so I could rewrite it on my word processor.

Was the editing and cutting for a new publisher painful?

That phase, which took three and a half months, actually went rather smoothly. Since scanning introduces minor typographical errors, going through every word of the long manuscript meticulously was good discipline and helped me find more clarity. The Capra book was the first I wrote on a word processor; all my previous books and scripts had been written on my sturdy 1940 Royal upright typewriter, which finally couldn't be repaired any longer. Although my early-model Radio Shack personal computer caused me some problems, I found that my writing improved with the electronic process, since it made editing easier, more inviting and more creative. I wound up cutting about thirty percent of the text, bringing it down to about 300,000 words, or 768 printed pages. As I write in *Frankly*, "Cutting any more would have hurt the book, but when my editing with Bender was finished, I felt it was significantly improved by being more concise and pointed.... I donated the original uncut manuscript to the Wisconsin Historical Society as part of the collection of my papers and will eventually donate the galley proofs of the *American Madness* version."

The book gained from that long gestation process. It was as well-written as I could have managed, and in terms of research, it dotted every "i" and crossed every "t." While demonstrating that there is a lengthy paper trail of documentation on all of us, *Frank Capra: The Catastrophe of Success* also benefited from my interviews with a total of 175 people, many of whom had died before the book was published. In addition to covering Capra's filmmaking, political controversies, World War II service as a maker of propaganda movies for the U.S. Army, and involvement with the Screen Directors Guild and the Academy of Motion Picture Arts and Sciences in the labor battles of the 1930s, I was able to paint a complete picture of the part of a subject's life that usually is lost, his upbringing, with the help of his boyhood friends, schoolmates, and many family members. The opposition I faced from Capra's three surviving children prevented me from covering his life as a father as thoroughly as I would have wished. But though his son Tom said in a 1997 interview on the *Today Show* that he considered the book "a hatchet job," he had to admit, "His research was really good." And Frank Jr. told the British paper *The Guardian*, "I recognise it's very complete. Perhaps there's some reality to it."

I can understand your reluctance to write a book that detailed your brutal battle to get the biography published.

I had been thinking for quite a while about writing *Frankly: Unmasking Frank Capra*. I finally was prompted to do so by Gottlieb publishing his mendacious, self-serving 2016 autobiography, *Avid Reader,* with flap copy that asks, "How does someone become the most celebrated editor of his time?" Since his prefatory note states, "naturally it's one's successes one tends to remember," there's nothing about his debacle with my Capra book. But Gottlieb blithely rhapsodizes over his long and somewhat mystifying friendship with Basinger. I found that rather brazen and couldn't let it go unanswered.

After recalling his fruitful work with one of his other authors, Gottlieb writes, "I've had an even more collaborative relationship with the distinguished Jeanine Basinger, head of the Wesleyan film department and film archive, scholar, expert, and always a joy to be with. The laughs!" (*The laughs*, indeed.) Gottlieb boasts, "I've published her totally satisfying book on *It's a Wonderful Life* (her Wesleyan archive holds all the Frank Capra material)." Gottlieb's memoir also mentions other books by Basinger that Knopf has published (as well as her book on musicals that would come out in 2019), while recounting the joys of their travels together to various distant film archives to watch obscure movies: "Jeanine and I can gab away for hours, and we do, not only about movies but about family, diners, detective stories.… Hollywood has few surprises for her."

Since *Frankly* was published, with positive reviews in *Sight and Sound* and *Cineaste*, Basinger and Gottlieb (who died in 2023 at the age of 92) have nevertheless maintained falsely inflated reputations in most quarters. Basinger, who continues to publish books with Knopf and other publishers, retired from teaching in 2020 and is a professor emerita at Wesleyan, which named a building after her, the Jeanine Basinger Center for Film Studies, the home of the

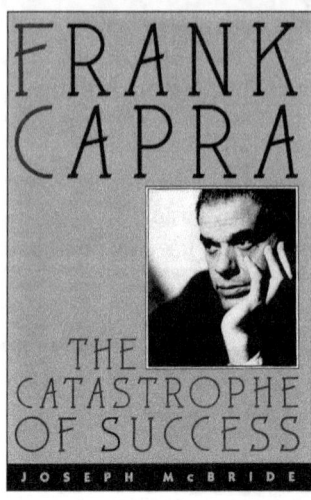

Covers of the first editions of
my biographies
*Frank Capra:
The Catastrophe of Success* (1992),
*Steven Spielberg:
A Biography* (1997), and
Searching for John Ford (2001).
(Simon & Schuster for the first
two/St. Martin's Press
for the third)

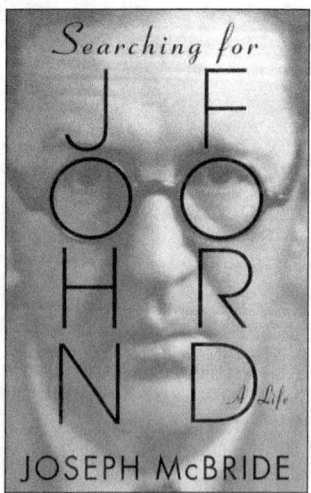

archives. Gottlieb's daughter, Lizzie, celebrated him in a 2022 documentary, *Turn Every Page: The Adventures of Robert Caro and Robert Gottlieb.*

Has there been film interest in Capra's life story?

Tom and Frank Jr. put me into a 1997 documentary feature that whitewashed their father's life, *Frank Capra's American Dream,* which they produced for Sony Pictures (the successor to Capra's longtime home studio, Columbia). They lured me into it through an intermediary without revealing their participation, but I was approached by an Associated Press reporter who debriefed me in a lengthy article about my criticisms of that documentary, which covered Capra's work fairly well but hid most of the darker side of his personality. Much of the same obfuscation was evident when Sony made another, only marginally better documentary in 2023, *Frank Capra: Mr. America,* which at least acknowledged his informing. But I regret I allowed myself to be conned into that film as another talking head. The moral of the story is the old one of "Fool me once, shame on you; fool me twice, shame on me." Whenever I get overtures to make a feature film or a documentary or a TV miniseries from *Frank Capra: The Catastrophe of Success,* the idea continues to be unthinkable.

For me the pinnacle of the book's success, after all the turmoil, was the thoughtful appreciation from Barry Gewen in the lead review of the *New York Times Book Review.* But even more gratifying was a response from one of the blacklisted writers who had worked with Capra, the novelist, historian, and *Why We Fight* screenwriter John Sanford, a lifelong member of the Communist Party. Capra had offered John an officer's commission in his U.S. Army unit but dropped him when Army Intelligence objected, a situation I chronicle in the book with the help of letters between them at the time. I came to know John well as a friend and admirer of his books.

After leaving *Daily Variety* and returning from a trip to Texas to research the assassination of President Kennedy, I spent several months in 1993 writing a lengthy essay about Sanford's work, doing my best to rescue him from his undeserved obscurity. "John Sanford's Personal History of America" shows what my career would have been like if I had pursued my early interest in literary criticism instead of concentrating on film. I finally published my essay on Sanford in *Two Cheers for Hollywood* after my intended outlet, *The New York Review of Books,* rejected it. To my disgust, editor

Barbara Epstein told me simply that Sanford was, quote, "an old lefty." (I also include in *Two Cheers* my profile from *Written By* of John's wife, screenwriter Marguerite Roberts.)

Shortly before *Frank Capra: The Catastrophe of Success* was published in April 1992, John sent me this letter:

> I just finished your biography of Frank Capra, and I want you to know without delay that I think it excellent. Over the past several years, in connection with my own writing, I've read biographies by the dozen, but none that I can recall did more than acquaint me with the story of a life. You made me feel that I was witnessing a tragedy made inevitable by reason of Capra's very nature. I'd known little of him before-hand, and it was your writing that made me perceive a man of great ability brought down by his innate fatal flaws. It wasn't the times, it wasn't the stars, it wasn't the ways of the world—it was Capra himself that was Capra's undoing, and relentlessly and truly you chronicled his fall.
>
> I say truly because I mean truly. I don't think you rejoiced in the fall; I think you deplored it. I think you deeply wished that there could've been a better second half to Capra's life, but knowing that it was otherwise, you chronicled it with sadness but with a clear eye. In doing so, you accomplished a wonder: you made me pity a man much of whose character I despised. That's art, Joe, and I congratulate you. It's a first-rate book, and I hope it's widely read.

That Aristotelian dimension of classical tragedy is what I was trying to achieve.

Steven Spielberg

What made you choose Steven Spielberg as your next biographical subject after Frank Capra? Your previous bios were about directors who were revered by most critics, but at the time, before he made Schindler's List, *Spielberg was not. Did you see a connection between Spielberg and Capra, as you did between Welles and Ford?*

There's a videotaped conversation of Capra and Spielberg meeting in the 1970s, in which the first thing Capra asks the younger director is, "What's with you, except success?"

Good question; I set out to answer it. The way Spielberg handles success so much better than Capra managed to do was one of the elements of his life that intrigued me. Writing a biography of Spielberg appealed to me as a much more pleasant job than writing the tragic life of Frank Capra for seven and a half years. And it was an intriguing change to write about a subject who's less than a year older than I am. Spielberg and I have many cultural experiences in common, including boyhood crushes on the same three female members of *The Mickey Mouse Club*: Karen (Pendleton), Darlene (Gillespie), and Annette (Funicello). Spielberg's relative youth also meant that I would be able to access so many people from his early life, which makes the book of increasing value as other biographies are written. My *Steven Spielberg: A Biography* was published in 1997 by Simon & Schuster and has been updated twice, for 2010 and 2012 editions.

It was long after writing my biographies of Capra, Spielberg, and Ford that I realized I was subconsciously pursuing a common theme in all these books: How someone deals with his ethnicity. These three filmmakers were preoccupied with their ethnicity but had dealt with it in different ways—rejection of his Italian American roots by Capra; prideful embrace of his Irish American heritage by Ford; and in Spielberg's case, his boyhood ambivalence toward his Judaism eventually being resolved in adulthood. And I came to understand why I had focused on that theme. As a boy in Wisconsin, I was raised to be proud of being Irish American, and yet it was still a time when people were encouraged to lose their ethnic characteristics in the "melting pot" of American homogeneity. That flattening pressure to assimilate at all costs (to which Ford was immune, a rarity in his time) largely went out the door when Alex Haley's 1976 novel, *Roots: The Saga of an American Family*, caused people of every background to feel renewed pride in their ancestry.

I had never gone as far as believing wholeheartedly in the melting pot propaganda, but in my youth I suffered from discomfort about being a Midwesterner. As I mentioned earlier, while seeing myself as the sophisticated son of intellectual parents, I looked down snobbishly on some of my fellow Wisconsinites as hayseeds while I in turn was treated with disdain, as a supposed hick, by some fellow students from other parts of the country when I went to college in Madison and by some people I encountered in California. I had to overcome those feelings of snobbery and shame as I matured. I moved west partly to escape what I felt was the stigma of my geographical and cultural background. But I gradually came to accept my complex identity, not without a sense of defiance yet also with some equanimity. So my exploration of such themes in my three biographies and the disparate paths of my subjects struck a deep chord in me and, bearing out Leon Edel's theory, made them "choose" me as their biographer.

But most of all, what motivated me to write a biography of Spielberg was that though he is one of the greatest American directors, he was such a pariah with film reviewers and film scholars when I decided in the early 1990s to write my book.

Before you wrote your book, Spielberg had directed a bunch of great films that also happened to be box-office blockbusters—Jaws, Close Encounters of the Third Kind, Raiders of the Lost Ark, E.T. The Extra-Terrestrial, *and* Jurassic Park. *Many serious critics made the mistake of disdaining films that were commercial hits even when they were also works of art. And many weren't swayed when he made a* great noncommercial *film such as* Empire of the Sun. *So I was delighted that you, a very serious critic, came to his defense in your 1997 biography.*

He was routinely dismissed and often denigrated by reviewers in the harshest terms for his subject matter, including his thematic concentration on broken families, his yearning for the reconstruction of nuclear families, his fascination with children, and other cultural crimes, but especially because he was so popular. The charge that he achieved such popularity by allegedly "manipulating" his audience even led some critics to smear this Jewish filmmaker by viciously comparing him with Nazi propagandist Leni Riefenstahl. Such intemperate attacks reminded me of the contempt American popular filmmakers such as Hitchcock, Hawks, and Ford provoked in American reviewers before our generation of cinephiles came along in the late 1960s and reversed that tendency. I felt that the mistreatment of Spielberg was reminiscent of that cultural myopia I thought we had dispelled.

So I was driven to right the wrong being done to Spielberg and to film history. As with most of my books, I was motivated to write this biography both because I thought it was needed but also because I was angry over the overall injustice being done to the subject. I felt like John Ford when he was asked by Emanuel Eisenberg in a 1936 interview for *New Theatre,* "Then you do believe, as a director, in including your point of view in a picture about

My biography of Steven Spielberg extensively covers his early filmmaking activities in Phoenix, Arizona, including at his home, which
his parents said wryly he had converted into a studio. He shot parts
of his first feature, the 1964 sci-fi film *Firelight*, in the carport. I paid
another visit to their former home in 1997 while promoting the book.
(Kendall Hailey)

things that bother you?" Ford replied, "What the hell else
does a man live for?" As an author, what I have always lived
for is that same spirit of compulsion to include my point
of view on a wrong I find being perpetrated or a situation
of neglect or misunderstanding. Before I began writing my
critical biography *Steven Spielberg: A Biography* in 1993,
there had been no full-scale Spielberg biography and had
never even been an adequate critical study. There were some
children's biographies, and for adults there was a slender
volume by British author Tony Crawley in 1983, *The
Steven Spielberg Story: The Man Behind the Movies*, which
was based mostly on quotes from previously published
interviews with Spielberg.

I knew that here was another story that had never been
told properly. As with the untold true story of Capra's
life, I felt that by writing a serious, in-depth biography of
Spielberg, with ample research including the viewpoints of
many other people who knew him, I would be inventing
the wheel. The British scholar Nigel Morris, who wrote
the best critical study of Spielberg in 2007, *The Cinema
of Steven Spielberg: Empire of Light*, has called me "the
godfather of Spielberg studies." I earned that designation
because I had the chutzpah to defy the conventional critical
wisdom of the 1990s and write about him with the same
scholarly approach I had devoted to Capra's life and to
the work of Welles and Ford. I hoped that by doing so I

would not only elevate the attitude of reviewers and others toward Spielberg, encouraging them to treat his work with the respect it was due, but also, by examining the sources of his work and treating it analytically in my biography, to prompt other scholars to write critical studies of him.

Although it was *Schindler's List*, released in 1993 a few months after I began work on my book, that made most reviewers see Spielberg in a different light (even if that great film was not without its mostly misguided detractors, whom I answer in my biography), I was pleased to find that my influence on the critical community was largely as I had hoped. My work helped lead to Morris's book as well as to thoughtful critical studies by Lester D. Friedman, Warren Buckland, Linda Ruth Williams, et al. Morris and Friedman were among those who invited me to be the keynote speaker at the first international conference on Spielberg at the University of Lincoln in the UK, "Spielberg at Sixty," in 2007. That gratifying event drew younger participants who discussed the director appreciatively, without the defensiveness that a few years earlier might have colored such an undertaking. I adapted my address into a 2009 essay on what Morris's book calls the "extraordinary vindictiveness" of Spielberg's enemies, or what I call the phenomenon of Spielberg hatred, "A Reputation: Steven Spielberg and the Eyes of the World," for the *New Review of Film and Television Studies*. I include material from that essay in the third edition of my biography, which was published in the UK by Faber and Faber as well as in China.

How far back does your interest in Spielberg go?

It began early. I had read about this unusually young director in *Variety* and thought of calling him for an interview when I went to Hollywood for the second time in the spring of 1971 to work on *The Other Side of the Wind* but unfortunately ran out of time. And when I saw his TV movie *Something Evil* in January 1972, I recognized in its flamboyantly surrealistic visual imagery that this was a major talent behind the camera. Revisiting that film many years later, I was most struck by Spielberg's seldom-recognized talent with actors, since he brought out a startlingly real performance from Sandy Dennis as a deranged mother, one of the early examples of his off-and-on fascination with that theme, which he also follows in his tragicomic 1974 feature starring Goldie Hawn, *The Sugarland Express*. Although *Something Evil*, which deals with demonic possession, evidently was designed as a takeoff on Roman Polanski's

1968 film, *Rosemary's Baby* (from the novel by Ira Levin), and William Peter Blatty's bestselling 1971 novel, *The Exorcist, Something Evil* also seems like Spielberg's underrated precursor to Stanley Kubrick's 1980 horror film, *The Shining,* based on the Stephen King novel that locates evil within the family, as well as to William Friedkin's 1973 film version of *The Exorcist.*

I spent an hour in Spielberg's company one night in the summer of 1975 in the Universal commissary as part of a group of reporters talking with him about *Jaws,* and I attended the sensational first Hollywood screening of that landmark film on April 24 at the Cinerama Dome before its June opening, recognizing immediately that it would be a huge hit. I remember wistfully regretting that, as a member of the trade press, I couldn't invest in MCA stock, which was sure to jump in value. When I watched Hitchcock shooting *Family Plot* at Universal in 1975, I saw him eagerly getting daily reports on the box-office performance of *Jaws,* since he was a major stockholder in MCA. Even so, he refused Spielberg's request to let him kibitz during the filming; Spielberg earlier had been kicked off the set of *Torn Curtain.*

E.T. The Extra-Terrestrial was released in 1982 and surpassed *Star Wars* as the highest-grossing film in history, as well as making Spielberg a household name. During that time I thought of doing his biography but concluded it would be premature because he was only thirty-five when the film was released. (Around that time I was also considering writing a biography of Roman Polanski, but a woman I was dating told me she was planning to write one herself. So I unwisely deferred to her, and she never wrote her book. Don't tell anyone what book you are writing.)

What eventually tipped me over the edge in making me propose the Spielberg book to my editor, Bob Bender, to follow my Capra biography at Simon & Schuster was the news that Spielberg was finally going to shoot *Schindler's List,* the Holocaust film based on Thomas Kenneally's nonfiction novel. Spielberg had been anxiously hesitating to make the film ever since Sid Sheinberg, his mentor at Universal, purchased the film rights with him in mind when that book was published in 1982. I saw Spielberg's decision to go ahead with that profoundly challenging project as a culmination and turning point in his life and career and a reflection of his largely unappreciated character.

Until then the prospect of dealing with such harrowing material and handling it with the maturity it required was too daunting for Spielberg, even though he had made *Empire*

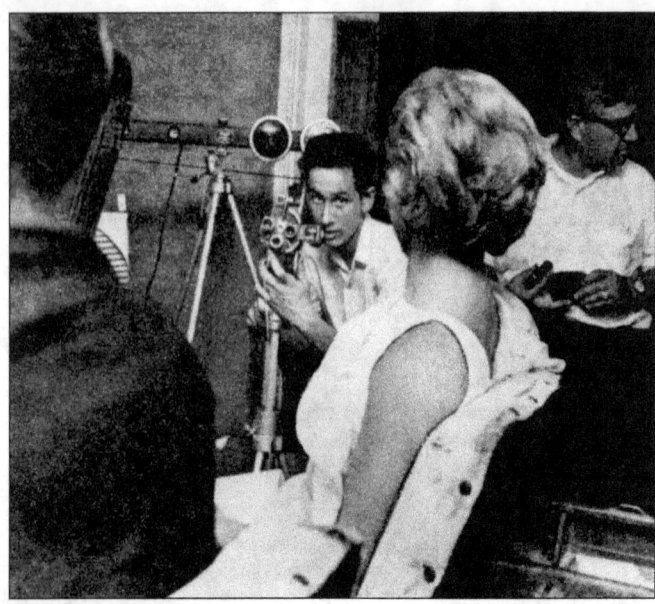

Spielberg shooting a night scene with his mother's Jeep in *Firelight*, his predecessor to *Close Encounters of the Third Kind*, in the family carport in 1963, as his father, Arnold, assists. After my biography was published in 1997, Steven began acknowledging his father's contributions to his early work. The leading lady of *Firelight* was Carol Stromme (foreground), but she quit and was replaced by Beth Weber Zelenski. (Ralph Camping, *The Arizona Republic*, Phoenix Newspapers, Inc.)

of the Sun, another searing film set in World War II. But he had internalized some of the criticism that he couldn't make a "serious, mature, adult film" even though he had been doing so since, at least, his 1971 television episode "Par for the Course." Spielberg's favorite of his episodic TV work was part of the series *The Psychiatrist* and deals with a golfer dying of cancer (played by Clu Gulager) and how his wife (played by Joan Darling) copes with her loss. Spielberg's trenchant Hollywood theatrical feature debut, *The Sugarland Express*, is also a serious, mature, adult work; it failed commercially because of its tragic ending and the casting against type of Goldie Hawn as the pathologically unfit mother, which angered members of the audience who were expecting a fluffy comedy.

When I made an exception in 1987 to my boycott of contemporary movies while writing the Capra book to see *Empire of the Sun*, Spielberg's masterful film from J. G. Ballard's semi-autobiographical novel about a British boy (Christian Bale) engulfed in the war, I thought the charge of artistic immaturity against the director was even more wrongheaded and baffling. So with the critical acclaim for the Capra biography behind me and my solid arguments about Spielberg's largely unrecognized importance, I did not find it difficult to convince Bender that it was time for a serious treatment of his life and work. When *Schindler's List* appeared to great critical acclaim and widespread commercial acceptance, Bob hailed my prescience in getting the book underway before that film started shooting.

That film also convinced Hollywood to "forgive" Spielberg, as he wryly put it in 1986 to a reporter from an Israeli newspaper: "When I'm sixty, Hollywood will forgive me—I don't know for what, but they'll forgive." He won his first Oscars for producing and directing *Schindler's List* (a film made when he was forty-six), and though he richly deserved those awards, I could not help wishing he had not been so emotionally overwhelmed on that occasion after the Academy had so cruelly snubbed him in the past. Spielberg's candid accounts while being interviewed about his psychological journey in shedding his youthful shame over being Jewish and coming to embrace his ethnic heritage with *Schindler's List* helped influence my thematic concentration on that evolution. I found that his acceptance of his identity provided a marked contrast with Capra's flight from his identity as an Italian American immigrant and helped account for why Spielberg is a more integrated personality, less at odds with himself and more successful in coping with the stresses of his profession and his obligations to the world.

How did Spielberg react to your writing an unauthorized biography about him?

Because I was still traumatized by the experience of writing and getting the Capra biography published—the PTSD from that experience will never leave me entirely—I took the precaution of interviewing a hundred people about Spielberg before I wrote his in-house publicist, Marvin Levy, in March 1994 to request an interview with the director. I made the point of stressing that I was writing an unauthorized, strictly independent biography. As I wrote in my acknowledgments, Levy, a gentlemanly fellow I knew from my trade press days, "replied in a telephone call on March 18 that while Spielberg knew my work and realized that I was writing a serious book, he had a policy of not talking with anyone writing a book about him because of his plans to write his autobiography. 'He'd be happy if there are *no* books' about him, Levy pointed out, but added, 'He's not going to stop *you* from writing a book.'"

Spielberg was largely true to his word: His office helpfully told people who called asking if they should cooperate with me that I was "kosher," which opened doors. I've still never spoken with Spielberg about my book, which is mostly favorable but also candidly criticizes his flaws, including a serious misdeed involving his lying about his age, a complicated story I discovered in my research that provoked a successful lawsuit against him. But a director who worked with Spielberg told me that because of the book's serious and mostly positive treatment, "Steven loves you, loves you, loves you, *loves* you."

I would guess that the crucial subject of his parents' divorce was foremost among the topics Spielberg wouldn't want to talk about with a biographer. How did your research for your book allow you to anticipate their later public revelations on the family breakup?

Spielberg's Amblin Entertainment and DreamWorks staff did ask a few people to save their reminiscences for his autobiography, which he still has not written all these years later, unless you count his semi-autobiographical 2022 film, *The Fabelmans*, which he wrote with Tony Kushner. But not all of those people followed their wishes. Spielberg asked his mother, Leah Adler, not to talk to me, and she was graciously apologetic. I had already interviewed his father, Arnold, who had rarely spoken with interviewers, and he was generous in providing background on the family history as well as commenting on his relationship with his son. The saddest experience I had while doing the book came when Arnold told me, "You know more about Steve than I do."

In my three years of work on the book, I interviewed 327 people, including many who knew the Spielbergs when they lived in Phoenix from 1957 to 1964 and launched his career as an amateur filmmaker. Before interviewing his father, I had already learned from other interviewees that Arnold had participated far more actively and positively in his son's upbringing than Steven cared to remember, including as a collaborator in their early filmmaking activities. The family breakup due to his parents' divorce had long been the traumatic engine that fueled Spielberg's film work, and previous reporting on the subject had been distorted, partly because of Steven's selective memory of those events. He had become estranged from his father and publicly blamed the divorce on Arnold's absorption in his work as a computer engineer, which was a factor in the family breakup but not the whole story. While uncovering a fuller picture of what had happened, I sought with my book to encourage Steven's reconciliation with his father, which was such an epochal event that it made the cover of *Life* magazine in 1999.

As part of my research, I obtained his parents' 1966 divorce records, which surprisingly revealed that Arnold and Leah agreed he would have custody of Steven and would support his son when the two of them moved to Southern California and shared an apartment in Brentwood. The property division provided that Arnold would keep sentimental items such as his mother's samovar. A samovar can be seen in the father and son's apartment in *The Fabelmans*. All of Steven's possessions went with them to southern California, including what is noted in the settlement agreement as "Steven's camera 'dolly.'"

I was able to piece together in my book much of the actual story about the parents' breakup, although I had to be somewhat circumspect with it. I found that when his mother fell in love with another man, Bernie Adler, Steven had primarily blamed *her* at the time for the resulting family breakup and not his father, contrary to what had been reported elsewhere over the years. And his understanding that his mother was mostly responsible is how the rupture is shown in *The Fabelmans*. The film's centerpiece is Spielberg's youthful surrogate, Sam Fabelman, played by Gabriel LaBelle, accidentally capturing with his camera his mother's casual intimacy on a family camping trip with the man she loved—"Mitzi" and "Bennie" are played by Michelle Williams and Seth Rogen—and Sam's subsequent stunned recognition of its implications when he edits the footage in his bedroom. It's a telling juxtaposition of scenes that captures how that trauma has haunted Spielberg's filmmaking ever since.

But over the years, Steven had been influenced by his father's assumption of blame for the divorce, which had been said to have resulted from his being a workaholic and neglecting his wife. Although that was true enough, the problem ran deeper than Arnold had admitted at the time. "I think I was just protecting her, because I was in love with her," Arnold revealed in a 2012 interview on *60 Minutes*. Leah confessed in that interview with Lesley Stahl that she had prompted the divorce by falling in love with Bernie, Arnold's best friend and fellow computer engineer, whom she married not long after the divorce. (Arnold, called "Burt" in the movie, is played by Paul Dano.) What I did not know, however, was the dramatic way Steven figured out what was happening, which is depicted in that powerful centerpiece of *The Fabelmans*; he has confirmed that is how he actually learned the truth.

Steven's falling-out with his father came later, partly due to his belief that Arnold was to blame for the divorce but also due to their friction while living together in Brentwood. As Tom Tugend reported after interviewing Arnold in 2012 for *Jewish Journal*, "Steven was working on his short film *Amblin'*, which later became his introductory card to Universal Studios, and commandeered the father's living room to store and edit his footage. Arnold, at the time recently divorced, was beginning to see other women and objected to Steven barging into the living room for his editing chores when the father was entertaining a date. There was a heated argument, and Steven moved out and relocated to Long Beach, where he was attending the local state university." Steven said in the *Life* feature about their reconciliation, "And when my father remarried, it separated us even further. I didn't like the person he married." So he stopped telephoning his father. "In my heart, I loved my Dad. But resentment can build up layers and barriers, and I just felt more comfortable not thinking about it." He eventually began rethinking the situation after his mother told him, "You know, this was not all your Dad's fault. It was my fault, too."

Early in his professional career, Steven featured irresponsible or distracted mother figures in his films (*Duel*, *Something Evil*, *The Sugarland Express*, *Close Encounters*, *E.T.*), but he gradually turned to concentrating on flawed father figures who neglect their families and need a dramatic comeuppance. His eventual reconciliation with his father is incorporated cinematically in one of his most underrated films, *Amistad*, which was released in 1997, later in the same year my Spielberg biography was published. In a scene that takes on a dual meaning and goes beyond the immediate text, former President John Quincy Adams (movingly played by Anthony Hopkins) invokes the memory of his late father, our second president, John Adams, in his closing argument defending a group of African captives before the U.S. Supreme Court in 1841. In doing so, he alludes to an insight the captive Cinqué (played by Djimon Hounsou) has given him about the importance of summoning one's ancestors in times of crisis.

Surrounded by busts and paintings of John Adams and the other Founding Fathers, whose stated ideals in the Declaration of Independence became compromised in practice, the aged John Quincy Adams addresses the founders: "We have long resisted asking you for guidance.

Spielberg dramatized his youthful filmmaking in Phoenix in
The Fabelmans, the semiautobiographical 2022 film he wrote with
Tony Kushner. Gabriel LaBelle plays Steven's alter ego,
Sam Fabelman, in this scene recreating the shooting of the
award-winning 1962 World War II film, *Escape to Nowhere*.
(Amblin Entertainment/Reliance Entertainment/Universal)

Perhaps we have feared in doing so, we might acknowledge that our individuality, which we so, so revere, is not entirely our own. Perhaps we've feared an appeal to you might be taken for weakness. But we have come to understand, finally, that this is not so. We understand now, we've been made to understand, and to embrace the understanding, that who we are *is* who we were." As I write in my book, the camera tracks in toward Adams as he reaches that key line in his speech, and "The emphatic camera movement, the gravity of the performance, and the centrality of the idea to Spielberg's body of work come together to make this the climactic moment of his career. The filmmaker's obsessive, career-long theme of struggle with flawed father figures is, symbolically, put to rest in this moment of intergenerational acceptance."

And it is no coincidence that Spielberg followed *Amistad* with a tribute to his father's generation of World War II veterans, *Saving Private Ryan,* and that his films soon went back to focusing on irresponsible mother figures rather than father figures. Such films as *A.I. Artificial Intelligence*, *Catch Me If You Can*, *Munich*, and *Lincoln* give us troubled mother figures who exhibit the disturbing centrifugal force Mitzi displays in *The Fabelmans*. The son's extreme emotional reaction to Mitzi's behavior in the camping sequence hints at why the family separation is so enduringly powerful for the director. There is a strong erotic component to Sam's anger over what he perceives as his mother's betrayal. That camping sequence in which her secret is revealed also includes the mother's sexy dance in a diaphanous gown, provoking disapproval of her display from one of his sisters as Sam films it, mesmerized by the spectacle.

The Fabelmans has an underlying and sometimes overt emphasis on what I learned while writing *The Broken Places*: the element of growth that Eugene O'Neill said is a necessary step toward full adulthood, forgiving your parents. And as Spielberg achieved more acceptance with his peers, began putting his youthful trauma in perspective, became more comfortable with his Jewishness, and had all the worldly success anyone could need, his drive to be popular, the drive that made him a filmmaker, lessened, and he has been able to pursue his more idiosyncratic creative impulses. In the process of his maturation as a man and a filmmaker, he has to some degree lost his audience or left it behind. The later Spielberg work—which broadened its focus after the events of 9/11 to concentrate for a time on the most anguished meditations by any filmmaker on the changes in our country—has gone off in fascinatingly different directions as he explores other facets of his creative interests.

My only partial reconstruction of the complex events surrounding Steven's key youthful experience, despite my strenuous efforts, reveals the limits of the biographical enterprise, especially when it involves a living subject and people around him who are still alive when the book is being written. Perhaps that is one reason Steven told his mother not to talk with me, although she had been interviewed so frequently that I was able to incorporate her voice into the book. It took Spielberg a long time to overcome his reluctance to tell the whole story of the family breakup in *The Fabelmans*, although he had dealt with aspects of the divorce or echoes of that romantic situation in most of his films, most notably in *Catch Me If You Can*. That story—as adapted for the 2002 movie from a dubious memoir of a con-man about his youthful scams and fraught relationship with his parents—was also regarded by Spielberg as partly autobiographical.

In another example of the intricate interplay between myth and reality, however, I learned the truth behind what I call the "creation myth" Spielberg relates about how he supposedly broke into filmmaking by impersonating a studio employee and setting himself up in an empty office at Universal. It was a story he retold in relation to the protagonist's impersonations in *Catch Me If You Can*. I found that the story is a significant embellishment on his mundane activities as an intern for studio film librarian Chuck Silvers, his first Hollywood mentor, from the summer of 1964 onward. The "creation myth" is also a way of concealing the fact that Steven's father helped him get his *entrée* into the studio, a more common way people break into the business. Such creation myths are so seductive that despite my debunking of Spielberg's yarn, many people still cling to it, and Spielberg himself seems to have come to believe it.

But he leaves that fable out of *The Fabelmans* and focuses instead on the wonderful scene of his meeting as a teenager with John Ford—a story Spielberg had told before on film and videotape—and a portrayal of the veteran director by David Lynch that I can personally attest seems authentic. I had an hour with Ford, and Spielberg had only a few minutes, but in both encounters, our idol was the same mixture of gruffness and parting kindness. When Ford gives Sam Fabelman his benediction, it marks the young filmmaker's acceptance by Hollywood.

His film is not called The Spielbergs, *but* The Fabelmans, *so how closely did Spielberg duplicate other actual events?*

As I found in my research for the biography, Spielberg became a filmmaker because he desperately needed acceptance into the mainstream society, and he made films with the other kids to fit in and receive approval, as well as to neutralize bullies and jocks whom he cleverly cast in his films in order to control them and his environment. He always felt like an outsider because he was Jewish and living in progressively more WASPy environments, from his Cincinnati origins in a Jewish neighborhood to New Jersey to Phoenix to Saratoga (California) to Los Angeles. That meant five sets of interviewing and other research for me, and I enjoyed following Spielberg's journey. His drive for acceptance was hampered by the increasing anti-Semitism he faced in Phoenix and Saratoga, which complicated his drive but also intensified it.

But in *The Fabelmans*, the anti-Semitism is limited to a handful of punks in a fictionalized version of Saratoga, not Phoenix. Although the Phoenix section memorably shows the making of Spielberg's award-winning World War II film *Escape to Nowhere*, it also leaves out his major youthful achievement in 1963 and '64, *Firelight*, perhaps because the making of his first feature deserves a movie in itself. In an article I was asked to write by the online magazine *Slant* about how closely *The Fabelmans* does and does not follow

Spielberg's actual life story, I wrote that *The Fabelmans* is a "lightly fictionalized autobiography" like *The 400 Blows* by François Truffaut, a Spielberg role model he directed in *Close Encounters of the Third Kind*.

With that "protective coloration," as I wrote in the article, *The Fabelmans* "provides another layer of mythification in Spielberg's life, or, to put it more positively, imaginative rewriting.... The fictional veneer, in these cases, also allows the filmmakers to accuse some of the guilty parties who made their adolescences 'hell on Earth.' That was the phrase Spielberg used to describe the year he spent at Saratoga High School in Northern California, where he suffered his most acute episodes of antisemitic bullying, painfully reenacted.... Altering reality to heighten one's life story, explore deeper truths, and make it come out the way one wishes it might have happened are among the purposes of autobiographical dramatization. Mostly Spielberg hews closely to the events and spirit of his youth, albeit with the compression, omission, and conflation that's necessary even in a movie that runs 151 minutes."

I pointed out that among the mysteries I ran up against in writing Spielberg's life story were "the identities of the antisemitic bullies who tormented him" not only in Saratoga but also in Phoenix. I noted that in the Phoenix section of *The Fabelmans* about Spielberg making his amateur war movie *Escape to Nowhere* on Camelback Mountain, we "see a John Wayne—like jock [played by Stephen Matthew Smith] being coaxed into acting in *Escape to Nowhere* but miss the social context that preceded it." That scene, however, offers a key to Spielberg's development because it shows how he learned to direct actors, which I argue in my book is his most underrated ability. The confrontation between a northern California bully (played by Sam Rechner) and Sam Fabelman in the school hallway—caused by the jock's anger at how he thinks he is mocked in ironic footage of a graduation beach party in Sam's movie *Senior Ditch Day*—seems fictionalized for dramatic effect, as a further motivating factor in the Spielberg surrogate's drive for success. Spielberg earlier recalled that the actual tormentor, after seeing his film *Senior Sneak Day*, "came over a changed person. He said the movie had made him laugh and that he wished he'd gotten to know me better."

Your research helped uncover the fact that Steven was lying about his age. What's the story on that and why is it so significant?

Even Arnold Spielberg wondered in our interview why "Steve lies about his age." While separating myth from fact in Spielberg's life, I performed the most basic task of a biographer, finding out the subject's birthdate. I dispelled his longtime lie that he had been born in 1947, not 1946. A former girlfriend of mine, journalist Patricia Goldstone, had discovered the correct date from college records while researching an article for the *Los Angeles Times* in 1981, and it had appeared occasionally in some publications earlier in his career before the false date was accepted. But why did Spielberg maintain the pretense that he was born a year later?

I figured there was a complicated story involved, and it turned out to be a sad one that explains certain mysterious events about his early life. Practicing Journalism 101, I called the Cincinnati Board of Health in 1994 and sent eight dollars for Spielberg's birth certificate, which verified that he had been born on December 18, 1946. Then I pieced together the story from my interviews with people who had known and worked with the young Spielberg at Universal.

Chuck Silvers was the only person at the studio willing to watch the 8mm films Steve made in Phoenix or the 16mm films he was making at California State College at Long Beach. Silvers told his intern that to be taken seriously, he had to make a professional-looking film in 35mm. Julie Raymond, a purchasing agent who worked with Steve in the office, knew a young man named Denis C. Hoffman who owned an optical and title company, had a small commercial studio, managed a rock band, and had $20,000 to invest in making a short film that would be Denis's own calling-card production as well as Steve's (back then he was called Steve, not Steven).

Steve made the short *Amblin'* for Hoffman in the summer of 1968, when he was twenty-one. That fine film is a lyrical and bittersweet romance about two youthful hitchhikers, played by Pamela McMyler and Richard Levin. Levin bears a strong resemblance to Spielberg, and the film is autobiographical in dealing with the young man's ruthless ambition to get to Los Angeles and, according to his sister Anne, who worked as the script supervisor, in Steve's depiction of Levin as a square masquerading as a hippie. After Silvers arranged for Sid Sheinberg, then the vice-president of production for Universal TV, to see *Amblin'*, it brought Spielberg his first contract with Universal as a TV director that December, shortly before he turned twenty-two on December 18, 1968. *Amblin'* had a theatrical release, debuting on that birthday of Spielberg's, with Hoffman throwing a premiere party for the director, but the *Los Angeles Times* reported the next day that Spielberg was twenty-one. Spielberg later suppressed this remarkably beautiful twenty-six-minute silent film (with music by Hoffman's rock group, October Country). Spielberg has unfairly disparaged *Amblin'* in retrospect as "a great Pepsi commercial" with "as much soul and content as a piece of driftwood," but it's the most mature love story he has ever filmed, as well as a thoughtful reflection on the changing mores of that turbulent period.

When Hoffman and Spielberg signed their September 1968 agreement for Spielberg to make *Amblin'*, Spielberg, although he wasn't paid for that job opportunity, had to promise to direct, for a modest fee, a feature film Hoffman would produce during the next ten years. But a lawsuit Hoffman filed in 1995 alleged that he was defrauded by "a deliberate and outrageous lie perpetrated by defendant Spielberg in a calculated and malicious scheme to avoid his legal obligations." After Spielberg's professional career took off, he avoided Hoffman's attempts for years to make a feature together, according to the lawsuit. Eventually, after *Jaws* became a blockbuster hit in June 1975, Spielberg and his attorney, Bruce Ramer, allegedly told Hoffman that the director had been a minor, only twenty, when he had signed their contract, making him unable to enter into a contract under California law. Believing that assertion, Hoffman, in 1977, accepted a $30,000 buyout offer from Spielberg for all rights to *Amblin'*, including the right to use the title of the film for the name of his production company.

Then I came along in 1994 and, deciding to spill my scoop about Spielberg's age in order to get more information for my book, I told Hoffman that Spielberg was *not* underage when he signed the contract but was actually twenty-one. Hoffman was stunned and asked me for a copy of the birth certificate. Wanting to keep my name out of it, I told him how to obtain that public record. Hoffman did so and sued Spielberg in 1995 for "fraud and deceit" and sought damages for the "many millions of dollars" a producing credit on a Spielberg feature might have been worth to his career. When the story broke in the press, Spielberg received a lot of head-wagging publicity wondering why he had been lying about his age; *Premiere* magazine joked that his film *1941* would now be known as *1942*. But the director never explained why he had lied, and I suggested why in the book.

Eventually, as the case wound its way through court, a judge ruled in Hoffman's favor. Hoffman called me from Acapulco and thanked me for making him a millionaire. The case did turn up more revelations that helped my book, and I was glad to have brought some justice for Hoffman. Yet he seemed saddened by the turn of events, evidently because he had felt Spielberg was his friend and had not expected him to be deceitful about the contract they had signed. Hoffman had spent his life running a Hollywood doughnut shop (with Spielberg's financial participation) but never got to produce a feature film, let alone a Spielberg feature.

What else did you learn through research?

The story surrounding Spielberg lying about his age was just one of many revelations I turned up in my research, which led me into much previously uncovered terrain, although most of it reflected well on him. Many of the people from Spielberg's boyhood whom I approached for interviews told me they had been waiting thirty years for the doorbell to ring. Like me, they wondered why this wonderful story of a kid filmmaker who taught himself how to become a genius had never really been told before. Billy Wilder quipped, not inaccurately, that Steven Spielberg was a great filmmaker when he was ten years old. I had fun tracing the colorful origin story of what had already been a forty-year film career (by the time of the book's publication in 1997) with the enthusiastic help of the men and women he had coaxed as boys and girls into being actors in and crew members on the increasingly ambitious amateur films he made while growing up in Phoenix, culminating in *Firelight*.

I love the scenes in The Fabelmans *of young Sam making amateur films with his classmates. Did your interview subjects remember him that way?*

The most spectacular story was the one I open the book with, the making of *Firelight*, a sci-fi prototype of *Close Encounters*. Spielberg wrote the corny script for his first feature—I obtained a copy from his leading lady, Beth Weber Zelenski—and shot the film with his father's help in 1963 in the desert, on Camelback Mountain. Steve used his family carport as a studio and hand-crafted ingenious special effects with his father. Allen Daviau, the cinematographer who shot such Spielberg films as *Amblin'*, *E.T.*, *The Color Purple*, and *Empire of the Sun*, was shown *Firelight* by Spielberg in the late 1960s. Daviau told me, "It's what you expect with a kid's film, the acting and so on, but oh, God! Some of it was so audacious. The effects were what was really amazing—that's what his heart was in. What he did with crumpled aluminum foil and bits of Jell-O on a kitchen table was pretty amazing." *Firelight*, complete with dubbed dialogue, music, and sound effects, triumphantly premiered at the Phoenix Little Theatre in March 1964 and made back its under-$600 cost, on the night before the Spielbergs moved to northern California.

One of the kids who worked on an earlier Spielberg film, a World War II short called *Fighter Squad*, was Steve Suggs. He was a jock and not close to Spielberg before he was asked to go to the local airport. Suggs told me,

> Somehow Steve had arranged access to a fighter and a bomber! He took a shot of me in the fighter with ketchup coming out of my mouth when I was shot. He had a script; he knew what he was doing. It wasn't just the boys going out and screwing around—he knew how to deal with people.
>
> I remember telling my mom about it afterward. Here was this kid who was sort of a nerd and wasn't one of the cool guys; he got out there and suddenly he was *in charge*. He became a totally different person, so much so that I as a seventh grader was impressed. He had all the football players out there, all the neat guys, and he was telling *them* what to do. An hour ago at home or on the campus he was the guy you kicked dirt in his eyes.
>
> It was miraculous. It just blew me away. It's as if you hear this nerd play piano and suddenly he's Van Cliburn.

What were the advantages and drawbacks of writing about a living subject?

There were many benefits, because if your subject is alive, so are many people who knew him, going back to his childhood. I was able to talk with Steven's father, schoolteachers, adult neighbors who knew him as a child, even babysitters. (What I would give to have been able to talk with Capra's parents!) But there are some drawbacks. Despite being able to paint an extraordinarily rich and detailed portrait of the Artist as Young Filmmaker and thoroughly documenting his apprenticeship in television, it became increasingly difficult, as the account of Spielberg's career advanced, to find colleagues who were willing to talk about him. The longer ago people worked with Spielberg—such as on his episodic television shows and TV movies, including his groundbreaking and career-making 1971 classic *Duel*—

the more accessible they were, since they generally didn't expect to work with him again and wanted to ensure that posterity knew of their contributions.

But it was hit-and-miss dealing with his colleagues in feature films. I was able to give a remarkably full account of the making of *Jaws,* complete with the kind of details that are elided from the standard sanitized reports. The film's production executive, William S. Gilmore Jr., gave me revealing accounts of the angry clashes he had with Spielberg over the failures of the mechanical shark. "I knew a lot better than he did," Gilmore said about the time Spielberg "went bananas" when ordered to move on when a key shot didn't work. "He could be there till *today* and it would never be any better." And Richard D. Zanuck vividly explained how he and his producing partner, David Brown, ran interference with the anxious studio on behalf of the beleaguered director as the film went way over schedule and budget. Zanuck said, "Steven will never know the severe beating we would take every night when we would report the day's activities."

But the closer in time people had worked with Spielberg, the harder it was for me to get them to sit for interviews, because they were afraid of provoking the wrath of Hollywood's most powerful individual and possibly losing another job with him. I found a pattern in the turndowns I received directly and the failure of people to reply to my letters: Actors were by far the most timid of people in the industry about speaking with an unauthorized biographer. Screenwriters, by contrast, were usually the most accessible sources (as I explained in my *Written By* article on screenwriters as "secret weapons" for biographers), and, as on my Capra book, I learned much about the director's working methods by talking with key crew people, such as cinematographers and editors. Those categories of people generally feel neglected and are grateful that a film historian cares enough to be interested in their contributions.

I also interviewed thirty-five Holocaust survivors as part of my research into *Schindler's List,* to find out how authentic they thought the film is. They unanimously thought it felt as real as being back in that time and place, a great compliment to the filmmakers, but also found it less violent than the actuality, as Spielberg admitted was necessary to keep viewers from fleeing the theater. And they were bothered that Ralph Fiennes was handsome, unlike the commandant of the Plaszów forced-labor camp, Amon Goeth, whose physical loathsomeness seemed to express his inner ugliness. A Plaszów camp survivor I interviewed, whom I found when I went for a haircut at his barbershop, had the job as a teenaged boy of caring for the German shepherds Goeth used to attack the inmates. That man told me the worst Holocaust story I have ever heard, so hideous I have never wanted to repeat it to anyone out of consideration for their sensibilities.

You've revised and updated your Spielberg biography over the years, but do you feel that another edition is called for, since he keeps working?

As *Steven Spielberg: A Biography* went along in the updating process, it began more and more to resemble a critical study. In updating the book twice, I was able to quote some revealing interviews that actors and others, including Spielberg, had given to the media in promoting the films. But I did not attempt to do any additional interviews. Publishers won't pay for the work an author does on a revised edition, so those new chapters by necessity are even more focused on the work.

So far, however, despite the gradual proliferation of serious critical studies of Spielberg, no other major, in-depth rival biography has turned up. Molly Haskell wrote a thoughtful short biography in 2017, *Steven Spielberg: A Life in Films*, for the Yale Jewish Lives series, drawing on data from my book with appropriate credit. Richard Schickel (the other film historian who came from Wauwatosa, Wisconsin) published a fawning coffee-table study/interview book in 2012, the authorized *Steven Spielberg: A Retrospective*, which was updated in 2024 without the subject's first name in the title. Schickel had died in 2017, so some ghostly hand perfunctorily added the new material. Its corporate nature was indicated anyway by Schickel's Author's Note stating that "this book has very little to say about Spielberg's life away from his work, about which I know next to nothing. This is as it should be, I think. He is a private man and he is entitled to his privacy." Spielberg's Foreword adds, "Richard agrees that what someone of public prominence owes to his audience is an accounting of those activities—in my case movies—that he offers to them for their approval.... I am not ruling out the possibility of someday writing some sort of memoir about my life, but I don't think that I'll be doing that in the very near future."

Among the other books Spielberg & Co. has turned out is Susan Goldman Rubin's *Steven Spielberg: Crazy for Movies*, an authorized 2001 biography that benefited from access I didn't have to his other immediate family members.

Rubin's is the most substantial of the many Spielberg biographies that are aimed primarily at children, a subgenre whose abundance is a byproduct of his relative neglect by most film historians in contrast to more acceptable directors such as Hitchcock, Ford, and Welles. But like other books from the Spielberg stable, Rubin's is hampered by its auto-hagiographical slant.

Spielberg works hard to document his own working methods for extras on DVD and Blu-ray releases of his films, which is valuable for history, but his need to control most of what's written about him tends not to serve him well. It results in books that are mostly detached or technical in nature and don't go far in examining his personality and inner life. Before I wrote my biography, the best books about his career tended to be those that are more about the filmmaking process, notably *The "Jaws" Log*, the insightful, bestselling 1975 chronicle of the barely controlled craziness on Martha's Vineyard by Carl Gottlieb, who wrote the shooting script on location; as production executive Bill Gilmore told me in 1995, *Jaws* was "the most difficult film ever made, to this day." The author of the novel, Peter Benchley, is also credited on the script; both writers gave me valuable interviews. Spielberg himself is an exceptionally articulate and insightful self-analyst in his many interviews, which helped me tell his story. But there were some aspects of the psychological relationships between his life and his work that he had not discussed in depth, and those areas were left up to me as biographer, which is the way it should be in any case. I tell people that the reason Spielberg wouldn't give me an interview for my book is that one self-described "control freak" came up against another control freak.

Your Spielberg book was surely easier to write and publish than your Capra biography, but did you run into any serious problems along the way?

I ran into a problem with my editor late in the writing of my Spielberg biography. The manuscript was turning out to be considerably longer than originally planned, a result of my abundance of research and discoveries, as also happened with my Capra and Ford books. That caused Bob Bender to become angry when I submitted the Spielberg manuscript with all but the final chapter written. (I had literally put my head on my desk and fallen asleep as I finished the penultimate chapter.) He insisted I cut the manuscript myself without his help, which I did, although I was desperately

Among my most highly personal pieces of journalism collected in
my 2017 book, *Two Cheers for Hollywood*, is my appreciation of
Leo McCarey's *The Bells of St. Mary's*, his 1945 comedy-drama about
the uneasy relationship between a nun (Ingrid Bergman) and a priest
(Bing Crosby). I spent more than a quarter of a century trying to
write this essay, published in 2000 in *Irish America* magazine as "My
Guiltiest Pleasure: *The Bells of St. Mary's*: A Tribute to a Classic That
Humanizes Catholicism." (Rainbow Productions/RKO)

running out of money. I calculated that the advance I
received for three years of work on the biography was equal
to what Spielberg earned every four hours even while he
was asleep.

We ran into a more serious issue over the section on
Twilight Zone—The Movie. Spielberg produced that
notorious five-part 1983 feature, along with John Landis,
who was among four people charged with crimes but
acquitted after veteran actor Vic Morrow and two child
extras, Renee Shin-Yi Chen and My-Ca Dinh Le, were
killed while filming Landis's Vietnam War segment in July
1982. After the accident, Spielberg directed his segment
while distancing himself from Landis and the production.
Spielberg was given extraordinary leeway by not having
to testify in the case, never being interviewed by any
government agency, and never having to give a deposition
in the civil suits resulting from the accident. He simply was
allowed to deny in a two-sentence statement to the National
Transportation Safety Board that he had been on the location
"on the night of the accident or at any other time."

The section I wrote on Spielberg and his staff in relation
to the *Twilight Zone* incident was meticulously documented
and written. But Bender wanted to cut the entire section,
which runs seven pages in the book, since he was afraid that

Spielberg might sue us, and he claimed it is peripheral to Spielberg's story. When I refused, arguing that the book would lack integrity if it didn't address this issue, Bender reacted by refusing to send me the copyedited manuscript. That was an unprecedented experience in my career; it made me become concerned over what he was trying to do. I turned over the matter to Maury Muehle, since Bender was acting intractable, and I was operating without an agent in those years. Bender became irate that I had called in my attorney. Eventually he relented and sent me the copyedited manuscript, and the attorney who was vetting the book for Simon & Schuster, Felice Javit, decided in my favor. She told me she found that the section is documented fully, properly, and acceptably. She added that as a mother she shared my outrage over the death of the children. They were not film professionals but through their unsuspecting parents were lured into the film, on which they were worked illegally and riskily.

The *Twilight Zone* incident and the way Landis and his colleagues escaped serious consequences from it appalled me and contributed to my disgust with the film industry. As Javit and I predicted, no one sued us over the book. But I paid a price. I knew I was burning my relationship with Simon & Schuster to defend the integrity of the book. As a result of the flap with Bender, he stonewalled me when I attempted to sell him another book project. I stubbornly submitted thirteen separate book proposals that he rejected one after the other.

Around that time, I updated *High and Inside* for publication by Contemporary Books in 1997 and, to help pay my bills, cooked up another book for them, *The Book of Movie Lists: An Offbeat, Provocative Collection of the Best and Worst of Everything in Movies*, which was published in 1999. It was a frolic writing that book in two months, indulging myself by making it into a form of disguised autobiography by commenting on my tastes in movies.

Finally Bender wanted to know whether I still planned to write the John Ford biography I had been talking about. I said I was, but after checking around Simon & Schuster, he learned that another editor was already working with Scott Eyman on his Ford biography. So even if Bender had been willing to do that book with me, I had no choice but to go elsewhere. I submitted the Ford project to St. Martin's Press, and it was acquired by editor Calvert Morgan Jr., who guided it through its early stages there. Eventually, after Cal left, Tim Bent took over the book and completed the editing process expertly, if unhappily over my losing the ill-advised race with Eyman.

Although I was treated well by my new publisher, I regretted the unfortunate and, in my mind, unnecessary dispute that ended my relationship with Simon & Schuster, which declined, although for financial reasons, to publish the paperback edition of the Spielberg book. I took it to Da Capo Press, the first American publisher of my and Mike Wilmington's *John Ford*. Eventually I moved the Spielberg biography to the University Press of Mississippi for the updated second edition. Mississippi also acquired the reprint rights to my Capra and Ford biographies and has published trade press editions of all three, which is highly gratifying, and has kept them in print. The only publishers that would print the third edition of my Spielberg biography, though, were Faber and Faber in 2012 and Dook Media in Shanghai in 2021, and few people seem to know that edition exists. Since it ends with Spielberg about to shoot his 2012 film, *Lincoln*, and especially now that he has made *The Fabelmans*, I will have to find time to put together another updated edition; Spielberg and I are both nearing eighty.

Biographies of movie directors, as you know more than anyone else, are time-consuming to write and expensive to produce and then can have a limited market, so were you hoping your Spielberg book would hit paydirt for you?

That was not my motive for writing it, but Bender and I were surprised that *Steven Spielberg: A Biography* did not sell particularly well in its original hardcover edition. It sold about 12,000 hardcovers compared with about 7,500 for the original edition of *Frank Capra: The Catastrophe of Success*. And the Capra book benefited from almost unanimous rave reviews, while the Spielberg book predictably was used by most reviewers as a springboard for expounding their views on Spielberg himself, pro or con (mostly con). The less-than-expected sales figure was not much of an improvement, since Spielberg was, at the time, the world's most commercially successful filmmaker. I pondered the reasons and concluded, with only slight exaggeration, that people who liked Spielberg didn't read books, and people who read books didn't like Spielberg.

It's also symptomatic of the continuing resistance in some quarters to Spielberg that, unlike some of my other film books, that biography has never found a publisher on the European continent. Publishers are fond of using the excuse that long books are too expensive to translate. But that did not stop my massive Ford biography from being published in French translation as a book of 1,159 pages,

A la recherche de John Ford. That 2007 edition was chosen by the French film critics' group, le Syndicat Français de la Critique de Cinéma, as the best foreign film book of the year. (I spent a year revising that translation myself.) *Steven Spielberg: A Biography* has found publishers in mainland China, Taiwan, and South Korea. When I met in Los Angeles with the editor of film books for *Cahiers du Cinéma* in France, she rejected the Spielberg biography by telling me, incredibly, "Steven Spielberg is not an auteur." A similar bias continues to infect academia: During my twenty-two years at San Francisco State University, I was only once allowed to teach a course partly on Spielberg, and my department chair accused me of "pandering to the students" by choosing that subject. I didn't bother doing it again, because I was fed up with that attitude.

We've spoken about how your research uncovered some fabrications by Spielberg. Since I know you don't want to leave people with the impression that you have mostly negative feelings about him, can you tell us why you respect Spielberg so much as a person and are so impressed with his talent and films?

My respect and admiration for Spielberg as a filmmaker should be obvious from my book and the fact that I wrote it despite the prevailing hostility toward him in the critical circles of the time. Spielberg is one of the last directors in Hollywood with a classical style that keeps the audience oriented in terms of film geography and maintains a clarity of approach to portraying characters of increasing complexity. He thinks cinematically rather than in terms of literary or theatrical staging. David Lean, his greatest influence, recognized those qualities when he saw *Duel.* "I knew that here was a very bright new director," Lean said later. "Steven takes real pleasure in the sensuality of forming action scenes—wonderful flowing movements. He has this extraordinary size of vision, a sweep that illuminates his films. But then, Steven is the way the movies used to be."

Spielberg has always been a great popular artist who is able to translate his distinctive vision and personal obsessions to the screen in ways that the widest number of viewers can share. His scope has expanded over time to powerful and sophisticated historical films, such as *Empire of the Sun, Schindler's List*, and *Lincoln*, although he has limitations in his perspective due to his spotty education and somewhat simplistic liberalism, which leads him to make something as appallingly stupid as *The Post*, his worst film. But like Graham Greene, Spielberg has admirably managed to alternate light entertainments with his heavier works, while keeping the audience riveted in both.

Unlike Capra, Spielberg has handled success for the most part admirably and has maintained his leading position in the industry with only a few lapses of character. Those are significant, however, such as his mistreatment of Denis Hoffman and his behavior during the *Twilight Zone* controversy. No successful career is without some shameful episodes, unfortunately. But Spielberg overall has been a serious and dedicated man in his work and life. Although Steven has long been beset with fears and anxieties, Rabbi Albert Lewis, who taught him in Hebrew school, observed to me that when Steven learned to use the movie camera, it gave him "the strength or the courage to be what he was" and "made a *mensch* out of him."

In addition to his prodigious visual skills and versatility with stories and genres, I believe that Spielberg is one of the most underrated directors of actors in the cinema. When I interviewed Anson Williams, who acted for Spielberg in a TV show during their youth and later became a director himself, Williams observed, "Any director can get a great performance out of Al Pacino. Only Steven Spielberg can get a great performance out of a rubber puppet." I wrote my book to help convince people that Spielberg belongs in film history along with such masters as Hitchcock, Ford, and Hawks, and time has borne out the truth of that assertion. But the naysayers who continue to run down Spielberg's talents out of jealousy over his prodigious success will not recognize his greatness until after his death and perhaps not even then. In my work as a critic and biographer, I have always tried to champion popular artists, despite what my peers may think. Usually in time they come around.

The late French film historian and director Bertrand Tavernier said he thought that the best book on John Ford is G. K. Chesterton's 1906 book *Charles Dickens*. And in the third edition of my Spielberg biography, I quote Chesterton, who eloquently states the case for the popular artist in terms that also apply to Spielberg. Writing of "a man whose public success was a marvel and almost a monstrosity," Chesterton disagrees with the "purely artistic critic" who would contend, "The people like bad literature. If your object is to show that Dickens was good literature, you should rather apologize for his popularity, and try to explain it away. You should seek to show that Dickens's work was good literature, although it was popular."

Also in *Two Cheers* is my interview with Stepin Fetchit, the unfairly maligned comedian who slyly satirized racism but was attacked for supposedly perpetuating it. He candidly unburdened himself to me in the basement of a Madison strip club at which he was the opening act. The 1971 interview ran in *Film Quarterly* and helped inspire two respectful biographies. (L. Roger Turner)

To that argument Chesterton responds, "The public does not like bad literature. The public likes a certain kind of literature and likes that kind of literature even when it is bad better than another kind of literature even when it is good.... Ordinary people dislike the delicate modern work, not because it is good or because it is bad, but because it is not the thing that they asked for.... Dickens stands first as a defiant monument of what happens when a great literary genius has a literary taste akin to that of the community. For this kinship was deep and spiritual. Dickens was not like our ordinary demagogues and journalists. Dickens did not write what the people wanted. Dickens wanted what the people wanted.... Hence there was this vital point in his popularism, that there was no condescension in it.... Dickens never talked down to the people. He talked up to the people. He approached the people like a deity and poured out his riches and his blood. This is what makes the immortal bond between him and the masses of men. He had not merely produced something they could understand, but he took it seriously, and toiled and agonized to produce it."

Was the disappointment over the Spielberg's sales numbers one of the reasons you decided to switch from writing biographies to critical studies?

In my writing career I've had to face the general problem that relatively few members of the reading public, even film fans, are interested in books about directors, even Spielberg. Although books about stars sell better, I've never written a full book about a star, aside from my short volume on Kirk Douglas. For a while I considered a biography of my homeboy Spencer Tracy, but eventually James Curtis wrote a good one. Otherwise, I've never been tempted to write about stars rather than directors, since a director's work on a film is more pervasive than an actor's. But I've concluded that the work involved in writing a biography of a director and the tremendous expense is no longer worth it. After finishing *Searching for John Ford* in 2001, four years after my Spielberg biography was published, I found myself in such heavy debt that it took ten years to become solvent again, even while working fulltime as a university professor. So my further biographical projects have had to fall by the wayside, including ones I might have written on George Stevens, Spike Lee, and Stanley Kubrick.

Still, your critical studies that have followed require an equal amount of research and writing and are similar to your biographies in that they correct what was written before and provide us with the truth about your subjects.

That's an important part of my approach. In my critical studies I always dispel myths and misunderstandings about my subjects as well as bringing in fresh research about areas of their lives that are unknown or have been inadequately covered. That's part of the fun of writing critical studies; I go to places where the subjects have lived, talk with some of their collaborators, and in some cases am able to report on my interactions with the subjects in interviews and watching them make films, as I did with Wilder and Cukor. But those interactions are more limited in scope than with a biography, since the emphasis is primarily on the films rather than the life and the work. The fact that I can longer afford to write biographies makes me somewhat sad, since I am especially proud of those books, but I accept the situation as a reality.

So I have been happy to have gone back instead to my original *metier* of writing critical studies, from Lubitsch and Wilder to the Coen Bros. and Cukor. I enjoy critical studies and find them just as creative and much less stressful than biographies. They are more affordable, since on a professor's salary (and now pension), I can manage to travel a bit here and there and purchase research materials and so forth without the overwhelming burden of researching a biography, which becomes an endless maw sucking up all your resources and driving you deeply into debt. Life is too short now for more of that. And focusing on the work more than on the life of a filmmaker enables me to dig even more deeply into the films themselves.

PART IV
TEACHING AND WRITING

8. "World enough and time"

When you moved from Los Angeles to the San Francisco Bay Area in 2000, how did your career and your life change?

When I moved during the throes of finishing *Searching for John Ford*, I did so largely because my son, John, was living in Palo Alto with his mother, Dr. Ruth O'Hara. She and I had separated, and she had moved north to take a position as a research psychologist at Stanford University. So John and I would take plane trips back and forth periodically to see each other. But as he entered adolescence, I knew he would soon be too busy to keep doing so. It was an opportune time for me to move to a new area, even though I had just about become accustomed to living in L.A. after all those years of feeling out of place. So I loaded my belongings into a truck (while leaving some behind in storage) and drove north all night in June 2000 to arrive on the day John was graduated from Palo Alto High School.

The period of twenty-five years since I moved north has also been my most prolific as an author. It may seem paradoxical that I have been so active with my writing while spending twenty-two of those years working fulltime as a professor at San Francisco State University. Between 2002, when I joined the Cinema Department faculty, and my retirement at the end of 2024, I published eleven new books as well as revised and expanded editions of three others.

I'm interrupting you, but I must ask if you took time off from writing at any time?

When people ask me what my secret is for being prolific, I tell them simply, "Write every day." And I will add, "Write even if you don't feel good; soon you will forget that you aren't feeling good. And don't wait for 'inspiration' to strike but just get down to it and, as Hemingway put it, 'Write the truest sentence that you know.'"

Hemingway also advised writers to stop when they know what will come next, so they can hit the ground running the next day. I recommend the compilation by Larry W. Phillips, *Ernest Hemingway on Writing*, which is full of wise and practical tips that I've always followed. Another good piece of advice was from Somerset Maugham, who would start each day just writing his name over and over until something more original came into his mind. I put down whatever initial thoughts I have to get things started on that dreaded blank screen, and it's amazing how doing so will serve as an impetus to write something more substantial. I always made my students feel better by telling them that every writer has writer's block every day; the trick is just to get beyond it as soon as possible and stop worrying that you don't have what it takes to be a writer. I also learned over the years not to be a perfectionist, a preoccupation that used to make me sweat and anguish over my writing. In my dreams I often found myself writing with a fluidity I could not manage while awake. But eventually I came to follow the advice Joe Kennedy Sr. gave his children, "Do your best and then to hell with it."

My partner, Ann Cornell, had the best explanation for why I am so productive, when she called me "a member of the Andrew Marvell school of writing." I understood the allusion right away—in one of my favorite poems, "To His Coy Mistress," Marvell writes, "But at my back I always hear/Time's wingèd chariot hurrying near."

I have advanced from age fifty-two to seventy-eight in my Berkeley years, so I hear that chariot hurrying near, ever more insistently. I have become even more focused and concentrated in my writing regimen. It's surprising how many writers fail to write every day but wait until the "inspiration" strikes, or whatever their excuse for procrastination may be. The older you get, time obviously becomes more precious. This exchange between Carl Reiner and Mel Brooks's 2000-Year-Old Man captures how I've always felt about the demands of a writing career:

> *Reiner*: What was the means of transportation back then?
> *2000-Year-Old Man*: Mostly fear.
> *Reiner*: Fear transported you?
> *2000-Year-Old Man*: Fear, yes. You would see... an animal would growl, you'd go two miles in a minute. Fear would be the main propulsion.

When I first moved north, that fear was palpable. Not only was I exhausted from the move—all those books! three new storage facilities!—and was in the last intense stages of writing and editing my Ford biography, which continued in the Bay Area, but I was also nearly broke after two years freelancing so I could just manage to pay bills while working on the book. I was knocking out magazine articles while teaching part time at New College of California in San Francisco to start getting back on my feet financially and professionally.

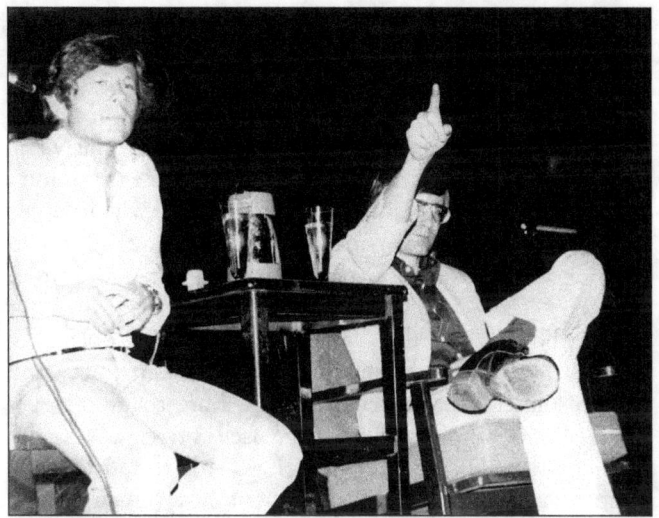

Among the guests at the first film course I taught, International Film
Directors, at Sherwood Oaks Experimental College in Hollywood
in 1974 was Roman Polanski, who was pleased that we showed his
favorite film, *Cul-de-Sac*. Our other guests were Howard Hawks,
Fritz Lang, Bob Rafelson, and Maximilian Schell.

My life with Ann in these years since I moved to
Berkeley has been delightful and fulfilling both emotionally
and intellectually. Along with all the other traits we have
in common, it is reassuring and comfortable to share life
with someone else who writes books and understands the
demands involved. Too often in the past I had to argue with
people in my life when I needed time to do my work; some
understood but most didn't.

*Did your move cause any problems with your work as a film
historian in making you more distant from the industry? Did
you miss that about L.A.?*

I miss friends and the wonderful venues to see films in
L.A., but especially difficult is not having easy access to
the Margaret Herrick Library of the Academy of Motion
Picture Arts & Sciences. Its books, periodical collections,
script and production files, and extensive clipping files are
invaluable for film historians. When I revise my Spielberg
biography, I go back down to the Academy library to update
my research. Not having it nearby is a handicap, though.
And Berkeley now is virtually bereft of movie theaters
other than a neighborhood theater called the Elmwood and
the Pacific Film Archive, where I have made appearances
for some of their film programs. I've also done events at

the San Francisco Silent Film Festival and other screening venues in the Bay Area. But it's not as rich a location for film study as L.A.

What I don't miss about L.A. is the materialism and the frantic ugliness of the place (which is more noticeable when I return for visits) and the fact that most people there don't read. After a while, I started pushing back when people would say they were too busy to read books. I would ask, "How often do you play tennis?" "Oh, a couple of times a week." "So you have time to play tennis but not to read books?" Silence. There are not such problems in the Bay Area, which is not only beautiful but funky and far more intellectually oriented. And I am relieved to get away from the insane focus on the useless trivia of the film industry that you encounter in L.A., where most of the mind-numbing discussions are about how much certain films grossed over the weekend. And most of all I am glad to escape the poisonous atmosphere, not just the smog but what Stanley Kubrick described in explaining why he left L.A., even though he conceded that "Hollywood is best" as a production center:

> I don't like living there.... When I lived there people would ask how it's going and you know that what they hoped to hear was that you were behind schedule or had trouble with the star.... You read books or see films that depict people being corrupted by Hollywood, but it isn't that. It's this tremendous sense of insecurity. A lot of destructive competitiveness. In comparison, England seems very remote. I try to keep up, read the trade papers, but it's good to get it on paper and not have to hear it every place you go. I think it's good to just do the work and insulate yourself from the undercurrent of low-level malevolence.

A major part of that malevolence is the *schadenfreude* one constantly encounters in Hollywood. You often hear a quote on the subject, attributed to various writers, and it's not used facetiously but seriously: "It is not enough that I should succeed—my friends must also fail." When one of my friends cited that maxim favorably, it redoubled my awareness that I needed to break free of the film business.

So what made you change your mind about teaching after resisting doing it for many years?

Leaving L.A. made me rethink my priorities and realize that continuing to be a freelance writer was an impractical and punishing way to live. I needed a regular job so I wasn't always scrambling for freelance work, living paycheck-to-paycheck, and going without health benefits and a pension plan, which become more serious concerns as you get older. I was ready psychologically to feel I could comfortably spend a substantial part of my time giving back what I knew to students. And I had to be practical as an author and shift from the financially ruinous profession of writing biographies to other kinds of books. But as Ruth pointed out, I couldn't have written my deeply researched and time-consuming biographies if I had been holding down a regular job as a teacher in those days.

I had been making occasional appearances at colleges and museums to talk about films since 1969 and taught my first film course in Hollywood in 1974 at Sherwood Oaks Experimental College. I also taught courses on Ford at the Santa Barbara Museum of Art and a film preview course, with Q&A sessions with the filmmakers, at the University of California, Irvine, Extension. But I shied away from a regular teaching career, despite the attractive offer I received from CalArts in the 1970s, until I felt ready to make that change. In the meantime, I began recognizing that in my biographies, teachers were often the heroes.

Especially in the Capra book: If it hadn't been for his grade school teacher Jean McDaniel, we never would have heard of Frank Capra. His parents were going to take him out of school to work in a brickyard like his older brother Tony. But as Miss McDaniel recalled about Frank, "He was such a bright little fellow and was so dependable that we interested ourselves in his behalf and succeeded in getting the Parent-Teachers Association to pay his parents what he could earn and let him go on to school." She taught him in two of his favorite subjects, history and mathematics. As he drew closer to graduation, she kept urging him to "Go on to high school," which not every youngster did in those days. His path to becoming a filmmaker was greatly influenced by his high school teacher Rob Wagner and his college English teacher, Clinton Kelly Judy. Capra went to the technical institute that later became known as Caltech and acknowledged that education was the key to his success in life.

My other biographical subjects also were deeply influenced by teachers. Ford's unparalleled skills in cinematic visual composition and aptitude for drawing were fostered by his grade school art teacher and principal

Marada F. Adams, who made annual trips to Italy to study art and brought that European influence to her students in Portland, Maine. While reminiscing to his grandson and biographer Dan Ford near the end of his life, Ford credited Miss Adams with instilling in him much of what he learned about the basic principles of art. Ford augmented those lessons by watching the renowned landscape painter Winslow Homer at his easel in nearby Prouts Neck.

Steven Spielberg's social studies teacher, Patricia Scott Rodney, gave the future director of *Schindler's List* his first exposure to film footage of German concentration camps by showing a documentary about Nazism called *The Twisted Cross*. And when Miss Scott assigned a "career exploration" project in eighth grade, encouraging students to show what they planned to do for a living, she let Steve go out in the desert with some classmates to make an 8mm Western, with a primitive soundtrack. She recalled, "We had a great time—we ran the movie forward and backward, and we all hollered. We all knew he had some special talent." When I asked how she felt when he became successful in Hollywood, his favorite grade-school teacher replied, "I wasn't a bit surprised by his filmmaking. *He was a filmmaker.* Always, from the early days."

And by embarking on a (partially) new career as a teacher, I was following my family tradition established by my grandfather John McBride, the longtime art teacher and "Mr. Chips" at Superior (Wisconsin) Central High School. Some of my siblings are also teachers, as are some of our younger generation, including my two children.

How did you get your first teaching gig in the Bay Area?

It was fortuitous that shortly after I arrived, I found a niche in teaching at New College, where I picked up some valuable experience. After giving a couple of guest lectures on films for their Irish Studies Program while visiting from L.A., I joined the faculty of that program, a thoughtful endeavor run by a maverick scholar of Irish culture named Danny Cassidy.

My entrée came through Ruth, who was teaching part time at New College while on the faculty at Stanford, and through her parents, Esther (Hetty) and Noel O'Hara, who also taught there. Noel was an electrical engineer in Ireland who eventually made a career of writing about and teaching literature and was planning to teach a course on Joyce's *Ulysses* that fall at New College. Unfortunately his life was cut short by leukemia at the time I moved north. Hetty taught

Teaching my basic screenwriting course at San Francisco State University, which I enjoyed each semester for twenty-two years from 2002 until my retirement. My teaching methods led to my 2012 book, *Writing in Pictures: Screenwriting Made (Mostly) Painless.* This is from my 2013 faculty profile by videographer Silvia Turchin. (San Francisco State Cinema Department/Documentary Film Institute/Sleeping Tree Pictures; frame enlargement)

the Irish language at New College and later with great success at the University of California, Berkeley.

New College was a flaky school overall, a degree mill in the San Francisco Mission District that had dubious practices and went under a few years later. But for me, teaching film courses under the aegis of the Irish Studies program for two years was like playing minor-league baseball before I moved up to the big leagues. At New College I taught courses on John Ford; Irish Literature/Irish Film; and the basics of screenwriting. Those experiences in my seminar-sized classes at the little school laid the foundation for my teaching of screenwriting and film history after I was hired for my first fulltime position in academia at San Francisco State University in fall 2002.

How did you think to apply there?

A former student tipped me off that SFSU's Cinema Department was searching for an associate professor of film studies, with a specific expertise in silent cinema. I applied at a fortuitous time, when their search had come up empty. My experience teaching at New College gave me some minor academic credibility, but it was my background as an author of books of film studies and a professional screenwriter that enabled an adventurous search committee to bring me aboard at SFSU. That sympathetic committee was composed of three veteran teachers: Jim Goldner, the founder of our department; Larry Clark, a director who came from the L.A. Rebellion group of filmmakers at UCLA; and Steve Kovacs, a Hungarian immigrant who was also a filmmaker and author. The search committee members saw beyond my lack of a conventional academic background and hired me.

Although my presentation for the job was mostly about silent cinema, with clips from Ford and Griffith films, it was ironic that I taught a class on that subject only once in my twenty-two years at San Francisco State, with a lively group of eleven students who soon became aficionados of silent films. Each semester, with few exceptions, I taught the regular course I designed on basic screenwriting and two film studies courses; sometimes I also taught an advanced feature-writing course for undergraduates. I generally avoided teaching graduate students, since I found most to be characterized by Alexander Pope's line "A little learning is a dangerous thing." Undergraduates, on the other hand, I found more open to learning.

Among the wide variety of studies courses I taught over the years were ones dealing with individual directors such as Ford, Welles, Renoir, Capra, Coppola, Hitchcock, Truffaut, Kubrick, Lubitsch, Wilder, and Spielberg. I also taught courses on Documentary Film, the Western, War Films, Film and Society (alternating my topics between films about American history and films about the media), and Film Dissent and Blacklisting. And I taught a potpourri course that focused on a producer-auteur (Selznick) and three disparate directors (Griffith, Cukor, and Spike Lee).

In response to a female professor urging us to have more courses on women, I designed and taught courses I especially enjoyed on Pioneering Women Directors (Lois Weber, Dorothy Arzner, Ida Lupino, Elaine May) and separate courses on women in the films of various directors (Truffaut, Ford, Lubitsch, Wilder). I was surprised to hear from my colleague that after her advocacy for courses on women, I was the only faculty member who stepped up and offered to teach them. She expressed gratitude, and yet she was often one of my adversaries. Go figure.

As the years wore on, however, waning student interest in cinephilia caused steady declines in the enrollment for our studies courses. When I first came to the school and taught a Hitchcock course, I had about eighty students; he used to be the single most popular director from classical Hollywood with contemporary film students. But over time, even the turnout for that course began declining to forty, thirty, twenty, and finally about a dozen students. That problem along with opposition from some of my fellow faculty members eventually forced me to resort to subterfuge to continue teaching film studies courses.

Your hiring as a university professor must have seemed fortunate, though, especially since you never finished college!

At first it was exhilarating. I found I had such a good time discussing films with students and presenting films in class. (If only that was all there was to a teaching job…) It took me back to my Madison days running the Wisconsin Film Society and enjoying the give-and-take with our young and ambitious film buffs. My students kept me on my toes and made me sharpen my views about movies. When a veteran teacher asked me early on how I found my new job, I found myself replying, "It's so easy." She bristled at what she took for my arrogance and snapped, "Wait until you have to lecture to 400 students." I didn't tell her I already *had* lectured to several hundred students regularly in Madison for the Wisconsin Film Society many years earlier, but our discussion abruptly ended when I mentioned that San Francisco State was breaking me in by having me teach classes of 400 students each for a freshman introductory course on Contemporary Cinema and an upper-level single-weekend course on Francis Ford Coppola.

What I meant by my candid but impolitic reply to her question was that I'd been preparing for this profession all my life. But I hadn't taken teacher's ed courses or earned a PhD and was winging it to some extent, with succinct and wise advice from John, Ruth, and Ann, as well as learning by doing. Although I enjoyed nothing more than lively exchanges about movies, with some students inevitably it was a struggle to stir up responses beyond a single sentence. Some put up fierce resistance to learning, which I'll soon expand on. But enjoying my interactions with the better students kept me devoted to the task for over two decades while I became increasingly disengaged from the department and its petty academic politics (to use an oxymoron). I remembered my high school teacher Thomas L. Book, a mentor of mine, telling me that if you have only one good student per semester, it makes teaching worthwhile.

What did you enjoy most about your students?

At a faculty meeting, a dean once asked us what we found most pleasing about our school. I replied it was the fact that many of our students are the first in their families to go to college. Since my mother had that distinction in her family, her high achievement after winning a scholarship from Marquette University made all the difference for her seven children (my Dad had two years of college in his hometown of Superior, Wisconsin, but was frustrated he didn't go farther). I found in my teaching that the most gratifying aspect was the difference you can make in the lives of receptive students who need confidence in their abilities (which many students lack). And I helped them learn more about the tools of the craft they were hoping to pursue or study professionally.

Fortunately, I found some students in each course who were eager to learn and receptive, and my most gratifying surprise was that I learned as much from them as they did from me. But I soon ran into opposition within my department from other professors who seized on the complaints of a minority of disaffected students as one of their ways of vilifying my teaching.

You allude to the snake pit academic politics can become. As a newcomer to the profession, how did you deal with that aspect of the job?

Before I entered my full-time teaching career, professors I knew had long warned me about the downside of university teaching, the academic politics, the onerous and trivial faculty meetings, and the small-minded, petty jealousies that are rife in the field. A quotation often attributed to Henry Kissinger points out that "The reason academic disputes are so acrimonious is that there is so little at stake." But I still had not counted on the vehemence of the resentment I faced from some of my fellow faculty members. In the eyes of a small but influential clique that opposed my hiring, I didn't qualify as one of them, since I had not come up through the traditional academic guidepath and therefore didn't have the requisite ideological orthodoxy. I have always been a maverick as a film scholar and critic, going my own way regardless of fashion, so it was inevitable that I would clash with the rigid barriers academia erects to maintain its exclusionary rules. It's ironic that my success in the field of film studies, which helped get me the job at SFSU, was held against me by some in our department. In my later years at the school, an emeritus professor said of our faculty, "They've always hated you because you've written more books than the rest of the department combined." That may be the basic reason for the opposition I faced from the beginning to the end at SFSU.

Didn't the chairman of your department approve of your hiring?

Like the committee, our chair at the time, Professor Stephen Ujlaki, valued my varied expertise, but I became a pawn in an internecine quarrel within the department over his own recent hiring. The fact that Steve was an erudite man who had a PhD from Harvard and had worked as a production assistant to Bergman and Godard didn't seem to matter to his adversaries, since he was also a Hollywood producer. Hollywood was still a dirty word in our department, which prided itself on its Bay Area bohemian artsiness and disdain for anything that smacked of helping students make a living in films. I actually proposed a mandatory course on that subject, with career advice from a wide variety of visiting professionals, but was shot down by our faculty.

And because I was such an unorthodox hire under Steve Ujlaki's sympathetic aegis, it was easy for some faculty members to stereotype me as a "Hollywood guy." I found that a joke, since if they only knew, I was more anti-Hollywood than they could possibly imagine. As a result of my hiring, they even pushed through a new rule that took hiring power away from the search committee and made its choice a mere recommendation to be voted on by the entire faculty. But it was too late to undo my hiring, even though my adversaries ostracized me within the department and used other harassment tactics. They didn't realize they had run up against an immovable object with long experience in withstanding punishment and fighting opposition.

What were the other harassment tactics?

For my first five years at SFSU, my principal nemesis, whom I shall refer to here as Professor Uriah Heep, and his allies did everything they could try to undermine my path to tenure, hoping to drive me away by casting unjust aspersions on my teaching and scholarly credentials. Auteurism is a dirty word in academic lingo, and one of their forms of attack was to stigmatize me as a hardcore auteurist, even though anyone who has read my writing should know that it has evolved over the years into a somewhat critical view of auteurism, with a stronger emphasis on collective or multiple authorship of films. I gave Professor Heep a copy of my Capra biography, but he must not have read it or chose to willfully ignore it, since it's largely a deconstruction of the auteurist mythology surrounding Capra's "one man, one film" claims to authorship. I argued instead that Robert Riskin was the principal author of "Capra's" films.

In my Capra, Spielberg, and Ford biographies and my other books, I concentrate on how individual artists— directors, writers, and others—could function effectively by working together. But what André Bazin called "the genius of the system," in referring to the classical period of Hollywood, has since become increasingly corporate, impersonal, and hostile to artists. And I find it ironic that in American academic circles, it is *de rigeur* to denigrate auteurism in theory, yet it seems that almost every film department, including the one I was in, slavishly follows auteurism in practice, organizing most courses around directors and seldom focusing on screenwriters and other contributors to the filmmaking process. Our department fostered what I consider the mistaken belief that students must both write and direct their own films. I tried to tell my students that not every writer should direct, and not every director should write, but that collaboration is essential to the filmmaking process, a lesson that too often escaped them because of the prevailing orthodoxy. One student said I was the only professor he ever had who even *mentioned* screenwriters.

Balancing books and teaching

You had so much going on at SFSU that it's hard to believe you were also busy writing many books. Did it take you a while to get back into gear with your writing after you made the big move to San Francisco and changed careers to some extent?

Yes, the first few years were a struggle for me as a writer until I hit my stride and figured out how to balance both occupations. Before I found some financial security at San Francisco State, I was eking out my marginal living teaching part time at New College and writing magazine articles. Meanwhile, I reached a kind of plateau when *Searching for John Ford* was published in 2001, and I took heart from both the *New York Times* and the *Irish Times* calling it the "definitive" Ford biography. Martin Scorsese, who read the book while directing *Gangs of New York* at Cinecittà, gave me a most gratifying blurb:

> Joseph McBride's book has the sweep, passion, complexity, and tragic grandeur of a great John Ford film. Thoroughly detailed and researched, McBride's book fills in the gaps and gives us the man in full: sentimental yet cruel, brilliant yet forever feigning illiteracy, politically liberal at one moment and conservative the next. Ultimately, McBride shows us that this artist, who balked at the very mention of the word *art,* could speak fully and honestly only through his films. For those of us who grew up on those films, the book is a treasure, and an eye-opener. For younger people who don't know his wok, who have yet to appreciate the timeless beauty of his greatest pictures, *Searching for John Ford* should be compulsory reading.

For a while after finishing the Ford biography, though, I was fumbling around half-heartedly with a misguided new book project about literary adaptations that I eventually abandoned. Although my full-time teaching job helped ease my financial anxieties, it ate up a lot of my time, especially in the first few years. Along with classes and the heavy load of grading, there were the chores and stresses of my pitched battle for tenure. But I also came up with an ambitious new writing project, my critical study/memoir *What Ever Happened to Orson Welles?: A Portrait of an Independent Career.* The needless distractions at SFSU were part of the reason my third book on Welles took five years to write. And during that period I was continually researching the assassination of President Kennedy, as I had been since 1982. The Welles book was published in 2006 by the University Press of Kentucky, qualifying it as my "tenure project" if such was needed.

Teaching is a natural profession for a writer, because it enables you to test your ideas in lectures and discussions with your students while learning from them. And teaching gives you three months off in the summers to do your writing, as well as a sabbatical semester every few years; I wrote two books during sabbaticals, my screenwriting manual, *Writing in Pictures: Screenwriting Made (Mostly) Painless*, which was published in 2012, and the critical study *George Cukor's People: Acting for a Master Director*, which came out in late 2024 as an e-book and early 2025 as a print book. At the start of my full-time teaching career,

I wrote books mostly on weekends and other time off from teaching. The tenure process occupied large parts of some summer "vacations" that I used to put together my voluminous personnel files. I felt the need of submitting much larger files to document my accomplishments than were actually necessary; it was a form of overkill, but it paid off. Eventually, after I achieved tenure, I found my rhythm and started writing every day again, which accelerated the pace of my books.

You said that another reason What Ever Happened to Orson Welles? *took so long to write was that it was hard to structure.*

Yes, that book was such a challenge to outline and organize because it is unconventional and follows a compressed, densely written narrative that I also designed to be enjoyable to read. It packs my account of Welles's entire life and work, along with my experiences with him in the last fifteen years of his life, into a relatively compact space, well under my goal of 400 pages. I wasn't writing a biography of Welles per se—that would take many more pages and involve a scope of research and travel I simply couldn't afford. Nor did I ever want to launch that kind of nearly impossible project. It's proven hard enough for his biographer Simon Callow, who has already written three volumes on Welles, taking him up to 1965, and in the midst of his busy acting career has been working on his fourth and avowedly final volume.

What Ever Happened to Orson Welles? began because I was bothered that most people knew little to nothing about what Welles was doing in the last part of his life. That happened to be the period when I knew and worked with him. I set out to correct the record (indeed, to *establish* the record) by reporting on and analyzing what he was making during those years and the roadblocks he was running up against even while he continued to shoot film virtually every day. I also examined his numerous unmade projects and scripts (some written with Oja Kodar), most of which had never been written about before. I traveled to the Munich Film Museum to watch numerous unfinished or rare Welles film and TV projects I still needed to see so I could tell the reader about all of his work and trace his artistic progression more clearly.

But as I mapped out that story, I realized that to fully understand what happened to Welles in his later years and why he finally became a fully independent filmmaker literally making "home movies" mostly with his own money, I would have to revisit his entire life and career and the bumpy road of independence that had carried him through. I borrowed that theme from a former Madison film mafia colleague, Douglas Gomery, an eminent film historian who argued that rather than seeing Welles as a failed Hollywood director, it's more accurate to see him as a career-long independent filmmaker who briefly used the resources of major studios before being expelled from Hollywood and following his independent path for the rest of his life.

Revisiting Welles's entire career to examine it in that light made the book much more complex to research and write. And as I get older and see life with more complexity than I did in my youth, that's why my books have gotten longer and more intricate: I have more to say. Another reason I wrote my third book on Welles was one I didn't mention in the book itself—to provide a road map for Callow in covering Welles's later life and work, the period about which there has been the most distortion by journalists and other biographers. Callow is a colorful writer who has a great deal of empathy with Welles and, as an actor himself, is able to evoke the sense of Welles's theater and radio work with brilliant immediacy. But he too has sometimes fallen prey to unfairly biased myths about Welles, such as the John Houseman version of their Mercury Theatre partnership and of Herman Mankiewicz's collaboration with Welles on the script of *Citizen Kane*. Callow's later volumes are better-informed and more sympathetic to Welles, but I wanted to alert him to certain pitfalls in covering the filmmaker's final years, such as why so much of the late work remained unfinished in his lifetime.

I decided to follow a loose memoir format on *What Ever Happened to Orson Welles?*, from my life-changing discovery of *Citizen Kane* as a young man onward to my study of his career, my overviews of its progression, and my experience of working for him. As a Welles chronicler who, late in the narrative, becomes a Welles character (Mister Pister), I felt an even more pressing need than usual to maintain the balance between participant and observer, as Leon Edel advises is so valuable to a biographer (or critic and memoirist, in my case). My intimate and revealing account of working with Welles on *The Other Side of the Wind* takes up about a third of the book, with his other late projects interwoven. In offering my perspective as a privileged insider, I wanted to keep a clear eye on what went awry with the project—why he made that film and what happened as it progressed, and what was holding it up—

as well as its qualities as a daringly experimental work of modernism filmed in two cinematic styles Welles had never explored before.

I also wanted to influence film history further by offering my perspective on how *Other Wind* could and should be finished, even though Peter Bogdanovich and Oja Kodar had shortsightedly fired me from producing the project soon after Gary Graver and I worked out the tentative deal with Showtime in 1998. The Showtime deal collapsed after my dismissal, but I had long since gotten beyond that injustice, so I gladly offered whatever help I could to the people who ultimately finished the film for Netflix in 2018, and I am credited onscreen as a consultant.

How did you go about keeping the Welles book as concise as possible and not let it get out of control?

Through extensive trial and error in outlining my book, I arrived at the unorthodox structure of starting with, in effect, two introductions. The first is highly personal, tracing the growth of my interest and involvement with Welles. The second (called the first chapter) starts from the vantage point of Welles launching the film in 1970 and goes on to analyze and critique the state of his reputation in his later years and up to the time of the book. With those joint introductions, I established my arguments and laid out the scope of the book for the reader. Then I go back to Welles's beginnings with *Kane* and in theater and radio and more or less follow a chronological path for the rest of the story.

In studying his career and legacy from the prism of seeing Welles as a lifelong independent, a maverick and radical, I was able to chose freely among the areas I felt necessary to discuss. I was under no obligation or need to engage in lengthy analysis of each film, especially since I'd already written a book doing that. Instead I focus on fresh revelations from my ongoing research to illuminate each phase of Welles's career and areas that had been the subject of distortions or lies in the media, as well as topics whose centrality to the development of his career had been misunderstood or, indeed, weren't known yet, such as my revelations about why he was fired by RKO from *It's All True* under false pretenses.

I tried to be as concise as possible throughout while not becoming simplistic, but when I felt it worthwhile to dilate upon a topic, I felt free to do so. *What Ever Happened?* is not a biography but an unusual hybrid, a critical study/memoir, and it still was a challenge to face the self-imposed discipline of what Lytton Strachey, in his preface to *Eminent Victorians,* calls "a becoming brevity—a brevity which excludes everything that is redundant and nothing that is significant— that, surely, is the first duty of the biographer."

I was influenced by how Strachey's highly compressed masterwork benefits from sticking closely to its main points in debunking, often wryly, the lives of its four compellingly odd but representative subjects. I have repeatedly re-read *Eminent Victorians* for guidance (along with Edel's *Writing Lives)* whenever I embark on a book about an artist, whether a biography or a critical study. I remember telling myself when I began writing *Searching for John Ford* to keep every section as concise as possible; that may seem ironic, since that book runs 838 pages, but Ford's life was such a vast subject that the biography could have spiraled out of control if I had not maintained that discipline. And I had to do some hard thinking and study and planning to write a relatively contained book on Welles. So Strachey's guidance about "a becoming brevity" was what I followed in confronting such a massive body of work as Welles's, which, contrary to the conventional wisdom that he was lazy and undisciplined, spans an astonishing 131 pages in the chronology of his career assembled by Jonathan Rosenbaum for *This Is Orson Welles.*

Strachey's counsel to the biographer "to maintain his own freedom of spirit" was second-nature to me from my experience writing Capra's life. And Strachey's short biographies (especially his thrilling and eloquent account of General "Chinese" Gordon) gain immeasurably in strength from having an impassioned and thoroughly supported point of view, as does my Capra biography. Although in *What Ever Happened?,* I was, to some extent, making a case for Welles against his detractors, I took pains not to indulge in hagiography but to deal with the role his own limitations and idiosyncrasies (such as his inability to charm the money men, as Charlton Heston put it) played in why certain projects were unfinished, imperfect, or mutilated by their backers. And while recalling the celebrated, oft-misquoted remark by Renoir's Octave in *The Rules of the Game*—"On this earth there is one thing that's terrible; it's that everyone has his reasons"—I bore in mind that every unfinished film by Orson Welles was unfinished for a different reason or reasons.

Avoiding facile judgments while recognizing what made Welles's life in the film industry so fraught with conflict, I wanted to convey why the attributes that made him a great cinematic artist were often the same characteristics that thwarted his ability to function at the peak of his talents. To answer the question I chose for my title, I wrote that "we need to understand both what Welles was doing in the little-known final years of his life and what happened before then to set the pattern of his career. Much of the answer lies in his still misunderstood early years as a film, theater, and radio director and progressive political activist, when he antagonized powerful adversaries in New York, Hollywood, and Washington and became a pawn in a studio power struggle that, he said later, forever 'branded' him as 'Crazy Welles.'"

Along the way I investigated with the aid of his FBI files and other sources his political blacklisting (a facet of his career that had been largely unacknowledged by scholars and by Welles himself), as well as how he coped with the demands of the studio system in his initially promising RKO years; his eventual marginalization in the industry; and the even more onerous problems of finding money to complete his films. That he was a poor and often dodgy businessman was one of his problems. As I wrote,

> In this "portrait of an independent career," I hope to stimulate a deeper public understanding of the complex circumstances that caused one of the twentieth century's major artists to become a pariah in Hollywood while still in his twenties, an exile from the United States for many years, and an artist laboring largely in obscurity during his final years. Despite all the difficulties Welles faced, his old age was far from being a tragic wasteland. It was a period of great artistic fecundity and daring, even if it was largely hidden from public view. What does that say about the nature of his artistic personality, and what does that say about our culture?

For a book with such an unusual structure, did you need to work from a strict outline?

After experimenting for quite a while and gradually getting the hang of it, I put together a detailed outline of the book in a loose-leaf binder that I filled in piece by piece, sometimes working on sections out of order. That was not my usual method of writing a book, but this was not a usual book. And when my original publisher demanded to see what I was writing before it was finished—a demand an author should always resist—I had to switch publishers because the first one didn't understand what I was doing. I knew I could pull it off and eventually, through the help of my old friend and fellow author Pat McGilligan, found a home for the book with the University Press of Kentucky.

The writing was an adventure, because I was captivated by the challenge of the subject and the need for economy in my style of writing and narrative line. Gradually it all went smoothly, and I had ample time to polish the text until any resemblance to the outline in the binder was deeply submerged, but the slow generation of the book proved the wisdom of the old adage that it takes more time to write a short letter than to write a long one.

Was it rewarding to get the book published and then have critics appreciate that you were providing previously uncovered Welles material?

The book has been influential in correcting the record about Welles and helping people realize that lamenting the roadblocks he faced is not as fruitful as celebrating the rich legacy of what he was able to accomplish. Martin Scorsese found the book particularly valuable in dispelling the most pervasive and pernicious misconception about Welles: "There has been so much written and said about Orson Welles over the years, and quite a bit of it has been fixated on the myth of his self-destruction at the expense of everything else: Welles had become the epitome of fallen genius, *our* fallen genius. Joseph McBride, who has a clearer understanding of Welles and his films than almost anyone, exposes that idea as the myth it is and always has been." And novelist Jonathan Lethem commented, "As with the invaluable accounts of Dickens written during Dickens's lifetime, McBride has charted a course through the smoke for all future scholarship (and, one prays, film restoration). Twenty-first-century Welles research begins here."

When the University Press of Kentucky decided to do a paperback edition of *What Ever Happened to Orson Welles?* in 2022, I expanded the book by adding an epilogue. I took its title from a poignant line of Everett Sloane's Mr. Bernstein in *Citizen Kane,* that he had been with Mr. Kane "From *before* the beginning, young fella—and now, it's after the end." My subheading is "Revelations from Welles's ongoing career." In that epilogue I write about two films people never thought would see the light of day. These serve as bookends for Welles's career, his rediscovered 1938 silent film, *Too Much Johnson,* and the 2018 release version of *The Other Side of the Wind.* But as I remind readers, Welles's career is not finished. More Welles films are yet to be found or finally completed, especially his *Don Quixote:* "Consciously or not, Welles left his body of work in a largely unfinished state in order to keep it alive, to keep his admirers wondering about his intentions, and to invite them to collaborate on his films after his death."

The teaching of writing made somewhat painless

Your teaching of screenwriting courses throughout your twenty-two years at San Francisco State led to your writing your screenwriting manual, Writing in Pictures: Screenwriting Made (Mostly) Painless. *That book, published in 2012, is based on how you designed your basic screenwriting course. But after your mostly depressing experience writing scripts in Hollywood, I would think you'd have been reluctant to teach screenwriting and bring back bad memories.*

Well, I did have my pleasurable moments working on films and the AFI shows. Especially the AFI shows. But I wondered about how my checkered experience might inhibit my teaching of screenwriting; I found that after all my years away from the industry, I had sufficient detachment from the field that I could enjoy teaching the craft to aspiring screenwriters and concentrate on helping them. The best advice I received when I started my teaching career came from my son, John, who was then a math major at Stanford. John said, "Remember how you taught yourself how to write screenplays. And then replicate that method for your students." John's advice on recalling my learning process and breaking it into components for my students became my basic organizing principle for every course I taught.

John has gone on to earn his master's degree in mathematics from SFSU and become a teacher himself, and I've learned a great deal from him over the years. Even when he was a boy, I would ask him to give me a five-minute or half-hour rundown on some scientific subject, such as relativity or radar, and he would do so with admirable precision and clarity that demystified the topic without oversimplifying it. As he was studying in high school and college, I kept getting helpful counsel from him about how to teach, including what students expect from their teachers. He told me that what students most want to hear is that they are making progress. So I tried to give them that reinforcement if they deserved it, while also taking pains to ensure that they *were* making progress.

When I joined the faculty at San Francisco State, I found that our students desperately needed to learn how to write. So my first job in any course was helping them learn basic writing skills. An outside Writing Task Force that came to study our student body early in my time at the school also determined that learning how to write was their most urgent need. And I was influenced by overhearing another faculty member say, "I teach every course as a writing course."

I devoted myself to helping my students develop the writing and reading skills they had not been taught in our sadly deficient K-12 public education system. I used my screenwriting courses as ways to teach those skills, and I used my film studies courses that way too. I found I had to teach many students the rudiments of grammar, spelling, and punctuation—i.e., remedial English. Most of the students I taught were juniors and seniors, but they generally wrote at what I considered a sixth-grade level, based on my own experience of schooling. Eventually I read that most California high school students actually *do* write on a sixth-grade level.

Student reading skills, not surprisingly, tended to be just as weak. Naturally there were numerous exceptions, and some students came to my classes already writing and reading well, often because they had attended private schools. But our university's point person on reading skills tested a class of mine and found they retained only seventy percent of two brief excerpts they had just read from speeches by John F. Kennedy and Dr. Martin Luther King Jr. As a remedy, I had my screenwriting students read classic short stories, the sophisticated kind of literature most of them were not taught in high school. They initially had trouble understanding and analyzing such stories, but when we worked on them together, it also greatly improved their writing skills. In film studies courses, I assigned books of history and criticism and often had the students read stories or screenplays on which the films were based. And without knowledge of fundamentals, many students are increasingly at a loss to write coherent, well-argued, well-structured papers.

Being a remedial English teacher was a job I hadn't counted on, but somebody had to do it. The students who accepted the challenge made rapid progress, learning to become much better writers in just a few months. Some of them informed me that no one had tried to help them before, and I told these college juniors and seniors that this was their last chance to learn how to write well before they went out to make a living, whether in the field of cinema if they were among the few who manage to do so, or in any other field that requires forms of writing.

How did your approach to teaching basic writing and reading skills go over at your school?

I found the general level of teaching at our university to be wanting. Our mandatory English courses didn't seem to do the job. Some fellow teachers simply tried to slough off their teaching responsibilities. Many professors in our Cinema Department didn't even assign books for the students to read. And some couldn't write well themselves (their email messages often made me wince, such as one by a writing teacher that went, "Here, here!"), so how could they teach writing? It was common in our department and in academia generally for professors to turn over the grading of papers to student teaching assistants, but after some failed early experiences relying on TAs, I realized that grading was one of my primary responsibilities, time-consuming though it is. Grading is a form of constructive dialogue with an individual student that goes beyond what can be taught in class.

Some students resented my efforts, especially those who didn't see why their writing skills needed improvement. They blamed me when they earned poor grades and tended to bail before they could succeed. Also, when I came to SFSU, Steve Kovacs advised me to share with my film studies students my experiences learning from interviewing great filmmakers and watching them at work, but that seemed to backfire, provoking mostly hostility. I put that down to a basic insecurity some students had about ever being able to enter the profession. But I kept doing so anyway and teaching the way I thought best.

My esteemed colleague Professor Jenny Lau, who is from Hong Kong, put these problems in a philosophical perspective. She told me Confucius said there are three kinds of students: (1) the ones who are so good you can't do anything to help them but give them encouragement; (2) the "teachables," who usually are the majority of students; (3) and the "unteachables," who can't be reached because they lack skills and preparation or because of bad attitudes or other problems. Unfortunately, the unteachables gradually became increasingly numerous over my years at San Francisco State.

When I complained about a disturbed student who disrupted a class, the man at our school in charge of students' psychological well-being told me in a state of agitation, "You have *no idea* how many of your students have serious psychological problems!" I told him I was concerned about the possibility of the kind of violence as had happened when thirty-two people were killed by a deranged student at Virginia Tech in 2007, and he shouted, "All you people are always talking about Virginia Tech!" Well, yeah. After the university balked at removing the student from my class, I had to refuse to enter the classroom for the sake of our safety until the school finally took action.

I did have one screenwriting student in Confucius's top category, a student I could only encourage because I consider her among the best in the field, Brie Williams. I may be biased, but I truly believe that her only peers today are Ethan and Joel Coen. Brie has won festival prizes for her daringly original, often surrealistic scripts. After her graduation, she wrote and directed (with John C. Clark) an incisive low-budget 2017 film about gay conversion therapy, *A Closer Walk with Thee.* I supported the production by investing a little money, but this well-made film unfortunately didn't go anywhere because of its hot-button theme and idiosyncratic approach. It's billed as "a homoerotic Evangelical exorcism film." Most of Brie's scripts haven't sold, because they are too original for an industry that shuns originality in favor of "safe" remakes and clones (even though William Goldman famously warned about the film industry, "NOBODY KNOWS ANYTHING"). After several frustrating years beating her head against the wall in Hollywood, Brie moved back to Oregon and began writing comedy-drama podcast series. You can't keep a good and determined writer down, but her example shows that one of the primary reasons Hollywood has gone so wrong is its systematic discouragement of genuine talent.

How did the majority of your "teachables" fare as you tried to help them become better writers?

Despite the fact that some students find it too onerous to be educated and fail to do the hard work involved, others are deeply grateful, even if in some cases it may take a few years for them to realize it and get back to you. One student wrote me in retrospect and said she couldn't do her job in TV, which required her to show up each day at 9 AM, if I hadn't been the only teacher who made her meet deadlines. A favorite student of mine, who is from Japan, came to me in her freshman year and worried that her English was not good enough to write papers. I said she spoke English well, so she could learn to write English well too, and I offered any help she needed. She took me seriously and enrolled in several of my classes, always did the extra-credit papers, often came to see me for counseling, and became an excellent writer in her second language.

I had been told by a couple of biased faculty colleagues that foreign students were especially bad in writing English. I found the opposite to be true: students from Japan and China, in particular, tend to be *better* writers in English than most American students. The foreign students have better training in how to write and structure an essay, even if they have the expected problems with word usage that can be easily rectified. To be allowed to study abroad, Japanese students need to be proficient in English, and they have at least five years of studying it. That is more training in English than students tend to get in the American public school system. My stellar student from Japan had the sense to go back home after her graduation with honors and become an international show business lawyer. Billy Wilder advised young people interested in a career in the modern film industry to become lawyers or stunt people, because that's where the work is. As a lawyer, my former student uses her knowledge of the American film industry to work on connections between companies in her country and the U.S.

I was also informed by a fellow faculty member that by the time a student is a junior in college, he or she can't learn anything anymore. That was a shocking dereliction of duty as well as patently absurd. I told my students that learning should be a lifelong process. One of my screenwriting students asked indignantly, "Does this mean I have to study writing *all my life?*" I replied, "Yes."

Another of my best students was a smart and industrious African American young man who did remarkable research for his screenplay, digging up background material for Flannery O'Connor's "A Late Encounter with the Enemy" that I hadn't seen before, but he struggled with verbal expression and took a while to learn to write better. He eventually succeeded admirably in the one semester we had together, and his mother came up to me with him at graduation and thanked me for being the only teacher who had ever taken the trouble to help her son. That was my most gratifying experience as a teacher.

When I became discouraged at one point late in my teaching career, Ruth told me, "Just remember, you've taught two generations of students to be better writers." In looking back I try to focus on the many success stories I helped foster rather than on disgruntled students who complained about my teaching and who were used as fodder by my adversaries in the department.

The Elements of Style

The pitched battles I fought in my first few years with my principal nemesis, Professor Heep, and others in the department often revolved around how rigorously I taught writing. Along with educating my students about literature, one basic tool I used was to have all my students read *The Elements of Style*, the classic writing manual by William Strunk Jr. and E. B. White. I quoted in my syllabi Stephen King, who declared, "Every aspiring writer should read *The Elements of Style*," and Dorothy Parker, who wrote, "If you have any young friends who aspire to become writers, the second-greatest favor you can do them is to present them with copies of *The Elements of Style*. The first-greatest, of course, is to shoot them now, while they're happy." That book, which we went through in class to some extent, was their refresher course on the basics of English prose they had not learned or had forgotten.

I first thought of teaching the book when I had a student in my basic screenwriting course who had imaginative visual ideas for his script but was semiliterate. Thinking about how I could help him, I gave him *The Elements of Style* and suggested that he write three extra-credit papers based on the book and meet with me regularly to discuss his writing. The results of his efforts were almost miraculous: By the end of the semester, he still had some writing problems but was writing much more clearly and communicating his visual ideas more effectively. That showed how quickly students can learn when given the opportunity.

That happy experience led me to assign *Elements* to all my classes. Many students read it with seeming enthusiasm, and the ones who wrote extra-credit papers drawing from it often told me the book had taught them much they had not learned in their previous schooling—for example, few of them had ever been taught anything about punctuation before—and they found that simply reading *Elements* had made them much better writers. The results demonstrated they were not shining me on. And I found that if only a professor insists on correct grammar, spelling, and punctuation (which one student wrote was "a most un–San Francisco State attitude"), rapid improvement will result.

But Professor Heep took it upon himself at a faculty meeting in September 2005 to attack me in highly personal terms for using *The Elements of Style* as a teaching tool. That meeting had been called to discuss the university's writing program that was formed as a result of the outside review of our students' needs. SFSU was undertaking what it called a "concerted campus-wide effort to live up to its commitment to make good writing a hallmark of its graduates." When I attempted to discuss ways our department could participate in that initiative and to explain some of my methods of teaching writing, Professor Heep called *Elements* outdated and ridiculed my use of a book that had first been published decades earlier. (He did not mention it was frequently updated, as recently as that fall.) I tried to explain that *Elements* is widely used in many high schools and colleges, including at Stanford, where it is assigned to every freshman, but he continually interrupted me, heatedly characterizing my teaching methods as "ridiculous" and "insane." At that point I walked out of the meeting to avoid further insults or confrontation. Later I was told that Professor Heep was willing to apologize to me privately in the chair's office, but I found that inadequate.

You would think explanations of why I taught basic writing skills would be superfluous at a university supposedly committed to improving student writing, but defending myself took up a great deal of my time and energy on my bumpy road to tenure. I found that someone posted on the Internet Movie Database that I was "Known at San Francisco State University for his high standards on essay work and requiring a manual of style in addition to other textbooks." I found it surprising and indicative of the low state of our educational system that having high standards and assigning *The Elements of Style* would be considered so remarkable as to bring attention on the worldwide web, but IMDb even added that I was considered a "grammar Nazi" by some at our school. I read that smear while visiting friends in Germany who were understandably baffled and alarmed by that reference (they didn't get the allusion to *Seinfeld*), and it took me a while to convince IMDb to remove the offensive language.

Responding to the outside Task Force that identified writing as our students' major problem, San Francisco State had made "writing in the discipline" courses mandatory for each department in what was called the GWAR program, short for the Graduate Writing and Reading Assessment Requirement. Working with my most sympathetic mentor, Steve Kovacs, I initially devised the course we taught to meet that requirement, Writing About Cinema. But another teacher, whom I shall call Professor Jane Murdstone, was awarded control of our GWAR program over me in what she heatedly told the faculty was a "personnel" matter. I later learned that she had been the first to object to my hiring;

perhaps that was because her entire body of published writing consisted of two journal articles. When she was told by our chair that she needed to publish more, she refused. Professor Murdstone tried to belittle my biographies by claiming they were merely "anecdotal," a silly slur common to the snobbish world of film studies, which tends to look down on what *Movie* magazine, in its review of my and Mike Wilmington's critical study of Ford, so hilariously called "the myth of personality."

Even though teaching the basics of writing ostensibly was the program's *raison d'être,* Professor Murdstone did not believe in grading students on grammar, spelling, and punctuation errors. Writing About Cinema continued to be taught after her death by lecturers or TAs who followed her benighted policy. Some of the GWAR instructors, I was told by my students, didn't even have their classes do *any* writing but just watched and discussed films!

Our GWAR program was something of a joke, as I soon learned at an orientation meeting for writing teachers. We were told, "You can't teach grammar," a remark that baffled me since, as I responded, "I do that successfully every semester." But the people running the program assured me that academic studies had demonstrated that grammar *cannot* be taught. I never went to another workshop but dug into academic articles and found there was indeed a school of thought dating back to the late 1960s that denigrated traditional teaching of literacy because it was considered unfair to minority students. A study in an academic journal showed that the teaching of grammar had been discouraged at some schools from that time onward, because it was claimed that to insist on "correct" grammar is a form of racist oppression. That notion, the author reported, was a byproduct of the drive to expunge dead white males and Western literature in general from college curricula. Of course, broadening the canon has been a worthy endeavor, and the teaching of English grammar needs to be respectful of cultural differences and the constant evolution of language. But it seems to me that it is misguided to refuse to help students from any background express themselves more clearly and precisely in the English language.

Using cultural oppression as an excuse for not teaching grammar strikes me as a cop-out by lazy teachers, and failing to teach linguistic skills to minority students, on the grounds that they can't or shouldn't be educated, is itself a form of racist discrimination. I rejected these classist and racist arguments and resolved all the more urgently to do what I could to remedy the situation. San Francisco State is a majority-minority school with large components of students from Latino/a and Asian backgrounds. So I went on trying to make up for my students' mistreatment by the educational system by teaching writing as best I could to help them improve their skills in expressing themselves.

Did the pushback against your teaching of writing continue as a result of that prevailing attitude that students can't be taught how to write?

That attitude may partly explain why I kept facing criticism over my teaching of writing from Professor Heep and some other faculty members. Students unhappy with their grades would often resort to Heepish complaints in their course evaluations, blaming their deficiencies on the instructor. I did my best to ignore such calumnies and faithfully do what I considered my job, at the cost of lowering my student evaluation scores to some extent, even though they came from a relatively small number of students. But those complaints and charges kept being brought into the tenure process in an attempt to discredit me.

I stopped reading evaluations after a while. In my view, the evaluation process, which is anonymous, harks back to the loyalty program of the Truman administration, McCarthyism, and the show business blacklist era. One of my brothers, a college dean, sent me an academic study showing convincingly that the student evaluation process is partly responsible for the decline in student learning, since it intimidates professors and makes them reluctant to give honest grades. I disregarded that concern even in the fraught period when I was advancing toward tenure, believing that a teacher has to bear the brunt of risking unpopularity to help students learn.

One of our deans told me when he reads student evaluations of instructors, he expects to see most in the middle range, which signifies to him that someone is teaching fairly, but when evaluations tend to be imbalanced in either the extremely positive or extremely negative range, that is cause for concern. But the dean's wise attitude was not shared by my adversaries in the department, who tended to cherry-pick some of the relatively few hostile evaluations I received and blow them out of proportion to generalize about my teaching. The problem was not so much those intemperate responses—my colleague Larry Clark advised me early on that we all have mentally ill students in our courses—but that my antagonists chose to automatically believe them. Still, some other faculty members on the retention and tenure committee came to my defense.

I succinctly explained the principles behind my teaching of writing in a letter to university officials in November 2005. Protesting Professor Heep's continual harassment and requesting that he be removed from his power base as head of the tenure committee before my case was decided, I pointed out,

> there was a false implication in Prof. [Heep's] attack on me at the faculty meeting that I am solely concerned with teaching grammar, spelling, and punctuation, to the exclusion of the other aspects of writing. Knowing the mechanics of writing is, of course, only one component of good writing. But if a screenwriting student cannot write clear and coherent English, that student will never be able to write a good screenplay. Only someone who has mastered the basic skills of writing can hope to succeed in the highly demanding fields of writing screenplays, fiction, or nonfiction, or, indeed, to succeed in any field that requires writing. So I insist on high standards in my writing classes to ensure that students learn how to express themselves most effectively. I work to help them communicate their thoughts and their imaginative ideas with the vigor that only sound writing skills can convey.

In that document I sent to the university hierarchy, I quoted a letter from one of my former screenwriting students, a graduate student who had written a script in my advanced class that was accepted in the Sundance screenwriting competition. I prize this student's words because she expresses so clearly what I was trying to achieve in working with someone as dedicated as her:

> I especially appreciated Professor McBride's demanding and invigorating approach to teaching. Though it should be obvious that excellent writing skills and habits are basic for any kind of success in the highly competitive screenwriting market, I think that many would-be writers seriously lack these tools. Professor McBride is emphatic and immovable about the necessity of mastering these basics. The material he presented and his expectations of students' response were of a consistently high and exacting caliber; I know that today I am a much better screenwriter because of his insistence on absolute professionalism in everything we did.

All writers want their work to be scrutinized by someone whose integrity, experience, and judgment they can trust implicitly; someone who will note absolutely everything, big stuff to little, and who will applaud the good and unhesitatingly rout out the bad. Professor McBride does all of this.... As a prolific, gifted writer and teacher, he provides in his classes an exemplary level of instruction, for students at either undergraduate or graduate level, to flourish in this difficult but exhilarating profession.

My fifteen-page letter to university officials, including our legal affairs department, detailing Professor Heep's abuses—which also included his misrepresentations of my teaching and his attempts to restrict my teaching of film studies courses—had the effect of bringing the dean to warn the committee against such bias. My protest ultimately led to Heep removing himself from membership on the committee just as I was about to go up for final consideration. That was the moment when I knew I would win tenure. I managed to do so in 2008. In my later years at the school, I tried to ignore the department and its trivial political games and just enjoy my classes and writing my books.

Along with using The Elements of Style *to help teach basic writing skills, how did you approach teaching the craft of writing for the screen?*

Cinematic storytelling was not among the skills being stressed in our department when I arrived. When I went to my first screening of our "best" student films, I found the sound and cinematography were OK, but the writing and acting were appalling. Because of the snobbishly anti-"Hollywood" bent of our department, telling a coherent story with capable actors evidently was considered vulgar. When I was named to the curriculum committee, I proposed a course on acting for cinema, but the other members wouldn't even discuss it. Years later, however, a talented professor who actually directed and wrote feature films and plays successfully instituted such a course. And eventually I had some success in raising general awareness of the need for good screenwriting. A fellow screenwriting teacher I helped bring to our school said later, "I can always tell a McBride student, because they know how to write a script."

When I taught screenwriting at New College in what amounted to my shakedown cruise in teaching, I had the students come in with their own (supposedly) original stories. But after I moved over to San Francisco State, I gradually began to approach my screenwriting courses differently. Having students bring in their own stories did not work very well, since most of the stories were not good film material. Many were rehashes of TV shows; one story that kept popping up in my early classes at San Francisco State had to do with two roommates at the school who suspect the third roommate of being a serial killer. As a result of such weak and formulaic material, about half of the students in those classes struggled to learn how to turn their ideas into screenplays.

So in coming up with a solution, I recalled how I had taught myself how to write screenplays by studying the *Citizen Kane* screenplay and later adapting existing works, starting with Hemingway's book about his youth in Paris, *A Moveable Feast,* and Jack London's "To Build a Fire." I realized that adaptation would be a better method than expecting students to start with their own stories before they knew how to write a screenplay. I recalled a fresh idea Jean Renoir had mentioned to Jacques Rivette in one of their interviews filmed for television in 1961:

> I know one way we can save films, and it's extremely simple. It would be to have the producers from a place like Hollywood or Paris decide that one year everyone would do one subject. Hollywood would decide, for example, that a certain Western would be made, that all the directors would make the same Western, and you would see the originality, the differences among the films. But instead of this, we pretend to be different by having different stories. In the end, though, we're producing exact copies. People tell a different story, but with the same faces, the same makeup, the same vocal expressions, the same emotions, but... But it's monotonous, don't you think?

That clicked as the solution I had been seeking to help all my students learn to write a good script. I would have each student adapt the same story, Hemingway's "Big Two-Hearted River." I was able to exercise my literary bent by teaching Hemingway as a model storyteller as I helped my students shape their adaptations of that classic short story into cinematic language. "Big Two-Hearted River" until 2021 was not a public-domain story like "To Build a Fire," but it could be adapted as a class exercise. I regard that story, which appears in Hemingway's 1925 collection of short stories, *In Our Time,* as his best piece of writing, the epitome of the terse, allusive, elliptical style with which he had revolutionized fiction. He carried it as far as it could go with "Big Two-Hearted River."

The author's alter ego, Nick Adams, is trying to recover his bearings on a solitary fishing expedition in the woods of Upper Michigan. After drafting the story, Hemingway excitedly wrote his mentor Gertrude Stein in 1924 that he had "finished the long one I worked on before I went to Spain where I am doing the country like Cézanne and having a hell of a time and sometimes getting it a little bit. It is about 100 pages long and nothing happens and the country is swell. I made it all up." With his exaggerated claim that "nothing happens," Hemingway was placing the focus on how the real action of the story takes place not so much in the taut fishing drama but in the psyche of the protagonist. Nick is struggling to keep his mind from falling apart while he convinces himself that he can still successfully do things he used to do well and that made him happy. I discussed with my students how this story draws from a theory Hemingway explained in his 1932 book on bullfighting, *Death in the Afternoon:*

> If a writer of prose knows enough about what he is writing about he may omit things that he knows and the reader, if the writer is writing truly enough, will have a feeling of those things as strongly as though the writer had stated them. The dignity of movement of an ice-berg is due to only one-eighth of it being above water. A writer who omits things because he does not know them only makes hollow places in his writing.

What Hemingway omitted in "Big Two-Hearted River" is what the story is about. While describing in *A Moveable Feast* how he was writing that story in a café, he comments, "The story was about coming back from the war but there was no mention of the war in it." Nick is a returning World War I veteran with what was then called shell shock but was called psycho-neurotic disorder in World War II and later became widely known as Post-Traumatic Stress Disorder (PTSD). To demonstrate the realities of PTSD, I showed my classes John Huston's 1945-1946 documentary *Let There Be Light,* the film I had helped liberate from the U.S. Army.

The Hemingway story is deceptively simple and a challenge to adapt because, as I had learned in trying to adapt *A Moveable Feast,* just following the surface action of the literary source is not enough. A cinematic equivalent has to be found to convey the psychological drama pulsing beneath the surface of Hemingway's prose style. The first thing a screenwriter jettisons in adapting a story is the style of the author, although it is possible to find cinematic equivalents of the prose in "Big Two-Hearted River," with its short sentences turning longer and freer in their syntax as Nick's tension loosens in the river and he becomes more confident, relaxed, and able to function.

That story, with both its clarity and its mysterious lacunae, proved ideal for beginning screenwriting students to adapt, and most found it a compelling challenge. Partly that was because everyone has some experience of trauma, and the increased focus on that topic today is seen in its prominence in academic writing on film. I spent a semester working with a student on an excellent paper she wrote on the trauma in Hitchcock's masterful, unfairly maligned *Marnie,* a paper that helped her get into grad school.

How did you convince your students that what you were asking them to do with the Hemingway short story would benefit them?

There are a number of major advantages in teaching the fundamentals of screenwriting by having everyone adapt the same story. First, as I told the students, it relieved them of the burden of having to come up with a solid original story, as most were not qualified to do before they learned how to write a screenplay. And it gave them the benefit of collaborating with a great writer on a story that has proven qualities (and has never been adapted for the screen, so they couldn't just copy what someone else had done). The story provides a vivid case for understanding exactly what screenwriting entails. And, equally important, since they all were working on the same story, that meant our classroom discussions about how to adapt it would keep everyone's attention.

I had found in teaching at New College that when one student was discussing her original story, the other students often stopped paying attention. The same problem arose when I taught advanced screenwriting courses at San Francisco State, in which students were expected to write a feature-length script (usually an original) in two semesters. It is possible to work hard to keep everyone interested in the various stories the students bring in, although it takes up time that in a beginning class can more profitably be invested in teaching the fundamentals of screenplay formatting, structure, imagery, and cinematic dialogue. Those are the elements that don't come naturally to students who may have written short stories in high school or college but have not tackled screenwriting.

I began my basic screenwriting course at SFSU each semester by promising the students, "If you do the assignments diligently and show up for classes, by the end of the semester you will be able to write a professional-quality screenplay. That's quite an achievement in only one semester." I told them I was not pulling their legs, and that the basics *could* be learned in that relatively short time. Only the students who failed to turn in assignments or show up for classes—I quoted Woody Allen's line that "Eighty percent of life is showing up"—would not be successful in learning the craft. For quite a while, only a couple of students would drop the ball, although that eventually changed due to other circumstances. The ones who finished the course successfully, I told them, would not (yet) be Robert Towne, but who among us is? Still, they could write a script that would pass muster professionally. My favorite student evaluation was by a screenwriting student who wrote, "Finally I learn a marketable skill."

In today's world, that is crucial, and as Paul Schrader observed in the 1990s, film schools are to some extent a scam, because those who earn a degree aren't assured of a job in the industry. The situation has only worsened over time. I told the students that the field is overcrowded, most professional screenwriters are out of work or make only a middle-class income, and if you want a steady, reliable income, you should go into another field. If you go to dental school, after a few years you will make a good living as a dentist, but it might not be as exciting as working in the arts can be. I quoted Kurt Vonnegut:

> Go into the arts. I'm not kidding. The arts are not a way to make a living. They are a very human way of making life more bearable. Practicing an art, no matter how well or badly, is a way to make your soul grow, for heaven's sake. Sing in the shower. Dance to the radio. Tell stories. Write a poem to a friend, even a lousy poem. Do it as well as you possibly can. You will get an enormous reward. You will have created something.

Did your students appreciate your method of teaching screenwriting?

Most found it enjoyable, although I usually had to overcome the kneejerk objection that adapting a story was not as "creative" as writing an original. I persuaded most, but not all, that it is just as creatively challenging to write an adaptation. And I pointed out that most films are adaptations of one kind or another, whether of an existing film or literary work, a story the writer has read in the newspaper, or a story from his or her personal experience. When the students began "breaking the back" of the Hemingway story—a crass but useful Hollywood expression—they realized there is so much more than meets the eye and what a useful challenge it is to learn how to convey Nick's PTSD through his actions. There are only three lines of dialogue in the Hemingway story, which presents a further challenge but proved stimulating, since the students were essentially writing a silent film and had to learn the importance of behavior and body language in telling a story cinematically.

In later years, you said, you also gave your students the option of adapting the story "A Late Encounter with the Enemy" by Flannery O'Connor.

After a while, I thought that would give them some flexibility if they didn't want to do the Hemingway. I chose O'Connor's great short story about a blinkered Southern woman in 1951, a racist schoolteacher who clings to the "Lost Cause" myth of the Confederacy and masquerades as the granddaughter of a Confederate general. Her grandfather, who is moribund at age 104, was actually only a footsoldier in the war, and O'Connor's depiction of his dying fantasies at his granddaughter's long-delayed graduation from college is a literary tour de force. That story, which also has never been filmed, offers many different opportunities from the Hemingway tale, since O'Connor's is satirical and often comical as well as having rich dialogue and taking place in two different time periods.

Some students took the challenge and wrote excellent screenplays from her story, but the majority still opted for the Hemingway story, partly perhaps because it seemed easier, which they learned was a deceptive notion. Still, most of the scripts adapted from both stories turned out well, and my courses were quite successful until the final years of my teaching career when, to my surprise, fewer and fewer of our students seemed interested in screenwriting. We used to have three sections of that basic screenwriting course; one semester, when my chair attempted to shield me from the wrath of Professor Heep, I taught all three. But eventually, the demand for the single basic course dwindled from more than twenty-five to twenty to sixteen to ten or twelve students, and more and more stopped coming to class. After I left, the School of Cinema stopped teaching the course entirely.

I had students read other classic short stories by Hemingway, O'Connor, Guy de Maupassant, Rudyard Kipling, and James Joyce to help them learn how to understand and appreciate the art of storytelling. Studying film adaptations of those stories helped them realize how cinematic storytelling works and what it can do when you're not talking down to your audience, as filmmakers too often do today. I found that my students initially had trouble comprehending these stories, since most of them had not been exposed to much sophisticated literature in California public high schools. So I made a point of assigning Maupassant's "A Day in the Country," Joyce's "The Dead," and Kipling's "The Man Who Would Be King" and had them watch the superb film versions of those stories so we could discuss the source material and how they were adapted.

I consider *Partie de campagne/A Day in the Country,* the 1936/1946 Maupassant adaptation written and directed by Jean Renoir, the greatest short film ever made. When Robert Towne was asked how he would teach screenwriting, he said he would just show films by Renoir, since he was not only the greatest director in film history but also the greatest screenwriter. I was shocked to find that most of our students had never seen *La Grande Illusion;* I told them they should not get out of film school without seeing it, so I showed it to all my classes and often had them watch two other Renoir masterpieces, *The Rules of the Game* and *The River.*

Since I consider John Huston to be overall the cinema's most expert, creative, and adventurous adapter of literature, I made his film versions of *The Man Who Would Be King* and *The Dead* staples of my screenwriting courses. I had the students read an essay I wrote for *Oxford American* magazine in 2007, "Who is John Huston? The Riddle of Adaptation and Authorship," on how he approached adaptations of some of the most difficult or seemingly unfilmable works by many of the greatest authors. (That essay is reprinted in *Two Cheers for Hollywood.*) Huston's eclectic range also encompassed O'Connor, Herman Melville, Carson McCullers, B. Traven, Tennessee Williams, Dashiell Hammett, Stephen Crane, Malcolm Lowry, Richard Condon, and even the authors of the Bible.

That essay explains what I consider the paradoxical nature of the authorship involving in adapting a literary work to the screen. I do so by pointing out that Huston did not attempt to impose his personality on the works of those authors in an overt or heavy-handed way but instead respected and, indeed, channeled their styles. The paradox involved in that process is that channeling the original authors made all of his work "Hustonian," since he chose stories he felt were compatible with his wry, sardonic, yet bleak vision of the world. And they became "his" because "anyone who has adapted a literary work realizes not only that it takes skill and imagination to remain 'faithful' to the source but also that every adaptation, 'faithful' or not and consciously or not, winds up reflecting the viewpoint of the adapter as much as that of the original author."

"WIN THE LOTTERY"

Had you been thinking for a while, as you tend to do before starting a book, about writing an instructional manual on screenwriting?

Four publishers' representatives approached me in my office at SFSU during a six-month period to ask me to write a book on screenwriting. I took their interest as a sign that I should finally get around to work on *Writing in Pictures*, which had been germinating in my mind for years. My agent, Richard Parks, initially doubted the need for yet another book on screenwriting. But I pointed out that when I first started teaching the subject, I couldn't find a how-to book on screenwriting that was useful as a textbook.

In 2002 I went to the Barnes & Noble bookstore in Berkeley, which still existed in those days and even had an ample film section, and bought a bunch of books on screenwriting. They mostly were written to prop up the shaky enthusiasm of would-be screenwriters by making the profession seem like a gold mine just waiting to be tapped. That foolish attitude was summed up by a cartoon in *The New Yorker* around that time showing a bookstore section of screenwriting manuals with a sign overhead, "WIN THE LOTTERY." The content of the books I read was mostly geared around telling the readers how to write scripts according to Hollywood formulas so their work (supposedly) had a better chance of selling. I found that approach not only counterproductive but illusory and dishonest. And none of the books spent much time on the actual process of planning, researching, and writing a screenplay, which became the practical focus of my book. Oddly enough, that was the difference that made it unusual and saleable.

So in *Writing in Pictures* I urge aspiring screenwriters to avoid trying to follow trends, which is not only a recipe for mediocrity but is a fool's errand anyway. My agent Jeff Berg, the best in the business, once told me, "A trend is over when the first project is announced." That wise observation reinforced what I learned from covering the industry at *Daily Variety*: Even though studios crank out a lot of carbon copies of other films, it is misguided for a writer to imitate films that are already in the pipeline or in theaters, because there are enough of them out there to crowd newcomers out of the market. And newcomers have a disadvantage, since studios are more likely to hire experienced hacks to write their formula projects. And anyway, who wants to live like that? Early in my days in Hollywood, I heard what may have been an urban myth about a busily employed screenwriter who had kept selling scripts since 1964 but had never had one produced. I would rather be dead.

One publisher of how-to film books turned down *Writing in Pictures* because he considered it too negative in warning would-be writers about the pitfalls of the field, but I argued it is more helpful to be both encouraging and realistic. I took that to heart with my students when I told them that although I managed to teach myself how to write screenplays, I didn't have the benefit of having a teacher who could warn me what not to do when I went to Hollywood, so I made so many foolish mistakes out of ignorance and because of what then was my blind impulse to trust people. I stressed to my students that they needed to know those dangers as well as being thoroughly versed in the financial and legal aspects of the business so they could minimize the extent to which they could be cheated. But I saved the discussion of "How do I sell a script?" for the last class of the semester. I waited until then because at New College, one student put up her hand and asked that question in the first class. "Before we can think about that," I said, "you have to learn how to *write* a script." At the finale of my classes at SFSU, I often brought in my witty and erudite friend Sam Hamm, the principal screenwriter of the 1989 *Batman* and other films, to offer his perspective on writing scripts. Sometimes it differed from mine, since he is more amenable to compromising with the system than I was.

In *Writing in Pictures,* to let the reader bite the economic bullet, I started with Sam's advice to my students, "If you can do anything else, do it." I added, "Sam is right. Trying to earn a living as a screenwriter, or as a writer of any kind, often resembles the Myth of Sisyphus." And I go through how little respect screenwriters are given in the industry and how frustrating it can be to see your script turned into a film, even if you direct it yourself. As Woody Allen admitted in 2009 after making his delightful romantic comedy *Vicky Cristina Barcelona*,

> I almost always feel disappointed when I see my movies [when they are finished]. When you're conceiving them at home, it's only happening in your mind and everything's fabulous. Then you find out that Javier and Penelope are not available, you're not gonna be able to get Buckingham Palace and the cameraman doesn't quite get the lighting exactly as you want. By the time the thing is over, between your own mistakes and the compromises and the money that you don't have to reshoot scenes, you never think, "This is amazing." Instead it's: "Oh, God, if I take it back into the editing room, cut this, put this over here and add some music, I think I can save it." You start out convinced you're gonna make *The Bicycle Thieves* and, by the time you're in the editing room, you're just fighting for survival. You've given up all your aspirations, greatness is out the window, you just don't want to embarrass yourself and for it to be coherent.

But as I wrote:

> if you can minimize your illusions about screen-writing and treat it as a job like any other, as the honorable profession it is, it can be a rewarding adventure indeed. Hearing good actors speak the lines you write or seeing images you imagined come to life on-screen is thrilling. I will never forget the first time I heard an actor speak the lines I wrote—Henry Fonda speaking my words honoring Jimmy Stewart...—or the time I stood in a high school corridor watching the revolutionary chaos I conceived for *Rock 'n' Roll High School* erupting all around me. At moments like that, it's all worthwhile.... That creative excitement I experi-enced as a young writer can happen to you if you write a script you care about and find someone with even a small amount of money who's willing to bring it to the screen.

With misgivings, but at the urging of Richard Parks, I eventually took *Writing in Pictures* to Random House. Richard convinced me that most of the people who had tried to block my Capra biography were no longer there, and that the new book would be judged on its own, so I needed not to let the old trauma stop me. That turned out to be good advice. The editor who acquired the book, Zachary Wagman of the publisher's Vintage/Anchor imprint, was cordial and helpful with his suggestions, as was Diana Secker Tesdell, who inherited the project after Zack moved to another division of Random House. Zack did find the manuscript overly long and balked at making a deal for that reason, but I took it with me on a one-week research trip to Madison and managed to cut it on the plane flights and in my hotel room sufficiently for Zack to accept it for publication. Those cuts helped the book for the most part, although I still miss the chapter on how Huston excelled in the art of adaptation, which I based on my *Oxford American* article. Random House handled *Writing in Pictures* well and has kept it in print ever since.

Since Writing in Pictures *is based on your classroom teaching method, how did you go about structuring the book's agenda to achieve similar results?*

In deciding what story I should use as an example throughout the book to walk the reader through the screenplay adaptation process, I realized a public-domain work would be best. I soon settled on Jack London's "To Build a Fire," the first story I had tried to adapt in 1967, as the basis for the exercises in the book. It was a natural choice, since it's a terse, vivid, exciting story with powerful suspense and human drama, mostly silent storytelling, and London's prose is highly visual. He's not as difficult to adapt as Hemingway, but London's classic story of a man getting stranded in the Yukon and gradually freezing to death because of his inexperience and hubris is still a challenge to render in cinematic language.

The chapters in *Writing in Pictures* discuss the nature of screenwriting and how to choose a viable story for the screen and then go through all the logical steps in the professional development process of conceiving, breaking down, researching, outlining, formatting, and writing a screenplay. I also include chapters on the importance of actors and how to write dialogue, as well as an epilogue on how to break into professional filmmaking. The book builds up to a new screenplay adaptation I wrote of London's story.

I admit that I found myself feeling a bit anxious before writing that script, since it was a long time between screenplays for me, but I was pleased to find the work easy and enjoyable. I wrote the script in just four days, and like the last complete script I wrote back in the day, *No More Mr. Nice Guy*, I only wrote one draft (although with word processing, the concept of a draft is somewhat passé, since you're continually revising and improving your work). I use my sample script to demonstrate most of the various modes of cinematic storytelling, including added scenes involving flashbacks and fantasies as well as dialogue to supplement the mostly silent storytelling. The chapter on formatting explains each cinematic device in detail and gives examples of each as well as the rationales for how and why formatting is important to good screenwriting, a point on which some beginners need convincing.

I put a lot more stress on research in *Writing in Pictures* than I did when I was a beginning screenwriter. Back then I just winged it in writing my script of "To Build a Fire" without studying life in the Yukon in 1908, Jack London's background and career, or how death would come to someone who becomes lost in temperatures around seventy-five below zero. Studying that question made me realize that an important difference between the world when London's story takes place and today is that an outdoorsman now would have a cellphone and a GPS device, so I kept the story in its period.

And it was embarrassing but humorous to realize, when I dug out my first adaptation of "To Build a Fire," how clueless I was to write a shot list rather than a filmable or even readable screenplay. I read through my numbered and mind-numbing descriptions of how the camera moves and how the scenes cut together and in what directions the man looks, etc. That's not how a screenplay works. It took me a while to figure that out when I was starting without having a teacher. But I include part of my old shot list in *Writing in Pictures* to show what not to do. And though I was intending to film the story back then with my friend Bill Donnelly as the bearded, middle-aged protagonist in the snows of our Wisconsin winter—tough weather but nowhere near as sub-freezing as in London's story—I still abandoned the notion because of the hardships involved. But London's story is perfect for an exercise in the fundamentals of screenwriting. I didn't show my classes the 1969 BBC-TV version, which is pretty good in some respects but relies excessively on Orson Welles narrating from the short story as a substitute for just dramatizing the action.

And when you designed Writing in Pictures, *how did you keep in mind that all your readers weren't in an actual class with you?*

When used as a textbook, *Writing in Pictures* supplements and expands on lessons a teacher has time to discuss in class. And it is also designed to be read by someone at home who will learn how to write a screenplay if he or she does the exercises and follows my guidelines. Doing that, I promise in the book as I did in my classes, should make the diligent reader a professional-quality screenwriter in just a few months. The samples of each step along the way include a story outline, adaptation outline, character biography, treatment, step outline, and the final screenplay. (I had those samples set in typewriter-style lettering to resemble professional submissions written on word processors.) I was a bit chastened to find myself constantly going over the page limit in writing each sample assignment before cutting them down, so in giving that mea culpa to my students in classes, I told them it made me more sympathetic with their learning tasks and even more cognizant of the need for compression in writing a screenplay. Hitchcock said screenplays need compression, unlike novels, which can go on for a thousand pages, and that the primary quality a film needs is clarity.

I was aware that the two things you don't get from the book are being in a group discussion and watching the films I would use in the classroom to illustrate my lessons. So I amplify those lessons to give much more detailed advice in *Writing in Pictures* than I could give in class, and I take more advantage of the knowledge I've acquired in my professional career and what I've learned from teaching my students. Those fuller explanations of the process and the business and legal aspects of screenwriting help make up for the absence of class discussion. To compensate for the absence of film clips, I include many examples from films and TV shows (past and more current) and offer suggestions with detailed descriptions of how to learn from them. I recommend that students watch the films on their own, which I hope the more dedicated readers will do.

Since I worked hard to ensure that *Writing in Pictures* is practical for both classroom and private use, I'm pleased that the feedback I've had from readers and people in the business convinces me that it is. Peter Bogdanovich gave me this blurb: "Impressively readable, unpretentious, and remarkably useful. Based on a lifetime of experience and observation, Joe McBride's comprehensive yet very succinct work should become a standard text." My droll friend and SFSU colleague Julian Hoxter also has written a screenwriting manual, and when I asked him how he goes about using his own book in his teaching, he said, "I just tell different jokes."

A possible solution

What did you advise students who wanted to have screenwriting careers to do to get around the Hollywood system?

As a recovering screenwriter, I felt somewhat ambivalent about encouraging students to enter the film industry, especially by going to Hollywood, so I offered them the frank warning that I regard Hollywood as a "criminal enterprise." The business is not only thoroughly dishonest in its interpersonal transactions but financially rigged to avoid giving all but a few of the creative people their fair share of the profits. This is due in large part to the work of the anonymous accounting genius who invented "creative bookkeeping," the system that ensures most films, even the most successful, never show a profit on the studio books. My actual feelings about that company town make it even more ironic that some of my colleagues at SFSU regarded me as "too Hollywood." I could say what Orson Welles did in a twist on the signature line of columnist Sidney Skolsky, who used to write, "But don't get me wrong. I love Hollywood." Welles said, "I love movies. But don't get me wrong. I hate Hollywood."

But if a student was serious about turning professional, I was encouraging while taking care to lay out all the pitfalls they might find along the way. I remembered that when I was in the depths of my despondency over my screenwriting career in Hollywood, I was invited to speak at a small class at the UW Madison. I basically told the students a succession of horror stories about the profession. I wondered if I had been too harsh, but one woman in the class thanked me afterward for telling the truth. She said she still was going to become a screenwriter but found it valuable to hear the downsides so she could avoid them. I wish someone had done that for me before I naively went to Hollywood and dove into a shark tank and made some terrible mistakes. Someone who goes into the professional world fully aware of the pitfalls stands a better chance of surviving and succeeding.

I mean it in the epilogue to *Writing in Pictures* when I urge readers to make what are known as "no-budget" films. Today all you need is a digital camera (borrowed if necessary; or as Werner Herzog famously advised, "If you want to do a film, steal a camera"); some volunteer actors; a few crew helpers; and a little money so you can feed them during the shoot. I tell the readers (as I told my students) to follow the advice of Robert Rodriguez in his marvelous book *Rebel Without a Crew: Or How a 23-Year-old Filmmaker with $7,000 Became a Hollywood Player*, his diary of the making of his feature *El Mariachi*, and illustrated in his wise and amusing supplemental video on the DVD, *The Robert Rodriguez Ten Minute Film School*. Rodriguez tells us that "if you want to make a movie for a really low budget, you can't spend on anything. You have to *refuse* to spend. I mean, that's just basically how you do it. You refuse to spend on anything. You start spending a little bit, you start that money hose going, and you just can't stop it. Think of a creative way to get around your problem."

Welles similarly told Henry Jaglom that the less money a young filmmaker has, the more freedom he has, but the more he is given, the more people start telling him what to do. I told my students not to wait around for the phone to ring or waste their time knocking on doors in Hollywood (as I did for years) but to "just go out and make your no-budget film." If you want to break into professional filmmaking, you need what's called a "calling-card film" to show what you can do, because mere talk means nothing. I showed the students Steven Spielberg's 1968 calling-card film, *Amblin'*, which I call "the *Citizen Kane* of student films," but that 26-minute short, which won him his first professional contract at Universal, cost about $20,000 to make, and $20,000 then was the equivalent of $186,000 today. Back then, when I also started, you were stymied by having to buy film, which was expensive, but now you don't have to do so, because you shoot with a digital camera. Writing a script costs nothing, and if it's any good, it's better than most scripts filmed in Hollywood. Plan the project so it can be shot without spending anything, using whatever locations and resources you can beg or borrow, draw up brief agreements giving percentages to your cast and crew in case the film makes money, and start shooting.

Two students took my advice and made no-budget features that benefit from solid screenplays and have only so-so acting but are well-shot and well-directed. Trevor Walters went back to his home town of Kalamazoo, Michigan, to shoot an engaging comedy-drama he wrote in my advanced screenwriting course about a group of aimless buddies who become discomfited when a maverick among them gets some initiative. My son described that 2010 film, *Fairfield*, as "the truest film I've seen about my generation." Trevor has gone on to make commercials and industrial films for his own digital company and has also been a teacher of filmmaking. And my former student Brie Williams and her collaborator John C. Clark made their modestly budgeted feature satirizing gay conversion therapy by raising $35,000 through crowdfunding. Although Brie and John didn't break through with that well-made film, you can still try to use your modest feature as the calling-card film every aspiring filmmaker needs to get in the door with producers. Offer it to festivals and package it as a DVD to sell on Amazon.com.

Our so-called "studies faculty"

During your years as a teacher, you updated your Spielberg biography twice, for 2010 and 2012 editions, and you continued publishing critical studies of filmmakers, including Lubitsch, Wilder, the Coen Bros., and Cukor. You mentioned that your antagonists in the Cinema Department nevertheless kept trying to undermine your teaching of film studies courses. How so?

Even after earning tenure and having job security, I continued to be ostracized to some extent in what was pretentiously renamed our "School of Cinema" and often had to fight for what I wanted to teach. I mostly managed to work my way around that with the help of more sympathetic colleagues, including some chairs who were more or less successful in negotiating solutions. But it may seem incredible to report that all the way from the beginning of my time at SFSU until I retired at the end of 2024, I was never considered a member of our "studies faculty," as our chair informed my colleagues that fall at a faculty meeting. Even after I objected by pointing out to the faculty that I had regularly taught film studies courses at the school since 2002 and am considered a leading name in the field, the chair followed up by putting his claim in writing to my colleagues and omitting my name from the list of studies faculty.

Some colleagues who taught our other studies courses had regular meetings as the so-called "studies faculty" and exchanged emails as a clique that pointedly excluded me. I'd say they behaved like high schoolers except that my classmates in high school were above that kind of behavior; grade school–level bullying is more like it. One studies teacher who was outraged by that ostracization tried repeatedly to add me to their meetings and email ring but to no avail. Frankly, I was relieved to be excluded. I've always just gone my own way.

Contrast the shabby treatment I received within my department with a letter of recommendation sent to our department by Robin Wood, who was then Professor Emeritus at York University in Toronto, when I was applying for tenure in 2007. Wood was one of numerous major film scholars who wrote such letters on my behalf. His was among the most gratifying, since I had learned so much from his example as an author of critical studies and essays. He wrote that I was

> one of the most important figures in the history of American film criticism.... Everyone, whether critic, filmmaker, film historian, or simple lover of American cinema, must feel deeply indebted to him.... Anyone who doubts that Mr. McBride has earned the highest rewards for his contribution to American cinema need only pause and ask him/her self what film history would lack if he had never existed. Mr. McBride's encyclopedic knowledge has always been nourished by his untiring enthusiasm, the sheer love of his subject that shines throughout his work.

And while I was going up for tenure and promotion to full professor, four leading academic scholars in their letters of recommendation described me as one of the founders of the field of film studies. As I wrote in my Introduction to *Two Cheers for Hollywood*, "I was delighted to know that, and rather surprised. All that time I just thought I was just writing about what interested me." Our chair who helped hire me, Steve Ujlaki, in his letter recommending me for tenure, cited those experts' appraisal of my role in the studies field, for which I am grateful.

But a subsequent chair omitted that appraisal when he wrote his recommendation letter supporting my promotion to full professor, which I finally earned in 2013. When I objected to his removal of the experts' view of my historical role in the field, that chair claimed that no one can be considered a founder of the field of film studies. Although I began publishing articles and books about film from 1967 and '68, in the eyes of many academics the "field of film studies" did not exist until the subject became legitimized in academia in the 1970s, when it morphed into a subset of linguistics and Marxism and was more about film theory than film history. When I once said half-jokingly, "You have to be a Marxist to be a film professor," my son wisely replied, "No, you have to *pretend* to be a Marxist."

I was fortunate to be out of academia by the time that happened, working in Hollywood as a trade reporter and reviewer and a screenwriter, as well as writing my idiosyncratic books. I avoid the requisite film studies jargon that makes many academic film books grotesquely unreadable. Absurdly, a review of one of my recent books in a film journal complained that it is too easy to read. But there was a group of us in the late 1960s who helped blaze the trail, and the Tenure and Promotion Committee recommending my advancement to full professor wrote, "Simply put, he emerges as a giant in his field."

Meanwhile, however, our departmental website had no qualms in praising Professor Heep for his "pioneering work as founder" of a branch of film studies and as a scholar whose work "helped to establish film studies as an academic discipline." That claim, taken virtually word-for-word from Professor Heep's curriculum vitae, refers to his first book, which appeared in 1976, eight years after I began publishing books. The department's downgrading of my role in the field while inflating that of my nemesis was the final step in my alienation from the school.

Not only was Professor Heep antagonistic until he finally departed for another institution, but a younger faculty member, a protégé of his who later became chair of the department, routinely interrupted me at meetings for years, always after I had spoken for one minute, which seemed a concerted strategy to keep me from fully expressing myself. So I decided to make a silent protest by emulating, partly with tongue in cheek, Supreme Court Justice Clarence Thomas, who for some years on the court had notoriously remained mute, presumably also to express his disenchantment with his institution. I stopped going to faculty meetings for a while and soon developed a policy of not speaking at those meetings anymore unless directly called upon, a practice I maintained until the end of my days at the school.

Into the Nightmare

Before you were obsessed with Welles and Ford, there was John F. Kennedy. Your lifelong search for the truth as a writer was never more evident than when you self-published Into the Nightmare: My Search for the Killers of President John F. Kennedy and Officer J. D. Tippit.

That book took thirty-one years to research and the better part of seven years to write before it was published in 2013, in time for the fiftieth anniversary of those murders on November 22, 1963. I continue to pursue that mission relentlessly because of my loyalty to the candidate I had worked for and because his unsolved murder disrupted my belief system so radically that I have to do all I can to understand what happened to him and why.

As I told you, I began writing about his assassination two years before it happened. My October 1961 short story "The Plot Against a Country" was written when I was fourteen. Although it's prescient, it's callow and reflects my political naivete at the time and my indoctrination with Cold War beliefs. President Kennedy is poisoned in the Oval Office by licking an envelope planted by a cleaning lady, one of "a small band of fanatics in East Germany sympathetic with communism and intent on throwing our nation into chaos." I stole the murder method from a *Superman* comic book. But despite the puerile nature of much of the story, I was already a student of the Lincoln assassination and had the historical sense to realize that killing a president wouldn't have been just a random, senseless act, but a conspiracy against an entire country. The story also discusses the presidential autopsy and the investigation by the FBI and the Secret Service.

Why did I write such a story? I mentioned to you how I became concerned by Kennedy's lack of security when I had met him twice while volunteering in his 1960 Wisconsin presidential primary campaign at the small "Kids for Kennedy" rally in Wauwatosa and at the large campaign rally in Milwaukee. On the first occasion, he had no visible security and mingled easily with the attendees, chatting with us as we stood around him (one of my little brothers kept crawling back and forth between his legs); on the second occasion, some policemen were around but did not keep close to the candidate as he shook hands with me and many other rallygoers. I think it was my rudeness in blowing off a flashbulb three feet from Kennedy's face, causing him to briefly react in shock before regaining his composure, that made me realize how vulnerable he truly was at that event and led to my writing the story. So I worried about his security enough to compare his fictional murderers to "John Wilkes Booth and his gang, who now share the dubious distinction of successfully executing the most infamous crimes in American history." The height of my naivete was my conclusion that "the conspirators will be brought to justice," but I added that "we certainly hope that [the story] will never become a grim reality."

So I was not entirely surprised when Kennedy actually was shot two years later. I heard the news from a fellow student while in the cafeteria line after Mass at Marquette and immediately ran two blocks to a drugstore where I could listen to a radio. As I began hearing network reports ten minutes after the 12:30 shooting, they indicated the shots were fired from the front, from the railroad bridge and/or the hill to the right of the motorcade (soon to be known as the Grassy Knoll). But at 1 PM, the network radio reports abruptly changed the direction of the shots, stating that they were all fired from behind the presidential limousine, from a window in a building called the Texas School Book Depository.

No explanation was offered for this complete reversal of the source of the bullets. I was already a journalist, and when a story is changed so drastically without explanation, a red flag of doubt goes up in my mind, but in my state of shock I was slow to grasp its meaning. By that evening I was not believing the official story, when I heard Lee Harvey Oswald professing his innocence of shooting Kennedy and Officer Tippit by shouting into the TV cameras, "I haven't killed anybody!" and declaring, "I'm just a patsy!"

How did your views on the case develop after that?

My skepticism—like that of many other Americans who doubted the official story—was lulled by the release of the Warren Report in September 1964 and the lies and cover-up by the mainstream media that began on November 22 and have continued to the present day. But by 1966, when a spate of books were coming out questioning the official story and my skepticism about governmental lies was stimulated by the expansion of the Vietnam War, I was paying attention to the case again, and my disbelief returned. That December I wrote a letter to the editor of Madison's liberal newspaper, the *Capital Times,* stating,

Senator John F. Kennedy addresses the "Kids for Kennedy" rally my mother helped organize at the Wauwatosa Civic Center on March 31, 1960, as part of his Wisconsin presidential primary campaign. I met JFK at that casual event, during which he quipped after I answered a question, "I hope I don't have to run against you in 1964." (Joseph McBride)

> I wanted to believe in the commission's findings, to reassure myself, and I was suspicious of the researchers who began questioning the findings. But now, after many inaccuracies have been found in the report, and as new and disconcerting evidence (e.g., the string of post-assassination reports of [dead] witnesses and newspapermen) has been revealed, I am totally unable to assess the case.... I shall forever by haunted by the memory of Oswald, at 7:55 CST Friday night, shaking his handcuffed fists at the TV cameras and shouting, 'I haven't killed anybody!'... No dead man can be convicted of a crime, and no unprosecuted dead man's reputation should be such.

My letter showed some confusion, but my admission of doubt and confusion at least was the beginning of wisdom. My study of the dissenting literature and scrutiny of other books increased—although I don't recall reading until some time later Sylvia Meagher's lucid, methodical and magisterial deconstruction of the report, *Accessories After the Fact: The Warren Commission, The Authorities, and The Report*, which was published in 1967 and is still the best book about the case. But I remember being especially struck when William Manchester's *The Death of a President* revealed, also in 1967, that there had been a nearly violent battle between the Secret Service and Kennedy's aides, led by the late president's appointments secretary, Kenneth O'Donnell, against the Dallas County medical examiner, Dr. Earl Rose, over the illegal removal of the coffin from the hospital without Rose being able to perform the official autopsy required by Texas law. That was one of the watershed moments in my understanding of the case. When I saw the 1967 Emile de Antonio-Mark Lane documentary, *Rush to Judgment*, based on Lane's seminal 1966 book of that title demolishing the case against Oswald, my newfound attitude was summed up in the concluding words of the crusading small-town Texas newspaper editor W. Penn Jones Jr.: "I think all of us who love our—this country should be alerted that something is wrong in the land."

During the 1970s, the Watergate scandal and the Church Committee findings about CIA assassination plots gave me a deeper understanding of how the government actually works. That erased my earlier naivete about the myth of American exceptionalism, showing that we have been a rogue state since 1963. I bought a rare pristine set of the twenty-six supplemental volumes of Warren Commission hearings and records (a set that had been sent to the Commerce Department but evidently was never read) and paid close attention to the hearings of the House Select Committee on Assassinations. In 1979 I bought the twelve-volume set of HSCA findings on one of the research trips I had begun taking to the National Archives (in those days before the Internet) to study the paper files on the Kennedy assassination. And I began reading widely in the voluminous literature of the case, including press coverage over the years, and purchased copies of manuscripts and other documents as well as a print of the Zapruder film from a collector in Canada who served as an informal clearing-house for researchers.

My radicalization as a result of those understandings of the case and my disillusioning awakening to the realities of the capitalist system as epitomized in Hollywood gradually led me to agree with historical critiques such as Peter Dale Scott's analysis of the assassination and related events in his 1993-1996 book, *Deep Politics and the Death of JFK* (which I later used as a textbook in a course on historical films at SFSU). Scott wrote, "There have been four incapacitating political crises in Washington since World War II: McCarthyism, Dallas, Watergate, and Contragate.... [B]y their decadic regularity, they deserve to be regarded as periodic readjustments of the open political system in which we [purportedly] live. At the center of all four crises have been perceived threats to the prosecution of the Cold War."

In Madison, every lefty who saw the Zapruder film believed several men, probably other than Oswald, had shot Kennedy on 11/22/63, but did you find that people in L.A. and other places didn't share your beliefs?

Despite the widespread public loss of belief in the official version when I was getting more deeply involved in my research from the 1970s onward, most people I met didn't want to hear any more about the assassination. They didn't want to have their kneejerk beliefs, fostered by the media, thrown into question. It's too troubling for many people to contemplate the possibility of a governmental cover-up, or worse, of a president's murder. Those today who continue to cling to the official Warren Report myth that a lone gunman with no apparent motive shot Kennedy and Tippit are usually inarticulate about the case, unable to explain why they hold that belief, which is easy to tear apart. As I write *in Into the Nightmare,* "The Warren Report offers eight basic 'proofs' of its theory that Oswald was the lone assassin. Surprisingly, that's all its case comes down to.... Those who still believe that Oswald was the lone gunman, or a gunman at all, probably have not examined these 'proofs' closely or have chosen to disregard the actual evidence in the case." The true believers tend to resort to mockery and ad hominem attacks. Even the HSCA's findings of conspiracy tend to be dismissed out of hand.

So back then, it was much harder to talk about the case than it is now. You had to become accustomed to people giving you that blank look of incomprehension, rolling their eyes, or shutting down the discussion with insults and the use of the supposedly case-closing term "conspiracy theory." That term was spread pervasively into the public consciousness as a derogatory expression by the infamous 1967 CIA memo "Countering Criticism of the Warren Report."

How did you react to that memo? And do you think that the people who wrote and sent it knew the truth, which I guess would make them part of the conspiracy?

During my first of numerous research trips to Dallas for my book
*Into the Nightmare: My Search for the Killers of President John
F. Kennedy and Officer J. D. Tippit*, I visited Dealey Plaza on
November 22, 1983, the twentieth anniversary of JFK's murder there.
I had begun researching the book in earnest in 1982; it was finally
published in 2013.

The memo was written under a cover name by the CIA's
Cord Meyer, a propaganda and disinformation specialist
who was later accused by the Agency's E. Howard Hunt
of playing a key role in organizing the assassination of
President Kennedy for Lyndon Johnson. The 1967 memo
was directed partly at "propaganda assets" including
"liaison and friendly elite contacts (especially politicians
and editors)," and it urged "discrediting the claims of the
conspiracy theorists," popularizing that phrase as coded
language to stigmatize Kennedy assassination researchers as
crazy and thereby cut off discussion.

The memo states that because of the spate of books in
that period questioning the official story and the widespread
public doubt, "This trend of opinion is a matter of concern
to the U.S. government, including our organization.... Just
because of the standing of the Commissioners, efforts to
impugn their rectitude and wisdom tend to cast doubt on
the whole leadership of American society. Moreover, there
seems to be an increasing tendency to hint that President
Johnson himself, as the one person who might be said
to have benefited, was in some way responsible for the
assassination. Innuendo of such seriousness affects not only
the individual concerned, but also the whole reputation of
the American government."

As a result of such propaganda muddying the public
consciousness and spreading hostility against assassination

researchers, you would get to the point where you stopped bringing up the case with most people even though you were eager to discuss it. It was a frustrating and lonely situation in those years. There was a limited community of far-flung researchers and authors, but before the Internet there wasn't much opportunity to talk among ourselves, so the subject was driven underground and more deeply into private research. By necessity I became more of what Abe Polonsky called me — "a secret man" — as I ran my side track of assassination research quietly alongside my public identity as a film historian and screenwriter.

What convinced you to finally write Into the Nightmare? *And what was the reaction of people who knew you as a film critic?*

I made an effort in 1985 to sell the book that became *Into the Nightmare* by writing a proposal to show Robert Gottlieb, who was then my editor at Knopf on my Capra biography. He passed the proposal to another editor who supposedly knew more about history but thought it too speculative; I should have known that Knopf's parent Random House is hostile to such books and has long specialized in books debunking conspiracy theories. And when I pitched my book proposal on the media coverage of the assassination, an editor at Simon & Schuster told me that although he believed a conspiracy was involved in the case, he couldn't publish a book that attacks the *New York Times*, since the company needs the *Times* to review its books and can't afford to offend that powerful publication.

That in a nutshell is the problem with politically unorthodox books, especially on this subject, which remains a third rail in American politics and journalism, along with 9/11. Noam Chomsky, for example, has said those are the two topics he won't touch, although he's published books on both subjects; I gather he means that he refuses to seriously study the conspiracy theories about those events. Nearly all books on the assassination from major publishers slavishly support the Warren Commission theory, even though the subsequent U.S. government investigation by the House Select Committee on Assassinations found that President Kennedy was killed by a conspiracy involving two gunmen.

After beginning work on *Into the Nightmare* in 1982, I came to the conclusion that I should write it as a memoir because (1) it enabled me to track how I became drawn into the case and took steps to mount my own investigation; and (2) I felt that by following my progression from initial skepticism to psychological resistance to greater understanding, I would be able to demonstrate for an empathetic reader how a concerned citizen evolves in comprehending the murders of Kennedy and Tippit. I eventually wrote an outline of 150 pages, kept it in a binder, but never consulted it, since I had it in my head. The hardest part of the book to write was the chapter on what actually happened that day in Dallas, which I felt was needed to anchor my account of my investigation as well as to make the actual facts of the case clear to readers who aren't experts on it. I wrote four different versions of that chapter over a two-year period and ultimately divided it into two chapters. My late friend F. X. Feeney, a film historian and screenwriter, compared *Into the Nightmare* to Joyce's *Ulysses* in its microscopic narrative about the events of a single day.

Although it is heartening that a majority of Americans over the years have consistently told pollsters they doubt the Warren Commission version of the case, I was and am deeply troubled by the apparent willingness of most Americans to simply accept the official lies or shrug their collective shoulders helplessly in response. As I wrote in my 2021 book *Political Truth: The Media and the Assassination of President Kennedy*,

> I finally found an answer in psychiatrist E. Martin Schotz's 1996 book, *History Will Not Absolve Us*, which calls the Kennedy assassination "a window onto the reality of American democracy." Schotz argues that the reason the murder of a president at high noon on a public street has not inspired the mainstream media or the populace to active revolt was that the assassination was "politically acceptable."
>
> In reaching that harsh, sobering, and accurate conclusion, Schotz believes the public has accepted the violent overthrowing of the government in 1963 partly for psychological reasons. He attributes that to citizens being held in "a state of confusion in which anything can be believed but nothing can be known, nothing of significance that is. And the American people are more than willing to be held in this state because to *know* the truth—as opposed to only *believe* the truth—is to face an awful terror and to be no longer able to evade responsibility. It is precisely in moving from belief to knowledge that the citizen moves from irresponsibility to responsibility, from helplessness and hopelessness to action." Since not only the government but also

the media, supposedly the people's watchdogs, have been complicit as accessories to the crime and cover-up, that has the effect of "immobilizing the American people politically."

So as Schotz puts it, "What does that say? It says that a conspiracy to kill the President and its cover-up are acceptable. Not legal, mind you. Nor moral. Upsetting? Of course. But, in the end, acceptable. The government continues to function and everyone remains in place. This is American democracy."

Officer J. D. Tippit was seen as an incidental and often forgotten figure in the story, but you bring him to the forefront in Into the Nightmare.

The more I studied the events of November 22, 1963, the more my instincts as an investigative reporter were stirred by the strange dearth of information and scrutiny of the Tippit murder and Tippit's personal life in both the official investigations and the literature surrounding those events. David Belin, a Warren Commission counsel who became its most strident defender, called the Tippit murder the "Rosetta Stone" of the assassination. What he meant was that the unproven claim that Oswald killed Tippit while fleeing from the assassination somehow proved that Oswald had shot Kennedy, which is a non sequitur even if Oswald had shot Kennedy. But that supposition proved helpful in guiding public opinion to blame the supposed cop-killer for Kennedy's murder.

When Oswald was brought before the TV cameras at midnight that Friday and again denied shooting anyone, while asking "someone to come forward to give me legal assistance," he had been told only that he had been charged with the Tippit murder. The complaint in the charge of killing the president had been signed by Captain Will Fritz, the head of Homicide for the Dallas Police Department, about half an hour earlier, but it was not lodged until shortly after 1:30 AM Saturday. When Oswald was asked at the press conference, "Did you kill the president?," he replied, "No. I've not been charged with that. In fact, nobody has said that to me yet. The first thing I heard about it was when the newspaper reporters in the hall, uh, asked me that question." A reporter responded insistently, seemingly in anger, as if Oswald were lying, "You have been charged. You *have* been charged." Dallas Homicide Detective James R. Leavelle confirmed to me that the police had not notified Oswald of that charge before the press conference, "so he answered it truthfully. He knew he was a suspect, but he hadn't been charged with it. Now, that was the difference in the Tippit deal.… We had charged him with the Tippit thing." But as I put it in *Into the Nightmare,* "one of the strangest pieces of evidence that has emerged to cast a shadow on the supposed quick solution to the dual murders" is an FBI document I found stating that Oswald was arraigned only on the charge of murdering Tippit and was never arraigned for the presidential assassination.

With my longstanding belief that the events kept most resolutely hidden are often the key to understanding a story, I began to realize that the Tippit murder was indeed the "Rosetta Stone" of the case, but for the opposite reason from the one Belin argued so speciously. On my first visit to Dallas in November 1983 to begin my on-the-scene research there during the twentieth anniversary of the assassination, I met Penn Jones, the crusading editor of the small-town *Midlothian* (Texas) *Mirror,* one of the first and most tenacious researchers of the assassination of President Kennedy. Penn was leading his annual ceremony on the Grassy Knoll to commemorate the assassination. I was immediately drawn to Penn, the same way I felt as when I met Sam Fuller. They were both feisty, no-nonsense old newspaper guys who always were after scoops and were relentless truth-tellers. That's what I try to be as well, and they were inspirational. Penn Jones became a mentor of mine in Dallas in helping me understand the assassination, which I had begun researching in a more dedicated and methodical way in 1982, once I began focusing my attention on the relatively obscure and under-investigated Tippit murder.

Penn gave me the same advice he gave many other researchers, and it guided my work: "Take one aspect of the case, one that hasn't been studied sufficiently, and research the hell out of it." I realized that I could make a difference by investigating the Tippit murder as well as exploring its connections to the Kennedy case. Even Sylvia Meagher, while referring to the Warren Commission's "profound lack of interest in Tippit," described him as "unknown and unknowable." That was my challenge. The Dallas police had essentially dropped its investigation of the Tippit murder when Oswald was shot two days later, and subsequent official investigations were also inadequate. Two independent researchers who seriously examined the case unearthed some new evidence and leads but left the case tantalizingly unresolved—Henry Hurt as part of his 1986 book, *Reasonable Doubt: An Investigation into the Assassination of*

John F. Kennedy, and Gary Murr in his short but valuable unpublished 1971 monograph, *The Murder of Dallas Police Officer J. D. Tippit* (which can be found online). Eventually Dale K. Myers provided a useful foil by publishing in 1998 what I consider the Warren Report of the Tippit case, *With Malice: Lee Harvey Oswald and the Murder of Officer J. D. Tippit*. Myers's conclusion is stated in the title of his meretricious book, which systematically discounts all evidence to the contrary, usually by relegating it to footnotes at the end and simply dismissing them as false.

How did your research on the murders of Kennedy and Tippit progress once you began focusing specifically on their murders on that one day?

During the 1980s, while digging through FBI files to assemble a pathway into the case and its many mysteries and discrepancies, I began making discoveries. One caused quite a stir in the press. That was the first of two articles I wrote for *The Nation* in July and August 1988 revealing the unacknowledged early CIA connections of George H. W. Bush. They were based on previously overlooked FBI documents released in 1977-1978 through Freedom of Information Act suits, among a total of 98,755 pages of Bureau documents, and my other research into Bush's covert CIA connections. My articles, "The Man Who Wasn't There: 'George Bush,' CIA Operative" and "Where *Was* George? (cont.)," were widely covered by other media at the time and led to my being interviewed live for an hour by Brian Lamb on C-SPAN from Washington, D.C.

The articles were prompted by my discovery of a November 29, 1963, FBI document I found about how "Mr. George Bush of the Central Intelligence Agency" and others were briefed by the FBI about the possible reactions of anti-Castro Cubans to the assassination. FBI Director J. Edgar Hoover wrote the memo to summarize the briefing an FBI agent gave Bush and Captain William Edwards of the Defense Intelligence Agency on November 23, when Lee Harvey Oswald was still alive and available to be interrogated about his connections to Cuban exiles and the CIA. I discovered the memo in 1985 at the library at California State University, San Bernardino, while going methodically through microfilm of the FBI documents. Numerous other related documents also turned up in that search, which I made while living in Green Valley Lake and taking time out from researching my Capra biography. It was claimed that I "stumbled upon" those documents, but my discoveries were part of my methodical search for evidence. I knew enough to not recall ever hearing that Bush had been part of the CIA before he served as its director in 1976 and '77, appointed supposedly despite having no prior intelligence connections. I printed the 1963 FBI memo and some other documents and took them home for my files as material for further research.

When Vice President Bush was running for president in 1988, I brought out the memo and researched other official sources on him, including his suspiciously bland 1987 autobiography, *Looking Forward* (written with Victor Gold). I soon realized that none mentioned any pre-1976 CIA service by Bush. The most he admitted in his autobiography was, "I'd come to the CIA with some general knowledge of how it operated." I thought an article was called for, since little of substance was emerging during the campaign on Bush's early years. I called his office, and a spokesman told me, "Must be another George Bush." And when I asked the CIA about Bush's involvement with the agency in the early 1960s, a spokesman responded with the usual official language, "I can neither confirm nor deny." But I had a good source who knew of Bush's involvement with the CIA "in the late 1950s and through the 1960s" and gave me additional details that supplemented my documentation and other research, including more study of the microfilmed FBI documents at the Doheny Memorial Library on the University of Southern California campus.

I offered the article to *The Nation*. The track record of that supposedly left-wing journal in dealing with the assassination had been mostly dismal, with a few exceptions. They had been the first to turn down Mark Lane's seminal article "Oswald Innocent? A Lawyer's Brief," in late 1963, with editor Carey McWilliams telling him, "We cannot take it. We don't want it. I am sorry but we have decided not to touch that subject." After being rejected by other anxious mainstream and liberal publications, the article ran in the *National Guardian,* a small left-wing tabloid weekly, and caused a sensation. But *The Nation* agreed to run my article on Bush, not out of interest in the assassination but because the magazine opposed his candidacy for the presidency.

What kind of reaction did that article and your followup piece get, and did they have lasting impact?

There was a flurry of media interest when the first article ran in July, with AP coverage and many mentions in the press, including the *New York Times* but not, conspicuously, the

CIA-connected *Washington Post,* which went to the absurd lengths of censoring a syndicated *Bloom County* comic strip to remove a headline referring to my revelation. But the interest of the mainstream media soon evaporated when the vice president's office denied the story and the CIA claimed the 1963 briefing had gone to another George Bush. That was George William Bush, a former agency staffer the CIA implausibly claimed they could not find. With the unsolicited help of the National Security Agency, I located and interviewed the other George Bush, who said he was a lowly map analyst at the time and had not received the briefing from the FBI.

My second article with my interview with George William Bush also ran in *The Nation,* but even though the magazine found me a grant to continue my research in Washington, it refused to run a third well-researched article I submitted in October 1988 after additional research I conducted in Texas. That article documented how George H. W. Bush, as head of the Harris County GOP in Houston in 1963, had called the FBI a little more than an hour after the assassination to report that the head of the county's Young Republicans, James Parrott (who was part of a Houston-Dallas extremist group), had threatened to kill President Kennedy when he came to Houston. Naturally I wondered why Bush didn't contact the FBI or the Secret Service about Parrott *before* Kennedy was shot. In the files of the *Houston Chronicle,* I found a front-page article from November 21, 1963, with Bush calling for a "warm and cordial" reaction to Kennedy's visit that day in Houston, but he oddly added, "There may be some nuts around who might do something, but they won't be Republicans."

Victor Navasky, the editor of *The Nation,* despite having commissioned the further research that had led to that third article, told me to avoid writing about the assassination, which he called a "quagmire." By 1988, I was accustomed to the mainstream media dropping the ball but was confident that my Bush revelations would have long-term repercussions. I knew that within a few years, other researchers would begin using my revelations as a lens to start seeing his career in new ways, and that was what happened. My two principal articles in *The Nation* were run by Mark Lane as appendices of his bestselling 1991 book, *Plausible Denial: Was the CIA Involved in the Assassination of JFK?,* which brought them to a much wider audience. Calling me "obviously a relentless researcher," Lane recognized that my revelations opened a new avenue of research into the assassination through Bush's involvement with and knowledge of anti-Castro Cubans who are among the key suspects in the case. Gaeton Fonzi, the most intrepid of HSCA researchers, writes of the important leads he followed in his 1993 book *The Last Investigation*, which describes my Bush research as "a startling discovery."

The influence of my Bush articles eventually grew when authors of books found further verification as well as additional evidence of Bush's CIA connections. So my work set off a whole new way of looking at the Bush family and its clandestine involvement in American history in books by maverick authors on the Bushes, the CIA, and the assassination. Nevertheless, mainstream books still keep mum on Poppy Bush's early CIA activities. But in 2008, Russ Baker published *Family of Secrets: The Bush Dynasty, America's Invisible Government, and the Hidden History of the Last Fifty Years*, one of the first serious investigative books on the Bush family and their myriad connections with clandestine intelligence operations. Baker used my discovery of the Hoover memo as the springboard for his own investigation. Baker dug up further evidence that supported my articles' reporting of Bush's early CIA connections, and he established that Bush had been in Dallas on November 21 and 22, 1963.

And what you wrote about in your three articles was expanded on in your book Into the Nightmare *twenty-five years later.*

My own continued investigation of Bush's involvement with the assassination, tangential or otherwise, covers thirty-five pages of *Into the Nightmare*. My book devotes a great deal of attention to the hostile far-right climate in Texas that provided the context for the assassination, including additional revelations on the extremist group to which James Parrott belonged. I found that even though the FBI had quickly cleared Parrott of involvement in the assassination, it learned that he had threatened Kennedy's life in 1961, and the bureau conducted an eight-month investigation into the activities of his group. I discovered some documents about that investigation, but many had been removed from the National Archives in 1975 shortly after Bush was appointed CIA director by President Gerald Ford, a former member of the Warren Commission. And I found that the annual 10-K reports of Bush's oil company, Zapata Petroleum, documents that companies are required by law to file with the federal government, had been removed from the Securities and Exchange Commission headquarters shortly after Bush became vice president.

When I visited Houston in the fall of 1988, I tried to contact Parrott for an interview, but his wife told me the FBI had called her husband and told him not to talk to me. Someone must have leaked my travel plans, even though I kept them close to the vest. When I questioned her further, she hedged on whether it was "someone from the FBI, a government agent, or somebody doing a study, with a private group doing a study for a government group." In 1992, James Parrott denied to *Spy* magazine interviewer David Robb that he had threatened JFK. He described himself as "a Bush supporter" and worked for President Bush's unsuccessful reelection campaign that year.

What were some of your other discoveries through your research on the assassination and the Tippit murder?

In the same batch of FBI documents in which I found the Hoover memo about Bush, I found an extraordinarily revealing FBI memo that singlehandedly destroys the Warren Commission's theory that a lone gunman killed President Kennedy. The memo was written some time after 9:18 PM (presumably EST) on November 22, 1963, by A. H. Belmont, assistant director of the FBI in charge of investigative work. It states that a bullet was "lodged behind the President's ear" and that the FBI was arranging to get it. No such bullet was entered into evidence in the case or mentioned in the official autopsy report or the findings of the FBI, the Warren Commission, and the HSCA. But eyewitness testimony, photographic evidence, and ballistics evidence support Belmont's report of a bullet hitting Kennedy in the right side of his head. A frontal shot evidently fired from the Grassy Knoll blew the brains out the back of his head, the only head wound (about the size of a grapefruit) seen by the doctors and nurses at Parkland Hospital. When Kennedy was taken to Bethesda Naval Hospital for the autopsy, a smaller wound of entry was found at the top of his hairline on the right side of his head, which was either an indication of an additional shot or the entry point of the bullet "lodged behind the President's ear."

The Warren Report concluded that only three shots were fired, all from behind, and the autopsy doctors claimed to have found no bullets in Kennedy's body. But evidence assembled by David S. Lifton in his 1980 book, *Best Evidence: Disguise and Deception in the Assassination of John F. Kennedy*—one of the paradigm changers for me in the case—demonstrated that the president's body was altered to eliminate evidence of shots from the front. Douglas P. Horne, a staff member of the Assassination Records Review Board, later found witnesses to the pre-autopsy "surgery of the head area, namely, in the top of the skull" reported by two FBI agents who witnessed the official sham autopsy; the evidence found by Horne indicates that the pre-autopsy surgery was hurriedly performed at Bethesda to alter the body before the official autopsy. So the Belmont memo, another document that had been missed by the inattentive press as well as by Lifton in his otherwise extensive research, was sufficient to disprove the findings of the Warren Report about the number of shots and from where they were fired.

I wrote an article on the Belmont memo in 1985-1987 and tried to place it with several publications, all of which declined to run it, although none disputed any part of my research. Dale Myers included the memo in the document appendix of his 1998 book on the Tippit case but without comment on Belmont's statement about the bullet; and in 2009, Horne scooped the field by discussing the "explosive" significance of the memo in the third volume of his self-published five-volume study, *Inside the Assassination Records Review Board: The U.S. Government's Final Attempt to Reconcile the Conflicting Medical Evidence in the Assassination of JFK*. I had to wait until *Into the Nightmare* in 2013 to include a section on the Belmont memo and its significance in my book. I also put it in the context of several other bullets not entered into evidence in the case. The Belmont memo supports Horne's conclusion that the bullet "lodged behind the President's ear" may have been among the crucial evidence removed in the surreptitious pre-autopsy craniotomy. As I write in *Into the Nightmare*, the Belmont memo is "the smoking gun that provides explicit proof of the suppression of evidence by the federal government while supporting the extensive photographic and eyewitness evidence of a second gunman on the knoll."

What were the most important interviews you landed in Dallas?

Following my departure from my last tour of duty on *Daily Variety,* I spent several months in Dallas in 1992 and '93 doing my most intensive interviewing for *Into the Nightmare.* Although I was frustrated to find that some of the key witnesses had left the area or gone underground, I had success in landing important interviews that resulted in major revelations about the case. Two of my most eye-opening interviews were with former District Attorney Henry Wade and retired Detective Leavelle, who headed the

Former Dallas County District Attorney Henry Wade gave me a
candid interview in his law office in January 1993, conceding the
weaknesses of the case he was given to prosecute against Lee Harvey
Oswald, the patsy in the murders of President Kennedy and Officer
J. D. Tippit. Wade was also the defendant in the landmark abortion
case *Roe v. Wade*. (Joseph McBride)

investigation of the Tippit murder, such as it was, and
participated in the interrogation of Oswald. These two key
figures made significant admissions about the flimsiness of
the case against Oswald for killing the president and the
inadequate investigation of the Tippit murder.

When I asked Leavelle why the Tippit killing seemed
to take precedence over the presidential assassination
in charging and arraigning Oswald for that murder, the
detective made a revealing admission, "Now the thing was,
the Captain [Will Fritz] asked me if I had enough to make
a case on him for the Tippit killing. And I said, 'Oh, yeah,
I got plenty on that.'… I had him identified by about three
or four people. And so Cap said, 'Well, go ahead and make
a tight case on him in case we have trouble making this one
on the presidential shooting.' So that was one reason he was
arraigned early on the Tippit shooting." But Wade admitted
to me about the Tippit case, "We never worked any on his
murder."

J. Edgar Hoover himself told President Johnson on the
morning of November 23, "This man in Dallas [Oswald].
We, of course, charged him with the murder of the President.
The evidence that they have at the present time is not very
very strong." (Actually, it was the DPD that charged Oswald,
because assassinating a president was not then a federal
crime.) If the public had known what Hoover, Leavelle, and
Fritz were actually saying behind the scenes, we would have
had quite a different view of the case at the time. And my

interview with former DA Wade reinforced the impression he gave in his testimony to the Warren Commission of being ambivalent or downright doubtful of Oswald's guilt in the assassination. Wade's notoriously lax recital of the alleged evidence at the press conference the DA held after Oswald's death on November 24 was echoed in our interview. He seemed to know little about the case and was cavalier about many of what he claimed were facts, and he admitted to me, "I probably made a lot of mistakes."

Wade was still a practicing attorney when I interviewed him in his office in January 1993, when he was seventy-eight. Warren Commission Chief Counsel J. Lee Rankin had called him "a very canny, able prosecutor." But Wade was also reckless in his failure to administer justice and, as our interview demonstrated, he was almost brazenly ill-informed and indifferent about the way the Dallas police and his office had approached the case against Oswald. His reputation had taken tremendous hits over the years, especially when it was determined by a subsequent Dallas DA, Craig Watkins, that many of the defendants Wade's office had managed to convict of crimes were innocent. Watkins reinvestigated cases and cleared suspects who had been prosecuted on dubious evidence under a philosophy of what Watkins called "convict at all costs."

As I write in *Into the Nightmare* of Wade's Warren Commission testimony, "Speaking of what he had known on the night of November 22, Wade told the commission, 'I think they had some witnesses who had identified [Oswald] there at the scene [of the Tippit killing], but I was more worried about the assassination[,] of them filing on somebody that we couldn't prove was guilty.' The DA went so far as to admit that 'I wasn't sure I was going to take a complaint,' i.e., to file on Oswald for the assassination.... Wade told the commission that as early as November 23, with the police talking too freely to the media about the evidence they planned to present against Oswald, thereby prejudicing the case in the minds of potential jurors, he 'felt like nearly it was a hopeless case.'"

In my interview with Wade on the day Bill Clinton was inaugurated as president in 1993, I started carefully with some relatively soft questions for the former DA, planning to lead up to the tough ones, but after a while Wade impatiently urged me to ask "more interesting" questions. He was anxious about making a luncheon appointment. So I hit him with some tough cross-examination, and he made many surprising admissions. When I asked why there was such haste to pin the Tippit killing on Oswald, he said,

"The Tippit charge, you had *eyewitnesses.*" That seemed to concede a key weakness in the case against Oswald for killing Kennedy. And when I pressed Wade on how sure he was about Oswald killing Tippit, he said, "Well, I was sure as you could be, because when I talked to [the police] they showed three witnesses that identified him or more, at least three, some saw him after and one was there and saw all of it. I think he got killed in an accident or something. [Wade did not identify that alleged witness who 'saw all of it' when I asked.] They've had a rash of 'em were killed, you know, or died. But that's all. You don't need any more than that. And he killed him with a pistol, and they identified, they had the gun, he had the gun over there in the theater, a pistol."

I spent years trying to sort out the *Rashomon*-like confusion surrounding the witnesses from the scene of the Tippit murder, which appears to have been a planned ambush. The witnesses are an extraordinarily mixed bunch, some who claim to have identified Oswald—most of those doing so, however, under highly questionable circumstances—some who said they could not identify him as the killer, and some who said there were two gunmen, as seems to have been the case. Another researcher, Jerry Rose, argued plausibly that there seemed to have been two sets of witnesses and that Jack Ruby may have helped stage the crime scene with planted witnesses, since some of them had connections to Ruby. The ballistics evidence tends to exonerate Oswald as the killer, since the bullets and cartridges recovered from the scene cannot be matched with the revolver introduced into evidence as the murder weapon, as an honest FBI expert testified to the commission; nor can that revolver be conclusively linked to Oswald. And since Wade admitted the Tippit case had not been properly investigated, that left the burden of the prosecution in trying to prove that Oswald had shot Kennedy.

Wade tried to tell me the police had five witnesses "at one time" who could identify Oswald as shooting Kennedy, but on questioning he conceded there was nobody who could positively identify Oswald as being in the window of the Texas School Book Depository firing shots. When I steered Wade onto the physical evidence he thought they had against Oswald for shooting Kennedy—Oswald, speaking to his brother Robert on November 23, said, "Don't believe all this so-called evidence"—Wade seemed as poorly informed as he had been during his nationally televised press conference on the night of November 24 after Oswald's death, when he rattled off a host of erroneous claims. I noted that Wade subsequently "expressed doubts to the commission about the evidence assembled by the police against Oswald," and on the early morning of November 23 he had identified the murder weapon to the press as a 7.65 Mauser (as two lawmen first described the rifle found in the Depository) before it mysteriously metamorphosed into a 6.5 Mannlicher-Carcano. John Armstrong's book *Harvey & Lee: How the CIA Framed Oswald* contains extensively researched chapters demonstrating that Oswald possessed neither the Mannlicher-Carcano nor the revolver entered into evidence from the Tippit killing, and that a handgun the police claimed to have taken from Oswald when he was arrested at the Texas Theatre was a probable planted weapon.

On the chaotic weekend of the assassination, Wade and the police had trouble keeping their phony stories straight, and in retrospect he mostly blamed the police for his own misstatements. As I write in my account of our interview, Wade "went on to mention other pieces of evidence as important to the case that, in fact, have not held up, such as the paraffin test and the palmprints that were claimed to have been found on the inside of the rifle. I tried reminding Wade about the problems with these various pieces of evidence, but it seemed to no avail." The former DA displayed his damning lack of knowledge and a breezy attitude toward the events of the assassination weekend, including his jocularity when he took responsibility in our interview for the disastrous decision to allow the Secret Service and Kennedy aides to remove his coffin from Parkland Hospital without the legally required local autopsy. Wade said the official autopsy at Bethesda Medical Center was "probably the poorest autopsy I ever saw.... And we had a good medical examiner, Earl Rose. He did eight hundred a year. He was good. [Rose did the autopsies on Tippit and Oswald, which are regarded as models of good work.] But the reason he didn't do [the Kennedy autopsy] was kind of my fault, to some extent anyhow."

Oswald's intelligence connections, including his involvement with the CIA as a false defector to the USSR, have been well-documented, and shortly after the assassination, it was rumored that he had also been an FBI informant. Some of the "evidence" put forward to debunk that rumor at the time appears to have been disinformation introduced to discredit an accurate part of his complicated history. When the commissioners held "emergency" meetings in January 1964 to discuss Oswald's possible informant status with the FBI, Hale Boggs said, "I don't even like to see this being taken down," and Allen Dulles said, "Yes, I think this record ought to be destroyed." In my research, I found numerous indications that Oswald in fact had infiltrated the plot against Kennedy and was reporting on it to the Dallas FBI without realizing until too late that he would become its "patsy."

Wade, a former FBI agent, told me something not previously reported that, if accurate, could help support that theory: He said that Oswald had spoken with the Dallas FBI the day before the assassination. The former DA said that on November 22, FBI Agent James Hosty had told Lieutenant Jack Revill, the head of the DPD's Criminal Intelligence Section (the department's anti-"subversive" squad), "We know Oswald well. I talked with him yesterday." Revill claimed that Hosty admitted, "We had information that he was capable of this." It was likely that Revill's unit had Oswald under surveillance at the time of the assassination. The previous month when I had reached Revill on the phone, he declined to meet with me, saying cryptically that there were too many "bad memories" connected with those events. "So I'd rather not get involved. Good luck to you on your book." Hosty, who was disciplined by Hoover after the assassination, filed an affidavit in 1964 denying that he had told Revill or anyone else "that the FBI knew OSWALD was capable of assassinating the President or that OSWALD possessed any potential for violence."

When I asked Wade to clarify that account from Revill about Oswald meeting with the FBI the day before the assassination, Wade said, "Within a day or two, I don't know exactly." That was a startling claim. I also found a neglected piece of information in the November 24 edition of the *Dallas Morning News,* published before Oswald was shot later that morning by the mob-connected Dallas nightclub operator Jack Ruby. The paper reported that Oswald had spoken with the FBI on November 16. And it had been revealed earlier that Oswald went to the Dallas FBI office on about November 12, supposedly to deliver a threatening note. That note was destroyed by the FBI on November 24, shortly after Oswald was murdered on national television in the basement of the Dallas police station, surrounded by policemen, reporters, and camera crews.

What did you conclude Officer Tippit was doing when he was shot, and who shot him? And what was the most pivotal interview you did on the Tippit murder?

Tippit drove into an ambush set up by his own department. He pulled up his squad car partly blocking a driveway on the 400 block of East 10th Street in suburban Oak Cliff and encountered a pedestrian who shot him. There was a second police car in the alley, and one of the two people in the vehicle came out and administered a head shot to make sure Tippit was dead. As the HSCA Report comments, "This action, which is often encountered in gangland murders and is commonly described as a coup de grace, is more indicative of an execution than an act of defense intended to allow escape or prevent apprehension. Absent further evidence—which the committee did not develop—the meaning of this evidence must remain uncertain." Based on the timing of the shooting, which the police and the Warren Report distorted, Oswald could not have walked there from his rooming house with sufficient speed. And the ballistics evidence exonerates him. So I discuss other possible suspects in *Into the Nightmare*. The shooting brought dozens of policemen to Oak Cliff to arrest Oswald in the nearby Texas Theatre.

Why did the Dallas Police Department select Tippit to be killed?

The framing and entrapment of Oswald as a supposed cop-killer was one of the motives for the killing of Tippit. There may have been other reasons for eliminating Tippit, including his knowledge of the assassination plot and the role or roles he was playing in it.

Early on there was speculation in the press that Tippit had been trying to track down Oswald in Oak Cliff. I found corroboration and further information from a source who had never been interviewed by a researcher before, the officer's father, Edgar Lee Tippit. I drove to rural Clarksville in the desolate East Texas area where the vigorous ninety-year-old man still worked as a farmer. Mr. Tippit told me that shortly after his son was killed, another policeman came to Marie Tippit, the officer's widow, to tell her what happened. I was able to identify him as Sergeant William D. Mentzel, the officer who was actually assigned to the district where Officer Tippit was killed (Tippit's shooting occurred four miles from his own district).

Mentzel told Marie that he and Officer Tippit were both dispatched by the department to hunt down Oswald in Oak Cliff, who was identified to them by name. This was within fifteen minutes of the assassination, long before the department supposedly learned of Oswald's identity. Revill's anti-subversive squad evidently knew where Oswald lived and correctly surmised that he was heading there. Whether Tippit and Mentzel were supposed to arrest Oswald or kill him on the street is unclear, but I suspect the latter, since Oswald was soon shot to death in the police station and probably was going to be killed in the theater if he hadn't had the presence of mind to repeatedly shout in front of civilian witnesses, "I am not resisting arrest!"

Tippit, who also was given a suspicious alert on the police radio shortly after the assassination, was seen staking out the viaduct for traffic headed from downtown, departing at a high rate of speed, and frantically racing around Oak Cliff in the minutes before his shooting, making a phone call at a record store and stopping a car to search it before he reached the nearby location where he was shot. Edgar Lee Tippit told me, "They called J. D. and another policeman and said he [Oswald] was headed in that direction. The other policeman told Marie." Edgar Lee reported what Marie learned from that other policeman (whose name he did not know) about why he had not made it to the scene of the shooting on Tenth Street: "The other boy stopped—he would have got there but he had a little accident, a wreck. They both started, but J. D. made it. He'd been expecting something. The police notified them Oswald was headed that way."

In telling me what the second officer told Marie Tippit about the accident, Edgar Lee reported that "he said if he hadn't been stopped, he was closer to this place [the shooting site] than J. D. was, and he'd have been [instead of] J. D. there and he'd have gotten it." The official record is that Mentzel reported to the scene of a traffic accident eleven and a half blocks from the shooting but soon cleared the area. The accident was reported shortly after Tippit was shot; perhaps Mentzel actually *had* the accident. Ardyce Mentzel, the officer's widow—he had died in 2002—recalled in an interview with Dale Myers, "Bill told me how bad he felt about Tippit's death. He felt like Tippit had died for him, since he was killed in my husband's district."

The early pursuit of the scapegoat in itself was evidence of a conspiracy involving the DPD and these two officers. They were clandestinely dispatched to hunt down a suspect whose identity would not officially be known to the department until after he was arrested and taken downtown (by about 2:10 PM). When I compared Edgar Lee's account to other reliable documentation about the activities of his son and other officers in Dallas and Oak Cliff during that time period, I found that his account squared with that pertinent information, and that he provided the strongest evidence to explain what his son's mission was that afternoon and how it went awry. When I probed Henry Wade to find out when he and other officials learned of Oswald's identity, what he said backed up Edgar Lee Tippit's account: "Somebody reported to me that the police already knew who he was, and they were looking for him."

What do you think motivated J. D. Tippit to be part of a conspiracy?

Tippit was a mediocre cop who had never been promoted in eleven years, and a psychological evaluation from a Rorschach test he took in 1952, shortly after he joined the force, indicated serious emotional disturbance: "His grip on reality is below the average. Errors of judgment may be expected." He had serious PTSD from his World War II U.S. Army service as a paratrooper and light machine gunner that caused him trouble looking people in the eye, a potentially fatal flaw for a policeman that may have helped lead to his death. Although I did not find any evidence of political extremism in his background, or of the racism that was common in the department, Tippit worked part time as a security guard at a restaurant in Oak Cliff that was a hangout not only for many policemen but also for right-wing extremists.

Austin's Barbecue was run by a member of the far-right John Birch Society, Austin Cook, whom I interviewed, and Cook was acquainted with General Edwin Walker, Deputy DA Bill Alexander, and other Dallas extremists. Cook had at least tangential ties through a fellow business partner with Ralph Paul, a shadowy Dallas area nightclub and restaurant proprietor with connections to organized crime who was identified in the Warren Report as Jack Ruby's "close friend and financial backer." Austin's Barbecue had formerly been a restaurant co-owned by Paul.

That right-wing milieu, where Tippit worked in uniform on weekends to control unruly teenagers, would have made him well-known to those figures and others on the Dallas right. Tippit moonlighted because he was financially overburdened with mortgages on two homes, although he came into some money soon before his death. Contrary to the image put forth that he was a dedicated family man, he was actually a busy philanderer. His mistress Johnnie Maxie Witherspoon (Johnnie Maxie Thompson in 1963), a former Austin's Barbecue waitress who gave me a candid interview, may have learned around the time of the assassination that she was pregnant, although she insisted Tippit was not the

After the publication of *Into the Nightmare*, I went to Dallas for a Q&A at the Sixth Floor Museum on Officer Tippit's ninetieth birthday, September 18, 2014, with his widow, Marie, and her surviving children. She had not replied to my request for an interview for the book, but I asked if I could see her the next day, and she seemed agreeable. Her ubiquitous Dallas Police Department minder (seen approaching) nullified that plan. (Frank Caplett)

father of her daughter born in June 1964. Her estranged husband was reportedly following them around. Some have tried to point to that man as a possible suspect in the officer's murder, but I found that unlikely.

Do you think your book has made a difference or will the lone-gunman theory always be the "official" history of what happened that day?

I'm not optimistic that most of the media will come around to reality in this case. But I was gratified to find that whenever I discussed the assassination in my Film and Society courses at San Francisco State—with the aid of Oliver Stone's reconstruction from *JFK*, witness interviews from the *Rush to Judgment* documentary, and the Zapruder film, whose alteration by the CIA I discussed—the students were receptive to the subject and showed keen interest. That was a marked difference from many people in my Baby Boomer generation who were around in 1963 and seem phobic about facing the facts when they are presented with them.

People in Europe, who are more sophisticated about how political power works, have always been baffled that anyone in the U.S. could believe the official story, since it is so obviously fraudulent. When French President Charles de Gaulle, the survivor of numerous assassination attempts, was briefed by a reporter on the Warren Commission's creation of the single-bullet theory, he exclaimed, *"Vous me blaguez!* [You're kidding me!] Cowboys and Indians!"

When I asked Penn Jones in 1983 if he thought the assassination would ever be fully solved, he replied matter-of-factly, "I and several other people solved the case back in the Sixties." Although that sounds hyperbolic, Jones and other first-generation JFK researchers did establish many of the basic facts in the case. As I write in my 2021 book *Political Truth: The Media and the Assassination of President Kennedy*, unlike "Norman Mailer, who rather melodramatically proclaimed the assassination 'The Great American Mystery,' and the many members of the media who cop out by claiming that 'We'll never know' what really happened in Dealey Plaza, [another leading early researcher, Philadelphia lawyer] Vincent J. Salandria believed that the basic answers have been obvious almost from the beginning for those with eyes to see them, even if the identities of the perpetrators remain unknown or a matter of speculation." Salandria wrote in 2000, "The killing of President John F. Kennedy and its cover-up are not mysterious. Rather, the assassination was patently a Cold War killing—the bloody work of the U.S. military-intelligence-national-security system. That same power structure and its supporting civilian elite have, since the assassination, worked to cover up the reasons for the killing. Today, those institutions are alive, well and unchanged and continue to maintain and promote the U.S. global empire."

I believe *Into the Nightmare* has advanced knowledge of the case by linking Tippit conclusively to the conspiracy and demonstrating what he was doing in the pursuit of Oswald in Oak Cliff. My book also explores the possibility that Tippit might even have been the man in a policeman's uniform (known as "Badge Man") who appears to have been one of the shooters, the figure photographed by several still and motion-picture cameras while in an apparent firing position behind the concrete retaining wall on the Grassy Knoll. But my investigation of that possibility must remain inconclusive, partly because the photographs are not clear enough to identify the suspect conclusively and because Marie Tippit claimed to have served her husband lunch at home soon before he was shot. That would give J. D. Tippit an alibi for the Kennedy assassination, but her story changed numerous times over the years and is open to question.

I tried to get an interview with Mrs. Tippit, but she did not respond to my letter, even though she has given numerous press interviews I was able to quote. After *Into the Nightmare* was published, I went to Dallas in 2014 to meet her at an event at the Sixth Floor Museum commemorating what would have been her husband's ninetieth birthday. She seemed willing to give me an interview during my visit to Dallas, but Gary Mack, the curator of the museum (which pushes the lone-nut theory), and her ubiquitous DPD minder anxiously and unfortunately intervened to prevent that from happening.

I hoped that *Into the Nightmare* would open up the Tippit case for further research by other scholars, and that has happened. Australian researcher Gavan MacMahon has conducted resourceful interviews with family members of Helen Markham (the Warren Commission's star witness in the Tippit murder, whose account, however, was seriously flawed) and another Tippit witness, cab driver William Scoggins. McMahon's research contends that Markham and Scoggins were among the witnesses planted at the scene by Ruby to exert control over their accounts of the shooting. Ruby, in his testimony to the Warren Commission from inside the Dallas County Jail, tried to drop broad suggestions to Earl Warren that he was involved in the assassination conspiracy and "party to a plot to silence Oswald," but Warren refused to believe him. Warren told Ruby, "I think I can say to you that there has been no witness before this Commission out of the hundreds we have questioned who has claimed to have personal knowledge that you were a party to any conspiracy to kill our President." And Ruby replied, "Yes; but you don't know this area here."

John Armstrong, the author of *Harvey & Lee*, has broadened his research on the case with the help of my findings to put his focus on two Dallas policemen as suspects in the Tippit shooting. Armstrong theorizes that Captain

William R. Westbrook, the head of personnel, worked with Kenneth H. Croy, a reserve sergeant, not only to murder Tippit but also to plant evidence and lead other police to the Texas Theatre to arrest Oswald. Westbook left the DPD in 1966 to work as a CIA-sponsored adviser to the Saigon Police Department during the Vietnam War, and died in 1996. Croy also worked for other law enforcement agencies and died in 2012.

Armstrong has produced a wealth of convincing evidence that the CIA was running an "Oswald project" with two men sharing that identity. That highly controversial theory may sound outlandish to those unaware of the frequent use of doubles in the intelligence field. But I believe Armstrong has proven it, even if some of the details remain elusive. Armstrong argues that both Oswalds were present at the movie theater, one who was involved in the plot to kill Tippit and the other a patsy to be accused of committing that act, and claims that the one he calls Lee, reported to have been arrested in the balcony, was soon released in the alley behind the theater. The patsy in the case, whom Armstrong calls Harvey and is known to the public as Lee Harvey Oswald, was arrested on the ground floor and taken to the police station. I disagree with Armstrong about Lee Oswald shooting Tippit but respect his complex and extremely diligent research and have contributed feedback to his ongoing work at his request.

It heartens me that the study of this previously neglected case by serious researchers is continuing. And I am glad that *Into the Nightmare* has struck a chord with many readers around the world and has continued to sell steadily since 2013.

Political Truth

It took another eight years, but did you always intend to write a follow-up to Into the Nightmare?

I kept thinking while writing *Into the Nightmare* that I should do a chapter on how badly and systematically the mainstream media have lied to us about the case from the day it happened to the present. I did write a chapter for that book of political/media criticism on the blanket network TV coverage during the assassination weekend, what I call the four-day assassination docudrama. The networks received great praise for supposedly healing the country with their coverage: It started with a traumatic shock opening, then showed the arrest of the suspect, with his trial-by-media and conviction followed with his on-camera execution, and they wrapped it all up neatly with the grand emotional spectacle of the president's military funeral. A shared national tragedy was smoothly packaged as a docudrama with a catharsis at the end.

The unprecedented degree of viewership—93 percent of all available sets in the country—kept Americans off the streets, narcotized while sitting in front of the tube absorbing government propaganda designed to forestall political action. In other countries, the populace would have rebelled against the violent overthrow of their country's president. I don't see the TV coverage of the assassination weekend as the triumph the media congratulate themselves by claiming it was but as the beginning of the long, unrelenting series of lies the mainstream media have been telling us about this coup d'état ever since, to the terrible detriment of our country.

Dan Rather was foremost among the people who made their journalistic careers from their mendacious assassination coverage. On CBS's twenty-fifth anniversary documentary in 1988, *Four Days in November: The Assassination of President Kennedy*, Rather offered

> a personal note, based on the many years CBS News and I have spent investigating, thinking about these four days. It was a day we haven't shown that also has a lot of meaning for me—the fifth day, Tuesday [November 26]. On Tuesday, America went back to work. The Constitution of the United States provides for the orderly transition of the presidency, and that's what took place. So it is Tuesday I often think of. Some two hundred million people went about their business, and America continued on course.

As I write in *Into the Nightmare*,

> On the contrary, I remember that Tuesday as a day of the most profound bleakness and desolation. I returned to high school that day feeling utterly lost. The transition of the presidency I had seen on television was brutal, not "orderly." I felt no sense of order or reassurance or triumph. Nor did I have any sense that life was "returning to normal" or that America was continuing "on course." To believe that would have been a final insult to the memory of President Kennedy. Getting back to

our daily business in the wake of the president's murder evidently meant that we were expected to go on as if nothing had happened, in a world that had changed in ways we could not yet begin to imagine.

I eventually realized that this is too big a theme to get into a single chapter. In 2013, I recorded a short video version, "Political Truth: The Media and the Assassination," for Black Op Radio producer Len Osanic's ambitious fifty-part YouTube series on the assassination and related events, *50 Reasons...50 Years* (with Jeff Carter as the ace videographer). And I eventually took the sixty-page proposal I had written in 1993 for a separate book on the topic of the media coverage and spent a couple of years in 2020 and '21 expanding upon and updating it, pouring my thoughts and feelings of indignation about the media into *Political Truth: The Media and the Assassination of President Kennedy.* I believe in some ways that relatively little-read book is the most important I have written. I don't think I can ever do better than I did with the Capra biography, but as Capra said when he told me why he considered *Mr. Smith Goes to Washington* his most important film, *Political Truth* is "a story about our government, a lot of the internal workings of our government are revealed. I suppose that's why I like it better than the other ones—it's *big.*"

Not only do I cover the way the story of the assassination was misreported from the beginning, and what we didn't know about it at the time, how I began to doubt the official story, and how the mainstream media have continued to spin those events as a fable about America continuing "on course," I analyze how if you want the truth, you have to go to the alternative media, independently published books, and films, which have more freedom to dissent. I go into the deeper reasons why the media have followed the government's bidding by demonizing "conspiracy theorists" for telling the truth about what happened to our government. I analyze the tropes they use to ridicule, minimize, and marginalize the writers and regular citizens who continue to question the official story and study the case independently, making up as best we can for the malfeasance of professional journalists and historians.

"Crimestop"

Do you think many people in the media even today actually know better but are afraid to admit the truth?

I do. I think many keep their thoughts to themselves for fear of losing their access, their jobs, and their awards, which are given for works that reinforce the status quo. These so-called journalists cautiously remain in what Orwell called a state of "protective stupidity," while engaging in their habitual practice of "Crimestop," which he defined in *Nineteen Eighty-Four* as "the faculty of stopping short, as though by instinct, at the threshold of any dangerous thought. It includes the power of not grasping analogies, of failing to perceive logical errors, of misunderstanding the simplest arguments" if they are inimical to the dominant ideology.

An example of "Crimestop" is the case of my fellow journalist Jim Hougan, whom I knew from my Wisconsin newspaper days and who wrote the groundbreaking revisionist book *Secret Agenda: Watergate, Deep Throat, and the CIA*, published in 1984. Hougan told me in 1988 that he had thought of writing about the assassination of President Kennedy but "not very seriously" because "To do that takes an extraordinary act of courage. Historically, it's tantamount to professional suicide. There are few things more important in journalism, but few things more difficult. It takes a long-term commitment. There's not a lot of money in it. And it's immensely difficult." Hougan ducked meeting me when I went to Washington to continue my Bush research. When I conduct my investigation of the assassination, I don't care about the kinds of concerns he expressed, since I make my living in another field and pay for the investigation myself, and I am willing to take any consequences.

Stone's landmark 1991 film, *JFK*, reopened the case for a mass audience and led to the declassification of millions of pages of formerly classified government documents. The film was widely attacked by Washington and New York media heavyweights for supposedly being inaccurate, but the irony is that Stone's account is far closer to the truth than the mainstream media's false reporting on the case for the past sixty-plus years. Stone commented that the media furor over his film stemmed from the questions of "who owns reality" and who has the right to tell it. "Is it the press?... I think they blew it from day one." Stone called the official account "a myth that has sustained a generation of journalists and historians who have refused to examine it, who have refused to question it, and above all who close ranks to criticize and vilify those who do."

I discuss a few veteran journalists, such as Helen Thomas and Bill Moyers, who admitted the serious flaws in the media's coverage of the assassination. "We were all remiss, period," said Thomas, the veteran White House correspondent for United Press International before she was forced out of her job for her tough questioning of the Bush-Cheney regime. Moyers, who became an esteemed TV journalist, admitted in 1992, "When it came to [reporting on the assassination], the working press was a lobster in a trap. Back then, what government said was the news.... In the 1950s and early '60s, the official view of reality was the agenda for the Washington press corps.... I think it is quite revealing that it's Oliver Stone that's forcing Congress to open up the files and not *The Washington Post*, *The New York Times*, or CBS."

Moyers had been an advance man for JFK's Texas trip and an aide to Lyndon Johnson as vice president and his presidential press secretary. Moyers had his own crucial involvement in the events of the assassination, helping plan the Dallas motorcade route in violation of Secret Service protocol and giving the order to remove the bubbletop from JFK's limousine at Love Field. Moyers then became a middleman in helping Johnson set up the Warren Commission, including by receiving the infamous November 25 "MEMORANDUM FOR MR. MOYERS" from the acting attorney general, Nicholas deB. Katzenbach, outlining the coverup of the case. As Katzenbach wrote on the day of President Kennedy's funeral, the day after Oswald was murdered in the Dallas police station, "The public must be satisfied that Oswald was the assassin; that he did not have confederates who are still at large; and that the evidence was such that he would have been convicted at trial.... Speculation about Oswald's motivation ought to be cut off."

Since Moyers, who died in 2025, never wrote the memoir many people might have expected of him, he largely evaded scrutiny for his role in these events. Those who simply considered him a trusted liberal journalist might be surprised to learn about that controversial history, as well as Moyers's participation as an aide and spokesman in the Johnson administration during the escalation of the war in Vietnam. Moyers was ordained as a Baptist minister, and his often admirable journalism often appeared to me as an expiation of the price he paid for the way he rose to national prominence.

One of the surprises I found over the years was how many media outlets and so-called journalists were involved in the Dallas events *before* they happened. Dan Rather, for instance, convinced his superiors at CBS to have five full network TV production crews in Dallas at the time of the assassination, including the only live remote TV network hookup on the motorcade route, in contrast to NBC and ABC, which each had only the customary single crew following the president. Time-Life, which bought the rights to the Zapruder film and then refused to let the public see more than inadequately selected frame enlargements, had helped finance some of the covert operations against Cuba by the CIA prior to the assassination, as had Clare Boothe Luce, the playwright and diplomat and the wife of Time-Life publisher Henry Luce. She also supported the CIA-backed militant Cuban exile organization that Oswald attempted to infiltrate in the summer of 1963, the Directorio Revolucionario Estudiantil (DRE, or Student Revolutionary Directorate). Clare Boothe Luce also leaked supposedly incriminating disinformation about Oswald to the media immediately after the assassination.

How did Political Truth *evolve after you wrote your 1993 outline?*

Since I was writing the book in the age of Trump when the "fake news" he habitually promoted was crowding out real news more stridently than ever before, and in the wake of the attempted Trump coup of January 6, 2021, I realized I had to grapple with the longterm damage the false media coverage of the assassination has done to our country, by tracing the influence of the cynicism and confusion those lies have engendered. We were naive to believe what the government told us before 1963, but we usually did, and when President Eisenhower was caught lying to the world about the U-2 plane in 1960, it was a shock. Now (to exaggerate only slightly) it's a shock when the president is caught telling the truth.

Where did you get the title?

I borrowed the title from author Edward Jay Epstein, who may have lifted it from Harry S. Truman, who said in 1962, "The trouble with Adlai Stevenson is he has *never* understood the difference between real truth and political truth." Truman's interlocutor on that occasion, TV producer Robert Alan Aurthur, explained what he thought the former

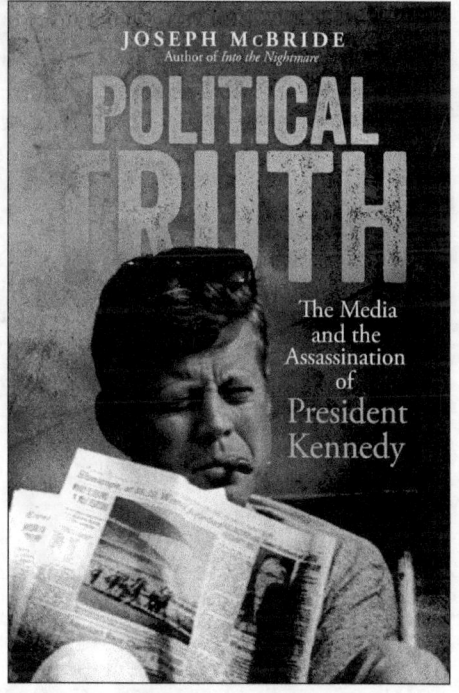

My long immersion in the events of November 22, 1963,
and their impact on our country led to these 2013 and 2021 books.
(Hightower Press)

president meant by that phrase: "Political truth, it developed, can be the biggest and damnedest lie ever, but if motivated toward a pragmatic political goal, preferably for reasons of national interest, and stated with total belief and fervor, it becomes true."

Epstein was an early Warren Commission critic who eventually turned into a pro-establishment writer soft-pedaling the CIA's manipulation of Oswald and attacking New Orleans District Attorney Jim Garrison, who did valuable work in trying to solve the case. A hint of that evolution (if evolution it was) can be found at the end of Epstein's revealing 1966 book, *Inquest: The Warren Commission and the Establishment of Truth,* when he offers a justification of sorts for the shoddy, lying investigation of the assassination he has just dissected in his book. Discussing the single-bullet theory, a demonstrable lie concocted to explain away the likelihood of a conspiracy involving more than one gunman, Epstein writes,

> It indicates that the conclusions of the Warren Report must be viewed as expressions of political truth.... Indeed, if the Commission had made it clear that very substantial evidence indicated the presence of a second assassin, it would have opened a Pandora's box of doubts and suspicions. In establishing its version of the truth, the Warren Commission acted to reassure the nation and protect the national interest.

What was the national interest in falsely reassuring the nation that, as NBC anchorman David Brinkley had declared on the very night of the assassination, the president was killed by "a punk with a mail-order rifle"? As I write in *Political Truth*, the more I have studied the Kennedy case and its historical context, the more "I have realized that in most of the major historical events in modern American history, from the early 1960s onward, the official explanations and verdicts do not make sense.

> Among those events are the assassinations of JFK, Malcolm X, Dr. Martin Luther King Jr., and Robert Kennedy; the Gulf of Tonkin incident; President Richard Nixon's fraudulent escalation of the war in Vietnam and expansion into Cambodia; Watergate; the October Surprise; Iran-Contra; the Gulf War; the 1993 bombing of the World Trade Center and the 9/11 attacks; the wars in Iraq and Afghanistan;

the systematic use of torture; the financial collapse of 2008; and the widespread loss of life resulting from the failed initial response of the federal government in the COVID-19 pandemic that began in 2020....

Naturally, this has exacerbated the confusion and divide in public opinion about these events. The public's growing awareness over the years that it is routinely misled about the most important matters and their consequences has prompted widespread skepticism about some, though not all, of these major events and about the structural integrity of our system.

A different book from the version I would have written in the 1990s, *Political Truth* turned into an overview of how the media have helped draw our country into a perilous situation in which two versions of history have been embraced by the opposing halves of the populace. Healthy skepticism is good for the country, but when half the country believes one version of reality, and the other half believes another, it fosters a situation approaching civil war. *Political Truth* studies how the mainstream media tried to minimize the impact of January 6 by spinning it as an "insurrection," "incursion," or "riot," partly to avoid using the fraught term "coup d'état" for fear of encouraging comparisons with the successful coup that was mounted from within the federal government in 1963.

When Jack Ruby was questioned by the Warren Commission in the Dallas County Jail on June 7, 1964, he told Chief Justice Earl Warren, "[A] whole new form of government is going to take over our country... it is a very serious situation. I guess it is too late to stop it, isn't it?" Warren pretended not to understand what Ruby was trying to tell him, including his desperate attempts to convey that he had been part of the conspiracy to kill the president. Ruby implored Warren to take him to Washington so he could speak more freely, out of the danger of Dallas County confinement. Warren refused. Ruby knew what he was talking about, and his prescient remarks about the course of American history have proven to be accurate. *Political Truth* discusses the inevitable denouement of the tragedy enacted in Dallas.

"My Own Stuff"

To me, all your books are somewhat autobiographical, because they are as much about you as your subjects, but of course the one that is most revealing and personal is The Broken Places. *Your memoir is the third book that you wrote during your time at SFSU that wasn't about film and like the two Kennedy books was self-published. I'm sure it reflects on how you think about the art of writing about lives, yours and others.*

In 1977 I interviewed the veteran actor George Coulouris for *Daily Variety* when he was preparing to play King Lear at Hollywood's Globe Theater. Coulouris is best known for his role as Walter Parks Thatcher, the banker who serves as the guardian of Charles Foster Kane after the boy's mother sells him to a bank. Despite our great difference in age, Coulouris and I hit it off because of our kinship as actors for Orson Welles; he had also worked with Welles in the theater and radio. Coulouris was as warm as Mr. Thatcher is chilly, and he slipped into a kind of guardianship role as we talked about our common experiences with the great man. He urged me to write a biography of Welles. I found myself replying haltingly, "I want to write my own stuff." Coulouris insisted, "This *would* be 'your own stuff.'"

That conversation helped put me on the road to becoming a biographer. I had been avoiding that form of writing because I foolishly considered it less creative than screenplays or novels. And I thought *real writing* was writing novels. A novelist constructs a world, after all. But I knew enough to recognize I wasn't yet capable of achieving that fullest reach of written storytelling. I took screenplays seriously but thought of them as a halfway approximation of novel-writing.

Coulouris made me reflect seriously on the craft of biography, its purposes and value. I had been one of those shortsighted people who, as Lytton Strachey observed in *Eminent Victorians,* "do not reflect that it is perhaps as difficult to write a good life as to live one." Why *couldn't* that form of literature be "my own stuff"? I immediately felt embarrassed over my glib dismissal of Coulouris's sage advice, but I think he recognized a glimmer of understanding dawning on me. After watching Coulouris play Lear with what I recall as paradoxically youthful energy, I never saw Kane's guardian again outside the movies, and he died in 1989, before I could get my Frank Capra biography into print and send him a copy with gratitude.

I came to see while writing the Capra biography from 1984 onward that everything a writer writes cannot help being "personal" and self-revealing, even if only inadvertently. If anything I've ever written reflected my thoughts and feelings about life all the way through, the Capra book surely does. Paradoxically, although that book is fiercely devoted to exposing the false story Capra constructed about his life with the help of the media, *Frank Capra: The Catastrophe of Success* also benefited greatly from my years of writing fiction in the form of screenplays. I had learned the techniques of constructing narrative, creating characters, and maintaining audience interest through suspense and mystery. My absorption and pleasure in the craft of writing helped sustain me during the four painful years of legal battles on that book. Every time I was writing a section of Capra's life story, I knew exactly what the next section would be; the transitions were seamlessly logical, so I knew I was on the right narrative track.

Even though I put aside my earlier attempts to write my autobiographical project *The Broken Places* as a screenplay and a novel, I could not give up on it. This was a story I had to tell. But *Into the Nightmare* was a story I felt just as strongly about, and that came first, since I wanted to get it out for the fiftieth anniversary of the assassination. Once that book was published in 2013, I turned my attention back to solving the problem of *The Broken Places*. By then I was a seasoned biographer who had acquired a respect for that form of writing; my three biographical subjects had shown me that their lives were as gripping as that of any fictional character. Now I could see I had been going down the wrong path all those years with *The Broken Places*: What the book needed to be was a memoir.

I finished the book in 2015 with relative ease, since it was finding the form it had always meant to be, my first-person account of my formative experiences during my breakdown in high school. In my lengthy introduction to *Two Cheers for Hollywood* about my misadventures in the world of movies, also titled "I Loved Movies, But... ," I wrote that "perhaps memoir is the next stage in a biographer's life, the final stage when you literally put yourself into it." I had also pursued the memoir form in *What Ever Happened to Orson Welles?* back in 2006 and even in my lighthearted but highly confessional *Book of Movie Lists* in 1999.

When I gave *The Broken Places: A Memoir* to my friend Laura Truffaut, the filmmaker's brilliant daughter who has a PhD in comparative literature from UC Berkeley, she astutely observed that the first part of the book—my subjectively immersive account of my childhood struggles with Catholicism and the abusive third-grade nun—reads like a novel, while the parts that dramatize my breakdown, recovery, and love story, read like a screenplay, despite my strenuous efforts to transform it. (Part of me still wants to give the novel form another try.) I incorporated some documentary research into the memoir, including the astute letter from the psychologist who examined me in 1956; clinical county hospital records that revealed aspects of myself and my parents I hadn't known before; a moving 1965 letter of advice from a friend of my mother's that I should have followed; and a poignant greeting card I received from the young woman who served as the model for Kathy in my memoir.

I found that I had to reshape some elements of reality to fulfill the demands of storytelling by condensing some elements of time, eliminating my second hospitalization in Madison, and inventing an episode of returning with Kathy to the reservation where she had grown up, a journey I *wished* we had taken. When I wanted to convey the hellishness of growing up in an alcoholic household, I condensed it to one archetypal quarrel between my parents, and when I wanted to portray Kathy's family background, I put it in the form of her monologue, to make clear it was her jaundiced viewpoint on her parents. Those solutions were a bit clumsy, but I could not figure out how to do otherwise. It was strange to realize that to tell my story truthfully, I had to interject some elements of fiction, but that illuminated the imaginative nature of the memoir form. Hemingway wrote in a fragment he removed from his greatest short story, "Big Two-Hearted River," that "The only writing that was any good was what you made up, what you imagined. That made everything come true."

The book's extensive dialogue between Kathy and me obviously was another element of artistic shaping, yet I have the strong sense of remembering vividly what we must have said to each other, even if that must be somewhat illusory or reshaped by the process of memory. When I was struggling with how to convey what had happened to Kathy in the years after we last saw each other, a period about which I had only bits of knowledge to extrapolate from and did not feel I could research like a biographer (for reasons of respecting her family's privacy), I had some valuable advice from my agent, Richard Parks. He suggested showing my character using my reporter's training to investigate her downfall as a framing story after the book begins with my learning of her death one night when I was proofreading *The Wisconsin State Journal,* as actually happened.

Literary shaping

My youthful character was influenced by my absorption in Hemingway during that time in my life, and when I wrote about our romance, I was trying to avoid the anxiety of influence from the Nick Adams stories but finding it irresistible. I often thought of Trudy, the Native American girl of whom the middle-aged Nick reflects, "Could you say she did first what no one has ever done better... " Nick is thinking about their first sexual encounter, but the similar feeling I harbored toward my girlfriend was not about our only sexual encounter, which was disastrous, but our passionate yet chaste make-out sessions along a riverbank and what she did for me emotionally and first that no one has ever done better.

I tried to recapture those enduring feelings in my prose, and in capturing her ghostly presence as of someone in a state between living and dead, I drew from James M. Barrie's play *Mary Rose,* the subject of an essay I had written in 2001 on a dream project Hitchcock was never able to consummate, even though he told me he slipped a bit of *Mary Rose* into the opening of *Family Plot,* as well as echoing the Barrie play in *Vertigo.* Another archetype I kept before me in writing *The Broken Places* was Ann Rutledge, the lost love of Abraham Lincoln, so indelibly alive and profoundly influential but just as quickly gone in John Ford's *Young Mr. Lincoln.* During my screenwriting days I worked on a film outline about Ann Rutledge and made a research trip with my daughter to Ann and Lincoln's homeland of New Salem, Illinois. Of course no one in Hollywood was interested in such a story in the early 1980s.

I read somewhere that some men have "an Ann Rutledge complex," and I certainly am one of those who keeps seeing my first love in other women I meet or only glimpse in public places. And her image is tied up in my memories with my fleeting glimpse of Jeanne Moreau's nudity during one of my guilty, lubricious excursions to the Princess Theater in downtown Milwaukee, which, as it happened, was near the seedy hotel where Kathy and I had our one lovemaking session, followed by her roughly telling me to get lost. The emotional violence of our relationship accounts for what one reviewer observed was my ambivalence toward Kathy in the book. One female reader of the screenplay told me the sex scene in the hotel alienated her because it was so unromantic and made her think of the "older Joe" rather than the teenaged boy having that jaded experience, but that was the point of my bluntly awful depiction of what actually happened when I was nineteen, a moment of truth that was both an end and a beginning in my life.

Those literary, dramatic, and cinematic influences were some of the guideposts that kept me focused during the writing of both the novel and the memoir, providing the sense of aesthetic distance that is necessary for a work of literature. In a deep sense the interplay between distancing and raw emotion was and remains part of the experience I had with her and try to convey in that book. I wondered during the final stretch of the forty-nine years I worked on *The Broken Places* whether the end result of the pain of remembering that I willingly put myself through would result in a catharsis.

Hemingway writes about the question of catharsis in one of his later Nick Adams stories, "Fathers and Sons," in obliquely discussing his father's suicide, the traumatic event I helped Welles work into the fabric of *The Other Side of the Wind*. In Hemingway's 1933 story, the middle-aged Nick drives back with his son into the Michigan landscape of his youth, the one explored in "Indian Camp" and other stories, where he had his tryst with Trudy. While Nick is recalling his experiences with his father through strong, clear sense memory, Hemingway observes, "If he wrote it he could get rid of it. He had gotten rid of many things by writing them. But it was still too early for that."

I wondered if would be cathartic to finish *The Broken Places*. But it wasn't. The book did help put me more at rest with my memories. The pain endures, though it has receded into the distant past, and I can now see the boy in the story as someone I used to know who resembles me, someone I wish I could talk with to give him fatherly advice. Writing the book also did not bring "closure," which I regard as an illusory concept, contrary to popular belief. People often seek "closure" on a painful experience, such as the loss of a loved one. Many Americans seem to have a harder time processing trauma and grief than people in other countries. But you are the sum of your experiences, and I believe instead that if you lose a loved one, you never get over it but only, hopefully, learn to live with the loss and what it makes of you. As Anthony Burgess put it, "What one loves about life are the things that fade. It's a sense of things passing— so regretful, regretful—of things being beautiful and yet mortal, that makes life worth living."

I published *The Broken Places* through my Hightower Press in 2015, illustrating it with photographs of the Milwaukee County Mental Health Center, North Division, where I had spent my months of healing. My brother Tim had taken the pictures a few years earlier when I went there to show him the rustic, decaying, abandoned facility, and I asked him to take pictures as part of my location scouting for the possible film version. By the time I put the book together, the facility had been razed, so it was fortunate we had commemorated the location in photographs, mostly of hauntingly desolate, no longer populated parts of the grounds and a couple showing me reflecting on the past events that occurred there.

I deliberately did not include the one photograph I have of Kathy's real-life model, a police mug shot my father had obtained, taken when she was arrested near the end of her life and given me by him without comment, although I knew and mostly resented what he meant to convey. I left it out of the book partly because I wanted to disguise her identity and partly because I wanted the reader to imagine her, but I often looked into her distraught, dazed eyes as I wrote the final version. My parents never understood what she meant to me, since they resisted, out of guilt and resentment, my attempts to confront them with the realities of that time. Their refusal to understand and my father's unjust hostility toward the young woman who rescued me were part of the story I was telling, further reasons for my alienation from my upbringing.

When *The Broken Places* was finally published after its forty-nine-year gestation period, some people remarked that "It would make a great movie," which made me want to scream. In recent years, though, I did consider making *The Broken Places* as an intimate low-budget movie. The older I get, the more fond I am of aesthetic minimalism, partly as a reaction against the elaborate meaningless of big-budget Hollywood moviemaking. But since it would be a period film, I finally concluded I don't have the money to do it right on my own, and maybe I'm too old to go through that process.

When I read it, I wished everyone you know personally would read it, too, because: who knew?

Unfortunately, *The Broken Places* hasn't found many readers, despite my efforts to promote it. Whatever its strengths or flaws, I've come to realize that in our culture, while memoirs of trauma by women are readily accepted and often sell well, memoirs of trauma by men tend not to be accepted. Although there are occasional exceptions for books whose problems have a more general application (such as drug addiction), by and large that kind of emotional sharing by men makes people uncomfortable and is considered "unmanly."

Nevertheless, *The Broken Places* was what matured me as a writer. My stubborn preoccupation with trying to sell that project helped destroy my Hollywood career and accelerated my disaffection with the industry. All that, in the end, was beneficial. And at the same time, overcoming the challenges the story presented spurred me along the path to writing my other highly personal books and enabled me to become a more ambitious and perceptive writer. I believe it was well worth the trade-off.

I know you are proponent of self-publishing. Why did you go the self-publishing route with The Broken Places, Into the Nightmare, Political Truth, *and others?*

The ease of self-publishing in the twenty-first century has been a boon to authors, especially with books that are difficult or impossible to market otherwise. These books are too controversial, idiosyncratic, and/or personal to find conventional publishers. The advent of personal computers has made it possible to set your own book in print-ready form, and after you hire a designer to make the book professional-looking and camera-ready, you find what's called a fulfillment house to print the book on demand. Since Amazon.com a few years ago began to accept self-published books, that makes it possible to get such work to the public and market your books to readers everywhere. People can also buy them directly from the fulfillment house, in my case from Vervante, a Utah company that does reliable print-on-demand work of high professional quality and ships the books to customers.

After *The Broken Places* was rejected by many publishers when I wrote it as a novel, I turned to self-publishing when I rewrote it as a memoir. Although I continue to publish some of my books through university presses—as I have with Columbia University Press on my recent critical studies of Lubitsch, Wilder, and Cukor—I've also taken the self-publishing route with my collection *Two Cheers for Hollywood* and *Frankly: Unmasking Frank Capra*. After trying ways of collecting my articles and interviews along various thematic lines, I decided to just put the ones I like best into *Two Cheers. Frankly,* an esoteric account of my misadventures with Knopf and Wesleyan over the Capra biography, is the kind of hot potato no regular publisher would touch, since it exposes wrongdoing in the publishing world.

Much has changed since my first book, *Persistence of Vision: A Collection of Film Criticism,* was self-published by our Wisconsin Film Society in 1968. We hired a local print shop to turn out what were intended as trade paperback copies, but as I realized belatedly, no bookstores would handle such a book; self-publishing existed in those days but was called "the vanity press" and looked down upon for that reason. Now, however, that stigma has mostly evaporated, and many self-published books sell well. The only drawback is that it's hard to get most mainstream magazines and newspapers to review self-published books, a barrier that eventually will have to fall. Film magazines, though, review my books, since I am a well-known author in my field. And I publicize my books successfully by sending review copies to bloggers, critics, and other journalists for online publications and to podcast interviewers. I do many podcasts and radio interviews on various topics related to my books and get some interviews and feature coverage in print publications. There are Internet forums to discuss and debate the Kennedy assassination and other specialized topics, so I use those to spread the word when my books are published as well as to keep finding new readers.

I named the imprint I created, Hightower Press, after one of my favorite film characters, Bob Hightower, the benign outlaw John Wayne plays in John Ford's ravishingly beautiful 1948 Western fable, *3 Godfathers;* I use a Fordian image of the Totem Pole rock spire in Monument Valley as my logo. Being able to print and sell these dream projects through Vervante has been made possible by the salary I earned from my full-time job as a professor at San Francisco State. The difficulty of supporting myself as a freelance writer, which I nevertheless managed to do intermittently for many years, and the necessity of obtaining advances from publishers for longterm projects made it hard to find the time and resources to write those dream books and get them into print. Now I have full control over the content to write as I wish, as well as control over the design and the printing process. And the profits, though modest, come in steadily, since there are no advances, and the fulfillment house gives a monthly accounting and payment.

I recommend self-publishing to any author with an offbeat book he or she wants to get out to the public. *Into the Nightmare,* in particular, the culmination of my thirty-plus years of research into the assassination and the Tippit murder, has kept selling remarkably well and steadily since 2013 to readers throughout the world. That is gratifying, although I will never earn back the more than $100,000 I estimate I put into my research expenses on the book (and counting, since my research continues). I have done that

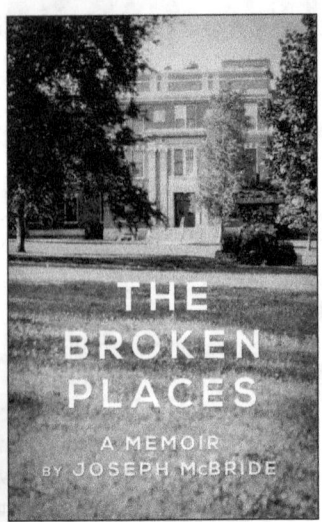

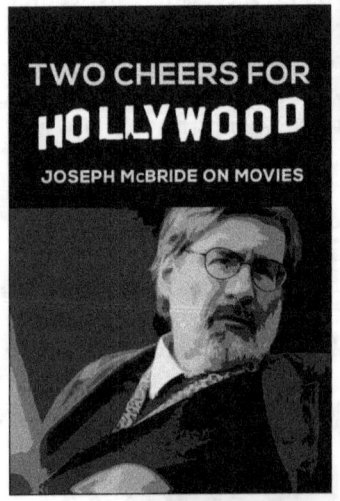

Three more of my "dream books," print-on-demand titles from Vervante and my Hightower Press: *The Broken Places: A Memoir* (2015); my collection of short pieces, *Two Cheers for Hollywood: Joseph McBride on Movies* (2017); and *Frankly: Unmasking Frank Capra* (2019).

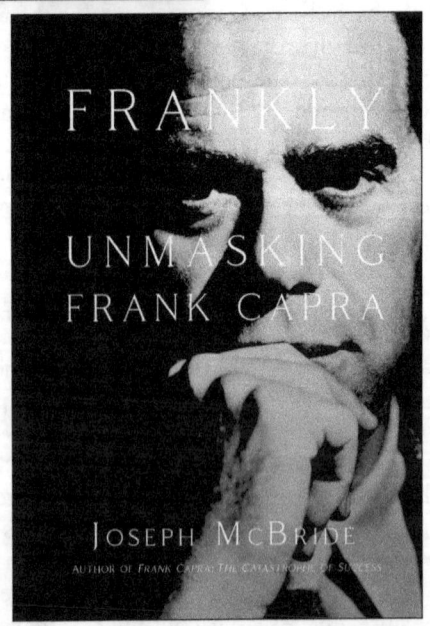

work as a labor of love, for the truth and for the memory of John F. Kennedy.

Despite all the hassles I encountered at San Francisco State, the teaching job was a godsend. It not only made me financially stable for the first time in a decade and earned me a reasonable pension, but it also gave me the enjoyable opportunity to keep in touch with young people and new developments in cinema, while enabling me to do some good by teaching them to hone their writing skills and become more informed and sophisticated cinephiles. And since I always maintain a double focus on immediate needs and more ambitious longterm plans, I viewed the teaching job as a pragmatic means of achieving my writing goals while practicing a profession I found worthwhile. I suffered a heart attack in 2017 but recovered well and actually wound up in much better physical shape than I had been since my youth, thanks to a healthier diet and regular workouts with a trainer. And as I mentioned earlier, the last couple of decades of my life have been my most prolific.

9. The decline of cinephilia

When we were in Wisconsin, we talked endlessly to each other, we members of the Madison film mafia, not only about aesthetics but also about how movies are a vital part of every country's political, social, and cultural history. I wonder if you had students like that at San Francisco State.

From time to time I was delighted to encounter students there who were devoted cinephiles, like we were during our college days. Some were passionate about classical and modern cinema and could more than hold their own in discussions, often including the sociohistorical dimensions of movies. It was enlightening to talk with them and hear their ideas. But I didn't find many such students, unfortunately. In Madison, we made up for the paucity of film courses at the UW by fanatically watching movies on our own every day, and I don't see much of that devouring appetite anymore. A happy exception was a young woman who became so passionate about *7 Women* after seeing it in my course on Women in the Films of John Ford that she watched Ford's great final feature on a streaming site ten more times that semester.

What has happened over the last few decades to the art form I loved—in this country it's been turned largely into moronic fodder for the adolescent male audience—is extremely disheartening. It makes me worry about the future of cinema. My introduction to *Two Cheers for Hollywood* is deeply pessimistic, although we can't envision the future of what used to be called "film." We just know that film as we knew it is over, though film history remains to be studied, even if much of it is lost. Now the world of cinema is changing so rapidly and unpredictably that no critic, historian, journalist, or teacher can have more than an educated hunch about where it is going.

When I heard Orson Welles talking with students at the University of Southern California in 1971 while we were shooting a scene there for (but not used in) *The Other Side of the Wind*, he was asked by a student how he would teach film. He said he wouldn't show films, since they've already seen enough films for one lifetime. That caused consternation. What then would he teach?, the student asked. Welles spread his arms wide and said, "I would teach the history of the world!" When my students would complain about having to take non-film classes, their GE (General Education) requirements, I told the prospective filmmakers that "your general education courses are the most important, because if all you know about are cameras and sound equipment, what are you going to make films about? This is a major reason why most films today are so bad." I've always liked movies because at their best they illuminate life by serving as a window onto the world, ideally showing us every possible facet of human nature and existence.

My interest in cinema has waned to some extent as I get older and spend more of my time studying history, my primary interest. My biographies of directors range widely into sociopolitical subjects, and I have branched out into books on other subjects besides movies. And that's how I have taught film, using it to enlighten students both aesthetically and to give them the knowledge they desperately need about the world. I took it upon myself to teach what I could about history, literature, science, and other subjects while also focusing on films.

You write in your Introduction to Two Cheers for Hollywood, *"We have to face the fact that we no longer live in an age of cinephilia. I would not be honest if I did not admit that makes me terribly sad." I find that at a time when so many old films are available but new generations of film fans—and filmmakers—don't bother to seek them out, my frustration runs neck and neck with my sadness.*

Soon after I began teaching at SFSU, I was taken aback when I mentioned to my students an influential modern classic, *Annie Hall,* and drew nothing but blank stares. I was rather naive in not realizing how complete our culture's Orwellian erasure of the past has become, but that was among the reasons I found it instructive to have contact with students. I'm not surprised by that kind of response anymore; the situation has only worsened over the years. When I came to our school, Steve Kovacs, the most sympathetic of my faculty mentors, told me, "Don't show any films made in the last five years, because they've already seen them. Show older films they haven't seen." But gradually I found with dismay that many young people don't even consider watching films that were made as recently as two or three years ago, or even last year.

I am sorry to report that most juniors and seniors came to my classes not having seen even some of the most celebrated and essential film classics, such as *Citizen Kane, Persona, Jules et Jim, Dr. Strangelove, The Conversation,* or other (formerly) canonical classics. They weren't helped much by our other professors. I found I was usually the only one introducing students to, say, Renoir, Ford, or

Bergman, let alone Kubrick or Coppola. But I would remind myself there was a time when I had never seen *Kane*, before I encountered it in my first film class, taught by Professor Byrne. And when I showed classic films I loved, most of the students responded favorably. I read somewhere that what a teacher can convey to his students is not so much information, which often goes in one ear and out the other, but enthusiasm, which can become a lasting influence. I was delighted when my students shared my enthusiasm for Lubitsch's *The Merry Widow* or Ford's *My Darling Clementine*, to mention two memorable examples when faces lit up with wonderment over cinematic riches and means of expression they hadn't known existed.

Peter Bogdanovich, who inspired me as a young writer and interviewer about film, said it's only films that are called "old"—people don't speak of "old symphonies" or "old novels." But it's not only "old" movies most of today's students find irrelevant. When I started at SFSU in 2002, on Mondays I would ask students what films they had seen over the weekend, and we had good discussions. Eventually, though, I found that few of them bothered to see films outside classes, even on streaming. When I asked about their visual entertainment, I found they tend to watch short videos on YouTube and other Internet sites that require only a limited attention span. I began to wonder why most of our students decide to major in Cinema, since they don't seem much interested in movies. And I wondered what *we* were doing trying to teach them about cinema. That brought about the same feeling of alienation I had from most people in Hollywood after I went there and realized they were there for reasons other than a love of movies.

Our department was partly remiss by not focusing enough on the "New Media" the students prefer to watch, but something crucial is missing if prospective filmmakers don't think in terms of sustained narrative storytelling or feature-length documentaries. When I asked my colleague Larry Clark a few years ago why documentaries had become so popular theatrically, he said, "They've learned to tell stories." If I were to enter the film industry today, I would go into the documentary field instead of fiction filmmaking, because there's more room for intelligent, adult subjects in that field, which has also outpaced mainstream journalism in digging incisively into controversial subjects.

Did you find that the decline in cinephilia reflects larger problems in the American cultural and political environment over recent decades?

Indeed. The students' malaise about cinematic knowledge and appreciation goes along with their general ignorance of history. It's far more shocking how little young people know about world and American history; a survey a few years ago showed that a majority of American high school students think we were fighting the Soviets in World War II and that Germany was our ally. Few know anything about what we used to be taught as "Civics." Many don't know what the three branches of our government are. That level of ignorance is dangerous, as we can see in our voting patterns, and it's not confined to younger Americans.

I believe this comes from a general collapse of our public education system that began with the so-called "tax revolt" of the 1970s. We had our infamous Proposition 13 in California enacted by a voters' initiative in 1978, a state constitutional amendment that lowered property taxes by freezing values at the 1976 level, limiting the taxation rate to one percent of the assessed value, with only minimal annual increases of the value restricted to an inflation factor not to exceed two percent annually. I knew that would lead to slashing the state education budget. But I remember when I said that at the time to a Hollywood film producer, she responded, "What do I care? I don't have children." That's the kind of shortsightedness even some supposed liberals brought to the issue at the time. The tax revolt was an excuse for a deliberate dumbing-down of the populace. Our national public education system has been systematically dumbed down from the mid-'70s onward. Right-wing power brokers want to keep the populace ignorant so they can to lie to them and put malleable ignoramuses such as George W. Bush and Donald Trump in power as figureheads for their schemes.

Here's an example of what the students don't learn in public schools: I always taught the Civil War, the Jim Crow era, and the civil rights movement when my screenwriting students adapted "A Late Encounter with the Enemy," the Flannery O'Connor story satirizing Southern racist nostalgia. In the early 2000s, some students always knew that history fairly well and were able to discuss it intelligently. But as ten or so years went by, I found that almost none knew anything about the civil rights movement. So I investigated and discovered that the state of California had stopped teaching that part of our national history in high schools. As a result, some of the students had trouble understanding the O'Connor story and recognizing that her protagonist is a racist.

I did my best to make up for that and other deficiencies of our K-12 schools, and I found that most students are eager to learn their history when given the chance. One student, however, called out in dismay during a Film and Society class—in which I showed and discussed films about American history or films about the media—"I didn't know this was going to be a *history* class!"

How were you coping with the decline of cinephilia? Did your approach to the teaching of film studies change in your later years at the school? You said you had to resort to subterfuge to keep teaching studies courses.

After I managed to achieve tenure in 2008, I still often had to fight for what I wanted to teach. I mostly managed to work my way around that, but it took help from some department chairs and required some ingenuity and subterfuge on my part. The sharply diminishing interest in film studies overall was a growing problem I faced in my later years at SFSU, reflected in the precipitous dropping of enrollment in such courses. Even though our department claimed to put equal stress on studies and production, in practice that was increasingly untrue. We gradually became, in effect, a trade school. That diminished our supposed mission. And it increased students' complaints about having to take non-film courses, even though they had chosen to attend a university, which is supposed to have a broader curriculum than a trade school. The department was always dominated by our production faculty, since most students myopically entered with dreams of becoming directors before many started facing the reality that (1) as Paul Schrader pointed out, a film school degree is of little to no help in finding professional employment; and (2) few people become directors, while even established directors these days have trouble finding work.

When I expressed chagrin as the enrollment in our studies courses began to decline in the early 2000s, Professor Heep told me he thought thirteen students was an ideal number for a course. Those were the days! Eventually, however, as overall enrollment at the university continued to plummet, the university started to economize by cancelling courses with low enrollment, which usually meant below ten or twelve students. I had to come up with roundabout ways to justify teaching film studies courses even on some of the filmmakers I wrote what are considered "definitive" books about, such as Ford and Welles.

I realized I could use the heading of a course I had originally proposed, Writing About Cinema, to teach courses on filmmakers while simultaneously helping students learn how to write about their work and film in general. That took double the amount of work, but the results were well worth it. In my later years at San Francisco State, an outside study of our department urged us to have senior tenured faculty members teach that vital course on writing rather than lecturers or TAs. So I seized on that opportunity. In addition to my basic screenwriting course, I offered to teach two sections of Writing About Cinema per semester, which benefited from mandatory enrollment that guaranteed sufficient class sizes, and covertly I designed them with the dual purpose of being studies courses.

I found it advantageous to teach courses that revolved around writing about a single film—one with rich historical content as well as landmark aesthetic qualities—so those I chose to build courses on were Ford's *The Searchers* and *The Man Who Shot Liberty Valance*, Welles's *The Magnificent Ambersons* and *The Other Side of the Wind*, Kubrick's *Dr. Strangelove*, *Fahrenheit 451* (the Truffaut version), and *The Manchurian Candidate* (the 1962 Frankenheimer/Axelrod version). I had the students read the literary source material and, when possible, the screenplays, and write analytical pieces about the films, taking into account their multiple authorship.

I enjoyed approaching studies courses as writing courses. Each semester, in addition to giving an exam on the film and reading material, I had my GWAR students write two drafts of their first and final papers, as well as outlining the final paper and giving an oral presentation on it to test their thesis and get feedback from me and their fellow students. Having students learn to outline and rewrite their papers greatly improved their study habits, since too many otherwise try to get away with dashing off papers at the last minute, as I was also guilty of doing in college. As you can glean from most of those titles, the films enabled me to be a history teacher, educating the classes about the American West, the Cold War, nuclear warfare policy, and the decline of agrarian America and the rise of cities, as well as discussing the collapse of the studio system followed by the brief flourishing of the New Hollywood.

How did the decline in cinephilia and the attrition that caused affect your view of teaching as a profession?

The problem I began to face toward the end of my time at San Francisco State was exacerbated by the widespread decline in national K-12 learning habits and ability due to the pandemic that began in 2020. Teachers everywhere saw noticeable drops in reading and writing skills.

To protect my health, which I felt necessary following my heart attack and in light of my history of respiratory illnesses, I taught online for my final four years. I found that my teaching improved as a result, since the flaw in my skills that most bothered me, my difficulty in generating sufficient class discussion, was alleviated. Online teaching meant that I could see the students' faces more easily (they could no longer hide out in the back of the classroom), and their names were displayed on the screen. I would make a point of calling on all of them each week, as my son's best English teacher at Palo Alto High School, Michael McNulty, told parents was his practice. I got along right away with Mr. McNulty because he even taught a course on sports literature and was so devoted to Robert Penn Warren's novel *All the King's Men* that he taught an entire semester's course around it, an example that encouraged my similar courses on individual films.

Although I found teaching online helpful in making classes more intimate and lively, nationwide reports showed that online teaching also has had mixed effects on student learning skills. Students drifted away during the pandemic. And our public university, faced with drastic declines in overall enrollment and severe cuts in our state budget allotment, began to admit 95 percent of those who applied (mostly from California high schools) rather than the previous 65 percent acceptance rate. That 30 percent degree of leniency made a major difference, sometimes causing the dropout rate in my writing courses to plunge below levels the university found acceptable in the new economic environment.

I was blamed for the falling enrollment in my courses, and the new environment encouraged the administration to treat the students as customers who were always right. When I was urged to be more lenient, I explained my methods and then did what I did when my *Daily Variety* editor told me to spend less time writing obituaries and crank them out "down and dirty": I declined. As a result of all this, I began to find our school no longer a viable place to teach. Tired of banging my head against an increasingly thick wall, I felt much the same way John Wayne's Captain Brittles does in *She Wore a Yellow Ribbon* when an order he protested leads to disaster: He says "it's about time I *did* retire." As a result, I took my retirement at the end of December 2024 with a well-earned pension and went back to writing books fulltime.

How gratifying was it for you to be named an Emeritus Professor after twenty-two years at San Francisco State?

That title, awarded in May 2025, is one of the few academic honors that means something to me. I especially appreciate it because I was expelled from the University of Wisconsin for failing to attend classes. So choosing to be an autodidact worked out well.

Have your views of any movies changed as a result of interacting with your students?

You'll recall that I passed up an opportunity to teach screenwriting at CalArts in my late twenties because I felt too wrapped up in on own screenwriting career to concentrate sufficiently on the students. But after I had been teaching at San Francisco State for more than a decade, I was interviewed for a 2013 faculty profile video directed by Silvia Turchin. When she asked how I felt about the profession, I replied, "The biggest surprise I got was you learn more from your students in a way than they do from you, because it's a real interchange, and you get your ideas tested, and they come up with insights you hadn't thought about. It's very exciting, and I think there's a time in life to get from people and then there's a time in life to give to people. And I think teaching is a form of giving, and it's a good feeling."

I'll mention truly stunning instances when my views of two films among those I most highly cherish were changed and heightened substantially by showing them to students and engaging in lively discussions. I have studied these films many times over the years, as well as written about them, which is why I was especially impressed by students who made me think more deeply about their meanings.

John Ford's *Fort Apache*, the film that launched my lifelong study of Ford, has always meant a great deal to me with its revisionist and sympathetic view of Native Americans. In a class I extolled Ford's paradoxically effective casting of John Wayne as Captain York, the cavalry officer who most deeply understands and cares about Native Americans. I discuss how York stands up to Henry Fonda's Colonel Thursday by vigorously protesting his suicidal order to charge, which causes most of their men to be massacred. I told the students that is the film's tragic climax, because Captain York's verbal defiance isn't sufficient, and he should have taken action by arresting or shooting his commanding officer. He fails to do so, although he is within his rights and duty and probably would have been exonerated by a court-martial. A student then commented about York that Dante reserves a place in Hell for "the good man who does nothing." I had read and translated some of the *Inferno* for my Italian course in college but had forgotten what the student called to my attention. That startled me into a deeper and more critical view of Captain York.

When I showed Frank Capra's *Mr. Smith Goes to Washington* and was praising Jimmy Stewart's idealistic junior senator for his crusade against corruption in Washington, a student observed that Mr. Smith is not only an "innocent," as I called him, but profoundly ignorant. Smith doesn't know anything about the political boss who actually runs his state, even though Smith publishes a statewide newspaper and therefore has no excuse. That observation fundamentally changed my view of Jefferson Smith and his culpable innocence. I began thinking of Smith in light of Graham Greene's comment in his 1955 novel *The Quiet American* about Pyle, the naive, innocent-appearing CIA officer who causes violent havoc in Saigon. As Greene puts it, "Innocence is a kind of insanity.… Innocence always calls mutely for protection when we would be so much wiser to guard ourselves against it: innocence is like a dumb leper who has lost his bell, wandering the world, meaning no harm."

What is a critical study?

After Searching for John Ford *in 2001, you stopped doing biographies and turned to critical studies again. It must be somewhat frustrating when some readers and even some reviewers continually fail to understand the difference between the two. People often call your critical studies biographies, but you are quick to correct them, even though they contain much biographical information on your subjects along with the analysis of their films. They're even longer!*

Yes, I'm surprised that many people don't understand what a "critical study" is anymore, even in the benighted world of cinema studies. During the SFSU ceremony when I was awarded my emeritus status in 2025, the presentation written by my department gave me credit for some biographies I hadn't written but are erroneously described books that are actually critical studies. I take pains in these later books and publicity to make sure they are labeled correctly. In writing what is known as a "critical biography" of Capra, Spielberg, or Ford—to reiterate, this means a biography that takes full account of the interplay between the life and the work, the only kind I feel is worth writing about an artist—I interweave analysis of their films throughout, but my primary focus is on how the work is affected by the subjects' actions and personality. On the other hand, a "critical study," such as the books I've written about Lubitsch, Wilder, the Coen Bros., and Cukor, concentrates primarily on the films while bringing in biographical and production data as background and context to shed light on the films.

But I still get that confusion from some reviewers who describe my critical studies of Welles, Ford, Lubitsch, Wilder, and Cukor as biographies, and I even get it occasionally from publishers. One prospective publisher wanted me to revise a critical study to take out my "opinions"! What?? I didn't respond, since I thought their response was crazy, and I heard that they were surprised not to hear back from me. As for my opinion about opinions, I always told my students that it's fine to put your opinions into your papers (even though they are taught in high school not to do so) but only if you can back them up with facts and examples. I quote Daniel Patrick Moynihan, who famously put it, "Everyone is entitled to his own opinion, but not his own facts." After starting my career writing critical studies on Welles and Ford back in Wisconsin, I have gone back to that form of writing in my old age partly because I can't afford to write biographies anymore and partly because I find critical studies give me even more room to delve in detail into the artists' work.

In my critical studies I interweave biographical information I turn up in my own research or find in the biographies I consider valuable (with appropriate citations and acknowledgments). If you look at Strachey's *Eminent Victorians*, you'll see that he also lists the biographies on which he relied for factual groundwork while writing his own idiosyncratic short biographies. My biographies are long because I turned up such a wealth of information and was writing about the work of prolific filmmakers who could fairly be called workaholics. As for writing longer books in my later years, I put that down partly to the fact that as I grew older, I started to view life and people in more complex ways than I did in my early books. Back then, I always knew where I was going with a book, and now I don't quite know where I am going or what I think about a subject until I write it. That makes the job more intriguing and the books more fluid in their approach and freer in their style.

Your critical studies are similar to your biographies in that they correct what was written before and are intended to provide the truth that you gather from your investigative research.

Yes, I confront false perceptions and challenge conventional wisdom in my critical studies as well, writing about careers that have been unfairly neglected, mischaracterized, or otherwise misunderstood. That has been the case with my recent critical studies of Ernst Lubitsch, Billy Wilder, Joel and Ethan Coen, and George Cukor.

How Did Lubitsch Do It?

When you began working on your 2018 book, How Did Lubitsch Do It?, *did you plan on writing many critical studies?*

I tend to keep various possible book projects in mind for a few years before I commit to writing one. In the early 2000s, I thought I had a nifty idea, to do a book on both Lubitsch and Wilder, since Wilder is Lubitsch's greatest acolyte and tried in various ways to follow in his tradition. And they are the leading examples of European filmmakers who came to America and transformed our industry in a more sophisticated, more continental direction, as well as commenting acutely on the U.S. from a European point of view. But after working on that Lubitsch/Wilder critical study for about a year, I realized that it not only would be way too long, but it would be cumbersome to keep switching back and forth from one to the other. Another key consideration was that the more I wrote about Lubitsch and Wilder, I could see their differences more clearly as well as their similarities. So I put my Wilder sections aside for a while and concentrated on finishing the Lubitsch book.

Why a book on Lubitsch?

One of my main motivations in writing that book was to make Lubitsch a household name again. He was still somewhat neglected, although he had passionately devoted fans here and there, so I was trying to bring him back to the prominence he deserves. The book has certainly helped do so, but he's still not taught as much in American universities as some of the other great directors, I suspect because he deals in such a sophisticated manner with sexuality. That makes academics nervous in our puritanical age, and since Lubitsch is far too sophisticated and complex in his attitudes to be pigeonholed as "politically correct," they tend to avoid him altogether.

But that's myopic. Lubitsch played the major role in inventing both the romantic comedy and the musical. In his prime he was a household name like Chaplin or Hitchcock. As Kristin Thompson points out in her book on Lubitsch, he was unique in that he was the leading director in two national cinemas, that of Germany and then the United States. And as Jean Renoir put it, "He invented the modern Hollywood.... This man was so strong that when he was asked by Hollywood to work there, he not only didn't lose his Berlin style, but he converted the Hollywood industry to his own way of expression." And I was always impressed by Welles's declaration in 1964 that Lubitsch "is a giant.... Lubitsch's talent and originality are stupefying."

I was tantalized back in the day by reading Herman G. Weinberg's piquant valentine to the director, his 1967 book *The Lubitsch Touch: A Critical Study,* which discusses so many marvelous films that I had no way of seeing, including some that no longer exist. Weinberg sent me an advance copy of the cover of his book, which I now see as a passing of the torch.

The first Lubitsch film I saw, in the late 1960s in Madison, was *Trouble in Paradise,* which made me think, "I've just seen this guy's masterpiece." It is one of the few films I would call perfect, along with *Citizen Kane* and Ozu's *Tokyo Story.* I rented the few Lubitsch films that were available on 16mm then to show our Wisconsin Film Society members but was frustrated I couldn't see the rest of his work. And now after managing to see all forty-eight extant Lubitsch films or fragments (out of sixty-nine features or shorts he directed, a relatively good survival rate for a director who began in the silent period), I still think I was right that *Trouble in Paradise* is this guy's masterpiece. And I found that he made so many other great films. The most influential film Lubitsch directed was his 1924 romantic comedy, *The Marriage Circle.* This work of consummate subtlety and wit is the film that transformed Hollywood with what Renoir called Lubitsch's "ironic approach to the big problems of life." It had a direct and profound influence

During my research trip to Berlin in 2014 to visit the old haunts of Ernst Lubitsch for my critical study *How Did Lubitsch Do It?*, I was able to enter the family apartments at 183 Schönhauser Allee with the resourceful help of my translator, actress Eszter Tompa. I was sick as a dog with stomach pains on this scorching-hot day but enjoyed exploring Lubitsch's beginnings. (Tompa)

on such disparate directors as Hitchcock, Douglas Sirk, and Yasujiro Ozu.

You wrote in the book's Introduction that you worked on it for nine years. I know how busy you were doing other things, so I ask with tongue in cheek: What took you so long? Did you begin the project thinking you were an expert on Lubitsch or were you happy to be learning about him?

I waited until I had seen most of the films to begin writing. And as usual with my books, I kept researching all through the writing process. One of the principal reasons I chose to write about Lubitsch is that I selfishly wanted to see all his films, and that gave me an excuse to travel to see them. So my Lubitsch book was a complex, self-financed research topic, involving three trips to Europe to see films and explore his roots in Berlin. I started by going to the Munich Film Museum, where the curator, Stefan Drössler, whom I knew from my work on Welles (the museum has most of Welles's unfinished work), brought me up to speed on Lubitsch's German films and his rare American films.

In recent years many of his films have been released on home video in the U.S. I've done audio commentaries on eight Lubitsch films for Kino Lorber. They have been doing admirable work in releasing some of his German work, but some of the German films and even some of the American silent films are still missing from home video. To mention one egregious example, *Kohlhiesels Töchter/ Kohlhiesel's Daughters*, a delightful 1920 Bavarian sex farce with Henny Porten (in a tour de force as both the pretty and the homely daughters) and Emil Jannings in a rare comedic role, has still never been released theatrically or on homevideo in the U.S., although it was posted on YouTube before its recent restoration. Lubitsch's first American film, *Rosita,* a charming 1923 period comedy-drama that its star and producer, Mary Pickford, inexplicably tried to destroy, and his wonderful 1924 Pola Negri romantic political satire, *Forbidden Paradise*, are two silent films that barely existed for years in bootlegged copies in poor condition from foreign archives. Since my book was published, both of those films have been restored by the Museum of Modern Art, with especially spectacular results in the case of *Rosita.* But for whatever reason, these two gems still have been shown only at festivals and in archives. I've tried to intervene but to no avail.

I was the curator of the Lubitsch retrospective at the 2010 Locarno International Film Festival in Switzerland, which gave me the invaluable opportunity to see the best possible 35mm prints in existence of most of the Lubitsch films, loaned from European and American archives. I contributed to a program booklet they published and introduced thirteen of the films as well as moderating panel discussions. The retrospective went over so well that I was even named "Al Personaggio più Significativo" (The Most Important Personage) of the festival by the independent critics covering it, which I took as more of a tribute to Lubitsch than to my efforts on his behalf.

Part of the joy as a reader of that book is that I sensed how much you enjoyed learning more than you knew about Lubitsch and how it made you appreciate him even more.

I thoroughly enjoyed discovering and re-watching and thinking about Lubitsch films: it was about as much fun as you can having writing a film book. One of my motives in writing books at this late stage of my life is simply to enjoy myself, even to indulge myself. So I'm glad to hear that I communicated that enthusiasm and excitement over what I found in Lubitsch's work.

Did you interview anyone who knew Lubitsch?

It wasn't that kind of a book, but I did have the good fortune after it was published to become friends with the director's delightful daughter, Nicola Lubitsch, who was a child when he died but remembers him well. We first spoke when she called to thank me after I wrote a column in *Daily Variety* paying tribute to her father on what would have been his hundredth birthday in 1992. When my book was published, she and I did some interviews together in Los Angeles, both on radio and at a screening of the restored print of his silent gem *So This Is Paris,* hosted by Jan-Christopher Horak at the Billy Wilder Theater of UCLA's Film and Television Archive. I was touched that Nicola wrote of the book that it is "Without doubt the best book ever written on my father. My bible on his work."

I also discussed Lubitsch during my trip to Berlin with Robert Fischer, the German filmmaker who made an excellent 2006 documentary feature on the director, *Ernst Lubitsch in Berlin: From Schönhauser Allee to Hollywood.* (Robert also did a video interview with me at the national film archive, *Perspectives on "Othello": Joseph McBride on Orson Welles,* for Blu-ray editions.) Robert told me how to find the apartment house in Berlin where Lubitsch and his family had lived as well as the location of the parents' business, a women's tailor shop. They had three floors in the apartment house: the first floor for the workers who made the clothing and separate floors for the parents and the children. Their business literally was the shop around the corner; by the time of my visit it had become a beauty parlor. The apartment house where Lubitsch had been born was right across the street from the shop but had since been torn down. There was a Cajun restaurant on the site, which I think Lubitsch would enjoy, since it's an American connection.

The neighborhood, Berlin's fabled Scheuneviertel, is now multiethnic, but in his youth it was a central location for Jewish residents of Berlin. During the Holocaust all of them were deported to death camps or killed in the local synagogue. His parents had died before then, and Lubitsch was safe in Hollywood. Having been stripped of his German citizenship by the Nazi regime, he became an American citizen. The U-Bahn (the subway) that runs through the neighborhood has large photographic murals of its days as a Jewish enclave, a haunting form of testimony that helps you feel the presence of those who are missing. This visit bore out the truth I always keep in mind of what Goethe wrote, "Whoever wishes to understand a poet/Must go into the poet's land."

I also did some research on Wilder during that trip to Berlin. My guide to translate rare films at the Deutsche Kinemathek, the national film archive, and to visit Lubitsch's old neighborhood was a bilingual young actress, Eszter Tompa, who has since gone on to success in films. She was resourceful, talking our way into the Lubitsch family apartment house by borrowing a key from the beauty shop. We were fortunate to find a young man who knew well about Lubitsch and was honored to live in the space where he grew up. The most fascinating revelation about the mazelike apartments was that there are so many doors, and doors within doors, which helps account for Lubitsch's trademark artistic method of using suggestive ellipses. That device also comes from the theater, where he was an apprentice for the great director Max Reinhardt for seven years. Eszter even talked our way into Reinhardt's Deutsches Theater by charming two guards who not only showed us the backstage area but let me stand on the stage where Lubitsch stood while they shone spotlights on me, which was thrilling.

Was seeing his early films how you best learned who he really was? Were there revelations?

Most of the books about him deal with his work in one or the other country, but my intention was to write the first in-depth study of his entire career and the evolution of his way of working. You can't fully understand Lubitsch's greatness as a director of comedy and drama without knowing how he developed from his early days as a knockabout comedian to a leading director of comedies, dramas, and spectacles in Berlin into a master of sophisticated comedies in Hollywood, such as *The Marriage Circle*, *Trouble in Paradise*, *Angel*, *Ninotchka*, *The Shop Around the Corner*, and the black comedy *To Be or Not to Be*.

The German films were a revelation and helped enlarge my views of his life and work. They opened up other ways of seeing Lubitsch's gradual development—I watched the films he acted in for other directors too—and he soon began directing as well as starring in such films. But he brought autobiographical elements into, for example, *Schuhpalast Pinkus/Shoe Salon Pinkus* in 1916. That's a ripoff of the 1914 comedy film that made him a star, *Der Stolz der Firma: Die Geschichte einer Lehrlings/The Pride of the Firm: The Story of an Apprentice*, which was directed by Carl Wilhelm, and in some ways Lubitsch's film is not as accomplished. Both films draw expressively from Lubitsch's own misadventures when he was grudgingly trying to follow his father's wishes to join him in the tailoring business.

Ernst's klutziness made him unsuited for that trade, as well as his penchant for hiding in corners reading plays when he was supposed to be working, but it established the comic type he made popular. There's a critical controversy over the Jewish humor he brought to the films he acted in, what were then called "Jewish milieu pieces." Their broad popularity with German audiences at the time has raised eyebrows in the post-Hitler era, especially since Lubitsch during the Third Reich became a target of anti-Semitic Nazi propaganda. I examine at length, in what I hope is an intelligently nuanced analysis, the arguments pro and con. Even though those films draw to some extent on the Jewish stereotypes of the time, I find they also are suffused with warmth and affection, with their ethnic humor "a sign of fellow feeling, a way of breaking down social barriers." That makes their humor seem largely congenial, if sometimes uncomfortable to watch today, especially in their moments of exaggerated, unsubtle lechery. I generally agree with Lubitsch, who said in his earliest known interview, in 1916, that he considered it a "quite incredible position" for people to take offense at his brand of Jewish humor. He added in that interview, "Jewish humor is, where it may appear, sympathetic and artistic."

Lubitsch also branched out into other kinds of films in Germany as he was trying to find his style, which he felt he finally achieved in 1919 with the raucous and expressionistic comic gem *Die Austernprinzessin/The Oyster Princess*. He also made an embryonic romantic comedy, *Wenn Vier Dasselbe Tun/When Four Do the Same;* a proto-feminist classic about cross-dressing, *Ich Möchte Kein Mann sein/I Don't Want to Be a Man*; expressionistic fantasies such as *Die Puppe/The Doll* and *Die Bergkatze/The Wildcat*; straight dramas such as *Rausch/Intoxication*, a Strindberg adaptation with Asta Nielsen that unfortunately is lost, and *Die Flamme/The Flame*, which only partially exists; and the "Orientalist" melodramas *Die Augen der Mumie Mâ/The Eyes of the Mummy* and *Sumurun*. His grand and racy spectacles *Madame DuBarry, Anna Boleyn, Das Weib des Pharaoh/The Wife of Pharaoh* brought him to the attention of Hollywood by breaking the taboo against the showing of German films internationally in the wake of the Great War.

Lubitsch's extraordinary range in these films illuminates so many facets of his work and shows the remarkable adaptability that would serve him well over the years as he was able to modulate his style to accommodate changing trends in the marketplace of two countries. That kept him commercially viable until his untimely death in 1947. As Truffaut movingly wrote of his style in his famous 1968 essay "Lubitsch Was a Prince," "The essential consideration here is never to treat the subject *directly*. So, if we are kept outside the closed doors of the bedroom when everything is happening inside... it's because Lubitsch has racked his brain during six weeks of writing so that the spectators can work out the plot along with him as they watch the film.... [He] has already examined all the previous solutions as to offer one that's never been used before—an unthinkable, bizarre, exquisite and disorienting solution." And to achieve such marvels of storytelling, Lubitsch "worked like a dog, bled himself white, died twenty years too early." (As did Truffaut himself, I can't help thinking while reading that.)

Seeing Lubitsch's German films and the Hollywood silent films—which also experimented with various styles and pioneered the romantic comedy genre—helped me greatly in understanding his genius and artistic personality. His better-known singing and talking classics grew from that fertile and diversified ground. I discovered along the way what my book was about. I came to see that his films are about much more than sophisticated sexual comedy, which is the outer layer of his work although one of the great pleasures they offer. I found more and more as I studied him that it is the underlying emotion, as much as the comedy, that I find compelling about his work, and the way the two interrelate. His comedies are not just farcical or naughty but have deeper dimensions. I can do no better than to quote Andrew Sarris on this subject. He wrote in *The American Cinema*, "A poignant sadness infiltrates the director's gayest moments, and it is this counterpoint between sadness and gaiety that represents the Lubitsch touch, and not the leering humor of closed doors." I came to understand how Lubitsch's films on a deeper level are about how men and women should treat each other.

When you watched Lubitsch's German silent films, were you thinking they were directed by a young version of the Lubitsch you knew from his American films? Or were they already the works of a mature, sophisticated filmmaker?

He grew a lot between 1914 and 1919. His earliest films as a director are rough-and-ready visually, with a lot of energy but some clumsiness and a not entirely sure-handed control of levels of comedy and how to mix them with drama. Before 1919, when he became a master with *The Oyster Princess,* he was doing promising apprentice work in both the comedy and spectacle formats. I like his German comedies better than the major spectacles of 1919 to 1922, although *Madame DuBarry,* with its lighter approach, holds up better than the ponderous *Anna Boleyn* and *The Wife of Pharaoh.* Those two are visually elegant and sometimes moving but tend to lack the humor and character nuances he brings to his best work. So while I think some of the comedies from that period are splendid, Lubitsch fully flowered in America.

The spectacles were treated respectfully by reviewers in the U.S., and his subsequent Hollywood comedies often received high praise from reviewers here, even from highbrow reviewers such as Edmund Wilson and Robert E. Sherwood, but there still was a tendency among some reviewers not to fully recognize Lubitsch's greatness. As still happens today, comedy itself is undervalued or not taken as seriously as films with obviously momentous social content. And yet ironically, Lubitsch's films that deal with political themes—such as *Trouble in Paradise, Ninotchka,* and *To Be or Not to Be*—were not recognized sufficiently as such in their day for the acuity of their political satire.

Were there writings about Lubitsch that you discovered? Did you have a translator?

I uncovered many forgotten interviews with Lubitsch and articles he wrote that were published in Germany and the U.S. and illuminate his way of working. Furthermore, Howard Prouty, an erudite librarian at the Academy of Motion Picture Arts & Sciences' Margaret Herrick Library, helped me obtain copies of numerous Paramount press releases that were either interviews with Lubitsch about his work and life or articles by him. These documents were remarkably valuable finds and, unlike most studio press releases from that period, they were thoughtful and well-grounded in reality. Whoever conducted the interviews and wrote the press releases was fully aware that Lubitsch was, as his star David Niven once put it, "the masters' master." Howard was a great help to me and went beyond the call of duty to send me copies of those materials. For German material, I hired translators.

My guess is that your book's title was inspired by the documentary about Wilder, Billy, How Did You Do It?, *by Volker Schlöndorff and Gisela Grischow.*

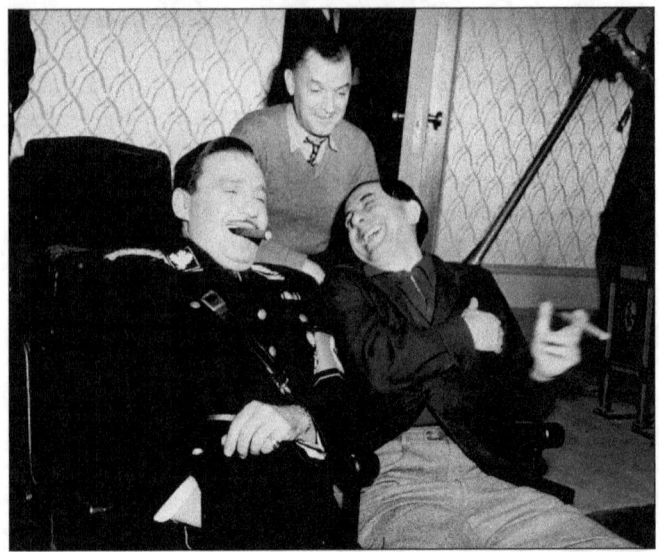

Lubitsch and Jack Benny, as a Polish actor masquerading as a Nazi officer in a plot to outwit Hitler and the Gestapo, share an uproarious laugh during the making of their daring and dazzlingly ingenious black comedy *To Be or Not to Be* (1942).
(United Artists/From the collections of the Margaret Herrick Library, Academy of Motion Picture Arts and Sciences)

Actually my title was inspired by a sign on the wall in Wilder's office reading, "How Would Lubitsch Do It?" That in turn inspired the title of the documentary about Wilder. Wilder said in 1989, "I made that sign. That way I never allow myself to write one sentence that I would be ashamed to show to my great friend, Ernst Lubitsch." I wanted to focus people's attention on Lubitsch's creative process and style—how he did it—since it's a critical study, not a biography. In so doing I also include a lot of information and background about his life and his working methods on the set.

How do you answer the question in your title? Did that entail your being forced to define "The Lubitsch Touch?"

Since Lubitsch's unique style, which as Wilder himself noted is impossible to replicate, relies on obliqueness and indirection, it respects the intelligence of the audience to put together the innuendoes. Attempting to define Lubitsch's style is the best way to analyze it. As my screenwriter friend Sam Hamm put it, "I have heard people say that it would probably take an entire book to explain 'the Lubitsch touch.' Well, it did, and this book is it."

But even though "The Lubitsch Touch"—a term that grew out of critical commentary on his work—became a publicity catchphrase like calling Hitchcock "the master of suspense," I like the phrase in Lubitsch's case much better, because it conveys the delicacy and lightness of his style. Nevertheless, I think people are overly fixated on "touches"; I believe an entire Lubitsch film is a "touch," and each film in the totality of its narrative partakes of his style and the worldview it expresses. That is a more illuminating way to look at them, particularly at the later films when his way of shooting and editing became more "invisible" in the classical Hollywood vein. This was partly because of tightened censorship after the Production Code began to be enforced after he made *The Merry Widow* in 1934, and partly because he had taken his style as far as it could go in 1932 with *Trouble in Paradise*.

The Lubitsch films that evaded censorship so ingeniously in the Code era, including *Angel*, *Ninotchka*, *The Shop Around the Corner*, and *To Be or Not to Be*, and the films made in what Sarris called "the mellow manner of later Lubitsch," *Heaven Can Wait* and *Cluny Brown*, are more focused on people and what they say to each other, and the camerawork is increasingly subtle. So I realized in my research that Lubitsch scholarship and criticism is not a matter of isolating "touches" and discussing them apart from the stories and characters, as too often had been done. I wanted to offer a fully integrated study of Lubitsch as an artist in all his facets.

You write, "Paradoxically, while subverting traditional moralism, Lubitsch made morality plays about sexuality and romance." I do think he made films about morality, but am I wrong in thinking he didn't really make "morality plays" because he wasn't a moralist and never judged his characters' suspect sexual and romantic behavior as being right or wrong?

Beneath the surface frivolity, Lubitsch is a profound moralist but one who is against conventional notions of morality. Lubitsch's work explores the highest sense of that often-misconstrued concept as it is defined by Amanda in Noël Coward's *Private Lives*: "Morals. What one should do and what one shouldn't." The opposite of a puritanical moralist, Lubitsch is tolerant of what is usually considered human misconduct or aberration but exacting yet generous in his analysis of male-female relations.

You quote Lubitsch saying shortly before leaving Germany that he intended to make "modern stories about American life," but do you think he set so few of his films in America because he thought sophisticated sexual themes worked better with European characters?

Yes, that seems to have been the case. Few of his films take place in America. He found it more congenial and easier in circumventing censorship to set his films in Europe, because audiences and censors were more tolerant of the sexual shenanigans of "those naughty Europeans." Some European critics, ironically, thought Lubitsch was pandering too much to our obsession with sexuality as a hypocritically puritanical country.

Would you say that Lubitsch was braver than most of his contemporaries even after the Code began to be rigidly enforced because, being a European, he advocated adultery as a way to make marriage tolerable and made it clear that sex is a major part of romance?

Certainly that is one of the most unusual aspects of his work, one that surprises audiences today. My students were particularly astonished by his films' attitude toward adultery. Adultery is virtually considered "un-American" in our still highly puritanical country. He somehow got away with making it mostly acceptable because of his more cosmopolitan and realistic view of marriage, although sometimes the adulterous situations in his films are painful, as in *The Marriage Circle*, *Angel*, and *The Shop Around the Corner*.

Lubitsch himself had a terribly traumatic experience when his first wife had an adulterous affair with Hanns Kräly, who was the screenwriter of most of his work in both Germany and the United States from 1915 through 1929. The simultaneous breakup of those two central relationships in Lubitsch's life is reflected in the shop owner's complex feelings of betrayal in the bittersweet *Shop Around the Corner*. After Kräly's expulsion from his life, Lubitsch had a fertile working relationship with the great screenwriter Samson Raphaelson, with whom he had a congenial but somewhat formal friendship. One of the sad ironies of Lubitsch's life, but part of the engine that drove his feverishly imaginative creativity, is that he was unlucky in love, unlike most of the characters in his deeply and alluringly romantic films.

I believe one reason his films are titillating is that Lubitsch really understood the sexual appeal of his actresses. I haven't seen his Pola Negri films, but no else better exploited the sexual appeal of Jeanette MacDonald, Miriam Hopkins, and Kay Francis. (And arguably Norma Shearer, Greta Garbo, and Carole Lombard.)

Lubitsch and his writers created a great gallery of female characters. He not only loved but understood women well. You only have to look at the films to see the richness and complexity of the roles those women play, and his comments on various actresses were both sympathetic and shrewd. *Photoplay* writer May Allison Quirk, after conducting an insightful interview with Lubitsch about his actresses in 1933, observed, "He knows more about feminine psychology than any man I have ever met."

Lubitsch seemed to love thieves and theater people, and my guess it was because they were proficient at deceit and deception—a trait shared by most of his lead characters.

Indeed. That was part of his ironic detachment from human foibles, which made him a comic artist, and part of his characteristic stance as an outsider, a byproduct of his role as a Jew in Germany with Russian roots and then as an immigrant to the United States. There are no saints in Lubitsch films, even if Satan points Henry Van Cleve "up there" after he presents himself in Hell in *Heaven Can Wait*. But Lubitsch loves most of his characters, and many of them are people we greatly admire for their audacity, independence, charm, and joie de vivre.

In Hollywood, Lubitsch moved away from his concentration on spectacles and no longer appeared as Jewish characters in his own films, and you can list other changes he made. Would you say he, perhaps deliberately, reinvented himself in Hollywood, or were there many connections between his American and German films?

His Hollywood debut film, *Rosita*, is a lavish period piece, and Lubitsch did make one more spectacle in Hollywood— *The Patriot* (1928), a part-sound, mostly-silent film that is mostly lost—but he concentrated instead on intimate stories. Most of his 1920s films in Hollywood are stylized and almost minimalist in their settings and costumes, which is among the reasons they seem less "dated" today.

After my Lubitsch book was published, I had the pleasure of becoming friends with his daughter, Nicola, seen here with UCLA archivist Jan-Christopher Horak before we did an event together at the Billy Wilder Theater. Nicola wrote of *How Did Lubitsch Do It?* that it is "Without doubt the best book ever written on my father. My bible on his work." (Ann Weiser Cornell)

Yes, he reinvented himself in Hollywood, quite consciously. He stopped making films with overtly Jewish characters, preferring to assimilate, like most foreign directors do, although as Joel Rosenberg notes, there are "implicit" Jewish characters in numerous Lubitsch films, including the Arab hunchback clown he plays in his 1920 film *Sumurun*, his last acting performance. Overtly Jewish characters returned in Lubitsch as World War II came, such as in his film about Nazism, *To Be or Not to Be*, and the other films with his Jewish alter ego, actor Felix Bressart, but even in those films Lubitsch was not allowed to use the word "Jew," which was a taboo in Hollywood then except for its use in Chaplin's *The Great Dictator*. Chaplin could get away with it because he owned his own studio.

Lubitsch is properly credited with inventing the Hollywood musical with The Love Parade *in 1929 and other films, including* The Merry Widow, *because he integrated the music into the story and used non-synchronized sound so he could move the camera without worrying about noise. Why did he stop making musicals in America?*

I think he felt he had done all he could in the genre once he had done *The Merry Widow*—it's a flamboyant visual and musical tour de force—but the changing marketplace was also a factor. That film was expensive and something of a flop. Audiences in the Depression were getting tired of musicals set in Europe or in mythical kingdoms. Proletarian comedies (such as Capra's) were more what audiences wanted. But then the Astaire-Rogers musicals came along with their glamorous escapism, and Busby Berkeley's musical extravaganzas also helped the audience distract itself from the Depression. But Lubitsch moved on to modern kinds of films that sometimes dealt more with how ordinary people lived, such as *The Shop Around the Corner.* His career was always influenced by the world around him, even though his films were highly artificial. He returned to the musical genre only once, with *That Lady in Ermine*, which he was directing when he died in November 1947. It was completed clumsily by Otto Preminger, and it's a weak imitation of Lubitsch's earlier musical classics.

What do you consider his "essential" German and American films that every Lubitsch devotee should see?

If I had to give a short list of his classics in the sound period to get people started or hooked on Lubitsch, I would say *Trouble in Paradise*, *Ninotchka*, *The Shop Around the Corner*, and *To Be or Not to Be.* Seeing those films would make a Lubitsch fan out of just about anybody. And from there I would recommend some of his best German silent films, such as *The Oyster Princess* and *I Don't Want to Be a Man*; and to sample one of his spectacles, *Madame DuBarry.* See also the masterpieces of his American silent period, *The Marriage Circle*, *Lady Windermere's Fan*, and *The Student Prince in Old Heidelberg.* But there is so much more to explore, some of it still hard to see, and I lay it all out in my book.

You chose not to self-publish with your Lubitsch book.

I went with Columbia University Press because going with a regular publisher ensures more review attention and sales in bookstores. I've done three books there, also including *Billy Wilder: Dancing on the Edge* in 2021 and *George Cukor's People: Acting for a Master Director* in 2024. I've benefited enormously from working with the erudite and sympathetic editors, John Belton and Philip Leventhal. John is a scholar I've long known and respected, and he has edited Columbia's invaluably rich Film and Culture series for many years. Philip, the executive editor, is a thoughtful reader and editor and, like John, is a champion of my work. It's a pleasure to work with a publishing company that has such integrity.

Billy Wilder: Dancing on the Edge

Could you have written a Billy Wilder critical study before an Ernst Lubitsch critical study?

Yes, but not with the same depth. Lubitsch had broken down many of the barriers against sexual maturity in American films during the 1920s before Wilder came to America, so it was a natural progression. Once I had tracked Lubitsch's career and clever circumvention of censorship, I could better study how Wilder came in and furthered the task of making the film audience more cosmopolitan. Wilder joked that Lubitsch was "one of the talented ones" who were called to Hollywood rather than having to flee Hitler, as Wilder did in 1933. Wilder continued in the tradition Lubitsch had begun but more bluntly shattered taboo after taboo in the '40s and '50s with his astringent frankness about sexual morality and other kinds of behavior.

And as I did while researching Lubitsch, I did an in-depth study of my subject's European background. I discuss Wilder's family in Austria and Poland and his loss of relatives in the Holocaust, his work as a reporter in Vienna and Berlin, his German screenwriting career, and his directing debut in Paris after escaping Nazism. It helped immensely that I had become grounded in that cultural context before I concentrated my full attention on Wilder's work. Again I felt it essential to study the filmmaker's entire career in both Berlin and Hollywood to understand his artistic development. That also included Wilder's work as a journeyman American screenwriter in the 1930s before he had the good fortune to team with the older and more experienced Charles Brackett and collaborate with Lubitsch on *Bluebeard's Eighth Wife* and, more meaningfully, *Ninotchka*. Not enough had been written before about Wilder's creative struggles and eventual triumphs as a screenwriter in Hollywood before he resumed his directing career here in 1942 with *The Major and the Minor,* and as always, I found an artist's evolution fascinating to study.

What was your first exposure to Wilder?

Oddly enough, *The Spirit of St. Louis.* As I've mentioned, that unusual Wilder film was the first film I liked enough to see it twice in my local theater, the Tosa in Wauwatosa. When I was ten in 1957, I responded naively to the heroic portrait of Charles Lindbergh as a young aviator and was amused by his talking to a fly in the cockpit on his way to Paris; I was already a fan of Jimmy Stewart, and I found the depiction of Lindbergh's flight thrilling. Later I found out that I had one thing in common with Lindbergh: We were both dropouts from the University of Wisconsin, Madison. Although the film seems somewhat stodgy dramatically and evasive today, neglecting the dark sides of Lindbergh that Wilder was not allowed to go near, the airplane stuff is still gripping. I was surprised to find that this film was an enormous flop, partly because few young people knew who Lindbergh was.

More influential in my life, though, was *Some Like It Hot* only two years later. And the reasons I call Wilder "my sex ed teacher" include, first of all, his stunning my youthful self with his outré depiction of cross-dressing and the barely-there dress Marilyn Monroe wears in the climactic scene of this wonderful comedy. But beyond the titillation factor in *Some Like It Hot*, it's a serious movie with a feminist slant about how a man learns to becomes a mensch by literally walking around in women's shoes. I like to think a bit of that understanding penetrated my murky consciousness as a boy. Somehow that film's B rating— "Morally Objectionable in Part for All"—from the Catholic Legion of Decency, which considered it "outright smut," didn't prevent me from learning its unorthodox moral lesson, with its Lubitschean theme of how men should treat women and vice versa. When my wife, Ruth, met Wilder with me, she thanked him for making a feminist film, which surprised and pleased him.

And in the fall of 1963, when I was a junior in high school, Wilder's *Irma La Douce* enabled me to make an even greater step in my sexual maturation, even if it took me three efforts to get through it. For all its bawdiness, *Irma* is actually a rather sweet and innocent movie. I didn't get to see *Kiss Me, Stupid*, which I now adore, when it opened in 1964, because a local priest had blocked it from coming to Milwaukee. But my boyhood friend Bob Kidera recently reminded me that when he came back for a visit that year after moving to New York, I "insisted" we go downtown to see a double bill of *Irma* and *Some Like It Hot.*

Thank you, Mr. Wilder, for helping me grow up, as you did for the whole of our puritanical country by breaking so many boundaries onscreen.

What was your relationship with Wilder, and did you always intend to write a book about him?

Billy Wilder: Dancing on the Edge, which came out in 2021, was the culmination of more than fifty years writing and thinking about him. By 1970 Wilder already was central enough in my filmic consciousness that I felt emboldened at age twenty-three to write the career profile essay with Mike Wilmington for *Film Quarterly*, "The Private Life of Billy Wilder." The same year, his *Private Life of Sherlock Holmes* was released, and we gave it a rave review in that journal. Our review of that mutilated masterpiece holds up rather well, even if the career piece is somewhat tentative and glib in its overview. We stood out of the critical crowd at the time with our enthusiasm for his late-career evolution, his veering away from the raunchy material for which he was known before the sexual revolution into surprisingly romantic terrain with *Sherlock Holmes* and his 1972 film, *Avanti!* My review of that delightful romantic comedy for *Film Heritage* was titled "The Importance of Being Ernst."

I interviewed Wilder twice at length and spoke with him on other occasions, and I spent a memorable day on a sound stage at Universal in 1974 watching him direct Jack Lemmon and Walter Matthau in *The Front Page,* based on the funniest American play, the 1928 newspaper comedy-melodrama by Ben Hecht and Charles MacArthur. Wilder and his writing partner I. A. L. Diamond turned it into a much darker, often bitter critique of the self-serving myths surrounding the press during the Watergate era when they made that film. With Todd McCarthy, I did a two-day interview with Wilder in 1978 for *Film Comment* that focused on his unjustly underappreciated late work. He told us how grateful he was for that lively discussion.

For quite a while I harbored the fantasy of doing an interview book with Wilder, but for reasons I could not quite comprehend, I never actually approached him with the idea. When I was talking with Wilder before presenting him with the Career Achievement Award from the Los Angeles Film Critics Association in 1995, my colleague and good friend Kirk Honeycutt of the *Hollywood Reporter* came over and mentioned to Wilder that I was hoping to do such a book. Neither Wilder nor I said anything. It was a very odd moment of silence. I didn't know then that Wilder

Talking with Billy Wilder before presenting him the Career Achievement Award from the Los Angeles Film Critics Association at a West Hollywood Hotel in 1995. I asked what he thought his best film is, and he said *The Apartment*, because it is his best blend of comedy and drama, the mixture he worked for throughout his career.
(Sam Robbins)

was doing an interview book with screenwriter-director Cameron Crowe, *Conversations with Wilder*, which was published in 1999. Any such book is valuable, but it is disorganized and rather gushy, with far too much concentration on Crowe's fanboy probing about Audrey Hepburn and Marilyn Monroe. A much better lengthy Wilder interview is that 1988/1991 documentary by Schlöndorff and Grischow, *Billy, How Did You Do It?*, but it disappointingly comes to an abrupt stop in 1960, which is symptomatic of the critical neglect of the later work.

As further background for my 2021 critical study, I was able to rely on several biographies, Ed Sikov's *On Sunset Boulevard: The Life and Times of Billy Wilder* and Kevin Lally's *Wilder Times: The Life of Billy Wilder*, as well as the German-language biographies *Billy Wilder: A European Career* by Andreas Hutter and Klaus Kamolz and Hellmuth Karasek's *Billy Wilder: A Close-up*, a book on which Wilder had some input. There is no necessity to write another Wilder biography, but I felt his work still needed to be explicated, since critical commentary on it often seemed confused or wrongheaded. Ultimately, through trial and error, I found the unconventional form my book needed to take. To quote Jonathan Lethem, this hefty critical study is done in a "free ruminative style, unbound by dutiful chronological study — instead, we have a sensibility, and a conversation."

You were undaunted by the realization that many younger film lovers had seen only Wilder's later critically panned films, and some older fans found his classics too cynical for their tastes.

The mistreatment by critics and audiences of Wilder's late work, including his deeply moving yet often hilarious *film maudit, The Private Life of Sherlock Holmes*, and his flawed but darkly fascinating fable about the movie business, *Fedora,* made me feel that a fresh study of his work was necessary. I wanted to take full cognizance of Wilder's largely unrecognized romanticism while putting to rest the outdated and myopic viewpoint that saw his unblinking realism reductively as the sign of a cynic, misogynist, and misanthrope.

Most reviewers were lambasting Wilder for his late films, and audiences largely stayed away, but I shared his distaste for the crudity of much of what Hollywood was turning out and enjoyed the perversity of Wilder's reaction when he upheld even more devotedly the elegant and subtle Lubitschean tradition. Mike Wilmington and I, with our immersion in the classical Hollywood, were able to recognize the virtues of Wilder's latent romanticism in 1970 as it emerged into the foreground of those elegant, against-the-grain works. That side of his nature, in retrospect, can be seen clearly now as the humane sensibility balancing the corrosive social satire of such films as *A Foreign Affair, Sunset Blvd., and The Apartment.* My book on Wilder takes as its main argument that his supposed "cynicism" was mostly a cover for his deep-seated romanticism. Wilder's recurrent fascination with modes of masquerading was also the survival mechanism of exile from his European background.

With his roots in the fallen Austro-Hungarian empire, Wilder was akin to the playwright and novelist Arthur Schnitzler, whose works, often breaking ground by dealing frankly with sexuality in ways that scandalized bluenoses, include the play *Reigen/La Ronde,* filmed by Max Ophüls, and *Traumnovelle/Dream Novella,* filmed by Stanley Kubrick. Wilder's longtime screenwriting partner I. A. L. Diamond, himself a European émigré, observed that the director was part of "an old Viennese tradition that comes down from Schnitzler. It is a Middle European attitude, a combination of cynicism and romanticism. The cynicism is sort of disappointed romanticism at heart—someone [Andrew Sarris] once described it as whipped cream that's gotten slightly curdled."

As I write in my book, "When I unthinkingly said to Wilder in 1978 that his romantic streak, more visible in his late work, had been 'disguised before under a certain cynicism,' he replied, 'But if *I'm* cynical, what adjective do you have for Peckinpah pictures?'" I said, "'Cynical' is another word in Hollywood for 'realistic.'" He responded, "I don't know. I think every play by Ibsen was cynical, right? Every play by Strindberg was cynical…. Now take, for instance, a picture like *The Apartment*. Did you really think that I went out of my way to dramatize things which did not exist? A society where things like this could not happen?" When I presented Wilder with the LAFCA award in 1995, I asked him what he thought his best picture is, and he said *The Apartment*, because he considered it his most successful blend of comedy and drama, the mixture he had been working for all his life.

So despite some people seeing him conveying an unrelentingly bleak view of human nature in his dramas, you call him a romantic.

The song that recurs most often in his films is "Isn't It Romantic?," which he uses with his most pointed irony in *A Foreign Affair* over shots of a GI Jeep driving through the ruins of his youthful haunt, Berlin. But it's even more striking that his favorite song was the 1931 ballad "I'm Thru with Love" by Fud Livingston, Matty Malneck, and Gus Kahn, the lament Marilyn sings at the climax of *Some Like It Hot*—"I've locked my heart/I'll keep my feelings there/ I've stocked my heart/With icy, frigid air"—just before her Sugar Cane discovers that love still exists, deeply hidden but still discoverable. As Wilder told a *Los Angeles Times* interviewer in 1986, "Anyone who knows me knows the cynicism hides my sentimentality."

Wilder's jaded concentration on "disappointed romanticism" (as Diamond put it) makes him explore the conflicts between materialism and love, prostitution and romance, sexual betrayal and exploitation. This theme explains all the kept men and women and prostitutes who abound in his work but also the way he puts them in situations that challenge their emotional aloofness. The major artistic loss in his career was the misguided cutting of the scene in *The Private Life of Sherlock Holmes* in which Sherlock (played by Robert Stephens) learns as an Oxford student that the beautiful young woman (played by Jenny Hanley) he worships from afar is actually a prostitute.

This flashback may have echoed an experience in Wilder's youth with his disillusionment over a girlfriend in Vienna named Ilse, although he denied that theory put forth by biographer Maurice Zolotow. Wilder told Todd McCarthy and me that the story was "Total bullshit." But in the uncut version of the film, Holmes tells the story about his experience at Oxford to explain his wariness of women to Gabrielle Vallladon/Ilse von Hoffmanstal (played by Geneviève Page), whom he is tempted by but is actually a German spy in the process of betraying him. "It was a very small price to pay for a very valuable lesson," Holmes tells her. "Any emotional involvement warps your judgment and clouds your reason."

The romantic relationships in Wilder's films are often blighted by such wariness and distrust, and the possible salvation they hold out for his male protagonists is lost as a result, such as when William Holden's screenwriter/kept man in *Sunset Blvd.* rejects the unquestioning love offered by the wholesome story editor played by Nancy Olson. Sometimes in his late films, though, such as in *The Apartment* and *Avanti!*, the couples are able to overcome the obstacles placed by materialism and cynicism, as the more tenaciously hopeful side of Wilder prevails.

And that hope underpins the emotional connection that develops in his unjustly reviled 1964 risqué comedy romance, *Kiss Me, Stupid*, between the goodhearted prostitute, Polly the Pistol, played by Kim Novak, and the man who had been crassly exploiting her, played by Ray Walston, before she helps him become a mensch. "Peculiarly enough, the theme of *Kiss Me, Stupid* was human dignity," Wilder said in 1966. "It was also about the sanctity of marriage." These tensions exist throughout his body of work in one form or another, and as his career progressed he became less jaded, even if many critics and audiences couldn't see that or wouldn't go along with him on that journey.

You write in your Introduction that "despite Wilder's considerable debt to Lubitsch, with whom critics often compare him, the differences in tone between their artistic signatures are as pronounced as their similarities." How so?

The clearest difference is how they attack social problems. Both do so, but Wilder is more of an overt social critic than Lubitsch, who approaches such issues more obliquely. As a former newspaperman, Wilder approached many of his films by making exposés of social problems. After he went to Germany at the end of the war to participate in the denazification effort, Wilder filmed the ruins of Berlin for his 1948 feature *A Foreign Affair*, and he helped edit and write narration for a documentary on the Holocaust called *Death Mills*. In a starkly contrasting way of dealing with trauma, Lubitsch never went back to Germany after his last visit in 1932 and refused to let German be spoken in his house after Hitler took over.

Lubitsch didn't make films as bluntly powerful as Wilder's *Ace in the Hole* (but really, nobody has, except Stroheim, Wilder's other master, and another ex-reporter, Samuel Fuller) or as shocking in its treatment of human vice as *Double Indemnity*. When Lubitsch tackled social issues, he tended to do so with irony, as in the treatment of the events leading up to the French Revolution through the racy story of a king's mistress in *Madame DuBarry*, or in what's been called his political trilogy of the sound era, *Trouble in Paradise*, *Ninotchka*, and *To Be or Not to Be*. Lubitsch satirizes capitalism by showing a jewel thief in love with a female factory owner, both of whom are sympathetic; communism by showing a Soviet commissar falling in love with a gigolo in capitalistic Paris; and Nazism by showing a clever theatrical troupe using stage magic to outwit the Gestapo.

Wilder kept getting drawn back to Europe in the postwar years, and late in his career he in effect resumed his career as a European filmmaker, even using German tax-shelter funding to make *Fedora* after Universal pulled out of the project. As he told me, "Look, I can't lose, because if this picture is a big hit [it wasn't], it's my revenge on Hollywood. If it is a total financial disaster, it's my revenge for Auschwitz." Though Lubitsch had made his own anti-Nazi film during the war, which took courage and brought down some flak on him for using black comedy as a weapon against Hitler, even if he had lived longer after the war, he probably would have avoided filming in Europe again.

But Wilder also learned from Lubitsch the virtues of obliqueness in dealing with social issues. Wilder daringly approached large political themes through romantic comedy, comedy-drama, or farce, as is shown by three films he set in Germany. *A Foreign Affair* uses the romantic comedy mode for dissecting the moral and political issues involved in the American postwar occupation. *Stalag 17* is a comedy-drama about the treachery of human conduct during World War II and, metaphorically, about informing during the Hollywood blacklist. *One, Two, Three* is a farce about the clash between communism and capitalism in Berlin. Wilder's penchant for blending genres paid creative dividends in his dissection of the corruption of American institutions through intimate, bitter, and sordid romantic situations in such films as *Sunset Blvd.* (about Hollywood) and *The Apartment* (about the insurance business, which is also the socially sanctioned racket practiced and manipulated in *Double Indemnity).*

Throughout his career Wilder kept returning obsessively to the task of trying to "do a Lubitsch" with romantic comedies of varying quality, from *The Emperor Waltz, Sabrina,* and *Love in the Afternoon* to his most successfully Lubitschean film, *Avanti!* That sublime film about a crass middle-aged American businessman (played by Jack Lemmon) being turned into a mensch by a sexually liberated yet neurotic younger Englishwoman (played by Juliet Mills) on the Italian island of Ischia remains largely unappreciated except by Wilder aficionados.

In making films that are mashups of different genres, Wilder kept himself amused and other people off-guard. He was so adroit at doing it that reviewers often missed what he was trying to do. That was especially true of reviewers who wanted films to fit neatly into their preconceptions, such as Hollis Alpert of *The Saturday Review,* who scoldingly called *The Apartment* a "dirty fairy tale," a putdown that irritated Wilder until he reflected that it is a fairly accurate description. As my book puts it, Wilder "resisted being pinned down, not wanting to be pigeonholed to one kind of film like Alfred Hitchcock or some other major directors.... His restless enjoyment of jumping from one kind of story to another is also a legacy of his work as a racing reporter."

Other than taking on critics who didn't appreciate Wilder's later films, was writing a book on Wilder a challenge? Did it turn out to be as fun to write as the Lubitsch book?

The most challenging aspect was my decision to break the usual chronological pattern when writing about the films Wilder directed in the U.S. from 1942 onward. Before that, the book mostly follows chronology in discussing his family and cultural background and early development as a journalist and screenwriter in Europe. I felt it was necessary to treat that period in a methodical, cumulative way, with some references to his later work. But I had become tired of the usual film-by-film method of writing about a director's career and felt that when I came to his American directing career, it would be more revealing to write in an essayistic way about Wilder's preoccupations, themes, and style, freely cross-cutting around his films. That proved a liberating and exciting experiment and, I think, captures how his creative personality worked.

I call Wilder "my sex ed teacher" because he opened my eyes to
unorthodox sexuality as well as Monroe's charms in
Some Like It Hot and in a raunchy romp with Shirley MacLaine as a
good-natured Parisian prostitute in his 1963 film,
Irma la Douce. It took me three anxious viewings to make it through
Irma; the second time I bailed when she is marrying her pimp (Jack
Lemmon) while going into labor. (Mirisch/United Artists)

Seeing the films Wilder made was not as much of a
challenge as it was in the case of Lubitsch. I did have to track
down rare copies of the German films he wrote and go to
the national archive in Berlin to see the first film on which
he is credited as a screenwriter, *Der Teufelsreporter: Im
Nebel der Grosstadt/The Devil's Reporter: In the Fog of the
Big City*, a zany 1929 chase film set in the newspaper world.
And it was there I also saw *Fanfaren der Liebe/Fanfares of
Love*, the 1951 German film about cross-dressing musicians
in a girls' band from which Wilder and Diamond adapted
their masterful *Some Like It Hot*. It was hard to see, because
Wilder disguised the fact that their gender-bending farce
(the funniest American sound film) is based, as the credits
obscurely put it, on a story by R. Thoeren and M. Logan.
Robert Thoeren and Michael Logan first worked out that
plot in their mildly amusing, less raucous 1935 French
original, *Fanfare d'amour/Fanfare of Love*, which I couldn't
find when I wrote my book but has since surfaced.

There are many things Wilder borrowed from those
writers despite his false claim that aside from the leading
characters going into drag to play in the girls' band in the
German version, "there was not one other thing that came
from this terrible picture" (they also cross-dress in the
French version). Nevertheless, he and Diamond made major
improvements while transferring the story to an American
setting. As Wilder put it, Diamond urged on him the need
for the "hammerlock" to make it impossible for the men to
switch out of their women's disguises, as they do too readily
when it's convenient in the German film. So they came up
with a daring life-or-death situation by having them witness

the St. Valentine's Day Massacre in a 1929 Chicago gang war. David O. Selznick told Wilder he was crazy to start a comedy with a bloodbath, but that stroke of genius is what made it work.

I always study the evolution of the story material in films, and it's vital in the case of Wilder and his collaborators Brackett and, later, Diamond, to analyze their carefully developed screenplays, which Wilder tended to follow carefully in his directing, albeit with some significant variations. In the case of *The Devil's Reporter* and some other films, I was able to trace the influence of Wilder's journalism on his film storytelling. That film not only has an intrepid reporter as its hero (Eddie Polo) but involves a kidnapped group of American millionaires' daughters visiting Berlin, the equivalent of a British girls' band and dance troupe, the Tiller Girls. Wilder wrote about those girls in the press with lubricious glee and later put their equivalents into *Some Like It Hot.*

My book studies Wilder's journalism career in detail, particularly his four-part 1927 series "'Waiter, Bring Me a Dancer!': From the Life of an *Eintänzer*," which was published in both Berlin and Vienna. That creative blend of fact and fiction—as he told me it was—deals with his job as an *eintänzer* (tea dancer) for hire by ladies at Berlin hotels, a demeaning situation he wrote about at the time and echoes in many of his films. That series could be made into a trenchant film in the vein of *Cabaret.* My shared newspaper background with Wilder helped me connect with him personally when we met on the set of *The Front Page* and gave me the opportunity to shed new light on that crucial part of his career.

Once you started analyzing Wilder's films, which ones proved to be more fascinating than you had realized?

Four examples are the 1932 German film *Ein blonder Traum/A Blonde Dream*; *Hold Back the Dawn*, released in 1941; and the 1948 releases *The Emperor Waltz* and *A Foreign Affair.* One of the most fascinating of the German scripts co-written by Billie Wilder (as he was known then) is *A Blonde Dream*, a film operetta starring the fetching Anglo-German actress-singer Lilian Harvey. It captures the uneasy lives of Berliners living on the margins of poverty in the period just before Hitler took power. The film celebrates the buoyant resilience of Harvey's wannabe actress and two male companions, who live together in an abandoned railway car. She dreams of going to Hollywood, which Wilder, his writing collaborator Walter

Reisch (who later worked with him on *Ninotchka*), and director Paul Martin portray in an expressionistic nightmare that prefigures Wilder's Hollywood noir *Sunset Blvd.* and is startlingly accurate in terms of what we would later call the #MeToo movement.

A song Harvey's Jou-Jou sings on a rooftop overlooking some of Berlin's most historic sites with potent political symbolism, "Somewhere in the World There's a Little Bit of Happiness," has great emotional resonance in retrospect, since it expresses the impossible fantasy of a better future at a time we know the country is doomed. The lyrics are by Robert Gilbert and Werner R. Heymann, with music by Heymann, who later worked on *Ninotchka* but regarded this song as his favorite work. *A Blonde Dream*, like other films Wilder wrote for the leading German studio, UFA, is somewhat compromised by infusions of right-wing corporate propaganda celebrating the unlikely happiness of ordinary workers in that precarious period. But the film is also subversive in its subtle use of the musical format to capture the *zeitgeist* of Berlin shortly before Wilder, who was Jewish, had to flee to Paris.

Hold Back the Dawn is the film Brackett & Wilder wrote that galvanized Wilder into directing again when their script was tampered with by director Mitchell Leisen. They had Charles Boyer's despondent European émigré comparing himself to a cockroach he smashes with a stick in his Mexican hotel room. The scene resonated deeply with Wilder through its echoes of Kafka and of Nazi propaganda equating Jews with vermin. But Boyer refused to film it, saying he didn't want to talk to a cockroach, and Leisen went along with the excision, instead showing Boyer's character lying in bed while contemplating suicide. Wilder and Brackett took revenge by cutting most of Boyer's remaining dialogue from the story.

This turns out to be Wilder's most directly autobiographical film. It deals with a Rumanian gigolo holed up in the border hotel waiting for an American visa as a resident alien. That reflects Wilder's experience in Mexico in the crucial period before he was allowed to return to stay in the U.S. thanks to the kindness of a consular official, whom I was able to identify as Willys A. Myers. The Boyer character's background is similar to that of Wilder, the former Berlin dancer-for-hire. And like Wilder, the Boyer character winds up as a Hollywood screenwriter (the film has a meta wraparound with Boyer selling the story to Leisen at Paramount).

The Emperor Waltz, which had seemed merely an oddly fizzled attempt at a Lubitschean musical set in Vienna during the reign of Emperor Franz Joseph I, proves to have much deeper resonance for his career when you realize (thanks to a brilliant essay by scholar Nancy Steffen-Fluhr) that it is a disguised metaphor for the Holocaust, which claimed the lives of Wilder's mother, stepfather, and grandfather. I trace echoes of the Holocaust that break through the façades of even some unlikely-seeming films such as this unfunny picture, which even Brackett and Wilder's wife Audrey couldn't fathom why he was making. "I was not up to making a musical," Wilder told Crowe. "I don't know, I should have gone to a hospital or something, after being in Germany and cutting [a] documentary about the concentration camps." The plot revolves around the brash American phonograph salesman Bing Crosby, one of the numerous "ugly American" characters in Wilder films, peddling his device to the emperor. Among the eleven commentaries I've done for Wilder films is one for *The Emperor Waltz*, and I was excited to find an actual phonograph recording of the emperor's voice to include with my audio track. But the Blu-ray of this obscure film still didn't attract much attention.

A Foreign Affair, another film for which I did a commentary, was neglected in its day partly because U.S. government opposition to its candid, non-propagandistic storyline about GI misbehavior caused Paramount to downplay its release. In retrospect it turns out to be one of Wilder's best films. This daring amalgam of bleak views of the bombed-out Berlin landscape with romantic comedy involving a prudish American congresswoman and a corrupt Army Intelligence officer (played by Jean Arthur and John Lund) provides the filmmaker with one of his most trenchant probes into sexual hypocrisy and moral compromise. The realism that leads Wilder to offer a relatively sympathetic portrait of a former Nazi collaborator (played by Marlene Dietrich, who was cast against her real-life role as an opponent of Nazism) enables the director to admire her character's survival skills and the generosity she shows to get her hapless American female rival out of trouble. While offering a satirical counterbalance to the extremely grim "rubble films" made by other directors in Germany during that period, Wilder challenges the audience with one of his most complex depictions of the stark conflict between naive idealism and harsh reality, the potent blend that permeates his work in various genres.

All four of those films I mentioned deserve closer examination by audiences wishing to understand Wilder and his milieu as a refugee from Europe and Nazism. Moreover, Wilder's empathy with the women and their predicaments with men in *Hold Back the Dawn* and *A Foreign Affair* shines a quite different light on the conventional view of him as a misogynist. Wilder pursued the theme of sexual exploitation throughout his career, and Olivia de Havilland's movingly portrayed Emmy Brown in *Hold Back the Dawn* is one of the many believably good women who I found proliferate in Wilder's supposedly misogynistic body of work. The initially unscrupulous gigolo in that film seduces an innocent American schoolteacher into marrying him so he can enter the U.S., but her goodness and his guilt over his deceit wind up turning him into a mensch (as the Jewish doctor neighbor of Jack Lemmon's C. C. Baxter urges him to become in *The Apartment*). Indeed, there are only four out-and-out villainous women in the films Wilder directed— Barbara Stanwyck in *Double Indemnity*, Jan Sterling in *Ace in the Hole*, Judi West in *The Fortune Cookie*, and Paula Prentiss in *Buddy Buddy*—yet his refusal to sentimentalize women in general has seemed harsh to some people used to sanitized Hollywood depictions.

I was pleased that the feminist critic Molly Haskell wrote of my book, "With his walk-on-the-dark-side comedies and refusal to sentimentalize, Wilder's reputation has only grown with time, and this magisterial critical study does full justice to his complex talent. McBride draws stunning connections between the life and the art, and his discussion of Wilder's treatment of women is especially fresh and persuasive."

We all like to champion unfairly neglected films by directors who made many masterpieces. For instance, you rave about Elia Kazan's Wild River *in* Two Cheers for Hollywood; *I'm sure you have found many of us who agree with you. But I'm not sure how many people have told you, "At last, someone else who thinks Billy Wilder's* Kiss Me, Stupid *is 'glorious!'"*

I discovered that Truffaut liked it very much! I have found a number of other "deviated preverts" (to quote the twisted line from *Dr. Strangelove*) who admire the Wilder film as well. I write in *Two Cheers* that *Kiss Me, Stupid* "was so far ahead of its time in satirizing American sexual hypocrisy." I adore the characters, who are deeply human and moving in their foolishness, and am entranced by how the outrageous situation is filmed with such visual elegance and verbal wit. When I told Wilder in 1978, "It's actually quite a romantic story," he agreed: "I thought it was very romantic. I'd like to do it again to show them what the thing was all about. But could you imagine going and telling people that I'm going to make *Kiss Me, Stupid* again?"

Joan Didion was the film's only U.S. critical champion at the time of its release. She wrote that Wilder "is not a funnyman but a moralist, a recorder of human venality.... The Wilder world is one seen at dawn through a hangover, a world of cheap double entendre and stale smoke and drinks in which the ice has melted: the true country of despair." After reading that review, which was published in *Vogue*, Wilder wrote her a note: "I read your piece in the beauty parlor while sitting under the hair dryer, and it sure did the old pornographer's heart good. Cheers, Billy Wilder."

Talk about the title choice of your book Billy Wilder: Dancing on the Edge *and how it reflects on how you saw Wilder.*

Wilder was always courting danger and breaking taboos by crossing boundaries in his work, between countries, between genres, between men and women, between opposite emotional poles. So I borrowed the image of him *Dancing on the Edge* from a study of the culture of Weimar Germany by Peter Gay. Wilder emerged from that tumultuous cultural period whose artists, Gay writes, were part of "a precarious glory, a dance on the edge of a volcano. Weimar culture was the creation of outsiders, propelled by history into the inside, for a short, dizzying, fragile moment." An exile several times over, Wilder was one of numerous filmmakers whose flight from Germany enriched American culture. He served as a cultural emissary from a more sophisticated yet also decadent past, helping lead us into a brash new view of reality that shattered (at least for a time) some of the remaining vestiges of our Puritan past.

Yet in his work there also remain what a mordant Frederick Hollander cabaret song performed by Marlene Dietrich in *A Foreign Affair* calls "the phantoms of the past" that continue to haunt and inspire the filmmaker from his days as a Jewish refugee from Hitler. For a while I used *The Phantoms of the Past* as the book's subtitle, but Columbia University Press felt we needed a title that captures both the precarious and buoyant nature of his work, so I proposed *Billy Wilder: Dancing on the Edge*.

What are your favorite Wilder films now?

Avanti!, Some Like It Hot, Sunset Blvd., A Foreign Affair, The Apartment, and *Kiss Me, Stupid,* along with *Hold Back the Dawn.*

Did Wilder's career end when he wanted it to?

Wilder was forced into what I call a period of internal exile at the end of his life. He couldn't get a job after the critical and box-office debacle of *Buddy Buddy* in 1981. Granted that remake of a French black comedy is an unmitigated disaster, but it shows him expressing his contempt for the coarse, juvenile marketplace Hollywood had become. In his waning days of bankability, in 1975, Wilder remarked, "Ernst Lubitsch, who could do more with a closed door than most of today's directors can do with an open fly, would have had big problems in this market."

The real turning point for Wilder and Diamond was their jaundiced portrait of the darkness descending on the industry in their 1978 film, *Fedora.* When I asked Wilder about the aging producer played by William Holden in that film, he said, "I could write *four* pictures about that character. Yeah, sure. That guy that's dragging his ass along Hollywood Boulevard." Note the location he mentions, a squalid descent from the already terminal setting of Sunset Blvd. I think Wilder could have found some humor in *Buddy Buddy* but chose to make it as grim as a Samuel Beckett play. He still had projects he wanted to film, but Hollywood, to its eternal shame, found him "unbankable" for the last twenty-two years of his life. I write about that period in detail in the sad denouement of my book on Wilder, but his long roster of great films has outlasted the industry that shortsightedly found him passé.

Audio commentaries

You mentioned doing audio commentaries for eight Lubitsch and eleven Wilder films, so before we move on to your later critical studies, tell me how you have become a go-to critic-historian for DVD/Blu-ray/HD audio commentaries for Kino Lorber and sometimes for Criterion. Did you consider your commentaries to be an extension of your teaching?

I consider audio commentaries a form of film criticism and history, with similarities to the books I've written on the filmmakers whose work I most often am asked to discuss. And they are a form of teaching I enjoy, especially since my retirement from my full-time teaching job. I have recorded audio commentaries for a few dozen films by now, including many by Ford (fourteen of his films to date), Lubitsch, and Wilder, and two by Welles. I also enjoy having the chance occasionally to talk about other filmmakers I haven't written books about, such as Leo McCarey, Elia Kazan, and Buster Keaton, but usually I get typecast. Since I love Ford, Lubitsch, and Wilder, I don't mind at all, for I appreciate the chance to examine their bodies of work even more thoroughly than I have done before. Also, doing an audio commentary helps raise awareness of my books.

How does the pay for doing commentaries compare to the pay for writing books?

The pay is OK but not commensurate with the level of work I put into preparing a commentary, which takes a few weeks of research and planning. When you write a critical study or a biography, you often don't have as much room to discuss an individual film, so I do additional research beyond what I've done on it for my books. But I consider it an honor to be part of the presentation of a film I admire. I've heard that some academics are willing to do commentaries without pay, to build up their CVs for the tenure process. I would find that exploitive. They are paying for my expertise, built up over years of research.

The only time I've made an exception about payment was when I lobbied Fox to reissue Ford's *Pilgrimage*, his 1933 masterwork that was virtually unknown at the time and had never been released on home video. Henrietta Crosman gives a powerful and heartrending performance as an insanely possessive mother who sends her son to his death in World War I rather than lose him to the woman he loves; she's the closest equivalent to John Wayne's Ethan Edwards in *The Searchers* in her assault on her own family. It's an amazing film that I consider Ford's first great work.

I persuaded Fox to include *Pilgrimage* in the *Ford at Fox* boxed set that was released in 2007. When they hesitated, I offered to do a commentary on *Pilgrimage* gratis; I felt a sense of accomplishment in getting that great film out to the public again. I only wish I had done a little more research and found out that Crosman, who was born during the Civil War, grew up on U.S. Army bases and was the daughter of a major and granddaughter of a general in that war, as well as a niece of the great songwriter Stephen Foster, whose works include "My Old Kentucky Home," the theme song of Ford's *The Sun Shines Bright* (her middle name was Foster). What she and Ford must have had to talk about! (Danny, don't let it get around that I did a commentary for free.)

I won't!

But I was well-paid for writing an essay on Ford's work for Fox in the companion book, and I had been sufficiently paid for my *Grapes of Wrath* and *How Green Was My Valley* commentaries on that bountiful set. My other contribution was appearing in and consulting on the splendid companion documentary by Nick Redman and Julie Kirgo, *Becoming John Ford*. The *Ford at Fox* set was a surprise bestseller and much-appreciated by reviewers.

What is the process for doing a commentary? Do you record whatever comes to mind as you watch the films or write it all out beforehand?

As I did when I taught classes, I work from detailed notes. I know that some people who do commentaries read from a script, and once in a while I've heard that done well, but usually it seems stiff. The rare times I've read a speech from a totally prepared text have been when I've given one that I find particularly important, such as my commencement address to the Department of Film & Media and the Department of Rhetoric at the University of California, Berkeley, in 2012.

That said, when I do an audio commentary, I write out some specific points I want to make and take off from those if such precision is called for; I rehearse lines in my head when I watch the film at home before doing the commentary. I want to have some spontaneity while I talk and react to a film, including responding to moments that strike me emotionally. I have the safety net of plenty of notes, as I always did while teaching, and I see the film repeatedly beforehand to work out the structure of what I will say about it (the companies provide screeners with time codes). For instance, if the ending of a film presents complex issues, I plan when I will start discussing it earlier to make sure I have enough time.

And sometimes my views of films evolve. When I was asked by Kino Lorber in 2025 to do a commentary on Ford's *Donovan's Reef*, it was a film I was never quite sure how I felt about. So that gave me the opportunity to work out my thoughts as I watched and discussed it. For that reason, I deliberately did not structure the commentary ahead of time as much as I usually do, and that worked out fine. It's often said, and I have found it truer as I get older, that you don't know what you think about something until you write about it, or in this case talk about it.

Do you turn down commentaries if you don't like the film that is offered to you?

Yes, and I remember that when I passed one up for a company other than Kino Lorber and Criterion, they were upset with me, but I told them I just didn't have enough regard for the film to say much about it. Usually, though, I get offered films by directors I admire, and even if a film is not one of the director's best, I still have a lot to discuss.

I'm interested in how you approach doing a commentary on a film by your favorite director, John Ford, that isn't universally appreciated, such as The Horse Soldiers, The Sun Shines Bright, The Hurricane, *and* Cheyenne Autumn. *Even* My Darling Clementine. *Do you concede there are things wrong with the film and try to strike a balance of praise and criticism, or do you try to convince listeners to feel as you do?*

It's crucial to be honest about a film's flaws, but I have a principle I've always followed, going back to my college days with the Wisconsin Film Society. When I introduce a film, I feel I am, in effect, the representative of the absent filmmaker, and I want to give the film its best shot. There would be no point in running it down too much beforehand, especially since you want people to have their own reactions to it. So when I did the audio commentary, for example, on Ford's problematic final Western, *Cheyenne Autumn*, I mentioned up front that it was a film he only managed to get made by accepting studio compromises on budget, color cinematography, and casting.

When Ford originally planned that film, he wanted to make it as a relatively inexpensive film in black-and-white like *The Grapes of Wrath* (another film about people escaping Oklahoma). He planned to have only actors with Native American ancestry playing the major Cheyenne roles, and have the Cheyenne speak their own language, with subtitles. Instead Warners insisted on a large-scale road-show epic in color and widescreen, with Mexican actors playing the lead Cheyenne roles and a glamorous leading lady. Carroll Baker is quite good in the role but distractingly beautiful, Ford thought, as a Quaker missionary. I told the listeners that instead of just lamenting that Ford could not make the film the way he wanted, let's try to understand and appreciate what the film does do and the virtues it actually has. I referred to flaws along the way without belaboring them unnecessarily.

I ran into some censorship problems on that job, since the lawyers at Warner Bros. cut ten parts of my discussion, all factual and well-documented points but inconvenient for the studio to acknowledge for various reasons. That was an unusual experience for me. I would have told Warners to pull the commentary but thought it was important to be the person speaking about that film. Now you know why there are some odd gaps in the commentary when you hear the film's soundtrack instead.

Is it hard to talk all the way through a film, or do you often stop and start?

I am amazed to recall that when I started doing audio commentaries in 2002, I sometimes would talk straight through them, though on *Cheyenne Autumn,* since it runs 154 minutes, I did the commentary in ten takes. Even that seems extraordinary to me today, since I have learned the value of doing retakes to fine-tune the commentary as I record it. Now when I do a commentary, I often rephrase lines that are seamlessly integrated through the expert work of the sound technician I work with, Alberto Hernandez. Alberto and I record the commentaries at his studio in the former Saul Zaentz postproduction facility near my house in Berkeley.

And when I work with the erudite film historian Bret Wood at Kino Lorber, who produces the film editions to which I contribute, I always have a short list of things to fix that he tidies up smoothly in post, such as bloopers or redundancies that crop up when you talk about a film for a couple of hours. I have learned the value of sound editing by working on features, such as when the team that finished *The Other Side of the Wind* had me re-loop my dialogue.

You spoke about how you want to teach history through film. When you did the audio commentary for My Darling Clementine, *how did you approach the parts of the film that are historically inaccurate?*

For that highly romanticized Fordian view of Wyatt Earp, I discussed at length the complex issues of legend vs. fact in Ford's Westerns, comparing *Clementine* to some extent with *The Man Who Shot Liberty Valance*, which as Mike Wilmington noted was something of an informal "remake" of that classic town-taming Western but from a more skeptical perspective. Nevertheless, although I admire *Liberty Valance* for its visual austerity and for acutely dissecting how "When the legend becomes fact, print the legend," I still appreciate *Clementine* for its pictorial beauty and mythic style, the grace and majesty of Henry Fonda's performance as an idealized Earp, and its sublime sequence of a church dedication in the rowdy town of Tombstone, Arizona. That sequence, though, is part of a disturbingly naive and romantic portrait of an embryonic white American civilization encroaching on the Native American land; it is filmed in Monument Valley, which belongs to the Navajo tribe. When the French critic Jean Mitry, who wrote a book about Ford, asked in 1954 whether *Clementine* was one of his favorite films, Ford said, "My children liked it a lot. But I—you know."

I suspect that as Ford aged and grew more skeptical about Western legend-making, he wished in retrospect he could have given a more authentic portrait of Wyatt Earp. As fine as Fonda is in embodying Earp's manner and temperament, the actual Earp was considerably more complex than he seems in *Clementine* as well as a somewhat unsavory character. Ford said he met Earp in the early days at Universal after his retirement to Los Angeles when he was hanging around the studios to schmooze with cowboys-turned-actors and others he had known in his wild days. Allan Dwan also told me he recalled Earp visiting his sets. Earp had less respect for most of the "damn fool dudes," as he called the filmmakers who swallowed his tall tales and were making the Westerns he found too fanciful, but he seemed to enjoy reminiscing to Ford, an earnest young prop boy at the time.

Ford told Bogdanovich, "I used to give him a chair and a cup of coffee, and he told me about the fight at the O.K. Corral. So in *My Darling Clementine*, we did it exactly the way it had been." As I say in my commentary, Ford's claim that his filming of the gunfight is authentic is "preposterous." *Clementine* presents an alluringly grandiose and self-consciously mythic confrontation on main street rather than what was in reality a quick, messy, confusing shootout in a corral located in a side street (I visited Tombstone and that mundane corral during my research for *Searching for John Ford*). And yet, as Ford acknowledges in *Fort Apache* and *Liberty Valance*, myths are also important to a society and how it views itself, although myths can be damaging to a society's sense of reality.

When you discuss a classic film with questionable elements, you need to be candid about its strengths and weaknesses and the controversies it raises. You should also discuss and debate what the filmmaker had in mind if you could have a genuine talk with him or her. A good audio commentary acknowledges and analyzes all these elements while suggesting further avenues of study. But I admire Ford for refusing to spend much time on such discussions with interviewers—that's our job, not his, to glean what he has in mind.

Are there other ways in addition to doing commentary that help promote your books?

Yes, such as by making appearances as a talking head in documentaries about films or the assassination of President Kennedy and the murder of Officer J. D. Tippit. Promoting your book is part of an author's duty, one I neglected in my early years but have learned to take seriously. Thanks for that lesson to my friend and fellow biographer Scott Berg, who relayed historian Theodore H. White's advice that an author should spend a month promoting his book for every year he spent working on it. At that rate, I need to spend thirty-one months promoting *Into the Nightmare* and forty-nine months promoting *The Broken Places,* if I live that long! So I keep at it. And seriously, it is also a pleasure to be asked to do an interview on a podcast, which is a valuable form of promotion as well as another form of teaching.

Two Cheers for Hollywood is, to me, as much a memoir as The Broken Places *and this book, because it takes us through your career on a deeply personal level. To add to your history, who would you want to interview for* Two More Cheers for Hollywood?

I am not interviewing many people these days, alas. These days I'm mostly being interviewed! I'm enjoying our process, Danny, which gives me insights about the trajectory I've followed in my life and work. This book helps me see a shape and logic beyond the tentative, aspirational dimensions my career seemed to have as I moved along. But being more of an interviewee than an interviewer feels strange and rather sad. Present company, of course, not included! It's just that I've been neglecting one of my best talents since I had to stop writing biographies. I guess that's the way life works. You do the stuff the best you can and then, if you are fortunate enough to have the time and the audience, you try to explain what the hell you've been doing.

Who Are the Coen Bros.?

Returning to your recent writing, do you consider you slim 2022 book, The Whole Durn Human Comedy: Life According to the Coen Brothers, *an outlier among your critical studies? What drew you to their work?*

I wrote in my introduction to *Two Cheers for Hollywood*, "The Coens, whom I regard as the equals of the major writer-directors of the past, are my favorite contemporary filmmakers along with Spielberg." One reason I'm attracted to the Coens is that they are our closest contemporary equivalents to Billy Wilder. I had long felt they are misunderstood and underrated for a variety of reasons, including their provocative nature, their unpredictability, and the remarkably diversity of their work. And like Wilder, Ethan and Joel Coen are often shortsightedly dismissed as too "cynical," "heartless," and contemptuous of their characters. I wanted to counteract those reductive and largely false impressions.

Much of *The Whole Durn Human Comedy* is drawn from the thirty-nine-page monograph I wrote for *Two Cheers* entitled "O Brothers, Who Art Thou?: Some Notes on the Coen Bros." It was written after I watched all their films again in an intense two-week period so I could reevaluate them in unexpected ways. It's one of five new pieces I added to the collection (besides the lengthy introduction) to help make *Two Cheers* fresh as well as a retrospective survey of my work. After a while I began thinking of turning the monograph into a book, partly because it wasn't getting enough attention since it was embedded in a long volume with many other pieces, and because I thought a stand-alone book on the Coen Bros. would attract new readers.

While doing some relatively minimal rewriting of the previous text, I added an essay on *The Ballad of Buster Scruggs*, which has the feeling of a summation of their work together. That brilliant six-part Western anthology film came out in 2018 but drew from scripts they wrote over a twenty-five-year period, so it spans much of their collaboration as well as encapsulating their varied themes and styles. Unusually for the Coens, the episodes tend not to combine styles but embody them in discrete ways, while the overall collection of tales has what Zoe Kazan (who movingly plays the title role of "The Gal Who Got Rattled" in the wagon train) calls an underlying "dream logic."

I did not realize, though, when I decided to turn my monograph into a separate book that Ethan and Joel Coen were on the verge of breaking up as a team so they could work separately on their individual pet projects. That was a somewhat distressing development for their admirers, although the Coens may eventually work together again and have numerous scripts they wrote together that still await filming, but that milestone was fortuitous timing for a critical study of their joint body of work.

Some of my readers were surprised that I turned to writing about contemporary filmmakers, since I'm mostly known for writing about classical filmmakers from the Golden Age of Hollywood, but that overlooks the biography I wrote of Steven Spielberg in 1997, when the critical consensus was strongly against him. It's good sometimes to analyze an artist or artists while they are still working and before critics make their minds up about them, a process that tends to congeal into conventional wisdom after an artist's retirement or death. When you write about somebody who is still working, you want to influence other critics and audience members while also hoping to be surprised by their future development. I am sure the Coens will continue to evolve in ways we haven't expected, including by heading off in their separate paths. Creative evolution is a sign of true artists; I find people who don't change frustrating, and I find it fascinating when anyone, including an artist, evolves.

And just as my abundant common ground with Spielberg prompted me to write a book about him, the Coens and I share a number of preoccupations and tendencies, including our being Midwesterners and having iconoclastic personalities and irreverent senses of humor. As I point out in my book, the Coens' humor stems from their being "existential comedians." I enjoy their provocative mixing of comedy and violence and the way they mash up genres, two of the traits that spark the most consternation from their critical adversaries. But people who can't relate to the Coens' worldview and find them too bleak and despondent tend to take offense at the absurdist humor of their films, especially when their subject matter is most pointedly serious.

How did you decide on the rhetorical approach of your book on the Coens, leading off each chapter with one of the most frequent "complaints" about their work?

When I broke the monograph into chapters, I structured them as responses to such complaints (setting those in italics). I often use the foremost Coen Bros. hater among American reviewers, J. Hoberman, as a foil. (Not coincidentally, Hoberman serves me that way in my Spielberg book too. Hoberman has written some good books but has blind spots with these filmmakers.) Citing an argument I find dubious and counteracting it is a valuable rhetorical device I learned from the Jesuits in high school. They taught us how to combat critics of the faith by first making them recite their positions and then counteracting their arguments in a logical way. That said, I share the view of Stephen Dedalus, the alter ego of the Jesuit-educated James Joyce in *A Portrait of the Artist as a Young Man,* when he is asked if his doubts about the teachings of the Catholic Church mean he intends to become a Protestant:

> —I said that I had lost the faith—Stephen answered—but not that I had lost selfrespect. What kind of liberation would that be to forsake an absurdity which is logical and coherent and to embrace one which is illogical and incoherent?—

The Jesuitical method of argument works for all occasions, including film criticism, and valid critical response to artists' work must be based on more than faith, as the Jesuits recognized to some extent about their belief system. And, as Stephen's friend Cranly "dispassionately" tells him, "It is a curious thing, do you know... how your mind is supersaturated with the religion in which you say you disbelieve." I see that is the case with me too, even though I've put that former Catholic belief system behind me, or, to put it in the words of Stephen Dedalus, although "I was someone else then.... I was not myself as I am now, as I had to become."

But the "supersaturated" nature of my mind helps explain why I still have an interest in art that deals with spiritual matters, matters that seem beyond our earthly ken. That is also why I respond in *The Whole Durn Human Comedy* with an entire chapter entitled "A Grand Design," about the way the Coens, who are falsely thought by some of their detractors to be *"merely nihilists and juvenile mockers without a belief system,"* have their characters "often talk in vaguely hopeful terms of finding some higher purpose in life, a 'plan' in nature, a 'grand design,' even if they never discover or achieve it. That yearning is an inchoate spiritual impulse, and given the filmmakers' skepticism, it is usually doomed to failure."

I recognized some of myself in Ethan Coen's revealing short story "The Old Country," which I describe as a "a scathing portrayal of Hebrew school, presumably reflecting the tedium and alienation he experienced as a youth while being forced to conform to the old ways in mostly Gentile Minneapolis." I analyze how that story relates to various characters in the Coens' films, and to the "state of dislocation" Joel points to in their work. That dilemma is reflected in the New York screenwriter Barton Fink (the title character played by John Turturro) with his "feeling of being a stranger in a strange new land" in their vision of Hollywood-as-Hell and in the biblically beleaguered Professor Larry Gopnik (played by Michael Stuhlbarg) in *A Serious Man*. That is the film stemming most directly from "the roots of the Coen Bros.' alienation in their upbringing," set as it is in the Jewish subculture of their native Minneapolis.

Their detractors feel the Coens are merely taking cruel amusement over the cosmic injustices meted out to such hapless figures as Barton Fink and Larry Gopnik, but *A Serious Man* is their modern-day version of the *Book of Job*. Larry's punishments seem particularly harsh, since he is such a good (if overly passive) man. But some of what the Coens affectionately call their "league of morons" seem more deserving of punishment they endure, such as the Minnesota car salesman Jerry Lundegaard (played by William H. Macy), who thinks it's a clever idea to hire thugs to stage a kidnapping of his wife for ransom in *Fargo*, or the motley, bumbling would-be traitors in the Coens' underrated black comedy about the CIA, *Burn After Reading*.

A black comedy, however high the body count, tends to suspend emotional identification with characters, although even in *Burn After Reading*, we can't help but enjoy the goofy characters played by Frances McDormand and Brad Pitt and half-wish they could get away with their scheming. But one of the ironies of the critical reception of the Coen Bros.' movies is that in their grimmer tales whose dark humor has prompted such critical consternation, our emotional identification with characters such as Larry Gopnik and Barton Fink is empathetically evoked by the Coens even as they also (and often literally) look down on the characters' struggles from a wryly detached perspective.

Such an Olympian viewpoint is found acceptable by literary critics in the works of the classic satirists such as Swift and Aristophanes and the anonymous author of *Job*. But filmmakers who express their pessimism in a mass-entertainment medium are held to a stricter standard by captious critics with Pollyanna tendencies or an inability to recognize that the Coens' supposed cynicism is, like Billy Wilder's, a mask over disappointed idealism. Hoberman in predictably glib and puerile fashion derides the Coens as looking at life from "the Olympian heights of a bunk bed in suburbia."

Being able to respond favorably or not to the Coens' dual perspective toward their characters largely depends on how much one's sense of humor can accommodate the ironic treatment of unjust suffering, mortality, and other bleak subject matter. I include myself in indicting the myopic folks to some extent, since my book criticizes the Coens because I felt that the black comedy in *A Serious Man* is "deeply buried and sticks in our throats." After re-seeing the film for this book, Danny, I find its "existential comedy" exquisitely and intelligently balanced throughout. But it's a measure of how truly disturbing that 2009 film is that my assessment of its dark vision of life and the failure of religion to provide meaningful answers to suffering humanity has continued to oscillate over the years.

"Flyover country"

You said you feel a connection to the alienated youth from Minneapolis in Ethan Coen's short story. How do you think your sense of kinship with both brothers comes partly from your shared Midwestern roots?

Some of the commonality of sardonic viewpoint and morbid humor I find with the Coen Bros. is a defiant byproduct of coming from what is derisively known in some parts of the U.S. as "flyover country," i.e., the Midwest. The Coens grew up as members of a minority Jewish community in a Minneapolis suburb and departed to live in New York and California, while I grew up as a Catholic in a mostly WASPish Milwaukee suburb and, after losing my faith and rebelling against my upbringing, departed to live in California. Perhaps it's because I've always seen myself as an outsider and rebel in alien landscapes that I have found such an affinity for several Jewish filmmakers—Spielberg,

Lubitsch, Wilder, and Cukor as well as the Coen Bros.— and have immersed myself in their works and worlds to write empathetic books about them. The Coens, like John Ford, who shares some of the traits I mention above, also deal incisively with ethnic humor while mocking ethnic stereotyping, a sophisticated approach that makes the Coens rare among modern filmmakers, who tend to run away from such issues out of cowardice.

I admire the Coens' daring and the way they manage to make highly personal, idiosyncratic films in a period when corporate filmmaking dominates Hollywood, but as I found, that is partly due to the Coens deriving some of their funding sources from Europe. In some ways, they are more European than American filmmakers, even though their subject matter tends to be American, and they are trenchant critics of our country's hypocrisy, as Wilder was. Wilder too, as I've pointed out, became a European filmmaker again in his later years after Hollywood mostly turned its back on him. Spielberg also functions with a considerable degree of independence, but that is a function of his great success within the system, although in recent years he has lost much of his audience; yet most of his films are still profitable, giving him a rare degree of freedom. The Coens resemble Ford in another way, their stubborn and sarcastic refusal to explain their work, which I respect. But it's noteworthy that they tend to engage more seriously with European interviewers, since they have more respect for the intelligence of those journalists.

Ethan and Joel Coen have respect for the audience's intelligence by refusing to play the game of spelling out their intentions but trusting us to understand why they are doing what they do. Nevertheless, as has also happened with Ford, that strategy has resulted in some glaring misunderstandings of their work, especially in regard to their use of ethnic humor, since we live today in such a simple-minded culture that tends to divide everything into good vs. bad, with little regard for nuances. In reading attacks on Ford and the Coens for their ethnic humor, I am reminded of what my favorite English teacher at Marquette High, the Jesuit scholastic Thomas L. Book, who supervised the school newsmagazine I edited, advised me. Mr. Book said, "Don't use irony, because most people won't understand it." He was right about how most people react, but I love irony and use it frequently, as do these filmmakers.

Was it difficult writing about films made by two individuals with strong, distinct personalities? I'd think you'd repeatedly

*write "the Coens did this or that," when it might have been
just one of them who is responsible.*

That is an unusual problem I faced in writing about them,
since not enough is known about them individually to draw
conclusions about who might have done what; we don't yet
have an ample enough biography of the Coens. But as I've
observed in regard to the collaborative art of filmmaking in
general, it's often hard to isolate who did what in a film, and
as I've discussed with you, my books have become more
and more focused on collaboration and joint authorship,
especially since I began laboring in the fields as a Hollywood
screenwriter.

   I've written extensively about directors whose teaming
with key writing collaborators is crucial to their work, such
as, to name a few, Capra and Riskin, Brackett & Wilder (as
their billing went), and Wilder & Diamond. Note that I use
an ampersand for writing teams, as the Writers Guild does
in film credits, while the "and" is reserved for people who
work separately and aren't members of a writing team per
se. As good directors often do with writers, Capra did work
with Riskin on preparing their stories, but it was Riskin
who did what's called in Hollywood, with unconsciously
bitter humor, "the actual writing," (I was once introduced
by a director on a set as "the actual writer.")

*I tell people that to fully appreciate the Coen Bros. they
should be aware that their films take place in an alternate—
often a movie—universe. Would you tell them that?*

Sure, because they are postmodernists with an advanced
taste for parody and a penchant for playing with genres and
genre conventions. I usually don't like postmodernism, but
they practice it in such a deft and witty way, visually and
verbally, that I am enthralled by their style.

*I find it interesting that different people have different
favorite Coen Bros. films, and regard some as minor that
others think are masterpieces. For instance: My favorite Coen
Bros. film is* Miller's Crossing, *and you call it "pretentious."
You also call it "grim," but I'm not sure that is criticism.*

My views on some of their films change when I re-see them.
I liked *Miller's Crossing* when I first saw it, but now find it
dismal in every way, as I do *The Hudsucker Proxy*. I don't
like *Intolerable Cruelty* as much as I once did. But I enjoy
Fargo a lot more than I did at first, when I didn't appreciate

their mockery of Midwesterners, until I found that my relatives in Wisconsin love the film because it captures their way of speaking and cultural ethos so perfectly. *Fargo* is perhaps the Coens' most seamless mixture of comedy and violence, and it has the most endearing performance in their body of work, Frances McDormand's complex and humane and Oscar-winning portrayal of the pregnant police chief, Marge Gunderson.

Burn After Reading, which was neglected by reviewers but popular with audiences (thanks in part to Brad Pitt), seems better every time, as does their highly personal portrait of a talented but self-destructive and commercially unsuccessful artist, *Inside Llewyn Davis*. I think it's a sign of the Coen Bros.' artistry and originality that our views of their work evolve, such as with my volatile view of *A Serious Man*. Maybe I will revisit *The Whole Durn Human Comedy* in a few years to see how my views have changed again.

Almost every Coen Bros. film has its own cult, but do you think the phenom-like cult status of The Big Lebowski *is partly because it is by them, or don't fans care who made it?*

It's a stoner bible. And it's simply a great film. I can't imagine why anyone wouldn't like it. And it's a tribute to Raymond Chandler in an ingenious modern way. The Coens have tried to alert people that they are more influenced by writers than by filmmakers. The other writers they mention as role models are Flannery O'Connor, James M. Cain, and Dashiell Hammett. Nevertheless, most film reviewers don't pick up on that strong hint and struggle to find filmic influences for Coen Bros. movies rather than drawing comparisons with their literary influences, as I do, for instance, by noting the similarities between the last segment of *Buster Scruggs*, "The Mortal Remains," with O'Connor's late story "Revelation," which was written when she was near death and was published shortly before she died.

I struggled for a while in trying to understand "The Mortal Remains" and its deliberately unreal style as it depicts a motley group of squabbling people crammed into a stagecoach, including a biased and querulous old lady, who end their journey by entering a spectral hotel. But when I compared it with "Revelation," O'Connor's savagely witty and exhilarating story about a motley group of squabbling people crammed into a doctor's office, including a racist woman who has a transformative vision of the afterlife, I understood what the Coens are doing, in their less hopeful but not entirely hopeless way, in "The

Mortal Remains." One of the many things that irritate me about some American film critics is that they can still get away with admitting (without apparent embarrassment or shame) that they haven't read the source material of a film they are writing about (or, when discussing the Coens, their literary role models). That may be excusable for a reviewer who has to cover films every week, but it's inexcusable for a film critic.

Do you find it weird that these outsider filmmakers would win Oscars, with No Country for Old Men, *from the Academy of Motion Picture Arts and Sciences? That's like Sam Fuller winning Oscars. In olden days, they would never have been welcomed into the mainstream.*

I find it refreshing that the Coens manage not only to keep making films in this generally mindless marketplace but also to win awards both here and in Europe. Their first Oscars were as the screenwriters of their 1996 film, *Fargo,* which is an original and won in that category (even though the film falsely and mischievously claims, "This is a true story"). For their 2007 film, *No Country for Old Men, th*e Coens won Oscars as producers, directors, and screenwriters; Javier Bardem won the supporting-actor award as the sociopathic serial killer, and the film received four other nominations, including for the Coens as editors. No doubt those multiple Academy honors were partly due to the film's basis in a critically acclaimed novel by Cormac McCarthy. Naysayers who might have attacked the film for its bleakness were checkmated by the film's literary cachet. The problem of a principled old-fashioned lawman (played by Tommy Lee Jones) recognizing his helplessness in the face of modern evil is a central preoccupation of the Coens, whose films, as I write in my book, confront us with "the nightmares behind the dreams we used to live by." (That phrase also describes some of my work.)

And *No Country* did well at the box office. Their only film that has outperformed it commercially is their 2010 remake of *True Grit,* based on the charmingly picaresque novel by Charles Portis. Although the remake is handsome to look at and retains the book's haunting epilogue, I regret that the Coens and Jeff Bridges don't offer a fresh take on Marshal Rooster Cogburn. Instead Bridges, with his half-soused mumbling through his beard, is allowed to do a parody of John Wayne's self-parody in the 1969 version (which unfortunately enabled Wayne to win his only Oscar rather than being honored for many splendid performances that were snobbishly overlooked). But occasional box-office successes helped keep the Coens bankable for their more adventurously idiosyncratic projects. Let's give the audience credit too for going along with their dark escapades, which demonstrates a yearning too rarely gratified in today's cliché-ridden marketplace.

Now that the Coens are working separately, at least for a while, have you liked their solo films as much?

Joel on his own directed *The Tragedy of Macbeth*, a project that didn't interest Ethan. They felt they had been on an exhausting treadmill making elaborate films together and were both interested in exploring new directions. Taking on his new (and pliable) writing partner, William Shakespeare, Joel made a striking, intensely focused film that draws powerful performances from Denzel Washington and Frances McDormand (Joel's wife and a key collaborator on Coen Bros. films who brings to life some of their most memorable characters). In the book I praise this 2021 adaptation of *Macbeth* for its "wondrously expressionistic visual poetry in conjunction with relatively naturalistic dialogue delivery and some extremely realistic violence, the kind of mixing of modes the Coens have always been known for in their work together."

Ethan's 2022 documentary, *Jerry Lee Lewis: Trouble in Mind*, is an entertaining look at an electrifying and deeply troubled artist. It rambles but intermittently touches on an intriguing theme, Lewis's transgressive sense that his work came from the deviltry he recognized within himself and his belatedly guilty sense that maybe he needed to find Jesus. That conflict—highlighted by the unstable dichotomy between Lewis and his controversial televangelist cousin, Jimmy Swaggart, a surprising pair of relations to say the least—is only sketchily presented, though. The film admirably lets Lewis's song numbers play largely intact but doesn't sufficiently explore his volatile personality. The film is edited with flair by Tricia Cooke, Ethan's wife, who had been collaborating with him and Joel since the late 1990s.

She and Ethan co-wrote *Drive-Away Dolls*, the 2024 comedy he directed with her as well, even though they weren't able to share that credit because she's not a member of the Directors Guild of America (it also took a while for Joel and Ethan to share directing credit). The film was originally titled *Drive-Away Dykes* before Coen and Cooke were forced to sanitize it. They reveal the original title at the end and prankishly frame the film as an adaptation of Henry James. It is part of what they call their ongoing "lesbian trilogy," which, so far, also includes *Honey Don't!*, released in 2025 (the third is supposed to be called *Go Beavers*). Cooke identifies as queer, and Ethan says they have an open, unconventional marriage.

Drive-Away Dolls, set in 1999, was written more than twenty years before it was filmed. It has some B-movieish verve but is mostly a rehash of earlier Coen Bros. shtick. The offbeat love story that develops between two contrasting friends on a road trip—Margaret Qualley plays the brassy Jamie and Geraldine Viswanathan the shy Marian—is the film's most enjoyable element. The cartoonish violence intercut with the lesbian sex and romance harks back to such Coen Bros. movies as *Raising Arizona* and *No Country for Old Men* but seems mostly formulaic. In *Honey Don't!*, Qualley is retro-stylish as a Chandleresque private eye stalking around a seedy, depressing milieu (baked-out Bakersfield, California, though the film was shot largely in New Mexico). The intermittent eruptions of brutal violence hark back to the Coens' relatively crude debut with *Blood Simple*, while the playful humor of Qualley's edgy relationships with an array of dead-end losers, sleazeballs, and psychos seems jarringly imbalanced with the blunt body count, unlike in the Coens' best films that pull off their dazzling balancing acts between playful comedy and existential dread.

If I miss the quirky, only seemingly digressive atmospheric flavor that characterizes the collaborations between Joel and Ethan, I'm willing to put that yen aside to let the brothers experiment with their own sensibilities. On the basis of their early experiments apart, it is still difficult to make facile generalizations about who was responsible for what in their previous collaborations, which seemed symbiotic. While going their own ways for a while may be necessary for the brothers, like other Coen Bros. admirers I've gotten somewhat restless in hoping they will either get back together or make increasingly bold, idiosyncratic bodies of work that reveal new dimensions in their separate creative strengths that previously were disguised in their seamless partnership.

The Jerry Lee Lewis documentary, *Drive-Away Dolls*, and *Honey Don't!* mostly lack the sure-handed bite the Coen Bros. were known for. And rather than this rather slight kind of doodling or the relatively abstract artistic exercise of Joel and Frances's *Tragedy of Macbeth*, we need more challenging reflections from them on our contemporary nightmares. The Coens are among the few contemporary film artists equipped to deal with those disturbing themes in a meaningful way.

George Cukor's People: Acting for a Master Director

A few years ago, you told me that George Cukor was, and I'll quote, "a great director, and I found him a lovable man, but I never quite got a handle on how to analyze his work. It's frustrating, but maybe someday I will figure out how." What changed so you could write George Cukor's People: Acting for a Master Director, *which was published in 2024 electronically and 2025 in hardcover?*

I bit the bullet and felt ready to take the challenge. Cukor, like Lubitsch, is another director whose work has been relatively neglected by people writing about movies. I'm talking about critical studies, because we are not lacking for biographical information on this partially closeted queer director whose byword was "discretion." Pat McGilligan wrote a superb, deeply researched 1991 biography, *George Cukor: A Double Life*, that answers the pertinent questions we need light on in order to draw connections between the life and the work. And there's the lively, witty, insightful, yet tantalizingly oblique 1972 interview book *On Cukor* by Gavin Lambert, the substitute for the autobiography Cukor never felt he could write.

But there have been few critical studies of Cukor. The best in English are Carlos Clarens's 1996 book in the BFI Cinema One series, *Cukor,* and *George Cukor: Hollywood Master*, a 2015 collection of essays edited by Murray Pomerance and R. Barton Palmer. The relative paucity of serious Cukor criticism is odd considering that many of his films are classics, and most cinephiles probably list two or three Cukor films among their favorites. François Truffaut, one of his critical champions in France in the 1950s, claimed, "The trouble is that Cukor isn't the kind of director you write about; he's someone to talk about with friends on the street or sitting in a café." I took that as a challenge, believing that the problem is not with the quality of Cukor's work but with the lack of a critical vocabulary to discuss the issues his work raises: the true nature of acting in cinema; the confusion surrounding authorship and collaboration; and how a director whose modesty in working "largely through his intimate collaborators with actors" prevented even sympathetic critics from evolving ways to write about him in sufficient depth.

At the 1975 American Film Institute L.A. premiere party for François Truffaut's *The Story of Adele H.*, I observe with delight the mutual admiration society between George Cukor and Truffaut, who as a young critic called him "that extraordinary man who makes, out of every five films, one masterpiece, three other very good ones, and the fifth still interesting." I took as a challenge what Truffaut also wrote in the 1950s, "The trouble is that Cukor isn't the kind of director you write about; he's someone to talk about with friends on the street or sitting in a café." (New World Pictures)

My introduction addresses these issues and sets out to explain how to deal with the challenges his work presents. It took me a long time to feel confident that I could tackle the job of explicating Cukor's methods, style, and artistic achievement. This is a book I could not have written in 1971, when I reviewed another critical study about Cukor in *Film Quarterly* and admitted that his work is "more difficult to evoke or analyze than that of almost any other major director." How to deal with a director whose self-expression is "a stream of sensations, intonations, and rhythms," conveyed through both actors and *mise-en-scène?* "The critic can describe the way Cukor gets from *this* to *this* to *this*, but how can he freeze each frame and tell you what *this* is?" I made a first, partly successful attempt to do so with a 1973 essay in *Film Comment* on Lowell Sherman's wry and subtle performance as a self-destructive alcoholic film director in Cukor's 1932 film *What Price Hollywood?*

I was only in my twenties when I made my first tentative attempts to write about Cukor, but even by 2000, when I was in my early fifties, I was still struggling. I was asked by the *New York Review of Books* to review a new edition of Lambert's interview book and submitted a lengthy career overview essay they rejected because they felt it overemphasized his queer sensibility. I thought building on McGilligan's foundation of knowledge of Cukor's personality—much of which the director had kept hidden from the public during his lifetime out of self-protection, part of the reason he is so little-known outside Hollywood—would provide a fresh way of analyzing his artistry. The magazine's rejection was shortsighted, in my view at the time, and it was a setback. After I published the essay in 2001 in Gary Morris's excellent online publication, *Bright Lights,* as "George Cukor: The Valor of Discretion," I still felt I hadn't cracked the critical dilemma.

When I look back at that overview after having written an entire book on Cukor's work, it does seem too sketchy. But when I felt the time finally had come to write a full-scale critical study two decades later, I submitted the more granular piece of analysis in my 1973 essay on Lowell Sherman as part of my proposal to Columbia University Press, to show how I intended to go about it, and that set the pattern for the book.

Did George Cukor's People *turn out to be a difficult book for you to write? Or did your varied Hollywood and SFSU experiences help prepare you for it?*

Ironically, after all that, I found it surprisingly easy to write. So what changed in the subsequent twenty-four years? My diverse and cumulative life experience made me well-prepared for the task. The various paths my career had taken enabled me to write what I consider an experiment in film criticism. Perhaps most valuable was my experience acting for Welles for more than five years on *The Other Side of the Wind* and collaborating with him on my dialogue. I was able to study how another great director worked with a mixture of diplomacy and firmness in collaboration with a cast of richly varied backgrounds, shaping our performances in individualized ways. Like Welles, Cukor excelled at the art of collaboration, not only with actors but also with screenwriters, cinematographers, art directors, and everyone else involved in the process. And what Bazin called "the genius of the system" is exemplified by the work of Cukor, showing classical Hollywood at its finest.

My involvement with many other directors and actors as a journalist and working with veteran stars as a writer of AFI shows expanded my knowledge of the craft. And my many years as a reviewer of both films and plays helped give me the basic vocabulary to understand acting and how those modes of performance differ. There's so much misunderstanding of what good film acting is; it's often confused with the *most* acting rather than restrained acting. Cukor generally evoked subtle performances from his casts, such as repeatedly coaxing Jack Lemmon to do "less, *less,* do less" in his first feature, *It Should Happen to You,* although the director sometimes encouraged flamboyant, even campy behavior when he felt it appropriate to the character, such as Katharine Hepburn's gender-bending title character in *Sylvia Scarlett* and Maggie Smith's outré Aunt Augusta in *Travels with My Aunt.* But overall, as he put it, "In films, it's what you *are* rather than what you *act.* "

I realize that I am indebted as well to my teaching experience. Cukor's work has a highly modern concentration on personal identity as role-playing, gender as performance, and what we now call gender-fluidity. Those preoccupations made him far ahead of his time and account for why his humorous, daring, and poignant treatment of cross-dressing with Hepburn posing as a young man for most of *Sylvia Scarlett* was rejected so vehemently by reviewers and audiences in 1935. Cukor and Hepburn ran up against a barrier they had to be more careful and covert in crossing with their future projects. Hepburn retreated from such overt game-playing with gender more decisively than Cukor, but he continued in subtle ways to explore these subversive themes for the rest of his career.

I was not as conversant in these areas when I left Los Angeles in 2000 for the San Francisco Bay Area—perhaps the most sexually avant-garde part of the United States—and began my late career in teaching. *George Cukor's People* benefited from my exposure to younger people navigating the shoals of gender roles with their brave mixture of excitement and trepidation. And my awareness of writing a tribute to such a profoundly civilized man as George Cukor while our culture was descending into the morass of the Trump era played an important role in how I shaped the book.

How did it help you to get to know Cukor over the years, from interviewing him and watching him at work on his last film, Rich and Famous?

I felt an immediate rapport with Cukor when I interviewed him in 1975 about the fiasco of a film he had made under trying conditions in the USSR, *The Blue Bird.* I was doing the interview for *Action,* the magazine of the Directors Guild of America, as we had lunch on the patio of the Polo Lounge of the Beverly Hills Hotel. I admired Cukor's philosophical humor about that experience, which would have sent lesser directors into retirement. I found Cukor's *élan* a refreshing contrast with the sour moods of other veteran directors I interviewed, since they weren't inclined to move with the times, but he was. He had a youthful enthusiasm and sense of adventure and actually welcomed the newfound freedoms and chance to experiment. What other old director was a fan of Paul Morrissey films, declaring that "I luxuriate in" *Lonesome Cowboys* and *Flesh*, and describing those casually raunchy bisexual films as "so bold and undiluted and really new"?

I also had the sense with Cukor that he was not a narcissist like most directors, even ones I greatly admired, but that he was genuinely interested in everyone he met—myself included. I felt we were having a real conversation, and I was impressed that he was able to size me up shrewdly on our first encounter when he said, "You're a very determined young man but deceptively mild-mannered. Keep that." His ability to see through my façade to a deeper level of personality most people failed to recognize demonstrated how uncommonly perceptive he was about the subtleties and subtexts of people's lives. That was part of what made him such an acutely insightful director of actors, who by their nature lead double lives. Cukor's own double life, as McGilligan calls it (borrowing the title of one of his films), helped him navigate cannily between social strata in Hollywood. As a gay man, a Jew, and the son of immigrants, Cukor was adept at the subtle rituals of "passing," and that enriched his personal and professional lives, helping give his films their rich layers of nuance.

With Todd McCarthy, I also conducted an interview with Cukor in 1981 that concentrated on his late work, which had been neglected by reviewers. After spending a day watching Cukor shooting his last film, *Rich and Famous*, with Candice Bergen and Jacqueline Bisset as longtime writer friends, on a soundstage at MGM, we went to Cukor's home to interview him for *Film Comment*. Cukor was in good form during the interview, sharp and focused and witty, and we captured his often hilariously profane way of talking. That irritated Gavin Lambert, who chided us for not cleaning up Cukor's language as he had in their interview book. I argued that it was more important to let Cukor speak naturally, but Gavin was not convinced. Having had a no-holds-barred conversation with Cukor helped me greatly when I came to write my book. Observing him at close range

Cukor at work, with his characteristically intimate intensity and the gesture of his right hand that seemed to coax deeper emotions from his actors. Here he is directing Audrey Hepburn in Eliza Doolittle's "draggled-tailed guttersnipe" period in his 1964 musical, *My Fair Lady*. (Warner Bros./From the George Cukor Papers of the Margaret Herrick Library, Academy of Motion Picture Arts and Sciences)

while getting a sense of his quicksilver mind and his emotional acuity and resilience gave me insights into how he functioned as an artist, even more than watching him at work so quietly and discreetly with Bergen and Bisset on the set of *Rich and Famous*.

Todd and I also interviewed Bisset separately, because we felt Cukor had been unfair to her when we asked about their relationship. The film's producer, William Allyn, who had developed the project with Bisset over a series of years, told me Cukor could not stand the idea of an actress trying to exert control over him. So he continually deflected our attempts to get him to say anything positive about what we considered Bisset's finely edgy, intelligent, restrained performance of a tormented character with a clandestine sexuality. Ironically, of the two lead characters, she is the one who more resembles Cukor, but he took more pleasure in indulging Bergen's campiness. When I was transcribing the interview, I realized that it seemed odd that Cukor was so neglectful of Bisset, so I called him and spent half an hour trying every way I could to coax him into saying something positive about her. I failed. It was a formidable demonstration of how stubborn he could be.

Nevertheless, as a result of that impasse, in writing my book I was able to interweave Bisset's thoughtful remarks about her skittish relationship with Cukor and how it affected her performance. That gives some rare insights into one of the key relationships he had with an actress, although their enmity was unusual in his career. When I asked him if Garbo hadn't been able to exert a similar power over *Camille*, he said, "Yes, but there was also good manners. You deferred; she deferred. It was very civilized." The problems Cukor had with Bisset were reflective of changes in the industry to which he had difficulty adjusting at the end of his career and perhaps a sense of insecurity he developed as a result.

How did you come up with your unusual approach to a critical study of a director, concentrating on his work with actors?

The breakthrough in my ability to write *George Cukor's People* was my decision to write about individual performances rather than conventional chapters analyzing films in their entirety. Over the years, as I had done in my Lubitsch book and especially in my Wilder book, in which I broke with the chronological approach, I had become restless with the usual way of writing about a director's career. Since, as Cukor said, "My work really begins and ends through the actors," even though his *mise-en-scène* is also lively and eloquent, that eventually helped me realize that it would make more sense to understand and appreciate what he does in his films by examining the performances with microscopic precision. So my critical study approaches Cukor primarily through his work with actors, his primary means of expressing himself with fidelity to the written texts his films were adapting. I felt the widespread lack of appreciation and understanding of the nature of film acting was largely responsible for Cukor's being undervalued, and I included a lengthy introduction giving my views of what film acting is and is not.

I watched Cukor's films over and over and took detailed notes to analyze and help convey the essential qualities of the key performances I wrote about. I wound up with several dozen examples, sometimes writing about more than one actor in a given film or even an ensemble, and I interwove insights from accounts of the actors' working relationships with Cukor. It was exhilarating work to meet this challenge in helping create a fresh vocabulary for understanding film acting.

While trying to find the verbal equivalents to capture Cukor's qualities on the printed page, I was influenced by two critics who have brought rare insights into the often misunderstood art of film acting. One is my friend James Naremore, whose 1988 book, *Acting in the Cinema*, is the groundbreaking text in the field, and who continued to show the way with his charming and perceptive 2022 book, *Some Versions of Cary Grant*. I was also struck in my research to discover Dan Callahan, whose incisive 2020 study, *The Camera Lies: Acting for Hitchcock*, provided me with another model.

While writing the text of my critical study, I was always aware of the need to be entertaining and lucid in my descriptions of the moments that make the performances in Cukor films as bright and complex as they are, while also being conscious of avoiding the pitfalls of plot description, which can be deadly. And as I had done while reviewing films for *Variety*, but with more space to make the descriptions breathe, I tried to be as specific about the performances as possible, bearing in mind the definition Arthur Penn gave of directing, "the reconstruction of processes," and the Hemingway quote I always cited for my students as the essence of screenwriting: "the real thing, the sequence of motion and fact which made the emotion."

When I regretted in my 1971 review of a book on Cukor how difficult it is to freeze moments in his films to complement verbal analysis, I was subconsciously looking forward to what is now much easier, the ability to make frame enlargements. It was possible then too—as Truffaut's Hitchcock book from the 1960s demonstrated—but it was impractical, taking a great deal of expensive work I was not yet able to muster. By the time I came to write my Cukor book, however, I was adept at using the computerized tools to make frame enlargements, and, as I had done with my Lubitsch book, I hired video experts to make them look as good as possible. John Belton and Philip Leventhal at Columbia fully understood the crucial importance of optimum illustrations for the Cukor book, as did the book's designer, Elliott S. Cairns. So we worked together diligently in our endeavor to make the book as elegant in its appearance as a Cukor film.

In your book you point out a prevalent Cukor theme that I found intriguing because it was autobiographical on his part. Like Lubitsch, Cukor had a number of his actors play actors, and those actors acted on and off the stage. Both Lubitsch and Cukor believed that actors, like most people, act their way through life, but do you believe that this theme was more serious and personal with Cukor?

While watching *My Fair Lady* repeatedly on weekend passes from
the hospital after my breakdown in 1965, I was emotionally struck
by this moment when Eliza (Hepburn) learns to express herself in a
more articulate way through the guidance of Professor Higgins (Rex
Harrison). Her character transformation not only echoed what I was
undergoing but also gave me encouragement.
(Warner Bros./frame enlargement)

Lubitsch came naturally to that theme since he had begun
as a stage actor. And as a Jew he was accustomed to living as
something of an outsider, even though his father ironically
had emigrated from Russia to Berlin because he considered
that city more hospitable to Jews; by the time the Holocaust
began, Ernst's parents were dead, and he was in America,
when the inhabitants of his old neighborhood were among
the millions of Jews who were slaughtered. Cukor, who was
also Jewish, grew up in New York City and spent his early
life directing in the theater, so he was similarly accustomed
to life as a minority group member and someone on the
fringe of so-called respectable society, even though he grew
up in a prosperous and well-connected family.

What made Cukor even more fascinated with role-
playing was that he was queer and hyper-conscious of
gender identity and the role-playing involved in both
masculinity and femininity and combinations thereof. So I
found it compelling to study Cukor partly because he was
far ahead of his time in his attention to and appreciation of
the complexities of sexual identity.

*Is there a Cukor film you write about that you think is
largely underappreciated although it reveals the most about
him?*

It may seem paradoxical that, as I write in the book, *The
Actress* is Cukor's most autobiographical film, since it's
actually Ruth Gordon's autobiographical work. *The Actress*
is her 1953 screen adaptation of her play *Years Ago,* about her
early life in New England, when she had to summon up the

courage with the support of her anxious mother to confront her father, a crusty former sailor, about her compulsion to go on the stage. What's most refreshing about the play and movie is that her father proves to be surprisingly supportive, unlike, say, Katharine Hepburn's father, who responded to her similar declaration by slapping her across the face. Cukor's parents were supportive of his decision to go into the theater, but as a fervent young theatergoer he could identify with Gordon's stagestruck behavior in her youth and said he admired her character's determination to succeed despite formidable odds.

Cukor also told Gavin Lambert, "I'm lost in admiration for people who come to New York or Hollywood with no money, only hopes. I had the enormous advantage of being born in New York and living at home when I first went out to fend for jobs in the theater.... After I graduated from high school[,] I said to my family, 'I want to go into the theater.' Nothing can shock parents today, of course, but then it was as if I'd said, 'Well, Mom and Dad, I'm going to become a pusher.'" Since I was one of those who came to Hollywood with no money and only hopes, I felt embraced by Cukor's understanding and welcoming complicity.

The title role in *The Actress* is played by the glamorous Jean Simmons, and Cukor admitted she was miscast to play a girl who overcame the stigma of not being conventionally attractive. But it is actually Spencer Tracy's movie. I was stunned to rediscover the film in my research on Cukor and to realize what a majestic performance he gives. I have never seen Tracy better than in playing this gruff but sympathetic man, Clinton Jones. That performance, one of six Tracy gave for Cukor, helps show how reductive was Cukor's longtime designation in the media as a "woman's director."

When Cukor is called a "woman's director," is that praise?

Although calling Cukor a "woman's director" may seem to be a tribute to his dazzling work with so many great actresses—to name a few of my favorites, Katharine Hepburn in ten films, Judy Holliday in five films, Greta Garbo in *Camille*, Ingrid Bergman and Angela Lansbury in *Gaslight*, Claire Bloom in *The Chapman Report*—the phrase "woman's director" was/is also disparaging code for "gay" and implies that he wasn't as good at directing men. How absurd when you look at the many superb male actors who give some of their best performances in Cukor films, including not only Tracy but also John Barrymore, Fredric March, Cary Grant, Lew Ayres, James Stewart,

Charles Boyer, James Mason, Rex Harrison, Dirk Bogarde, and Laurence Olivier, et al. Cukor became increasingly impatient and miffed over the years at that label.

And though Cukor notoriously was fired from *Gone With the Wind* partly because Clark Gable objected to being directed by a man he called "a fairy" and because Gable mistakenly thought Cukor might throw the picture to the female leads, the director who took over the picture, Victor Fleming, could not have praised Cukor more highly. Fleming's favorite screenwriter, John Lee Mahin, reported to Todd McCarthy and me that Fleming told him, "George would have done just as good a job as I. He'd probably have done a lot better on the intimate scenes. I think I did pretty well on some of the bigger stuff. George came from the stage and taught us what directing a dialogue scene was about. He knew. And nobody could direct a dialogue scene like George Cukor. It's bullshit that he's just a woman's director. He's not. He can direct anybody."

You once wrote about Cukor, "With his non-doctrinaire, instinctively feminist sensibility, Cukor usually filmed from the viewpoint of his female protagonist." I fear that back in the Sixties and Seventies we were all guilty of stating that Cukor had so many complex, interesting female leads because he was gay, when the truth was that he was a male Hollywood director who seemed to have a feminist sensibility.

That quote from my 2001 essay on Cukor shows that I too was somewhat under the influence of his "woman's director" reputation. Even though in the same essay I pointed out the inadequacy of that label, I was being simplistic about his viewpoint. Certainly Cukor is feminist in his understanding and sympathy with women's issues, but even that term seems an overgeneralization in approaching his rich and complex body of work. Ingmar Bergman once said that what makes great filmmaker is having a personal vision. Some directors who are good but perhaps not great have a vision that is overly slanted toward male characters, showing little interest in female characters or often restricting them to limited roles.

I'm thinking, for instance, of John Huston. In our AFI tribute, I had Lauren Bacall, our host, admit right at the top that Huston's world was "very much a man's world." Bacall made only one Huston film, *Key Largo*, with her husband Humphrey Bogart, and says on the show, "I was damn lucky to have done that." One reason I suggested Bacall as host is that we had trouble finding actresses who had made enough impact in his films to enlist them as speakers. (By the way, we pioneered the word "host" for a woman, since I pointed out that Bacall was a tough dame who hardly seemed like a "hostess." That wording caught on and is now common on TV shows.) Huston asked us to invite Mary Astor from the first feature he directed, *The Maltese Falcon*, and I inquired, but she was too infirm. Elizabeth Taylor had agreed to speak about their work together on *Reflections in a Golden Eye* but had to back out at the last minute because a film she was working on had a change of schedule. So in desperation we sent an SOS to Aileen Quinn, the talented but hardly stellar young actress from Huston's dreadful film *Annie.* And we could barely scrape up enough film clips of memorable women in Huston films to make a suitable montage. The dearth of women in Huston's world is a serious artistic limitation.

But in the bodies of work of the greatest male directors, such as Bergman, Ophüls, Ozu, or Cukor, male and female characters tend to be more evenly distributed, as they are in life itself. That's not to say that such directors don't make some female-centric films in which men are secondary—look at *Persona, Letter from an Unknown Woman, Late Autumn,* or *The Chapman Report*—and they choose such stories because they are more sensitive to women than most of their colleagues or because of marketplace demands, as happened when Hollywood studios tended to assign Cukor to women's vehicles. A case in point was *The Women*, MGM's adaptation of a gimmicky play by the reactionary Clare Boothe Luce with no men in the cast. Cukor and his writers—who included Anita Loos, Jane Murfin, F. Scott Fitzgerald, and Donald Ogden Stewart—transformed Luce's misogynistic diatribe into a droll and empathetic view of the many and complex social roles played by women in and around the upper-class society of 1939 New York City.

I mentioned that at San Francisco State I taught a course on Pioneering Women Directors, and though their work often focuses on women's issues, the men in their films are acutely observed as well, especially in the cases of Ida Lupino and Elaine May. The opening-up of cinema to more women directors in recent years has begun to rectify previous imbalances. But when it's sometimes said that men should not write or direct stories about women, as I heard when I was a Hollywood screenwriter, I disagree and always cite Tolstoy and *Anna Karenina.* Not only is that argument absurd, but it would mean that the obverse would logically apply; such restrictive edicts, which are often heard in ethnic contexts as well, are anti-art and, indeed, anti-human. The best directors do justice to all their characters, as Cukor does, say, in *Camille*, *Gaslight*, *A Star Is Born*, and *My Fair Lady*. Otherwise we wouldn't think of them so highly.

What George Cukor films must unretired film professors show to their eager students?

I'll mention a short course of five films to introduce Cukor to people who don't know him well. These are films of diverse kinds that carry his distinctive stamp and the daring originality of his sensibility: *Sylvia Scarlett*, *Holiday*, *A Star Is Born*, *Pat and Mike*, and *Love Among the Ruins*. If watching those five films doesn't make someone an admirer of Cukor, well then, to borrow the immortal words of the criminologist Dr. Henry Lee, "Something wrong."

Was Cukor and Katharine Hepburn's relationship unique? Did having hidden private lives draw them closer?

No doubt that was part of their rare level of mutual under-standing and protectiveness. (Cukor loved gossip, though not about her.) And Cukor not only discovered Hepburn for movies, going to bat for her with a starring role in her first film, the 1932 drama *A Bill of Divorcement*, he was so perceptive about her talents and androgynous idiosyncrasies that he shaped her career in a wide range of vehicles for the next forty-seven years. Along the way she starred in the film she considered her favorite and Cukor often cited as his favorite, the 1933 *Little Women*; the film that reestablished her shaky hold on stardom, *The Philadelphia Story*; and her underrated teaming with Tracy in *Pat and Mike*. I prefer *Pat and Mike* to the somewhat pretentious *Adam's Rib*, because it conveys the egalitarian relationship between the characters played by Tracy and Hepburn with deceptively offhand charm and uses Hepburn's impressive athletic skills in the neorealistic vein Cukor adventurously worked in during the early 1950s.

Love Among the Ruins, the magnificent romantic comedy-drama Cukor and Hepburn made in 1975 from a script by James Costigan, is the most nuanced performance of her late career. And Olivier, from whom Cukor evoked a performance of surpassing brilliance, called it "my happiest professional film experience." That Cukor at his late age was flexible enough to move enthusiastically into television was a refreshing sign of his modernity. The last film Hepburn and Cukor made together was a relatively routine adaptation for TV of Emlyn Williams's play *The Corn Is Green*, but Cukor, who prided himself for being a "survivor," wound up his career with *Rich and Famous*, which he made at the age of eighty-one. I wrote an article for *Daily Variety* at the time about how he was the oldest director ever to make a Hollywood studio film (this was before Clint Eastwood kept directing into his nineties), and rather than being miffed as some people in Hollywood would be to have their age broadcast, Cukor told me that reading the article made him "thrilled."

And then there is *Sylvia Scarlett*. Hepburn always dismissed that avant-garde film because of its disastrous reception in 1935. She couldn't recognize that she gives a delightful tour de force performance of transvestism while oscillating wittily between male and female identities. Their daring adventure was so far ahead of its time that Cukor too was somewhat defensive about it. But he also could recognize what they had achieved together, and he sometimes called *Sylvia Scarlett* his favorite film.

You wrote extensively about Hepburn's performances in your Cukor book. You mentioned you met her and interviewed her. What happened on those occasions?

I had a memorable telephone interview with Hepburn about her work with Frank Capra on their 1948 film, *State of the Union*. He managed to conceal from her how right-wing he was, but when I told her he hated Franklin D. Roosevelt, one of her heroes, she said, "Oh, dear!" But she gave me incisive observations of Capra and about the Red Scare in Hollywood. I also spent eight hours hanging out with her in the rain during the 1976 location shooting in the San Gabriel Valley of ending scenes for her dreadfully twee film *Olly Olly Oxen Free*. She wouldn't give me an interview on that occasion but would come over to me and chat from time to time, and once when she was massaging the neck of one of the little boys in the movie, she looked up at me and said flirtatiously, "I wish it were me." I also was an extra in the scene when Hepburn crashes a hot-air balloon into the stage of the Hollywood Bowl before striding briskly to a microphone, planting her hands on her hips, and announcing, "You see what you can do if you're crazy enough to try anything." We gave her a standing ovation. So when I wrote about her in the Cukor book, I was fortunate to have some direct and complex sense of her as a person.

Cukor directed the other great Hepburn as well, Audrey. Is it upsetting to you that so many of us don't appreciate My Fair Lady *as you do?*

Since that film means so much to me personally, as I've discussed earlier when I recalled the role it played in helping me back to life and a new level of maturity after my breakdown, I do tend to take it personally when people disparage the film. But passionate involvement always plays an important part in my film criticism. I also think that people who run down *My Fair Lady* because it is a popular musical based on two classic plays, and the only film that won Cukor an Oscar, are simply snobs. That's the bottom line of the brush-offs it tends to receive, although there are more rational grounds for disagreement. But Cukor brilliantly solved the aesthetic issues involved in how to stylize a play adaptation for the cinema—that was his forte throughout his career, and *My Fair Lady* is one of the last and best exemplars of classical Hollywood's musical genre—and the Pygmalion-Galatea theme carried over from George Bernard Shaw is central to Cukor's creative personality as a shaper of characters onscreen, a director who excels at uncovering layers beneath the surfaces of people.

And since so little serious criticism has been written about *My Fair Lady*, I found myself writing one of the fullest analyses of any Cukor film in my book while defending it against its detractors. I believe I make a convincing argument and hope that restores the film to its rightful place among Cukor's masterworks. A film critic is a kind of teacher, and as I've mentioned, in that endeavor conveying enthusiasm is vital. In any case, I don't read critics because I necessarily agree with them but because I hope to learn something by having my horizons expanded. That's what I'm trying to do with critical studies of directors I admire.

Did Cukor agree with you (and me) that A Star Is Born *is his masterpiece?*

The mutilation of that film was so traumatic that he found it somewhat hard to talk about, but reading between the lines, you could tell that he regarded it as an artistic pinnacle in his career. In my view it's one of the best twenty or so films ever made. I wanted to write a whole book about it in 1972 for the British Film Institute's Cinema One series (I don't remember the response I received, if any, to that suggestion). I was thrilled when my friend Ronald Haver made it his mission to try to find the missing parts and restore *A Star Is Born* to the form in which it was originally released. Ron made some exciting discoveries, even if his restoration is incomplete. His 1988 account of his quest, *A Star Is Born: The Making of the 1954 Movie and Its 1983 Restoration*, is one of my favorite film books. I always have a protective spot in my heart for a *film maudit*; my favorite film of all remains *The Magnificent Ambersons*, even in its mutilated form, and *A Star Is Born* stands with it and the truncated *Greed* as among the foremost monuments to the crass self-destructiveness of the American film industry.

Beyond that, why do I respond more strongly to *A Star Is Born* than to any other Cukor film, even *My Fair Lady*, which has such personal resonance for me? *A Star Is Born* resembles that later musical in being another Pygmalion-Galatea story, so it evokes for me how I was rescued by Kathy in my own version of that archetypal fable, *The Broken Places*. And the story of Judy Garland's Esther Blodgett desperately trying to rescue James Mason's self-destructive Norman Maine revolves around alcoholism, perhaps the most emotionally powerful treatment of that theme I have seen in the cinema. A close second would be *Rio Bravo*, with its depiction of the alcoholic deputy, Dude (played by Dean Martin) and his regeneration through the help of his friend John T. Chance (John Wayne). Seeing Martin's startlingly real performance in 1959 preceded the even more powerful impact *A Star Is Born* would have on me when I saw it during my college years, when my own alcoholism was already apparent. Even though I initially tried to resist drinking because of our family troubles, I began in college and did not stop until 1991. My longevity and productivity have benefited from my abstinence.

My earliest piece on Cukor shows that *A Star Is Born* was the film that started me on the path to writing my book about the director more than fifty years later. In that article I asked myself about an especially shattering Cukor scene, "How is a critic to explain the workings of Judy Garland's broken monologue on her broken husband in *A Star Is Born*—sudden unveilings of hysterical agony twisting her childishly painted harlequin face into a tragic mask in the raw glow of dressing-room bulbs?" That question and my profound identification with Garland's character show that my own feeling of helplessness over my parents' alcoholic self-destruction was as strong as my identification with Norman's futile gallantry in recognizing but fatalistically succumbing to his disease. Cukor's ability to evoke equal empathy with both partners in that tragic love story perhaps is what has made that film resonate so deeply with me. And that's not even to begin addressing, as I try to do in my book, the breathtaking audacity and paradoxical beauty of the film's *mise-en-scène*, which represented such an advance in Cukor's career that *Cahiers du Cinéma* proclaimed at the time with pardonable hyperbole, "A DIRECTOR IS BORN!"

As I read your book, film by film, I was startled by how many of Cukor's actors play characters who are already in the throes of alcoholic self-destruction when we are introduced to them. You write about Cukor's relationship with John Barrymore as one influence on this theme.

Dan Callahan's 2004 essay on Cukor in the online publication *Senses of Cinema* is full of eye-opening observations, such as this one that cuts to the essence of why Cukor shows such fascination and empathy with alcoholics in many of his films: "This was an artist who understood the deepest kind of pain" but was "fascinated by alcohol and why people needed it, the loosening of social inhibitions that came with it, and the somewhat alluring self-destruction it portended.... Cukor solidifies his favorite theme: the glory of alcoholic, lunatic or sexual abandonment and breakdown, the sheer sensuality of it, and, at the end, its high price."

That insight helped me understand the deeper reasons for Cukor's preoccupation with alcoholic self-destruction and related interest in states of mental breakdown, themes that have sometimes been traced to his friendship with Barrymore, one of the models for Norman Maine. But as I observe in my book, these themes "are so pervasive in [Cukor's] work that they more likely are metaphors for a disruptive side of his own personality that he managed to hold in balance." I explore that powerful tension in Cukor's vision throughout my book in studying the way he so knowingly and shrewdly guided his actors in expressing states of breakdown or precarious balance. Besides the tragic couple in *A Star Is Born* and the lost but mostly not self-pitying young alcoholic played by Lew Ayres in *Holiday*, the other character in Cukor's work who haunts me the most is Claire Bloom's Naomi Shields, the alcoholic and sex addict in *The Chapman Report*. Watching this elegantly beautiful woman's fatal descent through a combination of self-destructive compulsion and brutal victimization is like watching my Kathy Wolf, and both of them tear my heart out.

What next?

If you write another critical study about a legendary director who has fallen from favor, I bet you'll consider George Stevens. You wrote in Two Cheers for Hollywood *that he is "the most underrated American director today."*

That comment evoked some smug head-wagging by reviewers of the book, a further sign that Stevens, who was once so highly regarded, is in serious need of reevaluation. I've admired his work since I went to see *The Diary of Anne Frank* in downtown Milwaukee in 1959 and even more since seeing *Shane* when Stevens brought his personal print to Madison in the late 1960s and talked with us about that film, which I consider the greatest Western ever made. That opinion evokes further surprise, since Ford is my favorite director, but I appreciate the self-consciously classical approach Stevens took in making his majestic summation of the genre, even if that's often unfairly held against him in the perverse way the field of film studies tends to operate.

I am fond of Stevens as a man as well as a director and had a couple of other memorable meetings with him, including the leisurely interview Pat McGilligan and I did at the Beverly Hills Brown Derby in 1974, not long before he died. George Stevens Jr. told me it was the interview that best captured how his father actually spoke. That was published in a 1979 issue of *Bright Lights*; it took me six months to edit the interview, since Stevens tended to ramble, and I worked hard to structure our discussion to bring out his most eloquent remarks. Stevens was the only filmmaker I knew who, when we said goodbye, called me "My friend."

I tried unsuccessfully in the 1990s to interest publishers in a Stevens biography and have since considered writing a critical study. But the 2019 critical study by Neil Sinyard, *George Stevens: The Films of a Hollywood Giant,* is eloquent, even if there's always room for another. I keep re-watching Stevens's films and may or may not put my mind to that task. Actually, I wish I could write his biography, since a good one still needs to be done, but I don't have many months to spend going through his papers at the Academy library in Beverly Hills, since I don't live there anymore. More likely that is one of the projects that will go down in my list of regrettably unwritten books, such as the one on the decline of the American movie industry; a critical study of Ida Lupino, whose work has been now been covered by numerous authors; and biographies of Abe Polonsky, over which I tarried too long; Ray Bradbury, one of the subjects

For my last four years at San Francisco State, I taught online, which I enjoyed. In my final week of teaching in December 2024, I am saying goodbye to the students in a Writing About Cinema course with John Ford as our subject matter. Behind me is a frame enlargement of Ben Johnson and Joanne Dru in my current favorite Ford film, the 1950 Western *Wagon Master.* (Argosy Pictures/RKO)

I couldn't sell; and the great cinematographer James Wong Howe, whom I met all too briefly and wish I had pursued. But I have some other projects in mind, long-term ones, as always, including a partially written novel I might revisit. There's more to say about Welles, Ford, and the Kennedy assassination. Life keeps getting shorter, though.

And in this country, where my work has been concentrated, the cinematic art form is in a nearly terminal crisis. Martin Scorsese observed in 2019 that "the most ominous change has happened stealthily and under cover of night: the gradual but steady elimination of risk. . . . [Most movies] lack something essential to cinema: the unifying vision of an individual artist. Because, of course, the individual artist is the riskiest factor of all. . . . For anyone who dreams of making movies or who is just starting out, the situation at this moment is brutal and inhospitable to art. And the act of simply writing those words fills me with terrible sadness."

I loved movies, but...

You end your introduction to your 2017 book, Two Cheers for Hollywood, *with these five words: "Yes, I love movies, but... " I'd like you to expand on that...*

I feel I was betrayed by the movies, as I was by the Catholic Church, my parents, my schooling, and our government. My anger over that betrayal and my need to discover the truth behind the false façade and expose the lies and injustice that surround us is what has always fueled my writing. Jonathan

Among the best of the many documentaries on film history in which I have been interviewed is David Kittredge's *Boorman and the Devil*, a thoughtful 2025 film about John Boorman's unfairly maligned 1977 masterpiece, *Exorcist II: The Heretic*. (Triple Fire Productions)

Lethem aptly calls that my "rage for truth." And as John Ford put it about his similar need to express his passion for justice, "What the hell else does a man live for?" It's hard not to continue loving the movies I once loved, though, as well as some occasional new ones.

My feelings about the medium today are highly ambivalent. I feel in a sense I went into the wrong profession. My father may have been right after all. But you have to do *something* with your life, and as Joel Coen said of the movie business, "I guess it beats throwing trash for a living." But my interests have always gone beyond cinephilia, and I've incorporated my preoccupations into my work in the world of films, which I value as a window onto the endlessly compelling spectacle of reality. My biographies of directors range widely into sociopolitical subjects, and with my books on the assassination of President Kennedy, I have branched out into other subjects besides movies. To recall what I told the interviewer who did the video profile of me at San Francisco State, "I'm an investigative reporter" at heart. So I can't regret the choices I made as a youth—anyway, once you make them, it's almost impossible to turn back.

Now that you have retired from teaching, at your age you could gracefully give up writing and spend your time on a rocking chair once occupied by Ol' Mose Harper or Satchel Paige. So is it at all coincidental that your latest book is about George Cukor, who refused to retire and continued working until the end of his days?

For a while I did contemplate giving up writing books after my retirement from teaching. I took ten days off. That's a long break for me. Then I got back to work on this book, and...

BIBLIOGRAPHY

Books by Joseph McBride, in chronological order of original publication; revised editions are also listed but not foreign translations or U.S. reprint editions.

Persistence of Vision: A Collection of Film Criticism (editor), Wisconsin Film Society Press, Madison, 1968.

Focus on Howard Hawks (editor), Prentice-Hall, Englewood Cliffs, New Jersey, 1972.

Orson Welles, British Film Institute Cinema One Series, Secker & Warburg, London, 1972; revised and expanded edition, Da Capo Press, New York, 1996.

John Ford (with Michael Wilmington), British Film Institute Cinema Two Series, Secker & Warburg, London, 1974; revised and expanded edition, University Press of Kentucky, Lexington, 2023.

Kirk Douglas, Pyramid Books, Harcourt Brace Jovanovich, New York, 1976.

Orson Welles: Actor and Director, Pyramid Books, Harcourt Brace Jovanovich, New York, 1977.

High & Inside: The Complete Guide to Baseball Slang, Warner Books, New York, 1980; revised and expanded edition, *High and Inside: An A-to-Z Guide to the Language of Baseball,* Contemporary Books, Chicago, 1997.

Hawks on Hawks, University of California Press, Berkeley, 1982 ; revised edition, University Press of Kentucky, Lexington, 2013.

Filmmakers on Filmmaking: The American Film Institute Seminars on Motion Pictures and Television, Vols. I and II (editor), the American Film Institute and J. P. Tarcher, Los Angeles, 1983.

Frank Capra: The Catastrophe of Success, Simon & Schuster, New York, 1992; revised and expanded edition, St. Martin's Press, New York, 2000.

Steven Spielberg: A Biography, Simon & Schuster, New York, 1997; revised and expanded second edition, University Press of Mississippi, Jackson, 2010, and Faber and Faber, London, 2011; revised and expanded third edition, Faber and Faber, 2012.

The Book of Movie Lists: An Offbeat, Provocative Collection of the Best and Worst of Everything in Movies, Contemporary Books, Chicago, 1999.

Searching for John Ford, St. Martin's Press, New York, 2001.

What Ever Happened to Orson Welles?: A Portrait of an Independent Career, University Press of Kentucky, Lexington, 2006; revised and expanded edition, 2022.

Writing in Pictures: Screenwriting Made (Mostly) Painless, Vintage, New York, and Faber and Faber, London, 2012.

Into the Nightmare: My Search for the Killers of President John F. Kennedy and Officer J. D. Tippit, Hightower Press, Berkeley, 2013.

The Broken Places: A Memoir, Hightower Press, Berkeley, 2015.

Two Cheers for Hollywood: Joseph McBride on Movies, Hightower Press, Berkeley, 2017.

How Did Lubitsch Do It?, Columbia University Press, New York, 2018.

Frankly: Unmasking Frank Capra, Hightower Press, Berkeley, 2019.

Billy Wilder: Dancing on the Edge, Columbia University Press, New York, 2021.

Political Truth: The Media and the Assassination of President Kennedy, Hightower Press, Berkeley, 2021.

The Whole Durn Human Comedy: Life According to the Coen Brothers, Anthem Press, London and New York, 2022.

George Cukor's People: Acting for a Master Director, Columbia University Press, New York, 2024/2025.

FILMOGRAPHY/ VIDEOGRAPHY

This listing, in chronological order of release, includes films, television shows, or videos on which Joseph McBride is credited as writer or co-producer or in other production capacities. Not listed are his many other credits as an interview subject or his credits as an actor except for those on which he worked in production capacities.

Blood & Guts (Quadrant Films, Canada/Melvin Simon Productions, US), screenwriter with John Hunter and William Gray; also story and actor, 1978.

Rock 'n' Roll High School (New World Pictures, Los Angeles), screenwriter with Richard Whitley & Russ Dvonch; story by Allan Arkush & Joe Dante; also actor, 1979.

The American Film Institute Salute to James Stewart (CBS-TV), scriptwriter with George Stevens Jr., 1980.

The American Film Institute Salute to Fred Astaire (CBS-TV), scriptwriter with Stevens, 1981.

Let Poland Be Poland (United States Information Agency), principal scriptwriter, 1982.

The American Film Institute Salute to Frank Capra (CBS-TV), scriptwriter with Stevens, 1982.

The American Film Institute Salute to John Huston (CBS-TV), scriptwriter with Stevens, 1983.

The American Film Institute Salute to Lillian Gish (CBS-TV), scriptwriter with Stevens, 1984.

Remembering Orson ..., organizer and writer (uncredited) with Richard Wilson of Orson Welles Memorial, Directors Guild of America Theater, Hollywood, 1985. Taped by producer Frank Beacham (on Wellesnet.com and YouTube).

Obsessed with "Vertigo": New Life for Hitchcock's Masterpiece (American Movie Classics/MCA Universal Home Video/Signal Hill Entertainment), co-producer (and writer, uncredited), 1997.

100 Years...100 Movies: "War and Peace" (AFI/TNT), scriptwriter for the segment on war movies for the AFI's ten-part series on film history, 1998.

Orson Welles's *Touch of Evil* (partly restored version) (Universal), "special thanks," 1998.

John Ford Goes to War (Starz/Encore True Stories), co-producer, 2002.

Becoming John Ford (Twentieth Century Fox Home Entertainment), consultant and interviewee, 2007.

50 Reasons...50 Years: "The Tippit Shooting" and "Political Truth: The Media and the Assassination," writer and narrator of two episodes (producer: Len Osanic; videographer: Jeff Carter) (Black Op radio.com), 2013.

Italian American Cinema from Capra to the Coppolas (Museo Italo Americano, San Francisco), scriptwriter (uncredited) (editor: Silvia Turchin), 2015.

Errol Morris's *American Dharma* (Fourth Floor Productions/Utopia), "thanks," 2018.

Orson Welles's *The Other Side of the Wind* (Royal Road Entertainment/Netflix), actor and consultant, 2018.

They'll Love Me When I'm Dead (Netflix), "special thanks" and interviewee, 2018.

The Assassination and Mrs. Paine (Journeyman Pictures/ Open Ranch Productions), "special thanks," 2022.

DVD/BLU-RAY
AUDIO COMMENTARIES

How Green Was My Valley (d. John Ford, 1941)
(Twentieth Century Fox Studio Classics), with cast
member Anna Lee, 2002; and Blu-ray edition, 2013.

An Affair to Remember (d. Leo McCarey, 1957)
(Twentieth Century Fox Studio Classics), with cast
member (singer) Marni Nixon, 2002, and Blu-ray Book
edition, 2011.

The Grapes of Wrath (d. Ford, 1940)
(Twentieth Century Fox Studio Classics),
with John Steinbeck scholar Susan Shillinglaw, 2004.

Cheyenne Autumn (d. Ford, 1964)
(Warner Bros Home Video), 2006.

The Complete Buster Keaton Short Films, 1917–1923
(d. Keaton et al.), Masters of Cinema [UK]), 2006.

Jane Eyre (d. Robert Stevenson, 1944)
(Twentieth Century Fox Studio Classics), with cast
member Margaret O'Brien, 2007; and Blu-ray edition
(Twilight Time), 2013.

Pilgrimage (d. Ford, 1933) (Twentieth Century Fox), 2007.

My Darling Clementine (d. Ford, 1946)
(Criterion Collection), 2014

The Hurricane (d. Ford, 1937) (Kino Lorber), 2015.

3 Bad Men (d. Ford, 1926) (Kino Lorber), 2016.

The Quiet Man (d. Ford, 1952) (Olive Films), 2016.

Young Mr. Lincoln (d. Ford) (Criterion Collection), 2018.

Irma la Douce (d. Billy Wilder) (Kino Lorber [US] and Masters of Cinema/Eureka Video [UK]), 2018–2019.

A Foreign Affair (d. Wilder) (Kino Lorber), 2019.

Angel (d. Ernst Lubitsch) (Kino Lorber), 2020.

Straight Shooting (d. Ford) (Kino Lorber), 2020.

Hell Bent (d. Ford) (Kino Lorber), 2020.

Five Graves to Cairo (d. Wilder) (Kino Lorber), 2020.

The Lost Weekend (d. Wilder) (Kino Lorber), 2020.

The Emperor Waltz (d. Wilder) (Kino Lorber), 2021.

The Fortune Cookie (d. Wilder) (Kino Lorber), 2021.

Broken Lullaby (aka *The Man I Killed*, d. Lubitsch) (Kino Lorber), 2021.

The Sun Shines Bright (d. Ford) (Eureka! Masters of Cinema [UK]), 2022.

Some Like It Hot (d. Wilder) (Kino Lorber), 2022.

The Apartment (d. Wilder) (Kino Lorber), 2022.

The Horse Soldiers (d. Ford) (Kino Lorber), 2022.

When I Was Dead (d. Lubitsch) (Kino Lorber), 2023.

Meyer from Berlin (d. Lubitsch) (Kino Lorber), 2023.

The Oyster Princess (d. Lubitsch) (Kino Lorber), 2023.

I Don't Want to Be a Man (d. Lubitsch) (Kino Lorber), 2023.

The Doll (d. Lubitsch) (Kino Lorber), 2023.

The Trial (d. Orson Welles) (Criterion Collection), 2023.

Stalag 17 (d. Wilder) (Kino Lorber), 2023.

The Last Tycoon (d. Elia Kazan) (Kino Lorber), 2023.

Witness for the Prosecution (d. Wilder) (Kino Lorber), 2024.

Madame DuBarry (d. Lubitsch) (Kino Lorber), 2024.

Macbeth (d. Welles, 1948) (Olive Films), 2016; (Kino Lorber), 2024.

Donovan's Reef (d. Ford, 1963) (Kino Lorber), 2025.

Sabrina (d. Wilder, 1954) (Kino Lorber), 2025.

INDEX

Note: * after a name indicates a pseudonym.

ABOUT THE AUTHOR AND THE INTERVIEWER

Joseph McBride is an emeritus professor of the School of Cinema at San Francisco State University. His twenty-five previous books include biographies of Frank Capra, Steven Spielberg, and John Ford; three books on Orson Welles; and critical studies of Ford (with Michael Wilmington), Ernst Lubitsch, Billy Wilder, the Coen Bros., and George Cukor. McBride plays a film critic and historian in Welles's *The Other Side of the Wind* (2018), and he co-wrote the cult classic *Rock 'n' Roll High School* (1979). He received a Writers Guild of America award, four other WGA nominations, and two Emmy nominations for co-writing American Film Institute Life Achievement Award CBS-TV specials. McBride met Danny Peary when they were part of the "Madison film mafia" at the University of Wisconsin. Photo credit: Locarno International Film Festival.

Danny Peary has been writing about film, music, and sports for almost sixty years. He was the writer for *The Tim McCarver Show* for seventeen years and coauthored three books with the former baseball All-Star and Hall of Fame broadcaster. He coauthored Ralph Kiner's autobiography, *Baseball Forever*, and biographies of Roger Maris and Gil Hodges, and edited the fifties baseball oral history *We Played the Game* and *Cult Baseball Players*. His film books include *Close-Ups: The Movie Star Book*, three volumes of *Cult Movies*, *Guide for the Film Fanatic*, and *Alternate Oscars*. Photo credit: Suzanne Rafer.

www.ingramcontent.com/pod-product-compliance
Lightning Source LLC
Chambersburg PA
CBHW060400130626
46555CB00005B/1955